The Newborn Christian

THE NEWBORN

114 Readings from

CHRISTIAN

J. B. PHILLIPS

Collier Books
Macmillan Publishing Company
NEW YORK

ACKNOWLEDGMENT IS MADE to Harold Shaw Publishers for permission to reprint material from *Ring of Truth*, North American edition, Harold Shaw Publishers, 1977, copyright © 1967 by J. B. Phillips, Hodder & Stoughton, Ltd., London, and to the following for excerpts from other of J. B. Phillips' works, as shown:

The Methodist Publishing House, London: *Appointment with God*, copyright © 1954 by J. B. Phillips; *Plain Christianity*, copyright © 1952 by J. B. Phillips and *Your God Is Too Small*, copyright © 1952 by J. B. Phillips;

The Highway Press, London: *Making Men Whole*, copyright © 1952 by J. B. Phillips;

Hodder & Stoughton, London: *New Testament Christianity*, copyright © 1956 by J. B. Phillips; and *For This Day*, copyright © 1974 by J. B. Phillips;

Collins Publishers, London: *Four Prophets*, copyright © 1963 by J. B. Phillips and *Good News*, copyright © 1960 by J. B. Phillips.

Library of Congress Cataloging in Publication Data
Phillips, J. B. (John Bertram), 1906–82.
The newborn Christian.
Bibliography: p.
1. Meditations. I. Title.
BV4832.2.P497 1984   242   83-19576
ISBN 0-02-088270-X (pbk.)

Collier Books
Macmillan Publishing Company
866 Third Avenue, New York, NY 10022
Collier Macmillan Canada, Inc.

First Paperback Edition 1984

10 9 8 7 6 5 4 3 2

Macmillan books are available at special discounts for bulk purchases for sales promotions, premiums, fund-raising, or educational use. For details, contact:

Special Sales Director
Macmillan Publishing Company
866 Third Avenue
New York, NY 10022

Printed in the United States of America

Contents

Foreword   xi

God Unfocused   1

Spiritual Values   2

Beauty, Goodness, and Truth   4

God Focused   5

The Incarnation Hypothesized   7

The Hypothesis Incarnated   9

False Gods—   11

    Resident Policeman   11

    Tyrannical Parent   13

    Grand Old Man   15

    Escape Artist   16

    Jack in the Box   18

Chairman of the Board	19
The Disappointer	21
Narcissus on the Silver Screen	23
Olympic Sprinter	24
Mystical Vision	25
The Ultimate Bundle of Highest Values	26
Idol of the Worshipping Animal	27
Four Prophets	27
The Visited Planet	31
Jesus' Strength as a Man	35
Jesus' Miracles	40
Jesus' Prophecy	44
What Jesus Says About:	45
The Character of God	45
The Purpose of Life	46
Pride, Self-Righteousness, and the Exploitation of Others	48
Beatitudes and Non-Beatitudes	49
Pain and Disease, Injustice and Evil	51
The Good Shepherd	54
The Crucifixion	57
The Act of Reconciliation	59
The Resurrection According to Paul	60
The Resurrection According to Luke	63
The Resurrection in the Gospels	67
The Revolution of the Resurrection	70
The Ascension	71
The Living Spirit of Truth in the New Testament	75
The Gospels	76
The Letters	83
The Greatness of Paul	85

Conversion of the Corinthians	87
Nine New Testament Serendipities	89
"Rich in Mercy"	89
"Casting All Your Care"	90
"Fear and Trembling"	91
"Pressed Out of Measure"	92
"Quit You Like Men"	93
"Everyone That Loveth . . . Knoweth God"	95
"Now Are We the Sons of God"	96
"Count It All Joy"	97
"If Our Heart Condemn Us"	98
Similes and Metaphors in the New Testament	99
Faith	102
Faith in the New Testament	104
Faith in the Young Church	106
Justification by Faith	108
Faith in Today's World	109
Hope	112
Hope in the New Testament and the Young Church	114
Hope in Today's World	116
The Love Commandments	118
Love in the New Testament and the Young Church	120
Four Temptations Against Love	121
Love in Today's World	124
Peace	125
Six Obstacles to Peace	127
Christian Maintenance	131
Quietude	132
Prayer	134
Liturgy	136

Worship	137
Sacraments in Life	138
Communion and Common Sense	141
The Living Tradition	142
Eucharistic Fellowship	143
Spiritual Nutrition	145
The Christ Within Us	146
Christ and the Real Self	148
Physical and Mental Preparation for Communion	150
Spiritual Preparation for Communion	154
Forgiveness and Forgivingness	156
The Church	157
Fellowship of the Church	158
Christian Service	160
Bible Reading	163
Christian Reading	164
Books, Films, and Plays	165
The Badness of Goodness	168
Competition in Goodness	170
Evil	171
Temptation	173
Guilt	174
Imperfection	175
Humiliation	175
Sin	176
Reconciliation	179
Christ's Act of Reconciliation	183
Perfection and Perfectionism	185
Spiritual Vitality	188
The Spirit	191

CONTENTS

Plain Christians	193
Plain Non-Christians	195
Christian Qualities	197
Non-Christian Qualities	199
Dark Tunnels	202
Darknesses and Depressions	203
Inklings of Eternity	204
Funerals	207
Eschatology, Realized and Unrealized	208
Life After Death	211
Communion of Saints	213
Second Coming	215
After Nineteen Centuries of Christianity	217
New Testament Christianity	218
God's Comprehensive Love	219
Bibliography	221
Sources	223

Foreword

Bombs fell, sirens wailed, and buildings collapsed as J. B. Phillips talked about beatings, stonings, and shipwrecks. What first-century Christians had to endure was not unlike what twentieth-century Londoners had thrust upon them. Descriptions of the first-century experience, however, couched as they were in the regal English of the sixteenth and seventeenth centuries, were not easy for twentieth-century parishioners to understand. To remedy the situation, the London vicar decided to try his hand at Englishing one of the epistles. "It's like seeing an old picture after it's been cleaned," said C. S. Lewis about the result, and he urged the vicar to do more.

Phillips's university education and pastoral experience admirably equipped him to be a translator. He was graduated from Cambridge with an honors degree in classics and English in 1927. He was ordained a priest of the Anglican Church in 1931. He served as curate at St. John's and St. Margaret's, both churches in London, in the decade that followed. He was appointed vicar of the Church of the Good Shepherd, also in London, in 1941, and began the work that would occupy the next thirty years of his life.

Between the two curacies Phillips came down with a disabling sickness. Hospitalization and surgery followed, and when he heard a doctor tell a nurse that he would not live through the night, he did not despair. He fell into a deep sleep in which he saw "a vista of indescribable beauty." The earth breathed sweetness, and as an arrow seeks the bull's-eye, he ran toward "a white shining bridge" that would cross him from this world to the next. At the bridge's edge, however, he was met by a figure in white who gently but firmly indicated that it was not yet the fullness of his time. Phillips woke up from his dream, weeping with disappointment. The crisis was past. From that moment on his health improved, and the conviction that a special providence was at work in his life increased.

Letters to Young Churches—the title was suggested by Lewis—was published in 1947. The Acts of the Apostles was published as *The Young Church in Action* in 1955. *The Book of Revelation* appeared in 1957. *The New Testament in Modern English* was published in 1958; a second, thoroughly revised edition was published in 1972. Both editions have had sales in the millions both in England and the United States. And his only foray into the Old Testament—*Four Prophets: Amos, Hosea, First Isaiah, Micah*—was published in 1963.

Phillips's pastoral work during the years of translation also resulted in books. Bible readings appeared as *Making Men Whole* (1952). Destructive and constructive conceptions of God were dealt with in *Your God Is Too Small* (1953). Lenten addresses on the subject of Holy Communion became *Appointment with God* (1954). Talks for the British Broadcasting Corporation and the Australian Broadcasting Commission were collected under the title *Plain Christianity* (1956). Lectures in England and the United States were gathered under the title *New Testament Christianity* (1957). A series of twenty-six radio plays for the BBC had the biographical title, *A Man Called Jesus* (1959). And an anthology of various materials was called *Good News: Thoughts on God and Man* (1963).

If there is one word to describe Phillips's Christianity, it would be *newborn*. The sort of faith professed by Christians in the first century—focused, vigorous, harmonious—is exactly the sort of faith he recommends to Christians in the twentieth century. Against the attacks of avant-garde theologians and skeptical Bible scholars in the 1950s and 1960s, he stood firm. Against a religionless Christianity and a demythologized Jesus, he struck back. In *Ring of Truth*, which was published in 1967, he gave his testimony as a translator that the epistles and gospels rang true, like silver shekels flung on a marble floor.

What a newborn Christian of the first and indeed of any other century believes, therefore, is the subject of this anthology. Selections have been taken from nine of J. B. Phillips's works. The readings are thematically arranged, informally systematized, and devotionally styled. Sources of the readings are given at the back of this book.

—WILLIAM GRIFFIN
Macmillan Publishing Company
June 1, 1978

God Unfocused

LET US FLING wide the doors and windows of our minds and make some attempt to appreciate the "size" of God. He must not be limited to religious matters or even to the "religious" interpretation of life. He must not be confined to one particular section of time nor must we imagine Him as the local god of this planet or even only of the Universe that astronomical survey has so far discovered. It is not, of course, physical size that we are trying to establish in our minds. (Physical size is not important. By any reasonable scheme of values a human being is of vastly greater worth than a mountain ten million times his physical size.) It is rather to see the immensely broad sweep of the Creator's activity, the astonishing complexity of His mental processes which science laboriously uncovers, the vast sea of what we can only call "God" in a small corner of which man lives and moves and has his being.

To meditate on this broadness and vastness will do much . . . but if we stop there we may get no further than sensing a vague "unfocused" God, a depersonalized "Something" which is after a while peculiarly unsatisfying.

Spiritual Values

By [SPIRITUAL VALUES] we mean the qualities of spirit, of personality, which are recognizable and assessable, but are incapable either of scientific weighing or measuring—and incapable of physical destruction. In the light of the probable ultimate fate of the planet and of the present (far more impressive) threat to human life, we are driven to reconsider whether after all there is reality beyond the physical, measurable reality. We begin to wonder whether the whole position is not now the reverse of what men once thought. They used to talk of the "spiritual" values as shadowy and unsubstantial, and the physical as solid and "real" and reliable. They are beginning to see that the opposite may well be true. We can certainly see evidence of the universal destructibility of matter: perhaps it is after all true that "reality" lies in another realm altogether, and that its values are not unsubstantial after all.

This, of course, is far more readily believed by some temperaments than by others. The poets, artists, and philosophers, as well as a great many other undistinguished people, of many ages, have probably been more or less acutely conscious that the "spiritual" is of vastly greater importance than the material. To all of them, speaking broadly, this present physical life is the visible and tangible stage or battlefield of spiritual forces. Universal values, such as truth, goodness, and beauty, were often considered to exist apart from, as well as being exhibited in, the life of this world. To some of them this present life is merely the prelude, lived under difficulty and handicap, to a free unfettered life of the spirit. The latter is reality—the former is an important but transitory incident.

This age-long intuition is now being forced upon humanity as a strong and workable hypothesis by the threatened disintegration of the merely physical. And there is enough inward assent to it in the hearts of most men to give them at any rate one powerful clue to reality. It makes the idea of God far more sensible and far more desirable.

After all, if it should be true that the nature of reality is spiritual and it is only quite temporarily and incidentally involved in matter, is it not unreasonable to want to know something of the Spiritual Being behind the Scheme of Things. And on those unimaginative people to whom the spiritual has always sounded fanciful and unreal, it is slowly dawning that the physical world which is so real and tangible to them is most uncomfortably unreliable. A man used to be able to reckon on a good number of years of active material life, which were a most efficient buffer between him and the naked spiritual realities which in his more vulnerable moments he suspected might be true. Now his buffer of material things has been shown to be far from dependable. At any moment he might be pitchforked into the world of the spirit. His anchors are slipping, and if he feels the need of anchorage (and who, at heart, does not?) he must find it in the world of the spirit—he must find God.

Beauty, Goodness, and Truth

IN ALL PROBABILITY everyone is sensitive to beauty, although obviously some are far more so than others. Yet experience shows that even those who are apparently most prosaic are touched, even to their own surprise, by certain forms of beauty. The line along which this half-melancholy, half-magic touch may come varies enormously with different people. For some it is the appealing grace of childhood, for some the surge and thunder of the sea, for some the dazzling splendor of mountain peak, for some the song of birds in spring, for some the smell of wood smoke or of frosty autumn evenings, for some—but the list is endless. All poetry and music, and art of every true sort, bear witness to man's continual falling in love with beauty, and his desperate attempt to induce beauty to live with him and enrich his common life.

The appeal of beauty which is universal, however distorted or debased it may have become, cannot be lightly dismissed. It is a pointer to something, and it certainly points to something beyond the present limitations of time and space. We can at any rate say that beauty arouses a hunger and a longing which is never satisfied (and some would say never can be satisfied) in this world.

Disabusing our minds of self-conscious righteousness, goody-goodyness, and mere absence of evil, there is something unavoidably attractive about the good. However far from the ideal our own practice may be, we have an automatic respect for such things as honesty, sincerity, faithfulness, incorruptibility, kindness, justice, and respect for other people. . . . Surely this recognition of good, so deeply rooted and so universal, is another far from negligible pointer to Reality.

Both beauty and goodness, then (no doubt in different ways), exert an effect upon man which cannot be explained in terms of the world that we know, and to this we may add his search for truth. He is not only wanting to know facts, though the careful dispassionate amassing of ascertained facts is surely one of his most admirable activities, but he also wants to find some meaning to the puzzle of life. Scientific research, philosophy, and religion, all in their different ways, attest this reaching out of man to grasp more and more truth. And yet—why should he? Why should he not rest content with what he has and what he knows? Why can he not accept death and evil and disease without worrying about them? Why does he, in all ages and in all countries, reach out to find Something—something which will harmonize and explain and complete life's bewildering phenomena? Here, too, is surely a pointer. Arguing, as we must, from what we know to what we don't know, we may fairly say that as food is the answer to hunger, water the answer to thirst, and a mate to sexual desire, this universal hunger for Truth is unlikely to be without its answer and fulfillment, however hard to find it may be.

God Focused

ALTHOUGH EVERYONE KNOWS what is meant by Beauty, Goodness, and Truth, it is impossible to visualize them as absolute values. We can visualize a beautiful thing, but not beauty; a good man, but not goodness; a true fact, but not truth. Yet once we have a beautiful thing held in our minds it is comparatively easy to fill the mind with other beauties; once we consider a truly good man we can expand and develop his qualities until we begin to get some idea of goodness; while if we are once convinced of a certain fact (particularly if we have discovered it ourselves), we can at once think of a world of truths—we begin to visualize the absolute quality of Truth.

We see beauty, then, when it is first focused for us in a beautiful thing; goodness when it is focused in a good man; truth when it is focused in a fact of which we are sure. Absolute values may exist as mental concepts for the trained philosopher; but the ordinary man must see his values focused in people or things that he knows before he can grasp them.

Let us now make a further step. The mystic claims to be able to grasp something of God in the Absolute. But the mystic is even more uncommon than the philosopher, and any attempt by the ordinary man to "imagine" God results in nothing but the "vague oblong blur" complained of by those modern people who make the attempt. Yet if a man can see God focused and be convinced that he is seeing God, scaled-down but authentic, he can, as in the case of Beauty, Truth, and Goodness, add all the other inklings and impressions that he has of the majesty, magnificence, and order of the Infinite Being, and "see God."

But can he so see God "focused"? There must be more than elusive sparks and flashes of the divine—there must be a flame burning steadily so that its light can be examined and properly assessed.

It is a fascinating problem for us human beings to consider how the Eternal Being—wishing to show men His own Character focused, His own Thought expressed, and His own Purpose demonstrated—could introduce Himself into the stream of human history without disturbing or disrupting it. There must obviously be an almost unbelievable "scaling-down" of the "size" of God to match the life of the planet. There must be a complete acceptance of the space-and-time limitations of this present life. The thing must be done properly—it must not, for example, be merely an act put on for man's benefit. If it is to be done at all God must *be* man. There could be no convincing focusing of real God in some strange semi-divine creature who enjoys supernatural advantages. Nor, though it is plain that many men have been "inspired" to utter truth, to create beauty, and to demonstrate goodness, could it suffice for a unique and authentic focusing to depend on one "super-inspired" man. For complete dependability, for universal appeal, for a personally guaranteed authenticity to which all other truth is to be related, God must do it Himself.

The Incarnation Hypothesized

SUPPOSE . . . THAT God does slip into the stream of history and is born as Baby *A. A* will, as far as the limitations of time, space, and circumstance allow, grow up as God "focused" in humanity, speaking a language, expressing thoughts, and demonstrating life in terms that men can understand. Having once accepted *A*'s claim to be God expressing Himself in human terms, men will have a great deal by which to live.

First, they will know now for certain what sort of "character" the eternal God possesses. For He is certain to inform them that the man who observes Him is observing God. Secondly, the facts about man and God, the perennial anxieties about such things as pain and sin and death, the dim hopes of a more permanent world to follow this one—these and scores of other clamant questions will now have a fixed reference point, by which they can be adjusted if not settled. Thirdly, man will be able to gain at first hand information as to "what life is all about" and as to how he can co-operate with the Plan and the Power behind time and space. Fourthly, if they are convinced, as we are assuming, that the one before them is really God-become-man, they will be able to observe something absolutely unique in the history of the world: God Himself coping with life on the very terms that He has imposed upon His creatures. They will be seeing God not seated high on a throne, but down in the battlefield of life.

A, of course, having genuinely entered the space-time world and having become a human being, must enter at some particular time and must live in some particular locality. He will thus, as far as some incidentals and externals are concerned, be to some extent moulded, modified, and limited. He cannot, therefore, be a *full* expression of God—there is neither time nor space enough for that. But within the limit he sets himself he will be a perfectly genuine and adequate focusing of the nature of God. He will not only be information and example, but the aperture through which men may see more and more of God. If men are once convinced of the genuineness of his extraordinary claim, they will probably find that God is, so to speak, visible through an *A*-shaped aperture. Knowledge, experience, and appreciation may all expand enormously as the years pass, but that will not mean that men "grow out of" God. For *A* will have supplied by his demonstration in time and space one sure Fact, around which everything else of Truth, Goodness, and Beauty may be appropriately and satisfactorily crystallized.

The Hypothesis Incarnated

QUITE A NUMBER of people in all parts of the world have come to the conclusion that the hypothetical *A* has appeared in history—that *A* in fact equals the man Jesus, who was born in Palestine some nineteen centuries ago. Most of the possibilities that we have suggested might occur if God were to enter this world humanly, and historically were, they feel reasonably certain, fulfilled in the life and teaching of Jesus. And there were some remarkable additional features which could hardly have been surmised, and which we will consider in due course.

It is, of course, a very big step intellectually (and emotionally and morally as well, it will be found) to accept this famous figure of history as the designed focusing of God in human life. It is not made any easier by the clinging mass of sentimentality, superstitious reverence, and traditional associations which surround Him. It is emphatically not an easy matter for the honest modern mind to pierce the accretions and irrelevancies and see the Person, the Character—particularly as the records, though they have been examined far more closely than any other historic documents, are undeniably meager. Further, many people who have a vague childish affection for a half-remembered Jesus, have never used their adult critical faculties on the matter at all. They hardly seem to see the paramount importance of His claim to be God. Yet, if for one moment we imagine the claim to be true, the mind almost reels at its significance. It can only mean that here is Truth, here is the Character of God, the true Design for life, the authentic Yardstick of values, the reliable confirming or correcting of all gropings and inklings about Beauty, Truth, and Goodness, about this world and the next. Life can never be wholly dark or wholly futile if once the key to its meaning is in our hands.

Although an honest adult study of the available records is essential, to decide that Jesus really was the embodiment of God in a human being is not a merely intellectual decision. Our unconscious minds will sense (even if the conscious mind does not) that to accept such a unique Fact cannot but affect the whole of our life. We may with complete detachment study and form a judgment upon a *religion,* but we cannot maintain our detachment if the subject of our inquiry proves to be God Himself. This is, of course, why many otherwise honest intellectual people will construct a neat bypass around the claim of Jesus to be God. Being people of insight and imagination, they know perfectly well that once to accept such a claim as fact would mean a readjustment of their own purposes and values and affections which they may have no wish to make. To call Jesus the greatest Figure in History or the finest Moral Teacher the world has ever seen commits no one to anything. But once to allow the startled mind to accept as fact that this man is really focused-God may commit anyone to anything! There is every excuse for blundering in the dark, but in the light there is no cover from reality. It is because we strongly sense this, and not merely because we feel that the evidence is ancient and scanty, that we shrink from committing ourselves to such a far-reaching belief as that Jesus Christ was really God.

False Gods —
Resident Policeman

To MANY PEOPLE conscience is almost all that they have by way of knowledge of God. This still small voice which makes them feel guilty and unhappy before, during, or after wrongdoing is God speaking to them. It is this which, to some extent at least, controls their conduct. It is this which impels them to shoulder the irksome duty and choose the harder path.

Now no serious advocate of a real adult religion would deny the function of conscience, or deny that its voice may at least give some inkling of the moral order that lies behind the obvious world in which we live. Yet to make conscience into God is a highly dangerous thing to do. For one thing, as we shall see in a moment, conscience is by no means an infallible guide; and for another it is extremely unlikely that we shall ever be moved to worship, love, and serve a nagging inner voice that at worst spoils our pleasure and at best keeps us rather negatively on the path of virtue.

Conscience can be so easily perverted or morbidly developed in the sensitive person, and so easily ignored and silenced by the insensitive, that it makes a very unsatisfactory god. For while it is probably true that every normal person has an embryonic moral sense by which he can distinguish right from wrong, the development, nondevelopment, or perversion of that sense is largely a question of upbringing, training, and propaganda.

As an example of the first, we may suppose a child to be

brought up by extremely strict vegetarian parents. If the child, now grown adolescent, attempts to eat meat, he will in all probability suffer an extremely bad attack of "conscience." If he is brought up to regard certain legitimate pleasures as "worldly" and reprehensible, he will similarly suffer pangs of conscience if he seeks the forbidden springs of recreation. The voice will no doubt sound like the voice of God; but it is only the voice of the early upbringing which has conditioned his moral sense.

As an example of the second influence on the moral sense, we may take a "sportsman" who has been trained from his youth that it is "wrong" to shoot a sitting bird. Should he do so, even accidentally, he will undoubtedly feel a sense of shame and wrongdoing; though to shoot a bird flying twenty yards in front of the muzzle of his gun will not produce any sense of guilt. His conscience has been artificially trained, and it is thus that "taboos" are maintained among the civilized and uncivilized alike. . . .

Many moralists, both Christian and non-Christian, have pointed out the decline in our moral sense observed in recent years. It is at least arguable that this is almost wholly due to the decline in the firsthand absorption of Christian ideals. True Christianity has never had a serious rival in the training of the moral sense which exists in ordinary people.

Yet there are many, even among professing Christians, who are made miserable by a morbidly developed conscience, which they quite wrongly consider to be the voice of God. Many a housewife overdrives herself to please some inner voice that demands perfection. The voice may be her own demands or the relics of childhood training, but it certainly is not likely to be the voice of the Power behind the Universe.

On the other hand, the middle-aged businessman who has long ago taught his conscience to come to heel may persuade himself that he is a good-living man. He may even say, with some pride, that he would never do anything against his conscience. But it is impossible to believe that the feeble voice of the half-blind thing which he calls a conscience is in any real sense the voice of God.

Surely neither the hectically overdeveloped nor the falsely-trained, nor the moribund conscience can ever be regarded as God, or even part of Him. For if it is, God can be made to appear to the sensitive an overexacting tyrant, and to the insensitive a comfortable accommodating "Voice Within" which would never interfere with a man's pleasure.

False Gods— Tyrannical Parent

MANY PSYCHOLOGISTS ASSURE us that the trend of the whole of a man's life is largely determined by his attitude in early years toward his parents. Many normal people, with happy childhoods behind them, may scoff at this, but nevertheless the clinics and consulting-rooms of psychiatrists are thronged with those whose inner lives were distorted in early childhood by their relationship toward their parents. Quite a lot of ordinary people, who would never dream of turning to psychiatry, nevertheless have an abnormal fear of authority, or of a dominating personality of either sex, which could without much difficulty be traced back to the tyranny of a parent. Conversely there are many who would be insulted by the name "neurotic," but who nevertheless are imperfectly adjusted to life, and whose inner sense of superiority makes them difficult to work or live with. It would again not be difficult to trace in their history a childhood of spoiling and indulgence, in which the child's natural self-love was never checked or directed outward into interest in other people. The child is truly "the father of the man."

But what has this to do with an inadequate conception of God? This, that the early conception of God is almost invariably founded upon the child's idea of his father. If he is lucky enough to have a good father this is all to the good, provided of course that the conception of God grows with the rest of his personality. But if the child is afraid (or, worse still, afraid and feeling guilty because he is afraid) of his own father, the chances are that his Father in Heaven will appear to him a fearful Being. Again, if he is lucky, he will outgrow this conception, and indeed differentiate between his early "fearful" idea and his later mature conception. But many are not able to outgrow the sense of guilt and fear, and in adult years are still obsessed with it, although it has actually nothing to do with their real relationship with the living God. It is nothing more than a parental hangover. Many priests and ministers with some knowledge of psychology will have met the person abnormally afraid of God, and will have been able to recognize the psychological, rather than the religious, significance of the fear. Some of them will have had the joy of seeing the religious faith blossom out into joy and confidence, when the psychological disharmony has been analyzed and resolved. . . . It is worth observing for the sake of those who may possibly suffer from an irrational fear of, or violent revolt from, the idea of God that the root of their trouble is probably not their "sin" or their "rebelliousness," but what they felt toward their parents when they were very young.

False Gods—
Grand Old Man

SOME SUNDAY-SCHOOL children were once asked to write down their ideas as to what God was like. The answers, with few exceptions, began something like this: "God is a very old gentleman living in Heaven . . ."! Whether this story is true or not, there is no doubt that in many children's minds God is an "old" person. This is partly due, of course, to the fact that a child's superiors are always "old" to him and God must therefore be the "oldest" of all. Moreover, a child is so frequently told that he will be able to do such-and-such a thing or understand such-and-such a matter "when he is older" that it is only natural that the Source of all strength and wisdom must seem to him very old indeed. In addition to this his mind has quite probably been filled with stories of God's activities which happened "long ago." He is in consequence quite likely to feel, and even visualize, God as someone very old.

It may be argued that there is no particular harm in this. Since the child must adapt himself to an adult world there can be nothing wrong in his concept of an "old" God. But there is nevertheless a very real danger that the child will imagine this God not merely as "old," but as "old-fashioned"; and may indeed be so impressed with God's actions in "times of old" that he may fail to grasp the idea of God operating with unimpaired energy in the present and leading forward into a hopeful future.

But even if it be admitted that to visualize God as "old"

will do a child no harm, the persistence of the idea of childhood beneath the surface of the mind may well make it difficult to develop and hold an adequate idea of God in later years. In order to test whether this "old-fashioned" concept was persisting in modern young people, a simple psychological test was recently applied to a mixed group of older adolescents. They were asked to answer, without reflection, the question, "Do you think God understands radar?" In nearly every case the reply was "No," followed of course by a laugh, as the conscious mind realized the absurdity of the answer. But, simple as this test was, it was quite enough to show that *at the back of their minds* these youngsters held an idea of God quite inadequate for modern days. Subsequent discussion showed plainly that while "they had not really thought much about it," they had freely to admit that the idea of God, absorbed some years before, existed in quite a separate compartment from their modern experience, knowledge, and outlook. It was as though they were revering the memory of a Grand Old Man, who was a great power in His day, but who could not possibly be expected to keep pace with modern progress!

False Gods—
Escape Artist

THE CRITICS OF the Christian religion have often contended that a religious faith is a form of psychological "escapism." A man, they say, finding the problems and demands of adult life too much for him will attempt to return to the comfort and dependence of childhood by picturing for himself a loving parent, whom he calls God. It must be admitted that there is a good deal of ammunition ready to hand for such an attack, and the first verse of a well-known and well-loved hymn provides an obvious example:

> Jesus, Lover of my soul,
>   Let me to Thy bosom fly,
> While the nearer waters roll,
>   While the tempest still is high:
> Hide me, O my Saviour, hide,
>   Till the storm of life be past;
> Safe into thy haven guide,
>   O receive my soul at last.

Here, if the words are taken at their face value, is sheer escapism, a deliberate desire to be hidden safe away until the storm and stress of life is over, and no explaining away by lovers of the hymn can alter its plain sense. It can hardly be denied that if this is true Christianity, then the charge of "escapism," of emotional immaturity and childish regression, must be frankly conceded. But although this "God of escape" is quite common, the true Christian course is set in a very different direction. No one would accuse its Founder of immaturity in insight, thought, teaching, or conduct, and the history of the Christian Church provides thousands of examples of timid half-developed personalities who have not only found in their faith what the psychologists call integration, but have coped with difficulties and dangers in a way that makes any gibe of "escapism" plainly ridiculous.

False Gods—
Jack in the Box

THE MAN WHO is outside all organized Christianity may have, and often does have, a certain reverence for God, and a certain genuine respect for Jesus Christ (though he has probably rarely considered Him and His claims with his adult mind). But what sticks in his throat about the Christianity of the Churches is not merely their differences in denomination, but the spirit of "churchiness" which seems to pervade them all. They seem to him to have captured and tamed and trained to their own liking Something that is really far too big ever to be forced into little man-made boxes with neat labels upon them. He may never think of putting it into words, but this is what he thinks and feels.

"If," the Churches appear to be saying to him, "you will jump through our particular hoop or sign on our particular dotted line then we will introduce you to God. But if not, then there's no God for you." This seems to him to be nonsense, and nasty arrogant nonsense at that. "If there's a God at all," he feels rather angrily, "then He's here in the home and in the street, here in the pub and in the workshop. And if it's true that He's interested in me and wants me to love and serve Him, then He's available for me and every other Tom, Dick, or Harry who wants Him, without any interference from the professionals. If God is God, He's *big*, and generous and magnificent, and I can't see that anybody can say they've made a 'corner' in God, or shut Him up in their particular box."

Of course, it is easy to leap to the defense of the Churches, and point out that every cause must be organized if it is to be effective, that every society must have its rules, that Christ Himself founded a Church, and so on. But if the Churches give the outsider the impression that God works almost exclusively through the machinery they have erected, and, what is worse, damns all other machinery which does not bear their label, then they cannot be surprised if he finds their version of God cramped and inadequate and refuses to "join their union."

False Gods— Chairman of the Board

IF A MAN is in charge of fifty other men he can fairly easily make himself familiar with the history, character, abilities, and peculiarities of each man. If he is in charge of five hundred he may still take a personal interest in each one; but it is almost impossible for him to know and retain in his memory personal details of the individual. If he is in charge of five thousand men he may in general be wise and benevolent; but he cannot, indeed he does not, attempt to know his men as individuals. The higher he is, the fewer his individual contacts. Because in our modern world we are tending more and more to see men amassed in large numbers, for various purposes, we are forced to realize that the individual care of the "one in charge" must grow less and less. This realization has permeated our unconscious minds, and we find it almost inevitably suggested to us that the Highest of All must have the fewest contacts with the individual. Indeed if He is Infinitely High the idea of contact with an infinitesimal individual becomes laughable.

But only if we are modeling God upon what we know of man. That is why it is contended here that what at first sight appears to be almost a superadequate idea of God is, in reality, inadequate—it is based on too tiny a foundation. Man may be made in the image of God; but it is not sufficient to conceive God as nothing more than an infinitely magnified man.

There are, for example, those who are considerably worried by the thought of God simultaneously hearing and answering the prayers and aspirations of people all over the world. That may be because their mental picture is of a harassed telephone operator answering callers at a switchboard of superhuman size. It is really better to say frankly, "I can't imagine how it can be done" (which is the literal truth), than to confuse the mind with the picture of an enlarged man performing the impossible.

All "lofty" concepts of the greatness of God need to be carefully watched lest they turn out to be mere magnifications of certain human characteristics. We may, for instance, admire the ascetic ultraspiritual type which appears to have "a mind above" food, sexual attraction, and material comfort, for example. But if in forming a picture of the Holiness of God we are simply enlarging this spirituality and asceticism to the "nth" degree we are forced to some peculiar conclusions. Thus we may find ourselves readily able to imagine God's interest in babies (for are they not "little bits of Heaven"?), yet unable to imagine His approval, let alone design, of the acts which led to their conception!

Similarly, it is natural and right, of course, that the worship we offer to God in public should be of the highest possible quality. But that must not lead us to conceive a musically "Third-Program" god who prefers the exquisite rendering of a cynical professional choir to the ragged bawling of sincere but untutored hearts.

To hold a conception of God as a mere magnified human being is to run the risk of thinking of Him as simply the Commander-in-Chief who cannot possibly spare the time to attend to the details of His subordinates' lives. Yet to have a god who is so far beyond personality and so far removed from the human context in which we alone can appreciate "values," is to have a god who is a mere bunch of perfect qualities—which means an Idea and nothing more. We need a God with the capacity to hold, so to speak, both Big and Small in His Mind at the same time. This, the Christian religion holds, is the true and satisfying conception of God revealed by Jesus Christ.

False Gods — The Disappointer

To SOME PEOPLE the mental image of God is a kind of blur of disappointment. "Here," they say resentfully and usually with more than a trace of self-pity, "is One whom I trusted, but He *let me down.*" The rest of their lives is consequently shadowed by this letdown. Thenceforth there can be no mention of God, Church, religion, or even parson without starting the whole process of association with its melancholy conclusion: God is a Disappointment.

Some, of course, rather enjoy this never-failing well of grievance. The years by no means dim the tragic details of the Prayer that was Unanswered or the Disaster that was Undeserved. To recall God's unfaithfulness appears to give them the same ghoulish pleasure that others find in recounting the grisly details of their "operation." Others find, of course, that a God who has Himself failed is the best possible excuse for those who do not wish to be involved in any moral effort or moral responsibility. Any suggestion of obeying or following God can be more than countered by another glance at the perennial Grievance. . . .

The people who feel that God is a Disappointment have not understood the terms on which we inhabit this planet. They are wanting a world in which good is rewarded and evil is punished—as in a well-run kindergarten. They want to see the good man prosper invariably, and the evil man suffer invariably, here and now. There is, of course, nothing wrong with their sense of justice. But they misunderstand the conditions of this present temporary life in which God withholds His Hand, in order, so to speak, to allow room for His plan of free will to work itself out. Justice will be fully vindicated when the curtain falls on the present stage, the houselights go on, and we go out into the Real World.

There will always be times when from our present limited point of view we cannot see the wood for the trees. Glaring injustice and pointless tragedy will sometimes be quite beyond our control and our understanding. We can, of course, postulate an imaginary God with less good sense, love, and justice than we have ourselves; and we may find a perverse pleasure in blaming Him. But that road leads nowhere. You cannot worship a Disappointment.

False Gods—
Narcissus on the Silver Screen

JUST AS THE cinema apparatus projects onto the screen a large image from a picture about the size of a postage stamp, so the human mind has a tendency to "project" onto other people ideas and emotions that really exist in itself. The guilty man, for example, will project onto other people suspicion and disapproval, even though they are completely ignorant of his guilt. This, of course, is an everyday psychological phenomenon.

We tend to do the same thing in our mental conception of God. . . . A harsh and puritanical society will project its dominant qualities and probably postulate a hard and puritanical god. A lax and easygoing society will probably produce a god with about as much moral authority as Father Christmas.

The same tendency is observable in individual cases. We have already noted . . . how a certain type of keen Churchman, for example, tends to produce a god of Impeccable Churchmanship. But, of course, the inclination goes farther than this, and there is always a danger of imagining a god with moral qualities like our own, vastly magnified and purified of course, and *with the same blind spots.* Thus the god whom we imagine may have his face set against drunkenness (an evil which, though it does not tempt us, fills us with horror and indignation), may turn a blind eye to our business methods because he feels, as we do, that "business is business"!

Obviously, unless the conception of God is something higher than a Magnification of our own Good Qualities, our service and worship will be no more and no less than the service and worship of ourselves. Such a god may be a prop to our self-esteem but is, naturally, incapable of assisting us to win a moral victory and will be found in time of serious need to fade disconcertingly away.

Moreover, we are so made that we cannot really be satisfied with a mere projection. Even Narcissus must at times have grown tired of admiring his own reflection! The very fact that in choosing a friend or a life-partner men frequently choose someone very different from themselves is enough to show that they are not only and forever seeking an echo of their own personalities. If we are to be moved to real worship and stirred to give of ourselves, it must be by Something not merely infinitely higher but Something "other" than ourselves. . . .

The god who is wholly, or even partially, a mere projection of ourselves is quite inadequate for life's demands and can never arouse in us true worship or service. Indeed he is as real a danger as the pool became at last to Narcissus.

False Gods— Olympic Sprinter

IF THERE IS one thing which should be quite plain to those who accept the revelation of God in Nature and the Bible it is that He is never in a hurry. Long preparation, careful planning, and slow growth would seem to be leading characteristics of spiritual life. Yet there are many people whose religious tempo is feverish. With a fine disregard for its context they flourish like a banner the text, "The King's business requireth haste," and proceed to drive themselves and their followers nearly mad with tension and anxiety! "Consider," cries the passionate advocate of foreign missions, "that every second, thousands of pagan souls pass into a Christless eternity." "Evangelize to a finish in this generation!" cries the enthusiastic young convert at his missionary meeting.

It is refreshing, and salutary, to study the poise and quietness of Christ. His task and responsibility might well have driven a man out of his mind. But He was never in a hurry, never impressed by numbers, never a slave of the clock. He was acting, He said, as He observed God to act— never in a hurry.

False Gods— Mystical Vision

IT IS CHARACTERISTIC of human beings to create and revere a "privileged class," and some modern Christians regard the mystic as being somehow spiritually a cut above his fellows. Ordinary forms of worship and prayer may suffice for the ordinary man, but for the one who has direct apprehension of God—he is literally in a class by himself. You cannot expect a man to attend Evensong in his parish church when there are visions waiting for him in his study!

The New Testament does not subscribe to this flattering view of those with a gift for mystic vision. It is always downright and practical. It is by their fruits that men shall be known: God is no respecter of persons: true religion is expressed by such humdrum things as visiting those in trouble and steadfastly maintaining faith despite exterior circumstances. It is not, of course, that the New Testament considers it a bad thing for a man to have a vision of God, but there is a wholesome insistence on such a vision being worked out in love and service.

It should be noted, at least by those who accept Christ's claim to be God, that He by no means fits into the picture of the "mystic saint." Those who are fascinated by the supposed superiority of the mystic soul might profitably compile a list of its characteristics and place them side by side with those of Christ. The result would probably expose a surprising conclusion.

There is, in fact, no provision for a "privileged class" in genuine Christianity. "It shall not be so among you," said Christ to His early followers, "all ye are brethren."

False Gods—the Ultimate Bundle of Highest Values

THIS CONCEPTION IS one of the most "enlightened" and "modern." God is completely depersonalized and becomes the Ultimate Bundle of Highest Values. Such an idea is usually held by those who lead sheltered lives and who have little experience of the crude stuff of ordinary human life. It is manifestly impossible for any except the most intellectual to hold in his mind (let alone worship and serve) a God who is no more than what we think to be the highest values raised to the "nth" degree.

False Gods—
Idol of the Worshipping Animal

MAN HAS RIGHTLY been defined as a "worshipping animal." If for some reason he has no God, he will unquestionably worship *something*. Common modern substitutes are the following: the State, success, efficiency, money, "glamor," power, even security. Nobody, of course, calls them "God"; but they have the influence and command the devotion which should belong to the real God. It is only when a man finds God that he is able to see how his worshipping instinct has been distorted and misdirected.

Four Prophets

I CHOSE THESE PROPHETS, Amos, Hosea, Isaiah, and Micah, partly because the period of their ministry was such a crucial time in the history of God's chosen people; and partly because they pierce through a great many falsities (including religious falsities). Time and again they touch the very heart of the matter—the way in which men behave toward each other and the way in which they worship God; and all of these prophets can see that those two things are inseparable. They are thus, as it were, clearing the ground for the revolutionary teaching that was to come with the Gospel of Jesus Christ.

The people of Israel had never been so affluent as they were when Amos attempted rudely to awaken them. But with prosperity had come inhumanity to man—"the rich got rich and the poor got poorer"—and the worship of the false gods of riches, success, and security. Moral values had slumped and even common honesty and decent neighborliness were being squeezed out by greed and corruption. These four prophets could clearly see this galloping spiritual deterioration, and they not only denounced it but declared in no uncertain terms the consequences of moral and social evil. As prophets they "saw the truth," and as prophets they were constrained to declare what they saw. They were not necessarily foretelling the future, although history proves what remarkably accurate prophets they were in that sense, but they had to warn, even in the most terrifying terms, a people grown deaf and blind to the truth.

All of these prophetic books include what we might call, if we only read superficially, "a happy ending." But this is because the prophets could see far ahead. As in the "apocalyptic" passages in the synoptic Gospels, or in the Revelation of St. John the Divine, the earthly time-sense is in abeyance. Immediate future and far distant future are equally in focus. I do not myself see any cogent reason for supposing that these visions of a later people returning purified to their own land must be the work "of a later hand." If these prophets could see, with remarkable accuracy, what lay a few years ahead, why not a few hundred or a few thousand years?

But despite their visions, or, if we think more deeply, perhaps because of them, these proclaimers of the truth are solidly down to earth. They will not permit religion to exist in a vacuum. Unless man's worship of God is matched by his just and fair treatment of his neighbor, then ceremonies, rituals, observances, and sacrifices are nauseating to God. And they are highly dangerous to the worshipper because he is attempting to stifle his moral and social conscience by all the "business" of religion. He is, in fact, attempting to bribe God. This is what moves all of these prophets, in their different ways, to such violent indignation.

This declaration of the indissoluble connection between the way in which we love God and the way in which we love our neighbor seems to me unique in the religions of the ancient world. Many religions, though not all, have taught mankind to be merciful and charitable, but the Hebrew prophets are, I believe, alone in declaring the uses of religion to be entirely null and void unless men are treating their fellow men with mercy and justice. To a prophet of the caliber of these men it is not enough to drop a coin into the beggar's palm; you must ask yourself, *"How far am I responsible for his being a beggar at all?"* And this is a thoroughly relevant question today.

This marriage of the love of God and the love of man was the backbone of Christ's teaching seven hundred years later. Sometimes I think we forget that he taught quite categorically that we cannot be forgiven by God unless we also forgive those who injure or offend us. And perhaps not enough notice is taken of the only picture Christ ever painted of the Last Judgment, recorded in the twenty-fifth chapter of St. Matthew's Gospel. Here it is most plainly stated that the way we treat our fellows is an exact replica of the way in which we are treating the Son of God himself— surely a piercing and devastating truth if ever there was one! I am myself not overblessed with a historical sense, but I am amazed that these bold men were declaring such vital truth in the days of Homer, long before the heyday of Athens, and when Rome, the so-called "eternal city," was little more than a village.

Despite the distance in time, the frequent unfamiliarity of

idiom and the imperfect state of the Hebrew text, these four men speak with uncommon authority. All four strongly convey the sense that they are seeing the truth about God and man. There is something peculiarly compelling about men who have the deepest possible reverence for God and yet can say, "This is what the Lord says."

In these books there are some crude anthropomorphisms which offend our modern minds, and, naturally, the conception of God is a pre-Christian one. Nevertheless we are left with an overwhelming conviction that God is God, right is right, and wrong is wrong; and that in itself is an iron tonic to us moderns. For most of us today are afraid of denouncing evil for fear of being called intolerant; we are not allowed to be morally indignant for "psychology says" that what is making us angry is an identical fault in ourselves! We are not allowed to have any definite values of right and wrong, for all things, we are told, are purely relative— though relative to *what* is not made clear. In these days we can scarcely spare a thought for the victim of vicious assault, for all our sympathy is needed for the brutal and callous aggressor. We are frightened of sharing our faith with a fellow human being for fear of interfering with the sanctity of his private beliefs; we are even scared of living out the principles of the Gospel lest we are labeled contemptuously as "do-gooders."

But here in this world of nearly three thousand years ago human beings are far less self-conscious. They can be noble, wise, brave, and good, but they can also be cruel, stupid, greedy, fickle, or just plain wicked. We are back in a world of real people, potentially sons and daughters of the Most High, but making tragically wrong choices and treating each other abominably. But these four prophets assume always that men have consciences and that they have the power to choose their path. If they are beyond the reach of messages of sweetness and light, then violent, indeed terrifying, threats and warnings must be used to crack their dreadful complacency.

These men were not in the least concerned to make their message "acceptable." They were not out to placate the people in power or to conciliate the clever; their whole purpose was to speak "the word of the Lord." Such voices of integrity, despite all the obscurities and difficulties of the text, still sound like a trumpet down the centuries.

It seems to me (and Heaven knows any honest man can observe this in his own spirit) that human beings are forever trying to evade moral responsibility, while God is eternally trying to make them accept it, and thus grow up into being His sons. Because of this human tendency the world of the Bible is bound to be an uncomfortable world. For here God, not man, is master. Here God speaks and man, if he is wise, will listen with a proper humility.

The Visited Planet

ONCE UPON A TIME a very young angel was being shown round the splendors and glories of the universes by a senior and experienced angel. To tell the truth, the little angel was beginning to be tired and a little bored. He had been shown whirling galaxies and blazing suns, infinite distances in the deathly cold of interstellar space, and to his mind there seemed to be an awful lot of it all. Finally he was shown the galaxy of which our planetary system is but a small part. As the two of them drew near to the star which we call our sun and to its circling planets, the senior angel pointed to a small and rather insignificant sphere turning very slowly on its axis. It looked as dull as a dirty tennis ball to the little angel whose mind was filled with the size and glory of what he had seen.

"I want you to watch that one particularly," said the senior angel, pointing with his finger.

"Well, it looks very small and rather dirty to me," said the little angel. "What's special about that one?"

"That," replied his senior solemnly, "is the Visited Planet."

" 'Visited'?" said the little one. "You don't mean visited by—"

"Indeed I do. That ball, which I have no doubt looks to you small and insignificant and perhaps not overclean, has been visited by our young Prince of Glory." And at these words he bowed his head reverently.

"But how?" queried the younger one. "Do you mean that our great and glorious Prince, with all these wonders and splendors of His Creation, and millions more that I'm sure I haven't seen yet, went down in Person to this fifth-rate little ball? Why should He do a thing like that?"

"It isn't for us," said his senior, a little stiffly, "to question His 'why's,' except that I must point out to you that He is not impressed by size and numbers as you seem to be. But that He really went I know, and all of us in Heaven who know anything know that. As to why He became one of them . . . how else do you suppose could He visit them?"

The little angel's face wrinkled in disgust.

"Do you mean to tell me," he said, "that He stooped so low as to become one of those creeping, crawling creatures of that floating ball?"

"I do, and I don't think He would like you to call them 'creeping crawling creatures' in that tone of voice. For, strange as it may seem to us, He loves them. He went down to visit them to lift them up to become like Him."

The little angel looked blank. Such a thought was almost beyond his comprehension.

"Close your eyes for a moment," said the senior angel, "and we will go back in what they call Time."

While the little angel's eyes were closed and the two of them moved nearer to the spinning ball, it stopped its spinning, spun backward quite fast for a while, and then slowly resumed its usual rotation.

"Now look!" and as the little angel did as he was told, there appeared here and there on the dull surface of the globe little flashes of light, some merely momentary and some persisting for quite a time.

"Well, what am I seeing now?" queries the little angel.

"You are watching this little world as it was some thousands of years ago," returned his companion. "Every flash and glow of light that you see is something of the Father's knowledge and wisdom breaking into the minds and hearts of people who live upon the earth. Not many people, you see, can hear His Voice or understand what He says, even though He is speaking gently and quietly to them all the time."

"Why are they so blind and deaf and stupid?" asked the junior angel rather crossly.

"It is not for us to judge them. We who live in the Splendor have no idea what it is like to live in the dark. We hear the music and the Voice like the sound of many waters every day of our lives, but to them—well, there is much darkness and much noise and much distraction upon the earth. Only a few who are quiet and humble and wise hear His Voice. But watch, for in a moment you will see something truly wonderful."

The Earth went on turning and circling round the sun, and then, quite suddenly, in the upper half of the globe there appeared a light, tiny, but so bright in its intensity that both the angels hid their eyes.

"I think I can guess," said the little angel in a low voice. "That was the Visit, wasn't it?"

"Yes, that was the Visit. The Light Himself went down there and lived among them; but in a moment, and you will be able to tell that even with your eyes closed, the light will go out."

"But why? Could He not bear their darkness and stupidity? Did He have to return here?"

"No, it wasn't that," returned the senior angel. His voice was stern and sad. "They failed to recognize Him for Who He was—or at least only a handful knew Him. For the most part they preferred their darkness to His Light, and in the end they killed Him."

"The fools, the crazy fools! They don't deserve—"

"Neither you nor I nor any other angel knows why they were so foolish and so wicked. Nor can we say what they deserve or don't deserve. But the fact remains, they killed our Prince of Glory while He was Man amongst them."

"And that, I suppose, was the end? I see the whole Earth has gone black and dark. All right, I won't judge them, but surely that is all they could expect?"

"Wait. We are still far from the end of the story of the Visited Planet. Watch now, but be ready to cover your eyes again."

In utter blackness the Earth turned round three times, and then there blazed with unbearable radiance a point of light.

"What now?" asked the little angel, shielding his eyes.

"They killed Him, all right, but He conquered death. The thing most of them dread and fear all their lives He broke and conquered. He rose again, and a few of them saw Him, and from then on became His utterly devoted slaves."

"Thank God for that!" said the little angel.

"Amen. Open your eyes now; the dazzling light has gone. The Prince has returned to His Home of Light. But watch the Earth now."

As they looked, in place of the dazzling light there was a

bright glow which throbbed and pulsated. And then as the Earth turned many times, little points of light spread out. A few flickered and died, but for the most part the lights burned steadily, and as they continued to watch, in many parts of the globe there was a glow over many areas.

"You see what is happening?" asked the senior angel. "The bright glow is the company of loyal men and women He left behind, and with His help they spread the glow, and now lights begin to shine all over the Earth."

"Yes, yes," said the little angel impatiently. "But how does it end? Will the little lights join up with one another? Will it all be light, as it is in Heaven?"

His senior shook his head. "We simply don't know," he replied. "It is in the Father's hands. Sometimes it is agony to watch, and sometimes it is joy unspeakable. The end is not yet. But now I am sure you can see why this little ball is so important. He has visited it; He is working out His Plan upon it."

"Yes, I see, though I don't understand. I shall never forget that this is the Visited Planet. . . ."

Jesus' Strength as a Man

WHAT HAPPENED TO me as [my translation of the Gospels] progressed was that the figure of Jesus emerged more and more clearly, and in a way unexpectedly. Of course I had a deep respect, indeed a great reverence, for the conventional Jesus Christ whom the Church worshipped. But I was not at all prepared for the *unconventional* man revealed in those terse Gospels. No one could possibly have invented such a person: this was no puppet-hero built out of the imagina-

tions of adoring admirers. "This man Jesus," so briefly described, rang true, sometimes alarmingly true. I began to
see now why the religious establishment of those days
wanted to get rid of him at all costs. He was sudden death
to pride, pomposity, and pretence.

This man could be moved with compassion and could be
very gentle, but I could find no trace of the "Gentle Jesus,
meek and mild." He was quite terrifyingly tough, not in a
Bulldog Drummond-James Bond sort of way, but by the
sheer strength of a unified and utterly dedicated personality. He once (at least) walked unscathed through a murder-
ous crowd. I have known a few—a very, very few—men
who could do that. But then I find that this sheer strength
was still his after hours of unspeakable agony in the garden
of Gethsemane. Those who were sent to arrest him "fell
back to the ground." Previous pious generations attribute
this to some supernatural power. I do not believe this for a
moment. Jesus was a man of such complete authority that
he could remain in command of a situation even when the
odds were heavily against him.

It was this strength of human character which struck me
again and again. We are not being told of a superman but of
someone supremely human. He could work so hard that his
followers begged him to stop. Yet he was fast asleep aboard
the little fishing boat while the others did the rowing. He
was awake and out praying in solitude while the others
were asleep, yet there were times when he was tired.
"Jesus, being wearied with his journey, sat down beside a
well," records John. He touched the untouchable leper, he
made friends with those who had lost their reputation and
self-respect. He denounced in vitriolic words the leaders of
so-called religion. He spoke fearlessly to the violently in-
sane. He wept in the presence of human sorrow. He also
wept over Jerusalem because its people utterly failed to recognize God's Messiah when he taught and preached among

them, and also because, with the true prophet's insight, he foresaw the city's hideous destruction. With even a little imaginative sympathy one could sense the agony of his frustration and near-despair. For the first time it seemed to me that it was because he was a human being almost at the end of his tether that this man cursed a fig tree and then in the garden called for swords instead of cloaks. He admitted that he was terrified as he went into the garden of Gethsemane, and he sweated there in fear and anguish.

The record of the behavior of Jesus on the way to the Cross and of the Crucifixion itself is almost unbearable, chiefly because it is so intensely *human*. If, as I believe, this was indeed God focused in a human being, we can see for ourselves that here is no play acting, this is the real thing. There are no supernatural advantages for this man. No celestial rescue party delivered him from the power of evil men, and his agony was not mitigated by any superhuman anesthetic. We can only guess what frightful anguish of mind and spirit wrung from him the terrible words, "My God, my God, why hast thou forsaken me?" But the cry "It is finished!" cannot be one of despair. It does not even mean, "It is all over." It means, "It has been completed"—and the terrifying task of doing God's will to the bitter end had been fully and finally accomplished.

Here, in the four Gospels, fragmentary as they sometimes are, emerges a real man, whose perfect integrity is compelling. He "spoke with authority," and "the common people heard him gladly," and even at the end of his public career, those who were sent to arrest him returned empty handed. "Never man spake like this man," was their comment.

But it would be a profound mistake to think that Jesus was merely an eloquent field preacher who had got on the wrong side of authority. His character was strange and unpredictable. He was meek in the way that only the strong can truly be, yet he called, demanded, and commanded without explanation or apology. What other man could call some fishermen to leave their skilled jobs or ask somebody else to give up the lucrative, even though despised, work of tax collecting and to follow him, and succeed? What other man could look straight at a ring of hostile faces and throw out the challenge, "Which of you convinces me of sin?" and yet give no impression of arrogance or self-righteousness?

Yet the flashes of light upon this character which the four Gospels reveal are often surprising. Jesus was not some penniless ascetic like John the Baptist before him. Luke records that there were many women who "ministered to him of their substance." We may be pretty sure that the house of Mary and Martha was not the only home where he could find rest and refreshment. His cloak, "woven without seam," was hardly the covering of a beggar. There can be no doubt that he was socially popular, and although we can discount the jibe that he was "a gluttonous man and a wine bibber," we can fairly infer that he enjoyed God's good gifts of food and wine.

It struck me again and again that some of the unexpected sayings and actions of Jesus were recorded just because they were unexpected. The routine work (if we might so describe it) is sometimes dismissed in a few words—"he went about doing good and healing all manner of sickness and disease among the people." But the other words and works, which no one could have anticipated, and which must have been nearly inexplicable at the time, are treasured and remembered with the utmost fidelity.

Yet woe betide any man who tries to fit this man into any political or humanitarian slot! Those pacifists who would claim him as their champion would do well to remember that it was a soldier, a Roman commissioned officer, who most evoked the admiration of Jesus. The parable of the talents is enough to show that Jesus recognized the fundamental *inequality* of men in ability and possessions. The stories of Jesus abound in such inequalities, in the difference between master and man, hard working and lazy, prudent and improvident. It is true that he denounced hypocrisy, exploitation, and lack of compassion. But he made no attempt, as probably Judas Iscariot hoped, to make himself a national champion. The "other-worldly" aspect of his teaching cannot be fairly ignored. "My kingdom," he insisted, "is not of this world." Yet it had already "come upon men unawares" and was even then "among" or "within" them. The way men treated one another in this world was of paramount importance, but Jesus recognized the obvious unfairness and injustice in the here-and-now. In the end, justice would be done and be seen to be done, but not in this time-and-space world. Jesus was no sentimental "do-gooder," and he spoke quite unequivocally about rewards and punishments "in the world to come." He declared that a man who harmed one of his "little ones" would be better off dead. Some of the most terrifying words ever written in the New Testament are put into the mouth of Jesus. Yet they are not threats or menaces but warnings given in deadly earnest by the incarnation of unsentimental love.

What I am concerned with here is not to write a new life of Jesus, but to set down my witness to the continued shocks which his words and deeds gave me as I approached the Gospels uninsulated by the familiar cover of beautiful language. The figure who emerged is quite unlike the Jesus of conventional piety, and even more unlike that imagined hero whom members of various causes claim as their champion. What we are so often confronted with today is a "processed" Jesus. Every element that we feel is not consonant with our "image" of him is removed, and the result is more insipid and unsatisfying than the worst of processed food.

Jesus' Miracles

IN THE PROCESS of translation, a definite and indeed authoritative human character emerged from the combined writings of the Evangelists. This man Jesus was much more of a human being than I had previously thought. I suppose that somewhere in the recesses of my mind I had stored a mixed-up impression of a being of supernatural perfection and certain supernatural powers. I believed, and indeed still do believe, that Jesus was both God and man. But the conclusion grew upon me that the Jesus of the Gospels really *was* man, not a demigod and certainly not God playing, however convincingly, the part of man. I have written of the mental and spiritual toughness which coexisted in Jesus with extraordinary sympathy and compassion. So that when I came to the "miracles" of the Gospels I did not find in them anything incompatible with his character or his declared mission. They did not give me the impression of being celestial conjuring tricks designed to produce faith. Indeed the records insist that Jesus did not want publicity for his acts of physical or mental healing. I think it is difficult for us today to appreciate the spiritual power of a man uniquely integrated and dedicated, and who spent many hours in solitary communion with God. The sense grew upon me with the years that such a man, so toughened and disciplined in following the path laid out for him by his Father, might quite easily possess qualities of insight into the cause of a man's sickness, as well as the power to make him whole. Again, we need not quarrel with the picture language. To those who saw the outward manifestations of an epileptic or some mental disorder which made a man violently destructive, it was not unnatural to think of him as possessing or being possessed by "a devil." Indeed those of us who have ever been in the presence of the violently deranged and looked into their eyes could easily agree that some evil power appears to be possessing the patient. It seems that Jesus was in many cases able to get to the storm center of the disturbance and resolve it with authoritative love. We do not know even yet how far the mind affects the body or the body the mind, or how far either of them are influenced by spiritual power—by intercessory prayer, for example. We know how to "cure" certain diseases with fair accuracy, but what we are really doing is removing the obstacles which are preventing a natural ability to heal itself which both the human body and mind possess. It does not seem to me in the least unreasonable that a man of concentrated spiritual power should be able to remove these obstacles instantaneously. The whole business of "spiritual" healing is a much debated one, and I do not propose to enter any controversy here. I am simply concerned to record my own conviction that the miracles of healing which Jesus performed were perfectly genuine, even though they may be described in the jargon of the day.

This brings me to another important point. What we read in the Gospels is, I believe, true, but it is not necessarily described in words which we should use today, nearly two thousand years afterwards. A simple example springs to mind. In the three hours of darkness which fell over the whole countryside at the crucifixion of Jesus, Luke says that the sun's light failed, using the very Greek word which we use when we talk about an eclipse. Luke gives me the impression of being a very careful writer who, to use our modern phrase, would "interview" people about what they remembered of the life and teaching of Jesus. Now *we* know that there could not have been an eclipse of the sun, because that cannot happen at the time of the full moon, which was when Jesus died. We do not know whether Luke himself knew this. But since he records the failure of the sun's light and goes on to describe the dismay and confusion it caused (for men had no means of telling that the unnatural event was to last no more than three hours), it is perfectly possible that an eyewitness of that eerie darkness at noon might well have described it to Luke as an eclipse of the sun. We may never know in this life the cause of the phenomenon, but I believe that it happened, and as a Christian I believe it to be a singularly impressive reflection in the natural world of what was happening on the Cross.

To me this applies to any of the "miracles" of Jesus. Whether we one day know the laws of the spiritual sphere in which he was moving or not, I believe that the Evangelists were setting down in terms of their own time what they actually observed. I am not therefore particularly worried when Mark reports that at the baptism of Jesus he (Jesus), "saw the heavens split open, and the Spirit coming down upon him like a dove. A voice came out of Heaven, saying, 'You are my dearly beloved Son, in whom I am well pleased!' " (Mark 1:10–11). Whether Jesus alone saw this sight and heard these words, and later told his disciples about the occurrence, or whether there were those of sufficient spiritual perception to see and hear what happened, I do not know. For myself, I believe it happened, but whether I should have heard any voice or seen anything beyond a flash of light is naturally open to question. It is very interesting to find that in John's Gospel, where a "voice from heaven" speaks to Jesus shortly before his suffering and death, John records, "When the crowd of bystanders heard this, they said it thundered, but some of them said, 'An angel spoke to him' " (John 12:29). What then, I am concerned about is my conviction that many extraordinary events accompanied the life of Jesus, but they are necessarily described in the language of those who were eyewitnesses.

There is a good deal in the New Testament about light and darkness, and I think we should constantly remind ourselves to what an extent we take artificial light for granted. Most of us live within touch of an electric light switch, many of us live in cities and towns whose streets and houses are illuminated, and the electric torch operated by a battery is a commonplace almost all over the world. But in the world of the first century A.D. light created a much greater impression of divine presence or divine happening than speed or size or physical power, which are the things which impress many of us today. The story of the Transfiguration is a particularly good example of this. The dazzling brightness of both the face of Jesus and his clothes filled Peter, James, and John with exalted awe. I find this story interesting for another reason. Peter, James, and John described what they saw, and they observed Moses and Elijah talking to Jesus. It seems to me it would be quite possible to relate the incident in a different way. Suppose that the limitations of time and earthly life were, so to speak, momentarily fixed. Peter, James, and John would then see Jesus radiantly bright, talking without the sightest sense of anachronism with the two men of the past who represented the Law and the prophets. Thus one could say not so much that Jesus was transfigured but that the disciples were temporary relieved of their earth-blindness. It must have been an ecstatic experience and one which Peter, quite understandably, but in a rather clumsy way, wanted to prolong. Once again, to me it bears the hallmark of a true happening, however shortly and naively described.

Jesus' Prophecy

CLOSELY ALLIED TO the miraculous elements in the life of Jesus is the authentic note of prophecy. Most people who know the Bible at all know that prophecy does not necessarily mean foretelling the future, although it may well include it. I have so far only made one excursion into the world of the Old Testament [*Four Prophets*] but a close study of the prophets' message shows that such men are primarily concerned to declare the "Word of the Lord." They saw, sometimes with startling and heartbreaking clarity, what would be bound to happen if the nation continued on a course contrary to the will of the Lord. The time sense was temporarily suspended, there is a dramatic "foreshortening" of things which were to come. More frequently than not, their vision was astonishingly accurate, even though twenty or a hundred years might elapse before what they foresaw came true. Their messages were "early warnings" rather than long-term threats. Prophecy is not necessarily prediction. For the warning contained in the vision might lead to a change of heart, and therefore of subsequent events.

I found this same prophetic note in the teaching of Jesus as recorded by the first three Evangelists. At first I was tempted to think that various warnings of persecution and trouble in the future made by Jesus at different times had been put by some first-century Christian Jew into the accepted apocalyptic form. Certainly there is a marked change of key; Jesus is not now giving definite teaching or even speaking in parables; he is speaking as the prophets spoke. He was, of course, on intimate terms with the prophetic writings of the Old Testament, and he must have known the special form in which much of that prophecy is set. So I came to change my view, and I believe now that there were times when Jesus, probably to the inner circle of the disciples, shared his insights about the future in the prophetic idiom which they would to some extent understand. He knew that terrible persecutions would follow his death, he could foresee the wars and famines, the terrible sufferings which were to befall humanity. He could see "men's hearts failing them for fear" as they saw the inevitable approach of terrible destruction. He also spoke of his own "coming" as being as unexpected as a thief in the night but as unmistakably conspicuous as a flash of lightning. He spoke of himself as "coming" to judge the world. He wondered whether there would still be "faith" in the world when he should finally come. He knew how men's faith in God can be eroded by the anxieties and the many apparent injustices as well as by the present prosperity of evil. "Because iniquity shall abound, the love of many shall wax cold" (Matthew 24:12).

What Jesus Says About the Character of God

WHAT SORT OF person is God? Christ's answer is quite unequivocal. He is "the Father." When we hear this familiar truth we nearly always read back into God's Character what we know of fatherhood. This is understandable enough, but it reverses the actual truth. If God is "the Father," in Nature and Character and Operation, then we derive (if we are parents) our characteristics from Him. We are reproducing, no doubt on a microscopic scale and in a thoroughly faulty manner, something of the Character of God. If once we accept it as true that the whole Power behind this astonishing Universe is of that kind of character that Christ could only describe as "Father," the whole of life is transfigured. If we are really seeing in human relationships fragmentary and faulty but real reflections of the Nature of God, a flood of light is immediately released upon all the life that we can see. People and our relationships with them at once become of tremendous importance. Much of life is seen to be merely its setting, its stage, its "props"—the *business* of it is in the realm of personality; it is people not things that matter. It is thus quite impossible to divorce Christianity from life. Those who attempted to divorce the religion of their day from ordinary life were called by Christ, "play-actors" (hypocrites), i.e., they were acting a part and not really living at all.

What Jesus Says About the Purpose of Life

WHAT IS THE purpose of life? Christ did not give an answer to this question in its modern cynical form which implies, "Is it worth living at all?"; but He did answer those who wanted to know what to do with the vitality, affections, and talents with which they were endowed. He also answered those who already saw intuitively that this present life was transitory and incomplete and wanted to know how to be incorporated into the main timeless Stream of Life itself. The questions are really much the same. In both cases men wanted to know how they could be at one with Life's real purpose. And of course they still do. He said that there were really two main principles of living on which all true morality and wisdom might be said to depend. The first was to love God with the whole of a man's personality, and the second to love his fellow men as much and in the same way as he naturally loved himself. If these two principles were obeyed Christ said that a man would be in harmony with the Purpose of Life, which transcends time.

These two principles, one of which deals with the Invisible and Unchanging, the other with the visible and variable, cover the total relationships of a man's life. Christ made them intensely practical and indissolubly connected. The expression of love for God did not lie in formal piety nor in mystical contemplation, but in obedience to what He believed to be the will of God, which very often meant, in fact, the succoring and service of other men. A man could not be "friends with" God on any other terms than complete obedience to Him, and that included being "friends with" his fellow men. Christ stated emphatically that it was quite impossible in the nature of things for a man to be at peace with God and at variance with his neighbor. This disquieting fact is often hushed up, but it is undeniable that Christ said it, and the truth of it is enshrined (or should we say more properly embalmed) in the petition for forgiveness in the all-too-familiar "Lord's Prayer."

The Purpose of Life would seem to be the gradual winning of men to a willing loyalty to these two principles, the establishing of the Rule of God. Christ labeled the first one "primary and most important," probably because unless principles and values are first established by loving the true God there will not be "enough love to go round." The world would go on loving its own selected circle, despising, exploiting, or hating those outside it unless their hearts were first attuned to "the Father." Those who have exalted the second principle to the neglect of the first have again and again proved the wisdom of Christ's choice of their order.

What Jesus Says About Pride, Self-Righteousness, and the Exploitation of Others

WHAT IS REALLY wrong with the world? This is an extremely important question if only because it is asked so often and answered in so many different ways. Christ answered it, not directly, but quite plainly by implication. It is here, in diagnosis, that it is perhaps most important of all to realize the paramount authority of what Christ said. None of us thinks or speaks or feels without bias, and all of us are prone to fit facts to a theory. Christ had no bias and no theory: He came to give us the facts, and they are quite plainly, that this "power-to-love" which He recommended should be expended on God and other people, has been turned in on itself. The basic problems of happiness are not intellectual, but emotional. It is "out of the heart," according to Christ, that there proceed all those things which spoil relationships whether between individuals or between groups of people.

It is obvious, if we accept Christ's two great principles, that "sin" will lie in the refusal to follow them. To Christ the most serious sin was not the misdirection of the love-energy, which might be due to ignorance or mere carelessness, but the deliberate refusal to allow it to flow out either to God or to other people. This accounts for some of His surprising reversals of conventional and moral judgment. It was pride and self-righteousness and the exploitation of others which called forth His greatest anger. Self-love in fact He saw as the arch enemy. It was this which must be recognized and deliberately killed if a man were to follow His way of constructive love.

A few moments' thought will show us how true was His insight. While there is no "sin" that we can name which does not spring from love of self, yet the sins which do most damage and cause most suffering are those which have the highest content of self-love.

Christ's time, in the circumstances, was short and He wasted none of it in dealing with mere symptoms. It was with the motive and attitude of the heart, i.e., the emotional center, that He was concerned. It was this that He called on men to change, for it is plain that once the inner affections are aligned with God the outward expression of the life will look after itself.

What Jesus Says About Beatitudes and Non-Beatitudes

WHAT SORT OF people does God intend men to be? To this question Christ gave an explicit answer which, if considered seriously, is a real shock to the mind. He gave a complete reversal of conventional values and ambitions, though many people miss this undoubted fact because of the poetic form and archaic language of what are now called the "Beatitudes." This revolutionary character becomes apparent at once, however, if we substitute the word "happy" for the word "blessed" (which is perfectly fair), and if we paraphrase the familiar cadences of the Authorized Version and put the thoughts more into the form in which we normally accept facts and definitions. We may further throw their real character into relief by contrasting each "beatitude" with the normal view of the man of the world throughout the centuries. We can do it like this:

Most people think:

> Happy are the pushers: for they get on in the world.
> Happy are the hard-boiled: for they never let life hurt them.
> Happy are they who complain: for they get their own way in the end.
> Happy are the blasé: for they never worry over their sins.
> Happy are the slave drivers: for they get results.
> Happy are the knowledgeable men of the world: for they know their way around.
> Happy are the troublemakers: for people have to take notice of them.

Jesus Christ said:

> Happy are those who realize their spiritual poverty: they have already entered the kingdom of Reality.
> Happy are they who bear their share of the world's pain: in the long run they will know more happiness than those who avoid it.
> Happy are those who accept life and their own limitations: they will find more in life than anybody.
> Happy are those who are ready to make allowances and to forgive: they will know the love of God.
> Happy are those who are real in their thoughts and feelings: in the end they will see the ultimate Reality, God.
> Happy are those who help others to live together: they will be known to be doing God's work.

It is quite plain that Christ is setting up ideals of different quality from those commonly accepted. He is outlining the sort of human characteristics which may fairly be said to be cooperating with the purpose of Life, and He is by implication exposing the conventional mode of living which is at heart based on self-love and leads to all kinds of unhappiness.

It should be noticed that this "recipe" for happy and constructive living is of universal application. It cuts across differences of temperament and variations in capacity. It outlines the kind of character which is possible for *any* man, gifted or relatively ungifted, strong or weak, clever or slow in the uptake. Once more we find Christ placing His finger not upon the externals, but upon the vital internal attitude.

It should also be noted that although we have called His definitions "revolutionary" they are not fanatic. Indeed a great many people would probably realize that in following them men would become their real selves and not the greedy, competitive, self-loving characters that cause so many of the world's troubles. Christ is restoring the true order, which man can recognize as true. He is not imposing a set of arbitrary regulations.

What Jesus Says About Pain and Disease, Injustice and Evil

WHAT ARE WE to make of pain and disease, injustice and evil? We find Christ accepting these things, which many people advance as the greatest hindrance to religious faith, as part of the stuff of life. He did not pretend that they do not exist: He coped with them personally by restoring, wherever possible, the true order of health, sanity, and constructive goodness. He made no promise that those who followed him in His plan of re-establishing life on its proper basic principles would enjoy special immunity from pain and sorrow—nor did He himself experience such immunity. He did, however, promise enough joy and courage, enough love and confidence in God to enable those who went His way to do far more than survive. Because they would be in harmony with the very Life and Spirit of God they would be able to defeat evil. They would be able to take the initiative and destroy evil with good.

Although Christ gave no explicit explanation of the existence of pain and evil in the world, He gave certain implied facts which are well worth our serious consideration.

1. The "breaking of the rules" means suffering. The operation of self-love on a huge scale, which means a wholesale breaking of His two fundamental rules for human life, cannot but mean a highly complex and widespread "infection" of suffering. Men are not isolated units and their every action in some degree affects other people. The multiplication of the effects of countless acts by millions of self-centered, instead of God-centered, individuals may reasonably be thought to be destroying the world. The only way of being rescued from the vicious sin-suffering-death circle in which the world is involved is for men to re-center their lives on God. This they can do by deliberately giving their confidence to the Character which Christ exhibited in person and thereby seeing that real living, in harmony with God, lies in following Him and His basic principles.

There is thus no easy answer to the evil and suffering problem and no easy road to its solution. But Christ tackled the matter radically and realistically by winning the allegiance of a few men and women to a new way of living. Most people, he said, were drifting along the broad road of conventional standards which has in it the threat of destruction. The narrow road of following the basic rules which, because it is in harmony with God, is not affected by what we call death, was being followed by comparatively few. His plan of rescue (or salvation, to use a much misused word) had to begin with a tiny minority. They were to be the spearhead of good against evil.

2. Christ definitely spoke of a power of spiritual evil, and, using the language of His contemporaries, He called this power "Satan," "the Devil," or "the Evil One." Now whatever mystery lies behind the existence of such an evil spiritual power—whether we accept a Miltonic idea of a fallen angelic power or whether we conceive the evil spirit in the world as arising out of the cumulative effects of centuries of selfish living—there can be no blinking the fact that Christ spoke, and acted, on the assumption that there is a power of evil operating in the world. If we accept as fact His claim to be God this must make us think seriously.

We are so accustomed by modern thought to regard evil as "error," as the "growing pains" of civilization, or simply as an inexplicable problem, that once more the mind does not readily accept what is in effect God's own explanation—that there is a spirit of evil operating in the world. We find Christ speaking quite plainly of this spirit as responsible for disease and insanity as well as being the unremitting enemy of those who want to follow the new, true order.

Modern man has a lust for full explanation and habitually considers himself in no way morally bound unless he is in full possession of all the facts. Hence, of course, the prevalence of noncommittal agnosticism. Yet it would seem that Christ, God-become Man, did not give men a full explanation of the origin and operation of the evil forces in this world. (It is perfectly possible that in our present space-time existence we could not comprehend it, anyway.) But He did recognize evil as evil, not as a mere absence of good: He did, wherever He found it possible, destroy evil. He did indicate the lines along which evil could be defeated and He did talk of the positive resources which would be necessary for such defeat, and these we must consider a little later.

The Good Shepherd

IN ST. JOHN 10 our Lord contrasts Himself as the Good Shepherd in whose care the sheep find food and security, with the thieves and robbers who came before Him. I have often wondered whom He had in mind, for the words as they stand, "All that came before me are thieves and robbers" (St. John 10:8) sound rather harsh. It is probable that in the contemporary situation Christ had in mind leaders of men, political, national, and even religious, who really, in the long run, destroyed or sold for their own ends the souls of men. There are many "thieves and robbers" in the situation today who are similarly exploiting and destroying personality. We think of the soul-destroying aims and methods of Communism, of false religions which ask so much of men and in the end give them nothing. We think of the blight of materialism which by flattering a man's importance in this life deprives him of his destiny as a son of God. We think of the reckless pursuit of pleasure which meets man's love of beauty and happiness with the tawdry and the meretricious.

Within a man's own personality there is no lack of "thieves and robbers." There is his driving ambition which without the influence of Christ becomes, sooner or later, a destructive tyrant; there is his pride which insulates him from his neighbor and sows enmity between his group and another. Above all, there is his fear, rooted of course in pride and self-love, which drives out the milk of human kindness and which in its extreme forms makes him behave far worse than the animal creation. We have to face the fact that in the individual man as well as in society there have always been these disintegr ting factors, the "thieves and robbers" who, though often unseen, are quietly at work. Yet wherever He is given the chance, there is the integrating factor, the Good Shepherd Himself, seeking to make men whole, seeking to integrate both human personality and the whole human family.

The problem of making men whole, of integrating them as persons and unifying them in a community, is much more difficult than some idealists might suppose. The "thieves and robbers," the disintegrating forces, have had very long innings. They are deeply entrenched, their cumulative infection is overwhelming, and they are by no means always recognized for what they are. It is quite literally a superhuman task to plunge into the welter of centuries of disintegration and begin to make men whole.

At the risk of repetition, it must be emphasized that what we are beginning to envisage nowadays is a much larger-scale and more widespread integration than our forefathers as a general rule imagined. The salvation of an individual soul is indeed important, but we are beginning to see that the work of the Good Shepherd goes deeper and wider than we ever supposed. It is true that His plan considers the importance of the single "sheep"; under the Good Shepherd the one sheep can be saved and "go in and go out and find pasture" (John 10:9). But the plan is far greater than that. There are the "other sheep" (John 10:16) at present astray, who must also be brought into the fold. It is not only the so-called contemporary pressures which make us feel that we are "all in this together"; to those who are sensitive to the breath of the Spirit it is surely God Himself who is widening our horizons, mentally and spiritually, and making us feel and see the breathtaking compass of His integrating purpose.

Nothing less than a worldwide principle of wholeness, a world-loving and world-loved King and Shepherd, will suffice for our modern need. In the past, so long as men were broken up into more or less self-contained units, it was not altogether impossible to secure an integration which was local and to some extent superficial. The rules and customs of a tribe, for example, the unquestioned but purely parochial authority of their king, priest, or leader produced such a limited "wholeness." In our own country, there sometimes existed in a village, for example, such a circumscribed integration. And no doubt in many countries a similar local harmony was often achieved. But the need today, as is obvious to anyone with eyes to see, is for something at once more penetrating and more far-reaching than that limited conception. Indeed, on examination we find that the apparent wholeness of little communities was due at least in part to fear of other communities; and the very loyalty which preserved the local cohesion would effectually prevent cooperation with similar communities. In our Lord's day, for example, there was a certain cohesive loyalty about the Jews which produced in both personality and community some magnificent results. Yet it was exclusive, "for Jews have no dealings with Samaritans" (John 4:9), and they regard the Gentiles with, at the best, a tolerant contempt. We hardly realize the explosive quality of St. Paul's inspiration when, under the influence of the new integrating force, he declared that in Christ there can be "neither Jew nor Greek, there can be neither bond nor free, there can be no male and female" (Galatians 3:28).

The Crucifixion

JESUS REGARDED HIS own approaching death as a bitter necessity. Yet we, like the disciples who "followed with fear in their hearts," as the Gospel tells us, may well feel puzzled as they. Why must the One whom they were beginning to recognize as God-in-human-form undergo such a frightful death? Surely, if ever this was a case for divine intervention, for the flashing down of the celestial army of rescue that men might know who had been in their midst. Yet nothing of the kind occurred. The travesty of justice took its course, and the Man who was God in human form was brutally flogged and nailed to a wooden cross to die in the blazing sun.

We can appreciate the heroism and we can feel something of the tragedy, but can we understand the necessity, the bitter necessity?

I think, in order to do this, we have to think a little of the nature of God and of man. So long as we are skirting round the edges of the Christian Faith, thinking of God as some vague distant Benevolence, we shall not see the clamant need for reconciliation between God and man. But once we attempt with our adult minds and hearts to lead a Christian life, we begin to see the difficulty. For the gulf between us and God is not merely an intellectual one—it is not that God is infinitely wise and we, by comparison, blundering fools, though that is true—but the real gulf lies in the moral realm. You and I, through our own sins and failures, as well as by the infection of the sins of other people, are separated from God by a moral gulf. All serious religions recognize this, and all of them attempt some bridgehead from sinful human nature towards the Beauty and Perfection of the Holiness of God. Yes, they all attempt bridgeheads, but just as it is impossible to build a bridge across a chasm without starting from both sides, so it proves impossible in this matter of a moral gulf to do more than erect a painful and desperate bridgehead, *unless Someone is also building from the other side.* And that is precisely what we believe Christ did for us men. Not only did He, who was by nature God, come down to be born as a human being, not only did He live a life of perfect sinlessness, not only did He give us the "blueprint" or "recipe" for happy and constructive living, but in Himself He built the Bridge to span the gulf between God and man. "God was in Christ reconciling the world unto Himself."

The whole of mankind is caught up in a vicious circle of sin, suffering, and death, and Jesus Christ, Himself God and Himself Man, deliberately allowed Himself to be caught up in that deadly process. Though personally He had never done anything but good, though personally He had had no dealings with any form of sin, He, as Representative Man (for that is what "Son of Man" means), took the rap for mankind. We cannot begin to understand what kind of horror and revulsion such an experience must have meant to Him. It was, of course, not merely the physical degradation and suffering, but the terrifying dark experience of allowing evil to close in upon Him and kill Him, that fills us with wonder and awe.

The Act of Reconciliation

IN ALL OUR MINDS, sometimes lurking deep beneath the conscious level, there lies a sense that there is this gulf between us and God, and that something ought to be done about it. We make our good resolutions, we turn over new leaves—or we try to laugh the whole thing off—but there remains the sense that we are a long way from God and that there is nothing that we can do to close the gap. Sometimes we feel a passing sympathy with those heathen religions which make sacrifices, or go through complicated rituals of atonement to make themselves right with God, but we of the twentieth century feel we have grown beyond that sort of thing, though we have not grown beyond the sense that something ought to be done to atone for our sins and failures.

When we look at the Cross, without sentimentality, but with a little thought and imagination, we realize that what we could never do, what we are always powerless to do, *has been done* by Christ. This is the Act of Reconciliation which we could never make, the Bridge which we could never build. No longer do we see God as the Fearful Judge isolated in splendid Majesty, but right down among us, taking upon Him our flesh and plunging into the heart of our insoluble difficulty. When we see what sort of a God the Cross reveals to us, it is no exaggeration to say that a revolution takes place in our thinking and our feeling. It is not too difficult to hurl defiance at a high and mighty God who, secure in His majesty, makes us mortals feel guilty and afraid. But it is impossible to be unmoved when we see our very Creator down in the sweat and dust of the arena, going to that awe-inspiring length to make the Reconciliation. It may come quietly into our hearts, or it may break over us like a wave, that the nature of God is not, as we supposed, that of a Tyrant, a Spoilsport, or a Jesting Fate, but Love— not sentimental love, but real Love, that would face the grim degradation of the Cross to reconcile us to Himself.

The Resurrection According to Paul

THE FIFTEENTH CHAPTER [of First Corinthians] which I have come to regard in some ways as the most important chapter in the New Testament . . . is the earliest evidence for the resurrection of Christ. We need to remind ourselves that so far there were no written gospels, and that these words were written some twenty years after the crucifixion of Jesus. There would still be many alive who knew and remembered Him, and Paul lists some of those who saw Christ alive after his very public death. I was struck again by the "over five hundred Christians" who saw Jesus simultaneously, "of whom," Paul comments, "the majority are still alive." The evidence for the Resurrection does not rest on hysterical visions in the half-light of early dawn but on actual "appearances," the last of which seems to have happened to Paul. I noticed the flat, matter-of-fact recital of known events. There is no attempt to persuade or prove, and certainly there is no artistic embellishment. Paul is, in effect, saying: these are the historic facts which we know.

Then, at verse 12, he does allow himself to be moved. Since the risen Christ convinced him, and since the risen Christ is the power behind the gospel he preaches, as well as the author of the faith which has grown up in the unlikely soil of Corinth, how *can* anyone, even for the sake of argument, deny that Christ really rose?

I confess that I was as much astonished as Paul that *Christians* should not believe in the life that is to follow this obviously incomplete and imperfect one. Since faith in the resurrection of Christ and the sharing of his timeless life has always been an integral part of the Gospel, I cannot help wondering why quite a proportion of those who accept Christianity stop short of its most valuable promise.

It may be that there is some lack of imagination. If we speak loosely of "eternity," some people think that we mean millions of years plus millions of years ad infinitum. They do not seem able to grasp the fact that once we are outside the time-and-space setup (in which we are in this life inescapably confined), neither "time" nor "space" has any meaning. There may be all kinds of "dimensions" of which we are at present ignorant, and for which there are no descriptive words.

But I believe Paul himself puts his finger on the nub of the matter in verse 35 of this same chapter. Some people then, as some people now, seemed to envisage this temporary corruptible body being magically revived, and to think that this is what is meant by "resurrection." Of course it is not. Paul is at pains to explain that even on this planet the "body" which contains the life is adapted to the environment—fish, birds, animals are all different, while the "celestial bodies" to be observed in the sky are completely and splendidly unlike anything earthly.

God gives us the "spiritual" body suitable for the new environment for which we are destined as sons of God. We can be sure of that, and the resurrection of Christ is our guarantee. We can be equally sure that "the transitory could never possess the everlasting" (verse 50). Indeed who would wish for this old, weary, diseased, and possibly maimed body to be somehow newly injected with life? We know perfectly well that human flesh eventually decays, quickly by fire or slowly by decomposition in the earth, whatever the "morticians" would have us believe.

Why, then, does Paul insist on a "body" at all? It is because he is concerned to defend the Christian belief in man's resurrection after the pattern of Christ's resurrection. The old Greek belief, and its Roman counterpart, held that once the body was dead the disembodied soul lived a miserable twilight existence in Hades. It was the place of shadows and shades, the dark and joyless limbo of the departed. The Hebrew idea of Sheol was very little different. Sadness, silence, and hopelessness seemed to brood over the life after death. The men and women of Corinth would probably have heard of both Hades and Sheol. They might also have heard vaguely of the Greek philosophers' concept of the immortality of the human soul.

But death was to men of those days the ultimate disaster. It may be that some of these Corinthians could not accept the miserable twilight of such places as Hades or Sheol and that the persistence of the "soul" seemed no more than a philosopher's speculation. It may be that to believe in annihilation at death seemed to them the best way to meet it.

This negative thinking Paul is determined to correct. The resurrection of Christ was always to him the key to the human dilemma. Christ had become man, Christ had died for man, and Christ had risen to open the door to the glories that human vocabulary has no words to describe. Paul knew that man's last enemy, death, was now defeated, and men would look forward, not to a shadowy half-life, but to a life fuller and more glorious than human imagination can conceive. No more nonsense, he urges, about what sort of "body" we shall possess when these mortal bodies perish. That we can safely leave to God, who has demonstrated the defeat of death by the raising up of Christ.

For me, the translator, this fifteenth chapter seemed alive and vibrant, not with pious hope, but with inspired certainty. Quite suddenly I realized that *no man had ever written such words before.* As I pressed on with the task of translation I came to feel utterly convinced of the truth of the Resurrection. Something of literally life-and-death importance had happened in mortal history, and I was reading the actual words of people who had seen Christ after his resurrection and had seen men and women deeply changed by his living power. Previously, although I had known something of the "comfort of the Scriptures" and had never thought them to be false, I must have been insulated from their reality simply because they were known as "Scripture." Now I was compelled to come to the closest possible terms with this writing, and I was enormously impressed, and still am. On the one hand, these letters were written over quite a period of years, but there is not the slightest discernible diminution of faith. And on the other hand, it was borne in upon me with irresistible force that these letters could never have been written at all if there had been no Jesus Christ, no Crucifixion, and no Resurrection.

The more I thought about it, the more unthinkable it became that any of this new, courageous, joyful life could have originated in any kind of concocted story or wishful thinking. There had been a stupendous Event, and from that was flowing all this strength and utter conviction.

The Resurrection According to Luke

STRANGELY ENOUGH, it was while translating that vibrant book commonly known as the Acts of the Apostles, and

which I renamed the "Young Church in Action," that the
full weight of Christian evidence, centered as it must be in
the Resurrection, fell upon me with renewed force. But I
must wait a little while before I expand this conviction. For
the patient, careful Luke, with his sensitive "feeling" for
words, has more to tell us about Christian beginnings. I
had already come to the conclusion that he was a careful
historian, the kind of man who would tactfully but firmly
persuade people to tell him what they had actually seen and
heard, and check his information. We do not know exactly
when Luke became a Christian. Apparently, once he had
embraced the Christian cause, he became Paul's close companion in all kinds of danger and hardship. But, if the
records are to be trusted, and I believe they are, he was far
more than "the beloved physician." He set himself out to
write for Theophilus, a real or imaginary character, as true
an account of the earthly life of Jesus as he could manage.
When we come to his second work, the Acts, it is obvious
that he has been asking further questions of eyewitnesses of
events which he himself had not seen. Thus, in the opening
chapter of Luke's second book, we get a more detailed and
expanded version of what we commonly call the Ascension.
Here I think the picture has been spoiled for us by some lit-
eral-minded people who confuse the noisy, wasteful, and
expensive business of blasting a man into "space" with the
quiet simplicity of the real acted parable of the Ascension.
There is no connection between the two; you might just as
profitably enquire about the actual candlepower used in the
Transfiguration or of the light intensity, brighter than the
noonday sun, which halted Saul in his tracks on his way to
Damascus.

I know that it takes a little time for human minds to as-
similate a stupendous new truth. Thus we find Jesus appearing and disappearing over a period of some six weeks.
During this time he is not only teaching his disciples, but

helping them to grow accustomed to the idea that he is *with* them, and indeed will be *in* them, whether he is visible or not. But eventually the time comes when he must show them as directly, simply, and kindly as possible that as a bodily presence, such as they knew in the streets and on the hills of Palestine, he is to be no more with them. What would more plainly and finally convey to the men of those days this departure than the simple event of the Ascension? There is no question of a "countdown" and a "blast-off"! In the act of blessing them, the man, whom they knew and loved, rose there on the hillside until "a cloud received him out of their sight." This is what they saw; this is what they later reported to Luke; but it is not to be explained or explained away in terms of modern physics. Nevertheless it must have been an extraordinarily satisfying experience for these early disciples, since they, according to Luke, "returned to Jerusalem with great joy." They knew now for certain that death had been conquered, they knew that their beloved Jesus was truly the Son of God, and ringing in their ears was the promise that they would be given power to go out and to tell the world.

I found Luke's account of the beginning of the young church strangely moving. This mere handful of early believers, who had deserted their Master the moment real danger threatened, and who had, apparently, taken so long to realize that he had really and demonstrably conquered death, are bidden to wait. They are convinced; they are full of joy. But they lack the power to breach the defenses of an unbelieving world. The story, all too familiar to many of us who have been Christians for years, is told with extraordinary simplicity and economy of words. There must be some God-given power given to that tiny band charged with the alarming (and seemingly impossible) task of "preaching the gospel to every creature." And there was, for the living Spirit of God came upon these men in a way no one could have anticipated. Luke is describing, perhaps thirty years later, something of what men told him had happened at that momentous Pentecost. I cannot believe that Luke, or anybody else, concocted such a story. It is superhuman but not magical, and I find it wholly credible. There is this curious mixture of the earthly and the heavenly, which is typical of most of the New Testament. We have not gone very far in reading the Acts when, in chapter 6, we come across a down-to-earth case of human grumbling, or possibly jealousy. Whereupon seven more men are chosen as "deacons," among them Stephen, the first to suffer death for his faith. But even here Luke has an eye for a small but significant detail. In verse 7 of the same chapter we read that "a great company of the priests were obedient to the faith." Frankly, I had never seriously considered this before. The established order of things ecclesiastical, which included "the priests," had always seemed to me to be implacably opposed to Jesus, and later to Paul, wherever he traveled to proclaim the gospel. Now I cannot believe that Luke made this up! It is one of those unexpected partial glimpses of truth which make the whole so convincing.

But as I continued to read Luke's fascinating story, I slowly realized that the message proclaimed was basically that of "Jesus and the Resurrection." (This was almost farcically true just before Paul preached, not altogether unsuccessfully, to the sermon-tasters on Mars Hill. Some Stoic and Epicurean philosophers thought he was proclaiming *two* "foreign deities," Jesus and Anastasis [resurrection!]). The young church had, apparently, no knowledge of what we nowadays call the Virgin Birth, or even of the Christmas story. The great point to them was that God had become a human being, had been publicly executed, and then had *conquered death*. He had shown himself to them alive "by many infallible proofs" (Acts I:3) and had even eaten and drunk with them! (Acts 10:41). Naturally they could never forget this, and, as the gospel was preached to the then-known world, "Jesus, the risen Lord" was the heart and core of the message. The resurrection of Jesus was, and indeed is, historic fact. I suppose I have studied the relevant documents, commentaries, and attempts to controvert the whole story as fully as most men, and I am utterly convinced that *this thing really happened.* I am deeply grateful to Luke for showing me that it was the resurrection from death of a man. God's chosen man, Jesus, which gave the early church its enormous drive, vitality, courage, and hope.

The Resurrection in the Gospels

THE STORIES OF the rising from the dead of the man Jesus are not mounted or arranged as evidence for any court of law—or for that matter for any critic. I should be highly suspicious of them if they were. People who are frightened and despairing, suddenly confronted with evidence which contradicts all their previous experience of life, can hardly be considered to be ideal witnesses. Wouldn't you be shaken to the marrow if a young man whom you had seen die publicly and in agony on Friday greeted you with a cheerful greeting on the following Sunday? Does it *matter* whether there was one "man in white" or two who spoke to the bewildered women at the opened sepulcher? Can we not understand that a woman, half-crazy with grief and with eyes nearly blind with weeping should mistake a male figure in the early morning light for the gardener? Have we never been so overwhelmed with grief or disappointment, or both, that we literally do not *see* anything else? I am therefore not in the least worried by the story of the walk to

Emmaus (recorded only by Luke, and possibly recovered by him in his patient researches). I see no difficulty in believing that the minds of Cleopas and his companion were so utterly preoccupied with the collapse of their hopes and dreams that they did not recognize Jesus. Obviously, all the time that they had been walking with him, their despair was melting and their faith in Jesus, God's Christ, was coming back to life. But the "psychological moment" came when they were relaxed at a friendly table, and a familiar gesture brought instant recognition. It all "clicked into place," as we say in modern slang, or, as Luke records, "their eyes were opened and they knew him." Now, no one makes up a story like this. No one ever has, or ever will. This rings true; this certainly happened.

There is an almost haphazard recording of the appearances of Jesus after his resurrection, which I find extraordinarily convincing. I think my favorite again occurs in Luke's work. When the two who were walking to Emmaus had rushed back to Jerusalem to report their astounding experience to the eleven, they found that they already knew that "the Lord is risen indeed and hath appeared to Simon." Again, according to Luke, while they are still talking excitedly, Jesus himself appears among them. They were, as we might say, scared out of their wits; they thought they were seeing a ghost. But Jesus reassures them, and as was his habit, he asks penetrating questions. "Why are you so worried? . . . Why do doubts arise in your minds? Look at my hands and my feet—it is really I myself! Feel me and see; ghosts have no flesh and bones, as you can see that I have." Then Luke makes his shrewd comment as a doctor and student of human nature. Some things are too good to be true, and the human mind cannot accept them at once. It is entirely natural to me that Luke should record that "they still could not believe it through sheer joy and were quite bewildered." Then follows this extraordinary, and in a way amusing, test of whether Jesus was really there in person. He asks them, "Have you anything here to eat?" We can imagine the frantic dash to a shelf or cupboard where they kept their food, and we can imagine that they saw no incongruity in offering him a piece of broiled fish and part of a honeycomb. But I myself cannot imagine that Jesus consumed this rather strange meal before their eyes without a smile! But this in a way clinched it; whoever heard of a ghost *eating*? Again, I find this is the kind of story which no man would invent, but which any man who was present would remember until his dying day. And Luke, bless him, records it.

John, writing considerably later, contents himself with remarking, "many other signs truly did Jesus in the presence of his disciples which are not written in this book" (John 20:30). We cannot help wishing he had written more.

Although it is clear that Jesus meant his friends to understand that he had truly conquered death and sometimes went to great pains to convince them of the fact (see especially John 20:27), even a cursory reading of the Gospel stories is enough to show that the "appearances" are not the same in quality. On some occasions Jesus, now the risen Christ, appears among his astonished disciples when they are met behind closed doors, and sometimes he appears in the open air. Apparently his visible presence could disappear instantly, yet apparently he could also make himself not only visible but tangible to human senses. In the earliest account of the Resurrection appearances, which Paul records in 1 Corinthians 15, Paul seems to make no distinction between different kinds of appearance. His own vision of the risen Lord is to him as valid as the experience of the Apostles, "the five hundred brethren assembled at once," and the others. Nevertheless I am pretty certain that, if pressed, Paul would be the first to admit that the appearances were different in kind. The important thing to him was that "this man Jesus" had been "raised" by God from the dead, and had been set above all power in heaven and earth.

It does not bother me in the least that the man whom God had proved to be his Christ, and to whom God had given "all power in heaven and earth" should use his "resurrection body" in any way that he chose. There are such things as visions, and there are hallucinations, but the more I study the evidence the more I am convinced that Jesus was raised from the dead, body and all, in a real sense, leaving an open tomb and empty grave clothes.

The Revolution of the Resurrection

EVEN THOUGH THE Gospels are not . . . biographies, they build up a picture of a man whose stature and quality are unsurpassed in history. Yet no man rescued him from humiliation, mockery, and a torturing death. No celestial rescue party intervened. This was not merely the end of all their hopes and dreams to the early Christians, but a cruel outrage to their sense of justice. If ever there was a case for divine intervention, surely it was here. Once, in a moment of inspiration, Simon Peter had said, "You are Christ, the Son of the Living God!" And we may fairly assume that the others had come to share this view to a greater or lesser extent. Yet it was not to a band of expectant hero worshipers that Jesus appeared, but to men and women stunned by bitter grief and shattering disappointment. We can only guess at the black cloud of disillusionment which must have swept over them. After this terrible, final, and public disaster they had, apparently, forgotten that he himself had foreseen and indeed forewarned them of what would happen.

It was against a background of broken hope and utter despair that the great miracle occurred. All four Evangelists spend quite a lot of their short narratives in recounting the betrayal, the mock trial, the final humiliations, and the criminal execution. I do not think this was done merely for dramatic effect. It was written to show that even the best of men could suffer in this evil world. It was written to show all who should follow Jesus that he was not God *pretending* to be a man, but God who had become a man.

Thus the resounding triumph of the Resurrection was all the more splendid and magnificent. Armed with no supernatural equipment, Jesus had conquered man's last enemy, death. He had shown beyond any possible doubt that the victory was complete. To live again was no longer a pious hope or a wishful thought; it was a certainty. No conspiracy, no trick, no hysterical vision was responsible for this new certainty. As Paul remarked crisply some years later to King Agrippa, "This thing was not done in a corner" (Acts 26:26).

The Ascension

IT HAS ALWAYS seemed to me that the Ascension of our Lord is something of a poor relation among the festivals of the Church year. I imagine that this is largely because the divine event is celebrated on a weekday, and unless one is a pupil at a school with Christian observances—when the holy day is chiefly remembered because it is a day's holiday—it is likely to pass almost unnoticed by many good Christian people, and its significance scarcely appreciated.

Paul was not merely uttering a truism when he said— "Now that he ascended, what is it but that he also descended first? . . ." If we really believe that human life was invaded from Heaven by God's becoming a human being, it is surely not unreasonable to believe that the complement to that celestial dive of rescue is an ascension back in triumph to Heaven. The man who was also God had accomplished his mission, he had founded the kingdom, he had affected the reconciliation between God and man, and he had defeated man's last enemy—death. The Ascension not only satisfies the mind by completing the divine work, but it also strengthens and encourages the Christian soul. . . .

Men of all religions, of even of none, speak of "high" ideals, "high" aspirations, or even of "high" positions of responsibility or command. This seems to be a normal human trait, even though it is logically absurd, quite as absurd as it is to call one musical note "higher" than another. It does not really matter that the man of prayer might lift up his eyes to the heavens in the northern hemisphere, while the man in the southern hemisphere lifts up his eyes in a completely opposite direction. The point really is that human beings look up to God and what Paul calls the "heavenly," whether they are aware that they live on a spherical globe or not. Thus it was natural for Jesus, his work accomplished, to leave his followers by this acted parable. The man whom the early Christians had seen die and rise again did not simply vanish from their sight, as he had done on several occasions since his resurrection, but visibly ascended. The simplest witness could understand the obvious meaning of this action, while the wisest could ponder long over its deeper significance.

There are two aspects of this, the last earthly action of Jesus Christ, on which I think we can profitably reflect. . . . The first is simply this: that Jesus, who was both man and God, was taking humanity in his own person into the heavenly realm. This, naturally, had never been done before. Of course it is true that the risen Christ was not in all respects the same person as the representative man who had died in agony on the cross. We have only to read the resurrection stories to realize this. Yet he had become a man, he had involved himself in the human predicament, and as the eldest of many sons he was taking humanity into the new, perfect world—which is not just another "layer" above the protective belts that lie around this planet, but a new dimension beyond time and space as we know them.

He left with the promise to those who believe in him that "where I am there ye may be also." And since flesh and blood cannot possibly survive in the eternal world, we are promised through the inspired words of Paul that "we shall all be changed" and we shall be given bodies of new quality which the new world will demand. (A fresh reading of the fifteenth chapter of the first epistle to the Corinthians will help our thinking here.)

This much I think I can fairly see and believe, and the Ascension of Christ after his triumphant resurrection is the historical guarantee for our faith.

But the second aspect of the Ascension puzzles me considerably. It is simply this: that Jesus Christ, even before his death, spoke of his return to the Father and said these enigmatic words—"I go to prepare a place for you." We cannot help wondering what this preparation could be. We have grown away from the idea, and rightly in my judgment, that Jesus Christ is, to put it crudely, the "cushion" between the angry Father and us sinful human beings. There can be no schizophrenia in the nature of God, and in any case the ascended Christ had made the reconciliation which we could never make. Behind those mysterious and dreadful words, "he hath made him to be sin for us who knew no sin" and "he should taste death for every man," there lies more than a hint of the personal cost of our redemption. But at the time of the Ascension this was over; the agony, the darkness, and the dereliction of Calvary had been endured; and the resurrection was the proof that the work was done. What now remains for the ascended Christ to do?

I think this promise of Christ's "preparation" for men was meant, and is meant, to convey comfort, love and reassurance. However sincerely we trust our Lord, however deeply we love him, there remains something alarming to the naked human soul who is transferred by death from this familiar sphere into the beauty and perfection of the eternal world. . . . We love and welcome flashes of beauty, truth and goodness, but who in his own imperfection could face their very presence? It is true, as Paul was inspired to write, that "eye hath not seen, nor ear heard . . . the things which God hath prepared for them that love him"; but anyone with any imagination at all can sense the shock to the imperfect when it meets the perfect, to the incomplete when it meets the complete. This is perhaps why we need these words of reassurance.

Without pressing the words too literally, surely we are meant to be both strengthened and reassured by Christ's promise. He who was God by nature became man by deliberate choice, and, having perfected his mission, he now takes the humanity which he shares with us into the world of unimaginable perfection. Whatever lies behind his mysterious promise of "preparation" surely he means that we shall be at home in the place which he has prepared. We may be amazed but we shall not be terrified; we may be dazzled but we shall not be blinded. And it is perfectly possible that the tears which God will wipe from our eyes will not only be tears of regret for our past failures but tears of joy and unspeakable relief.

I spoke above of Ascension Day having become a kind of poor relation. It should, in fact, remind us that in our Lord and Savior we have an infinitely rich relation! For he is rich in mercy, in love and in understanding. He has defeated all our enemies, and the welcome which he has prepared for those who love and trust him will certainly surpass our wildest dreams.

The Living Spirit of Truth in the New Testament

I BELIEVE IT TO be very important indeed that close examination of the New Testament should produce conviction of its truth. No one is going to take the trouble to read it if once the idea becomes accepted that all we have is a collection of myths—and that is what is suggested by some of our so-called experts. Thus the Christian Church (and by that I mean all the churches) is regarded by many as a collection of people blindly clinging to beliefs which everyone else knows are false and refusing to meet modern scientific truth. Obviously there are some Christians who are obscurantists in their outlook, but I have met a good many, of most denominations, in both England and America who are displaying the same Christian qualities as the people described in the New Testament. They are refusing to be secularized, and they are refusing to allow the state or humanism or anything else to occupy the place which belongs to God.

Naturally we cannot turn the clock back, and it would be stupid to pretend that life anywhere in today's world is the same as the life of New Testament times. But people are the same, and the basic problems of human relationships are the same. The Spirit which Jesus promised would lead his followers "into all truth" is very actively at work wherever he is allowed. Some of his work is painful in the extreme. There has often to be the breaking-up of old ways of thinking, the expansion of responsibility, and the checking of priorities. Anyone who opens his personality to the living Spirit takes a risk of being considerably shaken. It seems obvious to me that the Churches themselves are also being shaken, perhaps as they have not been for centuries.

But we need not fear. The Spirit of truth does not contradict himself. It is not that the essential faith revealed in the New Testament is shown to be wrong; it is much more that our eyes are opened and we see how much more deeply relevant that faith is to our modern days than we thought. So that we do not gain but lose if we dismiss what was written by the inspiration of the same Spirit as folktale or myth. He will certainly lead us into all truth, but he will not lead us into arrogance and a confusion between technical advance and spiritual wisdom. He will certainly help us to "communicate" the truth of God to other people, but he becomes our enemy the moment we attempt to modify the wisdom of God to fit the "cleverness" of the twentieth century. The stern words of Paul have a peculiar aptness to the modern situation when he says, "The foolishness of God is wiser than men" (1 Corinthians 1:25).

The Gospels

THE GOSPELS ARE NOT, in the modern sense, biographies. We have no idea of the physical stature or build of their chief subject, and no clue to his coloring. We do not know whether he had a powerful voice, although we may fairly infer that he was physically strong. Apart from one isolated incident, we have no information about his childhood, adolescence, or young manhood and no record of the influences which formed his character. If we are looking for biography in the modern sense, we are disappointed. Some, like the late Albert Schweitzer, came to the conclusion that we never could know Jesus as an historical figure. And quite a number of scholars today would hold much the same view. The most we can do is to understand the meaning behind the "myths" of the Hellenic-Semitic world of first-century Palestine. I cannot, as a translator, agree with this at all, except in one minor way, which I will return to later.

Suppose you are, as I was, translating with the mind emptied as far as possible of preconception. You cannot help noticing the differences between the hurried, almost breathless style of Mark, where almost everything seems to happen "straight away," and the much more elaborate Gospel of Matthew, who has a very definite purpose in view—to convince the Jews that Jesus was indeed the Messiah of whom the Old Testament prophets had spoken. Quite different again is the work of Luke, who appears to have made diligent research and unearthed some stories of Jesus which none of the other Evangelists mentions. Here, uniquely, are set down the concern of Jesus for women, for foreigners, and for the underprivileged. To me it had all the marks of careful writing. And then came the problematical fourth Gospel, which is a work of quite different character.

Suppose that you have spent many hundred hours in putting these four widely differing accounts of some of the sayings and doings of the man Jesus into today's English. Do you find yourself so confused that you conclude that there was no such person at all? I take leave to doubt it. It is, in my experience, the people who have never troubled seriously to study the four Gospels who are loudest in their protests that there was no such person. I felt, and feel, without any shadow of doubt that close contact with the text of the Gospels builds up in the heart and mind a character of awe-inspiring stature and quality. I have read, in Greek and Latin, scores of myths, but I did not find the slightest flavor of myth here. There is no hysteria, no careful working for effect, and no attempt at collusion. These are not embroidered tales: the material is cut to the bone. One sensed again and again that understatement which we have been taught to think is more "British" than Oriental. There is an almost childlike candor and simplicity, and the total effect is tremendous. No man could ever have invented such a character as Jesus. No man could have set down such artless and vulnerable accounts as these unless some real Event lay behind them.

Thus the only small point which I will concede to the demythologizers is that several times I got the impression that the first three Evangelists, naturally enough, did not quite realize what a world-shaking happening they were describing. But how could they? Their view of the world was small; their knowledge of history was limited. They did not know even what Paul knew of contemporary life around them. It is easy for us to feel that these men were ignorant peasants compared with ourselves, who have advanced in knowledge over nearly two thousand years. If we do, we underestimate their intelligence and overestimate our own. Obviously they could not have anything approaching our historical perspective, but against this we must set the fact that they were living very much nearer to the actual point of time when Jesus was alive. There seems singularly little point in their concocting mythical stories about someone who never lived when violent persecution against those who followed the way of Jesus was well under way.

When I say that the first three Gospels at any rate are not biographies in the modern sense at all, I do not mean to say for one moment that I regard them as untrue. On the contrary, I believe them to be the verbal distillation of some of the things which Jesus said and did which the early Evangelists felt constrained to put down in writing. It is impossible at this stage to say what their original sources were, and do not let us forget that in no case have we an original manuscript or anything like it. But from the major manuscripts and from the thousands of minor ones, the textual experts are able to reconstruct with fair certainty what the Evangelists wrote in the first instance. One thing is perfectly clear: these men were not in a conspiracy together, or they would have been careful to avoid minor contradictions and discrepancies. The scholars who work out with enormous pains, through the evidence of style and vocabulary as well as from the content, the sources from which the Evangelists worked are called form critics. Of course, the whole business of form criticism is as absorbing and exciting as the best of detective stories, and I think it would surprise the average layman to know, for example, to what lengths the form critics will go in order to "prove" that some part of Luke's Gospel belonged to another period of time, or indeed to another author than the rest of it.

I should not like it to be thought that I want to belittle the work of the form critics, even though I sometimes cannot resist a smile at the way their views have changed over the last thirty years. But to me, as a translator, their work was largely irrelevant. I was dealing with material which was startlingly alive, and I could not really be overmuch bothered whether Matthew "borrowed" part of his Gospel story from Mark, or whether he and Mark shared a common source of written or spoken information which the critics call "Q." I know it is a shock to us today, and perhaps especially if we are professional writers and conscious of the laws of copyright, but it was not in the least strange in the first century A.D. to say that a gospel was "according to Matthew," even though it might contain sentences which were not written by Matthew at all. As long as the incident or the teaching was in keeping with the main stream which he had established, it seemed perfectly all right to the early Church to include it under Matthew's name. . . .

What seems to have happened, and in this I think all Christian scholars agree, is that the first three Evangelists wrote down what had previously been an oral tradition. This is no more than intelligent guesswork, but it seems likely that in the early days of the Christian community there was no need to write down the stories of what Jesus said and did, especially as many Christians were apparently expecting his early personal return. But what is not a guess but a fact is the fantastic retentiveness of the Oriental mind. Stories are told by word of mouth again and again, and no verbal deviation or embellishment is allowed. It is a phenomenon rather like that which children exhibit when they are very young and have their favorite bedtime story. It must not vary in the slightest detail from the familiar pattern. Strangely enough, only this very year I have been in contact with a friend who worked for some twenty-five years in business in Malaya. He found to his astonishment that conversations of twenty years ago and more could be recalled perfectly, mistakes, faulty pronunciations, and all, even though he himself had forgotten everything but the merest outline of such talk. Now this, I am told, would have been true of the Mediterranean world, and to me it seems most likely that it is the recollection of these gems of speech and action which the first three Evangelists record. This would account for the loose chronology, for we are reading not history in the modern sense but events and sayings treasured and remembered over a generation.

If we accept that the Evangelists, or at any rate the first three, wrote down various oral traditions which had been passed on with scrupulous accuracy over the years, we shall be spared many unnecessary headaches. Is it not reasonable to suppose that Jesus gave his teaching in slightly different forms on various occasions to different groups of people and that these were separately remembered and cherished? Before the days of mass communication (and that was not long ago) the prophet, preacher, or politician was bound to repeat his message again and again. What he said would be couched in compressed, intelligible, and memorable terms, but no one need suppose that he always used precisely the same words with parrot-like precision.

It is probable that Jesus spoke in Aramaic (a popular form of Hebrew), and if this is so, then the Evangelists had the extremely difficult job of listening to slightly varying accounts of the same, or similar, incidents and then setting them down in the widely understood Greek of the time. They were not reporters in the modern sense, nor were they preparing a statement for any court of law. They were simply setting down in writing what had till then been memorized and repeated by word of mouth. It is highly unlikely that we shall get any more information about the life and teaching of Jesus than we have already. In a sense this is tantalizing; what would we not give for a full-scale biography of this extraordinary man? How immensely valuable would be accurate descriptions of all that he ever said, as well as a detailed account of the events of his life. Why, we may plaintively ask, are we left almost completely in the dark about the childhood and young manhood of Jesus? Why have we no information (which would be regarded as essential in any modern biography) about the formative influences which produced such a matchless character? Why do we know almost nothing of the period between what we commonly call the Resurrection and the Ascension? What was it that the now risen Christ then taught to his followers about the "things pertaining to the Kingdom," as Luke describes them with such maddening brevity in the first chapter of the Acts? The plain answer is that we do not know.

The discovery of many papyri written in the same kind of

Greek as the New Testament has certainly illuminated our understanding of many words and expressions of that time. The Dead Sea Scrolls may well fill in more of our knowledge of Palestinian life of about the time of Jesus. But it is highly unlikely that the small esoteric group who copied and preserved the scrolls will shed any fresh light upon the actual historic life of Jesus or even, as some suggest, of John the Baptist. . . .

The fourth Gospel . . . is different in style, in vocabulary, and in "atmosphere." Instead of the true nature of Jesus being discovered in the course of his ministry, it is asserted at the beginning. Almost the whole of the story is set in Jerusalem. There is little mention of the extensive healing ministry of mind and body which the first three Evangelists record. Instead of short parables, we have quite lengthy discourses. There are times (inevitably, since New Testament Greek did not use quotation marks) when we are not sure whether we are reading the remembered words of Jesus himself or the comment of the Evangelist. Nevertheless the impact of the whole Gospel is, one is tempted to say, greater than the other three put together. The author plainly knew Jesus and had had time to think and meditate on the significance of the "Word becoming flesh." Whether he knew the existing Gospels we do not know, but I do not get the impression that John was writing a deliberate correction. The feeling is that a man of more maturity and deeper insight is giving his account. He is in effect saying, "This is how I saw and heard Jesus Christ, and this is the significance of his coming to this earth." The result is the portrait of a character in no way different from the sketches supplied by Matthew, Mark, and Luke, but carrying an even deeper authority.

Naturally I have read a good number of commentaries on John's Gospel, and I am fairly familiar with the difficulties of deciding who was the author. I also know of the hard task awaiting anyone who tries to fit this work into a "harmony" with the other Gospels. But I was not primarily concerned with this sort of thing. My work was to translate for, not to confuse, the modern reader.

The Letters

I WAS, AND INDEED AM, impressed by the fact that the New Testament letters were written not in some holy retreat but sometimes from prison, sometimes from ordinary, probably Christian homes. Moreover, they were written to people who were called to live Christian lives in a thoroughly pagan world. Moral standards of all kinds were low, and there was nothing remotely resembling a Christian public opinion. There were no Sundays, no church buildings, and very little leisure for most people. Slavery was, of course, everywhere, and so was dire poverty and unrelieved sickness and disease. The great persecutions had not yet started, but the smaller ones had. A man could lose not only his friends but his livelihood in a place like Ephesus if it became known publicly that he did not believe in the goddess Diana. A man could easily be looked at askance if he disowned the local gods, and he could be considered very odd if he broke with his previous companions in alcoholic revelings. And it could have been very easy to frame a charge against a man who set Jesus Christ above the Emperor of the Roman Empire.

It was against such a background of mixed paganism that the Christian faith began to grow and expand. Even if I were not myself a convinced Christian, I should find it impossible to explain this strange phenomenon. If we had records of a few emotional meetings, the effects of which were merely transient, we could write the whole Christian movement off as one of those passing waves of superstition which did from time to time disturb the pagan world. But we have no such thing: we have as good, solid evidence of a strong and growing faith as any historian could require. Let us, for a moment, discount the Gospel stories as written-up histories of a hero long since dead. (I do not myself think of the four Gospels like this, as I hope to show.) Even without the evidence of the books attributed to the four Evangelists, we have the strongest possible evidence for the early days of Christianity from the letters of Paul, James, Peter, and John. It is *letters* which are of unique value to the historian who is trying to record the actual events of any period. Newspapers, and before them broadsheets and pamphlets, naturally have their worth, but they are likely to be slanted one way or another. But if the historian can lay his hands upon a packet of letters, he has priceless evidence for the period of which he is writing. For letters, speaking generally, are not written with any political axe to grind, nor are they usually written for posterity. They reflect accurately the times in which they are written.

So it is with the New Testament Epistles. I doubt very much whether any of their writers had any idea that he was writing "Holy Scripture." For the most part it was *"ad hoc"* writing: a particular situation, or even the behavior of a particular person or group, called for the writing of the letter. Yet all of them, from their different points of view, bear witness to the growing of a new society of men and women quite different from the Greek, Roman, Jewish, or pagan pattern. The whole movement is based on the fact (about which no New Testament writer argues) that Jesus Christ was God and man. He is now "the Lord," and every system of thinking and every way of action must be decided not merely by reference to his example and teaching but by the leading of his active living Spirit.

As I continued this close association with the New Testament Epistles (on one full morning each week, for there was plenty of other work to be done!), I found an extraordinary unanimity of spirit. I say "extraordinary" because superficially Paul, James, John, and Peter are poles apart in temperament, and widely different in their presentation of the Christian gospel. But this difference is only superficial; it soon becomes plain that they are all speaking of the same thing, and, further, that their messages are complementary rather than contradictory. I have heard professing Christians of our own day speak as though the historicity of the Gospels does not matter—all that matters is the contemporary Spirit of Christ. I contend that the historicity does matter, and I do not see why we, who live nearly two thousand years later, should call into question an Event for which there were many eyewitnesses still living at the time when most of the New Testament was written. It was no "cunningly devised fable" but an historic irruption of God into human history which gave birth to a young church so sturdy that the pagan world could not stifle or destroy it.

The Greatness of Paul

WHEN I STARTED translating some of Paul's shorter letters I was at first alternately stimulated and annoyed by the outrageous certainty of his faith. It was not until I realized afresh what the man had actually achieved and suffered, that I began to see that here was someone who was writing, not indeed at God's dictation, but by the inspiration of God himself. Sometimes you can see the conflict between the Pharisaic spirit of the former Saul (who could say such grudging things about marriage and insist upon the perennial submission of women) and the Spirit of God, who inspired Paul to write that in Christ there is neither "Jew nor Greek . . . male nor female"!

Paul had, and still has, his detractors. There are those who say he is like the man who says, "I don't want to boast, but . . ."—and then proceeds to do that very thing! Very well then, but let us look at his list of "boasting." We have only to turn up 2 Corinthians 2:23–27. Has any of us gone through a tenth of that catalogue of suffering and humiliation? Yet this is the man who can not only say that in all these things we are more than conquerors, but can also "reckon that the sufferings of this present time are not worthy to be compared with the glory which shall be revealed in us" (Romans 8:18). Here is no armchair philosopher, no ivory-tower scholar, but a man of almost incredible drive and courage, living out in actual human dangers and agonies the implications of his unswerving faith. . . . I myself found as I studied [Paul's] writings that his mind was far more accurate than I had thought, and his imagination quite extraordinary in a man of such immense moral and physical courage. I would further say that we moderns tend to underestimate the intelligence of people like Paul. Because such a man had never seen a bicycle, a typewriter, or a television set, we, perhaps unconsciously, look down on him as living in some sort of twilight ignorance. We forget that he lived in point of time very close to the historic events described in the New Testament, and that he had plenty of opportunity to check their authenticity from many eyewitnesses. We forget, too, that he knew the philosophies of Greece not merely as textbook subjects but as systems of thought being taught and practiced in his day. When he wrote to the Colossians and warned them of "philosophy and vain deceit," he was not being anti-intellectual. He knew from observation as well as from personal knowledge of human beings that philosophy, however attractive intellectually, is sterile and impotent when it comes to changing human disposition.

Conversion of the Corinthians

THE LETTER WHICH really struck me a blow from which I have never recovered was the one popularly known as First Corinthians. Let me explain. I had been doing some background reading, and I was reminded that Corinth was a byword, even in those wicked old days, for every kind of vice and depravity. The Greeks, as usual, had a word for it, and "to Corinthize yourself" was to live with the candle alight at both ends, with all scruples and principles thrown aside, and every desire indulged to the full. Because of its geographical position—Corinth was easily reached by sea, and was a most important port in the East-West Mediterranean traffic—it had a very mixed population with a large number of travelers, traders, and hangers-on. It was probably not intrinsically any more wicked than any other seaport, but its reputation for sexual license had largely grown because it had been for hundreds of years a center for the organized worship of the Goddess of Love (first Aphrodite and now, in Roman times, Venus). As always happens where there is such a widespread sexual license, there sprang up a host of vicious fellow travelers—greed, blackmail, cheating, slander, perversion, and the rest.

I had a fair picture of the sort of place it must have been, and indeed of what an unlikely place it must have seemed for the founding of a Christian church, when I suddenly came across the eleventh verse of the sixth chapter. Paul has just recounted some of the more repulsive sins to which human beings can sink, and has assured his hearers that the Kingdom of God cannot be the possession of people like that, when suddenly he writes, AND SUCH WERE SOME OF YOU!

I had never realized what an astonishing piece of Christian evidence this is. No one doubts that this is an authentic letter of Paul, probably written some ten years before the first Gospel was set down. And here, to people living in this center of idolatry and all kinds of human depravity, Paul can write, "and such were some of you"! What, I ask, and shall continue to ask of my non-Christian friends, is supposed to have changed these men and women so fundamentally? The personality of Paul? The most casual reading of his two surviving letters to Corinth will quickly show that even among his converts he was not universally admired. It seems obvious that something very unusual had happened and was happening. People, sometimes the most unlikely people, were being converted in heart and mind by *something*. To Paul and his fellow Apostles it was plainly the invasion of the human spirit by God's own Spirit. The power required to convert and to sustain the new life *naturally* was to Paul another manifestation of the power which God showed in raising Jesus from the dead. The "fruits of the Spirit" which Paul lists in the fifth chapter of his letter to the Galatians are not the result of fearful effort and tormenting self-denial. They are fruits: they grow naturally, once the living Spirit of God is allowed to enter a man's inner being.

Nine New Testament Serendipities

Just over two hundred years ago, in 1754 to be precise, Horace Walpole coined the word "serendipity," which has now come to be accepted into our language. The word, which is derived from the ancient name for Ceylon, is defined as "the faculty of making happy and unexpected discoveries by accident." Before I go on to discuss the work of translating the Gospels I feel I must mention some of the "happy and unexpected discoveries" which I made in the translation of the Epistles.

"Rich in Mercy"

THE FIRST ONE I will mention, which of course may all the time have been no secret to anybody else, was the expression "rich in mercy" (Ephesians 2:4). This struck me as a positive jewel. Just as we might say that a Texas tycoon is "rich in oil," so Paul writes it as a matter of fact that God is "rich in mercy." The pagan world was full of fear, and the Christian gospel set out to replace that fear of the gods or the fates, or even life itself, with love for and trust in God. "Rich in mercy" was good news to the ancient world and it is good news today.

"Casting All Your Care"

I THINK THE IDEA of God's personal care for the individual came upon me with a similar unexpected strength when I came to translate 1 Peter 5:7, which reads in the Authorized Version, "Casting all your care upon him; for he careth for you." In one sense it is quite plain that God wants us to bear responsibility; it is a false religion which teaches that God wants us to be permanently immature. But there is a sense in which the conscientious and the imaginative can be overburdened. This familiar text reminded me that such overanxiety can be "off-loaded" onto God, for each one of us is his personal concern. The "text" is commonplace enough, perhaps too commonplace, for it was not until I had to translate it that I realized something of its full force. The word used for "casting" is an almost violent word, conveying the way in which a man at the end of his tether might throw aside an intolerable burden. And the Christian is recommended to throw this humanly insupportable weight upon the only One who can bear it and at the same time to realize that God cares for him intimately as a person. "He careth for you" is hardly strong enough and I don't know that I did much better in rendering the words, "You are his personal concern." The Greek words certainly mean this, but probably more. It is not the least glory of the Christian gospel that the God revealed by Jesus Christ possesses wisdom and power beyond all human imagining but r.ever loses sight of any individual human being. It may seem strange to us, and it may seem an idea quite beyond our little minds to comprehend, but each one of us *matters* to God. It is of course the same sense of intimate concern which Jesus expressed poetically when he assured us that even the hairs on our head are numbered. It is the kind of inspired truth of which we have continually to remind ourselves, if only because life so often apparently contradicts it.

"Fear and Trembling"

I HAD FOR SOME time been worried about the expression "fear and trembling." It did not seem likely to me that Paul in writing to the Philippians could have meant literally that they were to work out their salvation in a condition of anxiety and nervousness. We all know that fear destroys love and spoils relationships, and a great deal of the New Testament is taken up with getting rid of the old ideas of fear and substituting the new ideas of love and trust. I realized that the Greek word translated "fear" can equally well mean "reverence" or "awe" or even "respect," but I was bothered about the "trembling." Surely the same Spirit who inspired Paul to write to Timothy that "God hath not given us the spirit of fear; but of power and of love and of a sound mind" could not also have meant us to live our entire lives in a state of nervous terror. I came to the conclusion, a little reluctantly, that the expression "in fear and trembling" had become a bit of a cliché, even as it has in some circles today. As I went on translating I found that this must be the case. For when Paul wrote to the Corinthians and reported that Titus had been encouraged and refreshed by their reception of him, he then went on to say that the Corinthian Christians received him with "fear and trembling" (2 Corinthians 7:15). Now this makes no sense, unless it is a purely conventional verbal form implying proper respect. For, little as we know of Titus, we cannot imagine any real Christian minister being encouraged and refreshed by a display of nervous anxiety. We get the same phrase occurring again in Paul's advice to Christian slaves (Ephesians 6:5), where the context makes it quite clear that faithfulness and responsibility are much more what Paul means than "fear and trembling." This much became plain, and then I realized that when Paul really did mean the words to be taken literally he amplified them to make sure they would be properly understood. I think we sometimes imagine that the incredibly heroic Paul suffered from no human weaknesses, except for the "thorn in the flesh" about which all New Testament commentators have written (2 Corinthians 12:7). But if we turn to 1 Corinthians 2:3, we find Paul writing that, "I was with you in weakness, and in fear, and in much trembling." Now this is a different thing altogether. Here we have a man honest enough to admit that he was frightened and that he was, or had been, ill. "Fear and trembling" here are perfectly legitimate. It is only when they are used as a phrase almost without literal meaning that we begin to feel uncomfortable.

"Pressed Out of Measure"

THIS LEADS ME to another heartening discovery, which I made in 2 Corinthians, chapter 1, verses 8 and following. I had not previously realized that even a man of such indomitable courage as Paul, filled as he undoubtedly was with the Spirit of the living God, could nevertheless be "pressed out of measure, above strength, insomuch that we despaired even of life." We lesser mortals, who live infinitely less adventurous lives, may sometimes experience something of this pressure. It is not that we, any more than Paul, despair of God as far as the ultimate outcome is concerned. But we can be overcome by the most terrifying darkness and reduced to a sense of inadequacy amounting to near desperation. Again, it was not until I came to the close study of this passage that I realized under what fearful pressure Paul must at times have been. I further came to see that the "stiff upper lip" business is not necessarily Christian; it sounds much more like a throwback to the Stoics than to early Christianity. For although the New Testament abounds in advice to men to be strong and to master their fears, it does not consider it disgraceful, for example, that a man might be moved even to tears, not indeed for himself but because he cared deeply for others. The letters tell no story of idealized human beings but reflect the life of people who are changed but by no means yet perfect.

"Quit You Like Men"

AT SOME STAGE in my life as a Christian I must have heard the total depravity of man heavily emphasized. I do not think I ever personally accepted this, because ordinary observation showed a good deal of kindness and generosity produced by people whether they had religious faith or not. But I have found among gatherings of Christians of various denominations a minority who seemed to get a perverse delight in this emphasis on man's utter hopelessness. And indeed we have not got to look far into devotional literature, whether Protestant or Catholic, to come across the idea that man is hopelessly sinful and incapable of good without the operation of the grace of God. . . . Now, to my joy, I found two delightful instances which could be quoted against the detractors of humanity if, as they sometimes do, they want to indulge in a text-slinging match! One comes from the first Epistle of John, where the writer reminds his hearers that no one should deceive them by any clever talk: "The man who lives a consistently good life is a good man as surely as God is good." This truth is no more and no less than the saying of Christ himself when He said, "You will recognize them by their fruit; a good tree cannot produce bad fruit, any more than a bad tree can produce good fruit." This was a pleasant refreshment, but there was another, wholly unexpected one at the end of the first Epistle to the Corinthians (16:13), where Paul urges his converts in the words "Quit you like men." (May I say in passing that these words from the Authorized Version are totally meaningless to the vast majority of young people.) The literal translation is, of course, "Be *men*." Now if it is true that man is so steeped in iniquity and incapable of goodness as some, especially in past centuries, would have us believe, there is no sense whatever in Paul's advice. But if it is true that the image of God is still present in man, however much it has been distorted or disfigured by evil, then it makes the most encouraging sense to be told to live like a man. At any rate, I must put it on record that this is the effect the inspired words had upon me.

"Everyone That Loveth...
Knoweth God"

A SIMILAR PLEASANT "DISCOVERY" came in 1 John 4:7, in the words "everyone that loveth is born of God, and knoweth God." Again, this inspired truth had naturally been there all the time, but I don't think I had ever heard a sermon preached on it. Throughout my years of experience it had struck me that the things that were really admirable in human behavior were those inspired by love. I had also noticed, like many others, that people could exhibit most remarkable compassionate love without any great religious profession, or indeed with none at all. But if it is true, as John declares, that "God is love," it would make sense that any action that sprang from love had its origin in God. It would also mean that those who did give themselves in love to others did in fact "know God," however loudly they might protest their agnosticism. I have never been happy with any ecclesiastical or theological system in which correctness of belief was of paramount importance. It is only too easy for some men to build up a certain theological structure which includes them and excludes others. But what we really believe in our heart of hearts may be quite different from what we outwardly profess. I saw then, and I have seen nothing in life to disturb this view, that when a man acts in response to love and compassion he is responding to God *whatever he thinks or says.* Conversely the man who refuses to become involved in the troubles and burdens of his fellows is rejecting God, however religious his outward profession may be.

"Now Are We the Sons of God"

"BELOVED," WROTE JOHN, "now are we the sons of God, and it doth not yet appear what we shall be: but we know that, when he shall appear, we shall be like him; for we shall see him as he is" (1 John 3:2). These words, familiar as I think they must have been to me for years, were yet another shock for me as I came to translate them. For what would normally be sheer effrontery, or even blasphemy, is here written with cool confidence and authority. No one to my knowledge has ever written like these New Testament writers. Yet I was constantly aware that I was dealing not with exhortations or homilies but with letters written to people living in the midst of this world's business, people who were tempted and tried as we are, blinkered and frustrated and limited just as we are, yet with the same unquenchable flame of hope in their hearts as Christians have today. The material in this single verse is quite extraordinarily compressed; there is enough here for half a dozen useful sermons! But it is the *authority* which stabs the spirit broad awake. Paul and John wrote because they *knew*. The Christian revelation was not to them a tentative hypothesis, but the truth about God and men, experienced, demonstrated, always alive, and powerful in the lives of men. The whole Christian pattern had to be lived against pagan darkness and frequently overt hostility. It required superhuman qualities to survive. Of course there were casualties—Demas was not the first nor the last deserter—but the amazing thing to me is that the Christian Gospel took root and flourished in many different, and indeed unlikely, places.

"Count It All Joy"

THERE WAS ANOTHER unexpected treasure waiting for me in the letter of James. I suppose we all look upon the disappointments and pains of this life as somehow hostile to us. We either fight, or we grimly endure. It was therefore a salutary surprise to me to discover that James recommends his Christian brothers to *welcome* the assorted trials and troubles to which we are all exposed. "Count it all joy," he writes, "when you fall into divers [all kinds of] temptations" (1:2). Frankly I had never even thought of thus turning our apparent losses into real gains! But I am convinced that it is the right attitude to adopt. This is no question of "being a martyr," as we said when we were children, but of accepting suffering and loss as an integral part of life. I think we moderns are influenced more than we know by current modes of thinking which assume that we have a "right" to be happy, a "right" to live without pain, and somehow, a "right" to be shielded from the ills which flesh is heir to. Evidently the early Christians thought no such thing. They quite plainly took it as an honor to suffer for Christ's sake, and here the advice is to accept all kinds of troubles, whether they are apparently for Christ's sake or not, as friends instead of resenting them as intruders. Now I know that this kind of teaching can easily degenerate into an unhealthy and perverse wallowing in trouble. But this is not, I think, the early Christian intention. It is just as much a Christian duty to rejoice with those who rejoice as it is to weep with those who weep; it is as important to enjoy what God has richly given to us as it is to accept good humoredly and patiently the troubles, setbacks, disappointments, and griefs which are also part of the human pattern.

"If Our Heart Condemn Us"

I HAVE KEPT THE best until last. It occurs in John's first letter, chapter 3, verse 20. Like many others, I find myself something of a perfectionist, and if we don't watch ourselves this obsession for the perfect can make us arrogantly critical of other people and, in certain moods, desperately critical of ourselves. In this state of mind it is not really that I cannot subscribe to the doctrine of the Forgiveness of Sins, but that the tyrannical super-Me condemns and has no mercy on myself. Now John, in his wisdom, points out in inspired words, "If our heart condemn us, God is greater than our heart, and knoweth all things." This is a gentle but salutary rebuke to our assumption that we know better than God! God, on any showing, is infinitely greater in wisdom and love than we are and, unlike us, knows all the factors involved in human behavior. We are guilty of certain things, and these we must confess with all honesty, and make reparation where possible. But there may be many factors in our lives for which we are not really to blame at all. We did not choose our heredity; we did not choose the bad, indifferent, or excellent way in which we were brought up. This is naturally not to say that every wrong thing we do, or every fear or rage to which we are subject today, is due entirely to heredity, environment, and upbringing. But it certainly does mean that we are in no position to judge ourselves; we simply must leave that to God, who is our Father and "is greater than our heart, and knoweth all things." It is almost as if John is saying, "If God loves us, who are we to be so high and mighty as to refuse to love ourselves?"

Similes and Metaphors in the New Testament

THERE IS AN idea current among some New Testament scholars that people like Paul had a primitive system of thought—that theirs was a three-decker universe, with "heaven" above, "hell" below, and "earth" in between. For myself I seriously doubt this. In the intensive reading which translation requires I formed the strong impression that, far from trying to fit ideas of God into any preconceived concept, Paul is struggling with human words to express something of the wonders which, he senses, lie beyond observable life. To him it is the things which are seen that are temporal; it is the unseen things which are eternal. I find it hard to be patient with modern critics who assume that when Paul speaks of Christ's ascending "up on high" or when he urges the Colossians to "seek those things which are above, where Christ sitteth at the right hand of God," he is really talking of some location a certain number of miles above the earth's surface. There is a disquieting confusion of thought here. I think I can understand the Russian astronaut who is reputed to have said on his return from orbit that now he knew that there was no God, since he had been out in space and there was no one there. This shows merely a peasant's-eye view of religion. But there are several modern writers who pour scorn upon any idea of God being *up* or *above*. They are confusing literal spatial position with a mental image which must be common to nearly all thinking human beings. Why should we talk of *high* ideals or a *high* purpose? Why should we talk of a *rise* in salary? Why should sales be *soaring?* Why should a boy be promoted from the *lower* to the *upper* fifth form? Why does an important person in our judiciary sit in a *high* court? And so we could go on. It is a common and quite understandable symbolic way of speaking, and naturally the converse of it is equally true. For example, in ordinary speech a man may *fall* in our estimation, a failing business is fast going *downhill,* some people are of *low* intelligence, and some unfortunates have sunk to the *depths,* etc.

As I studied Paul's letters I became convinced that he uses expressions of height and depth as useful symbols but not as geographical locations. When, for example, he writes that, "God raised Christ from the dead and set him at his own right hand in the heavenly places, far above all principality and power, and might, and dominion, and every name that is named, not only in this world, but also in that which is to come," does anyone seriously imagine that Paul, or the Ephesian Christians to whom he was writing, thought of this exaltation as being measurable in physical terms? Again, in the same letter to Ephesus, when Paul asserts that the Christian's real battle is against spiritual rather than physical enemies and mentions "spiritual wickedness in high places," does anyone seriously suggest that Paul meant demonic goings-on at the Emperor's court? Of course not! To Paul there was the heavenly reality which at present we may sense but not see, and the earthly reality which is discernible by the senses but doomed, like all creation, to ultimate decay. The "bright blue sky" stuff belongs to Victorian piety and not to the New Testament.

I feel I must record here my sense of injustice that the Christian religion should be singled out as a target for criticism because it uses, and is bound to use, "picture language." We all do it every day of our lives, and we are none the worse for it. No one blames the accountant for talking of a "balance," the economist for speaking of "frozen assets," the electronics engineer for talking of a magnetic "field," the traffic controller for referring to a "peak" period, the electrical engineer for speaking of "load-shedding," or the town-planner for talking of a "bottleneck." Not one of these words is literally true, but each conveys quickly, and pretty accurately, an idea which can be readily understood. I cannot see why we, who accept hundreds of such usages in everyday speaking and writing, should decide that an expression such as "seated at the right hand of the Father" is either literally true or totally false.

But just as there is a real situation behind each of the shorthand "pictures" which I have given above, so there is a reality behind every Christian expression. Because picture language is sometimes used, it does not follow that the actual events are unhistorical or "mythical." The strange thing to me is that so few New Testament expressions need explanation. There are obvious exceptions: the Epistle to the Hebrews was especially written for the Hebrew mind and necessarily contains many ideas and expressions which are strange to the non-Jew. But on the whole the technical expressions are few and the "pictures" easily understood. Given a good translation, there is little in the New Testament letters which the modern reader will find dated or irrelevant. Indeed, as I said in a slightly different context above, I have literally hundreds of letters written from all parts of the English-speaking world which prove this very point. And although the difficulties are very much greater, those who have, with enormous care and sympathy, translated the Epistle into many other languages have found a similar response. The British and the American Bible societies have an impressive record of the relevance of the New Testament Epistles to life as people of very different backgrounds and cultures have to live it today.

Faith

As I WRITE these words I am aware of various things through my physical senses. As it happens, at the moment these are chiefly the light and warmth of sunshine, the beauty of trees in full leaf, the varied songs of birds and the distant sound of children at play. I am also mentally aware of the truth I am trying to express, and of you, my imaginary reader, following the line of thought I am trying to make clear. Doubtless as you read you are taking in similar sense impressions, as well as having your thoughts guided by the complicated system of marks made upon paper which we call printing. But simultaneously, in the immediate world of you the reader and me the writer, there are radio programs of various kinds actually in our rooms with us. The "ether" (for that is the name given to this all-pervasive but intangible medium) is continually pulsing and vibrating, strongly or feebly, with perhaps a hundred or more near or distant radio transmissions. In common parlance we frequently say that a certain program is "on the air"; but that, of course, is quite inaccurate. Radio transmissions are not vibrations in the air. They would function just as well if there were no air at all, and they make their way, as we all know, with very little hindrance through such things as timber, stone, and concrete. It is only when they meet conductors or partial conductors of electricity that these inaudible, invisible vibrations become minute electrical currents and even then they are undetectable except by that commonplace but quite complicated piece of circuitry known as a radio set. In your body, as in my body, there are at this very moment minute electrical currents of which we are quite unaware. They are, in fact, an untuned jumble of electrical vibrations representing the assorted offerings of many radio transmissions. Now we are unaware of this and normally we take no notice of it. It is only when we want to hear a particular radio program that we tune in a certain band of these etheric vibrations and by means of the radio set turn them back into audible sound. For even if we disapprove of radio, even if we refuse to believe in its all-pervasive presence, it makes not the slightest difference to the *fact*. Whether we like it or not, or whether we believe it or not, we are permeated by this mysterious "ether," and that is a fact which can easily be demonstrated. Before the advent of radio less than a century ago, such an idea would have seemed in the highest degree improbable and even impossible. We know today that it is true, that simultaneously with our ordinary-world sense impressions there co-exists a world of mysterious "ether" of which we only become aware when certain apparatus is used.

Now, this seems to me a most helpful, if simple, analogy. Suppose it is possible that the whole material world and the whole psychological world are interpenetrated by what we may call the "spiritual." For some reason or other we are inclined to think of the physical world and even the demonstrable world of the "ether" as somehow real, while the "spiritual" is regarded as unreal and imaginary. I believe the opposite to be true. As Paul foresaw long ago, "The things which are seen are temporal; but the things which are not seen are eternal" (2 Corinthians 4:18). Suppose what we are seeing and measuring and observing are the outward expressions in the time and space setup of what is really eternal and spiritual! If we make such a supposition we are in for a revolution in our whole way of thinking. But New Testament Christians had already experienced this revolution.

To sense the reality of the God-dimension, to conform to its purpose and order, to perceive its working in and through the visible world system is, speaking broadly, what the Bible calls faith.

Faith in the New Testament

IN THE GOSPELS it would appear in general that the existence and use of [the faculty of faith] provided the link between the Divine Order and human life. The centurion who earned Jesus' commendation for his "faith" plainly took it as a matter of course that as he occupied a position of authority in the purely earthly realm, so Jesus was able to exercise authority in the unseen realm (Matthew 8:5; Luke 7:2). It was not so much personal admiration for Jesus, and probably not full recognition of Who he really was, so much as an intuitive perception that here was One Who was a Master over the unseen forces which influence observed life. His "faith" was nevertheless a sincere recognition that there was a Divine Order which was real and reliable. Again, in the case of those four young men who were prepared to take desperate measures to get their friend to Jesus, there was the same recognition of the unseen Divine Order and Power (Mark 2:3; Luke 5:18). In both these cases, and of course in many others, the use of the faith faculty was, so to speak, the agent which enabled Jesus' power to be released. The contrary was also true. Where men were imprisoned by the closed system and could not, for reasons of prejudice or sheer unwillingness to believe, break through into the real dimensions, even the power of Jesus was inhibited. In Nazareth, "He could do no mighty works there because of their unbelief" (Matthew 13:58). We read moreover that "he marveled because of their unbelief" (Mark 6:4), and surely we may fairly guess that his observation of men's failure to use their faculty of faith must have continually astonished him. To him the Unseen Dimension and Order were continuously real. The love, the generosity, and the power of the Father were constant realities, and it must not only have amazed but grieved him more than we can guess to find men either unwilling or unable to use the power of faith. Again and again, he urges men to "have faith in God," and both by his own teaching and his own example it is plain that he is continually urging men to put the weight of their confidence not in earthly schemes and values, but in the unseen Heavenly Order, of which the supreme Head is the Father. To live like this, to live as though the spiritual realities were infinitely more important than the appearance of things, might fairly be said to be a basic teaching of Jesus. To live "by faith" is to him the truly natural way of living, and although it may demand effort and persistence he does not hold it out as a way of living merely for the spiritual elite. It is only in the exceptional case, as in the case of the healing of the epileptic boy (Luke 9:39) that Jesus declares that training and discipline are necessary for faith to produce the requisite power for good. In general throughout the Gospels Jesus seems to be urging men to dare to use their faith faculty—to knock, to seek, to ask. His general implication is that there are boundless resources in the Unseen World available for men of faith.

Faith in the Young Church

WHEN WE COME to the book of the Acts of the Apostles or the letters of the New Testament, we are reading about what actually happened when men and women began to "believe in the Lord Jesus Christ." The burden of preaching in the Acts is not, so far as can be discovered, the emphasis on man's depravity, but on faith—the grasping by the faith faculty of the new order. Naturally, the focal point of this new apprehension is God's personal focusing of Himself in the Man Jesus Christ. The word translated "repentance" does not necessarily mean being sorry for our sins, though that will probably be included. *Metanoia* means a fundamental change of outlook. As far as we can discover in the early preaching of the Gospel, the Good News was not primarily the announcement of the fact that men were sinners, but that the real world had broken through into this world in visible, tangible form—in fact, in Christ. God was now knowable; His Plan of a universal Kingdom was manifest; death itself was of no account now that God had revealed Himself in Jesus. Simultaneously with this proclamation of Good News to Jews and Gentiles was the announcement that the living contemporary Spirit of God was alive and active. We have only to read the book of the Acts to see how He, the Holy Spirit, the Spirit of Jesus, empowered, transformed, and guided the early Christians. The Young Church was full of divine energy and wisdom; and it would seem that its members were so filled because they learned more and more to use the faculty of faith, and because they prayed, not indeed to persuade an unwilling

God, but to bring themselves into line with His Purpose so that the power could safely be given. No one could honestly read the book of the Acts with an adult mind without being impressed with this sense of suprahuman power, wisdom, and authority. God Himself is plainly at work in and through these new Christians who, for all their faults, were plainly exercising the faith faculty.

When we enter the world of the Letters, which reflect the life of the early Church, we are again faced with the phenomenon of people whose whole outlook and pattern of life are being transformed by the use of the same faculty of faith. If we examine even the letter of James, which is supposed to concern itself much more with "good works" than with "faith," we find on examination that the letter is merely a corrective against false ideas of what "faith" implies. "Of what use is it," says James in effect, "if you do see the unseen realities of God, His Kingdom, and His Order, unless that perception is expressed and worked out in ordinary human situations?" That is a very proper question, and it is part of the discipline of life that, although we may have our glimpses of the glory of God, though we may by faith thoroughly accept the truth of the "Incarnation," the "Atonement," and "Resurrection," and so on, all these shining revolutionary truths have to be expressed and worked out in the dust and darkness, even in the strain and squalor of the sinful human situation. Far from decrying the value of faith, James is concerned to prevent such a faculty from becoming romantically airborne. He is determined, and rightly determined, that just as the young Prince of Glory lived His matchless life in the dust and sweat of the human arena, so users of the faith faculty must not consider themselves above their Lord.

It is, of course, when we come to the Letters of Paul that we find the word "faith" used again and again. It is used in slightly different senses . . . but always it includes this idea of grasping a reality, a whole dimension of reality which we cannot see with our fleshly senses. Paul indeed draws the strong contrast between the man whose vision and outlook is limited to this world and the man who, by the action of the Spirit, becomes alive to spiritual realities.

Justification by Faith

ONE OF Paul's most important teachings, though it is only one, is the doctrine of what we call "justification by faith." It frequently appears to the non-Christian mind that this is an immoral or at least unmoral doctrine. Paul appears to be saying that a man is justified before God not by his goodness or badness, not by his good deeds or bad deeds, but by believing in a certain doctrine of the Atonement.

Of course, when we come to examine the matter more closely we can see that there is nothing unmoral in this teaching at all. For if "faith" means using a God-given faculty to apprehend the unseen divine order, and means, moreover, involving oneself in that order by personal commitment, we can at once see how different that is from merely accepting a certain view of Christian redemption. What Paul is concerned to point out again and again is that no man can reconcile himself to the moral perfection of God by his own efforts in this time-and-space setup. It is a foregone conclusion that he must fail. The truth is—and of course it is a truth which can only be seen and accepted by the faith faculty—that God has taken the initiative, that, staggering as it may seem, one of the main objects of the Personal Visit was to reconcile man to Himself. That which man in every religion, every century, every country, was powerless to effect, God has achieved by the devastating humility of His action and suffering in Jesus Christ. Now, accepting such an action as a *fait accompli* is only possible by this perspective faculty of "faith." It requires not merely intellectual assent but a shifting of personal trust from the achievements of the self to the completely undeserved action of God. To accept this teaching by mind and heart does indeed require a *metanoia*, a revolution in the outlook of both mind and heart. Although the natural human personality sometimes regards this generous fact of reconciliation as an affront to its pride, to countless people since Paul's day it has been, as it was meant to be, Good News.

The phrase "justification by faith," then, simply means acceptance of a forgiveness and a reconciliation made by God Himself, and the total abandonment of efforts at self-justification. God's action, His "grace," as Paul calls it, becomes effectual when the truth of the matter becomes real by "faith." That is why Paul repeats again and again in different words his great theme, "By grace are ye saved through faith; and that not of yourselves: it is the gift of God" (Ephesians 2:8).

Faith in Today's World

IF WE ARE genuinely willing to welcome the fresh wind of the Spirit and to experience once again the God-given vigor of the early Church, we must plainly begin by reusing the faculty of faith. Perhaps it would be not out of place here to make a few suggestions which for convenience sake may be numbered:

(1) Let us deliberately take time to consider our modern situation, not so much its problems but its attitude of mind

and spirit. A few chapters read from the Acts of the Apostles might help us to appreciate by contrast how closed we have grown on the God-ward side. Perhaps we might, with as fresh minds as we can, read some of the Gospel incidents as well so that we may become convinced afresh that the fault in our present-day Christianity lies not in God with His astonishing generosity, but in our own neglected capacity to believe, to reach out and appropriate His resources. Although we are not responsible for our talents or lack of them, we are very largely responsible for our own attitude of mind. Let us without morbid self-accusing confess that we have largely neglected to use our God-given faculty of faith. Let us freely admit that at heart our life attitude has been a long way from that of men attuned to unseen realities.

(2) Let us by conscious and deliberate effort begin to exercise the long-disused faculty. Whatever our circumstances may be, life is so arranged that there is never a lack of opportunity for such exercise. It is apparent that, both for considering our own position in relation to God and for deliberately using our power of faith, we need a quiet space in our lives. This is absolutely essential, and nothing is more important than securing this space amid all our busyness. No one is too busy to set aside a period of, say, a quarter of an hour each day for such quiet. (We are all rather ridiculous here. For if we knew for certain that a space of a quarter of an hour's quiet was essential for our physical health, for example, we should unhesitatingly make room for it. It would become a top priority. Can we not see that such a period, which should be regarded as a minimum, could be absolutely essential for our spiritual health?) For many people this period of quiet must of necessity be solitary; but since a great deal of the vigor of the early Church depended on Christian fellowship and was in fact given and demonstrated through Christian fellowship, there is

good reason to suppose that a small God-seeking group of people might help one another enormously in redeveloping the faith faculty.

(3) Study of the New Testament with as unbiased and unprejudiced a mind as possible will undoubtedly stimulate faith itself and the desire to develop the faculty more. Before long we cannot help realizing, if we "soak" ourselves in the meaning and spirit of these inspired pages, that this other world, which we have been in the habit of regarding as shadowy and far away, can, and in fact historically did, permeate ordinary human life. Further, we shall conclude that there is no valid reason for supposing that if the right conditions are fulfilled the same suprahuman quality and power could not penetrate life today.

(4) Jesus told men "to knock," "to seek," and "to ask," by which I understand him to mean that although the resources of God are always available, it is up to us men to make use of them. I think, too, that he may well have meant men to make spiritual experiments, to try out, as it were, the Divine resources. As we do this, we shall inevitably find that the values and fortunes of this passing world become less important and clamant. Nevertheless, I think we should be wise, by deliberately training ourselves, to see that real security does not, indeed cannot, rest in this world, however lucky or careful we may be. Moreover, all experiences of love and beauty, much as we may enjoy and appreciate them in this transitory life, are not rooted here at all. We should save ourselves a lot of disillusionment and heartbreak if we reminded ourselves constantly that here we have "no continuing city" (Hebrews 13:14). The world is rich with all kinds of wonders and beauties, but we only doom ourselves to disappointment if we think that the stuff of this world is permanent: its change and decay are inevitable. The rich variety of transitory beauty is no more than a reflection or a foretaste of the real and the permanent.

Something surely of this thought is included in Christ's words, "Lay up for yourselves treasures in Heaven, where neither moth nor rust doth corrupt, and where thieves do not break through nor steal" (Matthew 6:20).

(5) Finally, we must accept as one of the facts of life that to live on this level and to retain this attitude of mind and heart are not as easy as falling off a log. Sometimes, it is true, to do so is easy and natural, but there are other times when contemporary pressures and even our own lethargy make it difficult to rise and live as sons and daughters of the Most High. We must cheerfully accept the fact that, cost what it may, for the time being "we walk by faith, not by sight" (2 Corinthians 5:7). To exercise faith will often mean an effort on our part, a determined breaking through of the matted layers of this world's self-sufficiency, and a persistent reaching out to touch the living God.

Hope

HOPE RUNS HIGH in the inspired pages; it is not a superior form of pious wishful thinking but hope based solidly upon the character and purpose of God Himself. But for us, during the last fifty years particularly, the quality of hope has ebbed away from our common life almost imperceptibly. I say again that we are affected far more than we know, far more than we should be, by the prevailing atmosphere of thought around us. Christians, at any rate as far as western Europe is concerned, do not seem to exhibit much more hope than their non-Christian contemporaries. There is an unacknowledged and unexpressed fear in the hearts of many people that somehow the world has slipped beyond the control of God. Their reason may tell them that this cannot be so, but the constant assault of world tensions and the ever present threat of annihilation by nuclear weapons make people feel that the present setup is so radically different that the old rules no longer apply. Without realizing it, many of us are beginning to consent in our inmost hearts to the conclusion that we live in a hopeless situation. . . .

A very great deal of what passes for hope today is either wishful expectation or the expressed reaction of a mind which is not prepared to face realities. We shall not find in the New Testament, I think, a single instance of hope used in any but its genuine sense, that is, hope rooted in the good Purpose of God. You will remember how James in his New Testament letter is particularly severe in his condemnation of the "pious hope" for other people's good which does nothing practical to implement the wish (James 2:15–16). He says in effect that if you should see people cold or hungry or without proper clothes, and you say, "Well, God bless you—I hope you will soon be all right!" what on earth is the good of that? This sort of pious hope is still with us. People will say, for example, "I do hope they will soon find a cure for cancer," but many of them would not dream of giving a penny to any anticancer research fund. Or they will say, "I do hope something is done for all those thousands and thousands of poor refugees and homeless people over there in Europe." But not one in a hundred who expresses such a hope does anything to make it come true. We have to rid our minds of both pious hopes and wishful thinking before we get down to solid, genuine hope.

Hope in the New Testament and the Young Church

THE INSPIRED WRITINGS of the New Testament are neither optimistic nor pessimistic; they are very far from being the enthusiastic outpourings of people expressing their ideals and painting rosy pictures of a dream world which might one day be true. Nor, on the other hand, do the writers underline the sinfulness and depravity of human nature. We are reading what was written by men at firsthand grips with realities, and it is both astonishing and heartening to find how hopeful they are. Unless we happen to have studied ancient history, we may not have realized how remarkable are the bright hopes of the early band of Christians. The surrounding pagan world was dark; it was full of fear, cruelty, and superstition. For the most part the old religions had failed. Human life had become cheap; common morality was in many cases very lightly regarded; and belief in a world to come was almost nonexistent. . . . But in the Young Church there was gay and indomitable hope. Nothing could quench this hope, for these men and women now knew through Christ what God was like, and they now knew for certain that death was a defeated enemy. While the pagan world had largely become sodden with self-indulgence and ridden by the fear of death, the brave new fellowship of believers in Christ was a light and a flame in the darkness; it was a fellowship of hope.

All hope in the New Testament . . . rests upon the Nature and Purpose of God. These men and women are hopeful because, as Jesus Christ told men, "with God all things are possible" (Mark 10:27). Those who had come to believe with complete conviction that God loves the world, that He has visited it in Person and shown His power in transforming the lives of the most unlikely characters, were not readily disposed to lose hope in His ultimate Purpose. But of course that hope was not limited to the present temporary scene that we call life. The center of gravity of their hope was in the eternal and not in the temporal world. This was the quality which both baffled and infuriated their enemies as fierce persecution began to arise. The pagan world with its ever present horror of death could scarcely believe the evidence of their senses when they found in the Christian martyrs men and women to whom death was not a disaster at all. To the pagan mind to take a man's life was to take his all, but to attack Christians by sword, torture, or the atrocities of the arena was to invite defeat. Even if you killed them they slipped through your fingers to be with their Lord forever!

Although New Testament Christians doubtless prayed, as we do, "Thy Kingdom come, Thy Will be done on Earth, as it is in Heaven," and though they therefore doubtless worked and prayed for the improvement of the world in which they lived, their hope rested upon God, not merely upon what He could do in this world, but upon His high, mysterious Purpose. Of comparatively recent years the center of our faith has become, at any rate in some quarters, more and more earthbound. We are concerned with the Christian attitude to housing, to social problems, to juvenile delinquency, to international relationships, and indeed to every department of human life. This is fine as far as it goes, but sometimes one gets the impression that Christians are "falling over backwards" to disavow their other-worldliness. Yet to have the soul firmly anchored in Heaven rather than grounded in this little sphere is far more like New Testament Christianity.

Hope in Today's World

IT IS ESSENTIAL that we recapture and hold fast the New Testament idea that God is the "God of hope" (Romans 15:13). In the New Testament writings there is a continual sense not only of the immediacy but of the contemporaneousness of God. Their authors can write realistically of the God of hope because they are very close in point of time to God's act of intervention in what nowadays we call the Incarnation, and because the power of the Young Church is very plainly and demonstrably the power of the living Spirit. Many modern Christians are inclined to put God back into the past. How many times in visiting various churches does one hear of what used to happen in the old days! And, since Christians derive a great deal of their inspiration from reading the Bible, they can all too easily envisage God as thoroughly at home in the sacred pages but somehow no part of the modern picture at all. In [*New Testament Christianity*] I recalled how I tested a group of young people by asking them to give a quick answer to the question "Do you think God understands radar?" And how the answer was "No," to be followed of course by laughter as the absurdity became apparent. But I am still convinced that the unpremeditated answer was highly significant and revealing. Without admitting it in so many words, many Christians today cannot readily conceive of God operating in a world of television, washing machines, atomic fission, automation, psychiatry, electronic brains, glossy magazines, modern music, and jet propulsion. The complication and speed of present-day living make it extremely difficult for the mind to imagine the Biblical God interpenetrating such a system and operating within its pressures. The very word "God" seems out of key and even bizarre in our modern context.

Two things are necessary if we are to rediscover the buoyant hope of the New Testament. The first obvious step is to make certain that our hope is really hope and not either wishful thinking or merely pious hope. It must be closely allied to our faith and must ultimately be rooted in what we know for certain of the Nature and Purpose of God Himself. We might do well to study afresh the kind of hopes which sustained and inspired the Young Church and compare them with our own. This will naturally bring us to our next step, which is to rediscover the contemporaneousness of God. This may require a drastic revolution in our thinking, for we may discover that we have been thinking of God as Someone we can escape to, rather than Someone Who is actually not only in ourselves but in the noisy hurly-burly of everyday life. This does not mean to deny that modern life is distracting, complex, and difficult, but it does mean realizing afresh that God is not in the slightest degree baffled or bewildered by what baffles and bewilders us. It is no good longing for the monastic quiet of a past age or for the simplicity of life of a pastoral generation. Our urgent need is to discover God, the God of hope, in the present strain, in the complex problem, actually at work in the given situation. For He is either a present help or He is not much help at all.

The Love Commandments

To LOVE God with the whole of our personalities and powers is, according to the words of Christ recorded in Matthew 22:38, the "first and great commandment." Yet among the thousands of people outside the ranks of the Church there would be very few who could be found to agree with him. "Be a decent chap and don't worry your head too much about God"—this is the working philosophy of a good many people.

Those of us who profess and call ourselves Christians are committed to accept Christ's authority, though not unthinkingly; and when we come to look behind what appear at first to be arbitrary commands, we find that invariably He had good reasons for the principles He laid down. So it is here. . . .

Unless we believe in God and love Him, the qualities we value, the things we call "good" or "bad," are purely a matter of personal opinion. Your "good" may be my "bad" and vice versa. . . . But Christians have an influence on national thought and conscience out of all proportion to their numerical strength; and even today a very large part of our tradition of behavior is nothing less than the fruit of Christian ideals having percolated almost imperceptibly into our habits of thinking. . . .

It is comparatively easy for us to love those "neighbors" who are nice and friendly towards us. It is easy to love the attractive and charming personalities of our friends. But Christ made it quite clear that loving our "neighbor" did not stop at loving our particular circle, but loving all those with whom life brought us into contact.

You will remember His semi-humorous comment on those who thought that to love their particular friends was enough—"Do not even the publicans the same?" We might paraphrase that—"Aren't even the tax-collectors nice to their pals?" No, if there is ever to be a happy and peaceful world we have all of us got to learn to understand and to love the difficult, the exasperating, and the unlovable—and that is a superhuman task.

I use the word "superhuman" deliberately, for by ourselves, without the inspiration that comes from loving God, it is plainly impossible for us to love, in the sense that Christ uses the word, our fellow men.

A clergyman probably realizes this far more acutely than the average layman. There are many departments of life where obviously you possess more knowledge and experience than I do; but in this matter of living in love and charity with all kinds of people the parson has to know a good deal. Forgive my plain speaking, but is it not true that if you find someone who is "difficult" or conceited or annoying, it is quite the easiest thing in the world for you simply to withdraw yourself and make friends with just those with whom you get on? But such a course is not open to me. I have to learn to understand and work with all kinds of different temperaments and outlooks, and in consequence I get a unique opportunity of seeing just how difficult is Christ's second commandment—to love other people as we love ourselves.

Frankly, I see no prospect of our even wanting to obey the second commandment seriously until we have begun to obey the first. We don't really see other men and women as our brothers and sisters simply by talking airily about the brotherhood of man. We only see them as such when we begin to get a vision of God the Father. It is so fatally easy to talk highfalutin hot air about all the world being "one big family," and yet fail to "get on" with the members of our own families, or with those who live next door, or in the [apartment] above us. In sober fact, men do not really love their fellows, except their own particular friends, until they have seriously begun to love God. It is only then that we learn to drop the destructive attitude of hatred and contempt and criticism, and begin to adopt the constructive attitude of Christian love. So, then, the second reason for the command to love God being "the first and great commandment" is that we don't really keep the second until we have obeyed the first.

Love in the New Testament and the Young Church

"GOD" IN VARIOUS religions might be thought of as benevolent toward the mortal creation, but the reason that the Gospel was Good News when it first burst upon the world was simply that men had realized that God is Love. The revelation of character provided by Christ Himself, the awe-full brunt of suffering which He was prepared to bear in order to redeem mankind, His triumph over man's last enemy, His ascension to timeless reality, taking Human Nature with Him as it were; His continual coming by the Spirit to transform and reinforce men's lives—all these, the unshakable conviction of the Young Church, showed one thing: that God is by nature Love and that He loves mankind. Men who accepted this foundation truth found an indefinable endorsement of it in their own hearts. They also found that their own "love-energy," which had previously been turned in upon themselves or was being given to the wrong things, now became an outflowing love embracing their fellow men for whom Christ died. Further, this love not only changed in direction but in quality. It was something more than natural love; it began to resemble Divine Love. Indeed, it is hardly an exaggeration to say that Christianity gave the word "love" a new and deeper meaning. The new love was stimulated and developed by accepting the love of God as shown in Christ. "If God then so loved us we ought also to love our brethren," wrote John (1 John 4:11). The new life of faith and hope is made possible, according to Paul, "because the love of God is shed abroad in our hearts" (Romans 5:5).

I am quite sure that a great deal of the joyful experience and invincible courage of the Young Church is due simply to the fact that the early Christians believed these words to be literally true. To them nothing could alter this basic fact, and no experience of life could separate them from God's unremitting love.

Four Temptations Against Love

ALL THOSE WHO try to love are beset by certain temptations of which these are the chief:

(1) *The temptation to imitate love.* . . . It is perfectly possible for us to behave kindly, justly, and correctly toward one another and yet withhold that giving of the "self" which is the essence of love. Married people will perhaps more easily appreciate what I am trying to say. A husband may behave with perfect kindness and consideration toward his wife; he may give her a generous allowance; he may do more than

his share of the household chores, and indeed he may do all the things which an ideal husband is supposed to do. But if he withholds "himself" the marriage will be impoverished. Women who seem to know these things intuitively would infinitely prefer the husband to be less kind, considerate, and self-sacrificing if they were only sure that he with all his imperfections and maddening ways gave "himself" in love in the marriage. This principle applies to some extent to all human relationships, and I am quite certain that it is this costly, self-giving love which Paul had in mind in 1 Corinthians 13. Many, even among Christians, shrink from it, not I think because they are afraid to give but because they are afraid that their gift will not be appreciated; in short, that they may be hurt. But surely this is the risk that love must always take, and without this giving of the self with all the risks that that entails, love is a poor pale imitation. "Consider *him*" (Hebrews 12:3) writes the author of the Epistle to the Hebrews, and if we do we find this is precisely the sort of rejectable, vulnerable love Christ lived and died to prove.

(2) *The temptation to hate oneself.* The cheerful pagan takes himself as a rule very much for granted, but the Christian who is sooner or later brought face to face with Truth is disgusted and dispirited to find how self-loving and self-centered his life really is. The more he comes into contact with the living Christ, the more he realizes there is to be put right, and if he is not careful his normal pride and self-respect go suddenly "into reverse." The more he thinks of the standards of love and those who live by them, the more wrong he feels, until he ends with a thoroughgoing contempt for himself and all his doings. The self with whom he has lived for some years in reasonable comfort becomes an intolerable person; before long he has slipped into despising himself wholeheartedly. Now this, despite what some

religious books have said, is a thoroughly bad state of mind in which to live. The man who despises or hates himself will sooner or later, despite all his religious protestations, reveal hatred and contempt for his brother men. Whatever his profession of love for "sinners," the contempt for the sin which he has found in himself is all too easily projected onto those who sin.

(3) *The temptation to separate love of God from love of people.* "The more I see of some people, the more I love my dog," runs the modern half-humorous comment. Of course, it is far easier to love a devoted animal who more than rewards us by the utmost fidelity and affection than it is to love people who in addition to being much more complex beings often do not reward us at all. Similarly, it is easy to love humanity without loving people. Many of the greatest crimes against individual living people have been committed in the name of love for humanity. There are plenty of people with us today who will talk about world peace and the universal brotherhood of man but who cannot get on with their own families or neighbors. People, in fact, unless they happen to be our own special friends, are quite difficult to love.

Naturally, Jesus knew this very well and he connected inseparably the love of God with the love of other people. Indeed, it is part of the act of Incarnation that God and human beings are indissolubly wedded. This is the kind of fact which most of us would rather not have to face. It is comparatively easy for us to imagine God as the Perfection of all beauty, truth, and love and to respond with worship and adoration to such a Being. What we find almost too much to stomach is that this very same God has allied Himself through Christ with ordinary human beings. In Jesus' famous parable of the Last Judgment (Matthew 25:31–46), men find to their astonishment that their treatment of fellow human beings is adjudged to be the same thing as their treatment of Christ Himself. . . .

(4) *The temptation to feel that people are not worth loving.* The world is lamentably short of outgoing love. Part of the reason for this is that it is so much easier to love among our own circle or at least to love those who will return our love. Although we do not express it in so many words, I believe that one of the reasons so few people venture to give themselves for the sake of other people is that they feel that "people are not really worth it." But who are we, who call ourselves Christians, "saved," pillars of the Church, and so on? In what way do we think that we were "worth it," when Christ visited this earth to save us? In the eyes of Heaven this whole sin-infected, blundering human race could hardly have seemed worthy of the highest sacrifice which God Himself could make for its redemption. Yet Love took the initiative and bore unspeakable contradiction, misunderstanding, and humiliation to win us to Himself. To quote John's words again, "If God so loved us, we ought also to love one another" (1 John 4:11).

Love in Today's World

"THE GREATEST OF these is love" (1 Corinthians 13:13), wrote Paul long ago, and we all agree, with admiration. But how far do our lives endorse what we assent to so readily? "The greatest of these is success" might well be the motto of many people, even though they themselves are not successful. "The greatest of these is security" is the motto of countless thousands. "The greatest of these is knowledge" is the unexpressed opinion of many of our scientifically-minded generation. We have to become convinced afresh that Paul's inspired words are quite literally true. Love is the greatest because without it there is no worthwhile success and certainly no real security. Love is the greatest because men are never transformed at heart permanently except by love. Love is the greatest because without it knowledge can become dangerous and even suicidal. Above all, love is the greatest because it persists beyond the confines of this temporal existence. The success of the film star, the brilliance of the best-selling novelist, the speed of the record-breaking athlete, the awe-inspiring knowledge of the top-secret scientist—of what value will these and a hundred other highly prized worldly achievements amount to in the Real World to which we are bound? But what has been done in love—the problems that have been solved, the personalities redeemed, the situations changed, the actual growth of character beneath the influence of love—all these will stand as permanent and demonstrable evidence of the Divine Purpose of Life. All of us are inclined to be swayed more than we realize by the values of the world in which we live, but must we be so dazzled and blinded that we fail to see the paramount importance as well as the permanence of Love?

Peace

DESPITE THE FIRE, energy, daring, hope, and faith that distinguished the Young Church, there is no trace of hysteria or morbid excitement in its recorded life. Some of us have seen people do all sorts of extraordinary things under the influence of religious excitement, and those of us who are pastors of souls have sometimes been not a little perturbed at the dangers of arousing religious emotions and at their equally dangerous reactions. But as we study New Testament Christianity we are aware that there is an inner core of tranquility and stability. In fact, not the least of the impressive qualities which the Church could demonstrate to the pagan world was this ballast of inward peace. It was, I think, something new that was appearing in the lives of human beings. It was not mere absence of strife or conflict, and certainly not the absence of what ordinarily makes for anxiety; nor was it a lack of sensitivity or a complacent self-satisfaction, which can often produce an apparent tranquility of spirit. It was a positive peace, a solid foundation which held fast amid all the turmoil of human experience. It was, in short, the experience of Christ's bequest when He said, "Peace I leave with you, my peace I give unto you: not as the world giveth, give I unto you" (John 14:27).

Although essential human nature has not changed, outward circumstances have changed enormously since the early days of the Christian faith. I do not think that we can claim that life is either more difficult or more dangerous, but modern living is certainly more complex and is certainly conducted at a higher speed. The natural factors which tend to destroy peace and tranquility are greater than ever. All the more reason, then, for Christians to experience and, consciously or unconsciously, to show living evidence of the divine gift—of the unshakable inner core of peace.

"Peace with God" is sometimes rather carelessly used in religious circles as though it had only one connotation, as though all the problems of a complex human personality were solved if only a man would accept the redemptive sacrifice of Christ upon the Cross. Actually, this is an oversimplification, for although to accept the reconciliation which God has provided is an absolute essential, there are many other factors, especially among the more intelligent, which prevent the soul from being at peace. The divine peace, the steady centering of life upon God, is basically a gift from God and must be accepted, like our forgiveness, as His gift and not as something that we can achieve. Nevertheless there are elements within our own personalities which must be frankly faced before we can expect to experience that gift. If we want to enjoy inward tranquility amid this whirling, bewildering modern life, we must be prepared to do some honest self-examination. In the last resort we shall find that our only true peace is "peace with God," but it may not prove quite so simple to find it as we imagined.

Six Obstacles to Peace

(1) *Self-indulgence.* In all of us, to a greater or less degree, depending on heredity, upbringing, and temperament, there is a thrusting, self-pleasing element which normally regards the world as centering upon oneself. It is not a thing to be horrified at, for it is in us all, but the whole way of thinking and feeling which belongs to the self-centered man must be abrogated or denied before there can be peace with God. What we call "sins" are simply expressions of this self-pleasing, self-regarding, and self-indulgent inward attitude. The word which is translated in the New Testament as "repentance" really means a thorough change of heart and mind. It means realizing that the real center of everything is not my little self, but God, and that in order to serve the King Himself, I must quit the throne of my own precious little kingdom. To some people this comes easily,

almost naturally, as soon as they see the truth of it. To others it means a hard and even agonizing struggle. Such people do not readily surrender; they do not easily cooperate with someone else's plan, even if that Someone Else is God. Yet it is obvious that there can be no inward peace until the self-conscious inward kingdom willingly and wholeheartedly concedes its rights to the Creator, the real King. . . .

(2) *Inner conflicts and tensions.* If we are quiet before God and allow His Spirit to shine upon our inward state, we shall probably discover more than one conflict which is robbing us of inner peace. The man who lives apart from God may be largely unconscious of his inward conflicts and only aware of their tension. Of course, he may be driven by the sheer force of the tension to a psychiatrist who, if he is a wise one, will help the man to realize the sources of his disharmony. But he still will not be at peace with the Nature of things, with his own conscience and the Divine Purpose that is being worked out in this world, unless the psychiatrist is able to lead him to faith in God. But except in unusual cases, the Christian need not turn to the psychiatrist. Either alone with God or with the help of a trusted friend, priest, or minister, he can, if he wishes, see for himself the fierce hidden resentment, the carefully concealed self-importance, the obstinate and unforgiving spirit, and all the other things which prevent inward relaxation. As long as his personality is a battleground it is foolish to suggest to him that he accept the peace of God. His hidden desires, ambitions, and pride must first be brought to the surface, not only to the surface of his own consciousness but, as it were, to the light of God's love and understanding. God is not concerned to condemn; however ashamed and guilty the man himself may feel, God is concerned to heal and to harmonize.

(3) *Reluctance to pray for peace.* For sheer practical wis-

dom Paul's famous words have never been surpassed. He wrote: "Be careful for nothing; but in every thing by prayer and supplication with thanksgiving let your requests be made known unto God. And the peace of God, which passeth all understanding, shall keep your hearts and minds through Christ Jesus" (Philippians 4:6–7). It is when the love of God is allowed to penetrate every corner of a man's being that the peace of God comes as a positive gift, as a sturdy guardian of the soul's inward rest. The sharing of anxieties and fears, the intimate thankfulness for joys and beauties, bring the individual very close to the life of God. They must be habitual and they must be practiced, but their fruit is a relaxed spirit.

(4) *Fear of inadequacy.* Much of our tension and anxiety can be traced directly to a fear of inadequacy. We should meet this fear in two ways. First, by learning to accept ourselves. We probably are *not* adequate for all our ambitious schemes, and only at the cost of enormous nervous energy can we succeed in becoming momentarily what we really are not. This is a self-imposed tyranny which is very common. Suppose we accept ourselves good-humoredly, realizing our limitations and how much we have to learn, with cheerfulness and without envy of those who are, or appear to be, more adequate than ourselves. It is simply no use at all claiming the gift of God's peace if we are ridden by an overmastering desire to appear bigger or cleverer or more important than we really are. We must first learn to practice acceptance. The second step is to learn to accept life, as Jesus Himself did, at the Father's hands *day by day.* It was not a cynic but the Son of God Himself Who said, "One day's trouble is enough for one day" (Matthew 6:34). We are assured by many inspired promises that God will give us, as we require it, the ability to cope with life victoriously on this day-by-day basis. We must teach ourselves to get out of the habit of thinking too far ahead, of imagining our-

selves tomorrow or next week as inadequate for a situation which exists only in our minds. The sooner we can get it into our feverish souls that we are meant to live a day at a time, the more we shall be able to enjoy that sense of adequacy which spells peace of mind.

(5) *Peace cannot be earned.* I have mentioned above only a few of the psychological factors which may prevent us from enjoying the peace of God. To some simple natures it will appear as though I have overcomplicated the issue. But it is the fortunate few whose inward growth and life is so simple (and by that of course I do not mean stupid) that they can quite readily accept in unquestioning faith the peace of God within their hearts. To others it will naturally appear that I have done no more than touch upon their difficulties, which indeed is all that I have done. I can only recommend here that there must be a full, unashamed bringing to the surface of all the warring elements within the personality. In making such unravelings and adjustments as we can, we are not creating peace; we are only creating conditions for the coming of peace. When our hearts are possessed by this gift of God, we know for certain how true it is that it "passeth man's understanding." Outward circumstances may be tempestuous; common sense may tell us that it is absurd to be at peace under such a load or such a threat. But the gift is supranatural; it goes far beyond earthly common sense. It is, like faith, hope, and love, rooted in the Purpose of God.

(6) *Misalignment with God's purpose.* Peace with God is ¬ot a static emotion. It is a positive gift which accompanies .r living in harmony with God's Plan. Dante's oft quoted saying, "And in His will is our peace," is not to be understood as surrender, resignation, and quiescence. The Christian will discover that he knows God's peace as he is aligned with God's Purpose. He may be called upon to be strenuous, but he is inwardly relaxed because he knows he

is doing the Will of God. This sense of knowing that he is cooperating with the Purpose defies human analysis and is always found singularly irritating by the opponent of Christianity. But Christians of all ages, not excepting our own, have found it to be true. However painful or difficult or, on the other hand, however inconspicuous or humdrum the life may be, the Christian finds his peace in accepting and playing his part in the Master Plan. Here again we must ask ourselves, "Am I doing what God wants me to do?" It is not a question of what my friends or a particular Christian pressure group want me to do, but of what God Himself wishes. By sharing our life with God, by throwing open our personality to His love and wisdom, we can know beyond any doubting what is God's will for us. When we are at one with Him in spirit and at one with Him in purpose, we may know the deep satisfaction of the peace of God.

Christian Maintenance

In order to live a life of New Testament quality we shall find it necessary to work out some kind of practical plan to keep us alive and sensitive to the Spirit of the living God, which will keep us supplied day by day with the necessary spiritual reinforcement, and which will help us to grow and develop as sons and daughters of God. It is, unfortunately, only too easy to slip back into conformity with our immediate surroundings and to lose sight of the suprahuman way of living, except perhaps as a wistful memory. This does not in the least mean that real Christian living is a kind of spiritual tightrope walk, a fantastic and unnatural progress which can only be maintained by intense concentration. On the contrary, the Christian way of living is *real* living, and it carries all the satisfaction and exhilaration which living in reality can bring. It is quite simply because we are surrounded by unreal and false values, by a pattern of living divorced from and unconscious of spiritual realities, that we have to take time and trouble to maintain supranatural life, even though that life is in the truest sense the natural one. Experience shows that Christians whose lives are illuminated by the new quality of living only maintain that inner radiance by taking certain practical steps. Naturally, these will vary in individual cases, and there are people who, either by temperament or through long years of practice, can absorb God through the pores of their being, so to speak, as naturally and easily as most of us can breathe. But for the majority of us who are walking "by faith and not by sight" there are some essentials for the maintenance of real Christian living.

Quietude

THE HIGHER THE function of the human spirit, the more necessity for quietude. We cannot, for example, solve a difficult mathematical problem, neither can we appreciate good music, nor indeed art in any form, if we are surrounded by noisy distractions. It is imperative that somehow or other we make for ourselves a period of quiet each day. I know how difficult this is for many people in busy households, and for some even the bedroom is not quiet or private enough. But if we see the utter necessity for this period of quiet our ingenuity will find a way of securing it. Many churches are open for this purpose, among others, and there is no reason at all why we should not use the quiet of the reading room of the Public Library. But daily quiet we simply must secure, or the noise and pressure of modern life will quickly smother our longing to live life of the new quality.

What we must do in the period of quiet is to open our lives to God—to perfect understanding, wisdom and love. Perhaps it seems unnecessary to point this out, yet pastoral experience convinces me that people need to be reminded that we must be completely natural and uninhibited in our approach to the God "in Whom we live and move and have our being." Most practicing Christians have got beyond feeling that God must be addressed in Elizabethan English in deference to His Majesty, but there still lingers on an idea that we must be spiritually "dressed in our best" as we approach Him. I am far from suggesting that we should ever treat the awe-inspiring mystery of God with over-familiarity. Yet we know perfectly well, on the authority of Christ, that He is our heavenly Father, and our common sense tells us that, although He respects our individuality and our privacy, yet everything about us is quite open to His eyes. We are not addressing some superearthly King, some magnified Boss; we are not even addressing a purified and enlarged image of our own earthly fathers. We are opening our hearts and minds to Love, and we need have no fears, no reticences, and no pretenses. Strange as it undoubtedly is, He loves us as we are, and indeed we shall make no sort of progress unless we approach Him as we are.

Prayer

PRAYER HAS SO many aspects that it requires much longer treatment than I can give it here, and I will only mention three which seem to be the most important.

The first is the value of worship. For myself I do not think worship can be forced, nor can I imagine that God wants it so to be. But if we make a habit of associating all that is good, true, lovely, and heartwarming in our ordinary experience of life and people with Him Who is the Source of every good and perfect gift; if without forcing ourselves to be grateful we quietly recount those things for which we can be truly thankful; if we allow our own dreams and aspirations to lead us upward to the One from Whom they are in fact derived, we shall not infrequently find that the springs of worship begin to flow. Sometimes a consideration of the Character of Christ as revealed in the Gospels, sometimes a consideration of the whole vast Plan for man's redemption, and sometimes a consideration of the immense complexity and wisdom revealed in a dozen different departments by the researches of science will move us to wonder, admiration, awe, and worship.

The second important point I should like to make is that in our prayers we should not merely confess our sins and failures to God, but claim from Him the opposite virtue. If we stress again and again our own particular failings, we tend to accentuate and even to perpetuate them. Many of us Christians need to adopt a more positive attitude. We need to dare to draw upon the inexhaustible riches of Christ, not as though that were some poetic and metaphorical expression, but as though it were a fact. The Gospel is not Good News if it simply underlines our own sinfulness. That is either a foregone conclusion or it is Bad News! But the whole wonder and glory of the Gospel is that into people who have sinned and failed badly God can pour not only the healing of forgiveness but the positive reactivating power of goodness. It is not the mere overcoming of a fault that we should seek from God, but such an overflowing gift of the opposite virtue that we are transformed. I cannot believe that the miracles of personality transformation, which undoubtedly occurred in such places as Corinth and Ephesus nineteen centuries ago, are beyond the power of God's activity today. We are altogether too timorous and tentative. Why should we not make bold and far-reaching demands upon the spiritual riches which are placed at our disposal?

Thirdly, I should like to stress the value of intercession for other people. I do not pretend to understand the mystery of intercession, though I am sure it is never an attempt to bend the will of a reluctant God to do something good in other people's lives. But somehow in the mysterious spiritual economy in which we live we are required to give love, sympathy, and understanding in our prayers for others, and this releases God's power of love in ways and at depths which would otherwise prove beyond our reach. I confess I stand amazed at the power of intercessory prayer, and not least at what I can only call the "celestial ingenuity" of God. He does not, as a rule, directly intervene; He assaults no man's personality, and He never interferes with the free will which He has given to men. Yet, working within these apparently paralyzing limitations, God's love, wisdom, and power are released and become operative in response to faithful intercessory prayer. It is all part of the high Purpose, and all true Christians are responsibly involved in such praying.

Liturgy

IN THE PALMY days when I enjoyed the services of two first-class curates and an excellent lay reader, there were times when I was able to attend services at my own church by slipping quietly into a back pew.

I did this, in the first instance, with a critical professional eye and ear, so that our worship might be of the best possible quality. But, rather to my surprise, I found myself aware of an almost indescribable feeling among the congregation, which I can only describe as a wistful hunger to know more of God.

In the parish of which I am speaking, I should say that very few went to church out of mere habit or duty, and certainly none went because it was "the thing to do" (it wasn't!).

These people came to worship and to pray, but most of all (or so was my strong feeling) to hear more and learn more of the love of God.

Like anyone else who cares for the souls of men, I was moved almost to tears by the quiet receptiveness of ordinary people in church. For in the house of God, they have temporarily laid aside mundane pressures and responsibilities. For the time being at least they are set free from the rat race of competition and from the need to keep up appearances.

In a sense they are naked and vulnerable. More than a little puzzled, sometimes more than a little battered by life's problems, they are seeking news about God.

It is monstrous for the preacher to offer such people a theological digest on the latest book on demythologizing the Gospels. Neither have they come to church to hear the preacher thundering against the sins of those who are not within earshot.

> They simply want to know about God.
> They want to hear the Good News.
> May they always be given it!

Worship

IF YOU ACCEPT the Christian view of God . . . I think you'll find your desire to worship Him will come along two main lines.

First you'll trace to their source all the things that make you admire and love and wonder. It doesn't matter whether it's the beauty of nature, the loveliness of music or poetry, the fascinating charms of childhood, the wonder of falling in love, or any other of the thousand things that move us so deeply. We shall get into the habit of connecting them up with God and probably say a quiet "thank you" for them.

Sometimes, when I've read a book that has really touched me, or seen a picture that has shown some fresh beauty to me, I've felt I'd give a lot to meet the author or the painter and say a personal "thank you." I'm pretty sure you often feel the same.

The other day, looking at some white lilac and thinking what a miracle of beauty it is, I said to myself, "I wish I could meet the one who designed that . . ." and then, quite suddenly, I realized what I was saying! *It was God, my Father and your Father!* And I don't mind telling that I worshiped the Supreme Artist who designed and made white lilac.

That's the sort of thing I mean. Once you accept Christ's

teaching that God is our Father, hundreds of lovely and "wonderfull" things in everyday life make you want to say how thrilled and grateful you are. You'll want to *worship*.

The second way in which you'll want to worship goes rather deeper. . . . When "the penny drops," as we say, when you actually *realize* what sort of Person God must be to come to this earth as a baby, and live and die to show how genuinely He loves us men; and when you realize, as well, that even at this moment God is in the here and now, actually suffering and struggling with us and in us, I'm pretty certain you'll feel "that's the kind of God I could love, that's the kind of God I want to worship."

If I think of God as a kind of Superarchitect who planned this amazing universe from stars to atoms, I feel a bit dazed and awed, but I don't think I particularly want to love Him. It's only when I see God coming in Person into the stream of human living, when I see Him loving and cheering and healing and inspiring people not only when He was on earth in Person 1900 years ago, but *today* whenever He's given the chance, that I feel I want to love and work for and worship Him.

Once you get it, once you realize that *all the time*, even when you broke the rules or did something that you're bitterly ashamed of now, He loved you and was only waiting for the chance to get into touch with you, I think you'll want to worship too.

Sacraments in Life

HERE . . . ARE THREE ordinary things which have very little meaning as physical actions but which may carry with them something far beyond their apparently trivial significance.

(1) Two lovers kiss. To the observer who knows neither of them, this may seem a commonplace, meaningless, or indeed rather vulgar gesture. But to the lovers themselves it may convey a meaning far beyond ordinary means of expression.

(2) Two men who have long been at enmity finally shake hands in reconciliation. Again, to the observer the mere physical action is not worth noticing, but it may be full of the most profound significance, reaching out in time far beyond the few seconds of the handclasp.

(3) We may take the clapping of hands as a token of love, admiration, or appreciation of some great deed or difficult accomplishment. To a stranger to this planet the batting of hands together would appear ridiculous and would convey absolutely nothing of the emotional state which this rather odd action is expressing.

Then we may consider, not actions, but *things* which become highly charged with emotion, though scientifically speaking they remain exactly the same. Here are three examples:

First, a wedding cake, which is in outward appearance and by every scientific measurement exactly the same cake as it was when it stood in the confectioner's window. But it is now a wedding cake, used and consumed at the wedding of two people much in love with each other. In one sense, the scientific sense, the cake is not changed, but in the sense of experience it is now Bill and Joan's wedding cake, and to the friends, near or far, who eat it, it is quite a different thing from the same cake in a shop window.

Or, let us look at this old armchair. To the eyes of the secondhand furniture dealer it is worth perhaps only a few dollars, but to the sons and daughters of the family it is "mother's armchair." It is not merely special, but actually sacred to them because of its hallowed associations.

Or, we may take a Purple Heart, worth as metal not more than a dollar, but to the parents of the man who died winning it worth something beyond price.

Here, we see, are ordinary inanimate things invested with a particular significance and sanctity because of their association with the love and sacrifice of human beings.

Moreover, there are in this bewildering world in which we find ourselves set, things which strike deep spiritual chords within us, which are not explainable in scientific or rational terms. Music can be analyzed into all its resonances, fundamental and harmonic, and its rhythm and pattern explained, but there has never been any explanation of the ways in which it can stir and haunt a human soul. The surge and thunder of the sea, the smell of wood smoke, the woods carpeted with bluebells and a hundred other things can touch and move our spirits in a way science is powerless to explain. It is as though there was another dimension, perhaps several other dimensions, to which our human spirits in some degree respond.

From such things we see that the commonplace may be invested with the highest and purest emotion, and that there are depths and heights in our spirits which may be touched by the simplest of natural phenomena. Then we may well begin to suspect that this physical world is in fact shot through and through with spiritual realities. The physical is plainly often necessary in order to experience or express the spiritual, and what we call the physical may only be the outcrop in time and space of what are eternal realities.

Then we may begin to see the necessity of the Word becoming flesh. For since we cannot appreciate goodness, truth, or beauty until they are embodied in a thing or a person or an action, neither can we properly know the supreme Reality, God, until he becomes a Man and lives among us.

Communion and Common Sense

THE ADVICE THAT Jesus gave was always sound and practical. Reading the Gospels will show us that so far from urging men to retire from this world and contemplate God, the point that Jesus was continually trying to make was that men should see that the Kingdom of God was in the here and now. He pointed out that our relationship with God was intimately bound up with our relationship with our fellow men—that we could not expect, for example, the forgiveness of God unless we were prepared to extend forgiveness to those who had wronged us. The commonsense instincts were to be trusted. *"If you then for all your evil know how to give good gifts . . . how much more? . . ."* Life in the here and now was in one sense of eternal significance, for He Himself had linked Himself indissolubly to the life of Man: He said, *"Inasmuch as ye did it not . . . ye did it not unto Me"* (Matthew 25:31–46).

It was always actual human behavior that mattered to Jesus, and never rosy religious dreams. The young man who hoped to be told what he could add to the pyramid of his spiritual accomplishment was told to sell all he possessed and follow Christ. The man who sought to settle the nice point as to who really was his neighbor was told in effect that whatever human being was in need was his neighbor. The woman who cried out sentimentally, *"How wonderful it must be to have been your mother!"* was told, *"Yes, but still more wonderful to hear the Word of God and keep it"* (Luke 11:27–28).

There is always in the life and teaching of Jesus Christ a

note of downright common sense, of practical human living. We cannot therefore believe that, in instituting this great Sacrament of His own Body and Blood, He would for one moment forget the burden of His teaching. Doubtless . . . through this planned contact with Himself, there will be times when the spirit of man rises above the earthly things. But since this life is so constructed that we have always to return to the humdrum, the unpleasant, the difficult, and the ugly, surely this Sacrament was not primarily designed to enable us to take flight of the spirit. If it means, as it surely must, union with Christ Himself, it cannot avoid meaning sharing something of His outlook, His life, His work, in the here and now, so that in the midst of the mystery there will always be the keynote of common sense and practicality.

The Living Tradition

ALTHOUGH WE HAVE in Holy Communion far more than a tradition, because we have in it something which is alive in itself, yet it has of course a value simply as a tradition, that is, as something men consider worth passing on from generation to generation. But it is unique in that the other end of it is, so to speak, *alive,* intimately joined to the very life of the Son of God Himself. We may perhaps appreciate this better if we compare this living tradition which we possess with some dead relic which we might, but do not in fact, possess. If, for example, we possessed the actual clothes worn by Christ, a lock of His hair, a piece of furniture which He had made while He worked as a carpenter, or even the actual chalice used at the Last Supper, what should we, in fact, have? A relic of enormous historical value, even a piece of solid visible evidence. We may be sure that there would be those who would go into a kind of reverent trance before such objects. But it is almost certain that, as happens with people being confronted with, shall we say, a pair of shoes worn by George Washington or a pen used by Mark Twain, the mind and attention and heart of the beholder would be drawn *toward the past*. Our eyes would inevitably be drawn backward toward the fact of Christ's earthly existence instead of forward to His living Presence today. . . . But we have infinitely more than this, for instead of dead relics, however authentic and well preserved, we have a living lifeline, stretching unbroken to Christ Himself. We have all the comfort and security that comes from historic tradition; but instead of being given the sad nostalgia of looking at an object and saying: "Look, how wonderful! This is what He touched then," we are given an evergreen memorial which says in effect, *"This is what He touches now."*

Eucharistic Fellowship

THE FELLOWSHIP TO which we are called in this strange and honoring and humbling gift of God is inescapably a fellowship of Love which may easily mean a fellowship of suffering. There is joy and strength, of course, in this holy food and drink, but it is also an inevitable joining of forces with the vast Scheme of reconciliation and redemption. Now, there is something in our natural selves that may well make us wary of such a contact. The man who in his heart intends to go on being selfish or proud, or who has already decided how far his Christian convictions should carry him, is probably obeying a sound instinct when he keeps away from this glorious but perilous Sacrament. For, if the truth be told, men are often willing to put their trust in a god who in the end must be triumphant, simply because they want to be on the winning side; but they are not nearly so ready to bear any part of the cost of that winning. Yet the fellowship of the broken bread and the poured-out wine can mean no less than that. . . .

All meals have a fellowship value: we know people better when they have come to tea with us, for example. The man of the world who says to his friends, "Come and have a drink with me," is obeying a deep human instinct for the sacramental, however crudely we may think he expresses it. But this particular fellowship is naturally of a deeper and more important kind. We must not for a moment belittle the value of ordinary human social intercourse, whether it be held in connection with the Church or not. But here Christ Himself is inviting us to experience and enjoy normal human fellowship at a much deeper level. Together we are satisfying a common spiritual need; together we are rededicating our lives to the service of Christ with all that that may imply. Together we are making use of this Christ-appointed contact and opportunity. The fellowship may not express itself in a hearty backslapping way, but it should surely be expressed in a renewed sense of family solidarity. We are meeting together at one of the deepest levels open to us as human beings.

Holy Communion is surely always falling short of its true purpose if it fails to produce some sense of solidarity with our fellow worshippers. It must never be regarded as a luxury for the devout; high and mysterious though it is, it is also the ordained place of deepest fellowship for those who are committed to the Way of Christ, ordinary, faulty, and imperfect though they are.

Spiritual Nutrition

WE ARE ALL familiar with the mystery of ordinary physical digestion. Indeed, like a good many commonplace happenings of this life, we are so familiar with it that we fail to see its wonder. A, B, and C sit round a breakfast table and from the same packet of cornflakes, the same bowl of sugar, and the same pitcher of milk they all break their fast. By a very complex process and, in the last resort, by a mystery which no one can explain, the inanimate matter eaten by A becomes part of A, rebuilding his tissues, or providing him with energy, or slowly adding to his weight. Exactly the same inanimate physical materials become by a similar process part of B or C. A may be redhaired, B may be blond, C may be completely bald, yet the taking of precisely similar quantities of food makes no alteration in their characteristics, but simply becomes part of the physical bodies of A, B, and C. This sort of thing has happened so many million times that we have forgotten that it is not only a highly complex process but a very mysterious one. Now, here in this holy Sacrament we are asked to believe a greater wonder—greater not so much in degree as in quality. We are in fact asked to believe that through the commonplace miracle of physical absorption and nutrition God Himself quickens and nourishes the spiritual life within us. We cannot help thinking at once of the words of Christ in St. John's Gospel: "Except ye eat my flesh and drink my blood, ye have no life in you" (John 6:53). The absorption of Christ into the human soul is an utter necessity if a human being is to remain a Christian at all.

These words spoken by Christ have an obviously wider application than to the Sacrament of Holy Communion. A man may absorb Christ through meditation and contemplation, through the opening of his spirit to the Holy Spirit, by his communion and prayer and worship in his own private room with the living Christ. And yet it is difficult to avoid the conclusion that though Christ was speaking in the broadest possible way of feeding on Himself, He did have in mind the concentrated absorption of Himself which He appointed in the Memorial Meal.

The Christ Within Us

THE RECOLLECTION OF God, the worship of God with mind as well as heart, sincere prayer and thanksgiving, will all help to maintain the vigor of the Christ-life within us. But for inner nourishment can there be anything more appropriate than the bread and wine which Christ Himself declared to be His own Body and Blood?

It is obvious that the Christian life can be maintained without Holy Communion at all. Indeed, it is so maintained, for example, by both the Quakers and by the Salvation Army. But it is surely not the normal, surely not the "Catholic" way (in its proper sense), in which the Spirit has led the Church through the centuries. A man may lead a happy and useful life with only one lung, or with part of his internal organs removed by surgery, but that is not the norm. Obviously it is possible for God to give His grace in a dozen different ways, but it is difficult to see why Christ instituted this particular means of spiritual nutrition unless it had a particular point and purpose for the vast army of

His future followers. Indeed, it is true to say from experience that Christians, unless they are prejudiced, or conditioned by their upbringing, are drawn intuitively toward Holy Communion. Their own natural spiritual hunger draws them instinctively toward the holy provision of the Lord's Table.

All Christians know with sorrow the difference between their high vocation and their everyday failures. All Christians recognize the need for the continual reinforcement of the good and timeless element within their personalities. Here in this Sacrament, under cover of what is ordinary, Christ is prepared to do the extraordinary—to infuse fresh life, to heal, to stimulate, to provide that health of soul which is one of the important meanings of "holiness."

All healing of the body is really accomplished by the *vis medicatrix naturae*, the healing force of nature. The most that medicine and surgery can do is to give this natural force a chance to overcome disease. As we all know very well, in the healthy body there is a host of minor ills which is overcome by the natural force of healing without recourse to doctor or medicine. Similarly the healthy and vigorous mind rejects the unwholesome and copes valiantly with the difficult. It is surely not unreasonable to suppose that there is a *vis medicatrix naturae* of the soul which is quite capable of dealing with the temptations, the sins, and the setbacks of the spiritual life. But only a healthy, properly nourished soul can exert this force, and the Christ-life within us needs its own particular nourishment to retain its resilience and vigor. It surely follows then that to receive with faith this Holy Food is adding immeasurably to the health and strength of the innermost soul.

Christ and the Real Self

IT MIGHT BE questioned . . . whether we are to think of the Holy Food as nourishing the life of Christ within us or whether it is our own souls which are feeding on the "Bread of the world in mercy broken." Here let us put forward the bold suggestion that our "real selves," "our souls," and the "Christ within us" are essentially the same thing. We shall certainly find support for this view in the teaching of the New Testament. First, let us establish the fact that there is a "real self" within us all. If there were not, there would be nothing in Matthew, Peter, James, and John, and the millions since their day, to respond to the One Who says, "Follow Me." There is no need to stress here the reality of the other factors within us; we are only too well aware of them. But it would appear from the record of the Gospels that Christ invariably addressed Himself to the real person existing behind the facade presented to the world. Even His scathing onslaughts against the hypocrisy of the religious leaders may fairly be regarded as an "armor-piercing" method designed to reach the diminished but real person within.

Now, when that real person, either suddenly or gradually, decides to follow Christ, he experiences not only a sense of peace, forgiveness, and deep happiness, but also of being, in a previously unimagined way, in touch with the Infinite God. Small, poor, and flickering his flame may be, but in all humility he recognizes that it is a tiny part of the celestial Radiance.

Christ Himself plainly taught that His own life and those

of His close disciples were interwoven not only with each other but even with the eternal life of the Father. Familiarity has dulled for most of us that hitherto unheard-of intimacy between the life of God, the life of Christ, and the life of the disciples of Christ, which is spoken of as a plain matter of fact in, for example, Chapters 14, 15, and 16 of St. John's Gospel. Like many other of the New Testament promises, we tend to think of these things as too good to be true, and cannot see that they are both good and true. The life of the Vine, for example, and the life of the branches is of the same stuff, essence, and quality. It cannot therefore be impertinent for us to hold firmly to the belief that the life of our real selves is the same thing as the life of Christ within us.

The letters of the New Testament abound not with pious hopes but with audacious certainty. "Now are we the sons of God," "heirs of God and joint-heirs with Christ," "seated together with Christ"—these are the sort of expressions which sparkle on the sea of that early Christian confidence. God is now no longer aloof, separate—He is one with His sons. Confidence that man could never muster, certainty which he never dared to believe possible—all this and much more has come true in Christ, and shines from the pages of these unself-conscious writings.

But we, in our cautious reverence, forget how closely God in Christ has identified Himself with humanity. Because of our worldly set of values, we set God on the wrong kind of pedestal, so that the reality of the Incarnation becomes as impossible to conceive as the thought of a company president having tea with his janitor! If we do that sort of thing, and ascribe this world's dignity and privilege to God (which is a frightful piece of impertinence), we miss the whole point of God's pride-shattering humility. But there is no blinking the facts. God *did* become Man, God *did* accept the limitation and frustrations of human living, God *did* link

Himself indissolubly with poor blundering humanity. He did not shrink from calling Himself, and acting as though He were, Representative Man, which is what "Son of Man" means. Moreover, in that picture of the Last Judgment, commonly known as the Parable of the Sheep and Goats, He so far identifies Himself with needy suffering human beings as to state categorically that the way in which men treat each other is in solemn fact the way in which they treat Him (Matthew 25:40–46).

In the light then of God's deliberate identification of Himself with mortal man through Christ, we shall not go far wrong if we identify the Christ Who is formed and is developing within us with the real self which has heard and is responding to His call. We need this particular nourishment, for upon the health of this vital center depends the whole quality of our life.

Physical and Mental Preparation for Communion

IF THIS IS an occasion when man can in a unique way make contact with his God and Savior (and surely it must always be such an occasion, even when we ourselves are weary and depressed), there must be a certain deliberate preparation of body, mind, and soul. No one, of course, makes any social contact without taking the trouble to prepare; how much more ready should we be to prepare ourselves to meet God at these special points in our earthly pilgrimage? Let us consider our bodies first. Surely the best way of setting either mind or spirit free is to be as unaware of the body as possible. If the body is overtired or out of sorts, it will be a drag upon the mind and spirit. We should be sensible enough to see that the body is in as good condition as possible, so that for the time being we may forget it . . . .

Again, in posture we should aim at that position of the body which allows both relaxation and alertness of mind. No one would dream of attempting to tackle a difficult personal problem or even of solving a crossword puzzle while in a cramped and unnatural posture. Why should we expect the spirit to rise and worship and adore if the body is hideously uncomfortable?

We need also, as we have already said, to prepare the mind. Probably one of the greatest things that we can learn to do is to learn a holy relaxation. Sometimes we are unaware of the cause of our tensions, but often they are revealed to us as we deliberately open our mental life to the Spirit of God. We may find that we have been trying to preserve an inflated idea of ourselves; we may find that we have been childishly nursing a grudge against life or against someone else. There are innumerable causes of tension, but in the presence of perfect understanding they can be relaxed. We may need to apologize to God or to other people, we may need an honest laugh at our pretentious selves, or we may need quite simply to hand responsibility, too big for ourselves, into the hand of God. To remove these tensions, possibly with the help of a trusted friend, is one of the essentials of preparation.

Having eased the mind of its strains, most of us need some central thought by which we can focus our attention during the time of Holy Communion. Obviously there are innumerable lines of thought which we may profitably follow. Here we suggest only a few.

(1) We may let our mind range quite freely over the vastness and complexity of God's wisdom and power,

slowly allowing ourselves to realize that such a God focused Himself in the historic Person of Christ. From this point we let our minds dwell on the fact that Christ instituted this particular Sacrament; that though He is all about us, and indeed within us, yet it was no "bright idea" of mankind but Christ's own purpose that He should give Himself to us in the mystery of the holy Bread and Wine.

(2) Sometimes we may think of the vast unseen world existing quite independently of the time-and-space setup. We may think of the times when spiritual reality touches us very closely. We may use our imaginations freely, and not feel in the least ashamed that "we that are in this tabernacle do groan being burdened." We may remind ourselves that though we are citizens of the heavenly country, yet for the most part we walk by faith and not by sight. Our moments of illumination are few, yet here, so to speak, is a guaranteed point where the eternal reaches through and touches the temporal. This Sacrament is a pledge from generation to generation, not only of the Love of God but of the everlasting nearness of the spiritual in the material.

(3) Sometimes we may think of ourselves, small and feeble as we are, carrying out, in company with millions of others, the Will of God in a world disrupted and disorganized. We think of ourselves together as representing Christ, however imperfectly, to a world desperately in need of the very qualities which He can provide. We think of our own deep need for the strength and vitality needed to represent Christ in our particular circle. We need the nourishment of Christ within, His very Personality potent and operative within our personalities. Then we think of what this Sacrament provides—the very nourishment, the very Presence we need, ready to be absorbed into our own selves.

(4) Sometimes we may think of the memorial aspect of the Great Sacrifice. We may have been guilty, as so many are, of allowing our own sense of sinfulness, or our own

limited ideas of justice, to caricature our idea of God. We may see Him again "advertised" in this Sacrament as infinitely patient, vulnerable Love. The particular Communion we are attending is one end of a thread which leads back over the centuries unbroken to the Cross of Christ. "God was in Christ reconciling the world unto Himself." We may long reflect upon God's almost fantastic generosity in making reconciliation by this personal action and at this personal cost. Have we by any chance been trying to worship the wrong kind of God?

(5) Sometimes we may reflect upon the nature of sacrifice. How often no lasting good is achieved without considerable cost to someone! We think of the lives of truly great men and women and how their great deeds have not influenced the lives of others without sacrifice. There is no need to be morbid, for often the sacrifices were cheerfully made. But it seems to be a principle of life that the lower must be denied to gain the higher, that no situation or person is redeemed without cost. Naturally we think of the One Great Sacrifice, now represented for us in poignant symbols in the broken bread and poured-out wine. We are to receive these things, this very Person, not only for our comfort and inspiration, but that we too may share, in a minor way no doubt, in the whole vast work of costly redemption. In our receiving of the sacrificial food there lies not only a deliberate allying of ourselves with the work of Christ, but an acceptance of the strength and joy to make whatever sacrifices come our way with courage and good humor.

These five suggestions are but a few of the ways in which we can deliberately turn our minds from their normal preoccupation with earthly activities and become receptive to the Eternal Purpose.

Spiritual Preparation for Communion

MUCH AS A tiny gland may affect the whole functioning of the body, so what goes on in his innermost soul will affect the whole attitude and activity of a man's life. Only God has access to this inmost soul, and He through His chivalry only by our permission.

But most of us, if we come to Communion at all, desire to give that permission. We want to be touched by God. We know only too well that we are soiled and weary, infected by the world around us far more than we care to be, and we want to be touched afresh with the never-failing Spring of Life Himself. How then can we prepare our soul?

(1) Without morbid "muckraking" we can freely admit our prides and cowardices, our lack of charity and the poor quality of our faith. Then we can accept the cordial of God's free forgiveness and reinstatement. There is no question of our deserving such generous love, but it is a fact of life of which we can be quite sure. Then, if we have first relaxed the mind, we can allow our inmost selves to be both teachable and flexible. It is the hardest thing in the world for some people to admit that they have been wrong. But we really shall not get far in the spiritual life if, in the presence of Infinite Wisdom, we insist on being always right! God is the only one Who is always right, and His ways, though firm, are much gentler than we may suppose.

(2) Then, without whipping ourselves up into a false state of emotion, let us be expectant. What the Bible calls

"faith" appears to be the essential link between the boundless resources of God and our own feebleness. The life of God within us is limited far more often than we know because we do not really believe in how much becomes possible through faith in God. "Faith" is often like a faculty which has grown atrophied through disuse. It is that function of ours with which we can touch and hold the love and power of God.

(3) Lastly, we can gently train our souls to respond to the Love of God. We cannot force our own souls to love or to be grateful towards God any more than we can force anybody else to feel love or gratitude towards us. But we can at least put ourselves in the way of responding to God's Love. We can meditate upon it, upon the Nature and Character of God as revealed by Christ, and we can deliberately associate in our minds with God all those lovely and heartwarming things which, despite the evil, adorn our common life. It is only love that can beget love, and self-giving that can stimulate self-giving. We cannot force the pace here, but we can quietly look upon what sort of Person our God really is.

Now, it is obviously impossible for most people who live busy lives to make an elaborate preparation for Holy Communion, however desirable that may be. But if there is no preparation of mind and soul, what should be a tryst with God will in most cases degenerate into a "duty attendance." Of course, if we imagine that Holy Communion is some kind of magical prescription which can be received in regular doses to maintain spiritual health, preparation would hardly be necessary. But because it is no such thing, because it is the using of our highest faculties and the possible touching of our deepest springs of feeling, there must be at least a simple preparation of mind and soul. There will be times, naturally, when through ill-health or fatigue or that deadness of spirit which assails us all from time to time, there will be little emotional content. But this need not matter if in all honesty and sincerity of purpose we have confidently kept out appointment with God.

The Sacrament itself will vary in its emphasis according to different needs or temper or circumstances. Sometimes it may be a tonic; sometimes it may be an inestimable refreshment, sometimes a revitalizing of the very springs of spiritual life, sometimes a glimpse of Heaven and an unspeakable joy, sometimes a renewal of dedication in deepest fellowship and with the Unseen Presence, but always it will be to those who love and believe an appointment with God.

Forgiveness and Forgivingness

ONE OF THE most astonishing things that Jesus Christ ever said was that men cannot hope to be forgiven by God unless they are prepared to forgive the people who offend or hurt them. I sometimes think this very searching truth has been soft-pedalled, but it's very evident in the Gospels. Every time we say the Lord's Prayer we say, "Forgive us our trespasses as we forgive them that trespass against us," and Jesus added: "For if you forgive other people their failures your Heavenly Father will also forgive you: but if you will not forgive other people neither will your Heavenly Father forgive your failures" (Matthew 6:14–15).

If we could only see for a moment how much God is prepared to forgive us, and how comparatively little we are prepared to forgive other people, we might have a good laugh at ourselves, which would do us a lot of good, as well as help us to know much more of what being at peace with God means.

The Church

THE CHURCH BEGAN with the supernaturally inspired insight of Peter who cried, "Thou art the Christ, the Son of the living God" (Matthew 16:16). Up to that moment, if we may look at things reverently from Christ's point of view, there had been swirling tides of emotion among the people whom He met. Popular enthusiasm ran high; He was the great Healer, He was the wonderful Teacher, He was a reincarnation of one of the prophets of old. But all this was an unreliable floating tide of opinion. Then came Peter's inspired remark, and at once our Lord (God walking the earth as a human being) seized upon the solidity of real faith. "You are Peter, the Rock-man!" He cried out, in delight, I think, "and upon this rock I will build my church" (Matthew 16:18). To Christ's matchless insight here was the beginning of this worldwide fellowship of men and women of all races. Here was the tiny beginning of the society which would transcend all barriers of color, class and custom, yes, and even time and space as well. For Peter, in a moment of true faith, had seen who Christ really was.

To see and to recognize who Jesus Christ really was and is makes the whole vast work of rescue possible. Prophets, poets, idealists, all have their message to give, but until someone sees that God Himself has penetrated into human life at man's own level there can be no real beginning to the work of making men whole. Without this recognition there is no certainty, only a feeling. Without this recognition there is no observable purpose in all the ills and accidents, the injustices and the bitter disappointment in this transitory part of existence that we call life. But once this recognition has come to birth, the certainty is there, the guarantee is there, the power is there; the authority, the plan and the purpose are all there, and the building can begin. No wonder Christ said of Peter's outburst of faith, "upon *this* rock I will build my church."

Fellowship of the Church

IT IS VERY noticeable in the New Testament records of the early Church that Christianity existed in fellowship. Of course, it may easily be pointed out that a sect which was such a tiny minority in a pagan world would be forced to close its ranks and stand together if it were to survive at all. That is perfectly true, but it was surely more than mere expediency that kept the early Christians together. Surely part of their extraordinary strength and vitality was due to their being "of one heart and mind." They worshiped and prayed together; they shared in "the breaking of bread" (Acts 2:42). Even though, judging from the evidence of Paul's letters, it was not very long before factions and "splinter groups" arose, yet the overall picture is of the Young Church standing firm and fearless in fellowship.

Because human beings are for the most part gregarious by nature, they tend to join with others who have similar interests. There are clubs, associations, fraternities, and societies without number throughout the whole civilized world to join together in fellowship people whose common interest may be fly fishing, stamp collecting, bird watching, hiking, photography, gardening, interplanetary travel, or any of a host of widely assorted subjects. Since this is so, it would appear to the casual observer that the fellowship of the Church is simply another organization, in this case an association of people whose interests lie in the Christian religion. But this is very far from being the case, for the fellowship of Christians is the outward manifestation of a deep spiritual unity. Men and women have discovered through the living Spirit of God what they are meant to be and the Plan with which they are called to cooperate. They have discovered the reality of the spiritual order and, what is even more important, they have found that Jesus Christ is no mere Figure of history but a living contemporary Person Whose personality and power cleanses and invigorates their own. They have discovered beneath the surface of different temperaments and backgrounds that they belong to the same family—that they are all sons and daughters of the same Father. They are, in a world largely insensitive to the true order of things, "picked representatives" of the new humanity (Colossians 3:12). In a very real sense they are carrying on the work which Christ began so long ago, not so much in admiration and memory of Him, but as people dedicated to follow the leading of His contemporary Spirit. They form together, as Paul pointed out long ago, "the body of Christ" (1 Corinthians 12:27). They are not a human organization but a suprahuman organism. They are the life of the real world being expressed in human terms in the present temporary setup.

Of course, all the above may appear a pathetically or even a ridiculously idealistic picture of the modern Church. But surely the words fairly represent what the Church should be and could be, and they at least partly explain why Christian fellowship in the Church is far more essential than any human association for the promotion of this, that, or the other. Because Christians are "members one of another" they must work as an organic whole, different as their individual functions may be. All this means that a very large part of our Christian maintenance will consist of joining in with the fellowship of the Church, in its prayer and worship, in its work and service . . . .

If the Church is to make any worthwhile impact on the surrounding community, if it is even to speak with a voice worth hearing, it must have the active, committed support of all true Christians . . . .

This whole question of entering fully into the worship and work of the Church must be faced by all those who genuinely desire to serve Christ in this modern age. There is an immense amount of diffused goodwill and willingness to serve others in countries with a Christian tradition such as this. Such things are far from valueless to the community as a whole, but I am convinced they would be far more potent in coping with mankind's ills and necessities if they were part of the extramural work of the Church of Christ. The Christian Church should surely be the center of inspiration, as well as the meeting place for worship.

Christian Service

THE EARLY VIGOROUS Church was essentially a working, serving, and forward-looking Church. Partly because of a sensitivity to the Spirit's direction and partly because of the rising tide of persecution the Young Church did not have much chance of becoming self-satisfied and complacent. It expanded and spread into all sorts of unlikely places armed only with the Good News of the love and power of the Spirit. Throughout the New Testament letters we can see how insistent are Paul and the others that the love of God which has sprung up in men's hearts at the touch of Christ must be expressed in outward conduct toward a pagan and frequently hostile world. The early Christians were pioneers of a new way of life, and many of them plainly regarded themselves as expendable for the cause of the Kingdom. The time had not yet come for any church to become inward-looking, prosperous, or self-satisfied.

Sometimes nowadays one gets the impression that the Christian churches have largely ceased to look outward. It is almost as though Christians exist in a closed circle of fellowship, with all their members facing inward, while behind their backs there are the millions who long, albeit unconsciously, for the Gospel, and for the point and purpose in life that only the Gospel can bring. If the churches are to recover the vast power and influence of the Church of New Testament times, there must be a fundamental change of attitude in many churches, which means, of course, a fundamental change in the attitude of the churches' members. We must recover our sense of vocation, our sense that we are not, as I said above, an organization of people who have a common interest in religion, but the local representatives of the God Whom we serve and of the Heaven to which we belong.

We may be full of joy, but we are not here for our own amusement. We are here to be used as instruments in God's Purpose. It is a fine thing to know that we are "right with God," "converted," "born again," and all the rest of it, but after a while such experiences become stale and unsatisfying unless we are passing the Good News on to others, positively assisting the work of the Church, or definitely bringing to bear upon actual human situations the pattern of Christian living. This means in effect that each Christian must ask himself, "Am I myself outward-looking in my Christian experience, or am I content to remain in a safe 'Christian rut'?" The recovery of the Church's power rests ultimately upon the individual Christian's answer to such a question.

Coming down to actual practice, the Christian has to ask himself what he can do to express outwardly and effectively his inward spiritual certainty. Obviously his first duty is to live a Christian life in his home and in his place of work. This is where his witness is most effective, and frequently most difficult, but busyness in Church affairs is no substitute whatever for exhibiting Christian graces in the home or being known as a Christian in our place of work. But, assuming that we have seriously considered our ordinary Christian life and witness, we ought also as members of the Church to think seriously of what our contribution should be in terms of time, personality, and talent to the life of the church to which we belong. I have already referred to the horrifying paucity of *leaders* in most of our churches, of men and women who will take responsibility and work at a job for the love of Christ and His Church. The influence of the Christian fellowship upon children, upon adolescents, upon the community in which the Church's life is set would be vastly enhanced if even half the existing church members were to give a single hour of dedicated service every week to their church. Of course, to do such a thing even at the one-hour-per-week rate is costly, and a hundred different excuses crowd readily into the mind. But if the Church is to revive and become once more ablaze with the truth of God and full of the warmth of His love, its members must be prepared to meet the cost and make the sacrifice. The by-product will be of course the maintenance of a high level in the spiritual life of the individual members. For the real danger to professing Christians lies not in the more glaring and grosser temptations and sins, but in a slow deterioration of vision, a slow death to daring, courage, and the willingness to adventure.

I cannot refrain from bringing this to a personal point. Our gifts vary enormously; we cannot all be evangelists, pastors, or teachers. We cannot all be leaders or bear great responsibility, but there is certain to be something, some worthwhile piece of service, which only you the reader can do. It may be exciting, it may be humdrum, it may be participating in a new venture, or it may be a mere routine. The apparent importance of it does not really matter; what is of real consequence both to your church and to your own soul is whether you are willing to give yourself sacrificially.

Bible Reading

COUNTLESS MEN AND WOMEN throughout the centuries have found their inspiration and nourishment for the Christian life in reading the Word of God. Now, I am not at all sure that our modern way of living is suited to the old-fashioned methods of Bible study. It is not really going to help us to live today if we know, for example, the chronological order of the kings of Israel and Judah, or study verse by verse the book of Lamentations or the book of Esther. If we are pressed for time, and most of us are, what we chiefly need to do is to study the four Gospels and soak ourselves in their spirit, and then to study with imagination the Epistles or Letters, which reflect the life of the vigorous Young Church. I am far from writing off the Old Testament as useless; but to the modern follower of Christ, whose time is limited, it is infinitely more important that he should know intimately the four recorded lives of Christ and the message of the Letters of the New Testament than to possess cover-to-cover knowledge of the whole Bible, which is bound to be sketchy and superficial. To my mind the day of "proof texts" is over. It is not a matter of guiding our life and conduct by finding a particular verse or phrase. What is important is that we should really understand to the limit of our ability what sort of Person Christ was, what were His methods, and what were His aims. We need to know what He did in fact say about the important questions affecting life and death, which all of us have to face sooner or later. We need to use our minds, to be as unfettered as we possibly can be from prejudice and religious indoctrination. Let us see and feel for ourselves what Christ really was and really taught. Let us allow our minds and spirits to be thoroughly influenced, not by the traditions of men, but by what Christ Himself was, said, and taught. He is "the same yesterday, and today, and forever" (Hebrews 13:8), and as we read His recorded life we can reflect that it is not fancy but sober fact that He Himself stands beside us to guide and instruct us. We need His living Spirit to make the connection between the world of New Testament days and the world in which we have to live today.

This intelligent reading, particularly of the New Testament, will keep alive and alert our inmost spirits. The sacred pages are truly inspired, not I believe in any "verbal inspirational" sense but because they contain the Word of God or, in case that is a meaningless cliché, they contain truths of the Real World in the language of this. Again and again we shall find ourselves challenged, convicted, inspired, or comforted by truths that are not of man's making at all, but which are bright shafts of light breaking through into our darkness.

Christian Reading

IT IS A profound mistake to suppose that the Holy Spirit of God ceased to inspire writers when the New Testament had been completed. There are many Christians today who from one year's end to another never read a Christian book. They have little or no idea, for example, how Christianity is spreading throughout the world, of the triumphs and disappointments of the worldwide Church. They have given themselves no chance to know why there is a worldwide movement toward a once more united Church. They do not know the Christian answer to the challenge of Communism; they are even hazy about the very real and solid achievements of Christian men and women throughout the centuries. To be brutally frank, they are very ignorant both of the history and of the implications of their Faith. In other departments of life they may be highly competent, efficient, and knowledgeable, but over this, the very heart and center of their true life, they are frequently abysmally ignorant. These are, I know, harsh words; but the Church could be infinitely more powerful as God's instrument for the establishment of His Kingdom if its members were better informed in their minds as well as more devoted in their hearts.

Books, Films, and Plays

THERE ARE THREE main ways in which fiction (in which term we include books, films, and plays) can mislead us, and in consequence profoundly affect the idea we unconsciously hold of God and His operation in human life.

First, the tacit ignoring of God and all "religious" issues.

A vast amount of fiction presents life as though there were no God at all, and men and women had no religious side to their personalities whatever. We may for instance meet, in fiction, charming people who exhibit the most delightful qualities, surmount incredible difficulties with heart-stirring courage, make the most noble sacrifices and achieve the utmost happiness and serenity—all without the slightest reference to God. The reader is almost bound to reflect that all the fuss Christianity makes about "seeking God's strength" and so on is much ado about nothing.

Conversely, we not infrequently read of evil characters who, for all their lust, cruelty, meanness, or pride never seem to suffer the faintest twinge of conscience. There appears to be no spiritual force at work pointing out to them, at vulnerable moments, a better way of living; and repentance is unthinkable. The reader is again, unconsciously, likely to conclude that God does nothing to influence "bad" characters.

This bypass which neatly avoids God and the religious side of life is not characteristic perhaps of the very best fiction, but it is extremely common. In films in particular, with a few notable exceptions, "providence" is subject to almost cast-iron conventions. These include the socially desirable "crime-does-not-pay" ethic, and the inevitable happy ending. But any resemblance between the celluloid providence and the real actions of God in human affairs is purely coincidental.

In actual life, as any parson worth his salt well knows, ordinary people do at times consider God and spiritual issues. The evil, and even the careless, are occasionally touched by their consciences. Moreover, the tensions and crises which are the breath of life to the fiction writer are the very things which frequently stimulate the latent spiritual or religious sense. It is an extraordinary phenomenon that the modern writer who has, Heaven knows, few reticences and who is sometimes almost morbidly analytical of his characters' actions, should so frequently use the bypass road round the whole sphere of a man's relations with his God.

Second, the wilful misrepresentation of religion.

It can of course be argued that it is no part of the duty of a writer of fiction to provide Christian propaganda—and that is perfectly true. But it is equally no part of his work, which is "to hold up a mirror to life," to give the impression that Christianity and the Church are no more than a subject for ridicule. It may of course be great fun for him—he may be working off a childhood grudge against an Evangelical aunt—to represent clergymen as comic, bigoted, or childishly ignorant of life, and Christians as smug hypocrites. He may even feel that there is more dramatic value in the rector who is a domestic tyrant or the nonconformist deacon who is a secret sadist than in the genuine articles. But he is not, in so doing, being fair to the actual facts of life, even though his writing my prove highly gratifying to the reader who is only too ready to welcome this endorsement of his own feeling that "religion is all rot anyway."

Again, this criticism cannot fairly be leveled at the best fiction, but it is extremely common in the popular type, and slowly but surely affects the conception of religion and of God in the minds of many readers.

Third, the manipulation of providence.

The author of fiction (and this is not the least of the attractions of authorship) is in the position of a god to his own creatures. He can move in a mysterious way, or an outrageous way, or an unjust way, his wonders to perform; and no one can say him nay. If he works skillfully (as, for instance, did Thomas Hardy) he may strongly infect his reader with, for example, the sense of a bitterly jesting Fate in place of God. He can communicate heartbreak by the simplest of manipulations, because he is himself providence, *but he is not thereby providing any evidence of the workings of real life.*

The whole tragedy of King Lear might be said to depend on Shakespeare's manipulation of the character of Cordelia. Because she is unable to see (though every schoolgirl in the pit can see) the probable consequence of her blunt "Nothing," the tragedy is launched. But it would be a profound mistake to confuse the organized disasters of even the greatest writer of tragedy with the complex circumstances and factors which attend the sufferings of real life.

Conclusions as to the nature of Life and God can only in very rare instances be inferred from the artificial evidence of fiction. We need therefore to be constantly on our guard against the "secondhand god"—the kind of god which the continual absorption of fictional ideas nourishes at the back of our minds. One tiny slice of real life, observed at firsthand, provides better grounds for our conclusions than the whole fairy world of fiction.

The Badness of Goodness

THERE IS A chapter in Professor Thomas Jessop's book *Law and Love* with the provoking title "The Badness of Goodness"; it explains with the utmost clarity why it was not the publicans and sinners, but those whose lifelong purpose was to lead good lives, who, by a strange paradox, became the deadly enemies of God in human form. It is, I think, a mistake to suppose that all the Pharisees, for example, were self-righteous humbugs whose unreality and hypocrisy Jesus mercilessly exposed. It would be truer to say that they were men ruled by principle, often with a great many conspicuous virtues; but they differed from Christ fundamentally in that the mainspring of their lives lay in observing the law and keeping their own souls unspotted from the world, while His lay in loving His Father with the whole of His being, and His fellow men with the same love that He knew was eternally at the heart of His Father. Their religion was a kind of contract, a *quid pro quo* performance, while His was the spontaneous outliving of unadulterated love. It must often have looked to them as though He were ready to drive a coach and six through the law and the prophets. But in fact He went far above and beyond any "righteousness" that the law could produce. When directly challenged, He declared that the whole of the prophet's message and the law's morality depended upon the two most important commandments, namely, to love God with the whole of the personality, and to love one's neighbor as oneself (Matthew 22:38–40). St. Paul, seeing the same truth in a slightly different way—and not, I think, ever quite able, despite his protestations, to shake himself completely free from the Law in which he was nurtured—declared, "Love therefore is the fulfillment of the law" (Romans 13:10).

It would be a profound mistake to suppose that all the Pharisees disappeared soon after the death of Christ, or that they have no heirs and successors today. Indeed, it is true that there is much of the Pharisee in each one of us, and by that I do not mean that we are hypocrites, but simply that we would rather reduce religion to a code, both inward and outward, than take the tremendous risk of being invaded by and becoming part of vulnerable but relentless love. We do not have to look far to find Christians who have tamed and regulated something that can in fact neither be tamed nor regulated. We do not like risks; we do not like being hurt or disappointed; and there is in us all something of the spirit which would rather label and condemn and bewail than love and suffer and perhaps redeem. We smile as we read of Peter's attempt to regulate the illimitable. "If I have got to forgive," he said, "could we not regard seven times as the maximum?" (Matthew 18:21). But the same spirit is in us, and perhaps we have not yet seen how vast and humble and magnificent and generous is the love of God, nor have we realized that we are to be "perfect as He is perfect" (Matthew 5:48). Yet until we have some realization of this illimitable love of God, we shall never understand the conflict between "religion" and the Son of God, observed and recorded for our learning.

Competition in Goodness

IT'S A STRANGE thing, but a lot of people seem to imagine that life is a kind of competition in being good! They think that Christians and the people who go to church are saying to those who live without faith, without ever going to church—"Look at us, we're ever so much better than you!" Consequently, the non-Christian, the non-Church-goer, quite often says,—"I'm quite as good as So-and-so who calls himself a Christian and goes to church regularly." And then he thinks he's given a final and crushing reply to the whole Christian faith!

I really don't know where this idea of a "competition in being good" came from; it certainly isn't the Christian religion. After all, judging by ordinary standards, I can think straightaway of a dozen good decent people who would never claim to hold the Christian faith and certainly never go to church, and they're very nice people. At the same time I can think of an equal number of people who *do* hold the Christian faith and who *do* go to church. They're full of faults and failings, of which they're well aware and which they're trying to overcome with the help of God. And they're very nice people too!

This "competition in goodness" idea is really quite beside the point. The fact is that a lot of decent-living people never seem to have any need of God. While among any group of Christians you'd be bound to find people who have sought God because they needed Him, either because their own temperaments were too much for them, or because life faced them with overwhelming tragedy or difficulty, or simply because they found that, until they knew God, life was a pretty empty affair with no aim or purpose. The question of being "better" or "superior" to people outside the churches doesn't, in my experience, arise at all.

Evil

THE POWERS OF EVIL, whether outside or inside the human personality, are never nowadays taken to have any real existence. We willingly admit to being maladjusted or repressed or deprived, and we are quite willing to have psychiatry explain our delinquencies and sins, but we do not usually admit the existence of "evil." Now to men like Paul, John, Peter, and James right and wrong existed as surely as light and darkness. The Christian's way was a tough and difficult battle, and to win it he needed "the whole armor of God." Theirs was a spiritual struggle against the unseen forces of evil.

If we talk or preach today about the reality of evil, we are accused of "dualism," which is a technical term meaning that this world has really two gods, the God who is all that is good, and Satan, who is all that is evil. If one's critics mean that we believe in the permanent existence of Satan, the devil, or the powers of evil, they are wrong, for we do not. Once we have passed from this stage of existence into the one Christ has prepared for us, "Satan" ceases to exist. But for the time being, the power of evil to obstruct, confuse, corrupt, seduce, dissuade—all the unholy battery by which the Christian is assailed—is real, and is to be fought and defeated.

If someone cannot grasp how a fact of this life can cease to be a fact in some other mode of existence, we need look no further for an illustration than our own bodies. For the time being, they are real enough, and we must feed and clothe and wash and generally look after them. No one but a madman believes that his body has no reality, and even the strictest ascetic has to eat and drink unless he is bent on suicide. These bodies are real, but only temporarily so. As we have already seen, they are doomed to physical dissolution sooner or later. In another world they cease to be. So it is with the powers of evil. They are "temporary" in the sense that they are limited to this life, but to regard them as anything less than real in the here-and-now can be most dangerous.

All this is nonsense to the uncommitted agnostic, but it is sober truth to the man who is honestly committed to the way of Christ. I have never yet met a Christian who was not tempted, sometimes severely and for a long time. And I don't think I have ever met an agnostic who has any idea of what we mean by our battle against spiritual powers of evil. The New Testament view makes better sense to me than the best of humanism, as well as describing something far more like my own experience and that of the Christians I know. There *is* a struggle, sometimes a very bitter and difficult one, and it is not merely against "absence of good" or "ignorance" or "the amoral unconscious mind." Maybe it is against these, but the sense of conflict against actual evil which the Christian has to fight is as real in his experience as any other part of his observed existence.

Temptation

JESUS APPARENTLY SPOKE of "Satan," "the devil," "the prince of this world," and "the wicked one." Paul wrote of "Satan," "the god of this world," "the devil," and in the famous sixth chapter of his letter to the Ephesians he speaks of the battle of the Christian "against principalities, against powers, against the rulers of the darkness of this world, against spiritual wickedness in high places." Peter warned his readers that their "adversary the devil, as a roaring lion, walketh about, seeking whom he may devour." James gave the advice to "resist the devil, and he will flee from you." John refers several times to "the devil," the "children of the devil," and "the works of the devil," and in speaking of the Christian's battle, he reminds his readers that "greater is he that is in you than he that is in the world."

There is no need at all for us to revert to medieval crudity and to conjure up a whole picture gallery of devils. But it is quite as unrealistic to suppose that there is no adversary, no sower of doubts and fears, no tempter to corrupt our best endeavors. Jesus used the name Satan for this evil force, presumably because it was current in his day and his hearers would know what he was talking about. But, just as he never argued about the existence of God, so he accepted as a fact of life this evil power which can, at any time, destroy or corrupt. It is noteworthy that when Peter was once inspired to see who Jesus really was, Jesus congratulated him on the insight given to him, and almost at once rebuked him sternly as "Satan," for suggesting a course that would be contrary to the plan of God (Matthew 16:23). I quote here from a recent book: "Anyone who has ever tried to formulate a private prayer in silence, and in his own heart, will know what I mean by *diabolical interference*. The forces of evil are in opposition to the will of God. And the nearer a man's will approaches God's, the more apparent and stronger and more formidable this opposition is seen to be. It is only when we are going in more or less the same direction as the devil that we are unconscious of any opposition at all." [*Of Heaven and Hope* by David Bolt.] These sentences are completely true to my own experience of life and to that of my Christian friends and correspondents. The battle of which the New Testament speaks so realistically is still raging, and every Christian finds himself involved in it.

Guilt

WE ARE NOT concerned with artificial guilt or sin. . . . All religions, Christianity unfortunately not excepted, tend to excite in certain people an artificial sense of guilt, which may have little or no connection with a man's actual standing before God. Probably Pharisaism, which Christ attacked with bitter scorn, represents this tendency at its highest, but it is a mistake to think that Pharisaism disappeared after the death of Christ. The danger of such a system, and the reason why Christ attacked it so violently, is that its values are artificial. The proud and correct feel "right with God" just when they are not, and the sensitive humble man feels hopeless and overburdened *for the wrong reasons*. (Christ's little cameo of the Pharisee and the tax collector at their prayers is an unforgettable commentary on this point.)

Imperfection

WE ARE NOT concerned with mere comparison with perfection. . . . A great deal of the sense of sin and shame and guilt induced in certain types of people is simply due to their (imaginary) comparison of their human standards with what they conceive to be the Divine Standards. Of course they feel failures! You have only to raise the standard, and go on raising it, to make anyone feel a hopeless blundering idiot. This may be what we are in comparison with the wisdom of God, but, to put it at its crudest, it would be an extraordinarily ungentlemanly thing for Him merely to keep raising the standard! After all, it is a foregone conclusion that no man can compete with his Creator, and there is neither sense nor justice in thinking that the Creator intends His creatures to feel permanently inferior and humiliated compared with Himself! Yet this comparison, cloaked and disguised, is often made in a certain type of sermon and a certain type of religious book. But the feeling of hopelessness and inadequacy it engenders is quite wrongly taken to be "conviction of sin."

Humiliation

WE ARE NOT concerned with mere humiliation. Quite a lot of people, if psychologically tested, would react with resentment to the words "sin," "guilt," "disobedience," "punishment," and so on. This is by no means necessarily because their adult lives are so proud and complacent that they resent criticism, but because there still exists in their minds a tender, touchy area connected with the misdemeanors of childhood. Unless they were exceptionally lucky it is quite probable that, though they have long ago forgotten the circumstances, they still half-consciously remember the shame, rage, impotence, and humiliation of childish naughtiness and its punishment. It was not without strain and conflict that they won free from adult domination, and it *feels* to them like a voluntary resumption of the humiliations of childhood to confess themselves "guilty sinners." For a little boy to be smacked on his behind may be of little significance, but for an adult man to be beaten is an unspeakable degradation. It is of course not really a renascence of this childish guilt and humiliation that the reputable evangelist seeks to arouse, but he may seem to be doing so. To have a real sense of sin is by no means the same thing as being humiliated.

Sin

THE TRUE ADULT sense of sin, guilt, and shame, which contact with the real God appears invariably to arouse (though by no means always at once), seems to come along at least four different lines, which we will attempt to illustrate.

(1) We will suppose that a man who is rather proud of his ability to knock off a quick effective little painting discovers a bit of canvas fastened to a wall. For his own pleasure and the appreciation of his friends he rapidly paints in a bright,

effective, and amusing little picture. Stepping back to see his own handiwork better, he suddenly discovers that he has painted his little bit of nonsense on the corner of a vast painting of superb quality, so huge that he had not realized its extent or even that there was a picture there at all. His feelings are rather like what a man feels when he suddenly sees the vast sweep of God's design in life, and observes the cheap and discordant little effort his own living so far represents when seen against that background. That is real conviction of sin.

(2) To illustrate the second way in which a real sense of sin may come, we will use a story which we believe is true, though it has not been possible to check its source. A young man of the "incorrigibile" variety grows up work-shy, and by a certain native quickness of wit manages for years to escape serious trouble. His favorite saying is: "I live my own life, and I don't care tuppence for anybody." Eventually, however, his self-confidence overreaches itself and he is convicted of serious crime and goes to prison for three years. While in prison he is hard and quite unrepentant. "What I do with my life," he says defiantly, "is nobody else's business. I shan't make the same mistake twice." In due course he leaves prison and, since he has nowhere else to go, decides to spend a few nights at home while he "looks around." He hasn't seen his mother since he saw her, plump, rosy, and tearful, out of the corner of his eye, at his trial. But when the door of his home is opened to him by a worn, grey-haired old woman, he does not see at once what has happened. For a second or two he simply stares, then he cries, "Oh, mother, what *have I done to you?*" and bursts into the tears that neither punishment nor prison had ever wrung from him.

This story is simply an illustration of how a man may suddenly realize the hurt he does to others by his own self-centeredness. It does not, unfortunately, often happen that a man sees as vividly as in that story the consequences of his wrong actions. But when he does he may experience a genuine conviction of sin. When Saul Kane in Masefield's *Everlasting Mercy* had his eyes opened, he suddenly saw "the harm I done in being me." That is just it. When a man sees not merely that his life is out of harmony with God's purpose, but realizes that that disharmony has injured and infected the lives of other people, he begins to feel a "sinner" in earnest.

(3) To illustrate the next point we must tell a simple story which will no doubt make the sophisticated smile. Two young men of the same age choose divergent paths. A is determined to squeeze all the pleasure and enjoyment out of life that he can. B is equally determined to "get on." Despite the gibes of his friend, he attends "evening classes" and works hard in his spare time at his chosen subject. We will suppose that the friends go separate ways and do not meet for several years. When they do B has unquestionably "got on" and has a responsible well-paid position. A has advanced very little. His reaction on seeing B again may quite possibly be just unreasonable envy, but equally possibly A may say to himself: "What a fool I've been! What opportunities I threw away. B is *just the sort of man I could have been!"*

This naive little tale illustrates quite well how a genuine "conviction of sin" may arise. A man who has lived selfishly and carelessly meets someone who has plainly found happiness and satisfaction in cooperating with what he can see of God's purpose. The former may pass the whole thing off as a joke. "Of course, old so-and-so always was a bit religious"—but he may quite possibly see in the other man *the sort of person he himself might have been.* The standards he mocked and the God he kept at arm's length have produced in the other man something he really very badly wants. If his reflection is, "What a fool I've been," he, too, is beginning to get a genuine sense of sin.

(4) The fourth road along which the "conviction of sin" may come is rather harder to explain. It is really the discovery of the enormous and implacable strength of real goodness and real love. The insincere man hates and fears the real truth; the sexually irresponsible man affects to be cynical about real and enduring passion, but secretly he hates and fears it; the egocentric man hates and fears the incalculable force of the personality selflessly devoted to a cause. In short, self-centered and evil people really *fear* the good. They express their fear by mockery, cynicism, and, when circumstances allow, by active persecution.

Now when this sense of the strength of goodness and love touches a man, whether it be by someone else's life, by something he reads or sees, or by an inner touch in his soul, he is really convicted of sin. He knows that sooner or later the game is up—the Nature of Life is Good and not Evil. He suddenly sees that the goodness and love he has despised as weakness are in reality incredibly strong. Peter once felt this about Christ and in a moment of panic cried out: "Depart from me, for I am a sinful man, O Lord!" Some people, of course, succeed in keeping the fear of goodness (which is really the fear of God) at a safe distance all their lives, but they live in continual danger of reality breaking in. And when it does there will be a strong sense of sin.

Reconciliation

To ANYONE THEREFORE who takes the unique claim of Christ seriously it is of the very greatest interest and significance to observe how He dealt with the question of sin and man's reconciliation with God. The following facts emerge from the records:

(1) Christ very rarely called men "sinners" and as far as we know never attempted deliberately to make them feel sinners, except in the case of the entrenched self-righteous, where He used the assault and battery of scathing denunciation. (This, we may surmise, is an instance of what He saw to be a desperate ill requiring a desperate remedy.) Some evangelists, whose chief weapon is the production of a sense of sin, would find themselves extraordinarily short of ammunition if they were obliged to use nothing but the recorded words of Christ. This is not, of course, to say that the life and words of Christ did not produce that genuine sense of guilt and failure which it outlined above, but it is undeniable that He did not set out to impress a sense of sin on His hearers.

(2) We find Christ unequivocally claiming the right "to forgive sins," but the grounds on which the sin of man can be forgiven are not, in the recorded words of Christ, the conventional ones presupposed by many Christians. We find in Christ an intimate connection between the forgiveness of sins and the existence of love in a man's heart. "Forgive us our trespasses as we forgive them that trespass against us" is so familiar in our ears that we hardly grasp the fact that Christ joined fellowship with God and fellowship with other human beings indissolubly. "Except ye from your hearts forgive everyone his trespasses," He is reported to have said after a particularly telling parable, "neither will my heavenly Father forgive you your trespasses." Moreover, on one occasion he said of a woman who was apparently something of a notoriety that "her sins, *which are many*, are forgiven: for she loved much." It seems to me consonant with Christ's teaching to hold that love is a prerequisite of forgiveness, and I take His consequent little story to the Pharisee to be another of those apparent "non sequiturs" of which the reply to the question "Who is my neighbor?" is a classic example.

On the other hand, it would seem that there is a possibility of a man's putting himself outside forgiveness by the "sin against the Holy Spirit." This, from an examination of the context, would appear to be a combination of refusing to recognize truth and refusing to allow the heart to love others. If God Himself is both Truth and Love it would be logical to suppose that a deliberate refusal to recognize or harbor truth and love would result in an attitude that makes reconciliation with God impossible.

Now if it is true that God is both Truth and Love it will readily be seen that the greatest sins will be unreality, hypocrisy, deceit, lying, or whatever else we choose to call sins against truth, and self-love, which makes fellowship with other people and their proper treatment impossible. Forgiveness must then consist in a restoration to Reality, i.e., Truth and Love.

(3) We must now ask whether Christ had anything to say about the clamant question of "atonement" mentioned above. He certainly hinted at it. He spoke of giving his life as a "ransom for many," and at the last meal which He shared with His followers He spoke of breaking His own body and shedding His own blood "for the remission of sins."

Now it is surely possible that to this question of atonement (as to the question of surviving death) Christ, whom we are considering as God in human form, could give the best and most complete answer by actual demonstration. He personally, being both God and Man, effected the reconciliation that man alone was powerless to make.

There are innumerable theories centering around the death of Christ as the atonement for the world's sins, and many of them frankly do not commend themselves to the honest modern mind. May we suggest the following way of looking at the matter.

We have already spoken of the vicious sin-suffering-death circle in which the world is involved, and of the individual man's helplessness to free himself from the entanglement of his own wrong-doing, let alone cleanse himself from the cumulative infection of the world's selfish living.

Suppose now that God, who has become human and represents in one person both His own Godhood and Humanity, allows Himself, though personally guiltless, to be involved in the complex. God, now, who made the inexorable rules of cause and effect, deliberately exposes Himself to the consequences of the world's self-love and sin. Because He is God, to do such a thing once in time is indicative of an eternal attitude, and we view the Character of God in an entirely different light if we see Him not abrogating justice, not issuing a mandate of reversal of natural law and order, but overcoming a repugnance which we cannot begin to imagine by letting Himself *be* Representative Man and suffering in His own Person the logical and inevitable suffering and death which the world has earned. The Moral Perfection which a man quite rightly dreads, has deliberately consented to become under the limitations of humanity, the focal point of the assault of evil. We cannot imagine what this would involve, but even to begin to think that it might be true takes the breath away.

Christians believe that this act of reconciliation was the inner meaning behind the rather sordid historical fact of Christ's death. The unreality, the pseudoreligion, the bitter hatred, the greed and jealousy that lay behind the judicial murder of Christ were the mere *setting*. The *fact* would have been the same wherever and whenever Christ appeared: evil would clash with Incarnate Good, and whether it was a cross, a hangman's rope, a guillotine, or a gas chamber, Christ would choose to accept death for humanity's sake.

Christ's Act of Reconciliation

WE SHALL ATTEMPT here no theories of atonement, but simply record that it is a matter of indisputable fact that when a man sees that God took the initiative in establishing a *rapprochement* between Himself and Man and underwent the (for Him) indescribable ignominy of death, his attitude toward God is from then on profoundly changed. The inarticulate but incurable sense that "something ought to be done about it," to which we referred above, is almost miraculously set at rest. Though it may defeat his reason to define exactly what has been done, a man knows that the "something" has been done. The idea of God, which was almost certainly a discomfort and possibly a threat, however reason might argue the point, is entirely changed. The former inevitable Judge is seen to be Lover and Rescuer, and if the revision of ideas is at all sudden there is bound to be a considerable emotional release.

To assent mentally to the suggestion that "Jesus died for me" is unhappily only too easy for certain types of mind. But really to believe that God Himself cut the knot of man's entanglement by a personal and unbelievably costly act is a much deeper affair. The bigger the concept of God the more the mind staggers at the thought, but once it is accepted as true it is not too much to say that the whole personality is reoriented. For most men in whom a moral sense is operating at all, are, unconsciously perhaps, trying to "put up a case" to justify their own conduct. The effort may only rarely reach the conscious level of the mind, but it is there, and the real "conviction of sin" which we defined above, however much it may be held at arm's length, is always in the offing. To realize that the effort to justify oneself, the hopeless effort to repay the overdraft, can safely be abandoned, is an unspeakable relief. It was all based on a false idea, that the central confidence of life should be in the self. It is a blow to the face of pride and a wrench to the habits of the mind to transfer that central confidence to the One Real Perfect Man, who was, and is, also God. But if the changeover is effected the relief and release are enormous, and energy formerly repressed is set free. This is what the New Testament means by being saved by faith in Christ.

This is, of course, far from being mere theory. People in all ages, of all nations, and of widely differing temperaments, have reacted in much the same way to Christ's Act of Reconciliation. Indeed so great is the weight of evidence that it would be sensible to admit that, if we cannot understand what happened and are at a loss to explain it, there is a mystery here beyond our powers of definition. We might even have the humility to say that God-become-man did something incalculable, the greatness of which we can only appreciate in a very limited degree.

But, though we may well be awed, we need not cease to use our minds, and we cannot but admire the superb psychological accuracy with which this Act was designed to touch the characters of men. Those who already to some extent live in love and truth will see the force and point of the Act almost intuitively. Those who are set, however secretly, in pride and self-love, will see nothing to marvel at and little to admire—though the Act may haunt them strangely as though it were the key to some long-forgotten door into life's real meaning. It is those who realize their spiritual poverty who find in Christ's Act the way into fellowship with God: it is the "rich" who are "turned empty away."

Nevertheless, although we have here a touchstone to reveal existing character, we have a great deal more than that.

Should the proud and self-loving man once see that God is *like that*, there may be, and sometimes is, a revolution in his whole scale of values. Should the careless-living man once see that this Act is a crystallizing in time of what is always happening—that every kind of sin, including apathy, is at heart seeking to destroy God—he too may see life with very different eyes. God may thunder His commands from Mount Sinai and men may fear, yet remain at heart exactly as they were before. But let a man once see his God down in the arena as a Man, suffering, tempted, sweating, and agonized—finally dying a criminal's death, he is a hard man indeed who is untouched. For Christ's claim to be not only God but Representative Man has had an almost incredible magnetic power. Over nineteen centuries have passed since that judicial murder in that turbulent little country of Palestine, yet still men see the Death as a personal matter. It seems to be designed to meet their own half-conscious needs. "The Son of God who loved *me* and gave Himself for *me*," wrote St. Paul, as though for the moment the Act affected him alone; but the words have been echoed unprompted by an imposing number since his day. So wide has been the acceptance of this reconciliation that we simply cannot easily dismiss it, particularly as the only possible alternative way of thought is a simple denial of the impasse which is a "fact" to every spiritually sensitive person.

Perfection and Perfectionism

SINCE GOD IS Perfection, and since He asks the complete loyalty of His creatures, then the best way of serving, pleasing, and worshipping Him is to set up absolute one-hundred-percent standards and see to it that we obey them. After all, did not Christ say, "Be ye perfect"?

This one-hundred-percent standard is a real menace to Christians of various schools of thought, and has led quite a number of sensitive conscientious people to what is popularly called a "nervous breakdown." And it has taken the joy and spontaneity out of the Christian lives of many more who dimly realize that what was meant to be a life of "perfect freedom" has become an anxious slavery.

It is probably only people of certain backgrounds and temperaments who will find the "one-hundred-percent god" a terrible tyrant. A young athletic extrovert may talk glibly enough of being "one-hundred-percent pure, honest, loving, and unselfish." But being what he is, he hasn't the faintest conception of what "one hundred percent" means. He has neither the mental equipment nor the imagination to begin to grasp what perfection really is. He is not the type to analyze his own motives, or build up an artificial conscience to supervise his own actions, or be confronted by a terrifying mental picture of what one-hundred-percent perfection literally means in relation to his own life and effort. What *he* means by "one-hundred-percent pure, honest, etc." is just as pure and honest as he sincerely knows how. And that is a very different matter.

But the conscientious, sensitive, imaginative person who is somewhat lacking in self-confidence and inclined to introspection, will find one-hundred-percent perfection truly terrifying. The more he thinks of it as God's demand the more guilty and miserable he will become, and he cannot see any way out of his impasse. If he reduces the one hundred percent he is betraying his own spiritual vision, and the very God who might have helped him is the Author (so he imagines) of the terrific demands! No wonder he often "breaks down." The tragedy is often that the "one-hundred-percent god" is introduced into the life of the sensitive by the comparatively insensitive, who literally cannot imagine the harm they are doing.

What is the way out? The words of Christ, "Learn of Me," provide the best clue. Some of our modern enthusiastic Christians of the hearty type tend to regard Christianity as a performance. But it still is, as it was originally, a way of living, and in no sense a performance acted for the benefit of the surrounding world. To "learn" implies growth; implies the making and correcting of mistakes; implies a steady upward progress toward an ideal. The "perfection" to which Christ commands men to progress is this ideal. The modern high-pressure Christian of certain circles would like to impose perfection of one hundred percent as a set of rules to be immediately enforced, instead of as a shining ideal to be faithfully pursued. His short cut, in effect, makes the unimaginative satisfied before he ought to be and drives the imaginative to despair. Such a distortion of Christian truth could not possibly originate from the One who said His "yoke was easy" and His "burden light," nor by His follower St. Paul, who declared after many years' experience that he "pressed toward the mark not as though he had already attained or were already perfect."

Yet even to people who have not been driven to distraction by "one-hundred-percent" Christianity, the same fantasy of perfection may be masquerading in their minds as God. Because it is a fantasy it produces paralysis and a sense of frustration. The true ideal . . . stimulates, encourages, and produces likeness to itself.

If we believe in God, we must naturally believe that He is Perfection. But we must not think, to speak colloquially, that He cannot therefore be interested in anything less than perfection. (If that were so, the human race would be in poor case!)

Christians may truthfully say that it is God's "ambition"

to possess the wholehearted love and loyalty of His children, but to imagine that He will have no dealings with them until they are prepared to give Him perfect devotion is just another manifestation of the "god of one hundred percent." After all, who, apart from the very smug and complacent, would claim that they were wholly "surrendered" or "converted" to love? And who would deny the father's interest in the prodigal son when his Spiritual Index was at a very low figure indeed?

God is truly Perfection, but He is no Perfectionist, and one hundred percent is not God.

Spiritual Vitality

IF A MAN accepts the fact that the Character of God is focused in Christ, if he accepts as true the Act of Reconciliation and the Demonstration with Death; and if he himself is willing to abandon self-centered living and follow the way of real living which Christ both demonstrated and taught, he is still not out of the wood. For he finds that apart from exceptional effort or spasmodic resolution he is not spiritually robust enough to live life on the new level. He simply has not got it in him to live for long as a pioneer of the new humanity. He can see that it is right, and he can desire, even passionately, to follow the new way, but in actual practice he does not achieve this new quality of living. He may blame his own past, he may blame the ever-present effect of the God-ignoring world in which he has to live, he may even reach the melancholy conclusion that it is all a beautiful theory but that it cannot be worked in practice.

This very natural impasse was, of course, anticipated by

Christ. He knew very well, for example, that the followers of His own day would very quickly collapse when the support and inspiration of His own personality were removed by death. He therefore promised them a new Spirit who should provide them with all the courage, moral reinforcement, love, patience, endurance and other qualities which they would need. A fair reading of the New Testament writings apart from the four Gospels shows plainly enough that this promise was implemented. Ordinary people were not only "converted" from their previous self-loving attitude, but received sufficient spiritual vitality to cause no little stir among the world in which they lived. It is a mistake to think that in general the receiving of this gift led to excitable demonstration. Its normal function was to produce in human life the qualities which Paul catalogues in Galatians 5: love, joy, peace, patience, kindness, generosity, fidelity, adaptability, and self-control. These are in fact the very qualities which men so easily "run short of," and which, taken together, comprise a character corresponding to the Representative Man, Christ Himself.

It is this invasion of human life by something (or Someone) from outside which the modern mind finds difficult to accept. We are all "conditioned" by the modern outlook, which regards the whole of life as a closed system. A great many things may happen inside that system, but it is unthinkable that the whole huge cause-and-effect process should in any way be interfered with from "outside."

But when we suppose, even only for the sake of argument, that the teaching of Christ is true—that this little life is acted against an immeasurable backdrop of timeless existence—it does not appear in the least impossible that under certain conditions of harmony between *this* faulty existence and *that* Perfection of Life, contact might be established. The result would be, to us, in the literal sense, supernatural. Indeed, we have already seen that a man may, even accidentally, come upon something of beauty, truth, goodness, or love, and find the "other end" is connected with the Permanent. At such times the closed-system idea is quite plainly inadequate.

Now we may wish, especially if we are more than a little tired of the closed-system idea and faintly but definitely conscious of the Real World, that these invasions might be more frequent or more demonstrable. Nevertheless, this much we do know, and can reasonably expect, that if a man honestly wants to follow the way of Christ and, as it were, opens his own personality to God, he will without any doubt receive something of the Spirit of God. As his own capacity grows and as his own channel of communication widens he will receive more. John goes so far as to call this the receiving of God's own heredity (1 John 3:9). This does not, of course, turn a man into a spiritualist medium! The man's own real self is purified and heightened, and though he will come to bear a strong family likeness to Christ he will, paradoxically enough, be more "himself" than he was before.

We may here point out the great difference that has come to exist between the Christianity of the early days and that of today. To us it has become a performance, a keeping of rules, while to the men of those days it was, plainly, an invasion of their lives by a new quality of life altogether. The difference is due surely to the fact that we are so very slow (even though we realize our impotence) to discard the closed-system idea. We have so little of what the New Testament calls "faith." And since it is fairly obvious that "faith" is the first requisite in making contact between this and the Permanent World we can scarcely wonder at the enormous difference in quality between first-century and twentieth-century Christianity.

Without a power from outside, the teaching of Christ remains a beautiful idea, tantalizing but unattainable. With the closed-system sooner or later you have to say: "You can't change human nature." Ideals fail for very spiritual poverty, and cynicism and despair take their place.

But the fact of Christ's coming is itself a shattering denial of the closed-system idea which dominates our thinking. And what else is His continual advice to "have faith in God" but a call to refuse, despite all appearance, to be taken in by the closed-system type of thinking? "Ask and ye shall receive, seek and ye shall find, knock and it shall be opened unto you"—what are these famous words but an invitation to reach out for the Permanent and the Real? If we want to cooperate the Spirit is immediately available. "If ye then, for all your evil, know how to give good gifts unto your children, how much more shall your heavenly Father give the Holy Spirit to them that ask Him?"

The Spirit

THERE IS AN apparent capriciousness and arbitrariness about the working of the Spirit of God which laughs at our modern docketing. The Spirit, like the wind, said Jesus, "bloweth where it listeth" (John 3:8), and though we can fulfill conditions and, so to speak, set our sails to meet the wind of the Spirit, yet (to change the metaphor) we can never harness or organize the living Spirit of God. We are indeed sure of His gentle purpose, but the details of His plan lie beyond our understanding and it is at once more sensible and more fitting for us to cultivate a sensitivity to the leading of the Spirit rather than to arrange His work for Him!

This unpredictable and suprarational movement of the

Spirit is an element in God's working which makes the whole Christian enterprise on which we are engaged at once more exciting and more difficult. "There were many widows in Israel in the days of Elijah . . . and unto none of them was Elijah sent, but only to Zarephath . . . unto a woman that was a widow," said Jesus (Luke 4:25–26), and He offered no comment on the seeming arbitrariness of the Spirit's working. Those who are responsible for what nowadays we call missionary strategy have always the difficult task of keeping in touch with the tides and currents of the Spirit of God as He pursues His "immemorial plan."

Now this apparently fortuitous element in the grand work of redemption, and which incidentally can be seen on a small scale in the working of any local church in which the Spirit is operating at all, is singularly exasperating to the tidy-minded. What God works in one place or in one person ought, we feel, to work in all places and in all persons. But we are not dealing with, shall we say, an electrical circuit in which the power of electricity can always be relied upon to do the same thing under the same conditions. We are not using an impersonal force, and if there is any question of using, it is He who uses us and not we Him. God is of course really moving, with what, from His point of view, if I may say so reverently, I can only describe as celestial ingenuity. But to us, who at the most only know the superficial facts of the situation, His actions may at times appear arbitrary or even capricious. I do not think we need to go "all solemn" about this, or to overemphasize our own ignorance and sinfulness. It is surely far better to accept with good humor the situation as it is—that His thoughts are higher than our thoughts, and His ways higher than our ways (Isaiah 55:8–9); and to realize that though we are called to this tremendous task of cooperation with Him, and are no longer servants but friends, we still need to be most humble, teachable and flexible as we follow His leading.

Plain Christians

WHEN I TALK about the lives of plain Christians as being to me a proof of the reality of the Christian Faith, I am thinking of those who have taken that Faith seriously (and by that I do not mean solemnly!), and who have over a period of years lived their lives by that Faith. As a parson I am fortunate in meeting all sorts of people of all kinds of temperament, people of varying degrees of intelligence and in various walks of life; and the thing that impresses me about the genuine Christians is a certain quality of life which they all possess. It is rather difficult to put into words and, of course, I am not claiming that they are "saints" in the sense that they have no faults. But they all exhibit three particular characteristics which I think are quite remarkable.

The first is a kind of inward tranquillity, as though the very center of their personalities were relaxed and at peace. Many of them of course are busy people with all kinds of responsibilities to carry and often with heavy burdens to bear. But nevertheless they give me this strong impression that inside they are at peace—and that is a thing which I very rarely see in those without a religious faith.

The second characteristic which is common to all the best Christians is an unquenchable gaiety of spirit. Christians of course never expect, and certainly don't enjoy, any particular immunity from trouble; but I find in them the ability, not only to cope courageously with their particular difficulty, but very often to cope with it good-humoredly and even joyfully. I don't want you to think that I always and invariably observe this, but I must say that I have seen it so often, and in such unlikely places, that I cannot help being very much impressed.

The third thing that I notice which is common to all Christians, whatever their background or circumstances may be, is a quality for which we can only use the word "love." Unfortunately, as you know, we have misused the word "love" so many times that it has almost ceased to mean anything at all to us. But there is in the genuine Christian life not merely kindliness and charity, but what I would describe as a kind of outgoing love which really is concerned about other people. Of course there is a lot of imitation "love" about, and since there are hypocrites among Christians as there are in any other group of people, there is unhappily such a thing as hypocritical love—or "love in inverted commas," as I sometimes call it. But of course I am not talking about that, nor am I talking about some sentimental, vague feeling of goodwill towards all mankind. The love I see exhibited in the best Christians is a deeper thing than kindness; it is a warmer thing than charity; and I think it is a more costly thing than mere expressions or feelings of goodwill. In fact, it rather looks to me as though it is some divine quality, much deeper and more sustained than any human feeling, expressing itself in and through normal human beings.

Now these three characteristics, which impress me very much and which appear all over the place wherever Christianity is seriously accepted, are to my mind a very definite pointer to something beyond merely human experience. We all know peace of mind, when there is nothing to worry us; we all know joy, when our surroundings are happy; and we all know love, among our friends who love us. But the impressive thing about these qualities which I have noticed through the years is that the tranquillity exists in spite of harassing circumstances; and the gaiety and good humor in spite of worrying and depressing conditions; and the love is exhibited not only in a small circle where it is likely to be returned, but extends to places and people where it is certainly not asked for and where it may not even be appreciated! To me, therefore, there is something Godlike about these characteristics of real Christians, and I find myself believing that they have somehow begun to share the quality of the Life of God Himself.

Plain Non-Christians

THERE ARE THREE things which ought to be said quite kindly but firmly about good men without faith.

The first is this, that I think you will find, as I have found, that in the life history of these nice good people there has usually been genuine Christian influence. A man, for example, may grow up with no Christian faith of his own, but nevertheless with the whole of his life guided by internal principles implanted there by either one or both of his parents *who were themselves Christians.* Or sometimes you will find parents, who in their own childhood had an overdose of Church-going, bringing up their children without any form of religious faith. *But they will bring up those children according to the Christian principles which they themselves learned years ago.* This sort of phenomenon can happen of course only in a country where Christianity has been the tradition for several generations. I don't think you will find much evidence of people being naturally and spontaneously Christian where there is no Christian tradition or environment.

The second difference that I must point out between "nice people" and Christians is that the nice people have not really in practice *enough* "niceness." What I mean is that they are charming and tolerant and kind within certain limits, but it is very, very rare to find them coping effectively with the messes and muddles made by the sins and failures of other men. Their goodness and their love are excellent up to a point, but they do not, as with the genuine Christian, enable them to cope effectively, and indeed redemptively, with a situation that has gone badly wrong. Of course I am not claiming that all Christians invariably do deal with dark and difficult situations effectually, but I do claim that the quality of their lives is such that something makes them want to move out from their own circle of love and happiness and bear some part of the pain and cost of putting a wrong situation right. They are not always very good at it, and they by no means always succeed, but for myself I am very much impressed by the fact that they do try to do something about it. They have, as I said before, an outgoing love.

The third weakness of nice people without faith is that they have literally nothing to offer to those who are *not* nice people. They probably behave kindly and tolerantly towards selfish people, but they have no means of communicating their secret of "niceness." To the man who has an unpleasant background, or an inherent moral weakness, they have no gospel to offer. They cannot, as the Christian can, point to Someone stronger than themselves who is quite capable of transforming a disposition and a character. The Christian knows God, or should I say a little bit of God, through Christ, and he has learned through his own experience to tap the resources of God. He can, therefore, at least point the way to a better quality of life to someone who is not by nature a nice type or a good type or an honest type. This the good man without faith is quite unable to do, since he has no experience of the active, operative power of God.

Christian Qualities

MAY I TELL you what I have observed of the quality of the life of the Christians that I have known? Naturally I have known a lot in the twenty-odd years that I have been a parson, and as far as outward circumstances, gifts and temperaments go, they have been a very varied bunch of people. Nevertheless, I am left with a very strong impression of a better quality of life lived by these people who have faith in God. I certainly don't mean that they are all perfect, or even that they are all saintly in the commonly accepted sense of that term. But, though they may be unaware of it themselves, their lives have got a quality—yes, I would almost call it a superhuman quality—which people who try to live without God never possess. There are many ways in which this shows itself, and I am only going to mention briefly four of them.

First, I notice that Christian men and women with a living faith in the living God have learned how the power of God can help them to cope with their own difficult natures. I don't claim that they always succeed, but I do claim that they know where to turn for spiritual reinforcement, and I do claim that in most of them you can easily detect something, or perhaps I should say Someone, operating in their own personalities who is higher and better than they would be by themselves. To put it quite bluntly, I have known people who would be called what we popularly term "nasty bits of work" if there were not operating in them Someone making them into good bits of work—changing them in fact into sons and daughters of God. Even allowing for the failures, it is to me one of the biggest arguments for the existence of God that I see Him operating in lives which are open to Him. I am not speaking of the super-pious, but of the ordinary people who are open on the Godward side and to whom marriage or home life or business life has been made of quite a different quality by the unseen Spirit of God.

In the second place I notice that real Christian people have as a rule much more concern and much more love for those outside their immediate circle. People living without God are friendly towards those who are friendly with them, of course, but usually their friendliness and concern only operate within a very restricted circle. But when a man opens his life to God, something of the Love of God comes into his heart, and his sympathies grow both wider and deeper. This is only perhaps what you might expect since God loves every man, but it is wonderful to see how Christian people can give time and money and a very real love to those who are quite outside their ordinary circle of acquaintances. It may be that they have a special concern for the blind or other incapacitated people. It may be that they have a special concern for those who have never heard the Gospel of Jesus Christ. But the real point is that they have a concern for the well-being of others, and I find this very well marked in all true Christians.

The third thing that I must say about Christian people is something in the nature of a tribute. Christians do not, as some people foolishly suppose, imagine that they are specially protected from life's ills and accidents, from sickness, bereavement, anxiety and all the rest. Indeed, it sometimes looks as though some of the very best people get far more than their share of misfortune. And yet I can't help observing (and this is where I pay my tribute), that these grand people can bear disappointment and loss and ill-health and all the other things that get people down, not only without bitterness but with the most astonishing courage and good humor. Again, I don't wish to make extravagant claims. They don't all do this. But I have seen so many of them living out the truth of St. Paul's words, "In all these things we are more than conquerors," that I am most profoundly moved and impressed. You see, theirs is not just a defiant courage, but that miraculous brave acceptance of the situation that turns a thing which is in itself evil into a shining beacon of faith and light and courage. Such grand Christians—and, thank God, I have met many of them—give the rest of us enormous encouragement.

The last thing I would say about people who live their lives with faith in God is that they have a Gospel to pass on. Many of them may be quite rightly reticent about their faith, for after all it is the most intimate side of their lives. But when the opportunity and the need arise, they can and do say something like this: "I know Someone far greater and stronger than you or I, Someone who has helped me through some pretty rough patches, and I am sure He can help you." And then sometimes they are able to show someone else, who up till now has lived life without God, how it is possible to get to know the infinite God through Christ, and how it is possible to tap His boundless resources through His Spirit who is living and active today.

Non-Christian Qualities

LIFE LIVED WITHOUT God is of poor quality. Now that is not a favorite theory of mine. It is a conclusion based on a good deal of personal observation. I expect you've realized that a parson has an almost unique opportunity of getting to know people, people of all types and temperaments, of all classes and of varying degrees of intelligence. Not many people have that opportunity. Most people know their own circle and have only the haziest idea of how other people live, except of course through books and films. People who live in towns have very little knowledge of how country people live, and vice versa. Business people, as a rule, only know their business friends and acquaintances, and a few friends outside. People who work in shops get to know their own customers pretty well, but they don't have much time or opportunity for knowing many other people apart from their own friends. But people like doctors, nurses and parsons, who are allowed into the homes of all sorts of people, have, as a rule, a much wider knowledge of human nature. They are privileged really, and when they have been on the job for over twenty years, working amongst different kinds of people, they can't help noticing a difference in quality between people who have a real faith in God and people who have not. Oh, by the way, I am leaving out . . . the hypocrites, of whom there are a few in any community, who pretend to be very holy and devout, and who are really thoroughly self-centered. I am thinking of the contrast that I have observed between the people who attempt to live without God and the people who have a living faith in Him. . . .

Let us look first at the people who have no faith in God. Please remember I am not condemning them; I am just telling you what I have observed.

The first thing I notice about them is that they have not got any real purpose in life. So often they are just waiting for something—waiting for the children to grow up and be off their hands, waiting for the time when they can retire. Very rarely have they got any sense of joining in and helping with a Purpose bigger than themselves. Many of them are very nice kindly people, but if you ask them straight out: "What are you living for?" they can usually give you only the most hazy or most trivial answers. I don't think they are aware of it, but to me it is pathetically clear that they are not linked to anything or anyone bigger than themselves.

In the second place I notice that such people have no one and nothing to turn to when they reach the end of their own resources. For example, a man may be cursed with a bad temper. He may know perfectly well that it worries his wife and frightens his children and spoils the atmosphere of his home. When he is pretty young he may battle against it and sometimes succeed, but as time goes on and he is defeated more often than not, he is very apt to conclude that there is nothing that can be done about it. His bad temper, or whatever the fault may be, is just one of those things that can't be altered. And so he shrugs his shoulders and simply makes a compromise with the bad temper or the jealous spirit or the bitter tongue, or whatever else it is that is spoiling his life. He does not know of any source to which he can turn which can enable him to control his own nature, still less to transform it.

Then too, I have noticed again and again that people who live without God are all right as long as they are well and reasonably prosperous, but that illness or accident knocks them completely sideways. Oh, they are ready enough then with, "How can there be a God to allow this to happen to me?" But they have never learned to find God as a refuge and a strength in good times as well as bad. Many of them are remarkably brave, but many more are completely lost when, for example, health fails, or there is some tragic happening in the family. They have literally no one to whom to turn.

The third thing that I notice about people who live without God . . . is that they have nothing constructive to offer to the men or women who are defeated either by their own natures or by the circumstances of life. Of course, they can and do say things like: "Cheer up—it may not be as bad as you think" or "Pull yourself together" or even, "Why can't you be like me?" but what they can never say, what they are quite unable to say, is, "I know Someone who is far stronger than you or I, who has helped me and who can help you." In other words, because they have no experience of God, they have no experience of any power or resource or refuge or strength outside themselves. And I think that is a very impoverishing thing.

Dark Tunnels

MOST OF US, sooner or later in life, have to go through what we might call dark tunnels, whether of pain, or adverse circumstances, or bereavement, or natural anxiety over someone we love. And when it comes we say to ourselves, "I do hope I shall come through this all right." But do we mean hope, real hope, or is that just a wish? Have we any reason, any good, solid dependable reason for hope? Can we, so to speak, see the light at the other end of the tunnel? Believe me, I do know what I'm talking about here and I can tell you that if your whole life is honestly committed, body and soul, to your creator, who is also your Father and your Savior—in the best sense your true lover—you can have real hope. You need not be lonely any more, and you need not be afraid any more, for you have not got to rely on the tension of your own screwed-up courage. You can relax, instead, upon the God of hope.

Once, some years ago, I myself went through a very dark tunnel indeed. And the words which came into my mind were these—"When thou passest through the waters I will be with thee, and through the rivers they shall not overflow thee." I rested my full weight on that promise and God brought me through that tunnel. A great many times since then I have passed that promise on to people in hospital or at home and, as simply as I could, urged them to rest their whole weight upon the goodness and the love of God. That is where hope, real hope, springs from. And Paul is perfectly right in calling God "The God of hope."

Darknesses and Depressions

I HAVE SUFFERED FROM ill-health during the last few years. To a large extent this was my own fault, for I accepted hundreds of demands on my time which were out of all proportion to my real strength. I should have realized that sooner or later a reaction was bound to set in. Therefore, I must say briefly that I now know a great deal about the assorted darknesses and depressions that can afflict the human spirit. And I know very well indeed how faith in oneself and one's own integrity, let alone faith in an omnipotent God, can be severely shaken and tested.

Of one thing I am quite certain. There is nothing that can help a man through a lengthy period of recovery better than a sustained faith in God, whatever one's feelings may happen to be.

I have read a great deal during the last few years, but I have never discovered anything that even remotely helps those who have to endure such times of depression unless it be found in, or derived from, the teachings of Jesus Christ and the New Testament generally.

Friends have helped in my period of depression, but I

have to say, in all honesty, chiefly those who have themselves suffered. And what are they but agents of the living God? I cannot bring myself to say that "suffering" is, by itself, a good thing. Yet it remains mysteriously true that those who have, through faith, conquered or come to terms with suffering are the only ones who can either understand or offer constructive help.

To go into all the implications of what I have hinted at here would require a book, and I doubt if I should ever be competent to write it.

But I see no hope at all in any view of life but the Christian one.

Inklings of Eternity

I HAVE *always* been aware of the eternal world. It often seemed to me that I lived in the here-and-now involuntarily and perhaps a little impatiently!

The innumerably clear and sharp experiences of childhood gave me hints and clues to beauty and reality which plainly transcended earthly life. I could not believe that this little life was my permanent home.

The sweetness of music, the loveliness of nature, the beauties of color and form were, at times, intolerably sweet reminders of some permanent reality lying beyond immediate perception.

Doors opened momentarily but would shut again tantalizingly. But those moments left a fleeting glimpse of unutterable beauty.

At the age of twenty-seven, these inklings of eternity crystallized in a dream or vision so real and so convincing that I can never forget it.

Let me tell you about it.

I had been vaguely ill for some months, and indeed had been forced to resign my first job through ill-health. I lay in a hospital, exhausted after a severe and prolonged operation. Physically I was weaker than I had thought it possible for a human being to be and yet remain conscious. I could hear and see, but I could not so much as move a finger nor blink an eyelid by any effort of the will. Yet my mind was perfectly clear, and late one night I overheard a doctor murmur to the night nurse: "I am afraid he won't live till the morning."

In my state of utter exhaustion, this aroused no emotion at all, but I clearly remember making a mental note that patients who are gravely ill and apparently unconscious may yet be able to hear.

I would not say that I felt then the presence of God as a person. I knew Him rather as some kind of "dimension."

I was however a helpless human being resting entirely upon my Creator.

God seemed to be, as it were, the sea of being, supporting me.

I felt that God to be infinitely compassionate and infinitely kind.

I fell asleep. Immediately, as it seemed, I had this startlingly vivid dream.

I was alone, depressed and miserable, trudging wearily down a dusty slope. Around me were the wrecks and refuse of human living. There were ruined houses, pools of stagnant water, cast-off shoes, rusty tin cans, worn-out tires and rubbish of every kind.

Suddenly, as I picked my way through this dreary mess, I looked up. Not far away on the other side of a little valley, was a vista of indescribable beauty. It seemed as though all the loveliness of mountain and stream, of field and forest, of cloud and sky were all displayed with such intensity of beauty that I gasped for breath. The loveliest of scents were wafted across to me. Heart-piercing birdsongs could be clearly heard. The whole vision seemed to promise the answer to my deepest longings as much as does the sight of water to a desperately thirsty man.

I ran towards this glorious world. I knew intuitively that there lay the answer to all my questing, the satisfaction for all that I had most deeply desired. This shining fresh world was the welcoming frontier of my true and permanent home.

I gathered my strength and hurried down the dirty, littered slope.

I noticed that only a tiny stream separated me from all that glory and loveliness. Even as I ran some little part of me realized, with a lifting of the heart, that Bunyan's "icy river" was, as I had long suspected, only a figment of his imagination. For not only was the stream a very narrow one, but as I approached it, I found that a shining white bridge had been built across it.

I ran towards the bridge, but even as I was about to set foot on it, my heart full of expectant joy, a figure in white appeared before me. He seemed to me supremely gentle but absolutely authoritative. He looked at me smiling, gently shook his head, and pointed me back to the miserable slope down which I had so eagerly run.

I have never known such bitter disappointment, and although I turned obediently, I could not help bursting into tears. This passionate weeping must have awakened me, for the next thing that I remember was the figure of the night nurse bending over me and saying, rather reproachfully: "What are you crying for? You've come through tonight—now you're going to live!"

But my heart was too full of the vision for me to make any reply.

What could I say to someone who had not seen what I had seen?

It is nearly forty years since the night of that dream, but I can only say that it remains as true and as clear to me today as it was then.

Words are almost useless as a means to describe what I saw and felt, even though I have attempted to use them.

I can only record my conviction that I saw reality that night, the bright sparkling fringe of the world that is eternal.

The vision has never faded.

Funerals

I HAVE TAKEN OVER 5,000 funerals. Though, of course, many of the mourners on such occasions have a very sketchy faith, even in the case of those who are convinced Christians of some years' standing, I find a strange inability to grasp the transitory nature of our present life and the breathtaking magnificence of the life which is to come.

I have, for instance, frequently suggested that it would be more appropriate to refer to the one whose physical body has died as the "arrived" rather than as the "departed."

No doubt there is nothing particularly original about this, but the significance lies in the fact that to many Christian people this is quite a new thought! They simply have not considered, or so it appears, that we are living this painful and difficult life against a background of unimaginable splendor.

Most of them hold desperately to a belief of some kind of survival, but that "the sufferings of this present time are not worthy to be compared with the glory that shall be revealed in us" seems hardly to have entered their hearts and minds.

Eschatology, Realized
and Unrealized

"ESCHATOLOGY" IS THE doctrine or teaching about "the last things"—death, judgment, heaven and hell. Much of today's Christianity is almost completely earthbound, and the words of Jesus about what follows this life are scarcely studied at all. This, I believe, is partly due to man's enormous technical successes, which make him feel master of the human situation. But it is also partly due to our scholars and experts. By the time they have finished with their dissection of the New Testament and with their explaining away as "myth" all that they find disquieting or unacceptable to the modern mind, the Christian way of life is little more than humanism with a slight tinge of religion. For it is not only advertisers who attempt to deaden our critical faculties by clever words, there are New Testament scholars who, whether consciously or not, do the same thing. Thus, if you are to be thought up-to-date and "with it," you are expected to believe in current phrases. One of these is "realized eschatology," which means that all those things which Jesus foretold have happened, either at the destruction of Jerusalem in A.D. 70 or in the persecutions of the Church. In other words, the prophetic element in the teaching of Jesus is of no value at all to us in the twentieth century. Such a judgment makes Jesus less of a prophet than Amos, Isaiah, Micah, Jeremiah, and the rest. I find myself quite unable to accept this. There *is* an element of the prophecy of Jerusalem's terrible downfall and of the desecration of the

Temple—the horror of which we who are not Jews find hard to appreciate. But the prophetic vision goes far beyond this. It envisages the end of the life of humanity on this planet, when, so to speak, eternity irrupts into time. There is no time scale: there is rarely such an earthbound factor in prophetic vision. The prophet sees the truth in compelling terms, but he cannot tell the day or the hour of any event, still less the time of the final end of the whole human affair.

We are ourselves somewhere in the vast worldwide vision which Jesus foresaw, and for all we know, we may be near the end of all things. You simply cannot read the New Testament fairly and come to the conclusion that the world is going to become better and better, happier and happier, until at last God congratulates mankind on the splendid job they have made of it! Quite the contrary is true; not only Jesus but Paul, Peter, John, and the rest never seriously considered human perfectibility in the short span of earthly life. This is the preparation, the training ground, the place where God begins His work of making us into what He wants us to be. But it is not our home. We are warned again and again not to value this world as a permanency. Neither our security nor our true wealth are rooted in this passing life. We are strangers and pilgrims, and while we are under the pressure of love to do all that we can to help our fellows, we should not expect a world which is largely God-resisting to become some earthly paradise. All this may sound unbearably old-fashioned, but this is the view of the New Testament as a whole.

In a true and real sense the Kingdom of God was already established upon earth, but none of the New Testament writers expects the vast work of redeeming the whole world to take place either easily or quickly.

Some, at least, of the early Christians apparently expected the return of their risen Lord in power in a very short time, and both Peter and Paul had to remind their converts that the "time" was entirely a matter of God's choosing. Meanwhile the Christian life must be led with patience and courage, the true gospel must be proclaimed, and Christian worship continued. The light must shine in a dark and cruel world.

It might be thought that if a Man's hope and treasure lay in another, unseen world, he would have little contact with, or interest in, the world in which he is only a temporary resident. Of course there have been, and are, sects who live apart from the world, but that is not the general picture. It is not usually the atheists and agnostics who are to be found fighting disease, ignorance, and fear in the most dangerous and difficult parts of the world. And this is because the Christian faith, although inevitably rooted in "heaven," is incurably earthly. The seeds of this paradoxical attitude are scattered throughout the New Testament. "Religion" which does not express itself in compassion is a dead and, indeed, a dangerous thing. Yet the root of the relief of disease, the removal of ignorance, and the teaching of faith lies in the love of God. We love because God first loved us.

I feel I must stress this point because we seem to live in an atmosphere of "either/or," whereas it is really a matter of "both/and." Certainly it is useless to preach a gospel of the soul's redemption to a starving man. But it is equally valueless (and the world around us is full of examples) to make man affluent in this world and at the same time deprive him of any sense of God or of any meaningful life after death. "Compassion" and "charity" are both popular words today, while faith in God is regarded as largely irrelevant. But in fact both compassion and charity can be monstrously misused unless they are informed by the love of God. Hence we get situations in which compassion goes out to the violent thug who assaults an old lady for her meager savings, but none at all to her! Charity means instant social acceptance for the adulterer but little compassion for his deceived and deprived wife. To love God is the first and greatest commandment, said Jesus, and this is the priority insisted on throughout the New Testament.

Life After Death

THE "FOCUSED" God, Jesus Christ, revealed to man not merely adequate working-instructions for meeting life happily and constructively, but also the means by which he could be linked with the timeless Life of God. "Heaven" is not, so to speak, the reward for "being a good boy" (though many people seem to think so), but is the continuation and expansion of a quality of life which begins when a man's central confidence is transferred from himself to God-become-man. This "faith" links him here and now with truth and love, and it is significant that Jesus Christ on more than one occasion is reported to have spoken of "eternal life" as being entered into *now*, though plainly to extend without limitation after the present incident that we call life. The man who believes in the authenticity of His message and puts his confidence in it already possesses the quality of "eternal life" (John 3:36, 5:24, 6:47, etc.). He comes to bring men not merely "life," but life of a deeper and more enduring quality (John 10:10, 10:28, 17:3, etc.).

If we accept this we shall not be too surprised to find Christ teaching an astonishing thing about physical death: not merely that it is an experience robbed of its terror, but that as an experience *it does not exist at all.* For some reason or other Christ's words (which Heaven knows are taken literally enough when men are trying to prove a point about pacificism or divorce, for example) are taken with more than a pinch of salt when He talks about the common experience of death as it affects the man whose basic trust is in Himself: "If a man keep my saying *he shall never see death*" (John 8:51); "Whosoever liveth and believeth on Me *shall never die*" (John 11:26). It is impossible to avoid the conclusion that the meaning that Christ intended to convey was that death was a completely negligible experience to the man who had already begun to live life of the eternal quality.

"Jesus Christ hath abolished death," wrote Paul many years ago, but there have been very few since his day who appear to have believed it. The power of the dark old god, rooted no doubt in instinctive fear, is hard to shake, and a great many Christian writers, though possessing the brightest hopes of "Life Hereafter" cannot, it seems, accept the abolition of death. "The valley of the shadow," "Death's gloomy portal," "the bitter pains of death," and a thousand other expressions all bear witness to the fact that a vast number of Christians do not really believe what Christ said. Probably the greatest offender is John Bunyan, writing in his *Pilgrim's Progress* of the icy river through which the pilgrims must pass before they reach the Celestial City. Thousands, possibly millions, must have been influenced in their impressionable years by reading *Pilgrim's Progress*. Yet the "icy river" is entirely a product of Bunyan's own fears, and the New Testament will be searched in vain for the slightest endorsement of his idea. To "sleep in Christ," "to depart and be with Christ," "to fall asleep"—these are the expressions the New Testament uses. It is high time the "icy river," "the gloomy portal," "the bitter pains," and all the rest of the melancholy images were brought face to face with the fact: "Jesus Christ hath abolished death."

The fact seems to many to be too good to be true. But if it does seem so, it is because we have not really accepted the revolutionary character of God's personal entry into the world. Once it dawns upon us that God (incredible as it may well sound) has actually identified Himself with Man, that He has taken the initiative in effecting the necessary Reconciliation of Man with Himself, and has shown the way by which little human personalities can begin to embark on that immense adventure of Living of which God is the Center, death—the discarding of a temporary machine adapted only for a temporary stage—may begin to seem negligible.

We have so far spoken only of "death" as it affects the man whose inner confidence is in Christ, His Character, His Values, and above all His claim to be the expressed character of the Inexpressible God. There is no brightly cheerful note in either the Gospels or the rest of the New Testament for those whose real inward trust is in their own capabilities or in the schemes and values of the present world-system. It is (as St. Paul insists almost *ad nauseam*) only *"in"* Christ, *"in"* the Representative Man who was also God, that death can be safely ignored and "Heaven" confidently welcomed. We have no reason to suppose that death is anything but a disaster to those who have no grip on the timeless Life of God.

Communion of Saints

MANY OF US who believe in what is technically known as the Communion of Saints must have experienced the sense of nearness, for a fairly short time, of those whom we love soon after they have died. This has certainly happened to me several times. But the late C. S. Lewis, whom I did not know very well and had only seen in the flesh once, but with whom I had corresponded a fair amount, gave me an unusual experience. A few days after his death, while I was watching television, he "appeared" sitting in a chair within a few feet of me, and spoke a few words which were particularly relevant to the difficult circumstances through which I was passing. He was ruddier in complexion than ever, grinning all over his face and, as the old-fashioned saying has it, positively glowing with health. The interesting thing to me was that I had not been thinking about him at all. I was neither alarmed nor surprised nor, to satisfy the Bishop of Woolwich, did I look up to see the hole in the ceiling that he might have made on arrival! He was just *there*—"large as life and twice as natural." A week later, this time when I was in bed, reading before going to sleep, he appeared again, even more rosily radiant than before, and repeated to me the same message, which was very important to me at the time. I was a little puzzled by this, and I mentioned it to a certain saintly bishop who was then living in retirement in Dorset. His reply was, "My dear John, this sort of thing is happening all the time."

The reason why I mention this personal and memorable experience is that although "Jack" Lewis was real in a certain sense, it did not occur to me that I should reach out and touch him. It is possible that *some* of the appearances of the risen Jesus were of this nature, being technically known as veridical visions. But the writers of the Gospels, in their naive, unself-conscious way, make it plain that something much more awesome and indeed authoritative characterized Christ's "infallible proofs."

Second Coming

WE MAY FREELY admit that the early Christians were wrong in thinking that Christ would return in power within their lifetime. It is possible to detect in the writings of Paul, for example, a change of atmosphere in his letters to the Thessalonians (which were probably his earliest), and what is probably his last letter, the letter to Titus. But even in the latter Paul refers to the "looking for that blessed hope, and the glorious appearing of the great God and our Savior Jesus Christ" (Titus 2:13). The hope may have become deferred in its fulfillment, but it is still a very real hope. New Testament Christians may well have modified their early views as to the immediacy of Christ's return, yet the fact of His coming again in judgment of the world is always implicit in their thinking and hoping. We need to remember that among the early Christians were quite a number who were actually present when the Son of God ascended back to Heaven—a symbolic action, of course, but historically true. Such men would not readily forget the words of the heavenly messenger who told them quite plainly that "this same Jesus, which is taken up from you into heaven, shall so come in like manner as ye have seen him go into heaven" (Acts 1:11).

Unhappily for us, the whole subject of the Second Coming of Christ has been for many years the playground of cranks and fanatics. This has made us not only shy of dealing with the question ourselves but reluctant to believe in "the blessed hope" as a fact at all. Various people, especially within the last sixty years or so, have manipulated texts of Holy Scripture with little regard to context to prove that Christ would return on this or that day. For example, in my own experience I remember a man in 1934 hiring the Queen's Hall in London solemnly to warn the British Empire that Jesus Christ would return in Person on, I think, the 24th of June of that year. So convinced was he of his calculations that he stated at the time that if he were wrong he would "sink into well-merited obscurity." He left himself no loophole for later revision of the timetable as others have done, and I presume he still lives in his obscurity. This example is only one of hundreds of misguided people who have thought they could calculate what, on Jesus' own admission, was known only to the Father (Mark 13:32). But I really don't see why, because this important New Testament hope has been the stamping ground of the fanatical, we should be cheated altogether of what was essentially a part of early Christian teaching. . . .

Planners as we are, if we envisage the Second Coming of Christ at all, we see Him returning in triumph upon a scene already largely perfected. We think it would be a fine thing if the world were neat and tidy, all problems were solved, all tensions were relaxed, understanding and friendship were worldwide, health and wealth were at their highest peak, when Christ returned, not this time as a helpless babe, but as a King in power and glory. Of one thing we can be quite certain: this high, unfathomable wisdom of God works on quite a different plane from any human planning. The time of the irruption of eternity into time, the moment for God to call the end to the long experiment that we call life, will not be made in consultation with human planners! Judging from His previous action in human history, God is perfectly capable of choosing an unusual and unlikely moment, as it will appear to human beings. Indeed, if we are to take the words of Jesus seriously, His return to the world or the winding up of the time and space setup, whichever way we look at it, is to be in the middle of strife, tension, and fear. In the letters of the New Testament it is the same: the coming of Christ is a blessed hope of intervention, not a personal appearance at a Utopian celebration.

Now if our hopes, whatever we protest, really lie in this world instead of in the eternal Order, we shall find it difficult to accept the New Testament teaching of the Second Coming. In our eyes the job is not yet done, and such an action would be, though we would not put it so, an interference. But suppose our hope rests in the purpose of God; then we safely leave the timing of the earthly experiment to Him.

After Nineteen Centuries of Christianity

CRITICS OFTEN COMPLAIN that if the world is in its present state after nineteen centuries of Christianity, then it cannot be a very good religion. They make two ridiculous mistakes. In the first place Christianity—the real thing—has never been accepted on a large scale and has therefore never been in a position to control "the state of the world," though its influence has been far from negligible. And in the second place they misunderstand the nature of Christianity. It is not to be judged by its success or failure to reform the world which rejects it. If it failed *where it is accepted* there might be grounds for complaint, but it does not so fail. It is a revelation of the true way of living, the way to know God, the way to live life of eternal quality, and is not to be regarded as a handy social instrument for reducing juvenile delinquency or the divorce rate. Any "religion," provided it can be accepted by the majority of people, can exert that sort of restrictive pressure. The religion of Jesus Christ changes people (if they are willing to pay the price of being changed) so that they quite naturally and normally live as "sons and daughters of God," and of course they exert an excellent influence on the community. But if real Christianity fails, it fails for the same reasons that Christ failed—and any condemnation rightly falls on the world which rejects both Him and it.

New Testament Christianity

IF NEW TESTAMENT Christianity is to reappear today with its power and joy and courage, men must recapture the basic conviction that this is a Visited Planet. It is not enough to express formal belief in the "Incarnation" or in the "Divinity of Christ"; the staggering truth must be accepted afresh that in this vast mysterious Universe, of which we are an almost infinitesimal part, the great Mystery, Whom we call God, has visited our planet in Person. It is from this conviction that there spring unconquerable certainty and unquenchable faith and hope. It is not enough to believe theoretically that Jesus was both God and Man; not enough to admire, respect, and even worship Him; it is not even enough to try to follow Him. The reason for the insufficiency of these things is that the modern intelligent mind, which has had its horizons widened in dozens of different ways, has got to be shocked afresh by the audacious central Fact that as a sober matter of history *God became one of us.*

This primary Fact is the foundation of all New Testament certainty about God and life. But there is a second conviction which is almost equally important. For while it is true that the earliest Christians had personally witnessed the breakthrough of Eternity into time, they did not regard this as a solitary isolated action. The Young Church lived in the daily demonstrable conviction that this world was continually interpenetrated by the world of the Spirit. Indeed, though some of them had seen the Man Jesus ascend into the clouds before their astonished eyes, the fact that He was with them and in them became an increasing joyful certainty. To anyone who studies the book we call the Acts of the Apostles it becomes quite plain that the Holy Spirit is not a vague influence for good, not even just a powerful Wind of Heaven, but a Person with a purpose and ideas of His Own. The earth was once visited for a few years, visibly, audibly, and tangibly by God in human form, but thereafter it was (and, of course, is) continually subject to invasions by the Spirit of Jesus. Happily, the Young Church was sensitive, alert, and flexible, and we can read for ourselves to what miraculous triumphs the Spirit led them. Again, if we are to regain the buoyant God-consciousness of New Testament Christianity, we must not only accept afresh the planned Personal Visit but be ready for any number of subsequent invasions of the Spirit.

God's Comprehensive Love

WE MAY FIND IT difficult to hold all these thoughts in our mind simultaneously, but they fairly represent the way in which the New Testament writers looked at God, man and life. Paul, for example, with his Jewish upbringing and Pharisaic training, would have a higly exalted view of the one true God, but after his conversion he also knows that the same God whose wisdom is unsearchable is his Father, and he can speak personally and naturally of Jesus Christ as "the Son of God who loved me and gave himself for me." In my experience of people I have found that among committed Christians this "comprehensive" view of God both as the Creator of infinite wisdom and power and as the Father caring deeply for the individual is a quite ordinary phenomenon. It is the agnostic or the would-be atheist who produces and magnifies the intellectual difficulty. No one in his senses would pretend that God is anything but a vast unfathomable mystery, and nothing is more repugnant as well as impertinent than that attitude of overfamiliarity which suggests that we are now old enough to talk on equal terms with the Creator. Nevertheless, it remains true that a human being can in a real sense "know" God through Christ, and Christ himself can be truly alive to him. I have seen this recognition and knowledge of God in people of all denominations, in men and women of several different nationalities as well as in those who belong to various social strata. I have known extremely clever scientists as well as men of the highest caliber in literature or the arts who regard God with the deepest awe and at the same time know Him through Christ almost as a personal friend. I have also known people of a much simpler cast of mind, who would probably not be able to pass any formal examination, who have a sturdy and invincible faith in God their Father and similarly find Christ a real person. It is true that the comparatively unintelligent will sometimes use naive terms in speaking of God, but I have never found a true Christian without a profound sense of awe and wonder. I cannot help being impressed by what I have seen and by what people have told me. The laboratory check for spiritual experience is life itself, and it is exactly here, sometimes in the most appallingly dangerous and painful situations, that I have found faith both sure and radiant. In short, I have seen the experience of God described in the New Testament occurring again and again in our modern world.

Bibliography

The following is a list of J. B. Phillips' books published in the United States. When there has been a Macmillan paperback edition, the publication date appears in parentheses.

A Man Called Jesus: A Series of Short Plays from the Life of Christ. New York: Macmillan Publishing Co., Inc., 1959.

Appointment with God: Some Thoughts on Holy Communion. New York: Macmillan Publishing Co., Inc., 1954.

For This Day: 365 Meditations. Waco, Texas: Word Books, 1975. New York: Bantam Books, 1977.

Four Prophets—Amos, Hosea, First Isaiah, Micah: A Translation from the Hebrew. New York: Macmillan Publishing Co., Inc., 1963 (1969).

Good News: Thoughts on God and Man. New York: Macmillan Publishing Co., Inc., 1963.

The Gospels: A Translation into Modern English. New York: Macmillan Publishing Co., Inc., 1952.

Letters to Young Churches: A Translation of the New Testament Epistles. With an Introduction by C. S. Lewis. New York: Macmillan Publishing Co., Inc., 1957 (1960, 1968).

Making Men Whole. New York: Macmillan Publishing Co., Inc., 1958.

New Testament Christianity. New York: Macmillan Publishing Co., Inc., 1957.

The New Testament in Modern English. New York: Macmillan Publishing Co., Inc., 1958 (1965).

The New Testament in Modern English. Revised edition. New York: Macmillan Publishing Co., Inc., 1973 (1972).

Plain Christianity and Other Broadcast Talks. New York: Macmillan Publishing Co., Inc., 1956.

Ring of Truth. New York: Macmillan Publishing Co., Inc., 1967. Paperback edition, Harold Shaw Publishers, Wheaton, Illinois, 1977.

The Young Church in Action: A Translation of the Acts of the Apostles. New York: Macmillan Publishing Co., Inc., 1955 (1964, 1967).

Your God Is Too Small. New York: Macmillan Publishing Co., Inc., 1953 (1961).

Sources

After Nineteen Centuries of Christianity — *Your God Is Too Small*, 139–140 (123–124)

Beatitudes and Non-Beatitudes — *Your God Is Too Small*, 100–103 (92–94)

Beauty, Goodness, and Truth — *Your God Is Too Small*, 46–50 (72–75), (69–71)

Bible Reading — *New Testament Christianity*, 95–97

Books, Films, and Plays — *Your God Is Too Small*, 44–47

"Casting All Your Care" — *Ring of Truth*, 61–62

Chairman of the Board — *Your God Is Too Small*, 43–45 (42–43)

Christ and the Real Self — *Appointment with God*, 37–39

Christian Maintenance — *New Testament Christianity*, 87

Christian Qualities — *Plain Christianity*, 28–30

Christian Reading — *New Testament Christianity*, 97

Christian Service — *New Testament Christianity*, 98–100

Christ's Act of Reconciliation — *Your God Is Too Small*, 107–109

Communion and Common Sense — *Appointment with God*, 1–3

Communion of Saints — *Ring of Truth*, 118–119

Competition in Goodness — *Good News*, 69–70

Conversion of the Corinthians — *Ring of Truth*, 29–31

"Count It All Joy" — *Ring of Truth*, 69–70

Dark Tunnels — *Good News*, 103–104

Darknesses and Depressions — *For This Day* (204–205)

Escape Artist — *Your God Is Too Small*, 31–32 (33–34)

Eschatology, Realized and Unrealized — *Ring of Truth*, 102–106

Eucharistic Fellowship — *Appointment with God*, 26–28

"Everyone That Loveth . . . Knoweth God" — *Ring of Truth*, 67–68

Evil — *Ring of Truth*, 46–48

Faith — *New Testament Christianity*, 25–27

Faith in the New Testament — *New Testament Christianity*, 30–31

Faith in the Young Church — *New Testament Christianity*, 33–35

Faith in Today's World — *New Testament Christianity*, 39–42

False Gods — *Your God Is Too Small*, 9–64 (15–59)

"Fear and Trembling" — *Ring of Truth*, 62–64

Fellowship of the Church — *New Testament Christianity*, 91–95

Forgiveness and Forgivingness — *Good News*, 35–36

Four Prophets — *Four Prophets*, xv–xix (xv–xviii)

Four Temptations Against Love — *New Testament Christianity*, 77–78

Funerals — *For This Day*, 223–224

God Focused — *Your God Is Too Small*, 76–78 (72–73)

God Unfocused — *Your God Is Too Small*, 65–66 (63–64)

God's Comprehensive Love — *Ring of Truth*, 54–56

Grand Old Man — *Your God Is Too Small*, 19–21 (22–24)

Guilt — *Your God Is Too Small*, 107–108 (97–98)

Hope — *New Testament Christianity*, 43, 46–47

Hope in the New Testament and the Young Church — *New Testament Christianity*, 48–49

Hope in Today's World — *New Testament Christianity*, 58–59

Humiliation — *Your God Is Too Small*, 109–110

Idol of the Worshipping Animal — *Your God Is Too Small*, 63 (58)

"If Our Heart Condemn Us" — *Ring of Truth*, 70–73

Imperfection — *Your God Is Too Small*, 108–109 (98–99)

Inklings of Eternity — *For This Day* (21–24)

Jack in the Box — *Your God Is Too Small*, 37–38 (37–38)

Jesus' Miracles — *Ring of Truth*, 94–99

Jesus' Prophecy   *Ring of Truth*, 100–102
Jesus' Strength as a Man   *Ring of Truth*, 86–92
Justification by Faith   *New Testament Christianity*, 35–36
Life After Death   *Your God Is Too Small*, 114–117
Liturgy   *For This Day* (107–108)
Love in the New Testament and   *Ring of Truth*, 61–62
    the Young Church
Love in Today's World   *Ring of Truth*, 77–78
Mystical Vision   *Your God Is Too Small*, 60–61
                                        (56–57)
Narcissus on the Silver Screen   *Your God Is Too Small*, 57–59
                                        (53–55)
New Testament Christianity   *New Testament Christianity*, 21–22
Nine New Testament Serendipi-   *Ring of Truth*, 60–72
    ties
Non-Christian Qualities   *Plain Christianity*, 25–27
"Now Are We the Sons of God"   *Ring of Truth*, 68–69
Olympic Sprinter   *Your God Is Too Small*, 59–60
                                        (55–56)
Pain and Disease, Injustice and   *Your God Is Too Small*, 103–106
    Evil   (94–96)
Peace   *New Testament Christianity*, 79–80
Perfection and Perfectionism   *Your God Is Too Small*, 28–31
                                        (30–32)
Physical and Mental Preparation   *Appointment with God*, 51–55
    for Communion
Plain Christians   *Plain Christianity*, 12–14
Plain Non-Christians   *Plain Christianity*, 15–16
Prayer   *New Testament Christianity*, 89–91
"Pressed Out of Measure"   *Ring of Truth*, 64–65
Pride, Self-Righteousness, and the *Your God Is Too Small*, 99–100
    Exploitation of Others   (90–92)
Quietude   *New Testament Christianity*, 88–89
"Quit You Like Men"   *Ring of Truth*, 65–66
Reconciliation   *Your God Is Too Small*, 115–119
                                        (102–107)
Resident Policeman   *Your God Is Too Small*, 15–16, 18
                                        (9–13)
"Rich in Mercy"   *Ring of Truth*, 60–61
Sacraments in Life   *Appointment with God*, 18–20
Second Coming   *New Testament Christianity*, 52–54,
                                        57
Similes and Metaphors in the   *Ring of Truth*, 58–60
    New Testament
Sin   *Your God Is Too Small*, 110–114
                                        (99–102)
Six Obstacles to Peace   *Plain Christianity*, 81–88

Spiritual Nutrition — *Appointment with God*, 30–31

Spiritual Preparation for Communion — *Appointment with God*, 56–58

Spiritual Values — *Your God Is Too Small*, 69–71 (67–68)

Spiritual Vitality — *Your God Is Too Small*, 117–120

Temptation — *Ring of Truth*, 48–50

The Act of Reconciliation — *Plain Christianity*, 76–77

The Ascension — *Good News*, 204–210

The Badness of Goodness — *Making Men Whole*, 30–31

The Character of God — *Your God Is Too Small*, 96–97 (88–89)

The Christ Within Us — *Appointment with God*, 33–35

The Church — *Making Men Whole*, 29–31

The Crucifixion — *Plain Christianity*, 74–76

The Disappointer — *Your God Is Too Small*, 50–53 (48–50)

The Good Shepherd — *Making Men Whole*, 16–18

The Gospels — *Ring of Truth*, 75–85

The Greatness of Paul — *Ring of Truth*, 28–29, 51–52

The Hypothesis Incarnated — *Your God Is Too Small*, 88–90 (81–83)

The Incarnation Hypothesized — *Your God Is Too Small*, 78–79 (73–75)

The Letters — *Ring of Truth*, 37–41

The Living Spirit of Truth in the New Testament — *Ring of Truth*, 121–123

The Living Tradition — *Appointment with God*, 8–9

The Love Commandments — *Good News*, 129–130, 133–135

The Purpose of Life — *Your God Is Too Small*, 97–99 (89–91)

The Resurrection According to Luke — *Ring of Truth*, 107–111

The Resurrection According to Paul — *Ring of Truth*, 119–121

The Resurrection in the Gospels — *Ring of Truth*, 112–116

The Revolution of the Resurrection — *Ring of Truth*, 119–121

The Spirit — *Making Men Whole*, 63–65

The Ultimate Bundle of Highest Values — *Your God Is Too Small*, 62–63 (58)

The Visited Planet — *New Testament Christianity*, 15–19

Tyrannical Parent — *Your God Is Too Small*, 14–15 (19–20)

What Jesus Says About . . . . — *Your God Is Too Small*, 96–106 (88–96)

Worship — *New Testament Christianity*, 59–61

The Martyred Christian

THE MARTYRED

160 READINGS FROM

CHRISTIAN

Dietrich Bonhoeffer

Selected and Edited by Joan Winmill Brown

COLLIER BOOKS
MACMILLAN PUBLISHING COMPANY
New York

COLLIER MACMILLAN PUBLISHERS
London

Macmillan Publishing Company
866 Third Avenue, New York, N.Y. 10022
Collier Macmillan Canada, Inc.

Library of Congress Cataloging in Publication Data
Bonhoeffer, Dietrich, 1906-1945.
The martyred Christian.
Originally published: New York: Macmillan; London:
Collier Macmillan, c1983.
Bibliography: p. 220
1. Theology—Addresses, essays, lectures. I. Brown,
Joan Winmill. II. Title.
BR85.B725   1985   230′.044   85-5932
ISBN 0-02-084020-9

Macmillan books are available at special discounts for bulk purchases for sales promotions, premiums, fund-raising, or educational use. For details, contact:
Special Sales Director
Macmillan Publishing Company
866 Third Avenue
New York, N.Y. 10022

First Collier Books Edition 1985
10 9 8 7 6 5 4 3 2

Printed in the United States of America

The author gratefully acknowledges permission to reprint

Abridged excerpts from pages 64, 65, 104-106, 110 in *Christ the Center* by Dietrich Bonhoeffer. Translated by Edwin Robertson. Copyright © 1947 by Christian Kaiser Verlag in Bonhoeffer's *Gesammelte Schriften*, Vols. 1-4. Copyright © 1966, 1978 in the English translation as Christology by William Collins, Sons, & Co., Ltd., and Harper & Row, Publishers, Inc. Reprinted by permission of Harper & Row, Publishers, Inc., and William Collins, Sons, & Co., Ltd.

Abridged excerpts from pages 17, 20, 27–28, 40–41, 99 in *Life Together* by Dietrich Bonhoeffer. Translated by John W. Doberstein. Copyright, 1954, by Harper & Row, Publishers, Inc. Reprinted by permission of Harper and Row, Publishers, Inc.

Excerpts from *The Cost of Discipleship* by Dietrich Bonhoeffer, translation © SCM Press 1948, 1959; *Ethics* by Dietrich Bonhoeffer, translation © SCM Press 1955; *Letters and Papers from Prison* by Dietrich Bonhoeffer, The Enlarged Edition, translation © SCM Press 1953, 1967, 1971; *Creation and Fall* by Dietrich Bonhoeffer, translation © SCM Press 1959; *Creation and Temptation* by Dietrich Bonhoeffer, translation © SCM Press 1959, 1966 (containing *Creation and Fall* and *Temptation* in one volume). Reprinted by permission of SCM Press Ltd. and Macmillan Publishing Company.

Excerpt from *No Rusty Swords* by Dietrich Bonhoeffer, translated by Edwin Robertson and John Bowden, translation © William Collins Sons & Company Ltd., 1965. Published by William Collins Sons & Co., Ltd., and Christian Kaiser Verlag.

*This book is dedicated
to the Bonhoeffer family and all Christians
who suffered and were martyred,
during the years of the Third Reich.*

Also by Dietrich Bonhoeffer
The Cost of Discipleship
Ethics
Creation and Fall; Temptation
Letters and Papers from Prison

Contents

Foreword   xiii

Created in His Image   1

The Kingdom of God   4

The Strength of God   5

God's Faithfulness   8

God's Blessing   8

The Commandment of God   9

Christians and Pagans   12

God's Will   13

Access to God   13

God Is No Stop-gap   16

The Name of Jesus Christ   17

The Incarnate One   18

The Body of Jesus Christ   20

The Lordship of Jesus Christ   22

The Light of His Presence   25

'I Am the Life'   26

Ecce Homo!   28

The Cross of Christ   30

The Love of God   31

Easter   32

The Glory of His Resurrection   33

His Ascension   34

Challenge to Faith   35

The Word of God   36

The Cause Is Urgent   38

The Acceptance of Guilt   39

The Decision   41

The Call of Jesus   42

The Christian Life   44

Christ Our Hope   45

The Imparting of Grace   46

The New Life   47

The Past   49

Justification   52

Conformation   53

Christ and His Body   54

The Church   55

Christ the Center   57

The Preacher   58

The Saints   59

The Task of the Church   60

The Battlefield   62

Confession of Guilt   63

Costly Grace	64
The New Fellowship	66
The Followers of Christ	67
Pray for Forgiveness	68
Good Works	69
Through and in Jesus Christ	71
Christ Among Us	71
The Day's Beginning	72
Morning Prayers	73
Evening Prayers	76
The Hiddenness of Prayer	77
Baptism	78
The Gift of Baptism	79
From 'Thoughts on the Day of Baptism of Dietrich Wilhelm Rüdinger Bethge'	80
Vocation	82
The Image of Christ	83
Discipleship and the Cross	84
Christ Alone	85
Fellowship	86
The Work	87
'The Harvest Is Great'	89
The Fruit	90
The Ministry of Helpfulness	91
Fulfilling Our Tasks	92
The Sermon on the Mount	93
Visionary Dreaming	94
Christian Radicalism	95
Human Relationships	96
The Friend	97

Life Together 101

The Joy of Fellowship 101

Love 102

The Strength of the Other Person 103

Marriage 105

The Community of Love 106

Christ the Foundation 107

What God Has Joined Together 107

Home 108

The Security of Home 109

A Virtuous Woman 110

To His Mother 112

The Heritage of Children 113

Abortion 114

The Rights of Natural Life 115

The Rights of Bodily Life 117

The Value of a Life 118

Suicide 119

Fulfilment 120

Of Success 121

Of Folly 123

Confidence 125

Sympathy 126

Optimism 127

Gratefulness 128

Deputyship 129

Lust 130

Shame 132

Desire 133

Conscience 134

Humanity and Goodness	136
The Pharisee	137
Judgement	138
Single-minded Love	139
The Concept of Reality	140
Divine Reality	142
The Reality of God	143
The Reality of Jesus Christ	145
Christ, Reality and Good	146
What Is Meant By 'Telling the Truth'?	147
Satanic Truth	149
Who Am I?	150
Our Lives	151
Freedom from Anxiety	152
Are We Still of Any Use?	154
Who Stands Fast?	155
The Taking Over of the Temptations	157
Concrete Temptations and Their Conquest	159
The Legitimate Struggle	161
Protection and Help	163
Securitas	164
Tempted by Suffering	165
Sorrow and Joy	168
Physical Suffering	170
Pain	170
Prayers in Time of Distress	171
The Suffering Servant	172
The Suffering of the Messengers	172
Sharing in God's Sufferings	174
Night Voices in Tegel	176

Separation from Those We Love 183

Christ's Restoration 184

New Year 1945 186

Glorifying God 187

Call of Liberation 188

Freedom 189

Stations on the Road to Freedom 191

Obedience and Freedom 193

The World of Conflicts 194

Contempt for Humanity? 195

Immanent Righteousness 196

The Sense of Quality 197

The Penultimate 199

The Sovereignty of God in History 200

Present and Future 201

Christ and Antichrist 202

Justification as the Last Word 203

Blessing and Completion 204

Jonah 206

The Last Temptation 207

The Last Judgement 208

Insecurity and Death 208

The Idolization of Death 209

From The Last Letter 210

Like the Angels 211

His Mercy and Forgiveness 212

The Hour of Death 212

Victory 212

Sources 213

Bibliography 220

Foreword

AT DAWN, on April 9, 1945, Dietrich Bonhoeffer was led by his guards down the steps leading to the execution area at the Flossenburg concentration camp in Germany. Only a few days before the Allies were to liberate the camp, the Nazis, at the express order of Heinrich Himmler, hanged this so-called "enemy of the state."

The leaders of the Third Reich were mistaken, however, in thinking that they could ever silence Bonhoeffer. His writings live on to enrich us spiritually, and to tell us what was required of those who lived as Christians amid the horrors of Nazi Germany. For many people the Germans of the 1930s and 1940s represent the "complete enemy," and little thought is given to those Christians who suffered for their religious beliefs. But the prisons of Europe were filled with Christians who refused to obey Adolf Hitler. These men and women were martyred because of their stand for Jesus Christ and His Church. One such Christian was Dietrich Bonhoeffer.

Bonhoeffer was born in 1906 and was recognized as an accomplished scholar while still in his twenties. He received his licentiate in theology in Berlin in 1927 and served a brief pastorate in Barcelona. He returned to Germany and the academic world to finish his habilitation thesis, entitled *Act and Being,* before traveling to America as an exchange student in 1930. Bonhoeffer returned to his native country the following year and became a lecturer in theology at the Berlin University; the lectures he delivered on the first three chapters of the book of Genesis were to become the exceedingly popular *Creation and Fall.*

Bonhoeffer's sojourn in America had opened his eyes politically, and he began to see with concern that Nazi influence was seeping into the politics of Germany. Hitler despised Christians, saying, reportedly, "You can do anything you want with them. They will submit...they are insignificant little people, submissive as dogs...." When he became the Führer in 1933, Hitler began a campaign of persecution and demoralization of the German Christian Church. Resisting the members of the Reich Church who were loyal to Hitler was a small group that came to be called the "Confessing Church," and Dietrich Bonhoeffer was one of its most vocal ministers. This Confessing Church split off from the Reich Church, and became one of the few institutions to oppose Hitler.

Bonhoeffer's disgust for Hitler and the submissive Reich Church moved him to accept a pastorate in London, where he developed a close friendship with George Bell, the bishop of Chichester. Bonhoeffer felt that the opinion of the worldwide church could have tremendous influence on events in Germany, and he kept Bell informed about the political climate created by the Nazis. Six years before he would be executed, Bonhoeffer wrote, "When Christ calls a man, he bids him come and die." Bishop Bell said of him, "There are different kinds of dying, it is true; but the essence of discipleship is contained in these words." He went on to say, "Dietrich was a martyr many times before he died. He was one of the first as well as one of the bravest witnesses against idolatry. He understood what he chose, when he chose resistance...He was crystal clear in his convictions; and young as he was, and humble-minded as he was, he saw the truth, and spoke it with complete absence of fear..."

When Bonhoeffer returned to Germany in 1935, he founded an illegal seminary of the Confessing Church at Finkenwalde, and during this period he wrote *The Cost of Discipleship*. The book is a brilliant exposition on the Sermon on the Mount. Bonhoeffer believed that these words of Jesus Christ were a source of power that could destroy the Nazi Reich, provided that the Church lived uncompromisingly by them, preaching fearlessly against what was fast becoming a godless dictatorship. In *The Cost of Discipleship*, students heard for the first time the terms *cheap grace* and *costly grace*. "Cheap grace is the deadly enemy of the church," said Bonhoeffer. "We are fighting today for costly grace."

During the Finkenwalde period Bonhoeffer produced two other exceptional books. One, *Life Together*, reveals the secret to living together as Christians, and is characteristic of the apostle Paul in its direct and practical approach. The second is entitled *Temptation* and deals with the daily human struggle against temptation and with the assurance that it can be overcome through Jesus Christ.

As Bonhoeffer continued to work for the Confessing Church, he spoke out repeatedly against the discrimination and persecution of the Jews. Although the Nazis threatened anyone who dared to "interfere in politics," Bonhoeffer would not be silenced, and he implored the Church to exercise its commission, taking as his text Proverbs 31:8: "Open your mouth for the dumb!" But after the horror of the "Crystal Night," when synagogues were burned and the Jewish community terrorized, the Confessing Church lost the courage to make any more public statements.

At this time Bonhoeffer's brother-in-law, Hans von Dohnanyi, who was the personal assistant to the minister of justice, became active in a military plot to overthrow Hitler. Dohnanyi confided in Bonhoeffer, who thus became an accessory to the plan, a crime that carried the death penalty. When Hitler's armies marched into Bohemia and Moravia in 1939, Bonhoeffer was no longer able to speak in public, and he accepted an invitation to take a sabbatical in America. He hoped that there he could carry on the work of his Church and complete his study of ethics. Before long, however, he realized how much he missed his homeland and those who were actively resisting the Reich. Although it meant certain persecution, he decided to return to Germany. He felt he would have no right to participate in the reconstruction of his country if he did not share also in her tribulation.

Shortly after Bonhoeffer's return, his brother-in-law arranged for him to be sent to Munich, where he joined the staff of the Abwehr (the intelligence bureau) as a civilian employee. Now in the inner circle of the resistance movement, Bonhoeffer stayed in a Benedictine monastery at Ettal and worked on his study of ethics while awaiting Abwehr assignments, which allowed him to travel outside Germany; he seized every opportunity to work for the Confessing Church. Regarded highly in ecumenical circles, Bonhoeffer traveled to Switzerland, Sweden, Norway, and Italy. He also relayed news about the resistance to London and carried information back to Germany. On one of his trips to Switzerland he was able to take a small group of Jews to safety. While in Sweden, Bonhoeffer contacted his old friend Bishop Bell, to whom he gave information about the intended coup. The bishop communicated the details to Britain's foreign minister, Anthony Eden; Eden felt that the communication might disguise a peace feeler from the Nazis, and so refused to send any reply.

Plans were then made for the assassination of Hitler. Bonhoeffer was horrified at the thought of murder, but he knew he could not stand by to witness the annihilation of so many people. As a minister he said he felt he must do more than comfort the relatives of those killed by the drunken driver; he must seize the wheel.

In 1943 the net around Bonhoeffer began to tighten. An Abwehr conspirator was arrested, and under torture, revealed the names of the members of the resistance. Bonhoeffer was warned that his telephone was being tapped, and when on April 5 his father came to tell him that two men were waiting to speak to him, Bonhoeffer knew what would happen. Calmly he went to meet the representatives of the Gestapo and left with them, never to return to his family home.

On his desk were the copious notes for his work on ethics. His close friend, Eberhard Bethge, painstakingly pieced together these notes, and saw to their publication in 1945 under the title *Ethics*. In *Ethics*, Bonhoeffer presents the case for the spirit of Jesus Christ permeating the everyday lives of those who believe in Him. All decisions, actions, relationships with family and neighbors, must be inspired by His presence; responsibility cannot be excused away. As Christians we must stand for all our Saviour lived and died for, in the triumph of the Resurrection.

After his arrest Bonhoeffer was taken to Tegel Prison, where he was tortured and interrogated. Not once did he implicate any of his family or other members of the Abwehr. Of the sessions he would only say that they were "disgusting." At first he spent weeks in solitary confinement; although the guards were forbidden to talk to political prisoners, many of them befriended Bonhoeffer, smuggling letters in and out of prison. One guard even arranged a visit from Bonhoeffer's sister. Because of the guards and Eberhard Bethge, we are able to share Bonhoeffer's experiences in *Letters and Papers from Prison*. In his letters Bonhoeffer shows us that, although separated from those he loved—friends, family, and fiancée—he was still capable of joy. The narrow confines of his prison cell provided a frame for a rich intellectual Christian life. Nor did he lose his sense of humor: Bonhoeffer referred to his experience in prison as "an unexpected sabbatical term."

In Tegel Prison he was able to minister to his neighbors and to demonstrate that Jesus Christ was all that He had promised, even amid vileness and suffering. Others looked to him for help and comfort, seeing in him a tower of strength.

In October 1943 Bonhoeffer was transferred to the Gestapo bunker in Prinz-Albrecht-Strasse and underwent further interrogation, never betraying his fellow conspirators. While Bonhoeffer was in solitary confinement, the building above the bunker was destroyed in an Allied bombing raid. Bonhoeffer was transferred several more times, and was eventually taken to a detention camp at Schönberg on April 5, 1945. That day, Hitler decided that none of the remaining Abwehr group would live.

On April 8 Bonhoeffer conducted a service for his fellow prisoners. He chose as his texts Isaiah 53:5 ("With his stripes we are healed") and Peter 1:3 ("Blessed be the God and Father of our Lord Jesus Christ, which according to his abundant mercy hath begotten us again unto a lively hope by the resurrection of Jesus Christ from the dead"). As he came to the end of his message, the door was flung open and Bonhoeffer was ordered to collect his belongings. An English army officer who was present relayed Bonhoeffer's final greeting to Bishop Bell: "...This is the end, but for me, it is the beginning."

Bonhoeffer was taken to the Flossenburg concentration camp and sentenced to death after an all-night court-martial. The prison doctor saw him kneel in prayer shortly after the sentence was pronounced. The next morning, when he was taken to the scaffold, he knelt to pray once more. Then, courageously, he climbed the steps to the gallows, and at thirty-nine years of age Dietrich Bonhoeffer, a noble and dedicated disciple of Jesus Christ, was hanged.

There was no funeral. No gravestone marks the final resting place of this brilliant but humble theologian. His ashes were scattered to the winds—but the Nazis could not obliterate the memory or impact of this man.

Tertullian, a Roman converted to Christianity in A.D. 192, said, "The blood of the martyrs is the seed of the Church." Originally the word *martyr* meant "witness." This Bonhoeffer was, and his message is as relevant today as it was in Nazi Germany. His words bid us be dedicated witnesses in today's confusingly violent and needy world.

In compiling this anthology of Dietrich Bonhoeffer's writings, it has been my hope that those who are familiar with his works will find a further blessing in these excerpts. Those who are unacquainted with Bonhoeffer's thought-provoking and challenging words will find in this collection a rich encounter with a man who lived and died triumphantly, experiencing costly grace and close communion with his Lord and Savior.

JOAN WINMILL BROWN

Created in His Image

YAHWEH SHAPES MAN with his own hands. This expresses two things. First, the bodily nearness of the Creator to the creature, that it is really he who makes me—man—with his own hands; his concern, his thought for me, his design for me, his nearness to me. And secondly there is his authority, the absolute superiority in which he shapes and creates me, in which I am his creature; the fatherliness in which he creates me and in which I worship him. That is God himself, to whom the whole Bible testifies.

The man whom God has created in his image, that is in freedom, is the man who is formed out of earth. Darwin and Feuerbach themselves could not speak any more strongly. Man's origin is in a piece of earth. His bond with the earth belongs to his essential being. The "earth is his mother"; he comes out of her womb. Of course, the ground from which man is taken is still not the cursed but the blessed ground. It is God's earth out of which man is taken. From it he has his *body*. His body belongs to his essential being. Man's body is not his prison, his shell, his exterior, but man himself. Man does not "have" a body; he does not "have" a soul; rather, he "is" body and soul. Man in the beginning is really his body. He is one. He is his body, as Christ is completely his body, as the Church is the body of Christ. The man who renounces his body renounces his existence before God the Creator. The essential point of human existence is its bond with mother earth, its being as body. Man has his existence as existence on earth; he does not come to the earthly world from above, driven and enslaved by a cruel fate. He comes out of the earth in which he slept and was dead; he is called out by the Word of God the Almighty, in himself a piece of earth, but earth called into human being by God. "Awake, thou that sleepest, and arise from the dead, and Christ shall shine upon thee."[1] Michelangelo also meant this. Adam resting on the newly created ground is so closely and intimately bound up with the ground on which he lies that he himself, in his still dreaming existence, is strange and marvellous to the highest degree—but just the same he is a piece of earth. Surely, it is in this full devotion to the blessed ground of creation's earth that the complete glory of the first man becomes visible. And in this resting on the ground, in this deep sleep of creation, man experiences life through bodily contact with the finger of God—the same hand that has made man touches him tenderly as from afar and awakens him to life. God's hand does not hold man in its embrace any longer, but it sets him free, and its creative power becomes the demanding love of the Creator towards the creature. The hand of God portrayed by the picture in the Sistine Chapel reveals more wisdom about the creation than many a deep speculation.

[1]Ephesians 5:14

. . . And God breathed into his nostrils the breath of life; and man became a living being.

Here body and life enter into one another totally. God breathes his Spirit into the body of man. And this Spirit is life and makes man alive. God creates other life through his Word; where man is concerned he gives of his life, of his Spirit. Man as man does not live without God's Spirit. To live *as man* means to live as body in Spirit. Escape from the body is escape from being man and escape from the spirit as well. Body is the existence-form of spirit, as spirit is the existence-form of body. All this can be said only of man, for only in man do we know of body and spirit. The human body is distinguished from all non-human bodies by being the existence-form of God's Spirit on earth, as it is wholly undifferentiated from all other life by being of this earth. The human body really only lives by God's Spirit; this is indeed its essential nature. God glorifies himself in the body: in this specific form of the human body. For this reason God enters into the body again where the original in its created being has been destroyed. He enters it in Jesus Christ. He enters into it where it is broken, in the form of the sacrament of the body and of the blood. The body and blood of the Lord's Supper are the new realities of creation of the promise for the fallen Adam. Adam is created as body, and therefore he is also redeemed as body, in Jesus Christ and in the Sacrament.

Man thus created is man as the image of God. He is the image of God not in spite of but just because of his bodiliness. For in his bodiliness he is related to the earth and to other bodies, he is there for others, he is dependent upon others. In his bodiliness he finds his brother and the earth. As such a creature man of earth and spirit is in the likeness of his Creator, God.

The Kingdom of God

...GOD IS BEING increasingly pushed out of a world that has come of age, out of the spheres of our knowledge and life, and that since Kant he has been relegated to a realm beyond the world of experience. Theology has on the one hand resisted this development with apologetics, and has taken up arms—in vain—against Darwinism, etc. On the other hand, it has accommodated itself to the development by restricting God to the so-called ultimate questions as a *deus ex machina;* that means that he becomes the answer to life's problems, and the solution of its needs and conflicts. So if anyone has no such difficulties, or if he refuses to go into these things, to allow others to pity him, then either he cannot be open to God; or else he must be shown that he is, in fact, deeply involved in such problems, needs, and conflicts, without admitting or knowing it. If that can be done—and existentialist philosophy and psychotherapy have worked out some quite ingenious methods in that direction—then this man can now be claimed for God, and methodism can celebrate its triumph. But if he cannot be brought to see and admit that his happiness is really an evil, his health sickness, and his vigour despair, the theologian is at his wits' end. It's a case of having to do either with a hardened sinner of a particularly ugly type, or with a man of 'bourgeois complacency', and the one is as far from salvation as the other.

You see, that is the attitude that I am contending against. When Jesus blessed sinners, they were real sinners, but Jesus did not make everyone a sinner first. He called them away from their sin, not into their sin. It is true that encounter with Jesus meant the reversal of all human values. So it was in the conversion of Paul, though in his case the encounter with Jesus preceded the realization of sin. It is true that Jesus cared about people on the fringe of human society, such as harlots and tax-collectors, but never about them alone, for he sought to care about man as such. Never did he question a man's health, vigour, or happiness, regarded in themselves, or regard them as evil fruits; else why should he heal the sick and restore strength to the weak? Jesus claims for himself and the Kingdom of God the whole of human life in all its manifestations.

The Strength of God

THE DISPLACEMENT OF GOD from the world, and from the public part of human life, led to the attempt to keep his place secure at least in the sphere of the 'personal', the 'inner', and the 'private'. And as every man still has a private sphere somewhere, that is where he was thought to be the most vulnerable. The secrets known to a man's valet—that is, to put it crudely, the range of his intimate life, from prayer to his sexual life—have become the hunting-ground of modern pastoral workers. In that way they resemble (though with quite different intentions) the dirtiest gutter journalists—do you remember the *Wahrheit* and the *Glocke*,[1] which made public the most intimate

[1]Berlin papers from the Weimar period.

details about prominent people? In the one case it's social, financial, or political blackmail and in the other, religious blackmail. Forgive me, but I can't put it more mildly.

From the sociological point of view this is a revolution from below, a revolt of inferiority. Just as the vulgar mind isn't satisfied till it has seen some highly placed personage 'in his bath', or in other embarrassing situations, so it is here. There is a kind of evil satisfaction in knowing that everyone has his failings and weak spots. In my contacts with the 'outcasts' of society, its 'pariahs', I've noticed repeatedly that mistrust is the dominant motive in their judgment of other people. Every action, even the most unselfish, of a person of high repute is suspected from the outset. These 'outcasts' are to be found in all grades of society. In a flower-garden they grub around only for the dung on which the flowers grow. The more isolated a man's life, the more easily he falls a victim to this attitude.

There is also a parallel isolation among the clergy, in what one might call the 'clerical' sniffing-around-after-people's-sins in order to catch them out. It's as if you couldn't know a fine house till you had found a cobweb in the furthest cellar, or as if you couldn't adequately appreciate a good play till you had seen how the actors behave off-stage. It's the same kind of thing that you find in the novels of the last fifty years, which do not think they have depicted their characters properly till they have described them in their marriage-bed, or in films where undressing scenes are thought necessary. Anything clothed, veiled, pure, and chaste is presumed to be deceitful, disguised, and impure; people here simply show their own impurity. A basic anti-social attitude of mistrust and suspicion is the revolt of inferiority.

Regarded theologically, the error is twofold. First, it is thought that a man can be addressed as a sinner only after his weaknesses and meannesses have been spied out. Secondly, it is thought that a man's essential nature consists of his inmost and most intimate background; that is defined as his 'inner life', and it is precisely in those secret human places that God is to have his domain!

. . . The Bible does not recognize our distinction between the outward and the inward. Why should it? It is always concerned with *anthrōpos teleios*, the *whole* man, even where, as in the Sermon on the Mount, the decalogue is pressed home to refer to 'inward disposition'. That a good 'disposition' can take the place of total goodness is quite unbiblical. The discovery of the so-called inner life dates from the Renaissance, probably from Petrarch. The 'heart' in the biblical sense is not the inner life, but the whole man in relation to God. But as a man lives just as much from 'outwards' to 'inwards' as from 'inwards' to 'outwards', the view that his essential nature can be understood only from his intimate spiritual background is wholly erroneous.

I therefore want to start from the premise that God shouldn't be smuggled into some last secret place, but that we should frankly recognize that the world, and people, have come of age, that we shouldn't run man down in his worldliness, but confront him with God at his strongest point, that we should give up all our clerical tricks, and not regard psychotherapy and existentialist philosophy as God's pioneers. The importunity of all these people is far too unaristocratic for the Word of God to ally itself with them. The Word of God is far removed from this revolt of mistrust, this revolt from below. On the contrary, it reigns.

God's Faithfulness

...THERE IS HARDLY ANYTHING that can make one happier than to feel that one counts for something with other people. What matters here is not numbers, but intensity. In the long run, human relationships are the most important thing in life; the modern 'efficient' man can do nothing to change this, nor can the demigods and lunatics who know nothing about human relationships. God uses us in his dealings with others.

God's Blessing

...IN THE OLD TESTAMENT—e.g. among the patriarchs— there's a concern not for fortune, but for God's blessing, which includes in itself all earthly good. In that blessing the whole of the earthly life is claimed for God, and it includes all his promises. It would be natural to suppose that, as usual, the New Testament spiritualizes the teaching of the Old Testament here, and therefore to regard the Old Testament blessing as superseded in the New. But is it an accident that sickness and death are mentioned in connection with the misuse of the Lord's Supper ('The cup of blessing', I Cor. 10:16; 11:30), that Jesus restored people's health, and that while his disciples were with him they 'lacked nothing'? Now, is it right to set the Old

Testament blessing against the cross? That is what Kierkegaard did. That makes the cross, or at least suffering, an abstract principle; and that is just what gives rise to an unhealthy methodism, which deprives suffering of its element of contingency as a divine ordinance. It's true that in the Old Testament the person who receives the blessing has to endure a great deal of suffering (e.g. Abraham, Isaac, Jacob, and Joseph), but this never leads to the idea that fortune and suffering, blessing and cross are mutually exclusive and contradictory—nor does it in the New Testament. Indeed, the only difference between the Old and New Testaments in this respect is that in the Old the blessing includes the cross, and in the New the cross includes the blessing.

To turn to a different point: not only action, but also suffering is a way to freedom. In suffering, the deliverance consists in our being allowed to put the matter out of our own hands into God's hands. In this sense death is the crowning of human freedom. Whether the human deed is a matter of faith or not depends on whether we understand our suffering as an extension of our action and a completion of freedom. I think that is very important and very comforting.

The Commandment of God

EITHER GOD DOES NOT SPEAK at all or else He speaks to us as definitely as He spoke to Abraham and Jacob and Moses and as definitely as in Jesus Christ He spoke to the disciples and through His apostles to the Gentiles. Does this mean that at every moment of our lives we may be informed of the commandment of God by some special direct divine inspiration, or that at every moment, in an unmistakable and unequivocal manner, God causes what Karl Heim calls the 'accent of eternity' to rest on a particular action which He wills? No, it does not mean that, for the concreteness of the divine commandment consists in its historicity; it confronts us in a historical form. Does this mean, then, that we are utterly lacking in certainty in the face of the extremely varying claims of the historical powers, and that, so far as the commandment of God is concerned, we are groping in the darkness? No, the reason why it does not mean this is that God makes His commandment heard in a definite historical form. We cannot now escape the question where and in what historical form God makes His commandment known. For the sake of simplicity and clarity, and even at the risk of a direct misunderstanding, we will begin by answering this question in the form of a thesis. God's commandment, which is manifested in Jesus Christ, comes to us in the Church, in the family, in labour and in government.

It is a necessary premise which must never be lost sight of, even though for the time being it may not be fully intelligible, that the commandment of God is and always remains the commandment of God which is made manifest in Jesus Christ. There is no other commandment of God than that which is revealed by Him and which is manifested according to His will in Jesus Christ.

This means that the commandment of God does not spring from the created world. It comes down from above. It does not arise from the factual claim on men of earthly powers and laws, from the claim of the instinct of self-preservation or from the claim of hunger, sex or political force. It stands beyond all these as a demand, a precept and judgement. The commandment of God establishes on earth an inviolable superiority and inferiority which are independent of the factual relations of power and weakness. In establishing this superiority it confers that warrant for ethical discourse of which we have already spoken, or, more comprehensively, it confers the warrant to proclaim the divine commandment.

Christians and Pagans

1
Men go to God when they are sore bestead,
Pray to him for succour, for his peace, for bread,
For mercy for them sick, sinning, or dead;
All men do so, Christian and unbelieving.

2
Men go to God when he is sore bestead,
Find him poor and scorned, without shelter or bread,
Whelmed under weight of the wicked, the weak,
　　the dead;
Christians stand by God in his hour of grieving.

3
God goes to every man when sore bestead,
Feeds body and spirit with his bread;
For Christians, pagans alike he hangs dead,
And both alike forgiving.

God's Will

...THE WILL OF GOD is not a system of rules which is established from the outset; it is something new and different in each different situation in life, and for this reason a man must ever anew examine what the will of God may be. The heart, the understanding, observation and experience must all collaborate in this task. It is no longer a matter of a man's own knowledge of good and evil, but solely of the living will of God; our knowledge of God's will is not something over which we ourselves dispose, but it depends solely upon the grace of God, and this grace is and requires to be new every morning. That is why this proving or examining of the will of God is so serious a matter. The voice of the heart is not to be confused with the will of God, nor is any kind of inspiration or any general principle, for the will of God discloses itself ever anew only to him who proves it ever anew.

Access to God

...NOT EVERYTHING THAT HAPPENS is simply 'God's will'; yet in the last resort nothing happens 'without God's will' (Matt. 10:29), i.e. through every event, however unto-

Editor's note: Written in Tegel Prison to his friend Eberhard Bethge.

ward, there is access to God. When a man enters on a supremely happy marriage and has thanked God for it, it is a terrible blow to discover that the same God who established the marriage now demands of us a period of such great deprivation. In my experience nothing tortures us more than longing. Some people have been so violently shaken in their lives from their earliest days that they cannot now, so to speak, allow themselves any great longing or put up with a long period of tension, and they find compensation in short-lived pleasures that offer readier satisfaction. That is the fate of the proletarian classes, and it is the ruin of all intellectual fertility. It's not true to say that it is good for a man to have suffered heavy blows early and often in life; in most cases it breaks him. True, it hardens people for times like ours, but it also greatly helps to deaden them. When *we* are forcibly separated for any considerable time from those whom we love, we simply *cannot,* as most can, get some cheap substitute through other people—I don't mean because of moral considerations, but just because we are what we are. Substitutes repel us; we simply have to wait and wait; we have to suffer unspeakably from the separation, and feel the longing till it almost makes us ill. That is the only way, although it is a very painful one, in which we can preserve unimpaired our relationship with our loved ones. A few times in my life I've come to know what homesickness means. There is nothing more painful, and during these months in prison I've sometimes been terribly homesick. And as I expect you will have to go through the same kind of thing in the coming months, I wanted to write and tell you what I've learnt about it, in case it may be of some help to you. The first result of such longing is always a wish to neglect the ordinary daily routine in some way or other, and that means that our lives become disordered. I used to be tempted sometimes to stay in bed after six in the morning (it would have been perfectly possible), and to sleep on. Up to now I've always been able to force myself not to do this; I realized that it would have been the first stage of capitulation, and that worse would probably have followed. An outward and purely physical régime (exercises and a cold wash down in the morning) itself provides some support for one's inner discipline. Further, there is nothing worse in such times than to try to find a substitute for the irreplaceable. It just does not work, and it leads to still greater indiscipline, for the strength to overcome tension (such strength can come only from looking the longing straight in the face) is impaired, and endurance becomes even more unbearable...

Another point: I don't think it is good to talk to strangers about our condition; that always stirs up one's troubles—although we ought to be ready, when occasion arises, to listen to those of other people. Above all, we must never give way to self-pity. And on the Christian aspect of the matter, there are some lines that say

> ...that we remember what we would forget,
> that this poor earth is not our home.

That is indeed something essential, but it must come last of all. I believe that we ought so to love and trust God in our *lives*, and in all the good things that he sends us, that when the time comes (but not before!) we may go to him with love, trust, and joy. But, to put it plainly, for a man in his wife's arms to be hankering after the other world is, in mild terms, a piece of bad taste, and not God's will. We ought to find and love God in what he actually gives us; if it pleases him to allow us to enjoy some overwhelming earthly happiness, we mustn't try to be more pious than God himself and allow our happiness to be corrupted by presumption and arrogance, and by unbridled religious fantasy which is never satisfied with what God gives. God will see to it that the man who finds him in his earthly happiness and thanks him for it does not lack reminder that earthly things are transient, that it is good for him to attune his heart to what is eternal, and that sooner or later there will be times when he can say in all sincerity, 'I wish I were home.' But everything has its time, and the main thing is that we keep step with God, and do not keep pressing on a few steps ahead—nor keep dawdling a step behind. It's presumptuous to want to have everything at once—matrimonial bliss, the cross, and the heavenly Jerusalem, where they neither marry nor are given in marriage. 'For everything there is a season' (Eccles. 3:1); everything has its time: 'a time to weep, and a time to laugh;...a time to embrace, and a time to refrain from embracing;...a time to rend, and a time to sew;...and God seeks again what is past.' I suspect that these last words mean that nothing that is past is lost, that God gathers up again with us our past, which belongs to us. So when we are seized by a longing for the past—and this may happen when we least expect it—we may be sure that it is only one of the many 'hours' that God is always holding ready for us. So we oughtn't to seek the past again by our own efforts, but only with God....

God Is No Stop-gap

...HOW WRONG IT IS to use God as a stop-gap for the incompleteness of our knowledge. If in fact the frontiers of knowledge are being pushed further and further back (and that is bound to be the case), then God is being pushed back with them, and is therefore continually in retreat. We are to find God in what we know, not in what we don't know; God wants us to realize his presence, not in unsolved problems but in those that are solved. That is true of the relationship between God and scientific knowledge, but it is also true of the wider human problems of death, suffering, and guilt. It is now possible to find, even for these questions, human answers that take no account whatever of God. In point of fact, people deal with these questions without God (it has always been so), and it is simply not true to say that only Christianity has the answers to them. As to the idea of 'solving' problems, it may be that the Christian answers are just as unconvincing—or convincing—as any others. Here again, God is no stop-gap; he must be recognized at the centre of life, not when we are at the end of our resources; it is his will to be recognized in life, and not only when death comes; in health and vigour, and not only in suffering; in our activities, and not only in sin. The ground for this lies in the revelation of God in Jesus Christ. He is the centre of life, and he certainly didn't 'come' to answer our unsolved problems. From the centre of life certain questions, and their answers, are seen to be wholly irrelevant (I'm thinking of the judgement pronounced on Job's friends). In Christ there are no 'Christian problems'...

The Name of Jesus Christ

...IT IS ONLY WHEN ONE KNOWS the unutterability of the name of God that one can utter the name of Jesus Christ; it is only when one loves life and the earth so much that without them everything seems to be over that one may believe in the resurrection and a new world; it is only when one submits to God's law that one may speak of grace; and it is only when God's wrath and vengeance are hanging as grim realities over the heads of one's enemies that something of what it means to love and forgive them can touch our hearts. . . .

The Incarnate One

If Jesus Christ is to be described as God, we may not speak of this divine being, nor of his omnipotence, nor his omniscience; but we must speak of this weak man among sinners, of his manger and his cross. If we are to deal with the deity of Jesus, we must speak of his weakness. In christology, one looks at the whole historical man Jesus and says of him, that he is God. One does not first look at a human nature and then beyond it to a divine nature, but one has to do with the one man Jesus Christ, who is wholly God.

The accounts of the birth and of the baptism of Jesus stand side by side. In the birth story, we are directed totally towards Jesus himself. In the story of the baptism, we are directed towards the Holy Spirit who comes from above. The reason why we find it difficult to take the two stories together is because of the doctrine of the two natures. The two stories are not teaching two natures. If we put this doctrine aside, we see that the one story concerns the being of the Word of God in Jesus, while the other concerns the coming of the Word of God upon Jesus. The child in the manger is wholly God: note Luther's christology in the Christmas hymns. The call at the baptism is confirmation of the first happening, there is no adoptionism in it. The manger directs our attention to the man, who is God; the baptism directs our attention, as we look at Jesus, to the God who calls.

If we speak of Jesus Christ as God, we may not say of him that he is the representative of an idea of God, which possesses the characteristics of omniscience and omnipotence (there is no such thing as this abstract divine nature!); rather, we must speak of his weakness, his manger, his cross. This man is no abstract God.

Strictly speaking we should not talk of the incarnation, but of the incarnate one. The former interest arises out of the question, 'How?' The question, 'How?', for example, underlies the hypothesis of the virgin birth. Both historically and dogmatically it can be questioned. The biblical witness is ambiguous. If the biblical witness gave clear evidence of the fact, then the dogmatic obscurity might not have been so important. The doctrine of the virgin birth is meant to express the incarnation of God, not only the fact of the incarnate one. But does it not fail at the decisive point of the incarnation, namely that in it Jesus has not become man just like us? The question remains open, as and because it is already open in the Bible.

The incarnate one is the glorified God: 'The Word was made flesh and we beheld his glory'. God glorifies himself in man. That is the ultimate secret of the Trinity. The humanity is taken up into the Trinity. Not from all eternity, but 'from now on even unto eternity'; the trinitarian God is seen as the incarnate one. The glorification of God in the flesh is now at the same time, the glorification of man, who shall have life through eternity with the trinitarian God. This does not mean that we should see the incarnation of God as God's judgement on man. God remains the incarnate one even in the Last Judgement. The incarnation is the message of the glorification of God, who sees his honour in becoming man. It must be noted that the incarnation is first and foremost true revelation, of the Creator in the creature, and not veiled revelation. Jesus Christ is the unveiled image of God.

The incarnation of God may not be thought of as derived from an idea of God, in which something of humanity already belongs to the idea of God—as in Hegel. Here we speak of the biblical witness, 'We saw his glory'. If the incarnation is thus spoken of as the glorification of God, it is not permissible to slip in once again a speculative idea of God, which derives the incarnation from the necessity of an idea of God. A speculative basis for the doctrine of the incarnation in an idea of God would change the free relationship between Creator and creature into a logical necessity. The incarnation is contingent. God binds himself freely to the creature and freely glorifies himself in the incarnate one.

Why does that sound strange and improbable? Because the revelation of the incarnation in Jesus Christ is not visibly a glorification of God. Because this incarnate one is also the crucified.

The Body of Jesus Christ

GOD WAS MADE MAN, and while that means that he took upon him our entire human nature with all its infirmity, sinfulness and corruption, the whole of apostate humanity, it does not mean that he took upon him the man Jesus. Unless we draw this distinction we shall misunderstand the whole message of the gospel. The Body of Jesus Christ, in which we are taken up with the whole human race, has now become the ground of our salvation.

It is *sinful* flesh that he bears, though he was himself without sin (II Cor. 5:21; Heb. 4:15). In his human body he takes all flesh upon himself. "Surely he hath borne our griefs, and carried our sorrows." It is solely in virtue of the Incarnation that Jesus was able to heal the diseases and pains of human nature, because he bore upon his own body all these ills (Matt. 8:15–17). "He was wounded for our transgressions, he was bruised for our iniquities." He bore our sins, and was able to forgive them because he had "taken up" our sinful flesh in his Body. Similarly, Jesus received sinners and took them to himself (Luke 15:2) because he bore them in his own body. With the coming of Christ the "acceptable (δεκτόν) year of the Lord" had dawned (Luke 4:19).

. . . The earthly body of Jesus underwent crucifixion and death. In that death the new humanity undergoes crucifixion and death. Jesus Christ had taken upon him not a man, but the human "form," sinful flesh, human "nature," so that all whom he bore suffer and die with him. It is all our infirmities and all our sin that he bears to the cross. It is *we* who are crucified with him, and we who die with him. True, his earthly body undergoes death, but only to rise again as an incorruptible, glorious body. It is the same body—the tomb was empty—and yet it is a new body. And so as he dies, Jesus bears the human race, and carries it onward to resurrection. Thus, too, he bears for ever in his glorified body the humanity which he had taken upon him on earth.

How then do we come to participate in the Body of Christ, who did all this for us? It is certain that there can be no fellowship or communion with him except through his Body. For only through that Body can we find acceptance and salvation. The answer is, through the two sacraments of his Body, baptism and the Lord's Supper. Note how in recording the incident of the water and blood which issued from the side of the crucified body of Christ, St John refers unmistakably to the elements of the two sacraments (John 19:34, 35). St Paul corroborates this when he rivets our membership of the Body of Christ exclusively to the two sacraments.[1] The sacraments begin and end in the Body of Christ, and it is only the presence of that Body which makes them what they are. The word of preaching is insufficient to make us members of Christ's Body; the sacraments also have to be added. Baptism incorporates us into the unity of the Body of Christ, and the Lord's Supper fosters and sustains our fellowship and communion (κοινωνία) in that Body. Baptism makes us members of the Body of Christ. We are "baptized into" Christ (Gal. 3:27; Rom. 6:3); we are "baptized into one body" (I Cor. 12:13). Our death in baptism conveys the gift of the Holy Spirit, and gains the redemption which Christ wrought for us in his body. The communion of the body of Christ, which we receive as the disciples received it in the early days, is the sign and pledge that we are "with Christ" and "in Christ," and that he is "in us." Rightly understood, the doctrine of the Body is the clue to the meaning of these expressions.

[1]Eph. 3:6 likewise embraces the whole gift of salvation—the Word, Baptism, and the Lord's Supper.

The Lordship of Jesus Christ

Jesus Christ, the eternal Son with the Father for all eternity: this means that no created thing can be conceived and essentially understood without reference to Christ, the Mediator of creation. All things were created by Him and for Him, and have their existence only in Him (Col. 1:15ff.). It is vain to seek to know God's will for created things without reference to Christ. Jesus Christ, the incarnate God: this means that God has taken upon himself bodily all human being; it means that henceforward divine being cannot be found otherwise than in human form; it means that in Jesus Christ man is made free to be really man before God. The 'Christian' element is not now something which lies beyond the human element; it requires to be in the midst of the human element. The 'Christian' element is not an end in itself, but it consists in man's being entitled and obliged to live as man before God. In the incarnation God makes Himself known as Him who wishes to exist not for Himself but 'for us'. Consequently, in view of the incarnation of God, to live as man before God can mean only to exist not for oneself but for God and for other men.

Jesus Christ, the crucified Reconciler: this means in the first place that the whole world has become godless by its rejection of Jesus Christ and that no effort of its own can rid it of this curse. The reality of the world has been marked once and for all by the cross of Christ, but the cross of Christ is the cross of the reconciliation of the world with God, and for this reason the godless world bears at the same time the mark of reconciliation as the free ordinance of God. The cross of atonement is the setting free for life before God in the midst of the godless world; it is the setting free for life in genuine worldliness. The proclamation of the cross of the atonement is a setting free because it leaves behind it the vain attempts to deify the world and because it has overcome the disunions, tensions and conflicts between the 'Christian' element and the 'secular' element and calls for simple life and action in the belief that the reconciliation of the world with God has been accomplished.

...*Jesus Christ, the risen and ascended Lord:* this means that Jesus Christ has overcome sin and death and that He is the living Lord to whom all power is given in heaven and on earth. All the powers of the world are made subject to Him and must serve Him, each in its own way. The lordship of Jesus Christ is not the rule of a foreign power; it is the lordship of the Creator, Reconciler and Redeemer, the lordship of Him through whom and for whom all created beings exist, of Him in whom indeed all created beings alone find their origin, their goal and their essence. Jesus Christ imposes no alien law upon creation; but at the same time He does not tolerate any 'autonomy' of creation in detachment from His commandments. The commandment of Jesus Christ, the living Lord, sets creation free for the fulfilment of the law which is its own, that is to say, the law which is inherent in it by virtue of its having its origin, its goal and its essence in Jesus Christ. The commandment of Jesus does not provide the basis for any kind of domination of the Church over the government, of the government over the family, or of culture over government or Church, or for any other relation of over-lordship which may be thought of in this connexion. The commandment of Jesus Christ does indeed rule over Church, family, culture and government; but it does so while at the same time setting each of these mandates free for the fulfilment of its own allotted functions. Jesus Christ's claim to lordship, which is proclaimed by the Church, means at the same time the emancipation of family, culture and government for the realization of their own essential character which has its foundation in Christ.[1] The liberation which results from the proclamation of the lordship of Christ alone renders possible that relation of the divine mandates 'with', 'for' and 'against' one another....

---

[1]The antinomy of heteronomy and autonomy is here resolved in a higher unity which we may call Christonomy.

The Light of His Presence

ALL THAT WE MAY RIGHTLY EXPECT from God, and ask him for, is to be found in Jesus Christ. The God of Jesus Christ has nothing to do with what God, as we imagine him, could do and ought to do. If we are to learn what God promises, and what he fulfils, we must persevere in quiet meditation on the life, sayings, deeds, sufferings, and death of Jesus. It is certain that we may always live close to God and in the light of his presence, and that such living is an entirely new life for us; that nothing is then impossible for us, because all things are possible with God; that no earthly power can touch us without his will, and that danger and distress can only drive us closer to him. It is certain that we can claim nothing for ourselves, and may yet pray for everything; it is certain that our joy is hidden in suffering, and our life in death; it is certain that in all this we are in a fellowship that sustains us. In Jesus God has said Yes and Amen to it all, and that Yes and Amen is the firm ground on which we stand.

In these turbulent times we repeatedly lose sight of what really makes life worth living. We think that, because this or that person is living, it makes sense for us to live too. But the truth is that if this earth was good enough for the man Jesus Christ, if such a man as Jesus lived, then, and only then, has life a meaning for us. If Jesus had not lived, then our life would be meaningless, in spite of all the other people whom we know and honour and love. Perhaps we now sometimes forget the meaning and purpose of our profession. But isn't this the simplest way of putting it? The unbiblical idea of 'meaning' is indeed only a translation of what the Bible calls 'promise'.

'I Am the Life'

JESUS CHRIST SAID of Himself: 'I am the life' (John 14:6 and 11:25), and this claim, and the reality which it contains cannot be disregarded by any Christian thinking, or indeed by any philosophical thinking at all. This self-affirmation of Jesus is a declaration that any attempt to express the essence of life simply as life is foredoomed to failure and has indeed already failed. So long as we live, so long as we do not know the boundary of life, death, how can we possibly say what life is in itself? We can only live life; we cannot define it. Jesus's saying binds every thought of life to His person. 'I am the life.' No question about life can go further back than this 'I am'. The question of what is life gives place to the answer who is life. Life is not a thing, an entity or concept; it is a person, a particular and unique person, and it is this particular and unique person, not in respect of what this person has in common with other persons, but in the I of this person; it is the I of Jesus. Jesus sets this I in sharp contrast with all the thoughts, concepts and ways which claim to constitute the essence of life. He does not say 'I have the life' but 'I am the life.' Consequently life can never again be separated from the I, the person, of Jesus. In proclaiming this, Jesus does not merely say that He is life, in other words simply some metaphysical spirit which might possibly light upon me as well as upon others; He says that He is precisely my life, our life; St Paul describes this state of affairs very accurately, though also very paradoxically, in the words 'To me to live is Christ' (Phil. 1:21) and 'Christ who is our life' (Col. 3:4). My life is outside myself, outside the range of my disposal; my life is another than myself; it is Jesus Christ. This is not intended figuratively, as conveying that my life would not be worth living without this other, or that Christ invests my life with a particular quality or a particular value while allowing it to retain its own independent existence, but my life itself is Jesus Christ. That is true of my life, and it is true of all created things. 'In all things that were made—He was the life' (John 1:4).[1]

'I am the life.' This is the word, the revelation, the proclamation of Jesus Christ. Our life is outside ourselves and in Jesus Christ; this is not at all a conclusion which we derive from our knowledge of ourselves; it is a claim which comes to us from without, a claim which we may either believe or contradict. This word is addressed to us, and when we hear it we recognize that we have fallen away from life, from our life, and that we are living in contradiction to life, to our life. In this saying of Jesus Christ, therefore, we hear the condemnation, the negation, of our life; for our life is not life; or, if it is life, it is life only by virtue of the fact that, even though in contradiction to it, we still live through the life which is called Jesus Christ, the origin, the essence and the goal of all life and of our life. This negation of our apostate life means that between it and the life which is Jesus Christ there stands the end, annihilation, death. This negation, the 'no' that we hear, itself brings us this death. But in bringing us death this 'no' becomes a mysterious 'yes', the affirmation of a new life, the life which is Jesus Christ. This is the life that we cannot give to ourselves, the life that comes to us entirely from without, entirely from beyond; and yet it is not a remote or alien life, of no concern to ourselves, but it

---

[1]*Cf*: Bultmann, *Das Evangelium des Johannes*, p.21ff.

is our own real daily life. This life lies hidden only behind the symbol of death, the symbol of negation.

We live now in tension between the negation and the affirmation. Our life can be spoken of now only in this relation to Jesus Christ. If we leave Him out of the reckoning, as the origin, the essence and the goal of life, of our life, if we fail to consider that we are creatures, reconciled and redeemed, then we shall achieve no more than mere biological and ideological abstractions. Our life is created, reconciled and redeemed; it finds in Jesus Christ its origin, its essence and its goal....

Ecce Homo!

Ecce homo!—Behold the man! In Him the world was reconciled with God. It is not by its overthrowing but by its reconciliation that the world is subdued. It is not by ideals and programmes or by conscience, duty, responsibility and virtue that reality can be confronted and overcome, but simply and solely by the perfect love of God. Here again it is not by a general idea of love that this is achieved, but by the really *lived* love of God in Jesus Christ. This love of God does not withdraw from reality into noble souls secluded from the world. It experiences and suffers the reality of the world in all its hardness. The world exhausts its fury against the body of Christ. But, tormented, He forgives the world its sin. That is how the reconciliation is accomplished. *Ecce homo!*

The figure of the Reconciler, of the God-Man Jesus Christ, comes between God and the world and fills the centre of all history. In this figure the secret of the world is laid bare, and in this figure there is revealed the secret of

God. No abyss of evil can remain hidden from Him through whom the world is reconciled with God. But the abyss of the love of God encompasses even the most abysmal godlessness of the world. In a manner which passes all comprehension God reverses the judgement of justice and piety, declares Himself guilty towards the world, and thereby wipes out the world's guilt. God Himself sets out on the path of humiliation and atonement, and thereby absolves the world. God is willing to be guilty of our guilt. He takes upon Himself the punishment and the suffering which this guilt has brought on us. God Himself answers for godlessness, love for hatred, the saint for the sinner. Now there is no more godlessness, no more hatred, no more sin which God has not taken upon Himself, suffered for and expiated. Now there is no more reality, no more world, but it is reconciled with God and at peace. God did this in His dear Son Jesus Christ. *Ecce homo!*

. . . *Ecce homo!*—Behold the man sentenced by God, the figure of grief and pain. That is how the Reconciler of the world appears. The guilt of mankind has fallen upon Him. It casts Him into shame and death before God's judgement seat. This is the great price which God pays for reconciliation with the world. Only by God's executing judgement upon Himself can there be peace between Him and the world and between man and man. But the secret of this judgement, of this passion and death, is the love of God for the world and for man. What befell Christ befalls every man in Him. It is only as one who is sentenced by God that man can live before God. Only the crucified man is at peace with God. It is in the figure of the Crucified that man recognizes and discovers himself. To be taken up by God, to be executed on the cross and reconciled, that is the reality of manhood.

The Cross of Christ

...THE WHOLE STORY of death begins with Cain. Adam, preserved on the way to death and consumed with thirst for life, begets Cain, the murderer. The new thing about Cain, the son of Adam, is that as man *sicut deus* Cain himself lays violent hands on human life. The man who is not allowed to eat of the tree of life all the more greedily reaches out for the fruit of death, the destruction of life. Only the Creator can destroy life. Cain usurps this ultimate right of the Creator and becomes a murderer. Why does Cain murder? Out of hatred towards God. This hatred is great. Cain is great, he is greater than Adam, for his hatred is greater, and this means that his yearning for life is greater. The story of death stands under the mark of Cain.

Christ on the Cross, the murdered Son of God, is the end of the story of Cain, and thus the actual end of the story. This is the last desperate storming of the gate of paradise. And under the flaming sword under the Cross, mankind dies. But Christ lives. The stem of the Cross becomes the staff of life, and in the midst of the world life is set up anew upon the cursed ground. In the middle of the world the spring of life wells up on the wood of the Cross and those who thirst for life are called to this water, and those who have eaten of the wood of this life shall never hunger and thirst again. What a strange paradise is this hill of Golgotha, this Cross, this blood, this broken body! What a strange tree of life, this tree on which God himself must suffer and die—but it is in fact the Kingdom of Life and of the Resurrection given again by God in grace; it is the opened door of imperishable hope, of waiting and of patience. The tree of life, the Cross of Christ, the middle of the fallen and preserved world of God, for us that is the end of the story of paradise.

> He unlocks again the door
> Of paradise today:
> The angel guards the gate no more.
> To God our thanks we pay.

The Love of God

...CHRIST DIED FOR THE WORLD, and it is only in the midst of the world that Christ is Christ. Only unbelief can wish to give the world something less than Christ. Certainly it may have well-intentioned pedagogical motives for this course, but these motives always have a certain flavour of clerical exclusiveness. Such a course implies failure to take seriously the incarnation, the crucifixion and the bodily resurrection. It is a denial of the body of Christ.

If we now follow the New Testament in applying to the Church the concept of the body of Christ, this is not by any means intended primarily as representing the separation of the Church from the world. On the contrary, it is implicit in the New Testament statement concerning the incarnation of God in Christ that all men are taken up, enclosed and borne within the body of Christ and that this is just what the congregation of the faithful are to make known to the world by their words and by their lives. What is intended here is not separation from the world but the summoning of the world into the fellowship of this body of Christ, to which in truth it already belongs. This testimony of the Church is foreign to the world; the

Church herself, in bearing this testimony, finds herself to be foreign to the world. Yet even this is always only an ever-renewed consequence of that fellowship with the world which is given in the body of Christ. The Church is divided from the world solely by the fact that she affirms in faith the reality of God's acceptance of man, a reality which is the property of the whole world. By allowing this reality to take effect within herself, she testifies that it is effectual for the whole world.

The body of Jesus Christ, especially as it appears to us on the cross, shows to the eyes of faith the world in its sin, and how it is loved by God, no less than it shows the Church, as the congregation of those who acknowledge their sin and submit to the love of God.

Easter

EASTER? We're paying more attention to dying than to death. We're more concerned to get over the act of dying than to overcome death. Socrates mastered the art of dying; Christ overcame death as 'the last enemy' (I Cor. 15:26). There is a real difference between the two things; the one is within the scope of human possibilities, the other means resurrection. It's not from *ars moriendi,* the art of dying, but from the resurrection of Christ, that a new and purifying wind can blow through our present world. *Here* is the answer to δὸς μοὶ ποῦ στῶ καὶ κινήσω τὴν γῆν.[1] If a few people really believed that and acted on it in their daily lives, a great deal would be changed. To live in the light of the resurrection—that is what Easter means....

---

[1]'Give me somewhere to stand, and I will move the earth' (Archimedes).

The Glory of His Resurrection

IF WE ARE CONFORMED to his image in his Incarnation and crucifixion, we shall also share the glory of his resurrection. "We shall also bear the image of the heavenly" (I Cor. 15:49). "We shall be like him, for we shall see him even as he is" (I John 3:2). If we contemplate the image of the glorified Christ, we shall be made like unto it, just as by contemplating the image of Christ crucified we are conformed to his death. We shall be drawn into his image, and identified with his form, and become a reflection of him. That reflection of his glory will shine forth in us even in this life, even as we share his agony and bear his cross. Our life will then be a progress from knowledge to knowledge, from glory to glory, to an ever closer conformity with the image of the Son of God. "But we all, with unveiled face reflecting as a mirror the glory of the Lord, are transformed into the same image from glory to glory" (II Cor. 3:18).

This is what we mean when we speak of Christ dwelling in our hearts. His life on earth is not finished yet, for he continues to live in the lives of his followers. Indeed it is wrong to speak of the Christian life: we should speak rather of Christ living in us. "I live, and yet no longer I, but Christ liveth in me" (Gal. 2:20). Jesus Christ, incarnate, crucified and glorified, has entered my life and taken charge. "To me to live is Christ" (Phil. 1:21). And where Christ lives, there the Father also lives, and both Father and Son through the Holy Ghost. The Holy Trinity himself has made his dwelling in the Christian heart, filling his whole being, and transforming him into the divine image. Christ, incarnate, crucified and glorified is formed in every Christian soul, for all are members of his Body, the Church. The Church bears the human form, the form of Christ in his death and resurrection. The Church in the first place is his image, and through the Church all her members have been refashioned in his image too. In the Body of Christ we are become "like Christ."

His Ascension

SINCE THE ASCENSION, Christ's place on earth has been taken by his Body, the Church. The Church is the real presence of Christ. Once we have realized this truth we are well on the way to recovering an aspect of the Church's being which has been sadly neglected in the past. We should think of the Church not as an institution, but as a *person*, though of course a person in a unique sense.

The Church is One Man. All who are baptized are "one in Christ" (Gal. 3:28; Rom. 12:5; I Cor. 10:17). The Church is "Man," the "New Man" (καινός ἄνθρωπος). The Church is created as the new man through Christ's death on the cross. On the cross the enmity between Jew and Gentile was abolished, that enmity which rent the world in two, "that he might create in himself of the twain one new man, so making peace" (Eph. 2:15). The "new man" is one, not many. Beyond the confines of the Church, the new man, there is only the old humanity with all its divisions.

Challenge to Faith

IF CHRIST HAD PROVED HIMSELF by miracles, we would have believed in the visible *theophany* of deity, but that would not have been faith in Christ *pro me*. It would not have been inner conversion, but simply acknowledgement. Belief in miracles is no more than believing the evidence of one's eyes in visible Epiphany. When I acknowledge a miracle nothing happens to me. But faith is there when a man so surrenders himself to the humiliated God-Man that he bets his life on him, even when this seems against all sense. Faith is when the search for certainty out of visible evidence is given up. Then it is faith in God and not in the world. The only assurance which faith accepts is the Word itself, which comes to me through Christ.

Whoever seeks signs to establish his faith remains with himself. Nothing is changed. Whoever recognizes the Son through the stumbling block is a believer in the sense of the New Testament. He sees the Christ *pro nobis*, he is reconciled and become new. The stumbling block which the incognito presents and the ambiguous form of the Christ *pro nobis* pose at the same time the continuing challenge to faith. Yet, this challenge teaches us to pay attention to the Word (Isaiah 28:19). And from the Word comes faith.

The Word of God

WE LIVE BY RESPONDING to the word of God which is addressed to us in Jesus Christ. Since this word is addressed to our entire life, the response, too, can only be an entire one; it must be given with our entire life as it is realized in all our several actions. The life which confronts us in Jesus Christ, as a 'yes' and a 'no' to our life, requires the response of a life which assimilates and unites this 'yes' and this 'no'.

We give the name responsibility to this life in its aspect as a response to the life of Jesus Christ as the 'yes' and the 'no' to our life. This concept of responsibility is intended as referring to the concentrated totality and unity of the response to the reality which is given to us in Jesus Christ, as distinct from the partial responses which might arise, for example, from a consideration of utility or from particular principles. In the face of the life which confronts us in Jesus Christ these partial responses are not enough and nothing less can suffice than the entire and single response of our life. Responsibility means, therefore, that the totality of life is pledged and that our action becomes a matter of life and death.

In this way we invest the concept of responsibility with a fulness of meaning which it does not acquire in everyday usage, even when it is placed extremely high on the scale of ethical values, as it was, for example, by Bismarck and Max Weber. Even in the Bible we scarcely find such great prominence given to this concept, though when it does appear it displays quite decisive characteristics. Responsibility in the biblical sense is, in the first place, a verbal response given at the risk of a man's life to the question asked by another man with regard to the event of Christ (II Tim. 4:16; I Pet. 3:15; Phil. 1:7 and 17). I answer with words at the risk of my life for that which has taken place through Jesus Christ. I do not therefore answer primarily for myself, for my own action; I do not justify myself (II Cor. 12:19); I answer for Jesus Christ and thereby also indeed for the commission which has been encharged to me by Him (I Cor. 9:3). Job presumptuously desires to answer for his own ways before God (Job 13:15), and God's words to Job put an end to any such temerity: 'He that reproveth God, let him answer it. Then Job answered the Lord, and said, Behold, I am vile; what shall I answer thee? I will lay mine hand upon my mouth' (Job 40:2–4). We are continuing along the lines of the Bible if we say that in answering for Christ, for life, before men, and only thus, I am at the same time accepting responsibility for men before Christ; I stand for Christ before men and for men before Christ. The responsibility which I assume for Christ in speaking to men is also my responsibility for men in speaking to Christ. My answering to men for Christ is my answering to Christ for men, and only in this is it my answering for myself to God and to men. When I am called to account by men and by God I can answer only through the witness of Jesus Christ who interceded for God with men and for men with God. There is responsibility to God and for God, to men and for men; it is always responsibility for the sake of Jesus Christ, and in this alone it is responsibility for my own life. A man can answer for himself only in confessing Jesus Christ with his lips and with his life.

The Cause Is Urgent

THE KING STANDS at the door, and he may come in at any moment. Will you bow down and humbly receive him, or do you want him to destroy you in his wrath? Those who have ears to hear have heard all there is to hear. They cannot detain the messengers any longer, for they must be off to the next city. If, however, men refuse to hear, they have lost their chance, the time of grace is passed, and they have pronounced their own doom. "To-day if ye shall hear his voice, harden not your hearts" (Heb. 4:7). That is evangelical preaching. Is this ruthless speed? Nothing could be more ruthless than to make men think there is still plenty of time to mend their ways. To tell men that the cause is urgent, and that the kingdom of God is at hand is the most charitable and merciful act we can perform, the most joyous news we can bring. The messenger cannot wait and repeat it to every man in his own language. God's language is clear enough. It is not for the messenger to decide who will hear and who will not, for only God knows who is "worthy"; and those who are worthy will hear the Word when the disciple proclaims it. But woe to the city and woe to the house which rejects the messenger of Christ. They will incur a dreadful judgement; Sodom and Gomorrah, the cities of unchastity and perversion, will be judged more graciously than those cities of Israel who reject the word of Jesus. Vice and sin may be forgiven, according to the word of Jesus, but the man who rejects the word of salvation has thrown away his last chance. To refuse to believe in the gospel is the worst sin imaginable, and if that happens the messengers can do nothing but leave the place. They go because the Word cannot remain there. They must recognize in fear and amazement both the power and the weakness of the Word of God. But the disciples must not force any issue contrary to or beyond the word of Christ. Their commission is not a heroic struggle, a financial pursuit of a grand idea or a good cause. That is why they stay only where the Word stays, and if it is rejected they will be rejected with it, and shake off the dust from their feet as a sign of the curse which awaits that place. This curse will not harm the disciples, but the peace they brought returns to them. "This is a great consolation for ministers of the Church when they are troubled because their work seems void of success. You must not be depressed, for what others refuse will prove an even greater blessing for yourselves. To such the Lord says: 'They have scorned it, so keep it for yourselves'" (Bengel).

The Acceptance of Guilt

...JESUS IS NOT CONCERNED with the proclamation and realization of new ethical ideals; He is not concerned with Himself being good (Matt. 19:17); He is concerned solely with love for the real man, and for that reason He is able to enter into the fellowship of the guilt of men and to take the burden of their guilt upon Himself. Jesus does not desire to be regarded as the only perfect one at the expense of men; He does not desire to look down on mankind as the only guiltless one while mankind goes to its ruin under the weight of its guilt; He does not wish that some idea of a new man should triumph amid the wreckage of a humanity whose guilt has destroyed it. He does not wish to acquit Himself of the guilt under which men die. A love which left man alone in his guilt would not be love for the real man. As one who acts responsibly in the historical existence of men Jesus becomes guilty. It must be emphasized that it is solely His love which makes Him incur guilt. From His selfless love, from His freedom from sin, Jesus enters into the guilt of men and takes this guilt upon Himself. Freedom from sin and the question of guilt are inseparable in Him. It is as the one who is without sin that Jesus takes upon Himself the guilt of His brothers, and it is under the burden of this guilt that He shows Himself to be without sin. In this Jesus Christ, who is guilty without sin, lies the origin of every action of responsible deputyship. If it is responsible action, if it is action which is concerned solely and entirely with the other man, if it arises from selfless love for the real man who is our brother, then, precisely because this is so, it cannot wish to shun the fellowship of human guilt. Jesus took upon Himself the guilt of all men, and for that reason every man who acts responsibly becomes guilty. If any man tries to escape guilt in responsibility he detaches himself from the ultimate reality of human existence, and what is more he cuts himself off from the redeeming mystery of Christ's bearing guilt without sin and he has no share in the divine justification which lies upon this event. He sets his own personal innocence above his responsibility for men, and he is blind to the more irredeemable guilt which he incurs precisely in this; he is blind also to the fact that real innocence shows itself precisely in a man's entering into the fellowship of guilt for the sake of other men. Through Jesus Christ it becomes an essential part of responsible action that the man who is without sin loves selflessly and for that reason incurs guilt.

The Decision

THE POWER which men enjoy for a brief space on earth is not without the cognizance and the will of God. If we fall into the hands of men, and meet suffering and death from their violence, we are none the less certain that everything comes from God. The same God who sees no sparrow fall to the ground without his knowledge and will, allows nothing to happen, except it be good and profitable for his children and the cause for which they stand. We are in God's hands. Therefore, "Fear not."

The time is short. Eternity is long. It is the time of decision. Those who are true to the word and confession on earth will find Jesus Christ standing by their side in the hour of judgement. He will acknowledge them and come to their aid when the accuser demands his rights. All the world will be called to witness as Jesus pronounces our name before his heavenly Father. If we have been true to Jesus in this life, he will be true to us in eternity. But if we have been ashamed of our Lord and of his name, he will likewise be ashamed of us and deny us.

The final decision must be made while we are still on earth. The peace of Jesus is the cross. But the cross is the sword God wields on earth. It creates division. The son against the father, the daughter against her mother, the member of the house against the head—all this will happen in the name of God's kingdom and his peace. That is the work which Christ performs on earth. It is hardly surprising that the harbinger of God's love has been accused of hatred of the human race. Who has a right to speak thus of love for father and mother, for son and daughter, but the destroyer of all human life on the one hand, or the Creator of a new life on the other? Who dare lay such an exclusive claim to man's love and devotion, but the enemy of mankind on the one hand, and the Saviour of mankind on the other? Who but the devil, or Christ, the Prince of Peace, will carry the sword into men's houses? God's love for man is altogether different from the love of men for their own flesh and blood. God's love for man means the cross and the way of discipleship. But that cross and that way are both life and resurrection. "He that loseth his life for my sake shall find it." In this promise we hear the voice of him who holds the keys of death, the Son of God, who goes to the cross and the resurrection, and with him takes his own.

The Call of Jesus

IF CHRIST IS THE LIVING LORD of my life, my encounter with him discloses his word for me, and indeed I have no other means of knowing him, but through his plain word and command. You may of course object that our trouble is that we should like to know Christ and believe on him, but have no means of knowing his will. But such an objection only shows that our knowledge of him is neither genuine nor clear. To know Christ means to know him by his word as the Lord and Saviour of my life. But that knowledge includes a recognition of his plain word directed to me.

Suppose then we say finally that whereas the commandment the disciples received was plain and clear enough, *we* have to decide for ourselves which of his words applies to our particular case. That again is a complete misunderstanding of the situation of the disciples, and of our own situation too. The object of Jesus' command is always the same—to evoke wholehearted faith, to make us love God and our neighbour with all our heart and soul. This is the only unequivocal feature in his command. Every time we try to perform the commandment of Jesus in some other sense, it is another sign that we have misunderstood his word and are disobeying it. But this does not mean that we have no means whatever of ascertaining what he would have us do in any concrete situation. On the contrary, we are told quite clearly what we have to do every time we hear the word of Christ proclaimed; yet in such a way that we understand that there is no other way of fulfilling it, but by faith in Jesus Christ alone. Thus the gift Jesus gave to his disciples is just as available for us as it was for them. In fact it is even more readily available for us now that he has left the world, because we know that he is glorified, and because the Holy Spirit is with us.

It is therefore abundantly clear that we cannot play off the various accounts of the calling of the disciples against other parts of the gospel narrative. It is not a question of stepping into the shoes of the disciples, or of any other of the New Testament characters. The only constant factor throughout is the sameness of Christ and of his call then and now. His word is one and the same, whether it was addressed during his earthly life to the paralysed or the disciples, or whether it is speaking to us to-day. Here, as there, we receive the gracious summons to enter his kingdom and his glory. It is dangerous to ask whether we are to draw a parallel between ourselves and the disciples or ourselves and the paralytic. We may not compare ourselves to either. All we have to do is to hear the word and obey the will of Christ, in whatever part of the scripture testimony it is proclaimed. The scriptures do not present us with a series of Christian types to be imitated according to choice: they preach to us in every situation the one Jesus Christ. To him alone must I listen. He is everywhere one and the same.

To the question—where to-day do we hear the call of Jesus to discipleship, there is no other answer than this: Hear the Word, receive the Sacrament; in it hear him himself, and you will hear his call.

The Christian Life

JESUS ASKED IN GETHSEMANE, 'Could you not watch with me one hour?' That is a reversal of what the religious man expects from God. Man is summoned to share in God's sufferings at the hands of a godless world.

He must therefore really live in the godless world, without attempting to gloss over or explain its ungodliness in some religious way or other. He must live a 'secular' life, and thereby share in God's sufferings. He *may* live a 'secular' life (as one who has been freed from false religious obligations and inhibitions). To be a Christian does not mean to be religious in a particular way, to make something of oneself (a sinner, a penitent, or a saint) on the basis of some method or other, but to be a man— not a type of man, but the man that Christ creates in us. It is not the religious act that makes the Christian, but participation in the sufferings of God in the secular life. That is *metanoia:* not in the first place thinking about one's own needs, problems, sins, and fears, but allowing oneself to be caught up into the way of Jesus Christ, into the messianic event, thus fulfilling Isa. 53. Therefore 'believe in the gospel', or, in the words of John the Baptist, 'Behold, the Lamb of God, who takes away the sin of the world' (John 1:29). (By the way, Jeremias has recently asserted that the Aramaic word for 'lamb' may also be translated 'servant'; very appropriate in view of Isa. 53!) This being caught up into the messianic sufferings of God in Jesus Christ takes a variety of forms in the New Testament. It appears in the call to discipleship, in Jesus' table-fellowship with sinners, in 'conversions' in the narrower sense of the word (e.g. Zacchaeus), in the act of the woman who was a sinner (Luke 7)—an act that she performed without any confession of sin, in the healing of the sick (Matt. 8:17; see above), in Jesus' acceptance of children. The shepherds, like the wise men from the East, stand at the crib, not as 'converted sinners', but simply because they are drawn to the crib by the star just as they are. The centurion of Capernaum (who makes no confession of sin) is held up as a model of faith (cf. Jairus). Jesus 'loved' the rich young man. The eunuch (Acts 8) and Cornelius (Acts 10) are not standing at the edge of an abyss. Nathaniel is 'an Israelite indeed, in whom there is no guile' (John 1:47). Finally, Joseph of Arimathea and the women at the tomb. The only thing that is common to all these is their sharing in the suffering of God in Christ. That is their 'faith'. There is nothing of religious method here. The 'religious act' is always something partial; 'faith' is something whole, involving the whole of one's life. Jesus calls men, not to a new religion, but to life.

Christ Our Hope

THE IMPORTANCE OF ILLUSION to one's life should certainly not be underestimated; but for a Christian there must be hope based on a firm foundation. And if even illusion has so much power in people's lives that it can keep life moving, how great a power there is in a hope that is based on certainty, and how invincible a life with such a hope is. 'Christ our hope'—this Pauline formula is the strength of our lives.

The Imparting of Grace

CHRIST COMES INDEED, and opens up His own way, no matter whether man is ready beforehand or not. No one can hinder His coming, but we can resist His coming in mercy. There are conditions of the heart, of life and of the world which impede the reception of grace in a special way, namely, by rendering faith infinitely difficult. We say that they impede it and render it difficult, but not that they make it impossible. And we are well aware also that even the levelling of the way and the removal of the obstacles cannot compel the imparting of grace. The merciful coming of Christ must still 'break the gates of brass and cut the bars of iron' (Ps. 107:16); grace must in the end itself prepare and make level its own way and grace alone must ever anew render possible the impossible. But all this does not release us from our obligation to prepare the way for the coming of grace, and to remove whatever obstructs it and makes it difficult. The state in which grace finds us is not a matter of indifference, even though it is always by grace alone that grace comes to us. We may, among other things, make it difficult for ourselves to attain to faith. For him who is cast into utter shame, desolation, poverty and helplessness, it is difficult to have faith in the justice and goodness of God. For him whose life has become a prey to disorder and indiscipline, it will be difficult to hear the commandments of God in faith. It is hard for the sated and the mighty to grasp the meaning of God's judgement and God's mercy. And for one who has been disappointed in mistaken belief, and who has become inwardly undisciplined, it is hard to attain to the simplicity of the surrender of the heart to Jesus Christ. That is not said in order either to excuse or to discourage those whom these things have befallen. They must know, on the contrary, that it is precisely to the depths of downfall, of guilt and of misery, that God stoops down in Jesus Christ; that precisely the dispossessed, the humiliated and the exploited, are especially near to the justice and mercy of God; that it is to the undisciplined that Jesus Christ offers His help and His strength; and that the truth is ready to set upon firm ground those who stray and despair.

The New Life

JESUS CHRIST WHO ROSE AGAIN—this means that God out of His love and omnipotence sets an end to death and calls a new creation into life, imparts new life. 'Old things are passed away' (II Cor. 5:17). 'Behold, I make all things new' (Rev. 21:5). Already in the midst of the old world, resurrection has dawned, as a last sign of its end and of its future, and at the same time as a living reality. Jesus rose again as a man, and by so doing He gave men the gift of the resurrection. Thus man remains man, even though he is a new, a risen man, who in no way resembles the old man. Until he crosses the frontier of his death, even though he has already risen again with Christ, he remains in the world of penultimate, the world into which Jesus entered and the world in which the cross stands. Thus, so long as the earth continues, even the resurrection does not annul the penultimate, but the eternal life, the new life, breaks in with ever greater power into the earthly life and wins its space for itself within it.

We have tried to make clear the unity and the diversity of the incarnation, the cross and the resurrection. Christian life is life with the incarnate, crucified and risen Christ, whose word confronts us in its entirety in the message of the justification of the sinner by grace alone. Christian life means being a man through the efficacy of the incarnation; it means being sentenced and pardoned through the efficacy of the cross; and it means living a new life through the efficacy of the resurrection. There cannot be one of these without the rest.

The Past

O HAPPINESS BELOVED, and pain beloved in heaviness,
you went from me.
What shall I call you? Anguish, life, blessedness,
part of myself, my heart—the past?
The door was slammed;
I hear your steps depart and slowly die away.
What now remains for me—torment, delight, desire?
This only do I know: that with you, all has gone.
But do you feel how I now grasp at you
and so clutch hold of you
that it must hurt you?
How I so rend you
that your blood gushes out,
simply to be sure that you are near me,
a life in earthly form, complete?
Do you divine my terrible desire
for my own suffering,
my eager wish to see my own blood flow,
only that all may not go under,
lost in the past?

Life, what have you done to me?
Why did you come? Why did you go?
Past, when you flee from me,
are you not still my past, my own?
As o'er the sea the sun sinks ever faster,
as if it moved towards the darkness,
so does your image sink and sink and sink
without a pause

into the ocean of the past,
and waves engulf it.
As the warm breath dissolves
in the cool morning air,
so does your image vanish from me,
and I forget your face, your hands, your form.
There comes a smile, a glance, a greeting;
it fades, dissolves,
comfortless, distant,
is destroyed, is past.

I would inhale the fragrance of your being,
absorb it, stay with it,
as on hot summer days the heavy blossoms
  welcoming the bees
intoxicate them,
as privet makes the hawk-moths drunken—
but a harsh gust destroys both scent and blossoms,
and I stand like a fool
seeking a past that vanished.
It is as if parts of my flesh were torn out with red-hot
  pincers,
when you, a part of my life that is past, so quickly
  depart.
Raging defiance and anger beset me,
reckless and profitless questions I fling into space.
'Why, why, why?' I keep on repeating—
why cannot my senses hold you,
life now passing, now past?
Thus I will think, and think anew,
until I find what I have lost.

But I feel
that everything around me, over, under me
is smiling at me, unmoved, enigmatic,
smiling at my hopeless efforts

to grasp the wind,
to capture what has gone.

Evil comes into my eye and soul;
what I see, I hate;
I hate what moves me;
all that lives I hate, all that is lovely,
all that would recompense me for my loss.
I want my life; I claim my own life back again,
my past, yourself.
Yourself. A tear wells up and fills my eye;
can I, in mists of tears,
regain your image,
yourself entire?
But I will not weep;
only the strong are helped by tears,
weaklings they make ill.

Wearily I come to the evening;
welcome are bed and oblivion
now that my own is denied me.
Night, blot out what separates, give me oblivion,
in charity perform your kindly office;
to you I trust myself.
But night is wise and mighty,
wiser than I, and mightier than day,
What no earthly power can do,
what is denied to thoughts and senses, to defiance, to
    tears,
night brings me, in its bounty overflowing.
Unharmed by hostile time,
pure, free, and whole,
you are brought to me by dream,
you, my past, my life,
Close to you I waken in the dead of night,
and start with fear—

are you lost to me once more? Is it always vainly that I
  seek you,
you, my past?
I stretch my hands out,
and I pray—
and a new thing now I hear:
'The past will come to you once more,
and be your life's enduring part,
through thanks and repentance.
Feel in the past God's forgiveness and goodness,
pray him to keep you today and tomorrow.'

Justification

...NOT FOR A MOMENT can faith and evil intention exist side
by side. When a man undergoes justification he is given
everything, but only faith brings justification. When a
man encounters Christ, everything that Christ is and has
is made the property of this man; yet my life is justified
solely by that which is the property of Christ and never by
that which has become my own property. Thus the
heaven opens over man's head and the joyful tidings of
God's salvation in Jesus Christ come down like a shout of
rejoicing from heaven to earth, and man believes, and, in
believing, he has already received Christ to himself; he
possesses everything. He lives before God.

He never knew before what life is. He did not understand
himself. Only by his own potentialities or by his own
achievement could he try to understand himself and to
justify his life. In this way he could justify himself to
himself and to a god of his own imagining, but he could
have no means of access to the potentialities and the works

of the living God; he could have no conception of a life which should proceed from these potentialities and works of the living God. He could not conceive of a life on a foundation other than himself, sustained by a power other than his own. Yet this is the life that he found when Christ justified him in His way. He lost his own life to Christ, and Christ became his life. 'I live; yet not I, but Christ liveth in me' (Gal. 2:20). Christian life is the life of Christ.

Conformation

TO BE CONFORMED with the Risen One—that is to be a new man before God. In the midst of death he is in life. In the midst of sin he is righteous. In the midst of the old he is new. His secret remains hidden from the world. He lives because Christ lives, and lives in Christ alone. 'Christ is my life' (Phil 1:21). So long as the glory of Christ is hidden, so long, too, does the glory of his new life remain 'hidden with Christ in God' (Col. 3:3). But he who knows espies already here and there a gleam of what is to come. The new man lives in the world like any other man. Often there is little to distinguish him from the rest. Nor does he attach importance to distinguishing himself, but only to distinguishing Christ for the sake of his brethren. Transfigured though he is in the form of the Risen One, here he bears only the sign of the cross and the judgement. By bearing it willingly he shows himself to be the one who has received the Holy Spirit and who is united with Jesus Christ in incomparable love and fellowship.

The form of Jesus Christ takes form in man. Man does not take on an independent form of his own, but what gives him form and what maintains him in the new form is always solely the form of Jesus Christ Himself. It is therefore not a vain imitation or repetition of Christ's form but Christ's form itself which takes form in man. And again, man is not transformed into a form which is alien to him, the form of God, but into his own form, the form which is essentially proper to him. Man becomes man because God became man. But man does not become God. It is not he, therefore, who was or is able to accomplish his own transformation, but it is God who changes his form into the form of man, so that man may become, not indeed God, but, in the eyes of God, man.

In Christ there was re-created the form of man before God. It was not an outcome of the place or the time, of the climate or the race, of the individual or the society, or of religion or of taste, but quite simply of the life of mankind as such, that mankind at this point recognized its image and its hope. What befell Christ had befallen mankind. It is a mystery, for which there is no explanation, that only a part of mankind recognize the form of their Redeemer. The longing of the Incarnate to take form in all men is as yet still unsatisfied. He bore the form of man as a whole, and yet He can take form only in a small band. These are His Church.

Christ and His Body

THROUGH HIS SPIRIT, the crucified and risen Lord exists as the Church, as the new man. It is just as true to say that his Body is the new humanity as to say that he is God incarnate dwelling in eternity. As the fulness of the Godhead dwells in Christ bodily, so the Christian believers are filled with Christ (Col. 2:9; Eph. 3:19). Indeed, they are themselves that fulness in so far as they are in the Body and in so far as it is he alone who filleth all in all.

When we have recognized the unity between Christ and his Body, the Church, we must also hold fast to the complementary truth of Christ's Lordship over the Body. That is why St Paul, as he comes to develop the theme of the Body of Christ, calls him the Head of the Body (Eph. 1.22; Col. 1:18; 2:19). This assertion symbolizes and preserves the truth that Christ stands over against his Church. The historical fact in the story of our redemption which makes this truth essential, and rules out any idea of a mystical fusion between Christ and his Church, is the Ascension of Christ (and his Second Coming). The same Christ who is present in his Church will also come again. It is the same Lord and the same Church in both places, and it is one and the same Body, whether we think of his presence on earth or of his coming again on the clouds of heaven. But it makes a great deal of difference whether we are here or there. So it is necessary to give due weight both to the unity of Christ and his Church and to their distinction.

The Church is one man; it is the Body of Christ. But it is also many, a fellowship of members (Rom. 12:5; I Cor. 12:12 ff).

The Church

IF GOD IN JESUS CHRIST claims space in the world, even though it be only a stable 'because there was no room in the inn' (Luke 2:7), then in this narrow space He comprises together the whole reality of the world at once and reveals the ultimate basis of this reality. And so, too, the Church of Jesus Christ is the place, in other words the space in the world, at which the reign of Jesus Christ over the whole world is evidenced and proclaimed. This space of the Church, then, is not something which exists on its own account. It is from the outset something which reaches out far beyond itself, for indeed it is not the space of some kind of cultural association such as would have to fight for its own survival in the world, but it is the place where testimony is given to the foundation of all reality in Jesus Christ. The Church is the place where testimony and serious thought are given to God's reconciliation of the world with Himself in Christ, to His having so loved the world that He gave His Son for its sake. The space of the Church is not there in order to try to deprive the world of a piece of its territory, but precisely in order to prove to the world that it is still the world, the world which is loved by God and reconciled with Him. The Church has neither the wish nor the obligation to extend her space to cover the space of the world. She asks for no more space than she needs for the purpose of serving the world by bearing witness to Jesus Christ and to the reconciliation of the world with God through Him. The only way in which the Church can defend her own territory is by fighting not for it but for the salvation of the world. Otherwise the Church becomes a 'religious society' which fights in its own interest and thereby ceases at once to be the Church of God and of the world. And so the first demand which is made of those who belong to God's Church is not that they should be something in themselves, not that they should, for example, set up some religious organization or that they should lead lives of piety, but that they shall be witnesses to Jesus Christ before the world. It is for this task that the Holy Spirit equips those to whom He gives Himself. It is, of course, to be assumed that this testimony before the world can be delivered in the right way only if it springs from a hallowed life in the congregation of God. But a genuine hallowed life in the congregation of God differs from any pious imitation of it in that it at the same time impels a man to testify before the world.

Christ the Center

CHRIST IS *the* new creature. Thereby he shows all other creatures to be old creatures. Nature stands under the curse which God laid upon Adam's ground. It was the originally created Word of God, proclaiming it freely. As the fallen creation it is now dumb, enslaved under the guilt of man. Like history, it suffers from the loss of its meaning and its freedom. It waits expectantly for a new freedom. Nature, unlike man and history, will not be reconciled, but it will be set free for a new freedom. Its catastrophes are the dull will to set itself free, to show its power over man and by its own right to be a new creature, which it has made anew itself.

In the sacrament of the Church, the old enslaved creature is set free to its new freedom. As the centre of human existence and of history, Christ was the fulfilment of the unfulfilled law, i.e. their reconciliation. But nature is creation under the curse—not guilt, for it lacks freedom. Thus nature finds in Christ as its centre, not reconciliation, but redemption. Once again, this redemption, which happens in Christ, is not evident, nor can it be proved, but it is proclaimed. The word of preaching is that enslaved nature is redeemed in hope. A sign of this is given in the sacraments, where elements of the old creation are become elements of the new. In the sacraments they are set free from their dumbness and proclaim directly to the believer the new creative Word of God. They no longer need the explanation of man. Enslaved nature does not speak the Word of God to us directly. But the sacraments do. In the sacrament, Christ is the mediator between nature and God and stands for all creation before God.

To sum up, we must continue to emphasize that Christ is truly the centre of human existence, the centre of history and now also the centre of nature. But these three aspects can only be distinguished from each other *in abstracto*. In fact, human existence is also and always history, always and also nature. The mediator as fulfiller of the law and liberator of creation is all this for the whole of human existence. He is the same who is intercessor and *pro me*, and who is himself the end of the old world and the beginning of the new world of God.

The Preacher

WHAT THE CHURCH PROCLAIMS is the word of the revelation of God in Jesus Christ. This word does not proceed from any man's own heart or understanding or character; it comes down to man from heaven, from the will and the mercy of God; it is a word commanded and instituted by Jesus Christ, and from this it follows that the word, by the manner of its coming, establishes a clearly differentiated relation of superiority and inferiority. Above there is the office of proclamation, and below there is the listening congregation. In the place of God and of Jesus Christ there stands before the congregation the bearer of the office of preaching with his proclamation. The preacher is not the spokesman of the congregation, but, if the expression may be allowed, he is the spokesman of God before the congregation. He is authorized to teach, to admonish and to comfort, to forgive sin, but also to retain sin. And at the same time he is the shepherd, the pastor of the flock. This office is instituted directly by Jesus Christ Himself; it does not derive its legitimation from the will of the congregation but from the will of Jesus Christ. It is established *in* the congregation and not *by* the congregation, and at the same time it is *with* the congregation. When this office is exercised in the congregation to its full extent, life is infused into all the other offices of the congregation, which can after all only be subservient to the office of the divine word; for wherever the word of God rules alone, there will be found faith and service. The congregation which is being awakened by the proclamation of the word of God will demonstrate the genuineness of its faith by honouring the office of preaching in its unique glory and by serving it with all its powers; it will not rely on its own faith or on the universal priesthood of all believers in order to depreciate the office of preaching, to place obstacles in its way, or even to try to make it subordinate to itself. The superior status of the office of preaching is preserved from abuse, and against danger from without, precisely by a genuine subordination of the congregation, that is to say, by faith, prayer and service, but not by a suppression or disruption of the divine order or by a perverse desire for superiority on the part of the congregation.

The Saints

THE ECCLESIA *Christi,* the disciple community, has been torn from the clutches of the world. Of course it still has to live in the world, but it is made into one body, with its own sphere of sovereignty, and its own claim to living-space. It is the holy Church (Eph. 5:27), the community of the saints (I Cor. 14:33), and its members are called to be saints (Rom. 1:7), sanctified in Jesus Christ (I Cor. 1:2), chosen and set apart before the foundation of the world (Eph. 1:4). The object of their calling in Jesus Christ, and of their election before the foundation of the world, was that they should be holy and without blemish (Eph. 1:4). Christ had surrendered his body to death that he might present his own holy and without blemish and unreproveable before him (Col. 1:22). The fruit of their liberation from sin through the death of Christ is that whereas they once surrendered their members' servants to iniquity, they may now use them in the service of righteousness unto sanctification (Rom. 6:19–22).

The Task of the Church

WHAT THE WEST is doing is to refuse to accept its historical inheritance for what it is. The west is becoming hostile towards Christ. This is the peculiar situation of our time, and it is genuine decay. Amid the disruption of the whole established order of things there stand the Christian Churches as guardians of the heritage of the Middle Ages and of the Reformation and especially as witnesses of the miracle of God in Jesus Christ 'yesterday, and today, and for ever' (He. 13:8). And at their side there stands the 'restrainer', that is to say the remaining force of order which still opposes effective resistance to the process of decay. The task of the Church is without parallel. The *corpus christianum* is broken asunder. The *corpus Christi* confronts a hostile world. The world has known Christ and has turned its back on Him, and it is to this world that the Church must now prove that Christ is the living Lord.

Even while she waits for the last day, the Church, as the bearer of a historical inheritance, is bound by an obligation to the historical future. Her vision of the end of all things must not hinder her in the fulfilment of her historical responsibility. She must leave not only the end to God's decision, but also the possibility of the continuance of history. She must set her mind on both. In devoting herself to her proper task, that is to say to preaching the risen Jesus Christ, the Church strikes a mortal blow at the spirit of destruction. The 'restrainer', the force of order, sees in the Church an ally, and, whatever other elements of order may remain, will seek a place at her side. Justice, truth, science, art, culture, humanity, liberty, patriotism, all at last, after long straying from the path, are once more finding their way back to their fountain-head. The more central the message of the Church, the greater now will be her effectiveness. Her suffering presents an infinitely greater danger to the spirit of destruction than does any political power which may still remain. But through her message of the living Lord Jesus Christ the Church makes it clear that she is not concerned merely for the maintenance and preservation of the past. Even the forces of order she compels to listen and to turn back. Yet she does not reject those who come to her and seek to place themselves at her side. She leaves it to God's governance of the world to decide whether He will permit the success of the forces of order and whether she, the Church, while still preserving the essential distinction between herself and these forces, even though she unreservedly allies herself with them, will be allowed to pass on to the future that historical inheritance which bears within it the blessing and the guilt of past generations.

The Battlefield

BECAUSE IT IS SANCTIFIED by the seal of the Spirit, the Church is always in the battlefield, waging a war to prevent the breaking of the seal, whether from within or from without, and struggling to prevent the world from becoming the Church and the Church from becoming the world. The sanctification of the Church is really a defensive war, for the place which has been given to the Body of Christ on earth. The separation of the Church and the world from one another is the crusade which the Church fights for the sanctuary of God on earth.

This sanctuary can only exist in the visible Church. But—and here we come to the second point—the very fact that it is separated from the world means that while the Church lives in the sanctuary of God something of the world still lives in the Church. That is why it is the duty of the saints to walk worthily of their calling and of the gospel in every sphere of life (Eph. 4:1; Phil. 1:27; Col. 1:10; I Thess. 2:12). But the only way to do this is by daily recalling the gospel on which their whole life depends. "Ye were washed, ye were sanctified, ye were justified" (I Cor. 6:11). It is by living daily on this recollection that the saints are sanctified. And the gospel of which they are to be worthy is that which proclaims the death of the world and the flesh, and their own crucifixion and death with Christ on the cross and through baptism, which proclaims that sin can no longer have dominion over them because its sovereignty has already been broken, and that it is no longer possible for the Christian to sin. "Whosoever is begotten of God doeth no sin" (I John 3:9).

Confession of Guilt

...EVEN THE MOST SECRET SIN of the individual is defilement and destruction of the body of Christ (I Cor. 6:15). From the desires that are in our bodily members come murder and envy, strife and war (Jas. 4:1ff.). If my share in this is so small as to seem negligible, that still cannot set my mind at rest; for now it is not a matter of apportioning the blame, but I must acknowledge that precisely my sin is to blame for all. I am guilty of uncontrolled desire. I am guilty of cowardly silence at a time when I ought to have spoken. I am guilty of hypocrisy and untruthfulness in the face of force. I have been lacking in compassion and I have denied the poorest of my brethren. I am guilty of disloyalty and of apostasy from Christ. What does it matter to you whether others are guilty too? I can excuse any sin of another, but my own sin alone remains guilt which I can never excuse. It is not a morbidly egotistical distortion of reality, but it is the essential character of a genuine confession of guilt that it is incapable of apportioning blame and pleading a case, but is rather the acknowledgement of one's own sin of Adam. And it is senseless to try to oppose this acknowledgement with an argument *ad absurdum* by pointing out that there are innumerable individuals each of whom must in this way be conscious of being to blame for the whole. For indeed these innumerable individuals are united in the collective personality of the Church. It is in them and through them that the Church confesses and acknowledges her guilt.

Costly Grace

CHEAP GRACE is the deadly enemy of our Church. We are fighting to-day for costly grace.

Cheap grace means grace sold on the market like cheapjacks' wares. The sacraments, the forgiveness of sin, and the consolations of religion are thrown away at cut prices. Grace is presented as the Church's inexhaustible treasury, from which she showers blessings with generous hands, without asking questions or fixing limits. Grace without price; grace without cost! The essence of grace, we suppose, is that the account has been paid in advance; and, because it has been paid, everything can be had for nothing. Since the cost was infinite, the possibilities of using and spending it are infinite. What would grace be if it were not cheap?

Cheap grace means grace as a doctrine, a principle, a system. It means forgiveness of sins proclaimed as a general truth, the love of God taught as the Christian "conception" of God. An intellectual assent to that idea is held to be of itself sufficient to secure remission of sins. The Church which holds the correct doctrine of grace has, it is supposed, *ipso facto* a part in that grace. In such a Church the world finds a cheap covering for its sins; no contrition is required, still less any real desire to be delivered from sin. Cheap grace therefore amounts to a denial of the living Word of God, in fact, a denial of the Incarnation of the Word of God.

. . . Cheap grace is the preaching of forgiveness without requiring repentance, baptism without Church discipline, Communion without confession, absolution without personal confession. Cheap grace is grace without discipleship, grace without the cross, grace without Jesus Christ, living and incarnate.

Costly grace is the treasure hidden in the field; for the sake of it a man will gladly go and sell all that he has. It is the pearl of great price to buy which the merchant will sell all his goods. It is the kingly rule of Christ, for whose sake a man will pluck out the eye which causes him to stumble, it is the call of Jesus Christ at which the disciple leaves his nets and follows him.

Costly grace is the gospel which must be *sought* again and again, the gift which must be *asked* for, the door at which a man must *knock.*

Such grace is *costly* because it calls us to follow, and it is *grace* because it calls us to follow *Jesus Christ.* It is costly because it costs a man his life, and it is grace because it gives a man the only true life. It is costly because it condemns sin, and grace because it justifies the sinner. Above all, it is *costly* because it cost God the life of his Son: "ye were bought at a price," and what has cost God much cannot be cheap for us. Above all, it is *grace* because God did not reckon his Son too dear a price to pay for our life, but delivered him up for us. Costly grace is the Incarnation of God.

Costly grace is the sanctuary of God; it has to be protected from the world, and not thrown to the dogs. It is therefore the living word, the Word of God, which he speaks as it pleases him. Costly grace confronts us as a gracious call to follow Jesus, it comes as a word of forgiveness to the broken spirit and the contrite heart. Grace is costly because it compels a man to submit to the yoke of Christ and follow him; it is grace because Jesus says: "My yoke is easy and my burden is light."

The New Fellowship

THE MEMBER of the Body of Christ has been delivered from the world and called out of it. He must give the world a visible proof of his calling, not only by sharing in the Church's worship and discipline, but also through the new fellowship of brotherly living. If the world despises one of the brethren, the Christian will love and serve him. If the world does him violence, the Christian will succour and comfort him. If the world dishonours and insults him, the Christian will sacrifice his own honour to cover his brother's shame. Where the world seeks gain, the Christian will renounce it. Where the world exploits, he will dispossess himself, and where the world oppresses, he will stoop down and raise up the oppressed. If the world refuses justice, the Christian will pursue mercy, and if the world takes refuge in lies, he will open his mouth for the dumb, and bear testimony to the truth. For the sake of the brother, be he Jew or Greek, bond or free, strong or weak, noble or base, he will renounce all fellowship with the world. For the Christian serves the fellowship of the Body of Christ, and he cannot hide it from the world. He is called out of the world to follow Christ.

The Followers of Christ

THE CHURCH of Jesus cannot arbitrarily break off all contact with those who refuse his call. It is called to follow the Lord by promise and commandment. That must suffice. All judgement of others and separation from them must be left to him who chose the Church according to his good purpose, and not for any merit or achievement of its own. The separation of Church and world is not effected by the Church itself, but by the word of its calling.

A little band of men, the followers of Christ, are separated from the rest of the world. The disciples are few in number, and will always be few. This saying of Jesus forestalls all exaggerated hopes of success. Never let a disciple of Jesus pin his hopes on large numbers. "Few there be...." The rest of the world are many, and will always be many. But they are on the road to perdition. The only comfort the disciples have in face of this prospect is the promise of life and eternal fellowship with Jesus.

The path of discipleship is narrow, and it is fatally easy to miss one's way and stray from the path, even after years of discipleship. And it is hard to find. On either side of the narrow path deep chasms yawn. To be called to a life of extraordinary quality, to live up to it, and yet to be unconscious of it is indeed a narrow way. To confess and testify to the truth as it is in Jesus, and at the same time to love the enemies of that truth, his enemies and ours, and to love them with the infinite love of Jesus Christ, is indeed a narrow way. To believe the promise of Jesus that his followers shall possess the earth, and at the same time to face our enemies unarmed and defenceless, preferring to incur injustice rather than to do wrong ourselves, is indeed a narrow way. To see the weakness and wrong in others, and at the same time refrain from judging them; to deliver the gospel message without casting pearls before swine, is indeed a narrow way. The way is unutterably hard, and at every moment we are in danger of straying from it. If we regard this way as one we follow in obedience to an external command, if we are afraid of ourselves all the time, it is indeed an impossible way. But if we behold Jesus Christ going on before step by step, we shall not go astray. But if we worry about the dangers that beset us, if we gaze at the road instead of at him who goes before, we are already straying from the path. For he is himself the way, the narrow way and the strait gate. He, and he alone, is our journey's end. When we know that, we are able to proceed along the narrow way through the strait gate of the cross, and on to eternal life, and the very narrowness of the road will increase our certainty. The way which the Son of God trod on earth, and the way which we too must tread as citizens of two worlds on the razor edge between this world and the kingdom of heaven, could hardly be a broad way. The narrow way is bound to be right.

Pray for Forgiveness

...WHEREVER IT BECOMES VISIBLE on a large scale, wherever the world looks at the Christians and feels obliged to say, as it said in the earliest days, "See how these Christians love one another," the saints must then take special care to keep their eyes on him alone, to ignore any good they may have achieved themselves, and to pray fervently for forgiveness. The same Christians who have claimed the privilege of being no longer under the dominion of sin, will confess: "If we say we have no sin, we deceive ourselves, and the truth is not in us. If we confess our sins, he is faithful and just to forgive us our sins, and to cleanse us from all unrighteousness. If we say that we have not sinned, we make him a liar, and his word is not in us. My little children these things I write unto you, that ye may not sin. And if any man sin, we have an advocate with the Father, Jesus Christ the righteous" (I John 1:8–2:1). This is exactly how the Lord himself taught us to pray—"Forgive us our trespasses." He charged us never to tire of forgiving one another (Eph. 4:32; Matt. 18:21ff). Brotherly forgiveness makes room for the forgiveness of Jesus to enter into their common life. Instead of seeing their neighbours as men who have injured them, they see them as men for whom Christ has won forgiveness on the cross. They meet on the basis of their common sanctification through the cross of Christ.

Good Works

THROUGH GOD'S OWN ACTION in Christ we have been saved and not through our own works. We can never boast about them, for we are ourselves his workmanship. Yet it remains true that the whole purpose of our new creation in Christ is that in him we might attain unto good works.

But all our good works are the works of God himself, the works for which he has prepared us beforehand. Good works then are ordained for the sake of salvation, but they are in the end those which God himself works within us. They are his gift, but it is *our* task to walk in them at every moment of our lives, knowing all the time that any good works of our own could never help us to abide before the judgement of God. We cling in faith to Christ and his works alone. For we have the promise that those who are in Christ Jesus will be enabled to do good works, which will testify for them in the day of judgement. They will be preserved and sanctified until the last day. All we can do is believe in God's Word, rely on his promise, and walk in the good works which he has prepared for us.

From this it follows that we can never be conscious of our good works. Our sanctification is veiled from our eyes until the last day, when all secrets will be disclosed. If we want to see some results here and assess our own spiritual state, and have not the patience to wait, we have our reward. The moment we begin to feel satisfied that we are making some progress along the road of sanctification, it is all the more necessary to repent and confess that all our righteousnesses are as filthy rags. Yet the Christian life is not one of gloom, but of ever increasing joy in the Lord. God alone knows our good works, all we know is his good work. We can do no more than hearken to his commandment, carry on and rely on his grace, walk in his commandments, and—sin. All the time our new righteousness, our sanctification, the light which is meant to shine, are veiled from our eyes. The left hand knows not what the right hand does. But we believe, and are well assured, "that he which began a good work in you will perfect it until the day of Jesus Christ" (Phil. 1:6). In that day Christ will show us the good works of which we were unaware. While we knew it not, we gave him food, drink and clothing and visited him, and while we knew it not we rejected him. Great will be our astonishment in that day, and we shall then realize that it is not our works which remain but the work which God has wrought through us in his good time without any effort of will and intention on our part (Matt. 25:31ff). Once again we simply are to look away from ourselves to him who has himself accomplished all things for us and to follow him.

Through and in Jesus Christ

CHRISTIANITY MEANS COMMUNITY through Jesus Christ and in Jesus Christ. No Christian community is more or less than this. Whether it be a brief, single encounter or the daily fellowship of years, Christian community is only this. We belong to one another only through and in Jesus Christ.

What does this mean? It means, first, that a Christian needs others because of Jesus Christ. It means, second, that a Christian comes to others only through Jesus Christ. It means, third, that in Jesus Christ we have been chosen from eternity, accepted in time, and united for eternity.

Christ Among Us

...IT IS THE MYSTERY of the community that Christ is in her and, only through her, reaches to men. Christ exists among us as community, as Church in the hiddenness of history. The Church is the hidden Christ among us. Now therefore man is never alone, but he exists only through the community which brings him Christ, which incorporates him in itself, takes him into its life. Man in Christ is man in community; where he exists is community. But because at the same time as individual he is fully a member of the community, therefore here alone is the continuity of his existence preserved in Christ. Therefore man can no longer understand himself from himself, but only from Christ. . . .

The Day's Beginning

"LET THE WORD OF CHRIST dwell in you richly" (Col. 3:16). The Old Testament day begins at evening and ends with the going down of the sun. It is the time of expectation. The day of the New Testament church begins with the break of day and ends with the dawning light of the next morning. It is the time of fulfilment, the resurrection of the Lord. At night Christ was born, a light in darkness; noonday turned to night when Christ suffered and died on the Cross. But in the dawn of Easter morning Christ rose in victory from the grave.

> Ere yet the dawn hath filled the skies
> Behold my Saviour Christ arise,
> He chaseth from us sin and night,
> And brings us joy and life and light.
>   Hallelujah

So sang the church of the Reformation. Christ is the "Sun of righteousness," risen upon the expectant congregation (Mal. 4:2), and they that love him shall "be as the sun when he goeth forth in his might" (Judges 5:31). The early morning belongs to the Church of the risen Christ. At the break of light it remembers the morning on which death and sin lay prostrate in defeat and new life and salvation were given to mankind.

Morning Prayers

O God, early in the morning I cry to you.
Help me to pray
And to concentrate my thoughts on you;
I cannot do this alone.

In me there is darkness,
But with you there is light;
I am lonely, but you do not leave me;
I am feeble in heart, but with you there is help;
I am restless, but with you there is peace.
In me there is bitterness, but with you there is patience;
I do not understand your ways,
But you know the way for me.

O heavenly Father,
I praise and thank you
For the peace of the night;
I praise and thank you for this new day;
I praise and thank you for all your goodness
and faithfulness throughout my life.

You have granted me many blessings;
Now let me also accept what is hard
from your hand.
You will lay on me no more
than I can bear.

Editor's note: Written for fellow prisoners Christmas 1943.

You make all things work together for good
for your children.

Lord Jesus Christ,
You were poor
and in distress, a captive and forsaken as I am.
You know all man's troubles;
You abide with me
when all men fail me;
You remember and seek me;
It is your will that I should know you
and turn to you.
Lord, I hear your call and follow;
Help me.

O Holy Spirit,
Give me faith that will protect me
from despair, from passions, and from vice;
Give me such love for God and men
as will blot out all hatred and bitterness;
Give me the hope that will deliver me
from fear and faint-heartedness.

O holy and merciful God,
my Creator and Redeemer,
my Judge and Saviour,
You know me and all that I do.
You hate and punish evil without respect of persons
in this world and the next;
You forgive the sins of those
who sincerely pray for forgiveness;
You love goodness, and reward it on this earth
with a clear conscience,

and, in the world to come,
with a crown of righteousness.

I remember in your presence all my loved ones,
my fellow-prisoners, and all who in this house
perform their hard service;
Lord, have mercy.

Restore me to liberty,
and enable me so to live now
that I may answer before you and before men.
Lord, whatever this day may bring,
Your name be praised.
Amen.

Evening Prayers

O Lord my God, thank you
for bringing this day to a close;
Thank you for giving me rest
in body and soul.
Your hand has been over me
and has guarded and preserved me.
Forgive my lack of faith
and any wrong that I have done today,
and help me to forgive all who have wronged me.

Let me sleep in peace under your protection,
and keep me from all the temptations of darkness.

Into your hands I commend my loved ones
and all who dwell in this house;
I commend to you my body and soul.
O God, your holy name be praised.
Amen.

The Hiddenness of Prayer

TRUE PRAYER is done in secret, but this does not rule out the fellowship of prayer altogether, however clearly we may be aware of its dangers. In the last resort it is immaterial whether we pray in the open street or in the secrecy of our chambers, whether briefly or lengthily, in the Litany of the Church, or with the sigh of one who knows not what he should pray for. True prayer does not depend either on the individual or the whole body of the faithful, but solely upon the knowledge that our heavenly Father knows our needs. That makes God the sole object of our prayers, and frees us from a false confidence in our own prayerful efforts.

> After this manner therefore pray ye: Our Father which art in heaven, Hallowed be thy name. Thy kingdom come. Thy will be done, as in heaven, so on earth. Give us this day our daily bread. And forgive us our debts, as we also have forgiven our debtors. And bring us not into temptation, but deliver us from the evil one. For if ye forgive not men their trespasses, neither will your Father forgive your trespasses. (Matt. 6:9–15)

Jesus told his disciples not only *how* to pray, but also *what* to pray. The Lord's Prayer is not merely the pattern prayer, it is the way Christians *must* pray. If they pray this prayer, God will certainly hear them. The Lord's Prayer is the quintessence of prayer. A disciple's prayer is founded on and circumscribed by it. Once again Jesus does not leave his disciples in ignorance; he teaches them the

Lord's Prayer and so leads them to a clear understanding of prayer.

Baptism

BAPTISM IS NOT AN OFFER made by man to God, but an offer made by Christ to man. It is grounded solely on the will of Jesus Christ, as expressed in his gracious call. Baptism is essentially passive—*being baptized, suffering* the call of Christ. In baptism man becomes Christ's own possession. When the name of Christ is spoken over the candidate, he becomes a partaker in this Name, and is baptized "*into* Jesus Christ" (εἰς, Rom. 6:3; Gal. 3:27; Matt. 28:19). From that moment he belongs to Jesus Christ. He is wrested from the dominion of the world, and passes into the ownership of Christ.

Baptism therefore betokens a *breach*. Christ invades the realm of Satan, lays hands on his own, and creates for himself his Church. By this act past and present are rent asunder. The old order is passed away, and all things have become new. This breach is not effected by man's tearing off his own chains through some unquenchable longing for a new life of freedom. The breach has been effected by Christ long since, and in baptism it is effected in our own lives. We are now deprived of our direct relationship with all God-given realities of life. Christ the Mediator has stepped in between us and them. The baptized Christian has ceased to belong to the world and is no longer its slave. He belongs to Christ alone, and his relationship with the world is mediated through him.

The breach with the world is complete. It demands and

produces the death of the old man.[1] In baptism a man dies together with his old world. This death, no less than baptism itself, is a passive event. It is not as though a man must achieve his own death through various kinds of renunciation and mortification. That would never be the death of the old man which Christ demands. The old man cannot will his own death or kill himself. He can only die in, through and with Christ. Christ is his death. For the sake of fellowship with Christ, and in that fellowship alone a man dies. In fellowship with Christ and through the grace of baptism he receives his death as a gift.[2] This death is a gift of grace: a man can never accomplish it by himself. The old man and his sin are judged and condemned, but out of this judgement a new man arises, who has died to the world and to sin.

[1] Even Jesus himself referred to his death as a baptism, and promised that his disciples would share this baptism of death (Mark 10:39; Luke 12:50).
[2] Schlatter also takes I Cor. 15:29 as a reference to the baptism of martyrdom.

The Gift of Baptism

IT IS THEIR BAPTISM into the Body of Christ which assures all Christians of their full share in the life of Christ and the Church. It is wrong, and contrary to the New Testament, to limit the gift of baptism to participation in the sermon and the Lord's Supper, i.e. to participation in the means of grace, or to the right to hold office or perform a ministry in the Church. On the contrary, baptism confers the privilege of participation in all the activities of the Body of Christ in every department of life. To allow a baptized brother to take part in the worship of the Church, but to refuse to have anything to do with him in everyday life, is to subject him to abuse and contempt. If we do that, we are guilty of the very Body of Christ. And if we grant the baptized brother the right to the gifts of salvation, but refuse him the gifts necessary to earthly life or knowingly leave him in material need and distress, we are holding up the gifts of salvation to ridicule and behaving as liars. If the Holy Ghost has spoken and we listen instead to the call of blood and nature, or to our personal sympathies or antipathies, we are profaning the sacrament. When a man is baptized into the Body of Christ not only is his personal status as regards salvation changed, but also the relationship of daily life.

From 'Thoughts on the Day of Baptism of Dietrich Wilhelm Rüdinger Bethge' May 1944

TODAY YOU WILL BE BAPTIZED A CHRISTIAN. All those great ancient words of the Christian proclamation will be spoken over you, and the command of Jesus Christ to baptize will be carried out on you, without your knowing anything about it. But we are once again being driven right back to the beginnings of our understanding. Reconciliation and redemption, regeneration and the Holy Spirit, love of our enemies, cross and resurrection, life in Christ and Christian discipleship—all these things are so difficult and so remote that we hardly venture any more to speak of them. In the traditional words and acts we suspect that there may be something quite new and revolutionary, though we cannot as yet grasp or express it. That is our own fault. Our church, which has been fighting in these years only for its self-preservation, as though that were an end in itself, is incapable of taking the word of reconciliation and redemption to mankind and the world. Our earlier words are therefore bound to lose their force and cease, and our being Christians today will be limited to two things: prayer and righteous action among men. All Christian thinking, speaking, and organizing must be born anew out of this prayer and action. By the time you have grown up, the church's form will have changed greatly. We are not yet out of the melting-pot, and any attempt to help the church prematurely to a new expansion of its organization will merely delay its conversion and purification. It is not for us to prophesy the day (though the day will come) when men will once more be called so to utter the word of God that the world will be changed and renewed by it. It will be a new language, perhaps quite non-religious, but liberating and redeeming—as was Jesus' language; it will shock people and yet overcome them by its power; it will be the language of a new righteousness and truth, proclaiming God's peace with men and the coming of his kingdom. 'They shall fear and tremble because of all the good and all the prosperity I provide for it' (Jer. 33:9). Till then the Christian cause will be a silent and hidden affair, but there will be those who pray and do right and wait for God's own time. May you be one of them, and may it be said of you one day, 'The path of the righteous is like the light of dawn, which shines brighter and brighter till full day' (Prov. 4:18).

Vocation

In the encounter with Jesus Christ man hears the call of God and in it the calling to life in the fellowship of Jesus Christ. Divine grace comes upon man and lays claim to him. It is not man who seeks out grace in its own place— God dwelleth in the light which no man can approach unto (I Tim. 6:16), but it is grace which seeks and finds man in *his* place—the Word was made flesh (John 1:14)— and which precisely in this place lays claim to him. This is a place which in every instance and in every respect is laden with sin and guilt, no matter whether it be a royal throne, the parlour of a respectable citizen or a miserable hovel. It is a place which is of this world. This visitation of man by grace occurred in the incarnation of Jesus Christ, and it occurs in the word of Jesus Christ which is brought by the Holy Ghost. The call comes to man as a Gentile or as a Jew, free man or slave, man or woman, married or single. At the precise place where he is he is to hear the call and to allow it to lay claim to him. This does not mean that servitude or marriage or celibacy in itself is thereby justified; but the man who has been called can in any of these places belong to God. It is only through the call which I have heard in Christ, the call of the grace which lays claim to me, that, as a slave or as a free man, married or celibate, I can live justified before God. From the standpoint of Christ this life is now my calling; from my own standpoint it is my responsibility.

... The calling is the call of Jesus Christ to belong wholly to Him; it is the laying claim to me by Christ at the place at which this call has found me; it embraces work with things and relations with persons; it demands a 'limited field of accomplishments', yet never as a value in itself, but in responsibility towards Jesus Christ. Through this relation to Christ the 'limited field of accomplishments' is freed from its isolation. Its boundary is broken through not only from above, that is to say by Christ, but also in an outward direction.

The Image of Christ

"WHOM HE foreknew, he also foreordained to be conformed to the image of his Son, that he might be the firstborn among many brethren" (Rom. 8:29). Here is a promise which passes all understanding. Those who follow Christ are destined to bear his image, and to be the brethren of the firstborn Son of God. Their goal is to become "as Christ." Christ's followers always have his image before their eyes, and in its light all other images are screened from their sight. It penetrates into the depths of their being, fills them, and makes them more and more like their Master. The image of Jesus Christ impresses itself in daily communion on the image of the disciple. No follower of Jesus can contemplate his image in a spirit of cold detachment. That image has the power to transform our lives, and if we surrender ourselves utterly to him, we cannot help bearing his image ourselves. We become the sons of God, we stand side by side with Christ, our unseen Brother, bearing like him the image of God.

Discipleship and the Cross

THE CROSS is laid on every Christian. The first Christ-suffering which every man must experience is the call to abandon the attachments of this world. It is that dying of the old man which is the result of his encounter with Christ. As we embark upon discipleship we surrender ourselves to Christ in union with his death—we give over our lives to death. Thus it begins; the cross is not the terrible end to an otherwise god-fearing and happy life, but it meets us at the beginning of our communion with Christ. When Christ calls a man, he bids him come and die. It may be a death like that of the first disciples who had to leave home and work to follow him, or it may be a death like Luther's, who had to leave the monastery and go out into the world. But it is the same death every time—death in Jesus Christ, the death of the old man at his call. Jesus' summons to the rich young man was calling him to die, because only the man who is dead to his own will can follow Christ. In fact every command of Jesus is a call to die, with all our affections and lusts. But we do not want to die, and therefore Jesus Christ and his call are necessarily our death as well as our life. The call to discipleship, the baptism in the name of Jesus Christ means both death and life. The call of Christ, his baptism, sets the Christian in the middle of the daily arena against sin and the devil. Every day he encounters new temptations, and every day he must suffer anew for Jesus Christ's sake. The wounds and scars he receives in the fray are living tokens of this participation in the cross of his Lord.

Christ Alone

THE LIFE of discipleship can only be maintained so long as nothing is allowed to come between Christ and ourselves—neither the law, nor personal piety, nor even the world. The disciple always looks only to his master, never to Christ *and* the law, Christ *and* religion, Christ *and* the world. He avoids all such notions like the plague. Only by following Christ alone can he preserve a single eye. His eye rests wholly on the light that comes from Christ, and has no darkness or ambiguity in it. As the eye must be single, clear and pure in order to keep light in the body, as hand and foot can receive light from no other source save the eye, as the foot stumbles and the hand misses its mark when the eye is dim, as the whole body is in darkness when the eye is blind; so the follower of Christ is in the light only so long as he looks simply to Christ and at nothing else in the world. Thus the heart of the disciple must be set upon Christ alone. If the eye sees an object which is not there, the whole body is deceived. If the heart is devoted to the mirage of the world, to the creature instead of the Creator, the disciple is lost.

Worldly possessions tend to turn the hearts of the disciples away from Jesus. What are we really devoted to? That is the question. Are our hearts set on earthly goods? Do we try to combine devotion to them with loyalty to Christ? Or are we devoted exclusively to him? The light of the body is the eye, and the light of the Christian is his heart. If the eye be dark, how great is the darkness of the body! But the heart is dark when it clings to earthly goods, for then, however urgently Jesus may call us, his call fails to find access to our hearts. Our hearts are closed, for they have already been given to another. As the light cannot penetrate the body when the eye is evil, so the word of Jesus cannot penetrate the disciple's heart so long as it is closed against it. The word is choked like the seed which was sown among thorns, choked "with cares and riches and pleasures of this life" (Luke 8:14).

The singleness of the eye and heart corresponds to that "hiddenness" which knows nothing but the call and word of Christ, and which consists in perfect fellowship with him. How can the disciple have dealings with earthly goods and yet preserve this singleness of heart? Jesus does not forbid the possession of property in itself. He was man, he ate and drank like his disciples, and thereby sanctified the good things of life. These necessities, which are consumed in use and which meet the legitimate requirements of the body, are to be used by the disciple with thankfulness.

Fellowship

THE FELLOWSHIP between Jesus and his disciples covered every aspect of their daily life. Within the fellowship of Christ's disciples the life of each individual was part of the life of the brotherhood. This common life bears living testimony to the concrete humanity of the Son of God. The bodily presence of God demands that for him and with him man should stake his own life in his daily existence. With all the concreteness of his bodily existence, man belongs to him who for his sake took upon him the human body. In the Christian life the individual disciple and the body of Jesus belong inseparably together.

All this is confirmed in the earliest record of the life of the Church in the Acts of the Apostles (Acts 2:42 ff; 4:32 ff). "They continued steadfastly in the apostles' teaching and fellowship, in the breaking of bread and the prayers."— "They that believed were of one heart and soul and...had all things in common." It is instructive to note that the fellowship (κοινωνία) is mentioned between Word and Sacrament. This is no accident, for fellowship always springs from the Word and finds its goal and completion in the Lord's Supper. The whole common life of the Christian fellowship oscillates between Word and Sacrament, it begins and ends in worship. It looks forward in expectation to the final banquet in the kingdom of God. When a community has such a source and goal it is a perfect communion of fellowship, in which even material goods fall into their appointed place. In freedom, joy and the power of the Holy Spirit a pattern of common life is produced where "neither was there among them any that lacked," where "distribution was made unto each according as anyone had need," where "not one of them said that aught of the things which he possessed was his own." In the everyday quality of these events we see a perfect picture of that evangelical liberty where there is no need of compulsion. They were indeed "of one heart and soul."

The Work

THESE TWELVE Jesus sent forth, and charged them, saying, Go not into any way of the Gentiles, and enter not into any city of the Samaritans; but go rather to the lost sheep of the house of Israel. (Matt. 10:5, 6)

All the activity of the disciples is subject to the clear precept of their Lord. They are not left free to choose their own methods or adopt their own conception of their task. Their work is to be Christ-work, and therefore they are absolutely dependent on the will of Jesus. Happy are they whose duty is fixed by such a precept, and who are therefore free from the tyranny of their own ideas and calculations.

In his very first word Jesus lays down a limitation of their work, a circumstance which they must inevitably have found strange and difficult. The choice of field for their labours does not depend on their own impulses or inclinations, but on where they are sent. This makes it quite clear that it is not their own work they are doing, but God's. How much they would have liked to go to the heathen and the Samaritans, who needed the glad tidings far more than anyone else. That may be quite true, but they receive no injunctions to go to them. The work of God cannot be done without due authorization, otherwise it is devoid of promise. Does it therefore follow that the promise and commission are not universally valid? Both are valid only where God authorizes them. But does not the very love of Christ constrain us to set no limit to its proclamation? The love of Jesus is something very differ- ent from our own zeal and enthusiasms because it adheres to its mission. What is the urge which drives us to proclaim the saving truths of the gospel? It is not just love for our fellow-countrymen or for the heathen in foreign lands: it is the Lord's commission as he delivered it in his missionary charge. It is only that commission which can show us the place where the promise lies. If Christ will not let us preach the gospel in any particular place, we must give up the attempt and abide by his will and word. Thus the disciples are bound to the word and to the terms of their commission. They can only go where the word of Christ and his commission direct them, "Go not into any way of the Gentiles, and enter not into any city of the Samaritans; but go rather to the lost sheep of the house of Israel."

'The Harvest Is Great'

...''FEED MY LAMBS'' was the last charge Jesus gave to Peter. The Good Shepherd protects his sheep against the wolf, and instead of fleeing he gives his life for the sheep. He knows them all by name and loves them. He knows their distress and their weakness. He heals the wounded, gives drink to the thirsty, sets upright the falling, and leads them gently, not sternly, to pasture. He leads them on the right way. He seeks the one lost sheep, and brings it back to the fold. But the bad shepherds lord it over the flock by force, forgetting their charges and pursuing their own interests. Jesus is looking for good shepherds, and there are none to be found.

The prospect grips his heart, and his divine pity goes out to this erring flock, these multitudes who surge around him. From the human point of view everything looks hopeless, but Jesus sees things with different eyes. Instead of the people maltreated, wretched and poor, he sees the ripe harvest field of God. ''The harvest is great.'' It is ripe enough to be gathered into the barns. The hour has come for these poor and wretched folk to be fetched home to the kingdom of God. Jesus beholds the promise of God descending on the multitudes where the scribes and zealots saw only a field trampled down, burnt and ravaged. Jesus sees the fields waving with corn and ripe for the kingdom of God. The harvest is great, but only Jesus in his mercy can see it.

There is now no time to lose: the work of harvest brooks no delay. "But the labourers are few." It is hardly surprising that so few are granted to see things with the pitying eyes of Jesus, for only those who share the love of his heart have been given eyes to see. And only they can enter the harvest field.

Jesus is looking for help, for he cannot do the work alone. Who will come forward to help him and work with him? Only God knows, and he must give them to his Son. No man dare presume to come forward and offer himself on his own initiative, not even the disciples themselves. Their duty is to pray the Lord of the harvest to send forth labourers at the right moment, for the time is ripe.

The Fruit

HE THAT RECEIVETH YOU receiveth me, and he that receiveth me receiveth him that sent me. He that receiveth a prophet in the name of a prophet shall receive a prophet's reward; and he that receiveth a righteous man in the name of a righteous man shall receive a righteous man's reward. And whosoever shall give to drink unto one of these little ones a cup of cold water only, in the name of a disciple, verily I say unto you, he shall in no wise lose his reward. (Matt. 10:40–42)

The bearers of Jesus' word receive a final word of promise for their work. They are now Christ's fellow-workers, and will be like him in all things. Thus they are to meet those to whom they are sent as if they were Christ himself. When they are welcomed into a house, Christ enters with them. They are bearers of his presence. They bring with them the most precious gift in the world, the gift of Jesus Christ. And with him they bring God the Father, and that means indeed forgiveness and salvation, life and bliss. That is the reward and fruit of their toil and suffering. Every service men render them is service rendered to Christ himself. This means grace for the Church and grace for the disciple in equal measure. The Church will be readier to give them its service and honour for with them the Lord himself has entered into their midst. But the disciples are given to understand that when they enter into a house they do not enter in vain. They bring with them an incomparable gift. It is a law of the kingdom of God that every man shall participate in the gift which he willingly receives as a gift from God. The man who receives a prophet and knows what he is doing will participate in the prophet's cause, his gift and his reward. He who receives a righteous man will receive the reward of a righteous man, for he has become a partner in his righteousness. He who offers a cup of cold water to the weakest and poorest who bears no honourable name has ministered to Christ himself, and Jesus Christ will be his reward.

Thus the disciples are bidden lastly to think, not about their own way, their own sufferings and their own reward, but of the goal of their labours, which is the salvation of the Church.

The Ministry of Helpfulness

WE MUST BE READY to allow ourselves to be interrupted by God. God will be constantly crossing our paths and canceling our plans by sending us people with claims and petitions. We may pass them by, preoccupied with our more important tasks, as the priest passed by the man who had fallen among thieves, perhaps—reading the Bible. When we do that we pass by the visible sign of the Cross raised athwart our path to show us that, not our way, but God's way must be done. It is a strange fact that Christians and even ministers frequently consider their work so important and urgent that they will allow nothing to disturb them. They think they are doing God a service in this, but actually they are disdaining God's "crooked yet straight path" (Gottfried Arnold). They do not want a life that is crossed and balked. But it is part of the discipline of humility that we must not spare our hand where it can perform a service and that we do not assume that our schedule is our own to manage, but allow it to be arranged by God.

Fulfilling Our Tasks

...I THINK WE MUST RISE to the great demands that are made on us personally, and yet at the same time fulfil the commonplace and necessary tasks of daily life. We must confront fate—to me the neuter gender of the word 'fate' (*Schicksal*) is significant—as resolutely as we submit to it at the right time. One can speak of 'guidance' only on the other side of that twofold process, with God meeting us no longer as 'Thou', but also 'disguised' in the 'It'; so in the last resort my question is how we are to find the 'Thou' in this 'It' (i.e. fate), or, in other words, how does 'fate' really become 'guidance'? It's therefore impossible to define the boundary between resistance and submission on abstract principles; but both of them must exist, and both must be practised. Faith demands this elasticity of behaviour. Only so can we stand our ground in each situation as it arises, and turn it to gain.

The Sermon on the Mount

EVERY ONE THEREFORE which heareth these words of mine, and doeth them, shall be likened unto a wise man, which built his house upon the rock: and the rain descended, and the floods came, and the winds blew, and beat upon that house; and it fell not: for it was founded upon the rock. And every one that heareth these words of mine, and doeth them not, shall be likened unto a foolish man, which built his house upon the sand: and the rain descended, and the floods came, and the winds blew, and smote upon that house; and it fell: and great was the fall thereof.

And it came to pass, when Jesus ended these words, the multitudes were astonished at his teaching: for he taught them as one having authority, and not as their scribes. (Matt. 7:24–29)

We have listened to the Sermon on the Mount and perhaps have understood it. But who has heard it aright? Jesus gives the answer at the end. He does not allow his hearers to go away and make of his sayings what they will, picking and choosing from them whatever they find helpful, and testing them to see if they work. He does not give them free rein to misuse his word with their mercenary hands, but gives it to them on condition that it retains exclusive power over them. Humanly speaking, we could understand and interpret the Sermon on the Mount in a thousand different ways. Jesus knows only one possibility: simple surrender and obedience, not interpreting it or applying it, but doing and obeying it. That is the only way to hear his word. But again he does not mean that it is to be discussed as an ideal, he really means us to get on with it.

This word, whose claim we recognize, this word which issues from his saying "I have known thee," this word which sets us at once to work and obedience, is the rock on which to build our house. The only proper response to this word which Jesus brings with him from eternity is simply to do it. Jesus has spoken: his is the word, ours the obedience. Only in the doing of it does the word of Jesus retain its honour, might and power among us. Now the storm can rage over the house, but it cannot shatter that union with him, which his word has created.

Visionary Dreaming

God hates visionary dreaming; it makes the dreamer proud and pretentious. The man who fashions a visionary ideal of community demands that it be realized by God, by others, and by himself. He enters the community of Christians with his demands, sets up his own law, and judges the brethren and God Himself accordingly. He stands adamant, a living reproach to all others in the circle of brethren. He acts as if he is the creator of the Christian community, as if his dream binds men together. When things do not go his way, he calls the effort a failure. When his ideal picture is destroyed, he sees the community going to smash. So he becomes, first an accuser of his brethren, then an accuser of God, and finally the despairing accuser of himself.

Because God has already laid the only foundation of our fellowship, because God has bound us together in one body with other Christians in Jesus Christ, long before we entered into common life with them, we enter into that common life not as demanders but as thankful recipients. We thank God for what He has done for us. We thank God for giving us brethren who live by His call, by His forgiveness, and His promise. We do not complain of what God does not give us; we rather thank God for what He does give us daily....

Christian Radicalism

RADICALISM ALWAYS SPRINGS from a conscious or unconscious hatred of what is established. Christian radicalism, no matter whether it consists in withdrawing from the world or in improving the world, arises from hatred of creation. The radical cannot forgive God His creation. He has fallen out with the created world, the Ivan Karamazov, who at the same time makes the figure of the radical Jesus in the legend of the Grand Inquisitor. When evil becomes powerful in the world, it infects the Christian, too, with the poison of radicalism. It is Christ's gift to the Christian that he should be reconciled with the world as it is, but now this reconciliation is accounted a betrayal and denial of Christ. It is replaced by bitterness, suspicion and contempt for men and the world. In the place of the love that believes all, bears all and hopes all, in the place of the love which loves the world in its very wickedness with the love of God (John 3:16), there is now the pharisaical denial of love to evil, and the restriction of love to the closed circle of the devout. Instead of the open Church of Jesus Christ, which serves the world till the end, there is now some allegedly primitive Christian ideal of a Church, which in its turn confuses the reality of the living Jesus Christ with the realization of a Christian idea. Thus a world which has become evil succeeds in making the Christians become evil too. It is the same germ that disintegrates the world and that makes the Christians become radical. In both cases it is hatred towards the world, no matter whether the haters are the ungodly or the godly. On both sides it is a refusal of faith in the creation. But devils are not cast out through Beelzebub.

Human Relationships

...THERE IS HARDLY ANYTHING that can make one happier than to feel that one counts for something with other people. What matters here is not numbers, but intensity. In the long run, human relationships are the most important thing in life; the modern 'efficient' man can do nothing to change this, nor can the demigods and lunatics who know nothing about human relationships. God uses us in his dealings with others.

The Friend

NOT from the heavy soil,
where blood and sex and oath
rule in their hallowed might,
where earth itself,
guarding the primal consecrated order,
avenges wantonness and madness—
not from the heavy soil of earth,
but from the spirit's choice and free desire,
needing no oath or legal bond,
is friend bestowed on friend.

Beside the cornfield that sustains us,
tilled and cared for reverently by men
sweating as they labour at their task,
and, if need be, giving their life's blood—
beside the field that gives their daily bread
men also let the lovely cornflower thrive.
No one has planted, no one watered it;
it grows, defenceless and in freedom,
and in glad confidence of life untroubled
under the open sky.
Beside the staff of life,
taken and fashioned from the heavy earth,
beside our marriage, work, and war,
the free man, too, will live and grow towards the sun.
Not the ripe fruit alone—
blossom is lovely, too.
Does blossom only serve the fruit,

or does fruit only serve the blossom—
who knows?
But both are given to us.
Finest and rarest blossom,
at a happy moment springing
from the freedom of a lightsome, daring, trusting
    spirit,
is a friend to a friend.

Playmates at first
on the spirit's long journeys
to distant and wonderful realms
that, veiled by the morning sunlight,
glitter like gold;
when, in the midday heat
the gossamer clouds in the deep blue sky
drift slowly towards them—
realms that, when night stirs the senses,
lit by the lamps in the darkness,
like treasures prudently hidden
beckon the seeker.

When the spirit touches
man's heart and brow
with thoughts that are lofty, bold, serene,
so that with clear eyes he will face the world
as a free man may;
when then the spirit gives birth to action
by which alone we stand or fall;
when from the sane and resolute action
rises the work that gives a man's life
content and meaning—
then would that man,
lonely and actively working,
know of the spirit that grasps and befriends him,
like waters clear and refreshing

where the spirit is cleansed from the dust
and cooled from the heat that oppressed him,
steeling himself in the hour of fatigue—
like a fortress to which, from confusion and danger,
the spirit returns,
wherein he finds refuge and comfort and
    strengthening,
is a friend to a friend.

And the spirit will trust,
trust without limit.

Sickened by vermin
that feed, in the shade of the good,
on envy, greed, and suspicion,
by the snake-like hissing
of venomous tongues
that fear and hate and revile
the mystery of free thought
and upright heart,
the spirit would cast aside all deceit,
open his heart to the spirit he trusts,
and unite with him freely as one.
Ungrudging, he will support,
will thank and acknowledge him,
and from him draw happiness and strength.

But always to rigorous
judgment and censure
freely assenting,
man seeks, in his manhood,
not orders, not laws and peremptory dogmas,
but counsel from one who is earnest in goodness
and faithful in friendship,
making man free.

Distant or near,
in joy or in sorrow,
each in the other
sees his true helper
to brotherly freedom.

At midnight came the air-raid siren's song;
I thought of you in silence and for long—
how you are faring, how our lives once were,
and how I wish you home this coming year.

We wait till half past one, and hear at last
the signal that the danger now is past;
so danger—if the omen does not lie—
of every kind shall gently pass you by.

Life Together

...IT IS NOT simply to be taken for granted that the Christian has the privilege of living among other Christians. Jesus Christ lived in the midst of his enemies. At the end all his disciples deserted him. On the Cross he was utterly alone, surrounded by evildoers and mockers. For this cause he had come, to bring peace to the enemies of God. So the Christian, too, belongs not in the seclusion of a cloistered life but in the thick of foes. There is his commission, his work....

The Joy of Fellowship

...THE PRISONER, the sick person, the Christian in exile sees in the companionship of a fellow Christian a physical sign of the gracious presence of the triune God. Visitor and visited in loneliness recognize in each other the Christ who is present in the body; they receive and meet each other as one meets the Lord, in reverence, humility, and joy. They receive each other's benedictions as the benediction of the Lord Jesus Christ. But if there is so much blessing and joy even in a single encounter of brother with brother, how inexhaustible are the riches that open up for those who by God's will are privileged to live in the daily fellowship of life with other Christians!

It is true, of course, that what is an unspeakable gift of

God for the lonely individual is easily disregarded and trodden under foot by those who have the gift every day. It is easily forgotten that the fellowship of Christian brethren is a gift of grace, a gift of the Kingdom of God that any day may be taken from us, that the time that still separates us from utter loneliness may be brief indeed. Therefore, let him who until now has had the privilege of living a common Christian life with other Christians praise God's grace from the bottom of his heart. Let him thank God on his knees and declare: It is grace, nothing but grace, that we are allowed to live in community with Christian brethren.

Love

...THE REVELATION OF GOD is Jesus Christ. 'In this was manifested the love of God toward us, because that God sent his only begotten Son into the world, that we might live through him' (I John 4:9). God's revelation in Jesus Christ, God's revelation of His love, precedes all our love towards Him. Love has its origin not in us but in God. Love is not an attitude of men but an attitude of God. 'Herein is love, not that we loved God, but that he loved us, and sent his Son to be the propitiation for our sins' (I John 4:10). Only in Jesus Christ do we know what love is, namely, in His deed for us. 'Hereby perceive we the love of God, because he laid down his life for us' (I John 3:16). And even here there is given no general definition of love, in the sense, for example, of its being the laying down of one's life for the lives of others. What is here called love is not this general principle but the utterly unique event of the laying down of the life of Jesus Christ for us. Love is inseparably bound up with the name of Jesus Christ as the revelation of God. The New Testament answers the question 'What is love?' quite unambiguously by pointing solely and entirely to Jesus Christ. He is the only definition of love. But again it would be a complete misunderstanding if we were to derive a general definition of love from our view of Jesus Christ and of His deed and His suffering. Love is not what He *does* and what He *suffers*, but it is what *He* does and what *He* suffers. Love is always He Himself. Love is always God Himself. Love is always the revelation of God in Jesus Christ.

The Strength of the Other Person

"It is not good that the man should be alone; I will make him a helper fit for him."

THE FIRST MAN is alone. Christ was also alone. And we are alone as well. Everyone is alone in his own way: Adam is alone in the expectation of the other person, the community. Christ is alone because only he loves the other person, because he is the way by which mankind has returned to its Creator. We are alone because we have pushed the other person from us, because we hated him. Adam was alone in hope, Christ was alone in the fullness of deity, and we are alone in evil, in hopelessness.

God creates a companion, a helpmeet, for Adam. It is not good that Adam is alone. For what purpose does man, living in the protection of God, need a companion? The answer is only revealed if we consider the story in its context again and again. In the Bible otherwise only God is a companion, a helpmeet to man. So if woman is here spoken of in this way it must mean something quite unusual. This follows from the description. First of all God forms animals out of the ground from which he formed man. According to the Bible men and animals have the same bodies! Perhaps he may find a companion among these brothers, for the animals really are of the same origin as he. The peculiar feature of this is that man must obviously know for himself whether these animals can be companions for him or not. Adam's companion was to be whichever creature he called his companion as the creatures were brought before him. There is Adam, the intelligent, calling all the animals by name—the brotherly world of the animals who have been taken from the same ground as he—and letting them pass by him. It was his first pain that these brothers whom he loved did not fulfill his own expectations: they remained a strange world to him. Indeed, in all good fellowship, they remain creatures subjected to him, whom he names and over which he rules. Adam remains alone. As far as I know, nowhere else in the history of religions have the animals been spoken of in such a significant context. When God desires to create for man, in the form of another creature, the helper he is himself, in the first place the animals are created; they are named and set in their places. Still Adam is alone. That which came out of the ground remains a stranger to him.

Marriage

...MARRIAGE IS THE UNION of two human beings as human beings, on the basis of the free decision of the individual. So long as human nature continues, it will continue to lay claim to this right. The denial of this right for any reason which lies neither on the entirely individual plane nor on the general human plane will sooner or later always prove ineffectual in the face of the power of natural life. The right of men and women to a child of their own, which implies the right to the choice of a partner in marriage, can never, in the long run, be overruled by considerations of class or of religious outlook or on economic or biological grounds. The human will to reproduce can never be interpreted as a purely social, economic, religious or biological obligation. All these factors may, and indeed must, be considered in making one's own choice, but they cannot replace the free decision. In marriage an individual unites himself with an individual, a human being with a human being. Economic, denominational, social and national ties all contribute to determining the decision of the individual, but they can neither obviate nor anticipate this decision. The reason for this lies in the fact that the desire for a child of one's own and the free choice of a mate which this implies, in other words human marriage, is the oldest of all human institutions and cannot therefore be conditional upon these secondary factors.

Human marriage existed before the development of any of the other bonds of human society. Marriage was given already with the creation of the first man. Its right is founded in the beginnings of mankind.

The Community of Love

Therefore a man leaves his father and his mother and cleaves to his wife, and they become one flesh.

IT COULD BE SAID that here the narrator is obviously stumbling. How can Adam, who knows nothing of a father or a mother, say such a thing? We could also say this is the narrator's practical application of the story, or something of the kind. Really, though, we recognize a basic fact here which has so far been hidden and which has now, as it were unintentionally, come to light. We ourselves are the Adam who speaks. We have a father and a mother and we know the uniqueness of belonging to one another in the love of man and woman, but for us this knowledge has been wholly spoilt and destroyed by our guilt. This passage does not justify running away from the worldly order or from our connexion with our father and mother. It is the profoundest way possible of describing the depth and seriousness of belonging to one another. This ultimate belonging to one another is undoubtedly seen here in connexion with man's sexuality. Very clearly sexuality is the expression of the two-sidedness of being both an individual and being one with the other person. Sexuality is nothing but the ultimate realization of our belonging to one another. Here sexuality has as yet no life of its own detached from this purpose. Here the community of man and woman is the community derived from God, the community of love glorifying and worshipping him as the Creator.

Christ the Foundation

God gives you Christ as the foundation of your marriage. 'Welcome one another, therefore, as Christ has welcomed you, for the glory of God' (Rom. 15[7]). In a word, live together in the forgiveness of your sins, for without it no human fellowship, least of all a marriage, can survive. Don't insist on your rights, don't blame each other, don't judge or condemn each other, don't find fault with each other, but accept each other as you are, and forgive each other every day from the bottom of your hearts.

What God Has Joined Together

God is guiding your marriage. Marriage is more than your love for each other. It has a higher dignity and power, for it is God's holy ordinance, through which he wills to perpetuate the human race till the end of time. In your love you see only your two selves in the world, but in marriage you are a link in the chain of the generations, which God causes to come and to pass away to his glory, and calls into his kingdom. In your love you see only the heaven of your own happiness, but in marriage you are placed at a post of responsibility towards the world and mankind. Your love is your own private possession, but marriage is more than something personal—it is a status, an office. Just as it is the crown, and not merely the will to rule, that makes the king, so it is marriage, and not merely your love for each other, that joins you together in the sight of God and man. As you first gave the ring to one another and have now received it a second time from the hand of the pastor, so love comes from you, but marriage from above, from God. As high as God is above man, so high are the sanctity, the rights, and the promise of marriage above the sanctity, the rights, and the promise of love. It is not your love that sustains the marriage, but from now on, the marriage that sustains your love.

God makes your marriage indissoluble. 'What therefore God has joined together, let no man put asunder' (Matt. 19:6). God joins you together in marriage; it is his act, not yours. Do not confound your love for one another with God. God makes your marriage indissoluble, and protects it from every danger that may threaten it from within and without; he wills to be the guarantor of its indissolubility. It is a blessed thing to know that no power on earth, no temptation, no human frailty can dissolve what God holds together; indeed, anyone who knows that may say confidently: What God has joined together, *can* no man put asunder. Free from all the anxiety that is always a characteristic of love, you can now say to each other with complete and confident assurance: We can never lose each other now; by the will of God we belong to each other till death.

Home

THE HOMES OF MEN are not, like the shelters of animals, merely the means of protection against bad weather and the night or merely places for rearing the young; they are places in which a man may relish the joys of his personal life in the intimacy and security of his family and of his property. Eating and drinking do not merely serve the purpose of keeping the body in good health, but they afford natural joy in bodily living. Clothing is not intended merely as a mean covering for the body, but also as an adornment of the body. Recreation is not designed solely to increase working efficiency, but it provides the body with its due measure of repose and enjoyment. Play is by its nature remote from all subordination to purpose, and it thus demonstrates most clearly that the life of the body is an end in itself. Sex is not only the means of reproduction, but, independently of this defined purpose, it brings with it its own joy, in married life, in the love of two human beings for one another. From all this it emerges that the meaning of bodily life never lies solely in its subordination to its final purpose. The life of the body assumes its full significance only with the fulfilment of its inherent claim to joy.

The Security of Home

IN THE REVOLUTIONARY TIMES ahead the greatest gift will be to know the security of a good home. It will be a bulwark against all dangers from within and without. The time when children broke away in arrogance from their parents will be past. Children will be drawn into their parents' protection, and they will seek refuge, counsel, peace, and enlightenment. You are lucky to have parents who know at first hand what it means to have a parental home in stormy times. In the general impoverishment of intellectual life you will find your parents' home a storehouse of spiritual values and a source of intellectual stimulation. Music, as your parents understand and practise it, will help to dissolve your perplexities and purify your character and sensibility, and in times of care and sorrow will keep a ground-bass of joy alive in you. Your parents will soon be teaching you to help yourself and never to be afraid of soiling your hands. The piety of your home will not be noisy or loquacious, but it will teach you to say your prayers, to fear and love God above everything, and to do the will of Jesus Christ. 'My son, keep your father's commandment, and forsake not your mother's teaching. Bind them upon your heart always; tie them about your neck. When you walk, they will lead you; when you lie down, they will watch over you; and when you awake, they will talk with you' (Prov. 6:20–22). 'Today salvation has come to this house' (Luke 19:9).

A Virtuous Woman

THE PLACE where God has put the wife is the husband's home. Most people have forgotten nowadays what a home can mean, though some of us have come to realize it as never before. It is a kingdom of its own in the midst of the world, a stronghold amid life's storms and stresses, a refuge, even a sanctuary. It is not founded on the shifting sands of outward or public life, but it has its peace in God, for it is God who gives it its special meaning and value, its own nature and privilege, its own destiny and dignity. It is an ordinance of God in the world, the place in which— whatever may happen in the world—peace, quietness, joy, love, purity, discipline, respect, obedience, tradition, and, with it all, happiness may dwell. It is the wife's calling, and her happiness, to build up for her husband this world within the world, and to do her life's work there. How happy she is if she realizes how great and rich a task and destiny she has. Not novelty, but permanence; not change, but constancy; not noisiness, but peace; not words, but deeds; not commands, but persuasion; not desire, but possession—and all these things inspired and sustained by her love for her husband—, that is the wife's kingdom. In the Book of Proverbs we read [31:11ff.]: 'The heart of her husband trusts in her, and he will have no lack of gain. She does him good, and not harm, all the days of her life. She seeks wool and flax, and works with willing hands.... She rises while it is yet night and provides food for her household and tasks for her maidens.... She opens her hand to the poor, and reaches out her hands to the needy...Strength and dignity are her clothing, and she laughs at the time to come...Her children rise up and call her blessed; her husband also, and he praises her...Many women have done excellently, but you surpass them all.' Again and again the Bible praises, as the supreme earthly happiness, the fortune of a man who finds a true, or as the Bible puts it, a 'virtuous' or 'wise' woman. 'She is far more precious than jewels' [Prov. 31:10]. 'A virtuous woman is the crown of her husband' [Prov. 12:4]....

To His Mother

[Prinz-Albrecht-Strasse]
28 December 1944

Dear mother,

I'm so glad to have just got permission to write you a birthday letter. I have to write in some haste, as the post is just going. All I really want to do is to help to cheer you a little in these days that you must be finding so bleak. Dear mother, I want you to know that I am constantly thinking of you and father every day, and that I thank God for all that you are to me and the whole family. I know you've always lived for us and haven't lived a life of your own. That is why you're the only one with whom I can share all that I'm going through. It's a very great comfort to me that Maria is with you. Thank you for all the love that has come to me in my cell from you during the past year, and has made every day easier for me. I think these hard years have brought us closer together than we ever were before. My wish for you and father and Maria and for us all is that the New Year may bring us at least an occasional glimmer of light, and that we may once more have the joy of being together. May God keep you both well.

With most loving wishes, dear, dear mother, for a happy birthday.

Your grateful Dietrich

The Heritage of Children

God has laid on marriage a blessing and a burden. The blessing is the promise of children. God allows man to share in his continual work of creation; but it is always God himself who blesses marriage with children. 'Children are a heritage from the Lord' (Ps. 127:3), and they should be acknowledged as such. It is from God that parents receive their children, and it is to God that they should lead them. Parents therefore have divine authority in respect of their children. Luther speaks of the 'golden chain' with which God invests parents; and scripture adds to the fifth commandment the special promise of long life on earth. Since men live on earth, God has given them a lasting reminder that this earth stands under the curse of sin and is not itself the ultimate reality. Over the destiny of woman and of man lies the dark shadow of a word of God's wrath, a burden from God, which they must carry. The woman must bear her children in pain, and in providing for his family the man must reap many thorns and thistles, and labour in the sweat of his brow. This burden should cause both man and wife to call on God, and should remind them of their eternal destiny in his kingdom. Earthly society is only the beginning of the heavenly society, the earthly home an image of the heavenly home, the earthly family a symbol of the fatherhood of God over all men, for they are his children.

Abortion

MARRIAGE INVOLVES acknowledgement of the right of life that is to come into being, a right which is not subject to the disposal of the married couple. Unless this right is acknowledged as a matter of principle, marriage ceases to be marriage and becomes a mere liaison. Acknowledgement of this right means making way for the free creative power of God which can cause new life to proceed from this marriage according to His will. Destruction of the embryo in the mother's womb is a violation of the right to live which God has bestowed upon this nascent life. To raise the question whether we are here concerned already with a human being or not is merely to confuse the issue. The simple fact is that God certainly intended to create a human being and that this nascent human being has been deliberately deprived of his life. And that is nothing but murder. A great many different motives may lead to an action of this kind; indeed in cases where it is an act of despair, performed in circumstances of extreme human or economic destitution and misery, the guilt may often lie rather with the community than with the individual. Precisely in this connexion money may conceal many a wanton deed, while the poor man's more reluctant lapse may far more easily be disclosed. All these considerations must no doubt have a quite decisive influence on our personal and pastoral attitude towards the person concerned, but they cannot in any way alter the fact of murder.[1]

---

[1]In view of the general practice serious thought must be provoked by the strong disapproval which the Roman Catholic Church expresses with regard to

the killing of the foetus in cases where the mother is in danger of losing her life. If the child has its right to life from God, and is perhaps already capable of life, then the killing of the child, as an alternative to the presumed natural death of the mother, is surely a highly questionable action. The life of the mother is in the hand of God, but the life of the child is arbitrarily extinguished. The question whether the life of the mother or the life of the child is of greater value can hardly be a matter for a human decision.

The Rights of Natural Life

...GOD'S HAVING CREATED the individual, and His having called him to eternal life, is a reality which is operative in natural life, and a reality which it is extremely dangerous to neglect. Within natural life, therefore, it is incumbent upon reason to take account of the right of the individual, even though the divine origin of this right is not recognized. Consequently the natural enemy of social eudemonism has always been reason, the organ which 'perceives' and introduces into consciousness the reality of the fallen world. Social eudemonism, for its part, allies itself with a blind voluntarism in an 'irrational', inconceivable overestimation of the power of the will in its encounter with the reality of natural life itself. It is a truth which lies beyond the reach of this voluntarism that reason is closer to reality than is the blind will, even though this blind will may claim to be closer to reality than anything else can be. The principle of *suum cuique* is the highest possible attainment of a reason which is in accord with reality and which, within the natural life, discerns the right which is given to the individual by God (of whom reason knows nothing).

In our discussion of the rights of natural life from the point of view of their contents the question of the guarantor of these rights will repeatedly demand an answer. Who is it that supports the rights of natural life with an effective guarantee? Here we must repeat what we have said already. It is in the first place God Himself who guarantees these rights. But for this purpose He continually makes use of life itself, which sooner or later gains the upper hand in spite of every violation of the natural. We have to reckon here with periods of time which may extend beyond the life span of the individual. The reason for this is that in the domain of natural life what matters is not so much the individual as the preservation of the life of man as a species. Natural life necessarily often rides rough-shod over the individual. If the right of the individual is destroyed, and perhaps not restored, this will augment the power of resistance of natural life and enable it to reassert itself in the next or next but one generation. It is the problem of a theodicy that presents itself here, but the solution of this problem must await a later occasion. If it is God, and through Him life itself, that intervenes effectively on behalf of the rights that are inherent in life, then any action of which the individual is capable in defence of his natural rights can only be of extremely restricted significance. What the individual does, in fact, do will depend on a large number of considerations which at present lie beyond the scope of our enquiry. But in any case he will always have to bear in mind that his most powerful ally is life itself. If one asks whether the individual is entitled to defend his natural rights, then the answer must clearly be yes. But in all circumstances he must defend the right in such a manner as to carry the conviction that it is not the individual but God who guarantees it.

The Rights of Bodily Life

THE LIFE OF THE BODY, like life in general, is both a means to an end and an end in itself. To regard the body exclusively as a means to an end is idealistic but not Christian; for a means is discarded as soon as the end is achieved. It is from this point of view that the body is conceived as the prison from which the immortal soul is released for ever by death. According to the Christian doctrine, the body possesses a higher dignity. Man is a bodily being, and remains so in eternity as well. Bodiliness and human life belong inseparably together. And thus the bodiliness which is willed by God to be the form of existence of man is entitled to be called an end in itself. This does not exclude the fact that the body at the same time continues to be subordinated to a higher purpose. But what is important is that as one of the rights of bodily life its preservation is not only a means to an end but also an end in itself. It is in the joys of the body that it becomes apparent that the body is an end in itself within the natural life. If the body were only a means to an end man would have no right to bodily joys. It would then not be permissible to exceed an expedient minimum of bodily enjoyment. This would have very far-reaching consequences for the Christian appraisal of all the problems that have to do with the life of the body, housing, food, clothing, recreation, play and sex. But if the body is rightly to be regarded as an end in itself, then there is a right to bodily joys, even though these are not necessarily subordinated to some higher purpose. It is inherent in the nature of joy itself that it is spoilt by any thought of purpose. We shall have to return to this later on when we come to deal with the right to happiness. Within the natural life the joys of the body are reminders of the eternal joy which has been promised to men by God. . . .

The Value of a Life

. . . THE IDEA OF DESTROYING a life which has lost its social usefulness is one which springs from weakness, not from strength.

But, above all, this idea springs from the false assumption that life consists only in its own usefulness to society. It is not perceived that life, created and preserved by God, possesses an inherent right which is wholly independent of its social utility. The right to live is a matter of the essence and not of any values. In the sight of God there is no life that is not worth living; for life itself is valued by God. The fact that God is the Creator, Preserver and Redeemer of life makes even the most wretched life worth living before God. The beggar Lazarus, a leper, lay at the rich man's gate and the dogs licked his sores; he was devoid of any social usefulness and a victim of those who judge life according to its social usefulness; yet God held him to be worthy of eternal life. And where if not in God should there lie the criterion for the ultimate value of a life? In the subjective will to live? On this rating many a genius is excelled by half-wits. In the judgement of society? If so it would soon be found that opinion as to which lives were socially valuable or valueless would be determined by the requirements of the moment and therefore by arbitrary decisions; one group of human beings after another would in this way be condemned to extermination. The distinction between life that is worth living and life that is not worth living must sooner or later destroy life itself. Now that we have made this principle clear, we must still say a word about the purely social utility of the seemingly useless and meaningless life. We cannot indeed ignore the fact that precisely the supposedly worthless life of the incurably sick evokes from the healthy, from doctors, nurses and relatives, the very highest measure of social self-sacrifice and even genuine heroism; this devoted service which is rendered by sound life to sick life has given rise to real values which are of the highest utility for the community.

Suicide

GOD, THE CREATOR and Lord of life, Himself exercises the right over life. Man does not need to lay hands upon himself in order to justify his life. And because he does not need to do this it follows that it is not rightful for him to do it. It is a remarkable fact that the Bible nowhere expressly forbids suicide, but that suicide appears there very often (though not always) as the consequence of extremely grave sin, so, for example, in the case of the traitors Ahithophel and Judas. The reason for this is not that the Bible sanctions suicide, but that, instead of prohibiting it, it desires to call the despairing to repentance and to mercy. A man who is on the brink of suicide no longer has ears for commands or prohibitions; all he can hear now is God's merciful summons to faith, to deliverance and to conversion. A man who is desperate cannot be saved by a law that appeals to his own strength; such a law will only drive him to even more hopeless despair. One who despairs of life can be helped only by the saving deed of another, the offer of a new life which is to be lived not by his own strength but by the grace of God. A man who can no longer live is not helped by any command that he should live, but only by a new spirit.

God maintains the right of life, even against the man who has grown tired of his life. He gives man freedom to pledge his life for something greater, but it is not His will that man should turn this freedom arbitrarily against his own life. Man must not lay hands upon himself, even though he must sacrifice his life for others. Even if his earthly life has become a torment for him, he must commit it intact into God's hand, from which it came, and he must not try to break free by his own efforts, for in dying he falls again into the hand of God, which he found too severe while he lived.

Fulfilment

ONLY THE TRIUMPHAL ENTRY of the Lord will bring with it the fulfilment of manhood and goodness. But a light is already shed by the coming Lord upon what is meant by being man and by being good in the way which is required for true preparation and expectation. It is only by reference to the Lord who is to come, and who has come, that we can know what it is to be man and to be good. It is because Christ is coming that we must be men and that we must be good. For Christ is not coming to hell, but to 'His own' (John 1:11); He is coming to His creation, which, in spite of its fall, is His creation still. Christ is not coming to devils but to men, certainly to men who are sinful, lost and damned, but still to men. That the fallen creation is still the creation, and that sinful man still remains man, follows from the fact that Christ is coming to them and that Christ redeems them from sin and from the power of the devil. It is in relation to Christ that the fallen world becomes intelligible as the world which is preserved and sustained by God for the coming of Christ, the world in which we can and should live good lives as men in orders which are established. But wherever man becomes a thing, a merchandise, a machine, wherever the established orders are arbitrarily destroyed, and wherever the distinction is lost between 'good' and 'evil', there the reception of Christ is impeded by an additional obstacle over and above the general sinfulness and forlornness of the world. There the world is destroying itself, so that it is in grave peril of becoming devilish. Even in the midst of the fallen, lost world, it makes a difference in God's sight whether a man observes or violates the order of marriage and whether he acts justly or arbitrarily. Certainly he is still a sinner, even though he is blameless in marriage and a protector of justice, but it still makes a difference whether the penultimate is attended to and taken seriously or not. The preparation of the way requires that the penultimate shall be respected and validated for the sake of the approaching ultimate.

Of Success

ALTHOUGH IT IS CERTAINLY NOT TRUE that success justifies an evil deed and shady means, it is impossible to regard success as something that is ethically quite neutral. The fact is that historical success creates a basis for the continuance of life, and it is still a moot point whether it is ethically more responsible to take the field like a Don Quixote against a new age, or to admit one's defeat, accept the new age, and agree to serve it. In the last resort success makes history; and the ruler of history repeatedly brings good out of evil over the heads of the history-makers. Simply to ignore the ethical significance of success is a short-circuit created by dogmatists who think unhistorically and irresponsibly; and it is good for us sometimes to be compelled to grapple seriously with the ethical problem of success. As long as goodness is successful, we can afford the luxury of regarding it as having no ethical significance; it is when success is achieved by evil means that the problem arises. In the face of such a situation we find that it cannot be adequately dealt with, either by theoretical dogmatic arm-chair criticism, which means a refusal to face the facts, or by opportunism, which means giving up the struggle and surrendering to success. We will not and must not be either outraged critics or opportunists, but must take our share of responsibility for the moulding of history in every situation and at every moment, whether we are the victors or the vanquished. One who will not allow any occurrence whatever to deprive him of his responsibility for the course of history—because he knows that it has been laid on him by God—will thereafter achieve a more fruitful relation to the events of history than that of barren criticism and equally barren opportunism. To talk of going down fighting like heroes in the face of certain defeat is not really heroic at all, but merely a refusal to face the future. The ultimate question for a responsible man to ask is not how he is to extricate himself heroically from the affair, but how the coming generation is to live. It is only from this question, with its responsibility towards history, that fruitful solutions can come, even if for the time being they are very humiliating. In short, it is much easier to see a thing through from the point of view of abstract principle than from that of concrete responsibility. The rising generation will always instinctively discern which of these we make the basis of our actions, for it is their own future that is at stake.

Of Folly

FOLLY IS A MORE DANGEROUS ENEMY to the good than evil. One can protest against evil; it can be unmasked and, if need be, prevented by force. Evil always carries the seeds of its own destruction, as it makes people, at the least, uncomfortable. Against folly we have no defence. Neither protests nor force can touch it; reasoning is no use; facts that contradict personal prejudices can simply be disbelieved—indeed, the fool can counter by criticizing them, and if they are undeniable, they can just be pushed aside as trivial exceptions. So the fool, as distinct from the scoundrel, is completely self-satisfied; in fact, he can easily become dangerous, as it does not take much to make him aggressive. A fool must therefore be treated more cautiously than a scoundrel; we shall never again try to convince a fool by reason, for it is both useless and dangerous.

If we are to deal adequately with folly, we must try to understand its nature. This much is certain, that it is a moral rather than an intellectual defect. There are people who are mentally agile but foolish, and people who are mentally slow but very far from foolish—a discovery that we make to our surprise as a result of particular situations. We thus get the impression that folly is likely to be, not a congenital defect, but one that is acquired in certain circumstances where people *make* fools of themselves or allow others to make fools of them. We notice further that this defect is less common in the unsociable and solitary than in individuals or groups that are inclined or condemned to sociability. It seems, then, that folly is a sociological rather than a psychological problem, and that it is a special form of the operation of historical circumstances on people, a psychological by-product of definite external factors. If we look more closely, we see that any violent display of power, whether political or religious, produces an outburst of folly in a large part of mankind; indeed, this seems actually to be a psychological and sociological law: the power of some needs the folly of the others. It is not that certain human capacities, intellectual capacities for instance, become stunted or destroyed, but rather that the upsurge of power makes such an overwhelming impression that men are deprived of their independent judgment, and—more or less unconsciously—give up trying to assess the new state of affairs for themselves. The fact that the fool is often stubborn must not mislead us into thinking that he is independent. One feels in fact, when talking to him, that one is dealing, not with the man himself, but with slogans, catchwords, and the like, which have taken hold of him. He is under a spell, he is blinded, his very nature is being misused and exploited. Having thus become a passive instrument, the fool will be capable of any evil and at the same time incapable of seeing that it is evil. Here lies the danger of a diabolical exploitation that can do irreparable damage to human beings.

But at this point it is quite clear, too, that folly can be overcome, not by instruction, but only by an act of liberation; and so we have come to terms with the fact that in the great majority of cases inward liberation must be preceded by outward liberation, and that until that has taken place, we may as well abandon all attempts to convince the fool. In this state of affairs we have to realize why it is no use our trying to find out what 'the people' really think, and why the question is so superfluous for the man who thinks and acts responsibly—but always given these particular circumstances. The Bible's words that 'the fear of the Lord is the beginning of wisdom' (Ps. 111:10) tell us that a person's inward liberation to live a responsible life before God is the only real cure for folly.

But there is some consolation in these thoughts on folly: they in no way justify us in thinking that most people are fools in all circumstances. What will really matter is whether those in power expect more from people's folly than from their wisdom and independence of mind.

Confidence

THERE IS HARDLY ONE OF US who has not known what it is to be betrayed. The figure of Judas, which we used to find so difficult to understand, is now fairly familiar to us. The air that we breathe is so polluted by mistrust that it almost chokes us. But where we have broken through the layer of mistrust, we have been able to discover a confidence hitherto undreamed of. Where we trust, we have learnt to put our very lives into the hands of others; in the face of all the different interpretations that have been put on our lives and actions, we have learnt to trust unreservedly. We now know that only such confidence, which is always a venture, though a glad and positive venture, enables us really to live and work. We know that it is most reprehensible to sow and encourage mistrust, and that our duty is rather to foster and strengthen confidence wherever we can. Trust will always be one of the greatest, rarest, and happiest blessings of our life in community, though it can emerge only on the dark background of a necessary mistrust. We have learnt never to trust a scoundrel an inch, but to give ourselves to the trustworthy without reserve.

Sympathy

WE MUST ALLOW for the fact that most people learn wisdom only by personal experience. This explains, first, why so few people are capable of taking precautions in advance— they always fancy that they will somehow or other avoid the danger, till it is too late. Secondly, it explains their insensibility to the sufferings of others; sympathy grows in proportion to the fear of approaching disaster. There is a good deal of excuse on ethical grounds for this attitude. No one wants to meet fate head-on; inward calling and strength for action are acquired only in the actual emergency. No one is responsible for all the injustice and suffering in the world, and no one wants to set himself up as the judge of the world. Psychologically, our lack of imagination, of sensitivity, and of mental alertness is balanced by a steady composure, an ability to go on working, and a great capacity for suffering. But from a Christian point of view, none of these excuses can obscure the fact that the most important factor, large-heartedness, is lacking. Christ kept himself from suffering till his hour had come, but when it did come he met it as a free man, seized it, and mastered it. Christ, so the scriptures tell us, bore the sufferings of all humanity in his own body as if they were his own—a thought beyond our comprehension—accepting them of his own free will. We are certainly not Christ; we are not called on to redeem the world by our own deeds and sufferings, and we need not try to assume such an impossible burden. We are not lords, but instruments in the hand of the Lord of history; and we can share in other people's sufferings only to a very limited degree. We are not Christ, but if we want to be Christians, we must have some share in Christ's large-heartedness by acting with responsibility and in freedom when the hour of danger comes, and by showing a real sympathy that springs, not from fear, but from the liberating and redeeming love of Christ for all who suffer. Mere waiting and looking on is not Christian behaviour. The Christian is called to sympathy and action, not in the first place by his own sufferings, but by the sufferings of his brethren, for whose sake Christ suffered.

Optimism

IT IS WISER to be pessimistic; it is a way of avoiding disappointment and ridicule, and so wise people condemn optimism. The essence of optimism is not its view of the present, but the fact that it is the inspiration of life and hope when others give in; it enables a man to hold his head high when everything seems to be going wrong; it gives him strength to sustain reverses and yet to claim the future for himself instead of abandoning it to his opponent. It is true that there is a silly, cowardly kind of optimism, which we must condemn. But the optimism that is will for the future should never be despised, even if it is proved wrong a hundred times; it is health and vitality, and the sick man has no business to impugn it.

There are people who regard it as frivolous, and some Christians think it impious for anyone to hope and prepare for a better earthly future. They think that the meaning of present events is chaos, disorder, and catastrophe; and in resignation or pious escapism they surrender all responsibility for reconstruction and for future generations. It may be that the day of judgement will dawn tomorrow; in that case, we shall gladly stop working for a better future. But not before.

Gratefulness

...I THINK we honour God more if we gratefully accept the life that he gives us with all its blessings, loving it and drinking it to the full, and also grieving deeply and sincerely when we have impaired or wasted any of the good things of life (some people denounce such an attitude, and think it is bourgeois, weak, and sensitive), than if we are insensitive to life's blessings and may therefore also be insensitive to pain. Job's words, 'The Lord gave etc. . . .' include rather than exclude this, as can be seen clearly enough from his teeth-clenching speeches which were vindicated by God (42:7ff.) in face of the false, premature, pious submission of his friends. . . .

Deputyship

THE FACT that responsibility is fundamentally a matter of deputyship is demonstrated most clearly in those circumstances in which a man is directly obliged to act in the place of other men, for example as a father, as a statesman or as a teacher. The father acts for the children, working for them, caring for them, interceding, fighting and suffering for them. Thus in a real sense he is their deputy. He is not an isolated individual, but he combines in himself the selves of a number of human beings. Any attempt to live as though he were alone is a denial of the actual fact of his responsibility. He cannot evade the responsibility which is laid on him with his paternity. This reality shatters the fiction that the subject, the performer, of all ethical conduct is the isolated individual. Not the individual in isolation but the responsible man is the subject, the agent, with whom ethical reflexion must concern itself. This principle is not affected by the extent of the responsibility assumed, whether it be for a single human being, for a community or for whole groups of communities. No man can altogether escape responsibility, and this means that no man can avoid deputyship. Even the solitary lives as a deputy, and indeed quite especially so, for his life is lived in deputyship for man as man, for mankind as a whole. And, in fact, the concept of responsibility for oneself possesses a meaning only in so far as it refers to the responsibility which I bear with respect to myself as a man, that is to say, because I am a man. Responsibility for oneself is in truth responsibility with respect to the man, and that means responsibility with respect to mankind. The fact that Jesus lived without the special responsibility of a marriage, of a family or of a profession, does not by any means set Him outside the field of responsibility; on the contrary, it makes all the clearer His responsibility and His deputyship for all men. Here we come already to the underlying basis of everything that has been said so far. Jesus, life, our life, lived in deputyship for us as the incarnate Son of God, and that is why through Him all human life is in essence a life of deputyship. Jesus was not the individual, desiring to achieve a perfection of his own, but He lived only as the one who has taken up into Himself and who bears within Himself the selves of all men. All His living, His action and His dying was deputyship. In Him there is fulfilled what the living, the action and the suffering of men ought to be. In this real deputyship which constitutes His human existence He is the responsible person *par excellence.* Because He is life all life is determined by Him to be deputyship. Whether or not life resists, it is now always deputyship, for life or for death, just as the father is always a father, for good or for evil.

Lust

What does the Bible say about the lust of men as the author of their temptation? "Let no man say when he is tempted, I am tempted of God: for God cannot be tempted with evil, and he himself tempteth no man: but each man is tempted, when he is drawn away by his own lust, and enticed. Then the lust, when it hath conceived, beareth sin: and the sin, when it is fullgrown, bringeth forth death" (James 1:31ff.).

First, he who transfers the guilt of the temptation to someone other than himself, thereby justifies his fall. If I am not guilty in my temptation, neither am I guilty when I perish in it. Temptation is guilt in so far as the fall is inexcusable. It is therefore impossible to put the guilt of temptation on to the devil; then all the more is it a blasphemy to make God answerable for it. It may appear pious, but in truth the statement implies that God is himself in some way open to evil. This would attribute division to God, which makes his Word and his will questionable, ambiguous, doubtful. Since evil has no place in God, not even the possibility of evil, temptation to evil must never be laid at God's door. God himself tempts no one. The source of temptation lies in my own self. Secondly, temptation is punishment. The place in which all temptation originates is my evil desires. My own longing for pleasure, and my fear of suffering, entice me to let go the Word of God. The hereditary depraved nature of the flesh is the source of the evil inclinations of body and soul, as are men and things, which now become temptation. Neither the beauty of the world, nor suffering, are in themselves evil and tempting, but our evil desires which win pleasure from all this and which let themselves be suborned and enticed, turn all this into temptation for us. While in the devilish origin of temptation the objectivity of temptation must become clear, here its complete subjectivity is emphasized. Both are equally necessary.

Thirdly, desire in itself does not make me sinful. But "when it hath conceived, it beareth sin, and the sin, when it is fullgrown, bringeth forth death." Desire conceives by the union of my "I" with it—when I abandon the Word of God which upholds me. As long as desire remains untouched by my self, it is an "It." But sin occurs only through the "I." Thus the source of temptation lies in the ἐπιθυμία, the source of sin is in myself, and in my self alone. Therefore I must acknowledge that mine alone is the guilt and that I deserve eternal death when in temptation I succumb to sin. Jesus indeed pronounces a terrible judgement on him who tempts the innocent, who offends one of the little ones; "Woe unto him who tempts another to sin"—that is what the Word of God says about every tempter. But yours alone is the guilt in your sin and your death, if you submit to the temptation of your desire. That is God's Word to the tempted.

Shame

INSTEAD OF SEEING GOD man sees himself. 'Their eyes were opened' (Gen. 3:7). Man perceives himself in his disunion with God and with men. He perceives that he is naked. Lacking the protection, the covering, which God and his fellow-man afforded him, he finds himself laid bare. Hence there arises shame. Shame is man's ineffaceable recollection of his estrangement from the origin; it is grief for this estrangement, and the powerless longing to return to unity with the origin. Man is ashamed because he has lost something which is essential to his original character, to himself as a whole; he is ashamed of his nakedness. Just as in the fairy-story the tree is ashamed of its lack of adornment, so, too, man is ashamed of the loss of his unity with God and with other men. Shame and remorse are generally mistaken for one another. Man feels remorse when he has been at fault; and he feels shame because he lacks something. Shame is more original than remorse. The peculiar fact that we lower our eyes when a stranger's eye meets our gaze is not a sign of remorse for a fault, but a sign of that shame which, when it knows that it is seen, is reminded of something that it lacks, namely, the lost wholeness of life, its own nakedness. To meet a stranger's gaze directly, as is required, for example, in making a declaration of personal loyalty, is a kind of act of violence, and in love, when the gaze of the other is sought, it is a kind of yearning. In both cases it is the painful endeavour to recover the lost unity by either a conscious and resolute or else a passionate and devoted inward overcoming of shame as the sign of disunion.[1]

[1]'Shame isn't spontaneous. . .it's artificial, it's acquired. You can make people ashamed of anything. Agonizingly ashamed of wearing brown boots with a black coat, or speaking with the wrong sort of accent. . . . The Christians invented it, just as the tailors in Savile Row invented the shame of wearing brown boots with a black coat' (Aldous Huxley, *Point Counter Point*, chapter x). To this it must be replied that first, embarrassment and diffidence are not to be confused with shame, and, secondly, shame may also find expression in quite external matters in a way which will depend on the character of the individual. The point is that shame may arise wherever there is experience of man's disunion—so why not also in connexion with dress?

Desire

IN OUR MEMBERS there is a slumbering inclination towards desire which is both sudden and fierce. With irresistible power desire seizes mastery over the flesh. All at once a secret, smouldering fire is kindled. The flesh burns and is in flames. It makes no difference whether it is sexual desire, or ambition, or vanity, or desire for revenge, or love of fame and power, or greed for money, or, finally, that strange desire for the beauty of the world, of nature. Joy in God is in course of being extinguished in us and we seek all our joy in the creature. At this moment God is quite unreal to us, he loses all reality, and only desire for the creature is real; the only reality is the devil. Satan does not here fill us with hatred of God, but with forgetfulness of God. And now his falsehood is added to this proof of strength. The lust thus aroused envelops the mind and will of man in deepest darkness. The powers of clear discrimination and of decision are taken from us. The questions present themselves: "Is what the flesh desires really sin in this case?" "Is it really not permitted to me, yes—expected of me, now, here, in my particular situation, to appease desire?" The tempter puts me in a privileged position as he tried to put the hungry Son of God in a privileged position. I boast of my privilege against God.

It is here that everything within me rises up against the Word of God. Powers of the body, the mind and the will, which were held in obedience under the discipline of the Word, of which I believed that I was the master, make it clear to me that I am by no means master of them. "All my powers forsake me," laments the psalmist. They have all gone over to the adversary. The adversary deploys my powers against me. In this situation I can no longer act as a hero; I am a defenceless, powerless man. God himself has forsaken me. Who can conquer, who can gain the victory?

None other than the Crucified, Jesus Christ himself, for whose sake all this happens to me; for he is by me and in me, and therefore temptation besets me as it beset him.

Conscience

JESUS CHRIST has become my conscience. This means that I can now find unity with myself only in the surrender of my ego to God and to men. The origin and the goal of my conscience is not a law but it is the living God and the living man as he confronts me in Jesus Christ. For the sake of God and of men Jesus became a breaker of the law. He broke the law of the Sabbath in order to keep it holy in love for God and for men. He forsook His parents in order to dwell in the house of His Father and thereby to purify His obedience towards His parents. He sat at table with sinners and outcasts; and for the love of men He came to be forsaken by God in His last hour. As the one who loved without sin, He became guilty; He wished to share in the fellowship of human guilt; He rejected the devil's accusation which was intended to divert Him from this course. Thus it is Jesus Christ who sets conscience free for the service of God and of our neighbour; He sets conscience free even and especially when man enters into the fellowship of human guilt. The conscience which has been set free from the law will not be afraid to enter into the guilt of another man for the other man's sake, and indeed precisely in doing this it will show itself in its purity. The conscience which has been set free is not timid like the conscience which is bound by the law, but it stands wide open for our neighbour and for his concrete distress. And so conscience joins with the responsibility which has its foundation in Christ in bearing guilt for the sake of our neighbour. Human action is poisoned in a way which differs from essential original sin, yet as responsible action, in contrast to any self-righteously high-principled action, it nevertheless indirectly has a part in the action of Jesus Christ. For responsible action, therefore, there is a kind of relative freedom from sin, and this shows itself precisely in the responsible acceptance of the guilt of others.

Humanity and Goodness

...WHATEVER HUMANITY and goodness is found in this fallen world must be on the side of Jesus Christ. It is nothing less than a curtailment of the gospel if the nearness of Jesus Christ is proclaimed only to what is broken and evil and if the father's love for the prodigal son is so emphasized as to appear to diminish his love for the son who remained at home. Certainly the humanity and goodness of which we are speaking are not the humanity and goodness of Jesus Christ; they cannot stand before the judgement; and yet Jesus loved the young man who had kept the commandments (Mark 10:17ff.). Humanity and goodness should not acquire a value on their own account, but they should and shall be claimed for Jesus Christ, especially in cases where they persist as the unconscious residue of a former attachment to the ultimate. It may often seem more in earnest to treat a man in this situation simply as a non-Christian and to urge him to confess his unbelief. But it will be more Christian to claim precisely that man as a Christian who would himself no longer dare to call himself a Christian, and then with much patience to help him to the profession of faith in Christ.

The Pharisee

IT IS IN JESUS' MEETING with the Pharisee that the old and the new are most clearly contrasted. The correct understanding of this meeting is of the greatest significance for the understanding of the gospel as a whole. The Pharisee is not an adventitious historical phenomenon of a particular time. He is the man to whom only the knowledge of good and evil has come to be of importance in his entire life; in other words, he is simply the man of disunion. Any distorted picture of the Pharisees robs Jesus' argument with them of its gravity and its importance. The Pharisee is that extremely admirable man who subordinates his entire life to his knowledge of good and evil and is as severe a judge of himself as of his neighbour to the honour of God, whom he humbly thanks for this knowledge. For the Pharisee every moment of life becomes a situation of conflict in which he has to choose between good and evil. For the sake of avoiding any lapse his entire thought is strenuously devoted night and day to the anticipation of the whole immense range of possible conflicts, to the reaching of a decision in these conflicts, and to the determination of his own choice. There are innumerable factors to be observed, guarded against and distinguished. The finer the distinctions the surer will be the correct decision. This observation extends to the whole of life in all its manifold aspects. The Pharisee is not opinionated; special situations and emergencies receive special considerations; forbearance and generosity are not excluded by the gravity of the knowledge of good and evil; they are rather an expression of this gravity. And there is no rash presumption here, or arrogance or unverified self-esteem. The Pharisee is fully conscious of his own faults and of his duty of humility and thankfulness towards God. But, of course, there are differences, which for God's sake must not be disregarded, between the sinner and the man who strives towards good, between the man who becomes a breaker of the law out of a situation of wickedness and the man who does so out of necessity. If anyone disregards these differences, if he fails to take every factor into account in each of the innumerable cases of conflict, he sins against the knowledge of good and evil.

Judgement

'JUDGE NOT, that ye be not judged' (Matt. 7:1). This is not an exhortation to prudence and forbearance in passing judgement on one's fellow-men, such as was also recognized by the Pharisees. It is a blow struck at the heart of the man who knows good and evil. It is the word of Him who speaks by virtue of his unity with God, who came not to condemn but to save (John 3:17). For man in the state of disunion good consists in passing judgement, and the ultimate criterion is man himself. Knowing good and evil, man is essentially a judge. As a judge he is like God, except that every judgement he delivers falls back upon himself. In attacking man as a judge Jesus is demanding the conversion of his entire being, and He shows that precisely in the extreme realization of his good he is ungodly and a sinner. Jesus demands that the knowledge of good and evil be overcome; He demands unity with God. Judgement passed on another man always presupposes disunion with him; it is an obstacle to action. But the good of which Jesus speaks consists entirely in action and not in judgement. Judging the other man always means a break in one's own activity. The man who judges never acts himself; or, alternatively, whatever action of his own he may be able to show, and sometimes indeed there is plenty of it, is never more than judgement, condemnation, reproaches and accusations against other men....

Single-minded Love

WHEN WE JUDGE other people we confront them in a spirit of detachment, observing and reflecting as it were from the outside. But love has neither time nor opportunity for this. If we love, we can never observe the other person with detachment, for he is always and at every moment a living claim to our love and service. But does not the evil in the other person make me condemn him just for his own good, for the sake of love? Here we see the depth of the dividing line. Any misguided love for the sinner is ominously close to the love of sin. But the love of Christ for the sinner in itself is the condemnation of sin, is his expression of extreme hatred of sin. The disciples of Christ are to love unconditionally. Thus they may effect what their own divided and judiciously and conditionally offered love never could achieve, namely the radical condemnation of sin.

If the disciples make judgements of their own, they set up standards of good and evil. But Jesus Christ is not a standard which I can apply to others. He is judge of myself, revealing my own virtues to me as something altogether evil. Thus I am not permitted to apply to the other person what does not apply to me. For, with my judgement according to good and evil, I only affirm the other person's evil, for he does exactly the same. But he does not know of the hidden iniquity of the good but seeks his justification in it. If I condemn his evil actions I thereby confirm him in his apparently good actions which are yet never the good commended by Christ. Thus we remove him from the judgement of Christ and subject him to human judgement. But I bring God's judgement upon my head, for I then do not live any more on and out of the grace of Jesus Christ, but out of my knowledge of good and evil which I hold on to. To everyone God is the kind of God he believes in.

Judgement is the forbidden objectivization of the other person which destroys single-minded love. I am not forbidden to have my own thoughts about the other person, to realize his shortcomings, but only to the extent that it offers to me an occasion for forgiveness and unconditional love, as Jesus proves to me. If I withhold my judgement I am not indulging in *tout comprendre c'est tout pardonner* and confirm the other person in his bad ways. Neither I am right nor the other person, but God is always right and shall proclaim both his grace and his judgement....

The Concept of Reality

Whoever wishes to take up the problem of a Christian ethic must be confronted at once with a demand which is quite without parallel. He must from the outset discard as irrelevant the two questions which alone impel him to concern himself with the problem of ethics, 'How can I be good?' and 'How can I do good?', and instead of these he must ask the utterly and totally different question 'What is the will of God?' This requirement is so immensely far-reaching because it presupposes a decision with regard to the ultimate reality; it presupposes a decision of faith. If the ethical problem presents itself essentially in the form of enquiries about one's own being good and doing good, this means that it has already been decided that it is the self and the world which are the ultimate reality. The aim of all ethical reflection is, then, that I myself shall be good and that the world shall become good through my action. But the problem of ethics at once assumes a new aspect if it becomes apparent that these realities, myself and the world, themselves lie embedded in a quite different ultimate reality, namely, the reality of God, the Creator, Reconciler and Redeemer. What is of ultimate importance is now no longer that I should become good, or that the condition of the world should be made better by my action, but that the reality of God should show itself everywhere to be the ultimate reality. Where there is faith in God as the ultimate reality, all concern with ethics will have as its starting-point that God shows Himself to be good, even if this involves the risk that I myself and the world are not good but thoroughly bad. All things appear distorted if they are not seen and recognized in God. All so-called data, all laws and standards, are mere abstractions so long as there is no belief in God as the ultimate reality. But when we say that God is the ultimate reality, this is not an idea, through which the world as we have it is to be sublimated. It is not the religious rounding-off of a profane conception of the universe. It is the acceptance in faith of God's showing forth of Himself, the acceptance of His revelation. If God were merely a religious idea there would be nothing to prevent us from discerning, behind this allegedly 'ultimate' reality, a still more final reality, the twilight of the gods and the death of the gods. The claim of this ultimate reality is satisfied only in so far as it is revelation, that is to say, the self-witness of the living God. When this is so, the relation to this reality determines the whole of life. The apprehension of this reality is not merely a gradual advance towards the discovery of ever more profound realities; it is the crucial turning-point in the apprehension of reality as a whole. The ultimate reality now shows itself to be at the same time the initial reality, the first and last, alpha and omega. Any perception or apprehension of things or laws without Him is now abstraction, detachment from the origin and goal. Any enquiry about one's own goodness, or the goodness of the world, is now impossible unless enquiry has first been made about the goodness of God. For without God what meaning could there be in a goodness of man and a goodness of the world? But God as the ultimate reality is no other than He who shows forth, manifests and reveals Himself, that is to say, God in Jesus Christ, and from this it follows that the question of good can find its answer only in Christ.

Divine Reality

THE PROBLEM of Christian ethics is the realization among God's creatures of the revelational reality of God in Christ, just as the problem of dogmatics is the truth of the revelational reality of God in Christ. The place which in all other ethics is occupied by the antithesis of 'should be' and 'is', idea and accomplishment, motive and performance, is occupied in Christian ethics by the relation of reality and realization, past and present, history and event (faith), or, to replace the equivocal concept by the unambiguous name, the relation of Jesus Christ and the

Holy Spirit. The question of good becomes the question of participation in the divine reality which is revealed in Christ. Good is now no longer a valuation of what is, a valuation, for example, of my own being, my outlook or my actions, or of some condition or state in the world. It is no longer a predicate that is assigned to something which is in itself in being. Good is the real itself. It is not the real in the abstract, the real which is detached from the reality of God, but the real which possesses reality only in God. There is no good without the real, for the good is not a general formula, and the real is impossible without the good. The wish to be good consists solely in the longing for what is real in God. A desire to be good for its own sake, as an end in itself, so to speak, or as a vocation in life, falls victim to the irony of unreality. The genuine striving for good now becomes the self-assertiveness of the prig. Good is not in itself an independent theme for life; if it were so it would be the craziest kind of quixotry. Only if we share in reality can we share in good.

The Reality of God

...CHRISTIAN BELIEF deduces that the reality of God is not in itself merely an idea from the fact that this reality of God has manifested and revealed itself in the midst of the real world. In Jesus Christ the reality of God entered into the reality of this world. The place where the answer is given, both to the question concerning the reality of God and to the question concerning the reality of the world, is designated solely and alone by the name Jesus Christ. God and the world are comprised in this name. In Him all things consist (Col. 1:17). Henceforward one can speak neither of God nor of the world without speaking of Jesus Christ. All concepts of reality which do not take account of Him are abstractions. When good has become reality in Jesus Christ, there is no more force in any discussion of good which plays off what should be against what is and what is against what should be. Jesus Christ cannot be identified either with an ideal or standard or with things as they are. The hostility of the ideal towards things as they are, the fanatical putting into effect of an idea in the face of a resisting actuality, may be as remote from good as is the sacrifice of what should be to what is expedient. Both what should be and what is expedient acquire in Christ an entirely new meaning. The irreconcilable conflict between what is and what should be is reconciled in Christ, that is to say, in the ultimate reality. Participation in this reality is the true sense and purpose of the enquiry concerning good.

In Christ we are offered the possibility of partaking in the reality of God and in the reality of the world, but not in the one without the other. The reality of God discloses itself only by setting me entirely in the reality of the world, and when I encounter the reality of the world it is always already sustained, accepted and reconciled in the reality of God. This is the inner meaning of the revelation of God in the man Jesus Christ. Christian ethics enquires about the realization in our world of this divine and cosmic reality which is given in Christ. This does not mean that 'our world' is something outside the divine and cosmic reality which is in Christ, or that it is not already part of the world which is sustained, accepted and reconciled in Him. It does not mean that one must still begin by applying some kind of 'principle' to our situation and our time. The enquiry is directed rather towards the way in which the reality in Christ, which for a long time already has comprised us and our world within itself, is taking effect as something now present, and towards the way in which life may be conducted in this reality. Its purpose is, therefore, participation in the reality of God and of the world in Jesus Christ today, and this participation must be such that I never experience the reality of God without the reality of the world or the reality of the world without the reality of God.

The Reality of Jesus Christ

...THERE IS NO PLACE to which the Christian can withdraw from the world, whether it be outwardly or in the sphere of the inner life. Any attempt to escape from the world must sooner or later be paid for with a sinful surrender to the world. It is after all a matter of experience that when the gross sins of sex have been overcome they are succeeded by covetousness and avarice, which are equally gross sins even though the world may treat them less severely. The cultivation of a Christian inner life, untouched by the world, will generally present a somewhat tragicomical appearance to the worldly observer. For the sharp-sighted world recognizes itself most distinctly at the very point where the Christian inner life deceives itself in the belief that the world is most remote. Whoever professes to believe in the reality of Jesus Christ, as the revelation of God, must in the same breath profess his faith in both the reality of God and the reality of the world; for in Christ he finds God and the world reconciled. And for just this reason the Christian is no longer the man of eternal conflict, but, just as the reality in Christ is one, so he, too, since he shares in this reality in Christ, is himself an undivided whole. His worldliness does not divide him from Christ and his Christianity does not divide him from the world. Belonging wholly to Christ, he stands at the same time wholly in the world.

Christ, Reality and Good

CHRIST AND HIS ADVERSARY, the devil, are mutually exclusive contraries; yet the devil must serve Christ even against his will; he desires evil, but over and over again he is compelled to do good; so that the realm or space of the devil is always only beneath the feet of Jesus Christ. But if the kingdom of the devil is taken to mean that world which 'lies in disorder', the world which has fallen under the devil's authority, then here, especially, there is a limit to the possibility of thinking in terms of spheres. For it is precisely this 'disordered' world that in Christ is reconciled with God and that now possesses its final and true reality not in the devil but in Christ. The world is not divided between Christ and the devil, but, whether it recognizes it or not, it is solely and entirely the world of Christ. The world is to be called to this, its reality in Christ, and in this way the false reality will be destroyed which it believes that it possesses in itself as in the devil. The dark and evil world must not be abandoned to the devil. It must be claimed for Him who has won it by His incarnation, His death and His resurrection. Christ gives up nothing of what He has won. He holds it fast in His hands. It is Christ, therefore, who renders inadmissible the dichotomy of a bedevilled and a Christian world. Any static delimitation of a region which belongs to the devil and a region which belongs to Christ is a denial of the reality of God's having reconciled the whole world with Himself in Christ.

That God loved the world and reconciled it with Himself in Christ is the central message proclaimed in the New Testament. It is assumed there that the world stands in need of reconciliation with God but that it is not capable of achieving it by itself. The acceptance of the world by God is a miracle of the divine compassion. For this reason the relation of the Church to the world is determined entirely by the relation of God to the world. There is a love for the world which is enmity towards God (Jas. 4:4) because it springs from the nature of the world as such and not from the love of God for the world. The world 'as such' is the world as it understands itself, the world which resists and even rejects the reality of the love of God which is bestowed upon it in Jesus Christ. This world has fallen under the sentence which God passes on all enmity to Christ. It is engaged in a life-and-death struggle with the Church. And yet it is the task and the essential character of the Church that she shall impart to precisely this world its reconciliation with God and that she shall open its eyes to the reality of the love of God, against which it is blindly raging. In this way it is also, and indeed especially, the lost and sentenced world that is incessantly drawn in into the event of Christ.

What Is Meant By 'Telling the Truth'?

FROM THE MOMENT IN OUR LIVES at which we learn to speak we are taught that what we say must be true. What does

Editor's note: Written after intensive interrogation.

this mean? What is meant by 'telling the truth'? What does it demand of us?

It is clear that in the first place it is our parents who regulate our relation to themselves by this demand for truthfulness; consequently, in the sense in which our parents intend it, this demand applies strictly only within the family circle. It is also to be noted that the relation which is expressed in this demand cannot simply be reversed. The truthfulness of a child towards his parents is essentially different from that of the parents towards their child. The life of the small child lies open before the parents, and what the child says should reveal to them everything that is hidden and secret, but in the converse relationship this cannot possibly be the case. Consequently, in the matter of truthfulness, the parents' claim on the child is different from the child's claim on the parents.

From this it emerges already that 'telling the truth' means something different according to the particular situation in which one stands. Account must be taken of one's relationships at each particular time. The question must be asked whether and in what way a man is entitled to demand truthful speech of others. Speech between parents and children is, in the nature of the case, different from speech between man and wife, between friends, between teacher and pupil, government and subject, friend and foe, and in each case the truth which this speech conveys is also different.

It will at once be objected that one does not owe truthful speech to this or that individual man, but solely to God. This objection is correct so long as it is not forgotten that God is not a general principle, but the living God who has set me in a living life and who demands service of me within this living life. If one speaks of God one must not simply disregard the actual given world in which one lives; for if one does that one is not speaking of the God who entered into the world in Jesus Christ, but rather of some metaphysical idol. And it is precisely this which is determined by the way in which, in my actual concrete life with all its manifold relationships, I give effect to the truthfulness which I owe to God. The truthfulness which we owe to God must assume a concrete form in the world. Our speech must be truthful, not in principle but concretely. A truthfulness which is not concrete is not truthful before God.

Satanic Truth

THERE IS A TRUTH which is of Satan. Its essence is that under the semblance of truth it denies everything that is real. It lives upon hatred of the real and of the world which is created and loved by God. It pretends to be executing the judgement of God upon the fall of the real. God's truth judges created things out of love, and Satan's truth judges them out of envy and hatred. God's truth has become flesh in the world and is alive in the real, but Satan's truth is the death of all reality.

Who Am I?

WHO AM I? They often tell me
I would step from my cell's confinement
calmly, cheerfully, firmly,
like a squire from his country-house.

Who am I? They often tell me
I would talk to my warders
freely and friendly and clearly,
as though it were mine to command.

Who am I? They also tell me
I would bear the days of misfortune
equably, smilingly, proudly,
like one accustomed to win.

Am I then really all that which other men tell of?
Or am I only what I know of myself,
restless and longing and sick, like a bird in a cage,
struggling for breath, as though hands were compres-
    sing my throat,
yearning for colours, for flowers, for the voices of
    birds,
thirsting for words of kindness, for neighbourliness,
trembling with anger at despotisms and petty
    humiliation,
tossing in expectation of great events,
powerlessly trembling for friends at an infinite
    distance,

weary and empty at praying, at thinking, at making,
faint, and ready to say farewell to it all?

Who am I? This or the other?
Am I one person today, and tomorrow another?
Am I both at once? A hypocrite before others,
and before myself a contemptibly woebegone
   weakling?
Or is something within me still like a beaten army,
fleeing in disorder from victory already achieved?

Who am I? They mock me, these lonely questions of
   mine.
Whoever I am, thou knowest, O God, I am thine.

Our Lives

...I THINK it is a literal fact of nature that human life
extends far beyond our physical existence. Probably a
mother feels this more strongly than anyone else. There
are two passages in the Bible which always seem to me to
sum the thing up. One is from Jeremiah 45: 'Behold, what
I have built I am breaking down, and what I have planted I
am plucking up...And do you seek great things for
yourself? Seek them not...but I will give your life as a
prize of war...'; and the other is from Psalm 60: 'Thou
hast made the land to quake, thou hast rent it open; repair
its breaches, for it totters.'

Freedom from Anxiety

(MATTHEW 6:25–34)

BE NOT ANXIOUS! Earthly possessions dazzle our eyes and delude us into thinking that they can provide security and freedom from anxiety. Yet all the time they are the very source of all anxiety. If our hearts are set on them, our reward is an anxiety whose burden is intolerable. Anxiety creates its own treasures and they in turn beget further care. When we seek for security in possessions we are trying to drive out care with care, and the net result is the precise opposite of our anticipations. The fetters which bind us to our possessions prove to be cares themselves.

The way to misuse our possessions is to use them as an insurance against the morrow. Anxiety is always directed to the morrow, whereas goods are in the strictest sense meant to be used only for to-day. By trying to ensure for the next day we are only creating uncertainty to-day. Sufficient unto the day is the evil thereof. The only way to win assurance is by leaving to-morrow entirely in the hands of God and by receiving from him all we need for to-day. If instead of receiving God's gifts for to-day we worry about to-morrow, we find ourselves helpless victims of infinite anxiety. "Be not anxious for the morrow": either that is cruel mockery for the poor and wretched, the very people Jesus is talking to who, humanly speaking, really will starve if they do not make provision to-day. Either it is an intolerable law, which men will reject with indignation; or it is the unique proclamation of the gospel of the glorious liberty of the children of God, who have a Father in heaven, a Father who has given his beloved Son. How shall not God with him also freely give us all things?

"Be not anxious for the morrow." This is not to be taken as a philosophy of life or a moral law: it is the gospel of Jesus Christ, and only so can it be understood. Only those who follow him and know him can receive this word as a promise of the love of his Father and as a deliverance from the thraldom of material things. It is not care that frees the disciples from care, but their faith in Jesus Christ. Only they know that we *cannot* be anxious (verse 27). The coming day, even the coming hour, are placed beyond our control. It is senseless to pretend that we can make provision because we cannot alter the circumstances of this world. Only God can take care, for it is he who rules the world. Since we *cannot* take care, since we are so completely powerless, we *ought* not to do it either. If we do, we are dethroning God and presuming to rule the world ourselves.

But the Christian also knows that he not only cannot and dare not be anxious, but that there is also no need for him to be so. Neither anxiety nor work can secure his daily bread, for bread is the gift of the Father. The birds and lilies neither toil nor spin, yet both are fed and clothed and receive their daily portion without being anxious for them. They need earthly goods only for their daily sustenance, and they do not lay up a store for the future. This is the way they glorify their Creator, not by their industry, toil or care, but by a daily unquestioning acceptance of his gifts. Birds and lilies then are an example for the followers of Christ. "Man-in-revolt" imagines that there is a relation of cause and effect between work and sustenance, but Jesus explodes that illusion. According to him, bread is not to be valued as the reward for work; he speaks instead of the carefree simplicity of the man who walks with him and accepts everything as it comes from God.

. . . Worldly cares are not a part of our discipleship, but distinct and subordinate concerns. Before we start taking thought for our life, our food and clothing, our work and families, we must seek the righteousness of Christ. This is no more than an ultimate summing up of all that has been said before. Again we have here either a crushing burden, which holds out no hope for the poor and wretched, or else it is the quintessence of the gospel, which brings the promise of freedom and perfect joy. Jesus does not tell us what we ought to do but cannot; he tells us what God has given us and promises still to give. If Christ has been given us, if we are called to his discipleship we are given all things, literally *all* things. He will see to it that they are added unto us. If we follow Jesus and look only to his righteousness, we are in his hands and under the protection of him and his Father. And if we are in communion with the Father, nought can harm us. We shall always be assured that he can feed his children and will not suffer them to hunger. God will help us in the hour of need, and he knows our needs.

After he has been following Christ for a long time, the disciple of Jesus will be asked "Lacked ye anything?" and he will answer "Nothing, Lord." How could he when he knows that despite hunger and nakedness, persecution and danger, the Lord is always at his side?

Are We Still of Any Use?

WE HAVE BEEN SILENT witnesses of evil deeds; we have been drenched by many storms; we have learnt the arts of equivocation and pretence; experience has made us suspicious of others and kept us from being truthful and open; intolerable conflicts have worn us down and even made us cynical. Are we still of any use? What we shall need is not geniuses, or cynics, or misanthropes, or clever tacticians, but plain, honest, straightforward men. Will our inward power of resistance be strong enough, and our honesty with ourselves remorseless enough, for us to find our way back to simplicity and straightforwardness?

Who Stands Fast?

THE GREAT MASQUERADE of evil has played havoc with all our ethical concepts. For evil to appear disguised as light, charity, historical necessity, or social justice is quite bewildering to anyone brought up on our traditional ethical concepts, while for the Christian who bases his life on the Bible it merely confirms the fundamental wickedness of evil.

The *'reasonable'* people's failure is obvious. With the best intentions and a naïve lack of realism, they think that with a little reason they can bend back into position the framework that has got out of joint. In their lack of vision they want to do justice to all sides, and so the conflicting forces wear them down with nothing achieved. Disappointed by the world's unreasonableness, they see themselves condemned to ineffectiveness; they step aside in resignation or collapse before the stronger party.

Still more pathetic is the total collapse of moral *fanaticism*. The fanatic thinks that his single-minded principles qualify him to do battle with the powers of evil; but like a bull he rushes at the red cloak instead of the person who is holding it; he exhausts himself and is beaten. He gets entangled in non-essentials and falls into the trap set by cleverer people.

Then there is the man with a *conscience*, who fights single-handed against heavy odds in situations that call for a decision. But the scale of the conflicts in which he has to choose—with no advice or support except from his own conscience—tears him to pieces. Evil approaches him in so many respectable and seductive disguises that his conscience becomes nervous and vacillating, till at last he contents himself with a salved instead of a clear conscience, so that he lies to his own conscience in order to avoid despair; for a man whose only support is his conscience can never realize that a bad conscience may be stronger and more wholesome than a deluded one.

From the perplexingly large number of possible decisions, the way of *duty* seems to be the sure way out. Here, what is commanded is accepted as what is most certain, and the responsibility for it rests on the commander, not on the person commanded. But no one who confines himself to the limits of duty ever goes so far as to venture, on his sole responsibility, to act in the only way that makes it possible to score a direct hit on evil and defeat it. The man of duty will in the end have to do his duty by the devil too.

As to the man who asserts his complete *freedom* to stand four-square to the world, who values the necessary deed more highly than an unspoilt conscience or reputation, who is ready to sacrifice a barren principle for a fruitful compromise, or the barren wisdom of a middle course for a fruitful radicalism—let him beware lest his freedom should bring him down. He will assent to what is bad so as to ward off something worse, and in doing so he will no longer be able to realize that the worse, which he wants to avoid, might be the better. Here we have the raw material of tragedy.

Here and there people flee from public altercation into the sanctuary of private *virtuousness*. But anyone who does this must shut his mouth and his eyes to the injustice around him. Only at the cost of self-deception can he keep himself pure from the contamination arising from responsible action. In spite of all that he does, what he leaves undone will rob him of his peace of mind. He will either go to pieces because of this disquiet, or become the most hypocritical of Pharisees.

Who stands fast? Only the man whose final standard is not his reason, his principles, his conscience, his freedom, or his virtue, but who is ready to sacrifice all this when he is called to obedient and responsible action in faith and in exclusive allegiance to God—the responsible man, who tries to make his whole life an answer to the question and call of God. Where are these responsible people?

The Taking Over of the Temptations

By the temptation of Jesus Christ the temptation of Adam is brought to an end. As in Adam's temptation all flesh fell, so in the temptation of Jesus Christ all flesh has been snatched away from the power of Satan. For Jesus Christ wore our flesh, he suffered our temptation, and he won the victory from it. Thus today we all wear the flesh which in Jesus Christ vanquished Satan. Both our flesh and we have conquered in the temptation of Jesus. Because Christ was tempted and overcame, we can pray: Lead us not into temptation. For the temptation has already come and been conquered. He did it in our stead. "Look on the temptation of thy Son Jesus Christ and lead *us* not into temptation." Of the granting of that prayer we may and should be certain; we should utter our amen to it, for it *is* granted in Jesus Christ himself. From henceforth *we* shall no longer be led into temptation, but every temptation which happens now is the temptation of Jesus Christ in his members, in his congregation. We are not tempted, *Jesus Christ is tempted in us.*

Because Satan could not bring about the fall of the Son of God, he pursues him now with all temptations in his members. But these last temptations are only the offshoots of the temptation of Jesus on earth; for the power of temptation is broken in the temptation of Jesus. His disciples are to let themselves be found in this temptation, and then the kingdom is assured to them. It is the fundamental word of Jesus to all his disciples. "But ye are they which have continued with me in my temptations, and I appoint unto you a kingdom" (Luke 22:28f.). It is not the temptations of the *disciples* which here receive the promise, but their participation in the life and the temptation of Jesus. The temptations of the disciples fall on *Jesus,* and the temptations of Jesus come upon the disciples. But to share in the atonement of Christ means to share also in Christ's overcoming and victory. It does not mean that the temptations of Christ had finished and that the disciples would no longer suffer them. They will indeed suffer temptations, but it will be the temptations of Jesus Christ which befall them. Christ has also won the victory over these temptations.

It is by the disciples sharing in the temptation of Jesus Christ that Jesus will protect his disciples from other temptation: "Watch and pray, that ye enter not into temptation" (Matt. 26:41). What temptation threatened the disciples in the hour of Gethsemane, if it was not that they should be offended at the passion of Christ, and they would not share in his temptations? So Jesus uses here the petition of the Lord's Prayer: "Lead us not into temptation." Finally, it is the same thing when it says in Hebrews 2:18: "For in that he himself hath suffered being tempted, he is able to succour them that are tempted." This is not only a question of the help which he alone can give who has learnt to know the need and suffering of the other man in his own experience. The true meaning is rather that in my temptations my real succour is only in his temptation; to share in his temptation is the only help in my temptation. Thus I ought not to think of my temptation other than as the temptation of Jesus Christ. In his temptation is my succour; for here only is victory and overcoming.

The practical task of the Christian must, therefore, be to understand all the temptations which come upon him as temptations of Jesus Christ in him, and thus he will be aided. But how does it happen? Before we can speak of the concrete temptations of Christians and their overcoming, the question of the author of the temptation of Christians must be put. Only when the Christian knows with whom he has to do in temptation, can he act rightly in the actual event.

Concrete Temptations and Their Conquest

IN THE CONCRETE TEMPTATION of Christ there is also, therefore, to be distinguished the hand of the devil and the hand of God, there is the question of resistance and of submission in the right place; that is, resistance to the devil is only possible in the fullest submission to the hand of God.

This must now be made clear in detail. Since all temptations of believers are temptations of Christ in his members, of the body of Christ, we speak of these temptations in the analogy of the temptation of Christ. (1)

Of fleshly temptation. (2) Of high spiritual temptation. (3) Of the last temptation. But I Cor. 10:12ff. is true of all temptations: "Wherefore let him that thinketh he standeth take heed lest he fall. There hath no temptation taken you but such as man can bear: but God is faithful, who will not suffer you to be tempted above that ye are able; but will with the temptation make also the way of escape, that ye may be able to endure it." Here St. Paul opposes first all false security and, secondly, all false despondency in face of temptation. No one can be sure even for a moment that he can remain free from temptation. There is no temptation which could not attack me suddenly at this moment. No one can think that Satan is far from him. "Be sober, be watchful: your adversary the devil, as a roaring lion, walketh about, seeking whom he may devour." (I Pet. 5:8). Not for one moment in this life are we secure from temptation and fall. Therefore do not be proud if you see another stumble and fall. Such security will be a snare for you. "Be not high-minded, but fear" (Rom. 11:20). Rather be at all time ready that the tempter find no power in you.

"Watch and pray, that ye enter not into temptation" (Matt. 26:41). Be on your guard against the crafty enemy, pray to God that he hold us fast in his Word and his grace—that is the attitude of the Christian towards temptation.

But the Christian must not be afraid of temptation. If it comes upon him in spite of watching and praying, then he should know that he can conquer every temptation. There is no temptation which cannot be conquered. God knows our abilities, and he will not let us be tempted beyond our power. It is *human* temptation which harasses us, that is to say, it is not too big for us men. God allots to every man that portion which he can bear. That is certain. He who loses courage because of the suddenness and the aw-fulness of temptation, has forgotten the main point, namely that he will quite certainly withstand the temptation because God will not let it go beyond that which he is able to endure. There are temptations by which we are particularly frightened because we are so often wrecked upon them. When they are suddenly there again, we so often give ourselves up for lost from the beginning. But we must look at these temptations in the greatest peace and composure for they can be conquered, and they are conquered, so certain is it that God is faithful. Temptation must find us in humility and in certainty of victory.

The Legitimate Struggle

ALL TEMPTATION is temptation of Jesus Christ and all victory is victory of Jesus Christ. All temptation leads the believer into the deepest solitude, into abandonment by men and by God. But in this solitude he finds Jesus Christ, man and God. The blood of Christ and the example of Christ and the prayer of Christ are his help and his strength. The Book of Revelation says of the redeemed: "They overcome...because of the blood of the lamb" (Rev. 12:11). Not by the spirit, but by the blood of Christ is the devil overcome. Therefore in all temptation we must get back to this blood, in which is all our help. Then, too, there is the image of Jesus Christ which we should look upon in the hour of temptation. "See the end of the Lord" (James 5:11). His patience in suffering is the death of the flesh, the suffering of our flesh is made to seem of small account, we are preserved from all pride and comforted in all sorrow. The prayer of Jesus Christ which he promised to Peter: "Simon, behold, Satan asked to have you, that he might sift you as wheat, but I made supplication for thee" (Luke 22:31) represents our weak prayer before the Father in heaven, who does not allow us to be tempted beyond our powers.

Believers suffer the hour of temptation without defence. Jesus Christ is their shield. And only when it is quite clearly understood that temptation must befall the Godforsaken, then the word can at last be uttered which the Bible speaks about the Christian's struggle. From heaven the Lord gives to the defenceless the heavenly armour before which, though men's eyes do not see it, Satan flees. *He* clothes us with the armour of God, *he* gives into our hand the shield of faith, *he* sets upon our brow the helmet of salvation, *he* gives us the sword of the spirit in the right hand. It is the garment of Christ, the robe of his victory, that he puts upon his struggling community.

The Spirit teaches us that the time of temptations is not yet ended, but that the hardest temptation is still to come to his people. But he promises also: "Because thou didst keep the word of my patience, I also will keep thee from the hour of trial, that hour which is to come upon the whole world, to try them that dwell upon the earth. I come quickly" (Rev. 3:10ff.), and "The Lord knoweth how to deliver the godly out of temptation" (II Pet. 2:9).

So we pray, as Jesus Christ has taught us, to the Father in heaven: "Lead us not into temptation" and we know that our prayer is heard, for all temptation is conquered in Jesus Christ for all time, unto the end. So together with James we say: "Blessed is the man that endureth temptation, for when he hath been approved, he shall receive the crown of life, which the Lord promised to them that love him" (James 1:12). The promise of Jesus Christ proclaims: "Ye are they which have continued with me in my temptations, and I appoint unto you a kingdom" (Luke 22:28f.).

Protection and Help

...THE BIBLE teaches us in times of temptation in the flesh to *flee:* "Flee fornication" (I Cor. 6:18)—"from idolatry" (I Cor. 10:14)—"youthful lusts" (II Tim. 2:22)—"the lust of the world" (II Pet. 1:4). There is no resistance to Satan other than flight. Every struggle against lust in one's own strength is doomed to failure. Flee—that can indeed only mean, Flee to that place where you find protection and help, flee to the Crucified. His image and his presence alone can help. Here we see the crucified body and perceive in it the end of all desire; here we see right through Satan's deceit and here our spirit again becomes sober and aware of the enemy. Here I perceive the forsakenness and abandonment of my fleshly condition and the righteous judgement of God's wrath on all flesh. Here I know that in this lost condition I could never have helped myself against Satan, but that it is the victory of Jesus Christ which I now share. But here also I find ground for the attitude in which alone I can conquer all temptations—for patience (James 1:2ff.). I ought not to rebel against the temptations of the flesh in unlawful pride, as though I were too good for them. I ought to and I can humble myself under the hand of God and endure patiently the humiliation of such temptations. So I discern in the midst of Satan's deadly work the righteous and merciful punishment of God. In the death of Jesus I find refuge from Satan and the communion of death in the flesh under temptation and of life in the spirit through his victory.

Securitas

THE DEVIL tempts us in the sin of spiritual pride, in that he deceives us about the seriousness of God's law and of God's wrath. He takes the word of God's grace in his hand and whispers to us, God is a God of grace, he will not take our sins so seriously. So he awakens in us the longing to sin against God's grace and to assign forgiveness to ourselves even before our sin. He makes us secure in grace. We are God's children, we have Christ and his cross, we are the true church, no evil can now befall us. God will no longer hold us responsible for our sin. What spells ruin for others has no longer any danger for us. Through grace we have a privileged position before God. Here wanton sin threatens grace (Jude 4). Here it says: "Where is the God of judgement?" (Mal. 2:17), and "we call the proud happy; yea, they that work wickedness are built up; yea, they tempt God, and are delivered" (Mal. 3:15). From such talk follows all indolence of the spirit in prayer and in obedience, indifference to the Word of God, the deadening of conscience, the contempt of the good conscience, "shipwreck concerning the faith" (I Tim. 1:19). (Man persists in unforgiven sin and daily piles up guilt upon guilt.) Lastly there follows the complete hardening and obduracy of the heart in sin, in fearlessness and security before God, hypocritical piety (Acts 5:3 and 9). There is no longer any room for repentance, man can no longer obey. This way ends in idolatry. The God of grace has now become an idol which I serve. This is clearly the tempting of God which provokes the wrath of God.

Spiritual pride arises from disregard of the law and of

the wrath of God; whether I say that I am able to stand in my own goodness according to the law of God (justification by works); or whether I, through grace, bestow upon myself a privilege to sin (Nomism and Antinomianism). God is tempted in both, because I put to the test the seriousness of his wrath and demand a sign beyond his Word.

Tempted by Suffering

IF THE CHRISTIAN should fall into serious sickness, bitter poverty or other severe suffering, he should know that the devil has his hand in the game. Stoical resignation, which accepts everything as inevitable, is a self-defence of the man who will not acknowledge the devil and God. It has nothing to do with faith in God. The Christian knows that suffering in this world is linked with the fall of man, and that God does not will sickness, suffering and death. The Christian perceives in suffering a temptation of Satan to separate him from God. It is here that murmuring against God has its origin. While God disappears from man's sight in the fire of lust, the heat of affliction easily leads him into conflict with God. The Christian threatens to doubt the love of God. Why does God allow this suffering? God's justice is incomprehensible to him. Why must it happen to me? What have I done to deserve it? By suffering God should become our joy. Job is the Biblical prototype of this temptation. Everything is taken from Job by Satan, in order that in the end he may curse God. Violent pain, hunger and thirst can rob man of all his strength and lead him to the edge of apostasy.

How does the Christian conquer the temptation of

suffering? Here the end of the Book of Job is a great help to us. In the face of suffering Job has protested his innocence to the last, and has brushed aside the counsels to repentance from his friends who try to trace his misfortune back to a particular, perhaps hidden sin of Job. In addition, Job has spoken high-sounding words about his own righteousness. After the appearance of God Job declares: "Therefore have I uttered that which I understood not. . . . wherefore I abhor myself, and repent in dust and ashes" (Job, 42:3, 6). But the wrath of God is not now turned against Job, but against his friends: "for ye have not spoken of me the thing that is right, as my servant Job hath" (Job 42:7). Job gets justice before God and yet confesses his guilt before God. That is the solution of the problem. Job's suffering has its foundation not in his guilt but in his righteousness. Job is tempted because of his piety. So Job is right to protest against suffering coming upon him as if he were guilty. Yet this right comes to an end for Job when he no longer faces man but faces God. Face to face with God, even the good, innocent Job knows himself to be guilty.

This means for the Christian, tempted by suffering, that he must and should protest against suffering in so far as, in doing so, he protests against the devil and asserts his own innocence. The devil has broken into God's order and is the cause of suffering (Luther on Lenchen's death!). But in the presence of God the Christian also sees his sufferings as judgement on the sin of all flesh, which also dwells in his own flesh. He recognizes his sin and confesses himself to be guilty. "Thine own wickedness shall correct thee, and thy backslidings shall reprove thee. Know therefore and see that it is an evil thing and a bitter, that thou hast forsaken the Lord thy God, and that my fear is not in thee, saith the Lord, the Lord of hosts" (Jer. 2:19; 4:18). Suffering, therefore, leads to the knowledge of sin, and thereby, to the return to God. We see our suffering as the judgement of God on our flesh, and because of that we can be grateful for it. For judgement on the flesh, the death of the old man is only the side turned towards the world of the life of the new man. Thus it is said: "He that hath suffered in the flesh hath ceased from sin" (I Pet. 4:1). All suffering must lead the Christian to the strengthening of his faith and not to defection. While the flesh shuns suffering and rejects it, the Christian sees his suffering as the suffering of Christ in him. For he has borne our griefs and carried our sorrows. He bore God's wrath on sin. He died in the flesh, and so we also die in the flesh, because he lives in us.

Now the Christian understands his suffering, also, as the temptation of Christ in him. That leads him into patience, into the silent, waiting endurance of temptation, and fills him with gratitude; for the more the old man dies, the more certainly lives the new man; the deeper man is driven into suffering, the nearer he comes to Christ. Just because Satan took everything from Job, he cast him on God alone. So for the Christian suffering becomes a protest against the devil, a recognition of his own sin, the righteous judgement of God, the death of his old man, and communion with Jesus Christ.

Sorrow and Joy

SORROW and joy,
striking suddenly on our startled senses,
seem, at the first approach, all but impossible
of just distinction one from the other,
even as frost and heat at the first keen contact
burn us alike.

Joy and sorrow,
hurled from the height of heaven in meteor fashion,
flash in an arc of shining menace o'er us.
Those they touch are left
stricken amid the fragments
of their colourless, usual lives.

Imperturbable, mighty,
ruinous and compelling,
sorrow and joy
—summoned or all unsought for—
processionally enter.
Those they encounter
they transfigure, investing them
with strange gravity
and a spirit of worship.

Joy is rich in fears;
sorrow has its sweetness.
Indistinguishable from each other
they approach us from eternity,
equally potent in their power and terror.

From every quarter
mortals come hurrying,
part envious, part awe-struck,
swarming, and peering
into the portent,
where the mystery sent from above us
is transmuting into the inevitable
order of earthly human drama.

What, then, is joy? What, then, is sorrow?
Time alone can decide between them,
when the immediate poignant happening
lengthens out to continuous wearisome suffering,
when the laboured creeping moments of daylight
slowly uncover the fullness of our disaster,
sorrow's unmistakable features.

Then do most of our kind,
sated, if only by the monotony
of unrelieved unhappiness,
turn away from the drama, disillusioned,
uncompassionate.

O you mothers and loved ones—then, ah, then
comes your hour, the hour for true devotion.
Then your hour comes, you friends and brothers!
Loyal hearts can change the face of sorrow,
softly encircle it with love's most gentle
unearthly radiance.

Physical Suffering

I BELIEVE. . . that physical sufferings, actual pain and so on, are certainly to be classed as 'suffering'. We so like to stress spiritual suffering; and yet that is just what Christ is supposed to have taken from us, and I can find nothing about it in the New Testament, or in the acts of the early martyrs. After all, whether 'the church suffers' is not at all the same as whether one of its servants has to put up with this or that. I think we need a good deal of correction on this point; indeed, I must admit candidly that I sometimes feel almost ashamed of how often we've talked about our own sufferings. No, suffering must be something quite different, and have a quite different dimension, from what I've so far experienced.

Pain

STIFTER once said 'pain is a holy angel, who shows treasures to men which otherwise remain forever hidden; through him men have become greater than through all joys of the world.' It must be so and I tell this to myself in my present position over and over again—the pain of longing which often can be felt even physically, must be there, and we shall not and need not talk it away. But it needs to be overcome every time, and thus there is an even holier angel than the one of pain, that is the one of joy in God.

Prayers in Time of Distress

O LORD God,
great distress has come upon me;
my cares threaten to crush me,
and I do not know what to do.
O God, be gracious to me and help me.
Give me strength to bear what you send,
and do not let fear rule over me;
Take a father's care of my wife and children.

O merciful God,
forgive me all the sins that I have committed
against you and against my fellow men.
I trust in your grace
and commit my life wholly into your hands.
Do with me according to your will
and as is best for me.
Whether I live or die, I am with you,
and you, my God, are with me.
Lord, I wait for your salvation
and for your kingdom.
Amen.

Editor's note: Written for fellow prisoners Christmas 1943.

The Suffering Servant

WE KNOW full well that the marks of the passion, the wounds of the cross, are now become the marks of grace in the Body of the risen and glorified Christ. We know that the image of the Crucified lives henceforth in the glory of the eternal High Priest, who ever maketh intercession for us in Heaven. That Body, in which Christ had lived in the form of a servant, rose on Easter Day as a new Body, with heavenly form and radiance. But if we would have a share in that glory and radiance, we must first be conformed to the image of the Suffering Servant who was obedient to the death of the cross. If we would bear the image of his glory, we must first bear the image of his shame. There is no other way to recover the image we lost through the Fall.

The Suffering of
the Messengers

NEITHER FAILURE NOR HOSTILITY can weaken the messenger's conviction that he has been sent by Jesus. That his word may be their strength, their stay and their comfort, Jesus repeats it. "Behold, I send you." For this is no way they have chosen themselves, no undertaking of their own. It is, in the strict sense of the word, a *mission*. With this the Lord promises them his abiding presence, even when they find themselves as sheep among wolves, defenceless, powerless, sore pressed and beset with great danger. Nothing can happen to them without Jesus knowing of it. "Be ye therefore wise as serpents, and harmless as doves." How often have the ministers of Jesus made wrong use of this saying! However willing they may be, it is indeed difficult for them to preserve a true understanding of this word, and to adhere to the path of obedience. How difficult it is to draw the line with certainty between spiritual wisdom and worldly astuteness! Are we not all prepared at heart to do without "worldly wisdom" and much prefer the harmlessness of the doves and thus again fall into disobedience? Who is there to let us know when we are running away from suffering through cowardice, or running after it through temerity? Who shows us the hidden frontier? It is just as bad to appeal to the commandment of simplicity against that of wisdom, as to appeal to the commandment of wisdom against that of simplicity. There is one in the world who has a perfect knowledge of his own heart. But Jesus never called his disciples into a state of uncertainty, but to one of supreme certainty. That is why his warning can only summon them to abide by the Word. Where the Word is, there shall the disciple be. Therein lies his true wisdom and his true simplicity. If it is obvious that the Word is being rejected, if it is forced to yield its ground, the disciple must yield with it. But if the Word carries on the battle, the disciple must also stand his ground.

Sharing in God's Sufferings

...THE CHRISTIAN is not a *homo religiosus,* but simply a man, as Jesus was a man—in contrast, shall we say, to John the Baptist. I don't mean the shallow and banal this-worldliness of the enlightened, the busy, the comfortable, or the lascivious, but the profound this-worldliness, characterized by discipline and the constant knowledge of death and resurrection. I think Luther lived a this-worldly life in this sense.

I remember a conversation that I had in America thirteen years ago with a young French pastor.[1] We were asking ourselves quite simply what we wanted to do with our lives. He said he would like to become a saint (and I think it's quite likely that he did become one). At the time I was very impressed, but I disagreed with him, and said, in effect, that I should like to learn to have faith. For a long time I didn't realize the depth of the contrast. I thought I could acquire faith by trying to live a holy life, or something like it. I suppose I wrote *The Cost of Discipleship* as the end of that path. Today I can see the dangers of that book, though I still stand by what I wrote.

I discovered later, and I'm still discovering right up to this moment, that it is only by living completely in this world that one learns to have faith. One must completely abandon any attempt to make something of oneself, whether it be a saint, or a converted sinner, or a churchman (a so-called priestly type!), a righteous man or an unrighteous one, a sick man or a healthy one. By this-

---

[1]Jean Lasserre.

worldliness I mean living unreservedly in life's duties, problems, successes and failures, experiences and perplexities. In so doing we throw ourselves completely into the arms of God, taking seriously, not our own sufferings, but those of God in the world—watching with Christ in Gethsemane. That, I think, is faith; that is *metanoia;* and that is how one becomes a man and a Christian (cf. Jer. 45!). How can success make us arrogant, or failure lead us astray, when we share in God's sufferings through a life of this kind?

Night Voices in Tegel

STRETCHED OUT on my cot
I stare at the grey wall.
Outside, a summer evening
That does not know me
Goes singing into the countryside.
Slowly and softly
The tides of the day ebb
On the eternal shore.
Sleep a little,
Strengthen body and soul, head and hand,
For peoples, houses, spirits and hearts
Are aflame.
Till your day breaks
After blood-red night—
Stand fast!

Night and silence.
I listen.
Only the steps and cries of the guards,
The distant, hidden laughter of two lovers.
Do you hear nothing else, lazy sleeper?

I hear my own soul tremble and heave.
Nothing else?
I hear, I hear
The silent night thoughts
Of my fellow sufferers asleep or awake,
As if voices, cries,

As if shouts for planks to save them.
I hear the uneasy creak of the beds,
I hear chains.

I hear how sleepless men toss and turn,
Who long for freedom and deeds of wrath.
When at grey dawn sleep finds them
They murmur in dreams of their wives and children.

I hear the happy lisp of half-grown boys,
Delighting in childhood dreams;
I hear them tug at their blankets
And hide from hideous nightmares.

I hear the sighs and weak breath of the old,
Who in silence prepare for the last journey.
They have seen justice and injustice come and go;
Now they wish to see the imperishable, the eternal.

Night and silence.
Only the steps and cries of the guards.
Do you hear how in the silent house
It quakes, cracks, roars
When hundreds kindle the stirred-up flame of their
hearts?

Their choir is silent,
But my ear is open wide:
'We the old, the young,
The sons of all tongues,
We the strong, the weak,
The sleepers, the wakeful,
We the poor, the rich,
Alike in misfortune,

The good, the bad,
Whatever we have been,
We men of many scars,
We the witnesses of those who died,
We the defiant, we the despondent,
The innocent, and the much accused,
Deeply tormented by long isolation,
Brother, we are searching, we are calling you!
Brother, do you hear me?'

Twelve cold, thin strokes of the tower clock
Awaken me.
No sound, no warmth in them
To hide and cover me.
Howling, evil dogs at midnight
Frighten me.
The wretched noise
Divides a poor yesterday
From a poor today.
What can it matter to me
Whether one day turns into another,
One that could have nothing new, nothing better
Than to end quickly like this one?
I want to see the turning of the times,
When luminous signs stand in the night sky,
And over the peoples new bells
Ring and ring.
I am waiting for that midnight
In whose fearfully streaming brilliance
The evil perish for anguish
And the good overcome with joy.

The villain
Comes to light
In the judgement.

Deceit and betrayal,
Malicious deeds—
Atonement is near.

See, O man,
Holy strength
Is at work, setting right.

Rejoice and proclaim
Faithfulness and right
For a new race!

Heaven, reconcile
The sons of earth
To peace and beauty.

Earth, flourish;
Man, become free,
Be free!

Suddenly I sat up,
As if, from a sinking ship, I had sighted land,
As if there were something to grasp, to seize,
As if I saw golden fruit ripen.
But wherever I look, grasp, or seize,
There is only the impenetrable mass of darkness.

I sink into brooding;
I sink myself into the depths of the dark.
You night, full of outrage and evil,
Make yourself known to me!
Why and for how long will you try our patience?
A deep and long silence;
Then I hear the night bend down to me:
'I am not dark; only guilt is dark!'

Guilt! I hear a trembling and quaking,
A murmur, a lament that arises;
I hear men grow angry in spirit.
In the wild uproar of innumerable voices
A silent chorus
Assails God's ear:

'Pursued and hunted by men,
Made defenceless and accused,
Bearers of unbearable burdens,
We are yet the accusers.

'We accuse those who plunged us into sin,
Who made us share the guilt,
Who made us the witnesses of injustice,
In order to despise their accomplices.

'Our eyes had to see folly,
In order to bind us in deep guilt;
Then they stopped our mouths,
And we were as dumb dogs.

'We learned to lie easily,
To be at the disposal of open injustice;
If the defenceless was abused,
Then our eyes remained cold.

'And that which burned in our hearts,
Remained silent and unnamed;
We quenched our fiery blood
And stamped out the inner flame.

'The once holy bonds uniting men
Were mangled and flayed,

Friendship and faithfulness betrayed;
Tears and rue were reviled.

'We sons of pious races,
One-time defenders of right and truth,
Became despisers of God and man,
Amid hellish laughter.

'Yet though now robbed of freedom and honour,
We raise our heads proudly before men.
And if we are brought into disrepute,
Before men we declare our innocence.

'Steady and firm we stand man against man;
As the accused we accuse!

'Only before thee, source of all being,
Before thee are we sinners.

'Afraid of suffering and poor in deeds,
We have betrayed thee before men.

'We saw the lie raise its head,
And we did not honour the truth.

'We saw brethren in direst need,
And feared only our own death.

'We come before thee as men,
As confessors of our sins.

'Lord, after the ferment of these times,
Send us times of assurance.

'After so much going astray,
Let us see the day break.

'Let there be ways built for us by thy word
As far as eye can see.

'Until thou wipe out our guilt,
Keep us in quiet patience.

'We will silently prepare ourselves,
Till thou dost call to new times.

'Until thou stillest storm and flood,
And thy will does wonders.

'Brother, till the night be past,
Pray for me!'

The first light of morning creeps through my window
    pale and grey,
A light, warm summer wind blows over my brow.
'Summer day,' I will only say, 'beautiful summer
    day!'
What may it bring to me?
Then I hear outside hasty, muffled steps;
Near me they stop suddenly.
I turn cold and hot,
For I know, oh, I know!
A soft voice reads something cuttingly and cold.
Control yourself, brother; soon you will have finished it,
soon, soon.
I hear you stride bravely and with proud step.
You no longer see the present, you see the future.
I go with you, brother, to that place,
And I hear your last word:
'Brother, when the sun turns pale for me,
Then live for me.'

Stretched out on my cot
I stare at the grey wall.
Outside a summer morning
Which is not yet mine
Goes brightly into the countryside.

Brother, till after the long night
Our day breaks
We stand fast!

Separation from Those We Love

FIRST: nothing can make up for the absence of someone whom we love, and it would be wrong to try to find a substitute; we must simply hold out and see it through. That sounds very hard at first, but at the same time it is a great consolation, for the gap, as long as it remains unfilled, preserves the bonds between us. It is nonsense to say that God fills the gap; he doesn't fill it, but on the contrary, he keeps it empty and so helps us to keep alive our former communion with each other, even at the cost of pain.

Secondly: the dearer and richer our memories, the more difficult the separation. But gratitude changes the pangs of memory into a tranquil joy. The beauties of the past are borne, not as a thorn in the flesh, but as a precious gift in themselves. We must take care not to wallow in our memories or hand ourselves over to them, just as we do not gaze all the time at a valuable present, but only at special times, and apart from these keep it simply as a hidden treasure that is ours for certain. In this way the past gives us lasting joy and strength.

Thirdly: times of separation are not a total loss or unprofitable for our companionship, or at any rate they need not be so. In spite of all the difficulties that they bring, they can be the means of strengthening fellowship quite remarkably.

Fourthly: I've learnt here especially that the *facts* can always be mastered, and that difficulties are magnified out of all proportion simply by fear and anxiety. From the moment we wake until we fall asleep we must commend other people wholly and unreservedly to God and leave them in his hands, and transform our anxiety for them into prayers on their behalf:

> With sorrow and with grief...
> God *will not* be distracted.

Christ's Restoration

> Let pass, dear brothers, every pain;
> What you have missed I'll bring again.

What does this 'I'll bring again' mean? It means that nothing is lost, that everything is taken up in Christ, although it is transformed, made transparent, clear, and free from all selfish desire. Christ restores all this as God originally intended it to be, without the distortion resulting from our sins. The doctrine derived from Eph. 1:10—that of the restoration of all things, ἀνακεφαλαίωσις, *recapitulatio* (Irenaeus)—is a magnificent conception, full of comfort. This is how the promise 'God seeks what has been driven away' is fulfilled. And no one has expressed this so simply and artlessly as Paul Gerhardt in these words that he puts into the mouth of the Christ-child: 'I'll bring again'. Perhaps this line will help you a little in the coming weeks. Besides that, I've lately learnt for the first time to appreciate the hymn 'Beside thy cradle here I stand'. Up to now I hadn't made much of it; I suppose one has to be alone for a long time, and meditate on it, to be able to take it in properly. Every word is remarkably full of meaning and beauty. There's just a slight flavour of the monastery and mysticism, but no more than is justified. After all, it's right to speak of 'I' and 'Christ' as well as of 'we', and what that means can hardly be expressed better than it is in this hymn. There are also a few passages in a similar vein in the *Imitation of Christ*, which I'm reading now and then in the Latin (it reads much better in Latin than in German); and I sometimes think of

from the Augustinian *O bone Jesu* by Schütz. Doesn't this passage, in its ecstatic longing combined with pure devotion, suggest the 'bringing again' of all earthly desire? 'Bringing again' mustn't, of course, be confused with 'sublimation'; 'sublimation' is σάρξ 'flesh' (and pietistic?), and 'restoration' is spirit, not in the sense of 'spiritualization' (which is also σάρξ), but of καινὴ κτίσις through the πνεῦμα ἅγιον, a new creation through the Holy Spirit. I think this point is also very important when we have to talk to people who ask us about their relation to their dead. '*I* will bring again'—that is, we cannot and should not take it back ourselves, but allow Christ to give it back to us.

New Year 1945

With every power for good to stay and guide me,
comforted and inspired beyond all fear,
I'll live these days with you in thought beside me,
and pass, with you, into the coming year.

The old year still torments our hearts, unhastening:
the long days of our sorrow still endure.
Father, grant to the soul thou hast been chastening
that thou hast promised—the healing and the cure.

Should it be ours to drain the cup of grieving
even to the dregs of pain, at thy command,
we will not falter, thankfully receiving
all that is given by thy loving hand.

But, should it be thy will once more to release us
to life's enjoyment and its good sunshine,
that we've learned from sorrow shall increase us
and all our life be dedicate as thine.

To-day, let candles shed their radiant greeting:
lo, on our darkness are they not thy light,
leading us haply to our longed-for meeting?
Thou canst illumine e'en our darkest night.

Editor's note: Composed during heavy air raids at the Gestapo prison in Berlin. Translated by Geoffrey Winthrop Young.

When now the silence deepens for our harkening,
grant we may hear thy children's voices raise
from all the unseen world around us darkening
their universal paean, in thy praise.

While all the powers of Good aid and attend us,
boldly we'll face the future, be it what may.
At even, and at morn, God will befriend us,
And oh, most surely on each new year's day!

Glorifying God

...PSALM 50 says quite clearly, 'Call upon me in the day of
trouble; I will deliver you, and you shall glorify me.' The
whole history of the children of Israel consists of such cries
for help. And I must say that the last two nights have
made me face this problem again in a quite elementary
way. While the bombs are falling like that all round the
building, I cannot help thinking of God, his judgement,
his hand stretched out and his anger not turned away (Isa.
5:25 and 9:11–10:4), and of my own unpreparedness. I
feel how men can make vows, and then I think of you all
and say, 'better me than one of them'—and that makes me
realize how attached I am to you all. I won't say anything
more about it—it will have to be by word of mouth; but
when all is said and done, it's true that it needs trouble to
shake us up and drive us to prayer, though I feel every
time that it is something to be ashamed of, as indeed it is.
That may be because I haven't so far felt able to say a
Christian word to the others at such a moment. As we

were again lying on the floor last night, and someone exclaimed 'O God, O God' (he is normally a very flippant type), I couldn't bring myself to offer him any Christian encouragement or comfort; all I did was to look at my watch and say, 'It won't last more than ten minutes now.' There was nothing premeditated about it; it came quite automatically, and perhaps I felt that it was wrong to force religion down his throat just then. (Incidentally, Jesus didn't try to convert the two thieves on the cross; one of them turned to him!)

Call of Liberation

...MAN CANNOT LIVE simultaneously in reconciliation and in disunion, in freedom and under the law, in simplicity and in discordancy. There are no transitions or intermediate stages here; it is one thing or the other. But it is impossible for a man by his own power to void and to overcome his knowledge of his own goodness, though he may deceive himself and mistake the methodical repression of this knowledge for the actual overcoming of it. That is why when Jesus speaks of the right hand which must not know what the left hand is doing, in other words of the concealment of a man's own goodness, it is once again the summons to forsake disunion, apostasy and the knowledge of good and evil, and to return to unity and to the origin, to the new life which is in Jesus alone. It is the call of liberation, the call to simplicity and to conversion; it is the call which nullifies the old knowledge of the apostasy and which imparts the new knowledge of Jesus, that knowledge which is entirely contained in the doing of the will of God....

Freedom

RESPONSIBILITY AND FREEDOM are corresponding concepts. Factually, though not chronologically, responsibility presupposes freedom and freedom can consist only in responsibility. Responsibility is the freedom of men which is given only in the obligation to God and to our neighbour.

The responsible man acts in the freedom of his own self, without the support of men, circumstances or principles, but with a due consideration for the given human and general conditions and for the relevant questions of principle. The proof of his freedom is the fact that nothing can answer for him, nothing can exonerate him, except his own deed and his own self. It is he himself who must observe, judge, weigh up, decide and act. It is man himself who must examine the motives, the prospects, the value and the purpose of his action. But neither the purity of the motivation, nor the opportune circumstances, nor the value, nor the significant purpose of an intended undertaking can become the governing law of his action, a law to which he can withdraw, to which he can appeal as an authority, and by which he can be exculpated and acquitted.[1] For in that case he would indeed no longer be truly free. The action of the responsible man is performed in the obligation which alone gives freedom and which gives entire freedom, the obligation to God and to our neighbour as they confront us in Jesus Christ. At the same time it is performed wholly within the domain of relativ-

---

[1]This makes it unnecessary to raise the fallacious question of determinism and indeterminism, in which the essence of mental decision is incorrectly substituted for the law of causality.

ity, wholly in the twilight which the historical situation spreads over good and evil; it is performed in the midst of the innumerable perspectives in which every given phenomenon appears. It has not to decide simply between right and wrong and between good and evil, but between right and right and between wrong and wrong. As Aeschylus said, 'right strives with right'. Precisely in this respect responsible action is a free venture; it is not justified by any law; it is performed without any claim to a valid self-justification, and therefore also without any claim to an ultimate valid knowledge of good and evil. Good, as what is responsible, is performed in ignorance of good and in the surrender to God of the deed which has become necessary and which is nevertheless, or for that very reason, free; for it is God who sees the heart, who weighs up the deed, and who directs the course of history.

Stations on the Road to Freedom

Discipline

If you set out to seek freedom, then learn above all
  things
to govern your soul and your senses, for fear that
  your passions
and longing may lead you away from the path you
  should follow.
Chaste be your mind and your body, and both in
  subjection,
obediently, steadfastly seeking the aim set before
  them;
only through discipline may a man learn to be free.

Action

Daring to do what is right, not what fancy may tell
  you,
valiantly grasping occasions, not cravenly doubting—
freedom comes only through deeds, not through
  thoughts taking wing.
Faint not nor fear, but go out to the storm and the
  action,
trusting in God whose commandment you faithfully
  follow;
freedom, exultant, will welcome your joy.

Suffering

A change has come indeed. Your hands, so strong
    and active,
are bound; in helplessness now you see your action
is ended; you sigh in relief, your cause committing
to stronger hands; so now you may rest contented.
Only for one blissful moment could you draw near to
    touch freedom;
then, that it might be perfected in glory, you gave it to
    God.

Death

Come now, thou greatest of feasts on the journey to
    freedom eternal;
death, cast aside all the burdensome chains, and
    demolish
the walls of our temporal body, the walls of our souls
    that are blinded,
so that at last we may see that which here remains
    hidden.
Freedom, how long we have sought thee in disci-
    pline, action, and suffering;
dying, we now may behold thee revealed in the Lord.

Obedience and Freedom

...JESUS STANDS BEFORE GOD as the one who is both obedient and free. As the obedient one He does His Father's will in blind compliance with the law which is commanded Him, and as the free one He acquiesces in God's will out of His own most personal knowledge, with open eyes and a joyous heart; He re-creates this will, as it were, out of Himself. Obedience without freedom is slavery; freedom without obedience is arbitrary self-will. Obedience restrains freedom; and freedom ennobles obedience. Obedience binds the creature to the Creator and freedom enables the creature to stand before the Creator as one who is made in His image. Obedience shows man that he must allow himself to be told what is good and what God requires of him (Micah 6:8); and liberty enables him to do good himself. Obedience knows what is good and does it, and freedom dares to act, and abandons to God the judgement of good and evil. Obedience follows blindly and freedom has open eyes. Obedience acts without questioning and freedom asks what is the purpose. Obedience has its hands tied and freedom is creative. In obedience man adheres to the decalogue and in freedom man creates new decalogues (Luther).

In responsibility both obedience and freedom are realized. Responsibility implies tension between obedience and freedom. There would be no more responsibility if either were made independent of the other. Responsible action is subject to obligation, and yet it is creative. To make obedience independent of freedom leads only to the Kantian ethic of duty, and to make freedom independent of obedience leads only to the ethic of irresponsible genius. Both the man of duty and the genius carry their justification within themselves. The man of responsibility stands between obligation and freedom; he must dare to act under obligation and in freedom; yet he finds his justification neither in his obligation nor in his freedom but solely in Him who has put him in this (humanly impossible) situation and who requires this deed of him. The responsible man delivers up himself and his deed to God.

The World of Conflicts

THE KNOWLEDGE of good and evil seems to be the aim of all ethical reflection.[1] The first task of Christian ethics is to invalidate this knowledge. In launching this attack on the underlying assumptions of all other ethics, Christian ethics stands so completely alone that it becomes questionable whether there is any purpose in speaking of Christian ethics at all. But if one does so notwithstanding, that can only mean that Christian ethics claims to discuss the origin of the whole problem of ethics, and thus professes to be a critique of all ethics simply as ethics.

Already in the possibility of the knowledge of good and evil Christian ethics discerns a falling away from the origin. Man at his origin knows only one thing: God. It is only in the unity of his knowledge of God that he knows

---

[1]For the purposes of our present discussion it makes no difference if modern ethics replaces the concepts of good and evil by those of moral and immoral, valuable and valueless or (in the case of existential philosophy) of actual or proper being and not actual or proper being.

of other men, of things, and of himself. He knows all things only in God, and God in all things. The knowledge of good and evil shows that he is no longer at one with this origin.

In the knowledge of good and evil man does not understand himself in the reality of the destiny appointed in his origin, but rather in his own possibilities, his possibility of being good or evil. He knows himself now as something apart from God, outside God, and this means that he now knows only himself and no longer knows God at all; for he can know God only if he knows only God. The knowledge of good and evil is therefore separation from God. Only against God can man know good and evil.

Contempt for Humanity?

THERE IS A VERY REAL DANGER of our drifting into an attitude of contempt for humanity. We know quite well that we have no right to do so, and that it would lead us into the most sterile relation to our fellow-men. The following thoughts may keep us from such a temptation. It means that we at once fall into the worst blunders of our opponents. The man who despises another will never be able to make anything of him. Nothing that we despise in the other man is entirely absent from ourselves. We often expect from others more than we are willing to do ourselves. Why have we hitherto thought so intemperately about man and his frailty and temptability? We must learn to regard people less in the light of what they do or omit to do, and more in the light of what they suffer. The only profitable relationship to others—and especially to our weaker brethren—is one of love, and that means the will to hold fellowship with them. God himself did not despise humanity, but became man for men's sake.

Immanent Righteousness

It is one of the most surprising experiences, but at the same time one of the most incontrovertible, that evil—often in a surprisingly short time—proves its own folly and defeats its own object. That does not mean that punishment follows hard on the heels of every evil action; but it does mean that deliberate transgression of the divine law in the supposed interests of worldly self-preservation has exactly the opposite effect. We learn this from our own experience, and we can interpret it in various ways. At least it seems possible to infer with certainty that in social life there are laws more powerful than anything that may claim to dominate them, and that it is therefore not only wrong but unwise to disregard them. We can understand from this why Aristotelian–Thomist ethics made wisdom one of the cardinal virtues. Wisdom and folly are not ethically indifferent, as Neo-protestant motive-ethics would have it. In the fullness of the concrete situation and the possibilities which it offers, the wise man at the same time recognizes the impassable limits that are set to all action by the permanent laws of human social life; and in this knowledge the wise man acts well and the good man wisely.

It is true that all historically important action is constantly overstepping the limits set by these laws. But it makes all the difference whether such overstepping of the appointed limits is regarded in principle as the superseding of them, and is therefore given out to be a law of a special kind, or whether the overstepping is deliberately regarded as a fault which is perhaps unavoidable, justified only if the law and the limit are re-established and respected as soon as possible. It is not necessarily hypocrisy if the declared aim of political action is the restoration of the law, and not mere self-preservation. The world *is*, in fact, so ordered that a basic respect for ultimate laws and human life is also the best means of self-preservation, and that these laws may be broken only on the odd occasion in case of brief necessity, whereas anyone who turns necessity into a principle, and in so doing establishes a law of his own alongside them, is inevitably bound, sooner or later, to suffer retribution. The immanent righteousness of history rewards and punishes only men's deeds, but the eternal righteousness of God tries and judges their hearts.

The Sense of Quality

UNLESS WE HAVE THE COURAGE to fight for a revival of wholesome reserve between man and man, we shall perish in an anarchy of human values. The impudent contempt for such reserve is the mark of the rabble, just as inward uncertainty, haggling and cringing for the favour of insolent people, and lowering oneself to the level of the rabble are the way of becoming no better than the rabble oneself. When we forget what is due to ourselves and to others, when the feeling for human quality and the power to exercise reserve cease to exist, chaos is at the door. When we tolerate impudence for the sake of material comforts, then we abandon our self-respect, the floodgates are opened, chaos bursts the dam that we were to defend; and we are responsible for it all. In other times it may have been the business of Christianity to champion the equality of all men; its business today will be to defend passionately human dignity and reserve. The misinterpretation that we are acting for our own interests, and the cheap insinuation that our attitude is anti-social, we shall simply have to put up with; they are the invariable protests of the rabble against decency and order. Anyone who is pliant and uncertain in this matter does not realize what is at stake, and indeed in his case the reproaches may well be justified. We are witnessing the levelling down of all ranks of society, and at the same time the birth of a new sense of nobility, which is binding together a circle of men from all former social classes. Nobility arises from and exists by sacrifice, courage, and a clear sense of duty to oneself and society, by expecting due regard for itself as a matter of course; and it shows an equally natural regard for others, whether they are of higher or of lower degree. We need all along the line to recover the lost sense of quality and social order based on quality. Quality is the greatest enemy of any kind of mass-levelling. Socially it means the renunciation of all place-hunting, a break with the cult of the 'star', an open eye both upwards and downwards, especially in the choice of one's more intimate friends, and pleasure in private life as well as courage to enter public life. Culturally it means a return from the newspaper and the radio to the book, from feverish activity to unhurried leisure, from dispersion to concentration, from sensationalism to reflection, from virtuosity to art, from snobbery to modesty, from extravagance to moderation. Quantities are competitive, qualities are complementary.

The Penultimate

IN JESUS CHRIST we have faith in the incarnate, crucified and risen God. In the incarnation we learn of the love of God for His creation; in the crucifixion we learn of the judgement of God upon all flesh; and in the resurrection we learn of God's will for a new world. There could be no greater error than to tear these three elements apart; for each of them comprises the whole. It is quite wrong to establish a separate theology of the incarnation, a theology of the cross, or a theology of the resurrection, each in opposition to the others, by a misconceived absolutization of one of these parts; it is equally wrong to apply the same procedure to a consideration of the Christian life. A Christian ethic constructed solely on the basis of the incarnation would lead directly to the compromise solution. An ethic which was based solely on the cross or the resurrection of Jesus would fall victim to radicalism and enthusiasm. Only in the unity is the conflict resolved.

Jesus Christ the man—this means that God enters into created reality. It means that we have the right and the obligation to be men before God. The destruction of manhood, of man's quality as man (*Menschsein*), is sin, and is therefore a hindrance to God's redemption of man. Yet the manhood (*Menschsein*) of Jesus Christ does not mean simply the corroboration of the established world and of the human character as it is. Jesus was man 'without sin' (Heb. 4:15); that is what is decisive. Yet among men Jesus lived in the most utter poverty, unmarried, and He died as a criminal. Thus the manhood of Jesus implies already a twofold condemnation of man, the absolute condemnation of sin and the relative condemnation of the established human orders. But even under this condemnation Jesus is really man, and it is His will that we shall be men. He neither renders the human reality independent nor destroys it, but He allows it to remain as that which is before the last, as a penultimate which requires to be taken seriously in its own way, and yet not to be taken seriously, a penultimate which has become the outer covering of the ultimate.

The Sovereignty of God in History

I BELIEVE that God can and will bring good out of evil, even out of the greatest evil. For that purpose he needs men who make the best use of everything. I believe that God will give us all the strength we need to help us to resist in all time of distress. But he never gives it in advance, lest we should rely on ourselves and not on him alone. A faith such as this should allay all our fears for the future. I believe that even our mistakes and shortcomings are turned to good account, and that it is no harder for God to deal with them than with our supposedly good deeds. I believe that God is no timeless fate, but that he waits for and answers sincere prayers and responsible actions.

Present and Future

WE USED TO THINK that one of the inalienable rights of man was that he should be able to plan both his professional and his private life. That is a thing of the past. The force of circumstances has brought us into a situation where we have to give up being 'anxious about tomorrow' (Matt. 6:34). But it makes all the difference whether we accept this willingly and in faith (as the Sermon on the Mount intends), or under continual constraint. For most people, the compulsory abandonment of planning for the future means that they are forced back into living just for the moment, irresponsibly, frivolously, or resignedly; some few dream longingly of better times to come, and try to forget the present. We find both these courses equally impossible, and there remains for us only the very narrow way, often extremely difficult to find, of living every day as if it were our last, and yet living in faith and responsibility as though there were to be a great future: 'Houses and fields and vineyards shall again be bought in this land' proclaims Jeremiah (32:15), in paradoxical contrast to his prophecies of woe, just before the destruction of the holy city. It is a sign from God and a pledge of a fresh start and a great future, just when all seems black. Thinking and acting for the sake of the coming generation, but being ready to go any day without fear or anxiety—that, in practice, is the spirit in which we are forced to live. It is not easy to be brave and keep that spirit alive, but it is imperative.

Editor's note: Written during resistance to Hitler.

Christ and Antichrist

THE OLDER THE WORLD GROWS, the more heated becomes the conflict between Christ and Antichrist, and the more thorough the efforts of the world to get rid of the Christians. Until now the world had always granted them a lodging-place by allowing them to work for their own food and clothing.... When the Christian community has been deprived of its last inch of space on the earth, the end will be near.

Thus while it is true that the Body of Christ makes a deep invasion into the sphere of secular life, yet at the same time the great gulf between the two is always clear at other points, and must become increasingly so. But whether in the world or out of it, the Christian's choice is determined by obedience to the same word: "Be not fashioned according to this world: but be ye transformed (μεταμορφοῦσθε) by the renewing of your mind, that ye may prove what is the good and acceptable and perfect will of God" (Rom. 12:2). There is a way of putting oneself on the same level as the world in the world as there is a way of creating one's own spiritual "world" in a monastery. There is a wrong way of staying in the world and a wrong way of fleeing from it. In both cases we are fashioning ourselves according to the world. But the Church of Christ has a different "form" from the world. Her task is increasingly to realize this form. It is the form of Christ himself, who came into the world and of his infinite mercy bore mankind and took it to himself, but who notwithstanding did not fashion himself in accordance with it but was rejected and cast out by it. He was not of this world. In the right confrontation with the world, the Church will become ever more like to the form of its suffering Lord.

Justification as the Last Word

THE ORIGIN and the essence of all Christian life are comprised in the one process or event which the Reformation called justification of the sinner by grace alone. The nature of the Christian life is disclosed not by what the man is in himself but by what he is in this event. The whole length and breadth of human life is here compressed into a single instant, a single point. The totality of life is encompassed in this event. What event is this? It is something final, something which cannot be grasped by the being or the action or the suffering of any man. The dark pit of human life, inwardly and outwardly barred, sinking ever more hopelessly and inescapably in the abyss, is torn open by main force, and the word of God breaks in. In the rescuing light man for the first time recognizes God and his neighbour. The labyrinth of the life he has so far led falls in ruin. Man is free for God and his brothers. He becomes aware that there is a God who loves him; that a brother is standing at his side, whom God loves as he loves him himself and that there is a future with the triune God, together with His Church. He believes. He loves. He hopes. The past and the future of his whole life are merged in one in the presence of God. The whole of the past is comprised in the word forgiveness. The whole of the future is in safe keeping in the faithfulness of God. Past sin is swallowed up in the abyss of the love of God in Jesus Christ. The future will be without sin, a life which proceeds from God (I John 3:9). Life knows now that it is held in tension between the two poles of eternity, that it extends from the choice made before the time of the world to the everlasting salvation. It knows itself to be a member of a Church and a creation which sings the praise of the triune God. All this takes place when Christ comes to men. In Christ all this is truth and reality, and just because it is not a dream, the life of the man who experiences the presence of Christ is henceforward no longer a lost life, but it has become a justified life, a life justified by grace alone.

Yet not only by grace alone, but also by faith alone. That is the teaching of the Bible and of the Reformation. A life is not justified by love or by hope, but only by faith. For indeed faith alone sets life upon a new foundation, and it is this new foundation alone that justifies my being able to live before God. This foundation is the life, the death and the resurrection of the Lord Jesus Christ. Without this foundation a life is unjustified before God. It is delivered up to death and damnation. To live by the life, the death and the resurrection of Jesus Christ is the justification of a life before God. And faith means the finding and holding fast of this foundation.

Blessing and Completion

IN THE BIBLE "rest" really means more than "having a rest." It means rest after the work is accomplished, it means completion, it means the perfection and peace of God in which the world rests, it means transfiguration, it means turning our eyes absolutely upon God's being God and towards worshipping him. It is never the rest of a lethargic God; it is the rest of the Creator. It is no relinquishing of the world, but the ultimate glorification of the world which is gazing upon the Creator. God must remain the Creator in his rest, too; "my Father worketh hitherto, and I work." God remains the Creator, but now as the one who has accomplished his work. We now understand God's rest to be at the same time the rest of his creation. His rest is our rest (as his freedom is our freedom, his goodness our goodness). Therefore God sanctifies the day of his rest for Adam and for us, whose heart is restless until it finds rest in God's rest. As far as we are concerned this rest is the promise which has been given to the people of God. It is unbelieving insolence either to want to snatch God's peace for ourselves prematurely in pious quietism or to reason impudently about the boredom of the peace of paradise, thereby combining and glorifying unrest and battle. This loud pleasure in one's own personal vitality might have to grow silent very quickly in the presence of the "living" God.

It is the day which in the New Testament is the day of the Lord's resurrection. It is the day of rest, the day of victory, of dominion, of perfection, of transfiguration; for us, the day of worship, the day of hope looking towards the day of final rest with God, the "rest of the people." All the days of the week have really only been created for its sake. Thou shalt keep holy the holiday and not sleep it away. For the sake of the final rest, for the sake of the resurrection of Jesus Christ, for the sake of the day of the final resurrection and the rest of the Creator with his creatures everything has been created, we have been created "that they may rest from their labours, for their works follow with them."

Jonah

'O GODS ETERNAL, excellent, provoked to anger,
help us, or give a sign, that we may know
who has offended you by secret sin,
by breach of oath, or heedless blasphemy, or murder,

who brings us to disaster by misdeed still hidden,
to make a paltry profit for his pride.'
Thus they besought. And Jonah said, 'Behold,
I sinned before the Lord of hosts. My life is forfeit.

Cast me away! My guilt must bear the wrath of God;
the righteous shall not perish with the sinner!'
They trembled. But with hands that knew no
        weakness
they cast the offender from their midst. The sea stood
        still.

In fear of death they cried aloud and, clinging fast
to wet ropes straining on the battered deck,
they gazed in stricken terror at the sea
that now, unchained in sudden fury, lashed the ship.

Editor's note: This poem was written after a plan to escape had been
abandoned.

The Last Temptation

...THE LAST ENEMY is death. Death is in Satan's hands. The sinner dies. Death is the last temptation. But even here where man loses everything, where hell reveals its terror, even here life has broken in upon the believer. Satan loses his last power and his last right over the believer. We ask once more: Why does God give Satan opportunity for temptation? First, in order finally to overcome Satan. Through getting his rights Satan is destroyed. As God punishes the godless man by allowing him to be godless, and allowing him his right and his freedom, and as the godless man perishes in this freedom of his (Rom. 1:19ff.), so God does not destroy Satan by an act of violence, but Satan must destroy himself. Second, God gives opportunity to Satan in order to bring believers to salvation. Only by knowledge of sin, by suffering and death, can the new man live. Third, the overcoming of Satan and the salvation of believers is true and real in Jesus Christ alone. Satan plagues Jesus with all sins, all suffering and the death of mankind. But with that his power is at an end. He had taken everything from Jesus Christ and thereby delivered him to God alone. Thus we are led to the knowledge from which we set out: Believers must learn to understand all their temptations as the temptation of Jesus Christ in them. In this way they will share in the victory.

The Last Judgement

...WHEN JESUS sits in judgement His own will not know that they have given Him food and drink and clothing and comfort. They will not know their own goodness; Jesus will disclose it to them. Then the time will have come for which there was no time here on earth, the time which will lay bare what is concealed so that it may then receive its public reward, the time of judgement. But even then all judging and all knowing will be on the part of God and of Jesus Christ, and we ourselves shall be filled with wonder at what we receive. The Pharisee, who thought that through impartial and earnest judgement of himself he could anticipate and prepare for the last judgement, cannot but regard as unintelligible and wrongful the message that he is to receive goodness solely from the knowledge, from the judgement and from the hand of Jesus.

Insecurity and Death

IN RECENT YEARS we have become increasingly familiar with the thought of death. We surprise ourselves by the calmness with which we hear of the death of one of our contemporaries. We cannot hate it as we used to, for we have discovered some good in it, and have almost come to terms with it. Fundamentally we feel that we really belong to death already, and that every new day is a miracle. It would probably not be true to say that we welcome death (although we all know that weariness which we ought to avoid like the plague); we are too inquisitive for that—or, to put it more seriously, we should like to see something more of the meaning of our life's broken fragments. Nor do we try to romanticize death, for life is too great and too precious. Still less do we suppose that danger is the meaning of life—we are not desperate enough for that, and we know too much about the good things that life has to offer, though on the other hand we are only too familiar with life's anxieties and with all the other destructive effects of prolonged personal insecurity. We still love life, but I do not think that death can take us by surprise now. After what we have been through during the war, we hardly dare admit that we should like death to come to us, not accidentally and suddenly through some trivial cause, but in the fullness of life and with everything at stake. It is we ourselves, and not outward circumstances, who make death what it can be, a death freely and voluntarily accepted.

The Idolization of Death

...WHEREVER IT IS RECOGNIZED that the power of death has been broken, wherever the world of death is illumined by the miracle of the resurrection and of the new life, there no eternities are demanded of life but one takes of life what it offers, not all or nothing but good and evil, the important and the unimportant, joy and sorrow; one neither clings convulsively to life nor casts it frivolously away. One is content with the allotted span and one does not invest earthly things with the title of eternity; one allows to death the limited rights which it still possesses. It is from beyond death that one expects the coming of the new man and of the new world, from the power by which death has been vanquished.

The risen Christ bears the new humanity within Himself, the final glorious 'yes' which God addresses to the new man. It is true that mankind is still living the old life, but it is already beyond the old. It still lives in a world of death, but it is already beyond death. It still lives in a world of sin, but it is already beyond sin. The night is not yet over, but already the dawn is breaking.

The man whom God has taken to Himself, sentenced and awakened to a new life, this is Jesus Christ. In Him it is all mankind. It is ourselves. Only the form of Jesus Christ confronts the world and defeats it. And it is from this form alone that there comes the formation of a new world, a world which is reconciled with God.

From *The Last Letter*

THESE WILL BE QUIET DAYS in our homes. But I have had the experience over and over again that the quieter it is around me, the clearer do I feel the connection to you. It is as though in solitude the soul develops senses which we hardly know in everyday life. Therefore I have not felt lonely or abandoned for one moment. You, the parents, all of you, the friends and students of mine at the front, all are constantly present to me. Your prayers and good thoughts, words from the Bible, discussions long past,

Editor's note: Written to his fiancée, Maria von Wedemeyer-Weller.

pieces of music, and books,—[all these] gain life and reality as never before. It is a great invisible sphere in which one lives and in whose reality there is no doubt. If it says in the old children's song about the angels: 'Two, to cover me, two, to wake me,' so is this guardianship (*Bewahrung*), by good invisible powers in the morning and at night, something which grown ups need today no less than children. Therefore you must not think that I am unhappy. What is happiness and unhappiness? It depends so little on the circumstances; it depends really only on that which happens inside a person. I am grateful every day that I have you, and that makes me happy (19 December 1944).

Like the Angels

I FEEL that I 'long to look', like the angels in I Peter to see how God is going to solve the apparently insoluble. I think God is about to accomplish something that, even if we take part in it either outwardly or inwardly, we can only receive with the greatest wonder and awe. Somehow it will be clear—for those who have eyes to see—that Ps. 58:11b and Ps. 9:19f[1] are true; and we shall have to repeat Jer. 45:5[2] to ourselves every day.

[1]'Surely there is a God who judges on the earth.' 'Arise, O Lord! Let not man prevail; let the nations be judged before thee.'
[2]'And do you seek great things for yourself? Seek them not; for, behold, I am bringing evil upon all flesh, says the Lord; but I will give you your life as a prize of war in all places which you may go.'

His Mercy and Forgiveness

...I AM SO SURE of God's guiding hand that I hope I shall always be kept in that certainty. You must never doubt that I'm travelling with gratitude and cheerfulness along the road where I'm being led. My past life is brim-full of God's goodness, and my sins are covered by the forgiving love of Christ crucified. I'm most thankful for the people I have met, and I only hope that they never have to grieve about me, but that they, too, will always be certain of, and thankful for, God's mercy and forgiveness....

The Hour of Death

...THE HOUR of a man's death is determined, and it will find him no matter where he may turn. We must be ready for it. But

> He knows ten thousand ways
> To save us from death's power.
> He gives us food and meat,
> A boon in famine's hour.

That's something we mustn't forget....

Victory

DEATH is the supreme festival on the road to freedom.

Sources

Abortion — *Ethics,* 175-176
Acceptance of Guilt, The — *Ethics,* 240-241
Access to God — *Letters and Papers from Prison,* 167-169

Are We Still of Any Use? — *Letters and Papers from Prison,* 16-17

Baptism — *Cost of Discipleship,* 256, 257
Battlefield, The — *Cost of Discipleship,* 315-316
Blessing and Completion — *Creation and Fall,* 42-43
Body of Jesus Christ, The — *Cost of Discipleship,* 265-267
Call of Jesus, The — *Cost of Discipleship,* 251-253
Call of Liberation — *Ethics,* 35
Cause Is Urgent, The — *Cost of Discipleship,* 233-235
Challenge to Faith — *Christ the Center,* 110
Christ Alone — *Cost of Discipleship,* 192-194
Christ Among Us — *No Rusty Swords,* 68
Christ and Antichrist — *Cost of Discipleship,* 299-300
Christ and His Body — *Cost of Discipleship,* 271-272
Christian Life, The — *Letters and Papers from Prison,* 361-362

Christian Radicalism — *Letters and Papers from Prison,* 386

Christians and Pagans — *Letters and Papers from Prison,* 348-349

Christ Our Hope — *Letters and Papers from Prison,* 372-373

Christ, Reality and Good — *Ethics,* 204-205
Christ's Restoration — *Letters and Papers from Prison,* 170-171

Christ the Center — *Christ the Center,* 64-65

Christ the Foundation — *Letters and Papers from Prison*, 46

Church, The — *Ethics*, 202-203
Commandment of God, The — *Ethics*, 278-279
Community of Love, The — *Creation and Fall*, 62-63
Concept of Reality, The — *Ethics*, 188-189
Concrete Temptations and Their Conquest — *Creation and Fall*, 115-116
Confession of Guilt — *Ethics*, 112-113
Confidence — *Letters and Papers from Prison*, 11-12

Conformation — *Ethics*, 82-83
Conscience — *Ethics*, 244-245
Contempt for Humanity — *Letters and Papers from Prison*, 9-10

Costly Grace — *Cost of Discipleship*, 45-48
Created in His Image — *Creation and Fall*, 46, 47
Cross of Christ, The — *Creation and Fall*, 93-94
Day's Beginning, The — *Life Together*, 40-41
Decision, The — *Cost of Discipleship*, 242-244
Deputyship — *Ethics*, 224-225
Desire — *Creation and Fall—Temptation*, 116-117

Discipleship and the Cross — *Cost of Discipleship*, 99
Divine Reality — *Ethics*, 190-191
Easter — *Letters and Papers from Prison*, 240

Ecce Homo! — *Ethics*, 70-71, 75
Evening Prayers — *Letters and Papers from Prison*, 141-142

Fellowship — *Cost of Discipleship*, 284-285
Followers of Christ, The — *Cost of Discipleship*, 210-212
Freedom — *Ethics*, 248-249
Freedom from Anxiety — *Cost of Discipleship*, 197-199, 201

Friend, The — *Letters and Papers from Prison*, 388-391

Fruit, The   *Cost of Discipleship,* 245-246
Fulfilling Our Tasks   *Letters and Papers from Prison,* 217-218
Fulfilment   *Ethics,* 139-140
Gift of Baptism, The   *Cost of Discipleship,* 286-287
Glorifying God   *Letters and Papers from Prison,* 199

Glory of His Resurrection, The   *Cost of Discipleship,* 343-344
God Is No Stop-gap   *Letters and Papers from Prison,* 311-312

God's Blessing   *Letters and Papers from Prison,* 374-375

God's Faithfulness   *Letters and Papers from Prison,* 387

God's Will   *Ethics,* 38
Good Works   *Cost of Discipleship,* 334-335
Gratefulness   *Letters and Papers from Prison,* 191-192

'Harvest Is Great, The'   *Cost of Discipleship,* 224, 225
Heritage of Children, The   *Letters and Papers from Prison,* 45-46

Hiddenness of Prayer, The   *Cost of Discipleship,* 183-184
His Ascension   *Cost of Discipleship,* 269-270
His Mercy and Forgiveness   *Letters and Papers from Prison,* 393

Home   *Ethics,* 158
Hour of Death, The   *Letters and Papers from Prison,* 306

Humanity and Goodness   *Ethics,* 142-143
Human Relationships   *Letters and Papers from Prison,* 386

'I Am the Life'   *Ethics,* 217-219
Idolization of Death, The   *Ethics,* 79
Image of Christ, The   *Cost of Discipleship,* 337
Immanent Righteousness   *Letters and Papers from Prison,* 10-11

Imparting of Grace, The   *Ethics,* 136-137

Incarnate One, The   *Christ the Center,*   104-106

Insecurity and Death   *Letters and Papers from*
    Prison,   16

Jonah   *Letters and Papers from*
    Prison,   398-399

Joy of Fellowship, The   *Life Together,*   20

Judgement   *Ethics,*   30-31

Justification   *Ethics,*   122

Justification As the Last Word

    Ethics,   120, 121

Kingdom of God, The   *Letters and Papers from*
    Prison,   341-342

Last Judgement, The   *Ethics,*   36

Last Letter, The   *Letters and Papers from*
    Prison,   419

Last Temptation, The   *Creation and*
    Fall—Temptation,   113,
    114

Legitimate Struggle, The   *Creation and*
    Fall—Temptation,   127-128

Life Together   *Life Together,*   17

Light of His Presence, The   *Letters and Papers from*
    Prison,   391

Like the Angels   *Letters and Papers from*
    Prison,   279

Lordship of Jesus Christ, The   *Ethics,*   296-297

Love   *Ethics,*   51

Love of God, The   *Ethics,*   206

Lust   *Creation and Fall,*   110-111

Marriage   *Ethics,*   173-174

Ministry of Helpfulness, The   *Life Together,*   99

Morning Prayers   *Letters and Papers from*
    Prison,   139-141

Name of Jesus Christ, The   *Letters and Papers from*
    Prison,   157

New Fellowship, The   *Cost of Discipleship,*   289-290

New Life, The   *Ethics,*   132-133

New Year 1945 — *Cost of Discipleship,* 20-21

Night Voices in Tegel — *Letters and Papers from Prison,* 349-356

Obedience and Freedom — *Ethics,* 252-253

Of Folly — *Letters and Papers from Prison,* 8-9

Of Success — *Letters and Papers from Prison,* 6-7

Optimism — *Letters and Papers from Prison,* 15-16

Our Lives — *Letters and Papers from Prison,* 105

Pain — *Letters and Papers from Prison,* 418

Past, The — *Letters and Papers from Prison,* 320-323

Penultimate, The — *Ethics,* 130-131

Pharisee, The — *Ethics,* 26, 27

Physical Suffering — *Letters and Papers from Prison,* 232

Prayers in Time of Distress — *Letters and Papers from Prison,* 142

Pray for Forgiveness — *Cost of Discipleship,* 323

Preacher, The — *Ethics,* 293-294

Present and Future — *Letters and Papers from Prison,* 14-15

Protection and Help — *Creation and Fall—Temptation,* 117-118

Reality of God, The — *Ethics,* 194-195

Reality of Jesus Christ, The — *Ethics,* 200-201

Rights of Bodily Life, The — *Ethics,* 156-157

Rights of Natural Life, The — *Ethics,* 154-155

Saints, The — *Cost of Discipleship,* 305

Satanic Truth — *Ethics,* 366

Securitas — *Creation and Fall—Temptation,* 123-124

Security of Home, The — *Letters and Papers from Prison,* 295-296

Sense of Quality, The — *Letters and Papers from Prison,* 12-13

Separation from Those You Love — *Letters and Papers from Prison,* 176-177

Sermon on the Mount, The — *Cost of Discipleship,* 218-219

Shame — *Ethics,* 20-21

Sharing God's Sufferings — *Letters and Papers from Prison,* 369-370

Single-minded Love — *Cost of Discipleship,* 204-205

Sorrow and Joy — *Letters and Papers from Prison,* 334-335

Sovereignty of God in History, The — *Letters and Papers from Prison,* 11

Stations on the Road to Freedom — *Letters and Papers from Prison,* 370-371

Strength of God, The — *Letters and Papers from Prison,* 344-346

Strength of the Other Person, The — *Creation and Fall,* 58-59

Suffering of the Messengers, The — *Cost of Discipleship,* 236-237

Suffering Servant, The — *Cost of Discipleship,* 340-341

Suicide — *Ethics,* 169-170

Sympathy — *Letters and Papers from Prison,* 13-14

Taking Over of the Temptations, The — *Creation and Fall,* 107-108

Task of the Church, The — *Ethics,* 108-109

Tempted by Suffering — *Creation and Fall—Temptation,* 118-120

'Thoughts on the Day of Baptism of Dietrich Wilhelm Rüdinger Bethge' — *Letters and Papers from Prison,* 299-300

Through and In Jesus Christ — *Life Together,* 21

To His Mother — *Letters and Papers from Prison,* 399-400

Value of a Life, The	*Ethics,* 163-164
Victory	*Letters and Papers from Prison,* 376
Virtuous Woman, A	*Letters and Papers from Prison,* 44-45
Visionary Dreaming	*Life Together,* 27-28
Vocation	*Ethics,* 254-255, 277
What God Has Joined Together	*Letters and Papers from Prison,* 42-43
What Is Meant By "Telling the Truth"?	*Ethics,* 363-364
Who Am I?	*Letters and Papers from Prison,* 347-348
Who Stands Fast?	*Letters and Papers from Prison,* 4-5
Word of God, The	*Ethics,* 222-223
Work, The	*Cost of Discipleship,* 228-229
World of Conflicts, The	*Ethics,* 17-18

Bibliography

Christ the Center. London: William Collins & Co., Ltd.; New York: Harper & Row, Publishers, Inc.

Creation and Fall—Temptation. New York: Macmillan Publishing Co., Inc., 1965.

Ethics. New York: Macmillan Publishing Co., Inc., 1965.

Letters and Papers from Prison. New York: Macmillan Publishing Co., Inc., 1972.

Life Together. New York: Harper & Row, Publishers, Inc.

The Cost of Discipleship. New York: Macmillan Publishing Co., Inc., 1963

No Rusty Swords. London: William Collins Sons & Co., Ltd.; New York: Harper & Row, Publishers, Inc.

The Joyful Christian

THE JOYFUL

127 Readings from

CHRISTIAN

C. S. LEWIS

COLLIER BOOKS

Macmillan Publishing Company

NEW YORK

Macmillan Publishing Company
866 Third Avenue, New York, N.Y. 10022

Extracts from *Mere Christianity, The Screwtape Letters, TheProblem of
Pain, Miracles,* and *The Abolition of Man* are reprinted by permission
of William Collins Sons & Company Limited. Copyright © Macmillan
Publishing Co., Inc. 1944, 1947. Copyright renewed 1972, 1975. Copyright
© Macmillan Publishing Co., Inc. 1943, 1944, 1945, 1952. Copyright
renewed 1972, 1973. Copyright © Macmillan Publishing Co., Inc. 1947.
Copyright renewed 1975. Published by Macmillan Publishing Co., Inc.
1940, 1943. Published by Macmillan Publishing Co., Inc. 1942, 1943.

Selections from *Letters to Malcolm: Chiefly on Prayer, The Four Loves,
Letters of C. S. Lewis, Reflections on the Psalms,* and *The World's Last
Night and Other Essays* are reprinted by permission of Harcourt Brace
Jovanovich, Inc.; copyright © 1958 by C. S. Lewis; copyright © 1960 by
Helen Joy Lewis; copyright © 1963, 1964, by the Estate of C. S. Lewis
and/or C. S. Lewis; copyright © 1966 by W. H. Lewis and Executors
of C. S. Lewis.

Selections from *A Grief Observed* are reprinted with permission of
The Seabury Press; © 1961 by N. W. Clerk [C. S. Lewis].

Selections from *Christian Reflections, God in the Dock,* and *Letters to an
American Lady* are reprinted with permission of Wm. B. Eerdmans Co.;
copyright © 1967 by the Executors of the Estate of C. S. Lewis;
copyright © 1970 by The Trustees of the Estate of C. S. Lewis;
copyright © 1967 by Wm. B. Eerdmans Publishing Co.

Library of Congress Cataloging in Publication Data
Lewis, C. S. (Clive Staples), 1898-1963.
  The joyful Christian.
  Reprint. Originally published: New York:
Macmillan, 1984.
  Bibliography: p.
  1. Church of England—Collected works.
2. Theology—Collected works—20th century.
3. Christian life—Anglican authors—Collected
works. I. Title.
[BX5037.L4 1984b]   230'.3   84-23084
ISBN 0-02-086930-4 (pbk.)

First Paperback Edition 1984

10   9   8   7

The Joyful Christian is also published in a hardcover edition by
Macmillan Publishing Company.

Printed in the United States of America

Contents

Foreword   xi

Right and Wrong   1

The Universe   3

Life on Other Planets   4

God in Outer Space   5

Atheism   7

Seeing and Believing   8

Miracle and the Laws of Nature   9

Morality   11

The Tao   14

Illustrations of the Tao   16

Joy   27

Theology   32

Divine Omnipotence	36
Divine Goodness	37
Begetting and Making	39
Spirit, Spirits, Spiritual	41
The Three-Personal God	43
The Trinity	45
The Fall of Man	48
The Incarnation	50
The Virgin Birth	56
Miracles of Fertility	58
Miracles of Healing	60
Miracles of Destruction	62
Miracle of the Resurrection	63
Miracle of the Walking on the Water	65
Miracle of the Raising of Lazarus	66
Miracle of the Transfiguration	67
Miracle of the Ascension	68
On Seeing a Miracle	69
The Second Coming	70
What Are We to Make of Jesus Christ?	72
"Putting on Christ"	74
Perfection	77
First Fervor	79
Scruples	80
Liturgy	80
Holy Communion	82
Devotions to Saints	83
Church Music	84
Ready-made Prayers	85
Festooning Ready-made Prayers	86
When and Where to Pray	88

CONTENTS

The Moment of Prayer	90
Mechanics of Meditation	92
Answered Prayers	95
The Efficacy of Prayer	96
Mysticism	100
Spiritual Reading	102
Reading the Gospels	104
Biblical Exegesis	106
Thought, Imagination, Language	107
Scripture	110
The Psalms	113
Prayer of Praise	115
Modern Translations of the Bible	121
Moral Choices	123
Virtue	124
Prudence	124
Temperance	125
Justice and Fortitude	126
Chastity	127
Belief	128
Belief and Disbelief	130
Faith	133
Faith and Good Works	135
Good Work and Good Works	136
Hope	138
Charity	139
Humility	141
Forgiveness	141
Almsgiving	143
Obedience	144
The Devil	145

Screwtape to Wormwood on

Prayer	146
War	147
Anxiety	149
Peaks and Troughs	150
Lust	151
Worldly Companions	152
Humility	153
Laughter	155
Irregular Churchgoing	157
Gluttony	158
Reinterpreting Jesus	159

Everythingism	162
Sins of Thought	163
Pride	164
Human Wickedness	167
Laziness	169
Guilt	169
Anxiety	171
Psychoanalysis	172
Social Morality	173
Christian Society	175
Ecumenism	176
Other Religions	177
Fascism and Communism	178
Is Christianity Hard or Easy?	178
Apologetics	183
Money	185
Gift-love and Need-love	186
Appreciative Love	187
Love of Nature	187

CONTENTS

Love of Country	*188*
Storge or Affection	*189*
Philia or Friendship	*191*
Eros and Venus	*192*
Agape or Charity	*194*
"Love Thy Neighbor"	*197*
Sex	*198*
Marriage	*198*
Divorce	*200*
Intercourse in the Afterlife	*201*
Christmas and Xmas	*203*
The Ego and the Self	*205*
The Airplane, the Wireless, and the Contraceptive	*206*
Human Pain	*209*
Animal Pain	*211*
Suffering	*212*
The Crown and the Cross	*214*
Death	*215*
Judgment	*218*
Resurrection of the Body	*220*
Purgatory	*222*
Hell	*222*
Heaven	*227*
Bibliography	*229*
Sources	*236*

Foreword

IF SALES ARE signs, then C. S. Lewis is one of the most popular Christian theologians being published in the United States today. He is already well known for such works as *The Screwtape Letters* (1942), a satiric correspondence in which a senior devil instructs a junior devil on the most salubrious ways to subvert a Christian; for *The Space Trilogy* (1938, 1943, 1945), a three-volume adventure into science fiction; and for *The Chronicles of Narnia* (1950–1956), a seven-volume sally into children's fiction. But it is the sales of his lesser-known theological works—*Miracles, The Problem of Pain, Reflections on the Psalms,* and *Letters to Malcolm, Chiefly on Prayer*—that have increased dramatically in the 1970s.

If sales are souls, then *Mere Christianity* is Lewis's most influential theological work. Not only have clerics and students been reading it since it was published in 1952—parts of it were published in 1942, 1943, and 1944—businessmen and politicians have also been picking it up and allowing it to influence their lives. Perhaps the most dramatic incident happened in 1973. The president of an American electronics firm handed a copy of the work to a lawyer who was then special counsel to the White House. After reading it, praying over it, discussing it with others, Charles W. Colson underwent a conversion to Christ that he was to describe in his best-selling *Born Again*.

Lewis himself was a convert. It happened on the way to a zoo. His brother was driving a motorcycle; he was riding in the sidecar. At the beginning of the trip he did not believe that Jesus Christ was the Son of God. Somewhere along the way—he was not blinded like St. Paul on the road to Damascus nor was he sprung from the sidecar by a piece of piano wire divinely strung across the roadway—he was, as he recounts in his autobiography, "surprised by joy." At the end of the trip he found himself believing what he thought he never could.

That was in 1931. At the time he was teaching English literature and language at Magdalen College, Oxford. In the mornings he would give lectures and tutorials; in the afternoons he would enjoy brisk walks and large cups of tea; in the evenings he would write and study. Some nights he would invite two or three students to his rooms for port, beer, and stimulating talk. One night a week for years he devoted to a group of friends who talked, read their latest compositions, and exchanged personal as well as literary criticisms. Two of his scholarly works have become classics: *The Allegory of Love* and *English Literature in the Sixteenth Century*—and one of his spiritual works got him on the cover of *Time* magazine: *The Screwtape Letters*. In the early 1940s he delivered twenty-five talks on various Christian topics over British radio; in the late 1950s he recorded ten lectures on love for use on American radio. In 1954 he was appointed Professor of Medieval and Renaissance English Literature at Cambridge University, a post he held until shortly before his death.

If there is one word to describe Lewis's life, it would be *joy*. The harmonizing of himself with the rest of the created world, the process that led him from atheism through theism and pantheism to Christianity, he has described as joy. His lectures and books, the ones dealing with things theological, can also be described as a sort of joy in that they attempt to attune the modern intellect to the facts and truths of Christianity. His marriage in 1957 was an intense, if very brief, joy of a different sort; Joy Davidman was her name; she died of cancer three years later. And since 1963, when he died at the age of sixty-five, he has no doubt been about the serious business of heaven, which he fully expected to be joy.

The sort of Christianity Lewis espoused throughout his life can be compared to his taste in food. As described by his brother, "His requirements were simply but strongly felt. Plain, domestic cookery was what he wanted, with the proviso that if the food was hot the plates should be hot as well. What he really disliked was 'messed up food,' by which he meant any sort of elaborately dressed dishes" (*Letters of C. S. Lewis*, 16).

What Lewis disliked about certain Christian doctrines were the elaborately prepared and elegantly served sauces, like transsubstantiation or consubstantiation for the Eucharist. "The command, after all, was Take, eat: not Take, understand" (*Letters to Malcolm*, 104). To him too much definition could disguise or even destroy the basic content of a doctrine. And he noted with distaste the bloodshed in the kitchen where theologians with contrary recipes have been sundering each other for centuries.

Although he thumped and thwacked every Christian communion for some excess of doctrinal enthusiasm, he also praised each of them for having one or another doctrine in its purest form. Discreetly, charitably, he almost never mentioned a denomination by name. Where historical or doctrinal controversies appeared, he was invariably to be found in the extreme middle. It is neither good actions nor faith in Christ that leads a Christian home—that's "like asking which blade of a scissors is [more] necessary" (*Mere Christianity*, 109)—it is both. This plainness, this mereness, of his theology makes him ecumenical *in excelsis* and helps explain why Christians of all sorts respond so enthusiastically to his work.

What a Christian can joyfully believe, therefore, is the subject of this anthology, and selections have been taken from fifteen of C. S. Lewis's works. The readings are thematically arranged, informally systematized, and devotionally styled. Sources of the readings are given at the back of this book; each source is readily available in a paperback edition; the bibliography tells the precise title and appropriate publisher.

With regard to the texts of the readings, no attempt has been made to produce a critical edition. The punctuation has merely been standardized, the spelling Americanized, the Latin abbreviations Englished, and the hyphens no longer deemed necessary by lexicographers deleted. Capitalizations of the divine pronoun and a variety of abstract nouns remain Lewis's own.

—WILLIAM GRIFFIN
Macmillan Publishing Company
July 15, 1977

The Joyful Christian

Right and Wrong

EVERYONE HAS HEARD people quarreling. Sometimes it sounds funny and sometimes it sounds merely unpleasant; but however it sounds, I believe we can learn something very important from listening to the kinds of things they say. They say things like this: "How'd you like it if anyone did the same to you?"—"That's my seat, I was there first"—"Leave him alone, he isn't doing you any harm"—"Why should you shove in first?"—"Give me a bit of your orange, I gave you a bit of mine"—"Come on, you promised." People say things like this every day, educated as well as uneducated, and children as well as grown-ups.

Now what interests me about all these remarks is that the man who makes them is not merely saying that the other man's behavior does not happen to please him. He is appealing to some kind of standard of behavior which he expects the other man to know about. And the other man very seldom replies: "To hell with your standard." Nearly always he tries to make out that what he has been doing does not really go against the standard, or that if it does there is some special excuse. He pretends there is some special reason in this particular case why the person who took the seat first should not keep it, or that things were quite different when he was given the bit of orange, or that something has turned up which lets him off from keeping his promise. It looks, in fact, very much as if both parties had in mind some kind of Law or Rule of fair play, or decent behavior, or morality, or whatever you like to call it, about which they really agreed. And they have. If they had not, they might, of course, fight like animals, but they could not *quarrel* in the human sense of the word. Quarreling means trying to show that the other man is in the wrong. And there would be no sense in trying to do that unless you and he had some sort of agreement as to what Right and Wrong are; just as there would be no sense in saying that a footballer had committed a foul unless there was some agreement about the rules of football.

Now this Law or Rule about Right and Wrong used to be called the Law of Nature. Nowadays, when we talk of the "laws of nature," we usually mean things like gravitation, or heredity, or the laws of chemistry. But when the older thinkers called the Law of Right and Wrong "the Law of Nature," they really meant the Law of *Human* Nature. The idea was that, just as all bodies are governed by the law of gravitation and organisms by biological laws, so the creature called man also had *his* law—with this great difference, that a body could choose either to obey the Law of Human Nature or to disobey it.

The Universe

WE WANT TO KNOW whether the universe simply happens to be what it is for no reason or whether there is a power behind it that makes it what it is. Since that power, if it exists, would be not one of the observed facts but a reality which makes them, no mere observation of the facts can find it. There is only one case in which we can know whether there is anything more, namely our own case, and in that one case we find there is. Or put it the other way round. If there was a controlling power outside the universe, it could not show itself to us as one of the facts inside the universe—no more than the architect of a house could actually be a wall, or staircase, or fireplace in that house. The only way in which we could expect it to show itself would be inside ourselves as an influence or a command trying to get us to behave in a certain way. And that is just what we do find inside ourselves. Surely this ought to arouse our suspicions? In the only case where you can expect to get an answer, the answer turns out to be Yes; and in the other cases, where you do not get an answer, you see why you do not.

Suppose someone asked me, when I see a man in a blue uniform going down the street leaving little paper packets at each house, why I suppose that they contain letters? I should reply, "Because whenever he leaves a similar little packet for me I find it does contain a letter." And if he then objected, "But you've never seen all these letters which you think the other people are getting," I should say, "Of course not, and I shouldn't expect to, because they're not addressed to me. I'm explaining the packets I'm not allowed to open by the ones I'm allowed to open."

It is the same about this question. The only packet I'm allowed to open is Man. When I do, especially when I open that particular man called myself, I find that I do not exist on my own, that I am under a law; that somebody or something wants me to behave in a certain way. I do not, of course, think that if I could get inside a stone or a tree I should find exactly the same thing, just as I do not think all the other people in the street get the same letters as I do. I should expect, for instance, to find that the stone had to obey the law of gravity—that whereas the sender of the letters merely tells me to obey the laws of my human nature, He compels the stone to obey the laws of its stony nature. But I should expect to find that there was, so to speak, a sender in both cases, a Power behind the facts, a Director, a Guide.

Life on Other Planets

I . . . FEAR THE PRACTICAL, not the theoretical, problems which will arise if ever we meet rational creatures which are not human. Against them we shall, if we can, commit all the crimes we have already committed against creatures certainly human but differing from us in features and pigmentation; and the starry heavens will become an object to which good men can look up only with feelings of intolerable guilt, agonized pity, and burning shame.

Of course, after the first debauch of exploitation we shall make some belated attempt to do better. We shall perhaps send missionaries. But can even missionaries be trusted? "Gun and gospel" have been horribly combined in the past.

The missionary's holy desire to save souls has not always been kept quite distinct from the arrogant desire, the busy-body's itch, to (as he calls it) "civilize" the (as he calls them) "natives." Would all our missionaries recognize a fallen race if they met it? Could they? Would they continue to press upon creatures that did not need to be saved that plan of Salvation which God has appointed for Man? Would they denounce as sins mere differences of behavior which the spiritual and biological history of these strange creatures fully justified and which God Himself had blessed? Would they try to teach those from whom they had better learn? I do not know.

What I do know is that here and now, as our only possible practical preparation for such a meeting, you and I should resolve to stand firm against all exploitation and all theological imperialism. It will not be fun. We shall be called traitors to our own species. We shall be hated of almost all men; even of some religious men. And we must not give back one single inch. We shall probably fail, but let us go down fighting for the right side. Our loyalty is due not to our species but to God. Those who are, or can become, His sons, are our real brothers even if they have shells or tusks. It is spiritual, not biological, kinship that counts.

God in Outer Space

THE RUSSIANS, I am told, report that they have not found God in outer space. On the other hand, a good many people in many different times and countries claim to have found God, or been found by God, here on earth.

The conclusion some want us to draw from these data is that God does not exist. As a corollary, those who think they have met Him on earth were suffering from a delusion.

But other conclusions might be drawn.

(1) We have not yet gone far enough in space. There had been ships on the Atlantic for a good time before America was discovered.

(2) God does exist but is locally confined to this planet.

(3) The Russians did find God in space without knowing it because they lacked the requisite apparatus for detecting Him.

(4) God does exist but is not an object either located in a particular part of space nor diffused, as we once thought "ether" was, throughout space.

The first two conclusions do not interest me. The sort of religion for which they could be a defense would be a religion for savages: the belief in a local deity who can be contained in a particular temple, island, or grove. That, in fact, seems to be the sort of religion about which the Russians—or some Russians, and a good many people in the West—are being irreligious. It is not in the least disquieting that no astronauts have discovered a god of that sort. The really disquieting thing would be if they had.

The third and fourth conclusions are the ones for my money. . . .

Space travel really has nothing to do with the matter. To some, God is discoverable everywhere; to others, nowhere. Those who do not find Him on earth are unlikely to find Him in space. (Hang it all, we're in space already; every year we go a huge circular tour in space.) But send a saint up in a spaceship and he'll find God in space as he found God on earth. Much depends on the seeing eye.

Atheism

MY ARGUMENT AGAINST GOD was that the universe seemed so cruel and unjust. But how had I got this idea of *just* and *unjust?* A man does not call a line crooked unless he has some idea of a straight line. What was I comparing this universe with when I called it unjust? If the whole show was bad and senseless from A to Z, so to speak, why did I, who was supposed to be part of the show, find myself in such violent reaction against it? A man feels wet when he falls into water, because man is not a water animal: a fish would not feel wet. Of course, I could have given up my idea of justice by saying it was nothing but a private idea of my own. But if I did that, then my argument against God collapsed too—for the argument depended on saying that the world was really unjust, not simply that it did not happen to please my private fancies. Thus in the very act of trying to prove that God did not exist—in other words, that the whole of reality was senseless—I found I was forced to assume that one part of reality—namely my idea of justice— was full of sense. Consequently atheism turns out to be too simple. If the whole universe has no meaning, we should never have found out that it has no meaning: just as, if there were no light in the universe and therefore no creatures with eyes, we should never know it was dark. *Dark* would be without meaning.

Seeing and Believing

IN ALL MY LIFE I have met only one person who claims to have seen a ghost. And the interesting thing about the story is that that person disbelieved in the immortal soul before she saw the ghost and still disbelieves after seeing it. She says that what she saw must have been an illusion or a trick of the nerves. And obviously she may be right. Seeing is not believing.

For this reason, the question whether miracles occur can never be answered simply by experience. Every event which might claim to be a miracle is, in the last resort, something presented to our senses, something seen, heard, touched, smelled, or tasted. And our senses are not infallible. If anything extraordinary seems to have happened, we can always say that we have been the victims of an illusion. If we hold a philosophy which excludes the supernatural, this is what we always shall say. What we learn from experience depends on the kind of philosophy we bring to experience. It is therefore useless to appeal to experience before we have settled, as well as we can, the philosophical question. If immediate experience cannot prove or disprove the miraculous, still less can history do so. Many people think one can decide whether a miracle occurred in the past by examining the evidence "according to the ordinary rules of historical inquiry." But the ordinary rules cannot be worked until we have decided whether miracles are possible, and if so, how probable they are. For if they are impossible, then no amount of historical evidence will convince us. If they are possible but immensely improbable, then only mathematically demonstrative evidence will convince us: and since history never provides that degree of evidence for any event, history can never convince us that a miracle occurred. If, on the other hand, miracles are not intrinsically improbable, then the existing evidence will be sufficient to convince us that quite a number of miracles have occurred. The result of our historical inquiries thus depends on the philosophical views which we have been holding before we even began to look at the evidence. The philosophical question must therefore come first.

Miracle and the Laws of Nature

THREE CONCEPTIONS of the "Laws" of Nature have been held. (1) That they are mere brute facts, known only by observation, with no discoverable rhyme or reason about them. We know *that* Nature behaves thus and thus; we do not know *why* she does and can see no reason why she should not do the opposite. (2) That they are applications of the law of averages. The foundations of Nature are in the random and lawless. But the numbers of units we are dealing with are so enormous that the behavior of these crowds (like the behavior of very large masses of men) can be calculated with practical accuracy. What we call "impossible events" are events so overwhelmingly improbable—by actuarial standards—that we do not need to take them into account. (3) That the fundamental laws of Physics are really what we call "necessary truths" like the truths of mathematics—in other words, that if we clearly understand what we are saying, we shall see that the opposite would be meaningless nonsense. Thus it is a "law" that when one billiard ball shoves another, the amount of momentum lost by the first ball must exactly equal the amount gained by the second. People who hold that the laws of Nature are necessary truths would say that all we have done is split up the single event into two halves (adventures of ball A, and adventures of ball B) and then discover that "the two sides of the account balance." When we understand this, we see that, of course, they *must* balance. The fundamental laws are in the long run merely statements that every event is itself and not some different event.

It will at once be clear that the first of these three theories gives no assurance against Miracles—indeed no assurance that, even apart from Miracles, the "laws" which we have hitherto observed will be obeyed tomorrow. If we have no notion why a thing happens, then, of course, we know no reason why it should not be otherwise, and therefore have no certainty that it might not some day be otherwise.

The second theory, which depends on the law of averages, is in the same position. The assurance it gives us is of the same general kind as our assurance that a coin tossed a thousand times will not give the same result, say, nine hundred times: and that the longer you toss it, the more nearly the numbers of Heads and Tails will come to being equal. But this is so only provided the coin is an honest coin. If it is a loaded coin, our expectations may be disappointed. But the people who believe in miracles are maintaining precisely that the coin *is* loaded. The expectation based on the law of averages will work only for *undoctored* Nature. And the question whether miracles occur is just the question whether Nature is ever doctored.

The third view (that Laws of Nature are necessary truths) seems at first sight to present an insurmountable obstacle to miracle. The breaking of them would, in that case, be a self-contradiction and not even Omnipotence can do what is self-contradictory. Therefore the Laws cannot be broken. And therefore, shall we conclude, no miracle can ever occur?

Morality

THERE IS A STORY about a schoolboy who was asked what he thought God was like. He replied that, as far as he could make out, God was "The sort of person who is always snooping round to see if anyone is enjoying himself and then trying to stop it." And I'm afraid that is the sort of idea that the word Morality raises in a good many people's minds: something that interferes, something that stops you having a good time. In reality, moral rules are directions for running the human machine. Every moral rule is there to prevent a breakdown, or a strain, or a friction, in the running of that machine. That is why these rules at first seem to be constantly interfering with our natural inclinations. When you are being taught how to use any machine, the instructor keeps on saying, "No, don't do it like that," because, of course, there are all sorts of things that look all right and seem to you the natural way of treating the machine, but do not really work.

Some people prefer to talk about moral "ideals" rather than moral rules and about moral "idealism" rather than moral obedience. Now it is, of course, quite true that moral perfection is an "ideal" in the sense that we cannot achieve it. In that sense every kind of perfection is, for us humans, an ideal; we cannot succeed in being perfect car drivers or perfect tennis players or in drawing perfectly straight lines. But there is another sense in which it is very misleading to call moral perfection an ideal. When a man says that a certain woman, or house, or ship, or garden is "his ideal," he does not mean (unless he is rather a fool) that everyone else ought to have the same ideal. In such matters we are entitled to have different tastes and, therefore, different ideals. But it is dangerous to describe a man who tries very hard to keep the moral law as a "man of high ideals" because this might lead you to think that moral perfection was a private taste of his own and that the rest of us were not called on to share it. This would be a dangerous mistake.

Perfect behavior may be as unattainable as perfect gear-changing when we drive; but it is a necessary ideal prescribed for all men by the very nature of the human machine just as perfect gear-changing is an ideal prescribed for all drivers by the very nature of cars. And it would be even more dangerous to think of oneself as a person "of high ideals" because one is trying to tell no lies at all (instead of only a few lies), or never to commit adultery (instead of committing it only seldom), or not to be a bully (instead of being only a moderate bully). It might lead you to become a prig and to think you were rather a special person who deserved to be congratulated on his "idealism." In reality you might just as well expect to be congratulated because, whenever you do a sum, you try to get it quite right. To be sure, perfect arithmetic is "an ideal"; you will certainly make some mistakes in some calculations. But there is nothing very fine about trying to be quite accurate at each step in each sum. It would be idiotic not to try; for every mistake is going to cause you trouble later on. In the same way every moral failure is going to cause trouble, probably to others and certainly to yourself. By talking about rules and obedience instead of "ideals" and "idealism," we help to remind ourselves of these facts.

Now let us go a step further. There are two ways in which the human machine goes wrong. One is when human individuals drift apart from one another, or else collide with one another and do one another damage, by cheating or bullying. The other is when things go wrong inside the individual—when the different parts of him (his different faculties, and desires, and so on) either drift apart or interfere with one another. You can get the idea plain if you think of us as a fleet of ships sailing in formation. The voyage will be a success only, in the first place, if the ships do not collide and get in one another's way; and, secondly, if each ship is seaworthy and has her engines in good order. As a matter of fact, you cannot have either of these two things without the other. If the ships keep on having collisions, they will not remain seaworthy very long. On the other hand, if their steering gears are out of order, they will not be able to avoid collisions. Or, if you like, think of humanity as a band playing a tune. To get a good result, you need two things. Each player's individual instrument must be in tune and also each must come in at the right moment so as to combine with all the others.

But there is one thing we have not yet taken into account. We have not asked where the fleet is trying to get to, or what piece of music the band is trying to play. The instruments might be all in tune and might all come in at the right moment, but even so the performance would not be a success if they had been engaged to provide dance music and actually played nothing but Dead Marches. And however well the fleet sailed, its voyage would be a failure it it were meant to reach New York and actually arrived at Calcutta.

Morality, then, seems to be concerned with three things. Firstly, with fair play and harmony between individuals. Secondly, with what might be called tidying up or harmonizing the things inside each individual. Thirdly, with the general purpose of human life as a whole: what man was made for: what course the whole fleet ought to be on: what tune the conductor of the band wants it to play.

The Tao

THE CHINESE . . . speak of a great thing (the greatest thing) called the *Tao*. It is the reality beyond all predicates, the abyss that was before the Creator Himself. It is Nature, it is the Way, the Road. It is the Way in which the universe goes on, the Way in which things everlastingly emerge, stilly and tranquilly, into space and time. It is also the Way which every man should tread in imitation of that cosmic and supercosmic progression, conforming all activities to that great exemplar. "In ritual," say the Analects, "it is harmony with Nature that is prized." The ancient Jews likewise praise the Law as being "true" (Psalm 119:151).

This conception in all its forms, Platonic, Aristotelian, Stoic, Christian, and Oriental alike, I shall henceforth refer to for brevity simply as "the *Tao*". . . . It is the doctrine of objective value, the belief that certain attitudes are really true, and others really false, to the kind of thing the universe is and the kind of things we are. Those who know the *Tao* can hold that to call children delightful or old men venerable is not simply to record a psychological fact about our own parental or filial emotions at the moment, but to recognize a quality which demands a certain response from us whether we make it or not. I myself do not enjoy the society of small children: because I speak from within the *Tao*, I recognize this as a defect in myself—just as a man may have to recognize that he is tone deaf or color blind. And because our approvals and disapprovals are thus recognitions of objective value or responses to an objective order, therefore emotional states can be in harmony with reasons (when we feel liking for what ought to be approved) or out of harmony with reason (when we perceive that liking is due but cannot feel it). No emotion is, in itself, a judgment: in that sense all emotions and sentiments are alogical. But they can be reasonable or unreasonable as they conform to Reason or fail to conform. The heart never takes the place of the head: but it can, and should, obey it. . . .

This thing which I have called for convenience the *Tao*, and which others may call Natural Law, or Traditional Morality, or the First Principles of Practical Reason, or the First Platitudes, is not one among a series of possible systems of value. It is the sole source of all value judgments. If it is rejected, all value is rejected. If any value is retained, it is retained. The effort to refute it and raise a new system of value in its place is self-contradictory. There never has been, and never will be, a radically new judgment of value in the history of the world. What purport to be new systems, or (as they now call them) "ideologies," all consist of fragments from the *Tao* itself, arbitrarily wrenched from their context in the whole and then swollen to madness in their isolation, yet still owing to the *Tao* and to it alone such validity as they possess. If my duty to my parents is a superstition, then so is my duty to posterity. If justice is a superstition, then so is my duty to my country or my race. If the pursuit of scientific knowledge is a real value, then so is conjugal fidelity. The rebellion of new ideologies against the *Tao* is a rebellion of the branches against the tree: if the rebels could succeed, they would find that they destroyed themselves. The human mind has no more power of inventing a new value than of imagining a new primary color, or, indeed, of creating a new sun and a new sky for it to move in.

Illustrations of the Tao

THE FOLLOWING ILLUSTRATIONS of the Natural Law are collected from such sources as come readily to the hand of one who is not a professional historian. The list makes no pretense of completeness. It will be noticed that writers . . . who wrote within the Christian tradition are quoted side by side with the New Testament. This would, of course, be absurd if I were trying to collect independent testimonies to the *Tao.* But (1) I am not trying to *prove* its validity by the argument from common consent. Its validity cannot be deduced. For those who do not perceive its rationality, even universal consent could not prove it. (2) The idea of collecting *independent* testimonies presupposes that "civilizations" have arisen in the world independently of one another; or even that humanity has had several independent emergences on this planet. The biology and anthropology involved in such an assumption are extremely doubtful. It is by no means certain that there has ever (in the sense required) been more than one civilization in all history. It is at least arguable that every civilization we find has been derived from another civilization and, in the last resort, from a single center—"carried" like an infectious disease or like the Apostolical succession.

I. THE LAW OF GENERAL BENEFICENCE

Negative

"I have not slain men." (Ancient Egyptian)

"Do not murder." (Ancient Jewish)

"Terrify not men or God will terrify thee." (Ancient Egyptian)

"In Nastrond (= Hell) I saw . . . murderers." (Old Norse)

"I have not brought misery upon my fellows. I have not made the beginning of every day laborious in the sight of him who worked for me." (Ancient Egyptian)

"I have not been grasping." (Ancient Egyptian)

"Who meditates oppression, his dwelling is overturned." (Babylonian)

"He who is cruel and calumnious has the character of a cat." (Hindu)

"Slander not." (Babylonian)

"Thou shalt not bear false witness against thy neighbor." (Ancient Jewish)

"Utter not a word by which anyone could be wounded." (Hindu)

"Has he . . . driven an honest man from his family? broken up a well cemented clan?" ' (Babylonian)

"I have not caused hunger. I have not caused weeping." (Ancient Egyptian)

"Never do to others what you would not like them to do to you." (Ancient Chinese)

"Thou shalt not hate thy brother in thy heart." (Ancient Jewish)

"He whose heart is in the smallest degree set upon goodness will dislike no one." (Ancient Chinese)

Positive

"Nature urges that a man should wish human society to exist and should wish to enter it." (Roman)

"By the fundamental Law of Nature Man [is] to be preserved as much as possible." (English: Locke)

"When the people have multiplied, what next should be done for them? The Master said, Enrich them. Jan Ch'iu said, When one has enriched them, what next should be done for them? The Master said, Instruct them." (Ancient Chinese)

"Speak kindness . . . show good will." (Babylonian)

"Men were brought into existence for the sake of men that they might do one another good." (Roman)

"Man is man's delight." (Old Norse)

"He who is asked for alms should always give." (Hindu)

"What good man regards any misfortune as no concern of his?" (Roman)

"I am a man: nothing human is alien to me." (Roman)

"Love thy neighbor as thyself." (Ancient Jewish)

"Love the stranger as thyself." (Ancient Jewish)

"Do to men what you wish men to do to you." (Christian)

II. THE LAW OF SPECIAL BENEFICENCE

"It is upon the trunk that a gentleman works. When that is firmly set up, the Way grows. And surely proper behavior to parents and elder brothers is the trunk of goodness." (Ancient Chinese)

"Brothers shall fight and be each others' bane." (Old Norse)

"Has he insulted his elder sister?" (Babylonian)

"You will see them take care of their kindred [and] the children of their friends . . . never reproaching them in the least." (American Indian)

"Love thy wife studiously. Gladden her heart all thy life long." (Ancient Egyptian)

"Nothing can ever change the claims of kinship for a right thinking man." (Anglo-Saxon)

"Did not Socrates love his own children, though he did so as a free man and as one not forgetting that the gods have the first claim on our friendship?" (Greek)

"Natural affection is a thing right and according to Nature." (Greek)

"I ought not to be unfeeling like a statue but should fulfill both my natural and artificial relations, as a worshipper, a son, a brother, a father, and a citizen." (Greek)

"This first I rede thee: be blameless to thy kindred. Take no vengeance even though they do thee wrong." (Old Norse)

"Is it only the sons of Atreus who love their wives? For every good man, who is right-minded, loves and cherishes his own." (Greek)

"The union and fellowship of men will be best reserved if each receives from us the more kindness in proportion as he is more closely connected with us." (Roman)

"Part of us is claimed by our country, part by our parents, part by our friends." (Roman)

"If a ruler . . . compassed the salvation of the whole state, surely you would call him Good? The Master said, It would no longer be a matter of 'Good.' He would without doubt be a Divine Sage." (Ancient Chinese)

"Has it escaped you that, in the eyes of gods and good men, your native land deserves from you more honor, worship, and reverence than your mother and father and all your ancestors? That you should give a softer answer to its anger than to a father's anger? That if you cannot persuade it to alter its mind you must obey it in all quietness, whether it binds you, or beats you, or sends you to a war where you may get wounds or death?" (Greek)

"If any provide not for his own, and specially for those of his own house, he hath denied the faith." (Christian)

"Put them in mind to obey magistrates." "I exhort that prayers be made for kings and all that are in authority." (Christian)

III. DUTIES TO PARENTS, ELDERS, ANCESTORS

"Your father is an image of the Lord of Creation, your mother is an image of the Earth. For him who fails to honor them, every work of piety is in vain. This is the first duty." (Hindu)

"Has he despised Father and Mother?" (Babylonian)

"I was a staff by my Father's side. . . . I went in and out at his command." (Ancient Egyptian)

"Honor thy Father and thy Mother."
(Ancient Jewish)

"To care for parents." (Greek)

"Children, old men, the poor, and the sick, should be considered as the lords of the atmosphere." (Hindu)

"Rise up before the hoary head and honor the old man." (Ancient Jewish)

"I tended the old man, I gave him my staff." (Ancient Egyptian)

"You will see them take care . . . of old men." (American Indian)

"I have not taken away the oblations of the blessed dead." (Ancient Egyptian)

"When proper respect toward the dead is shown at the end and continued after they are far away, the moral force of a people has reached its highest point." (Ancient Chinese)

IV. DUTIES TO CHILDREN AND POSTERITY

"Children, the old, the poor, etc., should be considered as lords of the atmosphere." (Hindu)

"To marry and to beget children." (Greek)

"Can you conceive an Epicurean commonwealth? . . . What will happen? Whence is the population to be kept up? Who will educate them? Who will be Director of Adolescents? Who will be Director of Physical Training? What will be taught?" (Greek)

"Nature produces a special love of offspring." "To live according to Nature is the supreme good." (Roman)

"The second of these achievements is no less glorious than the first; for while the first did good on one occasion, the second will continue to benefit the state forever." (Roman)

"Great reverence is owed to a child." (Ancient Chinese)

"The Master said, Respect the young." (Ancient Chinese)

"The killing of the women and more especially of the young boys and girls who are to go to make up the future strength of the people, is the saddest part . . . and we feel it very sorely." (American Indian)

V. THE LAW OF JUSTICE

Sexual Justice

"Has he approached his neighbor's wife?" (Babylonian)

"Thou shalt not commit adultery." (Ancient Jewish)

"I saw in Nastrond (= Hell) . . . beguilers of others' wives." (Old Norse)

Honesty

"Has he drawn false boundaries?" (Babylonian)

"To wrong, to rob, to cause to be robbed." (Babylonian)

"I have not stolen." (Ancient Egyptian)

"Thou shalt not steal." (Ancient Jewish)

"Choose loss rather than shameful gains." (Greek)

"Justice is the settled and permanent intention of rendering to each man his rights." (Roman)

"If the native made a 'find' of any kind (for example, a honey tree) and marked it, it was thereafter safe for him, as far as his own tribesmen were concerned, no matter how long he left it." (Australian Aborigines)

"The first point of justice is that none should do any mischief to another unless he has first been attacked by the other's wrongdoing. The second is that a man should treat common property as common property, and private property as his own. There is no such thing as private property by nature, but things have become private either through prior occupation (as when men of old came into empty territory) or by conquest, or law, or agreement, or stipulation, or casting lots." (Roman)

Justice in Court, etc.

"Who so takes no bribe . . . well pleasing is this to Samas." (Babylonian)

"I have not traduced the slave to him who is set over him." (Ancient Egyptian)

"Thou shalt not bear false witness against thy neighbor." (Ancient Jewish)

"Regard him whom thou knowest like him whom thou knowest not." (Ancient Egyptian)

"Do no unrighteousness in judgment. You must not consider the fact that one party is poor nor the fact that the other is a great man." (Ancient Jewish)

VI. THE LAW OF GOOD FAITH AND VERACITY

"A sacrifice is obliterated by a lie and the merit of alms by an act of fraud." (Hindu)

"Whose mouth, full of lying, avails not before thee: thou burnest their utterance." (Babylonian)

"With his mouth was he full of *Yea*, in his heart full of *Nay*?" (Babylonian)

"I have not spoken falsehood." (Ancient Egyptian)

"I sought no trickery, nor swore false oaths." (Anglo-Saxon)

"The Master said, Be of unwavering good faith." (Ancient Chinese)

"In Nastrond (= Hell) I saw the perjurers." (Old Norse)

"Hateful to me as are the gates of Hades is that man who says one thing, and hides another in his heart." (Greek)

"The foundation of justice is good faith." (Roman)

"[The Gentleman] must learn to be faithful to his superiors and to keep promises." (Ancient Chinese)

"Anything is better than treachery." (Old Norse)

VII. THE LAW OF MERCY

"The poor and the sick should be regarded as lords of the atmosphere." (Hindu)

"Who so makes intercession for the weak, well pleasing is this to Samas." (Babylonian)

"Has he failed to set a prisoner free?" (Babylonian)

"I have given bread to the hungry, water to the thirsty, clothes to the naked, a ferry boat to the boatless." (Ancient Egyptian)

"One should never strike a woman; not even with a flower." (Hindu)

"There, Thor, you got disgrace, when you beat women." (Old Norse)

"In the Dalebura tribe a woman, a cripple from birth, was carried about by the tribespeople in turn until her death at the age of sixty-six." "They never desert the sick." (Australian Aborigines)

"You will see them take care of . . . widows, orphans, and old men, never reproaching them." (American Indian)

"Nature confesses that she has given to the human race the tenderest hearts, by giving us the power to weep. This is the best part of us." (Roman)

"They said that he had been the mildest and gentlest of the kings of the world." (Anglo-Saxon)

"When thou cuttest down thine harvest . . . and hast forgot a sheaf . . . thou shalt not go again to fetch it: it shall be for the stranger, for the fatherless, and for the widow." (Ancient Jewish)

VIII. THE LAW OF MAGNANIMITY

A.

"There are two kinds of injustice: the first is found in those who do an injury, the second in those who fail to protect another from injury when they can." (Roman)

"Men always knew that when force and injury [were] offered they might be defenders of themselves; they knew that howsoever men may seek their own commodity, yet if this were done with injury unto others it was not to be suffered, but by all men and by all good means to be withstood." (English)

"To take no notice of a violent attack is to strengthen the heart of the enemy. Vigor is valiant, but cowardice is vile." (Ancient Egyptian)

"They came to the fields of joy, the fresh turf of the Fortunate Woods, and the dwellings of the Blessed . . . here was the company of those who had suffered wounds fighting for their fatherland." (Roman)

"Courage has got to be harder, heart the stouter, spirit the sterner, as our strength weakens. Here lies our lord, cut to pieces, our best man in the dust. If anyone thinks of leaving this battle, he can howl forever." (Anglo-Saxon)

"Praise and imitate that man to whom, while life is pleasing, death is not grievous." (Stoic)

"The Master said, Love learning and if attacked be ready to die for the Good Way." (Ancient Chinese)

B.

"Death is to be chosen before slavery and base deeds." (Roman)

"Death is better for every man than life with shame." (Anglo-Saxon)

"Nature and Reason command that nothing uncomely, nothing effeminate, nothing lascivious be done or thought." (Roman)

"We must not listen to those who advise us 'being men to think human thoughts, and being mortal to think mortal thoughts,' but must put on immortality as much as is possible and strain every nerve to live according to that best part of us, which, being small in bulk, yet much more in its power and honor surpasses all else." (Ancient Greek)

"The soul then ought to conduct the body, and the spirit of our minds the soul. This is therefore the first Law, whereby the highest power of the mind requireth obedience at the hands of all the rest." (English)

"Let him not desire to die, let him not desire to live, let him wait for his time . . . let him patiently bear hard words, entirely abstaining from bodily pleasures." (Ancient Indian)

"He who is unmoved, who has restrained his senses . . . is said to be devoted. As a flame in a windless place that flickers not, so is the devoted." (Ancient Indian)

C.

"Is not the love of Wisdom, a practice of death?" (Ancient Greek)

"I know that I hung on the gallows for nine nights, wounded with the spear as a sacrifice to Odin, myself offered to Myself." (Old Norse)

"Verily, verily I say to you unless a grain of wheat falls into the earth and dies, it remains alone, but if it dies it bears much fruit. He who loves his life loses it." (Christian)

Joy

IMAGINATION IS A VAGUE WORD and I must make some distinctions. It may mean the world of reverie, daydream, wish-fulfilling fantasy. . . . Invention is essentially different from reverie; if some fail to recognize the difference, that is because they have not themselves experienced both. . . . If we use the word imagination in a third sense, and the highest of all, this invented world was not imaginative. But certain other experiences were, and I will now try to record them. . . .

The first is itself the memory of a memory. As I stood beside a flowering currant bush on a summer day, there suddenly arose in me without warning, and as if from a depth not of years but of centuries, the memory of that earlier morning at the Old House when my brother had brought his toy garden into the nursery. It is difficult to find words strong enough for the sensation which came over me; Milton's "enormous bliss" of Eden (giving the full, ancient meaning to "enormous") comes somewhere near it. It was a sensation, of course, of desire; but desire for what? not, certainly, for a biscuit tin filled with moss, nor even (though that came into it) for my own past. . . . Before I knew what I desired, the desire itself was gone, the whole glimpse withdrawn, the world turned commonplace again, or only stirred by a longing for the longing that had just ceased. It had taken only a moment of time; and in a certain sense everything else that had ever happened to me was insignificant in comparison.

The second glimpse came through *Squirrel Nutkin;* through it only, though I loved all the Beatrix Potter books. But the rest of them were merely entertaining; it administered the shock, it was a trouble. It troubled me with what I can only describe as the Idea of Autumn. It sounds fantastic to say that one can be enamored of a season, but that is something like what happened; and, as before, the experience was one of intense desire. And one went back to the book, not to gratify the desire (that was impossible—how can one *possess* Autumn?) but to reawake it. And in this experience also there was the same surprise and the same sense of incalculable importance. It was something quite different from ordinary life and even from ordinary pleasure; something, as they would now say, "in another dimension."

The third glimpse came through poetry. I had become fond of Longfellow's *Saga of King Olaf:* fond of it in a casual, shallow way for its story and its vigorous rhythms. But then, and quite different from such pleasures, and like a voice from far more distant regions, there came a moment when I idly turned the pages of the book and found the unrhymed translation of *Tegner's Drapa* and read

> I heard a voice that cried,
> Balder the beautiful
> Is dead, is dead—

I knew nothing about Balder; but instantly I was uplifted into huge regions of northern sky, I desired with almost sickening intensity something never to be described (except that it is cold, spacious, severe, pale, and remote) and then, as in the other examples, found myself at the very same moment already falling out of that desire and wishing I were back in it.

The reader who finds these three episodes of no interest need read this book [*Surprised by Joy*] no further, for in a sense the central story of my life is about nothing else. For those who are still disposed to proceed, I will only underline the quality common to the three experiences; it is that of an unsatisfied desire which is itself more desirable than any other satisfaction. I call it Joy, which is here a technical term and must be sharply distinguished both from Happiness and from Pleasure. Joy (in my sense) has indeed one characteristic, and one only, in common with them; the fact that anyone who has experienced it will want it again. Apart from that, and considered only in its quality, it might almost equally well be called a particular kind of unhappiness or grief. But then it is a kind we want. I doubt whether anyone who has tasted it would ever, if both were in his power, exchange it for all the pleasures in the world. But then Joy is never in our power and pleasure often is. . . .

With my mother's death all settled happiness, all that was tranquil and reliable, disappeared from my life. There was to be much fun, many pleasures, many stabs of Joy; but no more of the old security. It was sea and islands now; the great continent had sunk like Atlantis. . . .

As for Joy, I labeled it "esthetic experience" and talked much about it under that name and said it was very "valuable." But it came very seldom and when it came it didn't amount to much. . . .

This discovery flashed a new light back on my whole life. I saw that all my waitings and watchings for Joy, all my vain hopes to find some mental content on which I could, so to speak, lay my finger and say, "This is it," had been a futile attempt to contemplate the enjoyed. All that such watching and waiting ever *could* find would be either an image (Asgard, the Western Garden, or what not) or a quiver in the diaphragm. I should never have to bother again about these images or sensations. I knew now that they were merely the mental track left by the passage of Joy—not the wave but the wave's imprint on the sand. The inherent dialectic of desire itself had in a way already shown me this; for all images and sensations, if idolatrously mistaken for Joy itself, soon honestly confessed themselves inadequate. All said, in the last resort, "It is not I. I am only a reminder. Look! Look! What do I remind you of?"

So far, so good. But it is at the next step that awe overtakes me. There was no doubt that Joy was a desire (and, insofar as it was also simultaneously a good, it was also a kind of love). But a desire is turned not to itself but to its object. Erotic love is not like desire for food, nay, a love for one woman differs from a love for another woman in the very same way and the very same degree as the two women differ from one another. Even our desire for one wine differs in tone from our desire for another. Our intellectual desire (curiosity) to know the true answer to a question is quite different from our desire to find that one answer, rather than another, is true. The form of the desired is in the desire. It is the object which makes the desire harsh or sweet, coarse or choice, "high" or "low." It is the object that makes the desire itself desirable or hateful. I perceived (and this was a wonder of wonders) that just as I had been wrong in supposing that I really desired the Garden of the Hesperides, so also I had been equally wrong in supposing that I desired Joy itself. Joy itself, considered simply as an event in my own mind, turned out to be of no value at all. All the value lay in that of which Joy was the desiring. And that object, quite clearly, was no state of my own mind or body at all. In a way, I had proved this by elimination. I had tried everything in my own mind and body; as it were, asking myself, "Is it this you want: Is it this?" Last of all I had asked if Joy itself was what I wanted; and, labeling it "esthetic experience," had pretended I could answer Yes. But that answer too had broken down. Inexorably Joy proclaimed, "You want—I myself am your want or—something other, outside, not you nor any state of you." I did not yet ask, Who is the desired? only What is it? But this brought me already into the region of awe, for thus I understood that in deepest solitude there is a road right out of the self, a commerce with something which, by refusing to identify itself with any object of the senses, or anything whereof we have biological or social need, or anything imagined, or any state of our own minds, proclaims itself sheerly objective. Far more objective than bodies, for it is not, like them, clothed in our senses; the naked Other, imageless (though our imagination salutes it with a hundred images), unknown, undefined, desired. . . .

It may be asked whether my terror was at all relieved by the thought that I was now approaching the source from which those arrows of Joy had been shot at me ever since childhood. Not in the least. No slightest hint was vouchsafed me that there ever had been or ever would be any connection between God and Joy. If anything, it was the reverse. I had hoped that the heart of reality might be of such a kind that we can best symbolize it as a place; instead, I found it to be a Person. For all I knew, the total rejection of what I called Joy might be one of the demands, might be the very first demand, He would make upon me. There was no strain of music from within, no smell of eternal orchids at the threshold, when I was dragged through the doorway. No kind of desire was present at all. . . .

But what, in conclusion, of Joy? For that, after all, is what the story has mainly been about. To tell you the truth, the subject has lost nearly all interest for me since I became a Christian.

Theology

EVERYONE HAS WARNED ME not to tell you what I am going to tell you. . . . They all say "the ordinary reader does not want Theology; give him plain practical religion." I have rejected their advice. I do not think the ordinary reader is such a fool. Theology means "the science of God," and I think any man who wants to think about God at all would like to have the clearest and most accurate ideas about Him which are available. You are not children: why should you be treated like children?

In a way I quite understand why some people are put off

by Theology. I remember once when I had been giving a talk to the R.A.F., an old, hard-bitten officer got up and said, "I've no use for all that stuff. But, mind you, I'm a religious man too. I *know* there's a God. I've *felt* Him: out alone in the desert at night: the tremendous mystery. And that's just why I don't believe all your neat little dogmas and formulas about Him. To anyone who's met the real thing they all seem so petty and pedantic and unreal!"

Now in a sense I quite agreed with that man. I think he had probably a real experience of God in the desert. And when he turned from that experience to the Christian creeds, I think he really was turning from something real, to something less real. In the same way, if a man has once looked at the Atlantic from the beach, and then goes and looks at a map of the Atlantic, he also will be turning from something real to something less real: turning from real waves to a bit of colored paper. But here comes the point. The map is admittedly only colored paper, but there are two things you have to remember about it. In the first place, it is based on what hundreds and thousands of people have found out by sailing the real Atlantic. In that way it has behind it masses of experience just as real as the one you could have from the beach; only, while yours would be a single isolated glimpse, the map fits all those different experiences together. In the second place, if you want to go anywhere, the map is absolutely necessary. As long as you are content with walks on the beach, your own glimpses are far more fun than looking at a map. But the map is going to be more use than walks on the beach if you want to get to America.

Now Theology is like the map. Merely learning and thinking about the Christian doctrines, if you stop there, is less real and less exciting than the sort of thing my friend got in the desert. Doctrines are not God: they are only a kind of map. But the map is based on the experience of hundreds of people who really were in touch with God—experiences compared with which any thrills or pious feelings you or I are likely to get on our own way are very elementary and very confused. And secondly, if you want to get any further, you must use the map. You see, what happened to that man in the desert may have been real, and was certainly exciting, but nothing comes of it. It leads nowhere. There is nothing to do about it. In fact, that is just why a vague religion—all about feeling God in nature, and so on—is so attractive. It is all thrills and no work; like watching the waves from the beach. But you will not get to Newfoundland by studying the Atlantic that way, and you will not get eternal life by simply feeling the presence of God in flowers or music. Neither will you get anywhere by looking at maps without going to sea. Nor will you be very safe if you go to sea without a map.

In other words, Theology is practical: especially now. In the old days, where there was less education and discussion, perhaps it was possible to get on with a very few simple ideas about God. But it is not so now. Everyone reads, everyone hears things discussed. Consequently if you do not listen to Theology, that will not mean that you have no ideas about God. It will mean that you have a lot of wrong ones—bad, muddled, out-of-date ideas. For a great many of the ideas about God which are trotted out as novelties today, are simply the ones which real Theologians tried centuries ago and rejected. To believe in the popular religion of modern England is retrogression—like believing the earth is flat.

For when you get down to it, is not the popular idea of Christianity simply this: that Jesus Christ was a great moral teacher and that if only we took his advice we might be able to establish a better social order and avoid another war? Now, mind you, that is quite true. But it tells you much less than the whole truth about Christianity and it has no practical importance at all.

It is quite true that if we took Christ's advice, we should

soon be living in a happier world. You need not even go as far as Christ. If we did all that Plato or Aristotle or Confucius told us, we should get on a great deal better than we do. And so what? We have never followed the advice of the great teachers. Why are we likely to begin now? Why are we more likely to follow Christ than any of the others? Because He is the best moral teacher? But that makes it even less likely that we shall follow Him. If we cannot take the elementary lessons, is it likely we are going to take the most advanced one: If Christianity only means one more bit of good advice, then Christianity is of no importance. There has been no lack of good advice for the last four thousand years. A bit more makes no difference.

But as soon as you look at any real Christian writings, you find that they are talking about something quite different from this popular religion. They say that Christ is the Son of God (whatever that means). They say that those who give Him their confidence can also become Sons of God (whatever that means). They say that His death saved us from our sins (whatever that means).

There is no good complaining that these statements are difficult. Christianity claims to be telling us about another world, about something behind the world we can touch and hear and see. You may think the claim false; but if it were true, what it tells us would be bound to be difficult—at least as difficult as modern Physics, and for the same reason.

Now the point in Christianity which gives us the greatest shock is the statement that by attaching to Christ we can "become Sons of God." One asks "Aren't we Sons of God already? Surely the fatherhood of God is one of the main Christian ideas?" Well, in a certain sense, no doubt we are sons of God already. I mean, God brought us into existence and loves us and looks after us, and in that way is like a father. But when the Bible talks of our "becoming" Sons of God, obviously it must mean something different. And that brings us up against the very center of Theology.

Divine Omnipotence

Omnipotence MEANS "power to do all, or everything." (The original meaning in Latin may have been "power *over* or *in* all." I give what I take to be current sense.) And we are told in Scripture that "with God all things are possible." It is common enough, in argument with an unbeliever, to be told that God, if He existed and were good, would do this or that; and then, if we point out that the proposed action is impossible, to be met with the retort, "But I thought God was supposed to be able to do anything." This raises the whole question of impossibility.

In ordinary usage the word *impossible* generally implies a suppressed clause beginning with the word *unless*. Thus it is impossible for me to see the street from where I sit writing at this moment; that is, it is impossible to see the street *unless* I go up to the top floor where I shall be high enough to overlook the intervening building. If I had broken my leg I should say "But it is impossible to go up to the top floor"—meaning, however, that it is impossible *unless* some friends turn up who will carry me. Now let us advance to a different plane of impossibility, by saying "It is, at any rate, impossible to see the street *so long as* I remain where I am and the intervening building remains where it is." Someone might add "unless the nature of space, or of vision, were different from what it is." I do not know what the best philosophers and scientists would say to this, but I should have to reply "I don't know whether space and vision *could possibly* have been of such a nature as you suggest." Now it is clear that the words *could possibly* refer to some absolute kind of possibility or impossibility which is different from the relative possibilities and impossibilities we have been considering. I cannot say whether seeing round corners is, in this new sense, possible or not, because I do not know whether it is self-contradictory or not. But I know very well that if it is self-contradictory it is absolutely impossible. The absolutely impossible may also be called the intrinsically impossible because it carries its impossibility within itself, instead of borrowing it from other impossibilities which in their turn depend upon others. It has no *unless* clause attached to it. It is impossible under all conditions, and in all worlds, and for all agents.

"All agents" here includes God Himself. His Omnipotence means power to do all that is intrinsically possible, not to do the intrinsically impossible. You may attribute miracles to Him, but not nonsense. This is no limit to His power. If you choose to say "God can give a creature free will and at the same time withhold free will from it," you have not succeeded in saying *anything* about God: meaningless combinations of words do not suddenly acquire meaning simply because we prefix to them the two other words "God can." It remains true that all *things* are possible with God: the intrinsic impossibilities are not things but nonentities. It is no more possible for God than for the weakest of His creatures to carry out both of two mutually exclusive alternatives; not because His power meets an obstacle, but because nonsense remains nonsense even when we talk it about God.

Divine Goodness

By the goodness of God we mean nowadays almost exclusively His lovingness; and in this we may be right. And by Love, in this context, most of us mean kindness—the desire to see others than the self happy; not happy in this way or in that, but just happy. What would really satisfy us would be a God who said of anything we happened to like doing, "What does it matter so long as they are contented?" We want, in fact, not so much a Father in Heaven as a grandfather in heaven—a senile benevolence who, as they say, "liked to see young people enjoying themselves," and whose plan for the universe was simply that it might be truly said at the end of each day, "a good time was had by all." Not many people, I admit, would formulate a theology in precisely those terms: but a conception not very different lurks at the back of many minds. I do not claim to be an exception: I should very much like to live in a universe which was governed on such lines. But since it is abundantly clear that I don't, and since I have reason to believe, nevertheless, that God is Love, I conclude that my conception of love needs corrections.

I might, indeed, have learned, even from the poets, that Love is something more stern and splendid than mere kindness: that even the love between the sexes is, as in Dante, "a lord of terrible aspect." There is kindness in Love: but Love and kindness are not coterminous, and when kindness (in the sense given above) is separated from the other elements of Love, it involves a certain fundamental indifference to its object, and even something like contempt of it. Kindness consents very readily to the removal of its object—we have all met people whose kindness to animals is constantly leading them to kill animals lest they should suffer. Kindness, merely as such, cares not whether its object becomes good or bad, provided only that it escapes suffering. As Scripture points out, it is bastards who are spoiled: the legitimate sons, who are to carry on the family tradition, are punished (Hebrews 12:8). It is for people whom we care nothing about that we demand happiness on any terms: with our friends, our lovers, our children, we are exacting and would rather see them suffer much than be happy in contemptible and estranging modes. If God is Love, He is, by definition, something more than mere kindness. And it appears, from all records, that though He has often rebuked us and condemned us, He has never regarded us with contempt. He has paid us the intolerable compliment of loving us, in the deepest, most tragic, most inexorable sense.

Begetting and Making

ONE OF THE CREEDS says that Christ is the Son of God "begotten, not created"; and it adds "begotten by his Father before all worlds." Will you please get it quite clear that this has nothing to do with the fact that when Christ was born on earth as a man, that man was the son of a virgin? We are not now thinking about the Virgin Birth. We are thinking about something that happened before nature was created at all, before time began. "Before all worlds" Christ is begotten, not created. What does it mean?

We don't use the words *begetting* or *begotten* much in modern English, but everyone still knows what they mean. To beget is to become the father of: to create is to make. And the difference is this. When you beget, you beget something of the same kind as yourself. A man begets human babies, a beaver begets little beavers, and a bird begets eggs which turn into little birds. But when you make, you make something of a different kind from yourself. A bird makes a nest, a beaver builds a dam, a man makes a wireless set—or he may make something more like himself than a wireless set: say, a statue. If he is a clever enough carver, he may make a statue which is very like a man indeed. But, of course, it is not a real man; it only looks like one. It cannot breathe or think. It is not alive.

Now that is the first thing to get clear. What God begets is God; just as what man begets is man. What God creates is not God; just as what man makes is not man. That is why men are not Sons of God in the sense that Christ is. They may be like God in certain ways, but they are not things of the same kind. They are more like statues or pictures of God.

A statue has the shape of a man but it is not alive. In the same way, man has (in a sense I am going to explain) the "shape" or likeness of God, but he has not got the kind of life God has. Let us take the first point (man's resemblance to God) first. Everything God has made has some likeness to Himself. Space is like Him in its hugeness: not that the greatness of space is the same kind of greatness as God's but it is a sort of symbol of it, or a translation of it into nonspiritual terms. Matter is like God in having energy: though, again, of course, physical energy is a different kind of thing from the power of God. The vegetable world is like Him because it is alive, and He is the "living God." But life, in this biological sense, is not the same as the life there is in God: it is only a kind of symbol or shadow of it. When we come on to animals, we find other kinds of resemblance to the unceasing activity and the creativeness of God. In the higher mammals we get the beginnings of instinctive affection. That is not the same thing as the love that exists in God: but it is like it—rather in the way that a picture drawn on a flat piece of paper can nevertheless be "like" a landscape. When we come to man, the highest of the animals, we get the completest resemblance to God which we know of. (There may be creatures in other worlds who are more like God than man is, but we do not know about them.) Man not only lives, but loves and reasons: biological life reaches its highest known level in him.

But what man, in his natural condition, has not got, is Spiritual life—the higher and different sort of life that exists in God. We use the same word *life* for both: but if you thought that both must therefore be the same sort of thing, that would be like thinking that the "greatness" of space and the "greatness" of God were the same sort of greatness. In reality, the difference between Biological life and Spiritual life is so important that I am going to give them two distinct names. The Biological sort which comes to us through Nature, and which (like everything else in Nature) is always tending to run down and decay so that it can only be kept up by incessant subsidies from Nature in the form of air, water, food, etc., is *Bios*. The Spiritual life which is in God from all eternity, and which made the whole natural universe, is *Zoë*. *Bios* has, to be sure, a certain shadowy or symbolic resemblance to *Zoë:* but only the sort of resemblance there is between a photo and a place, or a statue and a man. A man who changed from having *Bios* to having *Zoë* would have gone through as big a change as a statue which changed from being a carved stone to being a real man.

And that is precisely what Christianity is about. This world is a great sculptor's shop. We are the statues and there is a rumor going round the shop that some of us are some day going to come to life.

Spirit, Spirits, Spiritual

WHEN DEVOTIONAL WRITERS talk of the "spiritual life"—and often when they talk of the "supernatural life" or when I myself . . . talked of *Zoë*—they mean this *absolutely* Supernatural life which no creature can be given simply by being created but which every rational creature can have by voluntarily surrendering itself to the life of Christ. But much confusion arises from the fact that in many books the words "Spirit" or "Spiritual" are also used to mean the *relatively* supernatural element in Man, the element external to *this* Nature which is (so to speak) "issued" or handed out to him by the mere fact of being created as a Man at all.

It will perhaps be helpful to make a list of the senses in which the words "spirit," "spirits," and "spiritual" are, or have been, used in English.

1. The chemical sense, e.g. "Spirits evaporate very quickly."

2. The (now obsolete) medical sense. The older doctors believed in certain extremely fine fluids in the human body which were called "the spirits." As medical science this view has long been abandoned, but it is the origin of some expressions we still use; as when we speak of being "in high spirits" or "in low spirits" or say that a horse is "spirited" or that a boy is "full of animal spirits."

3. "Spiritual" is often used to mean simply the opposite of "bodily" or "material." Thus all that is immaterial in man (emotions, passions, memory, etc.) is often called "spiritual." It is very important to remember that what is "spiritual" in this sense is not necessarily good. There is nothing especially fine about the mere fact of immateriality. Immaterial things may, like material things, be good or bad or indifferent.

4. Some people use "spirit" to mean that relatively supernatural element which is given to every man at his creation—the rational element. This is, I think, the most useful way of employing the word. Here again it is important to realize that what is "spiritual" is not necessarily good. A Spirit (in this sense) can be either the best or the worst of created things. It is because Man is (in this sense) a spiritual animal that he can become either a son of God or a devil.

5. Finally, Christian writers use "spirit" and "spiritual" to mean the life which arises in such rational beings when they voluntarily surrender to Divine grace and become sons

of the Heavenly Father in Christ. It is in this sense, and in this sense alone, that the "spiritual" is always good.

The Three-Personal God

IN SPACE you can move in three ways—to left or right, backward or forward, up or down. Every direction is either one of these three or a compromise between them. They are called the three Dimensions. Now notice this. If you are using only one dimension, you could draw only a straight line. If you are using two, you could draw a figure: say, a square. And a square is made up of four straight lines. Now a step further. If you have three dimensions, you can then build what we call a solid body: say, a cube—a thing like a [die] or a lump of sugar. And a cube is made up of six squares.

Do you see the point? A world of one dimension would be a straight line. In a two-dimensional world, you still get straight lines, but many lines make one figure. In a three-dimensional world, you still get figures but many figures make one solid body. In other words, as you advance to more real and more complicated levels, you do not leave behind you the things you found on the simpler levels: you still have them, but combined in new ways—in ways you could not imagine if you knew only the simpler levels.

Now the Christian account of God involves just the same principle. The human level is a simple and rather empty level. On the human level one person is one being, and any two persons are two separate beings—just as, in two dimensions (say on a flat sheet of paper) one square is one figure, and any two squares are two separate figures. On the Divine level you still find personalities; but up there you find them combined in new ways which we, who do not live on that level, cannot imagine. In God's dimension, so to speak, you find a being who is three Persons while remaining one Being, just as a cube is six squares while remaining one cube. Of course, we cannot fully conceive a Being like that: just as, if we were so made that we perceived only two dimensions in space, we could never properly imagine a cube. But we can get a sort of faint notion of it. And when we do, we are then, for the first time in our lives, getting some positive idea, however faint, of something superpersonal—something more than a person. It is something we could never have guessed, and yet, once we have been told, one almost feels one ought to have been able to guess it because it fits in so well with all the things we know already.

You may ask, "If we cannot imagine a three-personal Being, what is the good of talking about Him?" Well, there isn't any good talking about Him. The thing that matters is being actually drawn into that three-personal life, and that may begin any time—tonight, if you like.

What I mean is this. An ordinary simple Christian kneels down to say his prayers. He is trying to get in touch with God. But if he is a Christian he knows that what is prompting him to pray is also God: God, so to speak, inside him. But he also knows that all his real knowledge of God comes through Christ, the Man who was God—that Christ is standing beside him, helping him to pray, praying for him. You see what is happening. God is the thing to which he is praying—the goal he is trying to reach. God is also the thing inside him which is pushing him on—the motive power. God is also the road or bridge along which he is being pushed to that goal. So that the whole threefold life of the three-personal Being is actually going on in that ordinary little bedroom where an ordinary man is saying his prayers. The man is being caught up into the higher kind of life—what I call *Zoë* or spiritual life: he is being pulled into God, by God, while still remaining himself.

The Trinity

I BEGIN . . . by asking you to get a certain picture clear in your minds. Imagine two books lying on a table one on top of the other. Obviously the bottom book is keeping the other one up—supporting it. It is because of the underneath book that the top one is resting, say, two inches from the surface of the table instead of touching the table. Let us call the underneath book A and the top one B. The position of A is causing the position of B. That is clear? Now let us imagine—it could not really happen, of course, but it will do for an illustration—let us imagine that both books have been in that position forever and ever. In that case B's position would always have been resulting from A's position. But all the same, A's position would not have existed before B's position. In other words, the result does not come *after* the cause. Of course, results usually do: you eat the cucumber first and have the indigestion afterward. But it is not so with all causes, and results. You will see in a moment why I think this important.

I said . . . that God is a Being which contains three Persons while remaining one Being, just as a cube contains six squares while remaining one body. But as soon as I begin trying to explain how these Persons are connected, I have to use words which make it sound as if one of them was there before the others. The First Person is called the Father and the Second the Son. We say that the First begets or produces the Second; we call it *begetting*, not *making*, because what He produces is of the same kind as Himself. In that way the word Father is the only word to use. But unfortunately it suggests that He is there first—just as a human father exists before his son. But that is not so. There is no before and after about it. And that is why I have spent some time trying to make clear how one thing can be the source, or cause, or origin, of another without being there before it. The Son exists because the Father exists: but there never was a time before the Father produced the Son.

Perhaps the best way to think of it is this. I asked you now to imagine those two books, and probably most of you did. That is, you made an act of imagination and as a result you had a mental picture. Quite obviously your act of imagining was the cause and the mental picture the result. But that does not mean that you first did the imagining and then got the picture. The moment you did it, the picture was there. Your will was keeping the picture before you all the time. Yet that act of will and the picture began at exactly the same moment and ended at the same moment. If there were a Being who had always existed and had always been imagining one thing, his act would always have been producing a mental picture; but the picture would be just as eternal as the act.

In the same way we must think of the Son always, so to speak, streaming forth from the Father, like light from a lamp, or heat from a fire, or thoughts from a mind. He is the self-expression of the Father—what the Father has to say. And there never was a time when He was not saying it. But have you noticed what is happening? All these pictures of light or heat are making it sound as if the Father and Son were two things instead of two Persons. So that, after all, the New Testament picture of a Father and a Son turns out to be much more accurate than anything we try to substitute for it. That is what always happens when you go away from the words of the Bible. It is quite right to go away from them for a moment in order to make some special point clear. But you must always go back. Naturally God knows how to describe Himself much better than we know how to describe Him. He knows that Father and Son is more like the relation between the First and Second Persons than anything else we can think of. Much the most important thing to know is that it is a relation of love. The Father delights in His Son; the Son looks up to His Father. . . .

The union between the Father and Son is such a live concrete thing that this union itself is also a Person. I know this is almost inconceivable but look at it thus. You know that among human beings, when they get together in a family, or a club, or a trade union, people talk about the "spirit" of that family, or club, or trade union. They talk about its "spirit" because the individual members, when they are together, do really develop particular ways of talking and behaving which they would not have if they were apart. It is as if a sort of communal personality came into existence. Of course, it is not a real person: it is only rather like a person. But that is just one of the differences between God and us. What grows out of the joint life of the Father and Son is a real Person, is in fact the Third of the three Persons who are God.

This third Person is called, in technical language, the Holy Ghost or the "spirit" of God. Do not be worried or surprised if you find it (or Him) rather vaguer or more shadowy in your mind than the other two. I think there is a reason why that must be so. In the Christian life you are not usually looking *at* Him: He is always acting through you. If you think of the Father as something "out there," in front of you, and of the Son as someone standing at your side, helping you to pray, trying to turn you into another son, then you have to think of the third Person as something inside you, or behind you. Perhaps some people might find it easier to begin with the third Person and work backward. God is love, and that love works through men—especially through the whole community of Christians. But this spirit of love is, from all eternity, a love going on between the Father and Son.

The Fall of Man

ACCORDING TO [the doctrine of the Fall], man is now a horror to God and to himself and a creature ill-adapted to the universe not because God made him so but because he has made himself so by the abuse of his free will. To my mind this is the sole function of the doctrine. It exists to guard against two sub-Christian theories of the origin of evil—Monism, according to which God Himself, being "above good and evil," produces impartially the effects to which we give those two names, and Dualism, according to which God produces good, while some equal and independent Power produces evil. Against both these views Christianity asserts that God is good; that He made all things good and for the sake of their goodness; that one of the good things He made, namely, the free will of rational creatures, by its very nature included the possibility of evil; and that creatures, availing themselves of this possibility, have become evil. Now this function—which is the only one I allow to the doctrine of the Fall—must be distinguished from two other functions which it is sometimes, perhaps, represented as performing, but which I reject. In the first place, I do not think the doctrine answers the question "Was it better for God to create than not to create?" . . . Since I believe God to be good, I am sure that, if the question has a meaning, the answer must be Yes. But I doubt whether the question has any meaning: and even if it has, I am sure that the answer cannot be attained by the sort of value judgments which men can significantly make. In the second place, I do not think the doctrine of the Fall can be used to show that it is "just," in terms of retributive justice, to punish individuals for the faults of their remote ancestors. Some forms of the doctrine seem to involve this; but I question whether any of them, as understood by its exponents, really meant it. The Fathers may sometimes say that we are punished for Adam's sin: but they much more often say that *we* sinned "in Adam." It may be impossible to find out what they meant by this, or we may decide that what they meant was erroneous. But I do not think we can dismiss their way of talking as a mere "idiom." Wisely, or foolishly, they believed that we were *really*—and not simply by legal fiction—involved in Adam's action. The attempt to formulate this belief by saying that we were "in" Adam in a physical sense—Adam being the first vehicle of the "immortal germ plasm"—may be unacceptable: but it is, of course, a further question whether the belief itself is merely a confusion or a real insight into spiritual realities beyond our normal grasp. At the moment, however, this question does not arise; for, as I have said, I have no intention of arguing that the descent to modern man of inabilities contracted by his remote ancestors is a specimen of retributive justice. For me it is rather a specimen of those things necessarily involved in the creation of a stable world. . . . It would, no doubt, have been possible for God to remove by miracle the results of the first sin committed by a human being; but this would not have been much good unless He was prepared to remove the results of the second sin, and of the third, and so on forever. If the miracles ceased, then sooner or later we might have reached our present lamentable situation: if they did not, then a world, thus continually underpropped and corrected by Divine interference, would have been a world in which nothing important ever depended on human choice, and in which choice itself would soon cease from the certainty that one of the apparent alternatives before you would lead to no results and was therefore not really an alternative.

The Incarnation

THE SON OF GOD became a man to enable men to become sons of God. We do not know—anyway, I do not know —how things would have worked if the human race had never rebelled against God and joined the enemy. Perhaps every man would have been "in Christ," would have shared the life of the Son of God, from the moment he was born. Perhaps the *Bios* or natural life would have been drawn up into the *Zoë*, the uncreated life, at once and as a matter of course. But that is guesswork. You and I are concerned with the way things work now.

And the present state of things is this. The two kinds of life are now not only different (they would always have been that) but actually opposed. The natural life in each of us is something self-centered, something that wants to be petted and admired, to take advantage of other lives, to exploit the whole universe. And especially it wants to be left to itself: to keep well away from anything better, or stronger, or higher than it, anything that might make it feel small. It is afraid of the light and air of the spiritual world, just as people who have been brought up to be dirty are afraid of a bath. And in a sense it is quite right. It knows that if the spiritual life gets hold of it, all its self-centeredness and self-will are going to be killed and it is ready to fight tooth and nail to avoid that.

Did you ever think, when you were a child, what fun it

would be if your toys could come to life? Well suppose you could really have brought them to life. Imagine turning a tin soldier into a real little man. It would involve turning the tin into flesh. And suppose the tin soldier did not like it. He is not interested in flesh; all he sees is that the tin is being spoiled. He thinks you are killing him. He will do everything he can do to prevent you. He will not be made into a man if he can help it.

What you would have done about that tin soldier I do not know. But what God did about us was this. The Second Person in God, the Son, became human Himself: was born into the world as an actual man—a real man of a particular height, with hair of a particular color, speaking a particular language, weighing so many stone. The Eternal Being, who knows everything and who created the whole universe, became not only a man but (before that) a baby, and before that a fetus inside a Woman's body. If you want to get the hang of it, think how you would like to become a slug or a crab.

The result of this was that you now had one man who really was what all men were intended to be: one man in whom created life, derived from his Mother, allowed itself to be completely and perfectly turned into the begotten life. The natural human creature in Him was taken up fully into the divine Son. Thus in one instance humanity had, so to speak, arrived: had passed into the life of Christ. And because the whole difficulty for us is that the natural life has to be, in a sense, "killed," He chose an earthly career which involved the killing of His human desires at every turn— poverty, misunderstanding from His own family, betrayal by one of His intimate friends, being jeered at and manhandled by the Police, and execution by torture. And then, after being thus killed—killed every day in a sense—the human creature in Him, because it was united to the divine Son, came to life again. The Man in Christ rose again: not only the God. That is the whole point. For the first time we saw a real man. One tin soldier—real tin, just like the rest— had come fully and splendidly alive.

One must be careful not to put this in a way which would blur the distinction between the creation of a man and the Incarnation of God. Could one, as a mere model, put it thus? In creation God makes—invents—a person and "utters"—injects—him into the realm of Nature. In the Incarnation, God the Son takes the body and human soul of Jesus, and, through that, the whole environment of Nature, all the creaturely predicament, into His own being. So that "He came down from Heaven" can almost be transposed into "Heaven drew earth up into it," and locality, limitation, sleep, sweat, footsore weariness, frustration, pain, doubt, and death, are, from before all worlds, known by God from within. The pure light walks the earth; the darkness, received into the heart of the Deity, is there swallowed up. Where, except in uncreated light, can the darkness be drowned?

The central miracle asserted by Christians is the Incarnation. They say God became Man. Every other miracle prepares for this, or exhibits this, or results from this. Just as every natural event is the manifestation at a particular place and moment of Nature's total character, so every particular Christian miracle manifests at a particular place and moment the character and significance of the Incarnation. There is no question in Christianity of arbitrary interferences just scattered about. It relates not a series of disconnected raids on Nature but the various steps of a strategically coherent invasion—an invasion which intends complete conquest and "occupation." The fitness, and therefore the credibility, of the particular miracles depends on their relation to the Grand Miracle; all discussion of them in isolation from it is futile.

The fitness or credibility of the Grand Miracle itself cannot, obviously, be judged by the same standard. And let us admit at once that it is very difficult to find a standard by which it can be judged. If the thing happened, it was the central event in the history of the Earth—the very thing that the whole story has been about. Since it happened only once, it is by Hume's standards infinitely improbable. But then the whole history of the Earth has also happened only once; is it therefore incredible? Hence the difficulty, which weighs upon Christian and atheist alike, of estimating the probability of the Incarnation. It is like asking whether the existence of Nature herself is intrinsically probable. That is why it is easier to argue, on historical grounds, that the Incarnation actually occurred than to show, on philosophical grounds, the probability of its occurrence. The historical difficulty of giving for the life, sayings, and influence of Jesus any explanation that is not harder than the Christian explanation is very great. The discrepancy between the depth and sanity and (let me add) *shrewdness* of His moral teaching and the rampant megalomania which must lie behind His theological teaching unless He is indeed God, has never been satisfactorily got over. Hence the non-Christian hypotheses succeed one another with the restless fertility of bewilderment. Today we are asked to regard all the theological elements as later accretions to the story of a "historical" and merely human Jesus: yesterday we were asked to believe that the whole thing began with vegetation myths and mystery religions and that the pseudohistorical Man was only fadged up at a later date. . . .

Since the Incarnation, if it is a fact, holds this central position, and since we are assuming that we do not yet know it to have happened on historical grounds, we are in a position which may be illustrated by the following analogy.

Let us suppose we possess parts of a novel or a symphony. Someone now brings us a newly discovered piece of manuscript and says, "This is the missing part of the work. This is the chapter on which the whole plot of the novel really turned. This is the main theme of the symphony." Our business would be to see whether the new passage, if admitted to the central place which the discoverer claimed for it, did actually illuminate all the parts we had already seen and "pull them together." Nor should we be likely to go very far wrong. The new passage, if spurious, however attractive it looked at the first glance, would become harder and harder to reconcile with the rest of the work the longer we considered the matter. But if it were genuine, then at every fresh hearing of the music or every fresh reading of the book, we should find it settling down, making itself more at home, and eliciting significance from all sorts of details in the whole work which we had hitherto neglected. Even though the new central chapter or main theme contained great difficulties in itself, we should still think it genuine provided that it continually removed difficulties elsewhere. Something like this we must do with the doctrine of the Incarnation. Here, instead of a symphony or a novel, we have the whole mass of our knowledge. The credibility will depend on the extent to which the doctrine, if accepted, can illuminate and integrate that whole mass. It is much less important that the doctrine itself should be fully comprehensible. We believe that the sun is in the sky at midday in summer not because we can clearly see the sun (in fact, we cannot) but because we can see everything else. . . .

In the Christian story God descends to reascend. He comes down; down from the heights of absolute being into time and space, down into humanity; down further still, if embryologists are right, to recapitulate in the womb ancient and prehuman phases of life; down to the very roots and seabed of the Nature He had created. But he goes down to come up again and bring the whole ruined world up with

Him. One has the picture of a strong man stooping lower and lower to get himself underneath some great complicated burden. He must stoop in order to lift, he must almost disappear under the load before he incredibly straightens his back and marches off with the whole mass swaying on his shoulders. Or one may think of a diver, first reducing himself to nakedness, then glancing in midair, then gone with a splash, vanished, rushing down through green and warm water into black and cold water, down through increasing pressure into the deathlike region of ooze and slime and old decay; then up again, back to color and light, his lungs almost bursting, till suddenly he breaks surface again, holding in his hand the dripping, precious thing that he went down to recover. He and it are both colored now that they have come up into the light: down below, where it lay colorless in the dark, he lost his color too.

In this descent and reascent everyone will recognize a familiar pattern: a thing written all over the world. It is the pattern of all vegetable life. It must belittle itself into something hard, small, and deathlike, it must fall into the ground: thence the new life reascends. It is the pattern of all animal generation too. There is descent from the full and perfect organisms into the spermatozoon and ovum, and in the dark womb a life at first inferior in kind to that of the species which is being reproduced: then the slow ascent to the perfect embryo, to the living, conscious baby, and finally to the adult. So it is also in our moral and emotional life. The first innocent and spontaneous desires have to submit to the deathlike process of control or total denial: but from that there is a reascent to fully formed character in which the strength of the original material all operates but in a new way. Death and Rebirth—go down to go up—it is a key principle. Through this bottleneck, this belittlement, the highroad nearly always lies.

The Virgin Birth

THE VIRGIN BIRTH is a doctrine plainly stated in the Apostles' Creed that Jesus had no physical father, and was not conceived as a result of sexual intercourse. It is not a doctrine on which there is any dispute between Presbyterians as such and Episcopalians as such. A few individual Modernists in both these churches have abandoned it; but Presbyterianism or Episcopalianism in general and in actual historical instances through the centuries both affirm it. The exact details of such a miracle—an exact point at which a supernatural enters this world (whether by the creation of a new spermatozoon, or the fertilization of an ovum without a spermatozoon, or the development of a fetus without an ovum) are not part of the doctrine. These are matters in which no one is obliged and everyone is free, to speculate.

I can understand the man who denies miracles altogether: but what is one to make of people who will believe other miracles and "draw the line" at the Virgin Birth? Is it that for all their lip service to the laws of Nature there is only one natural process in which they really believe? Or is it that they think they see in this miracle a slur upon sexual intercourse (though they might just as well see in the feeding of the five thousand an insult to bakers) and that sexual intercourse is the one thing still venerated in this unvenerating age? In reality the Miracle is no less, and no more, surprising than any others.

Perhaps the best way to approach it is from the remark I saw in one of the most archaic of our anti-God papers. The remark was that Christians believed in a God who had "committed adultery with the wife of a Jewish carpenter." The writer was probably merely "letting off steam" and did not really think that God, in the Christian story, had assumed human form and lain with a mortal woman, as Zeus lay with Alcmena. But if one had to answer this person, one would have to say that if you called the miraculous conception divine adultery, you would be driven to find a similar adultery in the conception of every child—nay, of every animal too. I am sorry to use the expression which will offend pious ears, but I do not know how else to make my point.

In a normal act of generation the father has no creative function. A microscopic particle of matter from his body, and a microscopic particle from the woman's body, meet. And with that there passes the color of his hair, and the hanging lower lip of her grandfather, and the form of humanity in all its complexity of bones, sinews, nerves, liver, and heart, and the form of those prehuman organisms which the embryo will recapitulate in the womb. Behind every spermatozoon lies the whole history of the universe: locked within it lies no inconsiderable part of the world's future. The weight or drive behind it is the momentum of the whole interlocked event which we call Nature up-to-date. And we know now that the "laws of Nature" cannot supply that momentum. If we believe that God created Nature, that momentum comes from Him. The human father is merely an instrument, a carrier, often an unwilling carrier, always simply the last in a long line of carriers—a line that stretches back far beyond his ancestors into prehuman and preorganic deserts of time, back to the creation of matter itself. That line is in God's hand. It is the instrument by which He normally creates a man. For He is the reality behind both Genius and Venus; no woman ever conceived a child, no mare a foal, without Him. But once, and for a special purpose, He dispensed with that long line which is

His instrument: once His life-giving finger touched a woman without passing through the ages of interlocked events. Once the great glove of Nature was taken off His hand. His naked hand touched her. There was, of course, a unique reason for it. That time He was creating not simply a man but the Man who was to be Himself: was creating Man anew: was beginning, at this divine and human point, the New Creation of all things. The whole soiled and weary universe quivered at this direct injection of essential life—direct, uncontaminated, not drained through all the crowded history of Nature. But it would be out of place here to explore the religious significance of the miracle. We are here concerned with it simply as Miracle—that and nothing more. As far as concerns the creation of Christ's human nature (the Grand Miracle whereby His divine nature enters into it is another matter), the miraculous conception is one more witness that here is Nature's Lord. He is doing now, small and close, what He does in a different fashion for every woman who conceives. He does it this time without a line of human ancestors: but even where He uses human ancestors, it is not the less He who gives life (Matthew 23:9). The bed is barren where that great third party, Genius, is not present.

Miracles of Fertility

THE EARLIEST of these was the conversion of water into wine at the wedding feast in Cana. This miracle proclaims that the God of all wine is present. The vine is one of the blessings sent by Jahweh: He is the reality behind the false god Bacchus. Every year, as part of the Natural order, God makes wine. He does so by creating a vegetable organism that can turn water, soil, and sunlight into a juice which will, under proper conditions, become wine. Thus, in a certain sense, He constantly turns water into wine, for wine, like all drinks, is but water modified. Once, and in one year only, God, now incarnate, short-circuits the process: makes wine in a moment: uses earthenware jars instead of vegetable fibers to hold the water. But uses them to do what He is always doing. The Miracle consists in the shortcut; but the event to which it leads is the usual one. If the thing happened, then we know that what has come into Nature is no anti-Natural spirit, no God who loves tragedy, and tears, and fasting *for their own sake* (however He may permit or demand them for special purposes) but the God of Israel who has through all these centuries given us wine to gladden the heart of man.

Other miracles that fall in this class are the two instances of miraculous feeding. They involve the multiplication of a little bread and a little fish into much bread and much fish. Once in the desert Satan had tempted Him to make bread of stones: He refused the suggestion. "The Son does nothing except what He sees the Father do"; perhaps one may without boldness surmise that the direct change from stone to bread appeared to the Son to be not quite in the hereditary style. Little bread into much bread is quite a different matter. Every year God makes a little corn into much corn: the seed is sown and there is an increase. And men say, according to their several fashions, "It is the laws of Nature," or, "It is Ceres, it is Adonis, it is the Corn King." But the laws of Nature are only a pattern: nothing will come to them unless they can, so to speak, take over the universe as a going concern. And as for Adonis, no man can tell us where he died or when he rose again. Here, at the feeding of the five thousand, is He whom we have ignorantly worshipped: the *real* Corn King who will die once and rise once at Jerusalem during the term of office of Pontius Pilate.

That same day He also multiplied fish. Look down into

every bay and almost every river. This swarming, undulating fecundity shows He is still at work "thronging the seas with spawn innumerable." The ancients had a god called Genius; the god of animal and human fertility, the patron of gynecology, embryology, and the marriage bed—the "genial" bed as they called it after its god Genius. But Genius is only another mask for the God of Israel, for it was He who at the beginning commanded all species "to be fruitful and multiply and replenish the earth." And now, that day, at the feeding of the thousands, incarnate God does the same: does close and small, under His human hands, a workman's hands, what he has always been doing in the seas, the lakes, and the little brooks.

Miracles of Healing

THE MIRACLES OF *Healing* . . . are now in a peculiar position. Men are ready to admit that many of them happened but are inclined to deny that they were miraculous. The symptoms of very many diseases can be aped by hysteria, and hysteria can often be cured by "suggestion." It could, no doubt, be argued that such suggestion is a spiritual power, and therefore (if you like) a supernatural power, and that all instances of "faith healing" are therefore Miracles. But in our terminology they would be miraculous only in the same sense in which every instance of human reason is miraculous: and what we are now looking for is miracles other than that. My own view is that it would be unreasonable to ask a person who has not yet embraced Christianity in its entirety to allow that all the healings mentioned in the Gospels were miracles—that is, that they go beyond the possibilities of human "suggestion." It is for the doctors to decide as regards each particular case—supposing that the narratives are sufficiently detailed to allow even probable diagnosis. . . . So far from belief in miracles depending upon ignorance of natural law, we are here finding for ourselves that ignorance of law which makes miracles unascertainable.

Without deciding in detail which of the healings must (apart from acceptance of the Christian faith) be regarded as miraculous, we can, however, indicate the kind of miracle involved. Its character can easily be obscured by the somewhat magical view which many people still take of ordinary and medical healing. There is a sense in which no doctor ever heals. The doctors themselves would be the first to admit this. The magic is not in the medicine but in the patient's body—in the *vis medicatrix naturae,* the recuperative or self-corrective energy of Nature. What the treatment does is to stimulate Natural functions or to remove what hinders them. We speak for convenience of the doctor, or the dressing, healing a cut. But in another sense every cut heals itself: no cut can be healed in a corpse. That same mysterious force which we call gravitational when it steers the planets and biochemical when it heals a live body, is the efficient cause of all recoveries. And that energy proceeds from God in the first instance. All who are cured are cured by Him, not merely in the sense that His providence provides them with medical assistance and wholesome environments, but also in the sense that their very tissues are repaired by the far-descended energy which, flowing from Him, energizes the whole system of Nature. But once He did it visibly to the sick in Palestine, a Man meeting with men. What in its general operations we refer to laws of Nature or once referred to Apollo or Asclepius thus reveals itself. The Power that always was behind all healings puts on a face and hands. Hence, of course, the apparent chanciness of the miracles. It is idle to complain that He heals those whom He happens to meet, not those whom He doesn't. To be a man means to be in one place and not in another. The world which would not know Him as present everywhere was saved by His becoming *local*.

Miracles of Destruction

CHRIST'S SINGLE MIRACLE of Destruction, the withering of the fig tree, has proved troublesome to some people, but I think its significance is plain enough. The miracle is an acted parable, a symbol of God's sentence on all that is "fruitless" and specially, no doubt, on the official Judaism of that age. That is its moral significance. As a miracle, it again does in focus, repeats small and close, what God does constantly and throughout Nature. We have seen . . . how God, twisting Satan's weapon out of his hand, had become, since the Fall, the God even of human death. But much more, and perhaps ever since the creation, He has been the God of the death of organisms. In both cases, though in somewhat different ways, He is the God of death because He is the God of Life: the God of human death because through it increase of life now comes—the God of merely organic death because death is part of the very mode by which organic life spreads itself out in Time and yet remains new. A forest a thousand years deep is still collectively alive because some trees are dying and others are growing up. His human face, turned with negation in its eyes upon that one fig tree, did once what His unincarnate action does to all trees. No tree died that year in Palestine, or any year anywhere, except because God did—or rather ceased to do—something to it.

Miracle of the Resurrection

IN THE EARLIEST DAYS of Christianity an "apostle" was first and foremost a man who claimed to be an eyewitness of the Resurrection. Only a few days after the Crucifixion when two candidates were nominated for the vacancy created by the treachery of Judas, their qualification was that they had known Jesus personally both before and after His death and could offer firsthand evidence of the Resurrection in addressing the outer world (Acts 1:22). A few days later St. Peter, preaching the first Christian sermon, makes the same claim—"God raised Jesus, of which we all (we Christians) are witnesses" (Acts 2:32). In the first Letter to the Corinthians St. Paul bases his claim to apostleship on the same ground—"Am I not an apostle? Have I not seen the Lord Jesus?"

As this qualification suggests, to preach Christianity meant primarily to preach the Resurrection. Thus people who had heard only fragments of St. Paul's teaching at Athens got the impression that he was talking about two new gods, Jesus and Anastasis (that is, Resurrection) (Acts 17:18). The Resurrection is the central theme in every Christian sermon reported in the Acts. The Resurrection, and its consequences, were the "gospel" or good news which the Christians brought: what we call the "gospels," the narratives of Our Lord's life and death, were composed later for the benefit of those who had already accepted the *gospel*. They were in no sense the basis of Christianity: they were written for those already converted. The miracle of the Resurrection, and the theology of that miracle, comes first: the biography comes later as a comment on it. Nothing could be more unhistorical than to pick out selected sayings of Christ from the gospels and to regard those as the datum and the rest of the New Testament as a construction upon it. The first fact in the history of Christendom is a number of people who say they have seen the Resurrection. If they had died without making anyone else believe this "gospel," no gospels would ever have been written.

It is very important to be clear about what these people mean. When modern writers talk of the Resurrection, they usually mean one particular moment—the discovery of the Empty Tomb and the appearance of Jesus a few yards away from it. The story of that moment is what Christian apologists now chiefly try to support and skeptics chiefly try to impugn. But this almost exclusive concentration on the first five minutes or so of the Resurrection would have astonished the earliest Christian teachers. In claiming to have seen the Resurrection they were not necessarily claiming to have seen *that*. Some of them had, some of them had not. It had no more importance than any of the other appearances of the risen Jesus—apart from the poetic and dramatic importance which the beginnings of things must always have. What they were claiming was that they had all, at one time or another, met Jesus during the six or seven weeks that followed His death. Sometimes they seem to have been alone when they did so, but on one occasion twelve of them saw Him together, and on another occasion about five hundred of them. St. Paul says that the majority of the five hundred were still alive when he wrote the First Letter to the Corinthians, that is in about 55 A.D.

The "Resurrection" to which they bore witness was, in fact, not the action of rising from the dead but the state of having risen: a state, as they held, attested by intermittent meetings during a limited period (except for the special, and in some ways different, meeting vouchsafed to St. Paul). This termination of the period is important, for, as we shall see, there is no possibility of isolating the doctrine of the Resurrection from that of the Ascension.

The next point to notice is that the Resurrection was not regarded simply or chiefly as evidence for the immortality of the soul. It is, of course, often so regarded today: I have heard a man maintain that "the importance of the Resurrection is that it proves *survival*." Such a view cannot at any point be reconciled with the language of the New Testament. On such a view Christ would simply have done what all men do when they die: the only novelty would have been that in His case we were allowed to see it happening. But there is not in Scripture the faintest suggestion that the Resurrection was new evidence for something that had *in fact* been always happening. The New Testament writers speak as if Christ's achievement in rising from the dead was the first event of its kind in the whole history of the universe. He is the "first fruits," the "pioneer of life." He has forced open a door that has been locked since the death of the first man. He has met, fought, and beaten the King of Death. Everything is different because He has done so. This is the beginning of the New Creation: a new chapter in cosmic history has opened.

Miracle of the Walking on the Water

IN THE WALKING ON THE WATER we see the relations of spirit and Nature so altered that Nature can be made to do whatever spirit pleases. This new obedience of Nature is, of course, not to be separated even in thought from spirit's own obedience to the Father of Spirits. Apart from that proviso such obedience by Nature, if it were possible, would result in chaos: the evil dream of Magic arises from finite spirit's longing to get that power without paying that price. The evil reality of lawless applied science (which is Magic's son and heir) is actually reducing large tracts of Nature to disorder and sterility at this very moment. I do not know how radically Nature herself would need to be altered to make her thus obedient to spirits, which spirits have become wholly obedient to their source. One thing, at least, we must observe. If we are in fact spirits, not Nature's offspring, then there must be some point (probably the brain) at which created spirit even now can produce effects on matter not by manipulation or technics but simply by the wish to do so. If that is what you mean by Magic, then Magic is a reality manifested every time you move your hand or think a thought. And Nature, as we have seen, is not destroyed but rather perfected by her servitude.

Miracle of the Raising of Lazarus

THE RAISING OF LAZARUS differs from the Resurrection of Christ Himself because Lazarus, so far as we know, was not raised to a new and more glorious mode of existence but merely restored to the sort of life he had had before. The fitness of the miracle lies in the fact that He who will raise all men at the general resurrection here does it small and close, and in an inferior—merely anticipatory—fashion. For the mere restoration of Lazarus is as inferior in splendor to the *glorious* resurrection of the New Humanity as stone jars are to the green and growing vine or five little barley loaves to all the waving bronze and gold of a fat valley ripe for harvest. The resuscitation of Lazarus, so far as we can see, is simple reversal: a series of changes working in the direction opposite to that we have always experienced. At death, matter which has been organic begins to flow away into the inorganic, to be finally scattered and used (some of it) by other organisms. The resurrection of Lazarus involves the reverse process. The general resurrection involves the reverse process universalized—a rush of matter toward organization at the call of spirits which require it. It is presumably a foolish fancy (not justified by the words of Scripture) that each spirit should recover those particular units of matter which he ruled before. For one thing, they would not be enough to go round: we all live in secondhand suits and there are doubtless atoms in my chin which have served many another man, many a dog, many an eel, many a dinosaur. Nor does the unity of our bodies, even in this present life, consist in retaining the same particles. My form remains one, though the matter in it changes continually. I am, in that respect, like a curve in a waterfall.

Miracle of the Transfiguration

THE TRANSFIGURATION or "Metamorphosis" of Jesus is . . . , no doubt, an anticipatory glimpse of something to come. He is seen conversing with two of the ancient dead. The change which His own human form had undergone is described as one to luminosity, to "shining whiteness." A similar whiteness characterizes His appearances at the beginning of the book of Revelation. One rather curious detail is that this shining or whiteness affected His clothes as much as His body. St. Mark indeed mentions the clothes more explicitly than the face, and adds, with his inimitable naivety, that "no laundry could do anything like it." Taken by itself this episode bears all the marks of a "vision"; that is, of an experience which, though it may be divinely sent and may reveal great truth, yet is not, objectively speaking, the experience it seems to be. But if the theory of "vision" (or holy hallucination) will not cover the Resurrection appearances, it would be only a multiplying of hypotheses to introduce it here. We do not know to what phase or feature of the New Creation this episode points. It may reveal some special glorifying of Chirst's manhood at some phase of its history (since history it apparently has), or it may reveal the glory which that manhood always has in its New Creation: it may even reveal a glory which all risen men will inherit. We do not know.

Miracle of the Ascension

WE FEEL SURE that the [New Testament writers] thought they had seen their Master setting off on a journey for a "local" Heaven where God sat in a throne and where there was another throne waiting for Him. And I believe that, for this reason, whatever they had actually seen (sense perception, almost by hypothesis, would be confused at such a moment), they would almost certainly have remembered it as a vertical movement. What we must not say is that they "mistook" local "Heavens," and celestial throne rooms, and the like for the "spiritual" Heaven of union with God and supreme power and beatitude. You and I have been gradually disentangling different senses of the word *Heaven*. . . . It may be convenient here to make a list. *Heaven* can mean (1) The unconditioned Divine Life beyond all worlds. (2) Blessed participation in that Life by a created spirit. (3) The Whole Nature or system of conditions in which redeemed human spirits, still remaining human, can enjoy such participation fully and forever. This is the Heaven Christ goes to "prepare" for us. (4) The physical Heaven, the sky, the space in which Earth moves. What enables us to distinguish these senses and hold them clearly apart is not any special spiritual purity but the fact that we are the heirs to centuries of logical analysis: not that we are sons to Abraham but that we are sons to Aristotle. We are not to suppose that the writers of the New Testament mistook Heaven in sense four or three for Heaven in sense two or one. You cannot mistake a half sovereign for a sixpence until you know the English system of coinage—that is, until you know the difference between them. In their idea of Heaven all these meanings were latent, ready to be brought out by later analysis. They never thought merely of the blue sky or merely of a "spiritual" heaven. When they looked up at the blue sky, they never doubted that He was "ascending" in what we should call a "spiritual" sense. . . . A man who really believes that "Heaven" is in the sky may well, in his heart, have a far truer and more spiritual conception of it than many a modern logician who could expose that fallacy with a few strokes of his pen. For he who does the will of the Father shall know the doctrine. Irrelevant material splendors in such a man's idea of the vision of God will do no harm, for they are not there for their own sakes.

On Seeing a Miracle

YOU ARE PROBABLY QUITE RIGHT in thinking that you will never see a miracle done: you are probably equally right in thinking that there was a natural explanation of anything in your past life which seemed, at the first glance, to be "rum" or "odd." God does not shake miracles into Nature at random as if from a pepper-caster. They come on great occasions: they are found at the great ganglions of history—not of political or social history, but of that spiritual history which cannot be fully known by men. If your own life does not happen to be near one of those great ganglions, how should you expect to see one? If we were heroic missionaries, apostles, or martyrs, it would be a different matter. But why you or I? Unless you live near a railway, you will not see trains go past your windows. How likely is it that you or I will be present when a peace treaty is signed, when a great scientific discovery is made, when a dictator commits suicide? That we should see a miracle is even less likely. Nor, if we understand, shall we be anxious to do so. "Nothing almost sees miracles but misery." Miracles and martyrdoms tend to bunch about the same areas of history—areas we have naturally no wish to frequent. Do not, I earnestly advise you, demand an ocular proof unless you are already perfectly certain that it is not forthcoming.

The Second Coming

In *King Lear* (III:vii) there is a man who is such a minor character that Shakespeare has not given him even a name: he is merely "First Servant." All the characters around him—Regan, Cornwall, and Edmund—have fine long-term plans. They think they know how the story is going to end, and they are quite wrong. The servant has no such delusions. He has no notion how the play is going to go. But he understands the present scene. He sees an abomination (the blinding of old Gloucester) taking place. He will not stand it. His sword is out and pointed at his master's breast in a moment: then Regan stabs him dead from behind. That is his whole part: eight lines all told. But if it were real life and not a play, that is the part it would be best to have acted.

The doctrine of the Second Coming teaches us that we do not and cannot know when the world drama will end. The curtain may be rung down at any moment: say, before you have finished reading this paragraph. This seems to some people intolerably frustrating. So many things would be interrupted. Perhaps you were going to get married next month, perhaps you were going to get a raise next week: you may be on the verge of a great scientific discovery; you may be maturing great social and political reforms. Surely no good and wise God would be so very unreasonable as to cut all this short? Not *now*, of all moments!

But we think thus because we keep on assuming that we know the play. We do not know the play. We do not even know whether we are in Act I or Act V. We do not know who are the major and the minor characters. The Author knows. The audience, if there is an audience (if angels and archangels and all the company of Heaven fill the pit and the stalls), may have an inkling. But we, never seeing the play from outside, never meeting any characters except the tiny minority who are "on" in the same scenes as ourselves, wholly ignorant of the future and very imperfectly informed about the past, cannot tell at what moment the end ought to come. That it will come when it ought, we may be sure; but we waste our time in guessing when that will be. That it has a meaning we may be sure, but we cannot see it. When it is over, we may be told. We are led to expect that the Author will have something to say to each of us on the part that each of us has played. The playing it well is what matters infinitely.

What Are We to Make of Jesus Christ?

WHAT ARE WE TO MAKE of Jesus Christ? This is a question which has, in a sense, a frantically comic side. For the real question is not what are we to make of Christ, but what is He to make of us? The picture of a fly sitting deciding what it is going to make of an elephant has comic elements about it. But perhaps the questioner meant what are we to make of Him in the sense of "How are we to solve the historical problem set us by the recorded sayings and acts of this Man?" This problem is to reconcile two things. On the one hand you have got the almost generally admitted depth and sanity of His moral teaching, which is not very seriously questioned, even by those who are opposed to Christianity. In fact, I find when I am arguing with very anti-God people that they rather make a point of saying, "I am entirely in favor of the moral teaching of Christianity"—and there seems to be a general agreement that in the teaching of this Man and of His immediate followers, moral truth is exhibited at its purest and best. It is not sloppy idealism, it is full of wisdom and shrewdness. The whole thing is realistic, fresh to the highest degree, the product of a sane mind. That is one phenomenon.

The other phenomenon is the quite appalling nature of this Man's theological remarks. You all know what I mean, and I want to stress the point that the appalling claim which this Man seems to be making is not merely made at one moment of His career. There is, of course, the one moment which led to His execution. The moment at which the High

Priest said to Him, "Who are you?" "I am the Anointed, the Son of the uncreated God, and you shall see Me appearing at the end of all history as the judge of the Universe."

But that claim, in fact, does not rest on this one dramatic moment. When you look into his conversation, you will find this sort of claim running through the whole thing. For instance, He went about saying to people, "I forgive your sins." Now it is quite natural for a man to forgive something you do to *him*. Thus if somebody cheats *me* out of £5, it is quite possible and reasonable for me to say, "Well, I forgive him, we will say no more about it." What on earth would you say if somebody had done *you* out of £5 and *I* said, "That is all right, I forgive him"?

Then there is a curious thing which seems to slip out almost by accident. On one occasion this Man is sitting looking down on Jerusalem from the hill above it and suddenly in comes an extraordinary remark—"I keep on sending you prophets and wise men." Nobody comments on it. And yet, quite suddenly, almost incidentally, He is claiming to be the power that all through the centuries is sending wise men and leaders into the world.

Here is another curious remark: in almost every religion there are unpleasant observances like fasting. This Man suddenly remarks one day, "No one need fast while I am here." Who is this Man who remarks that His mere presence suspends all normal rules? Who is the person who can suddenly tell the School they can have a half-holiday?

Sometimes the statements put forward the assumption that He, the Speaker, is completely without sin or fault. This is always the attitude. "You, to whom I am talking, are all sinners," and He never remotely suggests that this same reproach can be brought against Him. He says again, "I am begotten of the One God, before Abraham was, I am," and remember what the words "I am" were in Hebrew. They were the name of God, which must not be spoken by any human being, the name which it was death to utter.

Well, that is the other side. On the one side clear, definite moral teaching. On the other, claims which, if not true, are those of a megalomaniac, compared with whom Hitler was the most sane and humble of men. There is no halfway house and there is no parallel in other religions. If you had gone to Buddha and asked him, "Are you the son of Bramah?" he would have said, "My son, you are still in the vale of illusion." If you had gone to Socrates and asked, "Are you Zeus?" he would have laughed at you. If you had gone to Mohammed and asked, "Are you Allah?" he would first have rent his clothes and then cut your head off. If you had asked Confucius, "Are you Heaven?" I think he would probably have replied, "Remarks which are not in accordance with nature are in bad taste." The idea of a great moral teacher saying what Christ said is out of the question. In my opinion, the only person who can say that sort of thing is either God or a complete lunatic suffering from that form of delusion which undermines the whole mind of man. If you think you are a poached egg when you are looking for a piece of toast to suit you, you may be sane, but if you think you are God, there is no chance for you.

We may note in passing that He was never regarded as a mere moral teacher. He did not produce that effect on any of the people who actually met Him. He produced mainly three effects—Hatred—Terror—Adoration. There was no trace of people expressing mild approval.

"Putting on Christ"

UP TILL NOW, I have been trying to describe facts—what God is and what He has done. Now I want to talk about practice—what do we do next? What difference does all this theology make? It can start making a difference tonight. If you are interested enough to have read thus far, you are probably interested enough to make a shot at saying your prayers; and, whatever else you say, you will probably say the Lord's Prayer.

Its very first words are *Our Father*. Do you now see what those words mean? They mean, quite frankly, that you are putting yourself in the place of a son of God. To put it bluntly, you are *dressing up as Christ*. If you like, you are pretending. Because, of course, the moment you realize what the words mean, you realize that you are not a son of God. You are not being like The Son of God, whose will and interests are at one with those of the Father: you are a bundle of self-centered fears, hopes, greeds, jealousies, and self-conceit, all doomed to death. So that, in a way, this dressing up as Christ is a piece of outrageous cheek. But the odd thing is that He has ordered us to do it.

Why? What is the good of pretending to be what you are not? Well, even on the human level, you know, there are two kinds of pretending. There is a bad kind, where the pretense is there instead of the real thing; as when a man pretends he is going to help you instead of really helping you. But there is also a good kind, where the pretense leads up to the real thing. When you are not feeling particularly friendly but know you ought to be, the best thing you can do, very often, is to put on a friendly manner and behave as if you were a nicer person than you actually are. And in a few minutes, as we have all noticed, you will be really feeling friendlier than you were. Very often the only way to get a quality in reality is to start behaving as if you had it already. That is why children's games are so important. They are always pretending to be grown-ups—playing soldiers, playing shop. But all the time, they are hardening their muscles and sharpening their wits, so that the pretense of being grown-up helps them to grow up in earnest.

Now the moment you realize "Here I am, dressing up as

Christ," it is extremely likely that you will see at once some way in which at that very moment the pretense could be made less of a pretense and more of a reality. You will find several things going on in your mind which would not be going on there if you were really a son of God. Well, stop them. Or you may realize that, instead of saying your prayers, you ought to be downstairs writing a letter, or helping your wife to wash up. Well, go and do it.

You see what is happening. The Christ Himself, the Son of God who is man (just like you) and God (just like His Father) is actually at your side and is already at that moment beginning to turn your pretense into a reality. This is not merely a fancy way of saying that your conscience is telling you what to do. If you simply ask your conscience, you get one result: if you remember that you are dressing up as Christ, you get a different one. There are lots of things which your conscience might not call definitely wrong (specially things in your mind) but which you will see at once you cannot go on doing if you are seriously trying to be like Christ. For you are no longer thinking simply about right and wrong; you are trying to catch the good infection from a Person. It is more like painting a portrait than like obeying a set of rules. And the odd thing is that while in one way it is much harder than keeping rules, in another way it is far easier.

The real Son of God is at your side. He is beginning to turn you into the same kind of thing as Himself. He is beginning, so to speak, to "inject" His kind of life and thought, His *Zoë*, into you; beginning to turn the tin soldier into a live man. The part of you that does not like it is the part that is still tin.

Perfection

WHEN I WAS A CHILD I often had [a] toothache, and I knew that if I went to my mother she would give me something which would deaden the pain for that night and let me get to sleep. But I did not go to my mother—at least, not till the pain became very bad. And the reason I did not go was this. I did not doubt she would give me the aspirin; but I knew she would also do something else. I knew she would take me to the dentist next morning. I could not get what I wanted out of her without getting something more, which I did not want. I wanted immediate relief from pain: but I could not get it without having my teeth set permanently right. And I knew those dentists; I knew they started fiddling about with all sorts of other teeth which had not yet begun to ache. They would not let sleeping dogs lie; if you gave them an inch, they took an ell.

Now, if I may put it that way, Our Lord is like the dentists. If you give Him an inch, He will take an ell. Dozens of people go to Him to be cured of some one particular sin which they are ashamed of (like masturbation or physical cowardice) or which is obviously spoiling daily life (like bad temper or drunkenness). Well, He will cure it all right: but He will not stop there. That may be all you asked; but if you once call Him in, He will give you the full treatment.

That is why He warned people to "count the cost" before becoming Christians. "Make no mistake," He says, "if you let Me, I will make you perfect. The moment you put yourself in My hands, that is what you are in for. Nothing less, or other, than that. You have free will, and if you choose, you can push Me away. But if you do not push Me away, understand that I am going to see this job through. Whatever suffering it may cost you in your earthly life, whatever inconceivable purification it may cost you after death, whatever it costs Me, I will never rest, nor let you rest, until you are literally perfect—until my Father can say without reservation that He is well pleased with you, as He said He was well pleased with Me. This I can do and will do. But I will not do anything less."

And yet—this is the other and equally important side of it—this Helper who will, in the long run, be satisfied with nothing less than absolute perfection, will also be delighted with the first feeble, stumbling effort you make tomorrow to do the simplest duty. As a great Christian writer (George Macdonald) pointed out, every father is pleased at the baby's first attempt to walk: no father would be satisfied with anything less than a firm, free, manly walk in a grown-up son. In the same way, he said, "God is easy to please, but hard to satisfy."

The practical upshot is this. On the one hand, God's demand for perfection need not discourage you in the least in your present attempts to be good, or even in your present failures. Each time you fall He will pick you up again. And He knows perfectly well that your own efforts are never going to bring you anywhere near perfection. On the other hand, you must realize from the outset that the goal toward which He is beginning to guide you is absolute perfection; and no power in the whole universe, except you yourself, can prevent Him from taking you to that goal. That is what you are in for. And it is very important to realize that.

First Fervor

MANY RELIGIOUS PEOPLE lament that the first fervors of their conversion have died away. They think—sometimes rightly, but not, I believe, always—that their sins account for this. They may even try by pitiful efforts of will to revive what now seem to have been the golden days. But were those fervors—the operative word is *those*—ever intended to last?

It would be rash to say that there is any prayer which God *never* grants. But the strongest candidate is the prayer we might express in the single word *encore*. And how should the Infinite repeat Himself? All space and time are too little for Him to utter Himself in them *once*.

And the joke, or tragedy, of it all is that these golden moments in the past, which are so tormenting if we erect them into a norm, are entirely nourishing, wholesome, and enchanting if we are content to accept them for what they are, for memories. Properly bedded down in a past which we do not miserably try to conjure back, they will send up exquisite growths. Leave the bulbs alone, and the new flowers will come up. Grub them up and hope, by fondling and sniffing, to get last year's blooms, and you will get nothing. "Unless a seed die. . . ."

Scruples

ONE MUSTN'T MAKE the Christian life into a punctilious system of *law*, like the Jewish, [for] two reasons. (1) It raises scruples when we don't keep the routine. (2) It raises presumption when we do. Nothing gives one a more spuriously good conscience than keeping rules, even if there has been a total absence of all real charity and faith.

Liturgy

EVERY SERVICE is a structure of acts and words through which we receive a sacrament, or repent, or supplicate, or adore. And it enables us to do these things best—if you like it, it "works" best—when, through long familiarity, we don't have to think about it. As long as you notice, and have to count, the steps, you are not yet dancing but only learning to dance. A good shoe is a shoe you don't notice. Good reading becomes possible when you need not consciously think about eyes, or light, or print, or spelling. The perfect church service would be the one we were almost unaware of; our attention would have been on God.

But every novelty prevents this. It fixes our attention on the service itself; and thinking about worship is a different thing from worshipping. The important question about the Grail was "for what does it serve?" " 'Tis mad idolatry that makes the service greater than the god."

A still worse thing may happen. Novelty may fix our attention not even on the service but on the celebrant. You know what I mean. Try as one may to exclude it, the question "What on earth is he up to now?" will intrude. It lays one's devotion waste. There is really some excuse for the man who said, "I wish they'd remember that the charge to Peter was Feed my sheep; not Try experiments on my rats, or even Teach my performing dogs new tricks."

Thus my whole liturgiological position really boils down to an entreaty for permanence and uniformity. I can make do with almost any kind of service whatever, if only it will stay put. But if each form is snatched away just when I am beginning to feel at home in it, then I can never make any progress in the art of worship. You give me no chance to acquire the trained habit—*habito dell'arte.*

It may well be that some variations which seem to me merely matters of taste really involve grave doctrinal differences. But surely not all? For if grave doctrinal differences are really as numerous as variations in practice, then we shall have to conclude that no such thing as the Church of England exists. And anyway, the Liturgical Fidget is not a purely Anglican phenomenon; I have heard Roman Catholics complain of it too. . . .

As to the words of the service—liturgy in the narrower sense—the question is rather different. If you have a vernacular liturgy, you must have a changing liturgy: otherwise it will finally be vernacular only in name. The ideal of "timeless English" is sheer nonsense. No living language can be timeless. You might as well ask for a motionless river.

I think it would have been best, if it were possible, that necessary change should have occurred gradually and (to most people) imperceptibly; here a little and there a little; one obsolete word replaced in a century—like the gradual change of spelling in successive editions of Shakespeare.

Holy Communion

IT IS ALMOST impossible to state the negative effect which certain doctrines have on me—my failure to be nourished by them—without seeming to mount an attack against them. But the very last thing I want to do is to unsettle in the mind of any Christian, whatever his denomination, the concepts—for him traditional—by which he finds it profitable to represent to himself what is happening when he receives the bread and wine. I could wish that no definitions had ever been felt to be necessary; and, still more, that none had been allowed to make divisions between churches.

Some people seem able to discuss different theories of this act as if they understood them all and needed only evidence as to which was best. This light has been withheld from me. I do not know and can't imagine what the disciples understood Our Lord to mean when, His body still unbroken and His blood unshed, He handed them the bread and wine, saying *they* were His body and blood. . . .

I hope I do not offend God by making my Communions in the frame of mind I have been describing. The command, after all, was Take, eat: not Take, understand. Particularly, I hope I need not be tormented by the question "What is this?"—this wafer, this sip of wine. That has a dreadful effect on me. It invites me to take "this" out of its holy context and regard it as an object among objects, indeed as part of nature. It is like taking a red coal out of the fire to examine it: it becomes a dead coal. To me, I mean. All this is autobiography, not theology.

Devotions to Saints

THERE IS CLEARLY a theological defense for it; if you can ask for the prayers of the living, why should you not ask for the prayers of the dead? There is clearly also a great danger. In some popular practice we see it leading off into an infinitely silly picture of Heaven as an earthly court where applicants will be wise to pull the right wires, discover the best "channels," and attach themselves to the most influential pressure groups. But I have nothing to do with all this. I am not thinking of adopting the practice myself; and who am I to judge the practice of others? . . .

The consoling thing is that while Christendom is divided about the rationality, and even the lawfulness, of praying *to* the saints, we are all agreed about praying *with* them. "With angels and archangels and all the company of heaven." . . . One always accepted this *with* theoretically. But it is quite different when one brings it into consciousness at an appropriate moment and wills the association of one's own little twitter with the voices of the great saints and (we hope) of our own dear dead. They may drown some of its uglier qualities and set off any tiny value it has.

You may say that the distinction between the communion of the saints as I find it in that act and full-fledged prayer to saints is not, after all, very great.

Church Music

THERE ARE TWO musical situations on which I think we can be confident that a blessing rests. One is where a priest or an organist, himself a man of trained and delicate taste, humbly and charitably sacrifices his own (esthetically right) desires and gives the people humbler and coarser fare than he would wish, in a belief (even, as it may be, the erroneous belief) that he can thus bring them to God. The other is where the stupid and unmusical layman humbly and patiently, and above all silently, listens to music which he cannot, or cannot fully, appreciate, in the belief that it somehow glorifies God, and that if it does not edify him this must be his own defect. Neither such a High Brow nor such a Low Brow can be far out of the way. To both, Church Music will have been a means of grace; not the music they have liked, but the music they have disliked. They have both offered, sacrificed, their taste in the fullest sense.

But where the opposite situation arises, where the musician is filled with pride of skill or the virus of emulation and looks with contempt on the unappreciative congregation, or where the unmusical, complacently entrenched in their own ignorance and conservatism, look with the restless and resentful hostility of an inferiority complex on all who would try to improve their taste—there, we may be sure, all that both offer is unblessed and the spirit that moves them is not the Holy Ghost.

Ready-made Prayers

FOR MANY YEARS after my conversion I never used any ready-made forms except the Lord's Prayer. In fact, I tried to pray without words at all—not to verbalize the mental acts. Even in praying for others I believe I tended to avoid their names and substituted mental images of them. I still think the prayer without words is the best—if one can really achieve it. But I now see that in trying to make it my daily bread I was counting on a greater mental and spiritual strength than I really have. To pray successfully without words one needs to be "at the top of one's form." Otherwise the mental acts become merely imaginative or emotional acts—and a fabricated emotion is a miserable affair. When the golden moments come, when God enables one really to pray without words, who but a fool would reject the gift? But He does not give it—anyway not to me—day in, day out. My mistake was what Pascal, if I remember rightly, calls "Error of Stoicism"; thinking we can do always what we can do sometimes. . . .

For me words are . . . secondary. They are only an anchor. Or, shall I say, they are the movements of a conductor's baton: not the music. They serve to canalize the worship, or penitence, or petition, which might without them—such are our minds—spread into wide and shallow puddles. It does not matter very much who first put them together. If they are our own words they will soon, by unavoidable repetition, harden into a formula. If they are someone else's, we shall continually pour into them our own meaning.

At present—for one's practice changes and, I think, ought

to change—I find it best to make "my own words" the staple but introduce a modicum of the ready-made. . . .

Perhaps I shan't find it so easy to persuade you that the ready-made modicum has . . . its use: for me, I mean—I'm not suggesting rules for anyone else in the world.

First, it keeps me in touch with "sound doctrine." Left to one's self, one could easily slide away from "the faith once given" into a phantom called "my religion."

Secondly, it reminds me "what things I ought to ask" (perhaps especially when I am praying for other people). The crisis of the present moment, like the nearest telegraph post, will always loom largest. Isn't there a danger that our great, permanent, objective necessities—often more important—may get crowded out?

Finally, they provide an element of the ceremonial.

Festooning Ready-made Prayers

I DON'T VERY MUCH like the job of telling you "more about my festoonings"—the private overtones I give to certain petitions. . . .

I call them "festoons," by the way, because they don't (I trust) obliterate the plain, public sense of the petition but are merely hung on it. . . .

Thy kingdom come. That is, may your reign be realized here, as it is realized there. But I tend to take *there* on three levels. First, as in the sinless world beyond the horrors of animal and human life; in the behavior of stars and trees and water, in sunrise and wind. May there be *here* (in my heart) the beginning of a like beauty. Secondly, as in the best human lives I have known: in all the people who really bear the burdens and ring true, and in the quiet, busy, ordered life of really good families and really good religious houses. May that too be "here." Finally, of course, in the usual sense: as in Heaven, as among the blessed dead.

And *here* can of course be taken not only as "in my heart," but as "in this college"—in England—in the world in general. But prayer is not the time for pressing our own favorite social or political panacea. Even Queen Victoria didn't like "being talked to as if she were a public meeting."

Thy will be done. My festoons on this have been added gradually. At first I took it exclusively as an act of submission, attempting to do with it what Our Lord did in Gethsemane. I thought of God's will purely as something that would come upon me, something of which I should be the patient. And I also thought of it as a will which would be embodied in pains and disappointments. Not, to be sure, that I supposed God's will for me to consist entirely of disagreeables. But I thought it was only the disagreeables that called for this preliminary submission—the agreeables could look after themselves for the present. When they turned up, one could give thanks.

This interpretation is, I expect, the commonest. And so it must be. And such are the miseries of human life that it must often fill our whole mind. But at other times other meanings can be added. So I added one more.

The peg for it is, I admit, much more obvious in the English version than in the Greek or Latin. No matter: this is where the liberty of festooning comes in. "Thy will *be done.*" But a great deal of it is to be done by God's creatures; including me. The petition, then, is not merely that I may patiently suffer God's will but also that I may vigorously do it. I must be an agent as well as a patient. I am asking that I may be enabled to do it. In the long run I am asking to be given "the same mind which was also in Christ."

Taken this way, I find the words have a more regular

daily application. For there isn't always—or we don't always have reason to suspect that there is—some great affliction looming in the near future, but there are always duties to be done; usually, for me, neglected duties to be caught up with. "Thy will be *done*—by me—now" brings one back to brass tacks.

But more than that, I am at this very moment contemplating a new festoon. Tell me if you think it a vain subtlety. I am beginning to feel that we need a preliminary act of submission not only toward possible future afflictions but also toward possible future blessings. I know it sounds fantastic; but think it over. It seems to me that we often, almost sulkily, reject the good that God offers us because, at that moment, we expected some other good. Do you know what I mean? On every level of our life—in our religious experience, in our gastronomic, erotic, esthetic, and social experience—we are always harking back to some occasion which seemed to us to reach perfection, setting that up as a norm, and depreciating all other occasions by comparison. But these other occasions, I now suspect, are often full of their own new blessing, if only we would lay ourselves open to it. God shows us a new facet of the glory, and we refuse to look at it because we're still looking for the old one. And of course we don't get that. You can't, at the twentieth reading, get again the experience of reading *Lycidas* for the first time. But what you do get can be in its own way as good.

When and Where to Pray

No ONE in his senses, if he has any power of ordering his own day, would reserve his chief prayers for bedtime—obviously the worst possible hour for any action which needs concentration. The trouble is that thousands of unfortunate people can hardly find any other. . . . My own plan, when hard pressed, is to seize any time, and place, however unsuitable, in preference to the last waking moment. On a day of traveling—with, perhaps, some ghastly meeting at the end of it—I'd rather pray sitting in a crowded train than put it off till midnight when one reaches a hotel bedroom with aching head and dry throat and one's mind partly in a stupor and partly in a whirl. On other, and slightly less crowded, days a bench in a park, or a back street where one can pace up and down, will do.

A man to whom I was explaining this said, "But why don't you turn into a church?" Partly because, for nine months of the year, it will be freezingly cold, but also because I have had bad luck with churches. No sooner do I enter one and compose my mind than one or other of two things happens. Either someone starts practicing the organ. Or else, with resolute tread, there appears from nowhere a pious woman in elastic side-boots, carrying mop, bucket, and dustpan, and begins beating hassocks and rolling up carpets and doing things to flower vases. Of course (blessings on her) "work is prayer," and her enacted *oratio* is probably worth ten times my spoken one. But it doesn't help mine to become worth more.

When one prays in strange places and at strange times, one can't kneel, to be sure. I won't say this doesn't matter. The body ought to pray as well as the soul. Body and soul are both the better for it. Bless the body. Mine has led me into many scrapes, but I've led it into far more. If the imagination were obedient, the appetite would give us very little trouble. And from how much it has saved me! And but for our body one whole realm of God's glory—all that we receive through the senses—would go unpraised. For the beasts can't appreciate it and the angels are, I suppose, pure intelligences. They *understand* colors and tastes better than our greatest scientists; but have they retinas or palates? I fancy the "beauties of nature" are a secret God has shared with us alone. That may be one of the reasons why we were made—and why the resurrection of the body is an important doctrine.

But I'm being led into a digression. . . . The relevant point is that kneeling does matter, but other things matter even more. A concentrated mind and a sitting body make for better prayer than a kneeling body and a mind half asleep. Sometimes these are the only alternatives. . . .

A clergyman once said to me that a railway compartment, if one has it to one's self, is an extremely good place to pray in "because there is just the right amount of distraction." When I asked him to explain, he said that perfect silence and solitude left one more open to the distractions which come from within, and that a moderate amount of external distraction was easier to cope with. I don't find this so myself, but I can imagine it.

The Moment of Prayer

WE ARE ALWAYS, completely, and therefore equally, known to God. That is our destiny whether we like it or not. But though this knowledge never varies, the quality of our being known can. A school of thought holds that "freedom is willed necessity." Never mind if they are right or not. I want this idea only as an analogy. Ordinarily, to be known by God is to be, for this purpose, in the category of things. We are like earthworms, cabbages, and nebulae, objects of divine knowledge. But when we (a) become aware of the fact—the present fact, not the generalization—and (b) assent with all our will to be so known, then we treat ourselves, in relation to God, not as things but as persons. We have unveiled. Not that any veil could have baffled this sight. The change is in us. The passive changes to the active. Instead of merely being known, we show, we tell, we offer ourselves to view.

To put ourselves thus on a personal footing with God could, in itself and without warrant, be nothing but presumption and illusion. But we are taught that it is not; that it is God who gives us that footing. For it is by the Holy Spirit that we cry "Father." By unveiling, by confessing our sins and "making known" our requests, we assume the high rank of persons before Him. And He, descending, becomes a Person to us.

But I should not have said "becomes." In Him there is no becoming. He reveals Himself as Person: or reveals that in Him which is Person. For—dare one say it? in a book it would need pages of qualification and insurance—God is in some measure to a man as that man is to God. The door in God that opens is the door he knocks at. (At least, I think so usually.) The Person in Him—He is more than a person—meets those who can welcome or at least face it. He speaks as "I" when we truly call Him "Thou." (How good Buber is!)

This talk of "meeting" is, no doubt, anthropomorphic; as if God and I could be face to face, like two fellow creatures, when in reality He is above me and within me and below me and all about me. That is why it must be balanced by all manner of metaphysical and theological abstractions. But never, here or anywhere else, let us think that while anthropomorphic images are a concession to our weakness, the abstractions are the literal truth. Both are equally concessions; each singly misleading, and the two together mutually corrective. Unless you sit to it very tightly, continually murmuring "Not thus, not thus, neither is this Thou," the abstraction is fatal. It will make the life of lives inanimate and the love of loves impersonal. The naive image is mischievous chiefly insofar as it holds unbelievers back from conversion. It does believers, even at its crudest, no harm. What soul ever perished for believing that God the Father really has a beard?

Mechanics of Meditation

WHAT IS MORE NATURAL, and easier, if you believe in God, than to address Him: How could one not?

Yes. But it depends who one is. For those in my position—adult converts from the *intelligentsia*—that simplicity and spontaneity can't always be the starting point. One can't just jump back into one's childhood. If one tries to, the result will only be an archaizing revival, like Victorian Gothic—a parody of being born again. We have to work back to the simplicity a long way round.

In actual practice, in my prayers, I often have to use that long way at the very beginning of the prayer.

St. François de Sales begins every meditation with the command *Mettez-vous en la présence de Dieu*. I wonder how many different mental operations have been carried out in intended obedience to that?

What happens to me if I try to take it . . . simply, is the juxtaposition of two "representations," or ideas, or phantoms. One is the bright blur in the mind which stands for God. The other is the idea I call "me." But I can't leave it at that, because I know—and it's useless to pretend I don't know—that they are both phantasmal. The real I has created them both—or, rather, built them up in the vaguest way from all sorts of psychological odds and ends.

St. Ignatius Loyola (I think it was) advised his pupils to begin their meditations with what he called a *compositio loci*. The Nativity or the Marriage at Cana, or whatever the theme might be, was to be visualized in the fullest possible detail. One of his English followers would even have us look up "what good Authors write of those places" so as to get the topography, "the height of the hills and the situation of the townes," correct. Now for two different reasons this is not "addressed to my condition."

One is that I live in an archaeological age. We can no longer, as St. Ignatius could, believingly introduce the clothes, furniture, and utensils of our own age into ancient Palestine. I'd know I wasn't getting them right. I'd know that the very sky and sunlight of those latitudes were different from any my northern imagination could supply. I could no doubt pretend to myself a naiveté I don't really possess; but that would cast an unreality over the whole exercise.

The second reason is more important. St. Ignatius was a great master, and I am sure he knew what his pupils needed. I conclude that they were people whose visual imagination was weak and needed to be stimulated. But the trouble with people like ourselves is the exact reverse. We can say this to one another because, in our mouths, it is not a boast but a confession. We are agreed that the power—indeed, the compulsion—to visualize is not "Imagination" in the higher sense, not the Imagination which makes a man either a great author or a sensitive reader. Ridden on a very tight rein, this visualizing power can sometimes serve true Imagination; very often it merely gets in the way.

If I started with a *compositio loci*, I should never reach the meditation. The picture would go on elaborating itself indefinitely and becoming every moment of less spiritual relevance. . . .

I have called my material surroundings a stage set. A stage set is not a dream nor a nonentity. But if you attack a stage house with a chisel, you will not get chips of brick or stone; you'll only get a hole in a piece of canvas and, beyond that, windy darkness. Similarly, if you start investigating the nature of matter, you will not find anything like what imagination has always supposed matter to be. You will get mathematics. From that unimaginable physical reality my senses select a few stimuli. These they translate or symbolize into sensations, which have no likeness at all to the reality of matter. Of these sensations my associative power, very much directed by my practical needs and influenced by social training, makes up little bundles into what I call "things" (labeled by nouns). Out of these I build myself a neat little box stage, suitably provided with properties such as hills, fields, houses, and the rest. In this I can act.

And you may well say "act." For what I call "myself" (for all practical, everyday purposes) is also a dramatic construction; memories, glimpses in the shaving glass, and snatches of the very fallible activity called "introspection" are the principal ingredients. Normally I call this construction "me," and the stage set "the real world."

Now the moment of prayer is for me—or involves for me as its condition—the awareness, the reawakened awareness, that this "real world" and "real self" are very far from being rock-bottom realities. I cannot, in the flesh, leave the stage, either to go behind the scenes or to take my seat in the pit; but I can remember that these regions exist. And I also remember that my apparent self—the clown, or hero, or super—under his greasepaint is a real person with an off-stage life. The dramatic person could not tread the stage unless he concealed a real person: unless the real and unknown I existed, I would not even make mistakes about the imagined me. And in prayer this real I struggles to speak, for once, from his real being, and to address, for once, not the other actors, but—what shall I call Him: The Author, for He invented us all? The Producer, for He controls all? Or the Audience, for He watches, and will judge, the performance?

The attempt is not to escape from space and time and from my creaturely situation as a subject facing objects. It is more modest: to reawake the awareness of that situation. If that can be done, there is no need to go anywhere else. This situation itself is, at every moment, a possible theophany. Here is the holy ground; the Bush is burning now.

Answered Prayers

THE NEW TESTAMENT contains embarrassing promises that what we pray for with faith we shall receive. Mark 11:24 is the most staggering. Whatever we ask for, believing that we'll get it, we'll get. No question, it seems, of confining it to spiritual gifts; *whatever* we ask for. No question of a merely general faith in God, but a belief that you will get the particular thing you ask. No question of getting either it or else something that is really far better for you; you'll get precisely it. . . .

How is this astonishing promise to be reconciled (a) with the observed facts? and (b) with the prayer in Gethsemane, and (as a result of that prayer) the universally accepted view that we should ask everything with a reservation ("if it be Thy will")?

As regards (a), no evasion is possible. Every war, every famine or plague, almost every deathbed, is the monument to a petition that was not granted. . . .

But (b), though much less often mentioned, is surely an equal difficulty. How is it possible at one and the same moment to have a perfect faith—an untroubled or unhesitating faith as St. James says (1:6)—that you will get what you ask and yet also prepare yourself submissively in advance for possible refusal? If you envisage a refusal as possible, how can you have simultaneously a perfect confidence that what you ask will not be refused? If you have that confidence, how can you take refusal into account at all?

It is easy to see why so much more is written about worship and contemplation than about "crudely" or "naively" petitionary prayer. They may be—I think they are—nobler forms of prayer. But they are also a good deal easier to write about. . . .

It seems to me we must conclude that such promises about prayer with faith refer to a degree or kind of faith which most believers never experience. A far inferior degree is, I hope, acceptable to God. Even the kind that says "Help Thou my unbelief" may make way for a miracle. Again, the absence of such faith as insures the granting of the prayer is not even necessarily a sin; for Our Lord had no such assurance when He prayed in Gethsemane.

The Efficacy of Prayer

SOME YEARS AGO I got up one morning intending to have my hair cut in preparation for a visit to London, and the first letter I opened made it clear I need not go to London. So I decided to put the haircut off too. But then there began the most unaccountable little nagging in my mind, almost like a voice saying, "Get it cut all the same. Go and get it cut." In the end I could stand it no longer. I went. Now my barber at that time was a fellow Christian and a man of many troubles whom my brother and I had sometimes been able to help. The moment I opened his shop door he said, "Oh, I was praying you might come today." And, in fact, if I had come a day or so later, I should have been of no use to him.

It awed me; it awes me still. But, of course, one cannot

rigorously prove a causal connection between the barber's prayers and my visit. It might be telepathy. It might be accident.

I have stood by the bedside of a woman whose thighbone was eaten through with cancer and who had thriving colonies of the disease in many other bones as well. It took three people to move her in bed. The doctors predicted a few months of life; the nurses (who often know better), a few weeks. A good man laid his hands on her and prayed. A year later the patient was walking (uphill, too, through rough woodland) and the man who took the last X-ray photos was saying, "These bones are as solid as rock. It's miraculous."

But once again there is no rigorous proof. Medicine, as all true doctors admit, is not an exact science. We need not invoke the supernatural to explain the falsification of its prophecies. You need not, unless you choose, believe in a causal connection between the prayers and the recovery.

The question then arises, "What sort of evidence *would* prove the efficacy of prayer?" The thing we pray for may happen, but how can you ever know it was not going to happen anyway? Even if the thing were indisputably miraculous, it would not follow that the miracle had occurred because of your prayers. The answer surely is that a compulsive empirical proof such as we have in the sciences can never be attained.

Some things are proved by the unbroken uniformity of our experiences. The law of gravitation is established by the fact that, in our experience, all bodies without exception obey it. Now even if all the things that people prayed for happened, which they do not, this would not prove what Christians mean by the efficacy of prayer. For prayer is request. The essence of request, as distinct from compulsion, is that it may or may not be granted. And if an infinitely wise Being listens to the requests of finite and foolish creatures, of course He will sometimes grant and sometimes refuse them. Invariable "success" in prayer would not prove the Christian doctrine at all. It would prove something much more like magic—a power in certain human beings to control, or compel, the course of nature.

There are, no doubt, passages in the New Testament which may seem at first sight to promise an invariable granting of our prayers. But that cannot be what they really mean. For in the very heart of the story we meet a glaring instance to the contrary. In Gethsemane the holiest of all petitioners prayed three times that a certain cup might pass from Him. It did not. After that the idea that prayer is recommended to us as a sort of infallible gimmick may be dismissed.

Other things are proved not simply by experience but by those artificially contrived experiences which we call experiments. Could this be done about prayer? I will pass over the objection that no Christian could take part in such a project, because he has been forbidden it: "You must not try experiments on God, your Master." Forbidden or not, is the thing even possible?

I have seen it suggested that a team of people—the more the better—should agree to pray as hard as they knew how, over a period of six weeks, for all the patients in Hospital A and none of those in Hospital B. Then you would tot up the results and see if A had more cures and fewer deaths. And I suppose you would repeat the experiment at various times and places so as to eliminate the influence of irrelevant factors.

The trouble is that I do not see how any real prayer could go on under such conditions. "Words without thoughts never to heaven go," says the King in *Hamlet*. Simply to say prayers is not to pray; otherwise a team of properly trained parrots would serve as well as men for our experiment. You cannot pray for the recovery of the sick unless the end you have in view is their recovery. But you can have no motive for desiring the recovery of all the patients in one hospital and none of those in another. You are not doing it in order that suffering should be relieved; you are doing it to find out what happens. The real purpose and the nominal purpose of your prayers are at variance. In other words, whatever your tongue and teeth and knees may do, you are not praying. The experiment demands an impossibility.

Empirical proof and disproof are, then, unobtainable. But this conclusion will seem less depressing if we remember that prayer is request and compare it with other specimens of the same thing.

We make requests of our fellow creatures as well as of God: we ask for the salt, we ask for a raise in pay, we ask a friend to feed the cat while we are on our holidays, we ask a woman to marry us. Sometimes we get what we ask for and sometimes not. But when we do, it is not nearly so easy as one might suppose to prove with scientific certainty a causal connection between the asking and the getting.

Your neighbor may be a humane person who would not have let your cat starve even if you had forgotten to make any arrangement. Your employer is never so likely to grant your request for a raise as when he is aware that you could get better money from a rival firm and is quite possibly intending to secure you by a raise in any case. As for the lady who consents to marry you—are you sure she had not decided to do so already? Your proposal, you know, might have been the result, not the cause, of her decision. A certain important conversation might never have taken place unless she had intended that it should.

Thus in some measure the same doubt that hangs about the causal efficacy of our prayers to God hangs also about our prayers to man. Whatever we get we might have been going to get anyway. But only, as I say, in some measure. Our friend, boss, and wife may tell us that they acted because we asked and we may know them so well as to feel sure, first that they are saying what they believe to be true, and secondly that they understand their own motives well enough to be right. But notice that when this happens our assurance has not been gained by the methods of science. We do not try the control experiment of refusing the raise or breaking off the engagement and then making our request again under fresh conditions. Our assurance is quite different in kind from scientific knowledge. It is born out of our personal relation to the other parties; not from knowing things about them but from knowing *them*.

Our assurance—if we reach an assurance—that God always hears and sometimes grants our prayers, and that apparent grantings are not merely fortuitous, can only come in the same sort of way. There can be no question of tabulating successes and failures and trying to decide whether the successes are too numerous to be accounted for by chance. Those who best know a man best know whether, when he did what they asked, he did it because they asked. I think those who best know God will best know whether He sent me to the barber's shop because the barber prayed.

Mysticism

THE FOLLOWING POSITION is gaining ground and is extremely plausible. Mystics (it is said) starting from the most diverse religious premises all find the same things. These things have singularly little to do with the professed doctrines of any particular religion—Christianity, Hinduism, Buddhism, Neo-Platonism, etc. Therefore, mysticism is, by empirical evidence, the only real contact man has ever had with the unseen. The agreement of the explorers proves that they are all in touch with something objective. It is therefore the one true religion. And what we call the "religions" are either mere delusions or, at best, so many porches through which an entrance into transcendent reality can be effected.

> And when he hath the kernel eate,
> Who doth not throw away the shell?

I am doubtful about the premises. Did Plotinus and Lady Julian and St. John of the Cross really find "the same things"? Even admitting some similarity. One thing common to all mysticisms is the temporary shattering of our ordinary spatial and temporary consciousness and of our discursive intellect. The value of this negative experience must depend on the nature of that positive, whatever it is, for which it makes room. But should we not expect that the negative would always *feel* the same? If wineglasses were conscious, I suppose that *being emptied* would be the same experience for each, even if some were to remain empty, and some to be filled with poison, and some broken. All who leave the land and put to sea will find "the same things"—the land sinking below the horizon, the gulls dropping behind, the salty breeze. Tourists, merchants, sailors, pirates, missionaries—it's all one. But this identical experience vouches for nothing about the utility or lawfulness or final event of their voyages.

> It may be that the gulfs will wash them down,
> It may be they will touch the Happy Isles.

I do not at all regard mystical experience as an illusion. I think it shows that there is a way to go, before death, out of what may be called "this world"—out of the stage set. Out of this; but into what? That's like asking an Englishman "Where does the sea lead to?" He will reply, "To everywhere on earth, including Davy Jones's locker, except England." The lawfulness, safety, and utility of the mystical voyage depends not at all on its being mystical—that is, on its being a departure—but on the motives, skill, and constancy of the voyager, and on the grace of God. The true religion gives value to its own mysticism; mysticism does not validate the religion in which it happens to occur.

I shouldn't be at all disturbed if it could be shown that a diabolical mysticism, or drugs, produced experiences indistinguishable (by introspection) from those of the great Christian mystics. Departures are all alike; it is the landfall that crowns the voyage. The saint, by being a saint, proves that his mysticism (if he was a mystic; not all saints are) led him aright; the fact that he has practiced mysticism could never prove his sanctity.

Spiritual Reading

WHEREVER YOU FIND a little study circle of Christian laity, you can be almost certain that they are studying not St. Luke, or St. Paul, or St. Augustine, or Thomas Aquinas, or Hooker, or Butler, but M. Berdyaev, or M. Maritain, or Mr. Niebuhr, or Miss Sayers, or even myself.

Now this seems to me topsy-turvy. Naturally, since I myself am a writer, I do not wish the ordinary reader to read no modern books. But I would advise him to read the old. And I would give him this advice precisely because he is an amateur and therefore much less protected against the dangers of an exclusive contemporary diet. A new book is still on its trial and the amateur is not in a position to judge it. It has to be tested against the great body of Christian thought down the ages, and all its hidden implications (often unsuspected by the author himself) have to be brought to light. Often it cannot be fully understood without the knowledge of a good many other modern books. If you join at eleven o'clock a conversation which began at eight, you will often not see the real bearing of what is said.

Remarks which seem to you very ordinary will produce laughter or irritation and you will not see why—the reason, of course, being that the earlier stages of the conversation have given them a special point. In the same way sentences in a modern book which look quite ordinary may be directed "at" some other book; in this way you may be led to accept what you would have indignantly rejected if you knew its real significance. The only safety is to have a standard of plain, central Christianity ("mere Christianity" as Baxter called it) which puts the controversies of the moment in their proper perspective. Such a standard can be acquired only from the old books. It is a good rule, after reading a new book, never to allow yourself another new one till you have read an old one in between. If that is too much for you, you should at least read one old one to every three new ones.

✖

For a good ("popular") defense of our position against modern woffle, to fall back on, I know nothing better than G. K. Chesterton's *The Everlasting Man*. Harder reading, but very protective, is Edwyn Bevan's *Symbolism and Belief*. Charles Williams's *He Came Down from Heaven* doesn't suit everyone, but try it.

For meditative and devotional reading (a little bit at a time, more like sucking a lozenge than eating a slice of bread), I suggest *The Imitation of Christ* (astringent) and Traherne's *Centuries of Meditation* (joyous). Also my selection from Macdonald, *George Macdonald: An Anthology*. I can't read Kierkegaard myself, but some people find him helpful.

For Christian morals I suggest my wife's (Joy Davidman) *Smoke on the Mountain;* Gore's *The Sermon on the Mount* and (perhaps) his *Philosophy of the Good Life*. And possibly (but with a grain of salt, for he is too puritanical) William Law's *Serious Call to a Devout and Holy Life.* . . .

You'll want mouthwash for the *imagination*. I'm told that Mauriac's novels (all excellently translated, if your French is rusty) are good, though very severe. Dorothy Sayers' *Man Born to be King* (those broadcast plays) certainly is. So, to me, but not to everyone, are Charles Williams's fantastic novels. *Pilgrim's Progress,* if you ignore some straw-splitting dialogues on Calvinist theology and concentrate on the story, is first-class.

St. Augustine's *Confessions* will give you the record of an earlier adult convert, with many very great devotional passages intermixed.

Do you read poetry? George Herbert at his best is extremely nutritious.

I don't mention the Bible because I take that for granted. A modern translation is for most purposes far more useful than the Authorized Version.

As regards my own books, you might (or might not) care for *Transposition, The Great Divorce,* or *The Four Loves.* . . .

Have you read anything by an American Trappist called Thomas Merton? I'm at present on his *No Man Is an Island.* It is the best new spiritual reading I've met for a long time.

About prides, superiorities, and affronts, there's no book better than Law's *Serious Call to a Devout and Holy Life* where you'll find all of us pinned like butterflies on cards— the cards being little stories of typical characters in the most sober, astringent eighteenth-century prose.

Reading the Gospels

EVERYONE TOLD ME that [in the Gospels] I should find a figure whom I couldn't help loving. Well, I could. They told me I would find moral perfection—but one sees so very little of Him in ordinary situations that I couldn't make much of that either. Indeed some of His behavior seemed to me open to criticism, e.g. accepting an invitation to dine with a Pharisee and then loading him with torrents of abuse. Now the truth is, I think, that the sweetly-attractive-human-Jesus is a product of nineteenth-century skepticism, produced by people who were ceasing to believe in His divinity but wanted to keep as much Christianity as they could. It is not what an unbeliever coming to the records with an open mind will (at first) find there. The first thing you find is that we are simply not *invited* to speak, to pass any moral judgment on Him, however favorable; it is only too clear that He is going to do whatever judging there is; it is *we* who are *being* judged, sometimes tenderly, sometimes with stunning severity, but always *de haut en bas*. (Have you ever noticed that your imagination can hardly be forced to picture Him as shorter than yourself?) The first real work of the Gospels on a fresh reader is, and ought to be, to raise very acutely the question, "Who or What is this?" For there is a good deal in the character which, unless He really is what He says he is, is not lovable or even tolerable. If He *is*, then of course it is another matter; nor will it then be surprising if much remains puzzling to the end. For if there is anything in Christianity, we are now approaching something which will never be fully comprehensible. On this whole aspect of the subject I should go on . . . to Chesterton's *Everlasting Man*. You might also find Mauriac's *Vie de Jesus* useful. . . . If childish associations are too intrusive, in reading the New Testament it's a good idea to try it in some other language, or Moffatt's translation.

Biblical Exegesis

Scripture doesn't take the slightest pain to guard the doctrine of Divine Impassibility. We are constantly represented as exciting the Divine wrath or pity—even as "grieving" God. I know this language is analogical. But when we say that, we must not smuggle in the idea that we can throw the analogy away and, as it were, get in behind it to a purely literal truth. All we can really substitute for the analogical expression is some theological abstraction. And the abstraction's value is almost entirely negative. It warns us against drawing absurd consequences from the analogical expression by prosaic extrapolations. By itself, the abstraction "impassible" can get us nowhere. It might even suggest something far more misleading than the most naive Old Testament picture of a stormily emotional Jehovah. Either something inert, or something which was "Pure Act" in such a sense that it could take no account of events within the universe it had created.

I suggest two rules for exegetics. (1) Never take the images literally. (2) When the *purport* of the images—what they say to our fear, and hope, and will, and affections— seems to conflict with the theological abstractions, trust the purport of the images every time. For our abstract thinking is itself a tissue of analogies: a continual modeling of spiritual reality in legal, or chemical, or mechanical terms. Are these likely to be more adequate than the sensuous, organic, and personal images of Scripture—light and darkness, river and well, seed and harvest, master and servant, hen and chickens, father and child? The footprints of the Divine are more visible in that rich soil than across rocks or slag heaps. Hence what they now call "demythologizing"

Christianity can easily be "remythologizing" it—and substituting a poorer mythology for a richer.

Thought, Imagination, Language

WHEN I THINK about London, I usually see a mental picture of Euston Station. But when I think (as I do) that London has several million inhabitants, I do not mean that there are several million images of people contained in my image of Euston Station. Nor do I mean that several millions of real people live in the real Euston Station. In fact, though I have the image while I am thinking about London, what I think or say is not *about* that image, and would be manifest nonsense if it were. It makes sense because it is not about my own mental pictures but about the real London, outside my imagination, of which no one can have an adequate mental picture at all. Or again, when we say that the Sun is ninety-odd million miles away, we understand perfectly clearly what we mean by this number; we can divide and multiply it by other numbers and we can work out how long it would take to travel that distance at any given speed. But this clear *thinking* is accompanied by *imagining* which is ludicrously false to what we know that the reality must be.

To think, then, is one thing, and to imagine is another. What we think or say can be, and usually is, quite different from what we imagine or picture; and what we mean may be true when the mental images that accompany it are entirely false. It is, indeed, doubtful whether anyone except an extreme visualist who is also a trained artist ever has mental images which are particularly like the things he is thinking about.

In these examples the mental image is not only unlike the reality but is known to be unlike it, at least after a moment's reflection. I know that London is not merely Euston Station. Let us now go on to a slightly different predicament. I once heard a lady tell her young daughter that you would die if you ate too many tablets of aspirin. "But why?" asked the child, "it isn't poisonous." "How do you know it isn't poisonous?" said the mother. "Because," said the child, "when you crush an aspirin tablet you don't find horrid red things inside it." Clearly, when this child thought of poison, she had a mental picture of Horrid Red Things, just as I have a picture of Euston when I think of London. The difference is that whereas I know my image to be very unlike the real London, the child thought that poison was *really* red. To that extent she was mistaken. But this does not mean that everything she thought or said about poison was necessarily nonsensical. She knew perfectly well that a poison was something which killed you or made you ill if you swallowed it; and she knew, to some extent, which of the substances in her mother's house were poisonous. If a visitor to that house had been warned by the child, "Don't drink that. Mother says it is poison," he would have been ill-advised to neglect the warning on the ground that "This child has a primitive idea of poison as Horrid Red Things, which my adult scientific knowledge has long since refuted."

We can now add to our previous statement (that thinking may be sound where the images that accompany it are false) the further statement: thinking may be sound in certain respects where it is accompanied not only by false images but by false images mistaken for true ones.

There is still a third situation to be dealt with. In our two previous examples we have been concerned with thought and imagination, but not with language. I had to picture Euston Station, but I did not need to *mention* it; the child thought that poison was Horrid Red Things, but she could talk about poison without saying so. But very often, when we are talking about something which is not perceptible by the five senses, we use words which, in one of their meanings, refer to things or actions that are. When a man says that he grasps an argument, he is using a verb (*grasp*) which literally means to take something in the hands, but he is certainly not thinking that his mind has hands or that an argument can be seized like a gun. To avoid the word *grasp* he may change the form of expression and say, "I see your point," but he does not mean that a pointed object has appeared in his visual field. He may have a third shot and say, "I follow you," but he does not mean that he is walking behind you along a road. Everyone is familiar with this linguistic phenomenon and the grammarians call it metaphor. But it is a serious mistake to think that metaphor is an optional thing which poets and orators may put into their work as a decoration and plain speakers can do without. The truth is that if we are going to talk at all about things which are not perceived by the senses, we are forced to use language metaphorically. Books on psychology, or economics, or politics are as continuously metaphorical as books of poetry or devotion. There is no other way of talking, as every philologist is aware. Those who wish can satisfy themselves on the point by reading the books I have already mentioned [Mr. Owen Barfield's *Poetic Diction* and Mr. Edwyn Bevan's *Symbolism and Belief*] and the other books to which those two will lead them on. It is a study for a lifetime and I must here content myself with the mere statement; all speech about supersensibles is, and must be, metaphorical in the highest degree.

We have now three guiding principles before us. (1) That thought is distinct from the imagination which accompanies it. (2) That thought may be in the main sound even when false images that accompany it are mistaken by the thinker for true ones. (3) That anyone who talks about things that cannot be seen, or touched, or heard, or the like, must inevitably talk as *if they could be* seen, or touched, or heard (for example, must talk of "complexes" and "repressions" *as if* institutions could really grow like trees or unfold like flowers; of energy being "released" *as if* it were an animal let out of a cage).

Scripture

IF EVEN PAGAN UTTERANCES can carry a second meaning, not quite accidentally but because . . . they have a sort of right to it, we shall expect the Scriptures to do this more momentously and more often. We have two grounds for doing so if we are Christians.

(1) For us these writings are "holy," or "inspired," or, as St. Paul says, "the Oracles of God." But this has been understood in more than one way, and I must try to explain how I understand it, at least so far as the Old Testament is concerned. I have been suspected of being what is called a Fundamentalist. That is because I never regard any narrative as unhistorical simply on the ground that it includes the miraculous. Some people find the miraculous so hard to believe that they cannot imagine any reason for my acceptance of it other than a prior belief that every sentence of the Old Testament has historical and scientific truth. But this I do not hold, any more than St. Jerome did when he said that Moses described Creation "after the manner of a popular poet" (as we should say, mythically) or than Calvin did when he doubted whether the story of Job were history or fiction. The real reason why I can accept as historical a story in which a miracle occurs is that I have never found any philosophical grounds for the universal negative proposition that miracles do not happen. I have to decide on other grounds (if I decide at all) whether a given narrative is

historical or not. The Book of Job appears to me unhistorical because it begins about a man quite unconnected with all history or even legend, with no genealogy, living in a country of which the Bible elsewhere has hardly anything to say; because, in fact, the author quite obviously writes as a storyteller not as a chronicler.

I have therefore no difficulty in accepting, say, the view of those scholars who tell us that the account of Creation in Genesis is derived from earlier Semitic stories which were Pagan and mythical. We must, of course, be quite clear what "derived from" means. Stories do not reproduce their species like mice. They are told by men. Each reteller either repeats exactly what his predecessor had told him or else changes it. He may change it unknowingly or deliberately. If he changes it deliberately, his invention, his sense of form, his ethics, his ideas of what is fit, or edifying, or merely interesting, all come in. If unknowingly, then his unconscious (which is so largely responsible for our forgettings) has been at work. Thus at every step in what is called—a little misleadingly—the "evolution" of a story, a man, all he is and all his attitudes, are involved. And no good work is done anywhere without aid from the Father of Lights. When a series of such retellings turns a creation story which at first had almost no religious or metaphysical significance into a story which achieves the idea of true Creation and of a transcendent Creator (as Genesis does), then nothing will make me believe that some of the re-tellers, or some one of them, has not been guided by God. . . .

(2) The second reason for accepting the Old Testament in this way can be put more simply and is, of course, far more compulsive. We are committed to it in principle by Our Lord Himself. On that famous journey to Emmaus He found fault with the two disciples for not believing what the prophets had said. They ought to have known from their Bibles that the Anointed One, when He came, would enter

His glory through suffering. He then explained, from "Moses" (that is, the Pentateuch) down, all the places in the Old Testament "concerning Himself" (Luke 24:25–27). He clearly identified Himself with a figure often mentioned in the Scriptures; appropriated to Himself many passages where a modern scholar might see no such reference. In the predictions of His Own Passion which He had previously made to the disciples, He was obviously doing the same thing. He accepted—indeed He claimed to be—the second meaning of Scripture.

We do not know—or anyway I do not know—what all these passages were. We can be pretty sure about one of them. The Ethiopian eunuch who met Philip (Acts 8:27–38) was reading Isaiah 53. He did not know whether in that passage the prophet was talking about himself or about someone else. Philip, in answering his question, "preached unto him Jesus." The answer, in fact, was "Isaiah is speaking of Jesus." We need have no doubt that Philip's authority for this interpretation was Our Lord. . . . We can, again, be pretty sure, from the words on the cross (Mark 15:34), that Our Lord identified Himself with the sufferer in Psalm 22. Or when He asked (Mark 12:35,36) how Christ could be both David's son and David's Lord, He clearly identified Christ, and therefore Himself, with the "my Lord" of Psalm 110—was in fact hinting at the mystery of the Incarnation by pointing out a difficulty which only it could solve. In Matthew 4:6 the words of Psalm 91:11,12, "He shall give his angels charge over thee . . . that thou hurt not thy foot against a stone," are applied to Him, and we may be sure the application was His own since only He could be the source of the temptation story. In Mark 12:10 He implicitly appropriates to Himself the words of Psalm 118:22 about the stone which the builders rejected. "Thou shalt not leave my soul in hell, neither shalt thou suffer thy Holy One to see corruption" (Psalm 16:11) is treated as a prophecy of His resurrection in Acts 2:27, and was doubtless so taken by Himself, since we find it so taken in the earliest Christian tradition—that is, by people likely to be closer both to the spirit and to the letter of His words than any scholarship (I do not say, "any sanctity") will bring a modern. Yet it is, perhaps, idle to speak here of spirit and letter. There is almost no "letter" in the words of Jesus. Taken by a literalist, He will always prove the most elusive of teachers. Systems cannot keep up with that darting illumination. No net less wide than a man's whole heart, nor less fine of mesh than love, will hold the sacred Fish.

The Psalms

THE PSALMS ARE POEMS, and poems intended to be sung: not doctrinal treatises, nor even sermons. Those who talk of reading the Bible "as literature" sometimes mean, I think, reading it without attending to the main thing it is about; like reading Burke with no interest in politics, or reading the *Aeneid* with no interest in Rome. That seems to me to be nonsense. But there is a saner sense in which the Bible, since it is, after all, literature, cannot properly be read except as literature; and the different parts of it as the different sorts of literature they are. Most emphatically the Psalms must be read as poems; as lyrics, with all the licenses and all the formalities, the hyperboles, the emotional rather than logical connections, which are proper to lyric poetry. They must be read as poems if they are to be understood; no less than French must be read as French or English as English. Otherwise we shall miss what is in them and think we see what is not.

Their chief formal characteristic, the most obvious element of pattern, is fortunately one that survives in translation. Most readers will know that I mean what the scholars call "parallelism"; that is, the practice of saying the same thing twice in different words. A perfect example is "He that dwelleth in heaven shall laugh them to scorn: the Lord shall have them in derision" (2:4), or again, "He shall make thy righteousness as clear as the light; and thy just dealing as the noonday" (37:6). If this is not recognized as pattern, the reader will either find mares' nests (as some of the older preachers did) in his effort to get a different meaning out of each half of the verse or else feel that it is rather silly.

In reality it is a very pure example of what all pattern, and therefore all art, involves. The principle of art has been defined by someone as "the same in the other." Thus in a country dance you take three steps and then three steps again. That is the same. But the first three are to the right and the second three to the left. That is the other. In a building there may be a wing on one side and a wing on the other, but both of the same shape. . . . "Parallelism" is the characteristically Hebrew form of the same in the other, but it occurs in many English poets too: for example, in Marlowe's

> Cut is the branch that might have grown full straight
> And burned is Apollo's laurel bough,

or in the childishly simple form used by the *Cherry Tree Carol*,

> Joseph was an old man and an old man was he.

Of course, the Parallelism is often partially concealed on purpose (as the balances between masses in a picture may be something far subtler than complete symmetry). And, of course, other and more complex patterns may be worked in across it, as in Psalm 119, or in 107 with its refrain. I mention only what is most obvious, the Parallelism itself. It is (according to one's point of view) either a wonderful piece of luck or a wise provision of God's, that poetry which was to be turned into all languages should have as its chief formal characteristic one that does not disappear (as mere meter does) in translation.

If we have any taste for poetry, we shall enjoy this feature of the Psalms. Even those Christians who cannot enjoy it will respect it; for Our Lord, soaked in the poetic tradition of His country, delighted to use it. "For with what judgment ye judge, ye shall be judged; and with what measure ye mete, it shall be measured to you again" (Matthew 7:2). The second half of the verse makes no logical addition; it echoes, with variation, the first, "Ask, and it shall be given to you; seek, and ye shall find; knock, and it shall be opened unto you" (Matthew 7:7). The advice is given in the first phrase, then twice repeated with different images. We may, if we like, see in this an exclusively practical and didactic purpose; by giving to truths which are infinitely worth remembering this rhythmic and incantatory expression, He made them almost impossible to forget. I like to suspect more. It seems to me appropriate, almost inevitable, that when that great Imagination which in the beginning, for Its own delight and for the delight of men and angels and (in their proper mode) of beasts, had invented and formed the whole world of Nature, submitted to express Itself in human speech, that speech should sometimes be poetry. For poetry too is a little incarnation, giving body to what had been before invisible and inaudible.

Prayer of Praise

WHEN I FIRST BEGAN to draw near to belief in God and even for some time after it had been given to me, I found a stumbling block in the demand so clamorously made by all re-

ligious people that we should "praise" God; still more in
the suggestion that God Himself demanded it. We all despise the man who demands continued assurance of his
own virtue, intelligence, or delightfulness; we despise still
more the crowd of people round every dictator, every mil-
lionaire, every celebrity, who gratify that demand. Thus a
picture, at once ludicrous and horrible, both of God and of
His worshipers, threatened to appear in my mind. The
Psalms were especially troublesome in this way—"Praise
the Lord," "O praise the Lord with me," "Praise Him."
(And why, incidentally, did praising God so often consist
in telling other people to praise Him? Even in telling
whales, snowstorms, etc., to go on doing what they would
certainly do whether we told them or not?) Worse still was
the statement put into God's own mouth, "whoso offereth
me thanks and praise, he honoreth me" (Psalm 50:23). It was
hideously like saying, "What I most want is to be told that I
am good and great." Worst of all was the suggestion of the
very silliest Pagan bargaining, that of the savage who
makes offerings to his idol when the fishing is good and
beats it when he has caught nothing. More than once the
Psalmist seemed to be saying, "You like praise. Do this for
me, and you shall have some." Thus in Psalm 54 the poet
begins "save me" (verse 1), and in verse 6 adds an induce-
ment, "An offering of a free heart will I give thee, and
praise thy Name." Again and again the speaker asks to be
saved from death on the ground that if God lets His suppli-
ants die, He will get no more praise from them, for the
ghost in Sheol cannot praise (Psalm 30:10; Psalm 88:10;
Psalm 119:175). And mere quantity of praise seemed to
count; "seven times a day do I praise thee" (Psalm 119:164).
It was extremely distressing. It made one think what one
least wanted to think. Gratitude to God, reverence to Him,
obedience to Him, I thought I could understand; not this
perpetual eulogy. Nor were matters mended by a modern
author who talked of God's "right" to be praised.

I still think "right" is a bad way of expressing it, but I believe I now see what that author meant. It is perhaps easiest to begin with inanimate objects which can have no rights. What do we mean when we say that a picture is "admirable"? We certainly don't mean that it is admired (that's as may be) for bad work is admired by thousands and good work may be ignored. Nor that it "deserves" admiration in the sense in which a candidate "deserves" a high mark from the examiners—that is, that a human being will have suffered injustice if it is not awarded. The sense in which the picture "deserves" or "demands" admiration is rather this; that admiration is the correct, adequate or appropriate, response to it, that, if paid, admiration will not be "thrown away," and that if we do not admire we shall be stupid, insensible, and great losers, we shall have missed something. In that way many objects both in Nature and in Art may be said to deserve, or merit, or demand, admiration. It was from this end, which will seem to some irreverent, that I found it best to approach the idea that God "demands" praise. He is that Object to admire which (or, if you like, to appreciate which) is simply to be awake, to have entered the real world; not to appreciate which is to have lost the greatest experience, and in the end to have lost all. The incomplete and crippled lives of those who are tone deaf, have never been in love, never known true friendship, never cared for a good book, never enjoyed the feel of the morning air on their cheeks, never (I am one of these) enjoyed football, are faint images of it.

But, of course, this is not all. God does not only "demand" praise as the supremely beautiful and all-satisfying Object. He does apparently command it as lawgiver. The Jews were told to sacrifice. We are under an obligation to go to church. But this was a difficulty only because I did not . . . see that it is in the process of being worshiped that God communicates His presence to men. It is not, of course, the only way. But for many people at many times the "fair beauty of the Lord" is revealed briefly or only while they worship Him together. Even in Judaism the essence of the sacrifice was not really that men gave bulls and goats to God, but that by their so doing God gave Himself to men; in the central act of our own worship, of course, this is far clearer—there it is manifestly, even physically, God who gives and we who receive. The miserable idea that God should in any sense need, or crave for, our worship like a vain woman wanting compliments, or a vain author presenting his new books to people who never met or heard of him, is implicitly answered by the words "If I be hungry I will not tell *thee*" (Psalm 50:12). Even if such an absurd Deity could be conceived, He would hardly come to *us*, the lowest of rational creatures, to gratify His appetite. I don't want my dog to bark approval of my books. Now that I come to think of it, there are some humans whose enthusiastically favorable criticism would not much gratify me.

But the most obvious fact about praise—whether of God or anything—strangely escaped me. I thought of it in terms of compliment, approval, or the giving of honor. I had never noticed that all enjoyment spontaneously overflows into praise unless (sometimes even if) shyness or the fear of boring others is deliberately brought in to check it. The world rings with praise—lovers praising their mistresses, readers praising their favorite poet, walkers praising the countryside, players praising their favorite game—praise of weather, wines, dishes, actors, motors, horses, colleges, countries, historical personages, children, flowers, mountains, rare stamps, rare beetles, even sometimes politicians or scholars. I had not noticed how the humblest, and at the same time most balanced and capacious minds, praised most, while the cranks, misfits, and malcontents praised least. The good critics found something to praise in many imperfect works; the bad ones continually narrowed the list of books we might be allowed to read. The healthy and unaffected man, even if luxuriously brought up and widely experienced in good cookery, could praise a very modest meal: the dyspeptic and the snob found fault with all. Except where intolerably adverse circumstances interfere, praise almost seems to be inner health made audible. Nor does it cease to be so when, through lack of skill, the forms of its expression are very uncouth or even ridiculous. Heaven knows, many poems of praise addressed to an earthly beloved are as bad as our bad hymns, and an anthology of love poems for public and perpetual use would probably be as sore a trial to literary taste as *Hymns Ancient and Modern*. I had not noticed, either, that just as men spontaneously praise whatever they value, so they spontaneously urge us to join them in praising it: "Isn't she lovely? Wasn't it glorious? Don't you think that magnificent?" The Psalmists in telling everyone to praise God are doing what all men do when they speak of what they care about. My whole, more general, difficulty about the praise of God depended on my absurdly denying to us, as regards the supremely Valuable, what we delight to do, what indeed we can't help doing, about everything else we value.

I think we delight to praise what we enjoy because the praise not merely expresses but completes the enjoyment; it is its appointed consummation. It is not out of compliment that lovers keep on telling one another how beautiful they are; the delight is incomplete till it is expressed. It is frustrating to have discovered a new author and not to be able to tell anyone how good he is; to come suddenly, at the turn of the road, upon some mountain valley of unexpected grandeur and then to have to keep silent because the people with you care for it no more than for a tin can in the ditch; to hear a good joke and find no one to share it with (the perfect hearer died a year ago). This is so even when our expressions are inadequate, as, of course, they usually are. But how if one could really and fully praise even such things to perfection—utterly "get out" in poetry, or music, or paint the upsurge of appreciation which almost bursts you? Then indeed the object would be fully appreciated and our delight would have attained perfect development. The worthier the object, the more intense this delight would be. If it were possible for a created soul fully (I mean, up to the full measure conceivable in a finite being) to "appreciate," that is to love and delight in, the worthiest object of all, and simultaneously at every moment to give this delight perfect expression, then that soul would be in supreme beatitude. It is along these lines that I find it easiest to understand the Christian doctrine that "Heaven" is a state in which angels now, and men hereafter, are perpetually employed in praising God. This does not mean, as it can so dismally suggest, that it is like "being in Church." For our "services," both in their conduct and in our power to participate, are merely attempts at worship; never fully successful, often 99.9 percent failures; sometimes total failures. We are not riders but pupils in the riding school; for most of us the falls and bruises, the aching muscles, and the severity of the exercise, far outweigh those few moments in which we were, to our own astonishment, actually galloping without terror and without disaster. To see what the doctrine really means, we must suppose ourselves to be in perfect love with God—drunk with, drowned in, dissolved by, that delight which, far from remaining pent up within ourselves as incommunicable, hence hardly tolerable, bliss, flows out from us incessantly again in effortless and perfect expression, our joy no more separable from the praise in which it liberates and utters itself than the brightness a mirror receives is separable from the brightness it sheds. The Scotch catechism says that man's chief end is "to glorify God and enjoy Him forever." But we shall then know that these are the same thing. Fully to enjoy is to glorify. In commanding us to glorify Him, God is inviting us to enjoy Him.

ℳodern Translations of the Bible

I<small>T IS POSSIBLE</small> that the reader . . . may ask himself why we need a new translation of any part of the Bible. . . . "Do we not already possess," it may be said, "in the Authorized Version the most beautiful rendering which any language can boast?" Some people whom I have met go even further and feel that a modern translation is not only unnecessary but even offensive. They cannot bear to see the time-honored words altered; it seems to them irreverent.

There are several answers to such people. In the first place, the kind of objection which they feel to a new translation is very like the objection which was once felt to any English translation at all. Dozens of sincerely pious people in the sixteenth century shuddered at the idea of turning the time-honored Latin of the Vulgate into our common and (as they thought) "barbarous" English. A sacred truth seemed to them to have lost its sanctity when it was stripped of the polysyllabic Latin, long heard at Mass and at Hours, and put into "language such as men do use"— language steeped in all the commonplace associations of the nursery, the inn, the stable, and the street. The answer then was the same as the answer now. The only kind of sanctity which Scripture can lose (or, at least, New Testament Scripture) by being modernized is an accidental kind which it never had for its writers or its earliest readers. The New Testament in the original Greek is not a work of literary art: it is not written in a solemn, ecclesiastical language; it is written in the sort of Greek which was spoken over the

Eastern Mediterranean after Greek had become an international language and therefore lost its real beauty and subtlety. In it we see Greek used by people who have no real feeling for Greek words because Greek words are not the words they spoke when they were children. It is a sort of "basic" Greek; a language without roots in the soil, a utilitarian, commercial, and administrative language. Does this shock us? It ought not to, except as the Incarnation itself ought to shock us. The same divine humility which decreed that God should become a baby at a peasant woman's breast, and later an arrested field preacher in the hands of the Roman police, decreed also that He should be preached in a vulgar, prosaic, and unliterary language. If you can stomach the one, you can stomach the other. The Incarnation is in that sense an irreverent doctrine. When we expect that it should have come before the World in all the beauty that we now feel in the Authorized Version, we are as wide of the mark as the Jews were in expecting that the Messiah would come as a great earthly King. The real sanctity, the real beauty and sublimity of the New Testament (as of Christ's life) are of a different sort: miles deeper and *further in.*

In the second place, the Authorized Version has ceased to be a good (that is, a clear) translation. It is no longer modern English: the meanings of words have changed. The same antique glamor which has made it (in the superficial sense) so "beautiful," so "sacred," so "comforting," and so "inspiring," has also made it in many places unintelligible. Thus where St. Paul says, "I know nothing against myself," it translates "I know nothing by myself" (1 Corinthians 4:4). That was a good translation (though even then rather old-fashioned) in the sixteenth century: to the modern reader it means either nothing, or something quite different from what St. Paul said. The truth is that if we are to have translation at all, we must have periodical retranslation. There is no such thing as translating a book into another language once and for all, for a language is a changing thing. If your son is to have clothes, it is no good buying him a suit once and for all: he will grow out of it and have to be reclothed.

And finally—though it may seem a sour paradox—we must sometimes get away from the Authorized Version if for no other reason, simply *because* it is so beautiful and so solemn. Beauty exalts, but beauty also lulls. Early associations endear but they also confuse. Through that beautiful solemnity the transporting or horrifying realities of which the Book tells may come to us blunted and disarmed and we may only sigh with tranquil veneration when we ought to be burning with shame, or struck dumb with terror, or carried out of ourselves by ravishing hopes and adorations.

Moral Choices

PEOPLE OFTEN THINK of Christian morality as a kind of bargain in which God says, "If you keep a lot of rules, I'll reward you, and if you don't I'll do the other thing." I do not think that is the best way of looking at it. I would much rather say that every time you make a choice you are turning the central part of you, the part of you that chooses, into something a little different from what it was before. And taking your life as a whole, with all your innumerable choices, all your life long you are slowly turning this central thing either into a Heaven creature or into a hellish creature: either into a creature that is in harmony with God, and with other creatures, and with itself, or else into one that is in a state of war and hatred with God, and with its fellow creatures, and with itself. To be the one kind of creature is Heaven: that is, it is joy, and peace, and knowledge, and power. To be the other means madness, horror, idiocy, rage, impotence, and eternal loneliness. Each of us at each moment is progressing to the one state or the other.

Virtue

THERE IS A DIFFERENCE between doing some particular just or temperate action and being a just or temperate man. Someone who is not a good tennis player may now and then make a good shot. What you mean by a good player is the man whose eye and muscles and nerves have been so trained by making innumerable good shots that they can now be relied on. They have a certain tone or quality which is there even when he is not playing, just as a mathematician's mind has a certain habit and outlook which is there even when he is not doing mathematics. In the same way a man who perseveres in doing just actions gets in the end a certain quality of character. Now it is that quality rather than the particular actions which we mean when we talk of "virtue."

Prudence

PRUDENCE MEANS practical common sense, taking the trouble to think out what you are doing and what is likely to come of it. Nowadays most people hardly think of Prudence as one of the "virtues." In fact, because Christ said we could only get into His world by being like children, many Christians have the idea that, provided you are "good," it does not matter being a fool. But that is a misunderstanding. In the first place, most children show plenty of "prudence" about doing the things they are really interested in, and think them out quite sensibly. In the second place, as St. Paul points out, Christ never meant that we were to remain children in *intelligence:* on the contrary, He told us to be not only "as harmless as doves" but also "as wise as serpents." He wants a child's heart, but a grown-up's head. He wants us to be simple, single-minded, affectionate, and teachable, as good children are; but He also wants every bit of intelligence we have to be alert at its job, and in first-class fighting trim. The fact that you are giving money to a charity does not mean that you need not try to find out whether that charity is a fraud or not. The fact that what you are thinking about is God Himself (for example, when you are praying) does not mean that you can be content with the same babyish ideas which you had when you were a five-year-old. It is, of course, quite true that God will not love you any the less, or have less use for you, if you happen to have been born with a very second-rate brain. He has room for people with very little sense, but He wants everyone to use what sense they have. The proper motto is not "Be good, sweet maid, and let who can be clever," but "Be good, sweet maid, and don't forget that this involves being as clever as you can." God is no fonder of intellectual slackers than of any other slackers.

Temperance

TEMPERANCE IS, unfortunately, one of those words that has changed its meaning. It now usually means teetotalism. But in the days when the second Cardinal virtue was christened

"Temperance," it meant nothing of the sort. Temperance referred not specially to drink, but to all pleasures; and it meant not abstaining, but going the right length and no further. It is a mistake to think that Christians ought all to be teetotalers; Mohammedanism, not Christianity, is the teetotal religion. Of course it may be the duty of a particular Christian, or of any Christian, at a particular time, to abstain from strong drink either because he is the sort of man who cannot drink at all without drinking too much, or because he wants to give the money to the poor, or because he is with people who are inclined to drunkenness and must not encourage them by drinking himself. But the whole point is that he is abstaining, for a good reason, from something which he does not condemn and which he likes to see other people enjoying. One of the marks of a certain type of bad man is that he cannot give up a thing himself without wanting everyone else to give it up. That is not the Christian way. An individual Christian may see fit to give up all sorts of things for special reasons—marriage, or meat, or beer, or the cinema; but the moment he starts saying the things are bad in themselves, or looking down his nose at other people who do use them, he has taken the wrong turning.

Justice and Fortitude

JUSTICE MEANS much more than the sort of thing that goes on in law courts. It is the old name for everything we should now call "fairness"; it includes honesty, give and take, truthfulness, keeping promises, and all that side of life. And Fortitude includes both kinds of courage—the kind that faces danger as well as the kind that "sticks it" under pain. "Guts" is perhaps the nearest modern English. You will notice, of course, that you cannot practice any of the other virtues very long without bringing this one into play.

Chastity

CHASTITY IS the most unpopular of the Christian virtues. There is no getting away from it: the old Christian rule is, "Either marriage, with complete faithfulness to your partner, or else total abstinence." Now this is so difficult and so contrary to our instincts, that obviously either Christianity is wrong or our sexual instinct, as it now is, has gone wrong. One or the other. Of course, being a Christian, I think it is the instinct which has gone wrong.

But I have other reasons for thinking so. The biological purpose of sex is children, just as the biological purpose of eating is to repair the body. Now if we eat whenever we feel inclined and just as much as we want, it is quite true that most of us will eat too much: but not terrifically too much. One man may eat enough for two, but he does not eat enough for ten. The appetite goes a little beyond its biological purpose, but not enormously. But if a healthy young man indulged his sexual appetite whenever he felt inclined, and if each act produced a baby, then in ten years he might easily populate a small village. This appetite is in ludicrous and preposterous excess of its function.

Or take it another way. You can get a large audience together for a striptease act—that is, to watch a girl undress on the stage. Now suppose you came to a country where you could fill a theater by simply bringing a covered plate on to the stage and then slowly lifting the cover so as to let everyone see, just before the lights went out, that it contained a mutton chop or a bit of bacon, would you not think that in that country something had gone wrong with the appetite for food? And would not anyone who had grown up in a different world think there was something equally queer about the state of the sex instinct among us? . . .

Here is a third point. You find very few people who want to eat things that really are not food or to do other things with food instead of eating it. In other words, perversions of the food appetite are rare. But perversions of the sex instinct are numerous, hard to cure, and frightful. I am sorry to have to go into [this], but I must. The reason why I must is that you and I, for the last twenty years, have been fed all day long on good solid lies about sex. We have been told, till one is sick of hearing it, that sexual desire is in the same state as any of our other natural desires and that if only we abandon the silly old Victorian idea of hushing it up, everything in the garden will be lovely. It is not true. The moment you look at the facts, and away from the propaganda, you see that it is not.

Belief

ROUGHLY SPEAKING, the word Faith seems to be used by Christians in two senses or on two levels, and I will take them in turn. In the first sense it means simply Belief—accepting or regarding as true the doctrines of Christianity. That is fairly simple. But what does puzzle people—at least it used to puzzle me—is the fact that Christians regard Faith in this sense as a virtue. I used to ask how on Earth it can be a virtue—what is there moral or immoral about believing or not believing a set of statements? Obviously, I used to say, a sane man accepts or rejects any statement, not because he wants or does not want to, but because the evidence seems to him good or bad. If he were mistaken about the goodness or badness of the evidence, that would not mean he was a bad man, but only that he was not very clever. And if he thought the evidence bad but tried to force himself to believe in spite of it, that would be merely stupid.

Well, I think I still take that view. But what I did not see then—and a good many people do not see still—was this. I was assuming that if the human mind once accepts a thing as true it will automatically go on regarding it as true, until some real reason for reconsidering it turns up. In fact, I was assuming that the human mind is completely ruled by reason. But that is not so. For example, my reason is perfectly convinced by good evidence that anesthetics do not smother me and that properly trained surgeons do not start operating until I am unconscious. But that does not alter the fact that when they have me down on the table and clap their horrible mask over my face, a mere childish panic begins inside me. I start thinking I am going to choke, and I am afraid they will start cutting me up before I am properly under. In other words, I lose my faith in anesthetics. It is not reason that is taking away my faith: on the contrary, my faith is based on reason. It is my imagination and emotions. The battle is between faith and reason on one side and emotion and imagination on the other. . . .

Now just the same thing happens about Christianity. I am not asking anyone to accept Christianity if his best reasoning tells him that the weight of evidence is against it. That is not the point at which Faith comes in. But supposing a man's reason once decides that the weight of the evidence is for it. I can tell that man what is going to happen to him in the next few weeks. There will come a moment when there is bad news, or he is in trouble, or is living among a lot of other people who do not believe it, and all at once his emotions will rise up and carry out a sort of blitz on his belief. Or else there will come a moment when he wants a woman, or wants to tell a lie, or feels very pleased with himself, or sees a chance of making a little money in some way that is not perfectly fair: some moment, in fact, at which it would be very convenient if Christianity were not true. And once again his wishes and desires will carry out a blitz. I am not talking of moments at which any real new reasons against Christianity turn up. Those have to be faced and that is a different matter. I am talking about moments where a mere mood rises up against it.

Now Faith, in the sense in which I am here using the word, is the art of holding onto things your reason has once accepted, in spite of your changing moods. For moods will change, whatever view your reason takes. I know that by experience. Now that I am a Christian, I do have moods in which the whole thing looks very improbable: but when I was an atheist, I had moods in which Christianity looked terribly probable. This rebellion of your moods against your real self is going to come anyway. That is why Faith is such a necessary virtue: unless you teach your moods "where they get off," you can never be either a sound Christian or even a sound atheist, but just a creature dithering to and fro, with its beliefs really dependent on the weather and the state of its digestion. Consequently one must train the habit of Faith.

Belief and Disbelief

IN ACTUAL MODERN English usage the verb "believe," except for two special usages, generally expresses a very weak degree of opinion. "Where is Tom?" "Gone to London, I believe." The speaker would be only mildly surprised if Tom had not gone to London after all. "What was the date?" "430 B.C., I believe." The speaker means that he is far from sure. It is the same with the negative if it is put in the form "I believe not." ("Is Jones coming up this term?" "I believe not.") But if the negative is put in a different form, it then becomes one of the special usages I mentioned a moment ago. This is of course the form "I don't believe it," or the still stronger "I don't believe you." "I don't believe it" is far stronger on the negative side than "I believe" is on the positive. "Where is Mrs. Jones?" "Eloped with the butler, I believe." "I don't believe it." This, especially if said with anger, may imply a conviction which in subjective certitude might be hard to distinguish from knowledge by experience. The other special usage is "I believe" as uttered by a Christian. There is no great difficulty in making the hardened materialist understand, however little he approves, the sort of mental attitude which this "I believe" expresses. The materialist need only picture himself replying, to some report of a miracle, "I don't believe it," and then imagine this same degree of conviction on the opposite side. He knows that he cannot, there and then, produce a refutation of the miracle which would have the certainty of mathematical demonstration; but the formal possibility that the miracle might after all have occurred does not really trouble him any more than a fear that water might not be H and O. Similarly, the Christian does not necessarily claim to have demonstrative proof; but the formal possibility that God might not exist is not necessarily present in the form of the least actual doubt. Of course there are Christians who hold that such demonstrative proof exists, just as there may be materialists who hold that there is demonstrative disproof. But then, whichever of them is right (if either is) while he retained the proof or disproof would be not believing or disbelieving but knowing. We are speaking of belief and disbelief in the strongest degree, but not of knowledge.

Belief, in this sense, seems to me to be assent to a proposition which we think so overwhelmingly probable that there is a psychological exclusion of doubt, though not a logical exclusion of dispute.

It may be asked whether belief (and of course disbelief) of this sort ever attaches to any but theological propositions. I think that many beliefs approximate to it; that is, many probabilities seem to us so strong that the absence of logical certainty does not induce in us the least shade of doubt. The scientific beliefs of those who are not themselves scientists often have this character, especially among the uneducated. Most of our beliefs about other people are of the same sort. The scientist himself, or he who was a scientist in the laboratory, has beliefs about his wife and friends which he holds, not indeed without evidence, but with more certitude than the evidence, if weighed in the laboratory manner, would justify. Most of my generation had a belief in the reality of the external world and of other people—if you prefer it, a disbelief in solipsism—far in excess of our strongest arguments. It may be true, as they now say, that the whole thing arose from category mistakes and was a pseudo-problem; but then we didn't know that in the twenties. Yet we managed to disbelieve in solipsism all the same.

There is, of course, no question so far of belief without evidence. We must beware of confusion between the way in which a Christian first assents to certain propositions and the way in which he afterward adheres to them. These must be carefully distinguished. Of the second it is true, in a sense, to say that Christians do recommend a certain discounting of apparent contrary evidence, and I will later attempt to explain why. But so far as I know it is not expected that a man should assent to these propositions in the first place without evidence or in the teeth of the evidence. At any rate, if anyone expects that, I certainly do not. And in fact, the man who accepts Christianity always thinks he had good evidence; whether, like Dante, *fisici e metafisici argomenti,* or historical evidence, or the evidence of religious experience, or authority, or all these together. For of course authority, however we may value it in this or that particular instance, is a kind of evidence. All of our historical beliefs, most of our geographical beliefs, many of our beliefs about matters that concern us in daily life, are accepted on the authority of other human beings, whether we are Christians, Atheists, Scientists, or Men-in-the-Street.

Faith

THE QUESTION of Faith . . . arises after a man has tried his level best to practice the Christian virtues, and found that he fails, and seen that even if he could he would only be giving back to God what was already God's own. In other words, he discovers his bankruptcy. Now, once again, what God cares about is not exactly our actions. What he cares about is that we should be creatures of a certain kind of quality—the kind of creatures He intended us to be—creatures related to Himself in a certain way. I do not add "and related to one another in a certain way" because that is included: if you are right with Him, you will inevitably be right with all your fellow creatures, just as if all the spokes of a wheel are fitted rightly into the hub and the rim, they are bound to be in the right positions to one another. And as long as a man is thinking of God as an Examiner who has set him a sort of paper to do, or as the opposite party in a sort of bargain—as long as he is thinking of claims and counterclaims between himself and God—he is not yet in the right relation to Him. He is misunderstanding what he is and what God is. And he cannot get into the right relation until he has discovered the fact of our bankruptcy.

When I say "discovered," I mean really discovered: not simply said it parrot-fashion. Of course, any child, if given a certain kind of religious education, will soon learn to *say* that we have nothing to offer to God that is not already His own and that we find ourselves failing to offer even that without keeping something back. But I am talking of really discovering this: really finding out by experience that it is true.

Now we cannot, in that sense, discover our failure to keep God's law except by trying our very hardest (and then failing). Unless we really try, whatever we say there will always be at the back of our minds the idea that, if we try harder next time, we shall succeed in being completely good. Thus, in one sense, the road back to God is a road of moral effort, of trying harder and harder. But in another sense it is not trying that is ever going to bring us home. All this trying leads up to the vital moment at which you turn to God and say, "You must do this. I can't." Do not, I implore you, start asking yourselves, "Have I reached that moment?" Do not sit down and start watching your own mind to see if it is coming along. That puts a man quite on the wrong track. When the most important things in our life happen, we quite often do not know, at the moment, what is going on. A man does not always say to himself, "Hullo! I'm growing up." You can see it even in simple matters. A man who starts anxiously watching to see whether he is going to sleep is very likely to remain wide awake. As well, the thing I am talking of now may not happen to everyone in a sudden flash—as it did to St. Paul or Bunyan: it may be so gradual that no one could ever point to a particular hour or even a particular year. And what matters is the nature of the change in itself, not how we feel while it is happening. It is the change from being confident about our own efforts to the state in which we despair of doing anything for ourselves and leave it to God.

Faith and Good Works

CHRISTIANS HAVE often disputed as to whether what leads the Christian home is good actions, or Faith in Christ. I have no right really to speak on such a difficult question, but it does seem to me like asking which blade in a pair of scissors is [more] necessary. A serious moral effort is the only thing that will bring you to the point where you throw up the sponge. Faith in Christ is the only thing to save you from despair at that point: and out of that Faith in Him good actions must inevitably come. There are two parodies of the truth which different sets of Christians have, in the past, been accused by other Christians of believing: perhaps they may make the truth clearer. One set [was] accused of saying, "Good actions are all that matters. The best good action is charity. The best kind of charity is giving money. The best thing to give money to is the Church. So hand us over £10,000 and we will see you through." The answer to that nonsense, of course, would be that good actions done for that motive, done with the idea that Heaven can be bought, would not be good actions at all, but only commercial speculations. The other set [was] accused of saying, "Faith is all that matters. Consequently, if you have faith, it doesn't matter what you do. Sin away, my lad, and have a good time and Christ will see that it makes no difference in the end." The answer to that nonsense is that, if what you call your "faith" in Christ does not involve taking the slightest notice of what He says, then it is not Faith at all—not faith or trust in Him, but only intellectual acceptance of some theory about Him.

The Bible seems to clinch the matter when it puts the two things together into one amazing sentence. The first half is, "Work out your own salvation with fear and trembling"— which looks as if everything depended on us and our good actions: but the second half goes on. "For it is God who worketh in you"—which looks as if God did everything and we nothing. I am afraid this is the sort of thing we come up against in Christianity. I am puzzled, but I am not surprised. You see, we are now trying to understand, and to separate into watertight compartments, what exactly God does and what man does when God and man are working together. And, of course, we begin by thinking it is like two men working together, so that you could say, "He did this bit and I did that." But this way of thinking breaks down. God is not like that. He is inside you as well as outside: even if we could understand who did what, I do not think human language could properly express it. In the attempt to express it, different Churches say different things. But you will find that even those who insist most strongly on the importance of good actions tell you you need Faith; and even those who insist most strongly on Faith tell you to do good actions. At any rate that is as far as I go.

Good Work and Good Works

"Good works" in the plural is an expression much more familiar to modern Christendom than "good work." Good works are chiefly almsgiving or "helping" in the parish. They are quite separate from one's "work." And good works need not be good work, as anyone can see by inspecting some of the objects made to be sold at bazaars for charitable purposes. This is not according to our example.

When our Lord provided a poor wedding party with an extra glass of wine all around, he was doing good works. But also good work; it was a wine really worth drinking. Nor is the neglect of goodness in our "work," our job, according to precept. The apostle says everyone must not only work but work to produce what is "good."

The idea of Good Work is not quite extinct among us, though it is not, I fear, especially characteristic of religious people. I have found it among cabinetmakers, cobblers, and sailors. It is no use at all trying to impress sailors with a new liner because she is the biggest or costliest ship afloat. They look for what they call her "lines": they predict how she will behave in a heavy sea. Artists also talk of Good Work; but decreasingly. They begin to prefer words like "significant," "important," "contemporary," or "daring." These are not, to my mind, good symptoms.

But the great mass of men in all fully industrialized societies are the victims of a situation which almost excludes the idea of Good Work from the outset. "Built-in obsolescence" becomes an economic necessity. Unless an article is so made that it will go to pieces in a year or two and thus have to be replaced, you will not get a sufficient turnover. A hundred years ago, when a man got married, he had built for him (if he were rich enough) a carriage in which he expected to drive for the rest of his life. He now buys a car which he expects to sell again in two years. Work nowadays must *not* be good.

For the wearer, zip fasteners have this advantage over buttons: that, while they last, they will save him an infinitesimal amount of time and trouble. For the producer, they have a much more solid merit; they don't remain in working order long. Bad work is the *desideratum*.

We must avoid taking a glibly moral view of this situation. It is not solely the result of original or actual sin. It has stolen upon us, unforeseen and unintended. The degraded commercialism of our minds is quite as much its result as its cause. Nor can it, in my opinion, be cured by purely moral efforts.

Hope

HOPE IS ONE of the Theological virtues. This means that a continual looking forward to the eternal world is not (as some modern people think) a form of escapism or wishful thinking, but one of the things a Christian is meant to do. It does not mean that we are to leave the present world as it is. If you read history you will find that the Christians who did most for the present world were just those who thought most of the next. The Apostles themselves, who set on foot the conversion of the Roman Empire, the great men who built up the Middle Ages, the English Evangelicals who abolished the Slave Trade, all left their mark on Earth, precisely because their minds were occupied with Heaven. It is since Christians have largely ceased to think of the other world that they have become so ineffective in this. Aim at Heaven and you will get Earth "thrown in": aim at Earth and you will get neither. It seems a strange rule, but something like it can be seen at work in other matters. Health is a great blessing, but the moment you make health one of your main, direct objects you start becoming a crank and imagining there is something wrong with you. You are only likely to get health provided you want other things more— food, games, work, fun, open air. In the same way, we shall never save civilization as long as civilization is our main object. We must learn to want something else more.

Most of us find it very difficult to want "Heaven" at all— except insofar as "Heaven" means meeting again our friends who have died. One reason for this difficulty is that we have not been trained: our whole education tends to fix our minds on this world. Another reason is that when the real want for Heaven is present in us, we do not recognize it. Most people, if they had really learned to look into their own hearts, would know that they do want, and want acutely, something that cannot be had in this world. There are all sorts of things in this world that offer to give it to you, but they never quite keep their promise. The longings which arise in us when we first fall in love, or first think of some foreign country, or first take up some subject that excites us, are longings which no marriage, no travel, no learning, can really satisfy. I am not now speaking of what would ordinarily be called unsuccessful marriages, or holidays, or learned careers. I am speaking of the best possible ones. There was something we grasped at, in that first moment of longing, which just fades away in reality. I think everyone knows what I mean. The wife may be a good wife, and the hotels and scenery may have been excellent, and chemistry may be a very interesting job: but something has evaded us.

Charity

NATURAL LIKING OR AFFECTION for people makes it easier to be "charitable" toward them. It is, therefore, normally a duty to encourage our affections—to "like" people as much as we can (just as it is often our duty to encourage our liking for exercise or wholesome food)—not because this liking is itself the virtue of charity, but because it is a help to it. On the other hand, it is also necessary to keep a very sharp lookout for fear our liking for some one person makes us uncharitable, or even unfair, to someone else. There are even cases where our liking conflicts with our charity toward the person we like. For example, a doting mother may be tempted by natural affection to "spoil" her child; that is, to gratify her own affectionate impulses at the expense of the child's real happiness later on.

But though natural likings should normally be encouraged, it would be quite wrong to think that the way to become charitable is to sit trying to manufacture affectionate feelings. Some people are "cold" by temperament; that may be a misfortune for them, but it is no more a sin than having a bad digestion is a sin; and it does not cut them out from the chance, or excuse them from the duty, of learning charity. The rule for all of us is perfectly simple. Do not waste time bothering whether you "love" your neighbor; act as if you did. As soon as we do this, we find one of the great secrets. When you are behaving as if you loved someone, you will presently come to love him. If you injure someone you dislike, you will find yourself disliking him more. If you do him a good turn, you will find yourself disliking him less. There is, indeed, one exception. If you do him a good turn, not to please God and obey the law of charity, but to show him what a fine forgiving chap you are, and to put him in your debt, and then sit down to wait for his "gratitude," you will probably be disappointed. (People are not fools: they have a very quick eye for anything like showing off, or patronage.) But whenever we do good to another self, just because it is a self, made (like us) by God, and desiring its own happiness as we desire ours, we shall have learned to love it a little more or, at least, to dislike it less.

Consequently, though Christian charity sounds a very cold thing to people whose heads are full of sentimentality, and though it is quite distinct from affection, yet it leads to affection. The difference between a Christian and a worldly man is not that the worldly man has only affections or "likings" and the Christian has only "charity." The worldly man treats certain people kindly because he "likes" them:

the Christian, trying to treat everyone kindly, finds himself liking more and more people as he goes on—including people he could not even have imagined himself liking at the beginning.

Humility

IF ANYONE WOULD LIKE to acquire humility, I can, I think, tell him the first step. The first step is to realize that one is proud. And a biggish step, too. At least, nothing whatever can be done before it. If you think you are not conceited, it means you are very conceited indeed.

Forgiveness

EVERYONE SAYS FORGIVENESS is a lovely idea, until they have something to forgive, as we had during the war. And then to mention the subject at all is to be greeted with howls of anger. It is not that people think this too high and difficult a virtue: it is that they think it hateful and contemptible. "That sort of talk makes them sick," they say. And half of you already want to ask me, "I wonder how'd you feel about forgiving the Gestapo if you were a Pole or a Jew?"

So do I. I wonder very much. Just as when Christianity tells me that I must not deny my religion even to save myself from death by torture, I wonder very much what I should do when it came to the point. I am not trying to tell you . . . what I could do—I can do precious little—I am telling you what Christianity is. I did not invent it. And there, right in the middle of it, I find "Forgive us our sins as we forgive those that sin against us." There is no slightest suggestion that we are offered forgiveness on any other terms. It is made perfectly clear that if we do not forgive we shall not be forgiven. There are no two ways about it. What are we to do?

It is going to be hard enough, anyway, but I think there are two things we can do to make it easier. When you start mathematics you do not begin with calculus; you begin with simple addition. In the same way, if we really want (but all depends on really wanting) to learn how to forgive, perhaps we had better start with something easier than the Gestapo. One might start with forgiving one's husband or wife, or parents or children, or the nearest N.C.O., for something they have done or said in the last week. That will probably keep us busy for the moment. And secondly, we might try to understand exactly what loving your neighbor as yourself means. I have to love him as I love myself. Well, how exactly do I love myself?

Now that I come to think of it, I have not exactly got a feeling of fondness or affection for myself, and I do not even always enjoy my own society. So apparently "Love your neighbor" does not mean "feel fond of him" or "find him attractive." I ought to have seen that before, because, of course, you cannot feel fond of a person by trying. Do I think well of myself, think myself a nice chap? Well, I am afraid I sometimes do (and those are, no doubt, my worst moments) but that is not why I love myself. In fact it is the other way round: my self-love makes me think myself nice, but thinking myself nice is not why I love myself. So loving my enemies does not apparently mean thinking them nice either. That is an enormous relief. For a good many people imagine that forgiving your enemies means making out that they are really not such bad fellows after all, when it is quite plain that they are. Go a step further. In my most clear-sighted moments not only do I not think myself a nice man, but I know that I am a very nasty one. I can look at some of the things I have done with loathing and horror. So apparently I am allowed to loathe and hate some of the things my enemies do. Now that I come to think of it, I remember Christian teachers telling me long ago that I must hate a bad man's actions, but not hate the bad man: or, as they would say, hate the sin but not the sinner.

For a long time I used to think this a silly, straw-splitting distinction: how could you hate what a man did and not hate the man? But years later it occurred to me that there was one man to whom I had been doing this all my life—namely myself. However much I might dislike my own cowardice or conceit or greed, I went on loving myself. There had never been the slightest difficulty about it. In fact, the very reason why I hated the things was that I loved the man. Just because I loved myself, I was sorry to find that I was the sort of man who did those things. Consequently Christianity does not want us to reduce by one atom the hatred we feel for cruelty and treachery. We ought to hate them. Not one word of what we have said about them needs to be unsaid. But it does want us to hate them in the same way in which we hate things in ourselves: being sorry that the man should have done such things, and hoping, if it is anyway possible, that somehow, sometime, somewhere, he can be cured and made human again.

Almsgiving

IN THE PASSAGE where the New Testament says that everyone must work, it gives as a reason "in order that he may have something to give to those in need." Charity—giving to the poor—is an essential part of Christian morality: in the frightening parable of the sheep and the goats it seems to be the point on which everything turns. Some people nowadays say that charity ought to be unnecessary and that instead of giving to the poor we ought to be producing a society in which there were no poor to give to. They may be quite right in saying we ought to produce that kind of society. But if anyone thinks that, as a consequence, you can stop giving in the meantime, then he has parted company with all Christian morality. I do not believe one can settle how much we ought to give. I am afraid the only safe rule is to give more than we can spare. In other words, if our expenditure on comforts, luxuries, amusements, etc., is up to the standard common among those with the same income as our own, we are probably giving away too little. If our charities do not at all pinch or hamper us, I should say they are too small. There ought to be things we should like to do and cannot do because our charitable expenditure excludes them. I am speaking now of "charities" in the common way. Particular cases of distress among your own relatives, friends, neighbors, or employees, which God, as it were, forces upon your notice, may demand much more: even to the crippling and endangering of your own position. For many of us the great obstacle to charity lies not in our luxurious living or desire for more money, but in our fear—fear of insecurity. This must often be recognized as a temptation. Sometimes our pride also hinders our charity; we are tempted to spend more than we ought on the showy forms of generosity (tipping, hospitality) and less than we ought on those who really need our help.

Obedience

NEARLY EVERYONE will find himself in the course of his life in positions where he ought to command and in positions where he ought to obey. . . . Now each of them requires a certain training or habituation if it is to be done well; and indeed the habit of command or of obedience may often be more necessary than the most enlightened views on the ultimate moral grounds for doing either. You can't begin training a child to command until it has reason and age enough to command someone or something without absurdity. You can at once begin training it to obey; that is, teaching it the art of obedience *as such*—without prejudice to the views it will hold later on as to who should obey whom, or when, or how much . . . since it is perfectly obvious that every human being is going to spend a great deal of his life in obeying.

The Devil

THE COMMONEST QUESTION [I am asked about *The Screwtape Letters*] is whether I really "believe in the Devil."

Now, if by "the Devil" you mean a power opposite to God and, like God, self-existent from all eternity, the answer is certainly No. There is no uncreated being except God. God has no opposite. No being could attain a "perfect badness" opposite to the perfect goodness of God; for when you have taken away every kind of good thing (intelligence, will, memory, energy, and existence itself), there would be none of him left.

The proper question is whether I believe in devils. I do. That is to say, I believe in angels, and I believe that some of these, by the abuse of their free will, have become enemies to God and, as a corollary, to us. These we may call devils. They do not differ in nature from good angels, but their nature is depraved. *Devil* is the opposite of *angel* only as Bad

Man is the opposite of Good Man. Satan, the leader or dictator of devils, is the opposite, not of God, but of Michael.

I believe this not in the sense that it is part of my creed, but in the sense that it is one of my opinions. My religion would not be in ruins if this opinion were shown to be false. Till that happens—and proofs of a negative are hard to come by—I shall retain it. It seems to me to explain a good many facts. It agrees with the plain sense of Scripture, the tradition of Christendom, and the beliefs of most men at most times. And it conflicts with nothing that any of the sciences has shown to be true.

Screwtape to Wormwood on Prayer

THE BEST THING, where it is possible, is to keep the patient from the serious intention of praying altogether. When the patient is an adult recently reconverted to the Enemy's party, like your man, this is best done by encouraging him to remember, or to think he remembers, the parrotlike nature of his prayers in childhood. In reaction against that, he may be persuaded to aim at something entirely spontaneous, inward, informal, and unregularized; and what this will actually mean to a beginner will be an effort to produce in himself a vaguely devotional *mood* in which real concentration of will and intelligence have no part. One of their poets, Coleridge, has recorded that he did not pray "with moving lips and bended knees" but merely "composed his spirit to love" and indulged "a sense of supplication." That is exactly the sort of prayer we want; and since it bears a superficial resemblance to the prayer of silence as practiced by those who are very far advanced in the Enemy's service, clever and lazy patients can be taken in by it for quite a long time. At the very least, they can be persuaded that the bodily position makes no difference to their prayers; for they constantly forget, what you must always remember, that they are animals and that whatever their bodies do affects their souls. It is funny how mortals always picture us as putting things into their minds: in reality our best work is done by keeping things out.

If this fails, you must fall back on a subtler misdirection of his intention. Whenever they are attending to the Enemy Himself we are defeated, but there are ways of preventing them from doing so. The simplest is to turn their gaze away from Him toward themselves. Keep them watching their own minds and trying to produce *feelings* there by the action of their own wills. When they meant to ask Him for charity, let them, instead, start trying to manufacture charitable feelings for themselves and not notice that this is what they are doing. When they meant to pray for courage, let them really be trying to feel brave. When they say they are praying for forgiveness, let them be trying to feel forgiven. Teach them to estimate the value of each prayer by their success in producing the desired feeling; and never let them suspect how much success or failure of that kind depends on whether they are well or ill, fresh or tired, at the moment.

Screwtape to Wormwood on War

WAR IS ENTERTAINING. The immediate fear and suffering of the humans is a legitimate and pleasing refreshment for our myriads of toiling workers. But what permanent good does it do us unless we make use of it for bringing souls to Our Father Below? When I see the temporal suffering of humans who finally escape us, I feel as if I had been allowed to taste the first course of a rich banquet and then denied the rest. It is worse than not to have tasted it at all. The Enemy, true to His barbarous methods of warfare, allows us to see the short misery of his favorites only to tantalize and torment us—to mock the incessant hunger which, during this present phase of the great conflict, His blockade is admittedly imposing. Let us therefore think rather how to use, than how to enjoy, this European war. For it has certain tendencies inherent in it which are, in themselves, by no means in our favor. We may hope for a good deal of cruelty and unchastity. But, if we are not careful, we shall see thousands turning in this tribulation to the Enemy, while tens of thousands who do not go so far as that will nevertheless have their attention diverted from themselves to values and causes which they believe to be higher than the self. I know that the Enemy disapproves many of these causes. But that is where He is so unfair. He often makes prizes of humans who have given their lives for causes He thinks bad on the monstrously sophistical ground that the humans thought them good and were following the best they knew. Consider too what undesirable deaths occur in wartime. Men are killed in places where they knew they might be killed and to which they go, if they are at all of the Enemy's party, prepared. How much better for us if *all* humans died in costly nursing homes amid doctors who lie, nurses who lie, as we have trained them, promising life to the dying, encouraging the belief that sickness excuses every indulgence, and even, if our workers know their job, withholding all suggestions of a priest lest it should betray to the sick man his true condition! And how disastrous for us is the continual remembrance of death which war enforces. One of our best weapons, contented worldliness, is rendered useless. In wartime not even a human can believe that he is going to live forever.

Screwtape to Wormwood on Anxiety

THERE IS NOTHING like suspense and anxiety for barricading a human's mind against the Enemy. He wants men to be concerned with what they do; our business is to keep them thinking about what will happen to them.

Your patient will, of course, have picked up the notion that he must submit with patience to the Enemy's will. What the Enemy means by this is primarily that he should accept with patience the tribulation which has actually been dealt out to him—the present anxiety and suspense. It is about *this* that he is to say "Thy will be done," and for the daily task of bearing *this* that the daily bread will be provided. It is your business to see that the patient never thinks of the present fear as his appointed cross, but only of the things he is afraid of. Let him regard them as his crosses: let him forget that, since they are incompatible, they cannot all happen to him, and let him try to practice fortitude and patience to them in advance. For real resignation, at the same moment, to a dozen different and hypothetical fates, is almost impossible, and the Enemy does not greatly assist those who are trying to attain it: resignation to present and actual suffering, even where that suffering consists of fear, is far easier, and is usually helped by this direct action.

Screwtape to Wormwood on Peaks and Troughs

HAS NO ONE ever told you about the law of Undulation?

Humans are amphibians—half spirit and half animal. (The Enemy's determination to produce such a revolting hybrid was one of the things that determined Our Father to withdraw his support from Him.) As spirits they belong to the eternal world, but as animals they inhabit time. This means that while their spirit can be directed to an eternal object, their bodies, passions, and imaginations are in continual change, for to be in time means to change. Their nearest approach to constancy, therefore, is undulation— the repeated return to a level from which they repeatedly fall back, a series of Troughs and Peaks. If you had watched your patient carefully, you would have seen this undulation in every department of his life—his interest in his work, his affection for his friends, his physical appetites, all go up and down. As long as he lives on earth, periods of emotional and bodily richness and liveliness will alternate with periods of numbness and poverty. The dryness and dullness through which your patient is now going are not, as you fondly suppose, your workmanship; they are merely a natural phenomenon which will do us no good unless you make a good use of it.

Screwtape to Wormwood on Lust

I HAVE ALWAYS found that the Trough periods of the human undulation provide excellent opportunity for all sensual temptations, particularly those of sex. This may surprise you, because, of course, there is more physical energy, and therefore more potential appetite, at the Peak periods; but you must remember that the powers of resistance are then also at their highest. The health and spirits which you want to use in producing lust can also, alas, be very easily used for work or play or thought or innocuous merriment. The attack has a much better chance of success when the man's whole inner world is drab and cold and empty. And it is also to be noted that the Trough sexuality is subtly different in quality from that of the Peak—much less likely to lead to the milk-and-water phenomenon which the humans call "being in love," much more easily drawn into perversions, much less contaminated by those generous and imaginative and even spiritual concomitants which often render human sexuality so disappointing. It is the same with other desires of the flesh. You are much more likely to make your man a sound drunkard by pressing drink on him as an anodyne when he is dull and weary than by encouraging him to use it as a means of merriment among his friends when he is happy and expansive. Never forget that when we are dealing with any pleasure in its healthy and normal and satisfying form, we are, in a sense, on the Enemy's ground. I know we have won many a soul through pleasure. All the same, it is His invention, not ours. He made the pleasures:

all our research so far has not enabled us to produce one. All we can do is to encourage the humans to take the pleasures which our Enemy has produced, at times, or in ways, or in degrees, which He has forbidden. Hence we always try to work away from the natural condition of any pleasure to that in which it is least natural, least redolent of its Maker, and least pleasurable. An ever increasing craving for an ever diminishing pleasure is the formula. It is more certain; and it's better *style*. To get the man's soul and give him *nothing* in return—that is what really gladdens Our Father's heart. And the Troughs are the time for beginning the process.

Screwtape to Wormwood on Worldly Companions

I WAS DELIGHTED to hear . . . that your patient has made some very desirable new acquaintances and that you seem to have used this event in a really promising manner. I gather that the middle-aged couple who called at his office are just the sort of people we want him to know—rich, smart, superficially intellectual, and brightly skeptical about everything in the world. I gather they are even vaguely pacifist, not on moral grounds but from an ingrained habit of belittling anything that concerns the great mass of their fellow men and from a dash of purely fashionable and literary communism. This is excellent. And you seem to have made good use of all his social, sexual, and intellectual vanity. Tell me more. Did he commit himself deeply? I don't mean in words. There is a subtle play of looks and tones and laughs by which a mortal can imply that he is of the same party as those to whom he is speaking. That is the kind of betrayal you should specially encourage, because the man does not fully realize it himself; and by the time he does you will have made withdrawal difficult.

No doubt he must very soon realize that his own faith is in direct opposition to the assumptions on which all the conversation of his new friends is based. I don't think that matters much, provided that you can persuade him to postpone any open acknowledgment of the fact, and this, with the aid of shame, pride, modesty, and vanity, will be easy to do. As long as the postponement lasts, he will be in a false position. He will be silent when he ought to speak and laugh when he ought to be silent. He will assume, at first only by his manner, but presently by his words, all sorts of cynical and skeptical attitudes which are not really his. But if you play him well, they may become his. All mortals tend to turn into the thing they are pretending to be. This is elementary. The real question is how to prepare for the Enemy's counterattack.

Screwtape to Wormwood on Humility

YOUR PATIENT has become humble; have you drawn his attention to the fact? All virtues are less formidable to us once the man is aware that he has them, but this is specially true of humility. Catch him at the moment when he is really poor in spirit and smuggle into his mind the gratifying reflection, "By jove! I'm being humble," and almost immediately pride—pride at his own humility—will appear. If he awakes to the danger and tries to smother this new form of pride, make him proud of his attempt—and so on, through as many stages as you please. But don't try this too long, for fear you awake his sense of humor and proportion, in which case he will merely laugh at you and go to bed.

But there are other profitable ways of fixing his attention on the virtue of Humility. By this virtue, as by all the others, our Enemy want to turn the man's attention away from self to Him, and to the man's neighbors. All the abjection and self-hatred are designed, in the long run, solely for this end; unless they attain this end they do us little harm; and they may even do us good if they keep the man concerned with himself, and, above all, if self-contempt can be made the starting point for contempt of other selves, and thus for gloom, cynicism, and cruelty.

You must therefore conceal from the patient the true end of Humility. Let him think of it, not as self-forgetfulness, but as a certain kind of opinion (namely, a low opinion) of his own talents and character. Some talents, I gather, he really has. Fix in his mind the idea that humility consists in trying to believe those talents to be less valuable than he believes them to be. No doubt they *are* in fact less valuable than he believes, but that is not the point. The great thing is to make him value an opinion for some quality other than truth, thus introducing an element of dishonesty and make-believe into the heart of what otherwise threatens to become a virtue. By this method thousands of humans have been brought to think that humility means pretty women trying to believe they are ugly and clever men trying to believe they are fools. And since what they are trying to believe may, in some cases, be manifest nonsense, they cannot succeed in believing it, and we have the chance of keeping their minds endlessly revolving on themselves in an effort to achieve the impossible.

Screwtape to Wormwood on Laughter

I DIVIDE THE CAUSES of human laughter into Joy, Fun, the Joke Proper, and Flippancy. You will see the first among friends and lovers reunited on the eve of a holiday. Among adults some pretext in the way of Jokes is usually provided, but the facility with which the smallest witticisms produce laughter at such a time shows that they are not the real cause. What that real cause is we do not know. Something like it is expressed in much of that detestable art which the humans call Music, and something like it occurs in Heaven—a meaningless acceleration in the rhythm of celestial experience, quite opaque to us. Laughter of this kind does us no good and should always be discouraged. Besides, the phenomenon is of itself disgusting and a direct insult to the realism, dignity, and austerity of Hell.

Fun is closely related to Joy—a sort of emotional froth arising from the play instinct. It is very little use to us. It can sometimes be used, of course, to divert humans from something else which the Enemy would like them to be feeling or doing: but in itself it has wholly undesirable tendencies; it promotes charity, courage, contentment, and many other evils.

The Joke Proper, which turns on sudden perception of incongruity, is a much more promising field. I am not thinking primarily of indecent or bawdy humor, which, though much relied upon by second-rate tempters, is often disappointing in its results. The truth is that humans are pretty clearly divided on this matter into two classes. There are some to whom "no passion is as serious as lust" and for whom an indecent story ceases to produce lasciviousness precisely insofar as it becomes funny: there are others in whom laughter and lust are excited at the same moment and by the same things. The first sort joke about sex because it gives rise to many incongruities; the second cultivate incongruities because they afford a pretext for talking about sex. If your man is of the first type, bawdy humor will not help you—I shall never forget the hours which I wasted (hours to me of unbearable tedium) with one of my early patients in bars and smoking rooms before I learned this rule. Find out which group the patient belongs to—and see that he does *not* find out.

The real use of Jokes or Humor is in quite a different direction, and it is especially promising among the English, who take their "sense of humor" so seriously that a deficiency in this sense is almost the only deficiency at which they feel shame. Humor is for them the all-consoling and (mark this) the all-excusing, grace of life. Hence it is invaluable as a means of destroying shame. If a man simply lets others pay for him, he is "mean"; if he boasts of it in a jocular manner and twits his fellows with having been scored off, he is no longer "mean" but a comical fellow. Mere cowardice is shameful; cowardice boasted of with humorous exaggerations and grotesque gestures can be passed off as funny. Cruelty is shameful—unless the cruel man can represent it as a practical joke. A thousand bawdy, or even blasphemous, jokes do not help toward a man's damnation so much as his discovery that almost anything he wants to do can be done, not only without the disapproval but with the admiration of his fellows, if only it can get itself treated as a Joke. And this temptation can be almost entirely hidden from your patient by that English seriousness about Humor. Any suggestion that there might be too much of it can be represented to him as "Puritanical" or as betraying a "lack of humor."

But Flippancy is the best of all. In the first place it is very economical. Only a clever human can make a real Joke about virtue, or indeed about anything else; any of them can be trained to talk *as if* virtue were funny. Among flippant people the Joke is always assumed to have been made. No one actually makes it; but every serious subject is discussed in a manner which implies that they have already found a ridiculous side to it. If prolonged, the habit of Flippancy builds up around a man the finest armor plating against the Enemy that I know, and it is quite free from the dangers inherent in the other sources of laughter. It is a thousand miles away from joy; it deadens, instead of sharpening, the intellect; and it excites no affection between those who practice it.

Screwtape to Wormwood on Irregular Churchgoing

IF A MAN can't be cured of churchgoing, the next best thing is to send him all over the neighborhood looking for the church that "suits" him until be becomes a taster or connoisseur of churches.

The reasons are obvious. In the first place, the parochial organization should always be attacked, because, being a unity of place and not of likings, it brings people of different classes and psychology together in the kind of unity the Enemy desires. The congregational principle, on the other hand, makes each church into a kind of club, and finally, if all goes well, into a coterie or faction. In the second place, the search for a "suitable" church makes the man a critic where the Enemy wants him to be a pupil. What He wants of the layman in church is an attitude which may, indeed, be critical in the sense of rejecting what is false or unhelpful, but which is wholly uncritical in the sense that it does not appraise—does not waste time in thinking about what it rejects, but lays itself open in uncommenting, humble receptivity to any nourishment that is going. (You see how groveling, how unspiritual, how irredeemably vulgar He is!) This attitude, especially during sermons, creates the condition (most hostile to our whole policy) in which platitudes can become really audible to a human soul. There is hardly any sermon, or any book, which may not be dangerous to us if it is received in this temper. So pray bestir yourself and send this fool the round of the neighboring churches as soon as possible.

Screwtape to Wormwood on Gluttony

ONE OF THE GREAT achievements of the last hundred years has been to deaden the human conscience on [gluttony], so that by now you will hardly find a sermon preached or a conscience troubled about it in the whole length and breadth of Europe. This has largely been effected by concentrating all our efforts on gluttony of Delicacy, not gluttony of Excess. Your patient's mother, as I learn from the dossier . . . is a good example. She would be astonished—one day, I hope, *will* be—to learn that her whole life is enslaved to this kind of sensuality, which is quite concealed from her by the fact that the quantities involved are small. But what do the quantities matter, provided we can use a human belly and palate to produce querulousness, impatience, uncharitableness, and self-concern? . . . She is a positive terror to hostesses and servants. She is always turning from what has been offered her to say with a demure little sigh and a smile, "Oh, please, please . . . *all* I want is a cup of tea, weak but not too weak, and the teeniest-weeniest bit of really crisp toast." You see? Because what she wants is smaller and less costly than what has been set before her, she never recognizes as gluttony her determination to get what she wants, however troublesome it may be to others. At the very moment of indulging her appetite she believes that she is practicing temperance. In a crowded restaurant she gives a little scream at the plate which some overworked waitress has set before her and says: "Oh, that's far, far too much! Take it away and bring me about a quarter of it." If challenged, she would say she was doing this to avoid waste; in reality she does it because the particular shade of delicacy to which we have enslaved her is offended by the sight of more food than she happens to want.

Screwtape to Wormwood on Reinterpreting Jesus

A GOOD MANY Christian-political writers think that Christianity began going wrong, and departing from the doctrine of its Founder, at a very early stage. Now this idea must be used by us to encourage once again the conception of a "historical Jesus" to be found by clearing away later "accretions and perversions" and then to be contrasted with the whole Christian tradition. In the last generation we promoted the construction of such a "historical Jesus" on liberal and humanitarian lines; we are now putting forward a new "historical Jesus" on Marxian, catastrophic, and revolutionary lines. The advantages of these constructions, which we intend to change every thirty years or so, are manifold.

In the first place, they all tend to direct men's devotion to something which does not exist, for each "historical Jesus" is unhistorical. The documents say what they say and cannot be added to; each new "historical Jesus" therefore has to be got out of them by suppression at one point and exaggeration at another, and by that sort of guessing (*brilliant* is the adjective we teach humans to apply to it) on which no one would risk ten shillings in ordinary life, but which is enough to produce a crop of new Napoleons, new Shakespeares, and new Swifts in every publisher's autumn list.

In the second place, all such constructions place the importance of their "historical Jesus" in some peculiar theory He is supposed to have promulgated. He has to be a "great man" in the modern sense of the word—one standing at the terminus of some centrifugal and unbalanced line of thought—a crank vending a panacea. We thus distract men's minds from Who He is, and what He did. We first make Him solely a teacher, and then conceal the very substantial agreement between His teachings and those of all other great moral teachers. For humans must not be allowed to notice that all great moralists are sent by the Enemy, not to inform men, but to remind them, to restate the primeval moral platitudes against our continual concealment of them. We make the Sophists: He raises up a Socrates to answer them.

Our third aim is, by these constructions, to destroy the devotional life. For the real presence of the Enemy, otherwise experienced by men in prayer and sacrament, we substitute a merely probable, remote, shadowy, and uncouth figure, one who spoke a strange language and died a long time ago. Such an object cannot, in fact, be worshiped. Instead of the Creator adored by the creature, you soon have merely a leader acclaimed by a partisan, and finally a distinguished character approved by a judicious historian.

And fourthly, beside being unhistorical in the Jesus it depicts, religion of this kind is false to history in another sense. No nation, and few individuals, are really brought into the Enemy's camp by the historical study of the biography of Jesus, simply as biography. Indeed, materials for a full biography have been withheld from men. The earliest converts were converted by a single historical fact (the Resurrection) and a single theological doctrine (the Redemption) operating on a sense of sin which they already had— and sin, not against some new fancy dress law produced as a novelty by a "great man," but against the old, platitudinous, universal moral law which they had been taught by their nurses and mothers. The "Gospels" come later, and were written, not to make Christians, but to edify Christians already made.

The "historical Jesus," then, however dangerous he may seem to be to us at some particular point, is always to be encouraged. About the general connection between Christianity and politics, our position is more delicate. Certainly we do not want men to allow their Christianity to flow over into their political life, for the establishment of anything like a really just society would be a major disaster. On the other hand we do want, and want very much, to make men treat Christianity as a means; preferably, of course, as a means to their own advancement, but, failing that, as a means to anything—even to social justice. The thing to do is to get a man at first to value social justice as a thing which the Enemy demands, and then work him on to the stage at which he values Christianity because it may produce social justice. For the Enemy will not be used as a convenience. Men or nations who think they can revive the Faith in order to make a good society might just as well think they can use the stairs of Heaven as a shortcut to the nearest chemist's shop. Fortunately it is quite easy to coax humans round this little corner. Only today I have found a passage in a Christian writer where he recommends his own version of Christianity on the ground that "only such a faith can outlast the death of old cultures and the birth of new civilizations." You see the little rift? "Believe this, not because it is true, but for some other reason." That's the game.

Everythingism

I MEAN BY *Everythingism* the belief that "everything," or "the whole show," must be self-existent, must be more important than every particular thing, and must contain all particular things in such a way that they cannot be really very different from one another—that they must be not merely "at one," but one. Thus the Everythingist, if he starts from God, becomes a Pantheist; there must be nothing that is not God. If he starts from Nature he becomes a Naturalist; there must be nothing that is not Nature. He thinks that everything is in the long run "merely" a precursor or a development or a relic or an instance or a disguise, of everything else. This philosophy I believe to be profoundly untrue. One of the moderns has said that reality is "incorrigibly plural." I think he is right. All things come from One. All things are related—related in different and complicated ways. But all things are not one. The word "everything" should mean simply the total (a total to be reached, if we knew enough, by enumeration) of all the things that exist at a given moment. It must not be given a mental capital letter; must not (under the influence of picture thinking) be turned into a sort of pool in which particular things sink or even a cake in which they are the currants. Real things are sharp and knobbly and complicated and different. Everythingism is congenial to our minds because it is the natural philosophy of a totalitarian, mass-producing, conscripted age. That is why we must be perpetually on our guard against it.

Sins of Thought

[CHRISTIAN WRITERS] seem to be so very strict at one moment and so very free and easy at another. They talk about mere sins of thought as if they were immensely important: and then they talk about the most frightful murders and treacheries as if you had only got to repent and all would be forgiven. But I have come to see that they are right. What they are always thinking of is the mark which the action leaves on that tiny central self which no one sees in this life but which each of us will have to endure—or—enjoy— forever. One man may be so placed that his anger sheds the blood of thousands, and another so placed that however angry he gets he will only be laughed at. But the little mark on the soul may be much the same in both. Each has done something to himself which, unless he repents, will make it harder for him to keep out of the rage next time he is tempted, and will make the rage worse when he does fall into it. Each of them, if he seriously turns to God, can have that twist in the central man straightened out again: each is, in the long run, doomed if he will not. The bigness or smallness of the thing, seen from the outside, is not what really matters.

Pride

ACCORDING TO Christian teachers, the essential vice, the utmost evil, is Pride. Unchastity, anger, greed, drunkenness, and all that, are mere fleabites in comparison: it was through Pride that the devil became the devil: Pride leads to every other vice: it is the complete anti-God state of mind.

Does this seem exaggerated? If so, think it over. I pointed out a moment ago that the more pride one had, the more one disliked pride in others. In fact, if you want to find out how proud you are, the easiest way is to ask yourself, "How much do I dislike it when other people snub me, or refuse to take any notice of me, or shove their oar in, or patronize me, or show off?" The point is that each person's pride is in competition with everyone else's pride. It is because I wanted to be the big noise at the party that I am so annoyed at someone else being the big noise. Two of a trade never agree. Now what you want to get clear is that Pride is *essentially* competitive—is competitive by its very nature—while the other vices are competitive only, so to speak, by accident. Pride gets no pleasure out of having something, only out of having more of it than the next man. We say that people are proud of being rich, or clever, or good-looking, but they are not. They are proud of being richer, or cleverer, or better-looking than others. If everyone else became equally rich, or clever, or good-looking, there would be nothing to be proud about. It is the comparison that makes you proud: the pleasure of being above the rest. Once the element of competition has gone, pride has gone. That is why I say that Pride is essentially competitive in a way the other vices are not. The sexual impulse may drive two men into competition if they both want the same girl. But that is only by accident; they might just as likely have wanted two different girls. But a proud man will take your girl from you, not because he wants her, but just to prove to himself that he is a better man than you. Greed may drive men into competition if there is not enough to go round; but the proud man, even when he has got more than he can possibly want, will try to get still more just to assert his power. Nearly all those evils in the world which people put down to greed or selfishness are really far more the result of Pride.

Take it with money. Greed will certainly make a man want money, for the sake of a better house, better holidays, better things to eat and drink. But only up to a point. What is it that makes a man with £10,000 a year anxious to get £20,000 a year? It is not the greed for more pleasure. £10,000 will give all the luxuries that any man can really enjoy. It is Pride—the wish to be richer than some other rich man, and (still more) the wish for power. For, of course, power is what Pride really enjoys: there is nothing makes a man feel so superior to others as being able to move them about like toy soldiers. What makes a pretty girl spread misery wherever she goes by collecting admirers? Certainly not her sexual instinct: that kind of girl is quite often sexually frigid. It is Pride. What is it that makes a political leader or a whole nation go on and on, demanding more and more? Pride again. Pride is competitive by its very nature: that is why it goes on and on. If I am a proud man, then, as long as there is one man in the whole world more powerful, or richer, or cleverer than I, he is my rival and my enemy.

The Christians are right: it is Pride which has been the chief cause of misery in every nation and every family since the world began. Other vices may sometimes bring people together: you may find good fellowship and jokes and friendliness among drunken people or unchaste people. But Pride always means enmity—it *is* enmity. And not only enmity between man and man but enmity to God.

In God you come up against something which is in every respect immeasurably superior to yourself. Unless you know God as that—and, therefore, know yourself as nothing in comparison—you do not know God at all. As long as you are proud, you cannot know God. A proud man is always looking down on things and people: and, of course, as long as you are looking down, you cannot see something that is above you.

That raises a terrible question. How is it that people who are quite obviously eaten up with Pride can say they believe in God and appear to themselves very religious? I am afraid it means they are worshiping an imaginary God. They theoretically admit themselves to be nothing in the presence of this phantom God, but are really all the time imagining how He approves of them and thinks them far better than ordinary people: that is, they pay a pennyworth of imaginary humility to Him and get out of it a pound's worth of Pride toward their fellowmen. I suppose it was of those people Christ was thinking when He said that some would preach about Him and cast out devils in His name, only to be told at the end of the world that He had never known them. And any of us may at any moment be in this deathtrap. Luckily, we have a test. Whenever we find that our religious life is making us feel that we are good—above all, that we are better than someone else—I think we may be sure that we are being acted on, not by God, but by the devil. The real test of being in the presence of God is that you either forget about yourself altogether or see yourself as a small, dirty object. It is better to forget about yourself altogether.

It is a terrible thing that the worst of all the vices can smuggle itself into the very center of our religious life. But you can see why. The other, and less bad, vices come from the devil working on us through our animal nature. But this does not come through our animal nature at all. It comes direct from Hell. It is purely spiritual: consequently it is far more subtle and deadly. For the same reason, Pride can often be used to beat down the simpler vices. Teachers, in fact, often appeal to a boy's Pride, or, as they call it, his self-respect, to make him behave decently: many a man has overcome cowardice, or lust, or ill temper by learning to think that they are beneath his dignity—that is, by Pride. The devil laughs. He is perfectly content to see you becoming chaste and brave and self-controlled provided, all the time, he is setting up in you the Dictatorship of Pride—just as he would be quite content to see your chilblains cured if he was allowed, in return, to give you cancer. For Pride is spiritual cancer: it eats up the very possibility of love, or contentment, or even common sense.

Human Wickedness

CHRIST TAKES IT for granted that men are bad. Until we really feel this assumption of His to be true, though we are part of the world He came to save, we are not part of the audience to whom His words are addressed. We lack the first condition for understanding what He is talking about. And when men attempt to be Christians without this preliminary consciousness of sin, the result is almost bound to be a certain resentment against God as to one who is always making impossible demands and always inexplicably angry. Most of us have at times felt a secret sympathy with the dying farmer who replied to the Vicar's dissertation on repentance by asking "What harm have I ever done *Him?*" There is the real rub. The worst we have done to God is to leave Him alone—why can't He return the compliment? Why not live and let live? What call has He, of all beings, to be "angry"? It's easy for Him to be good!

Now at the moment when a man feels real guilt—moments too rare in our lives—all these blasphemies vanish away. Much, we may feel, can be excused to human infirmities: but not *this*—this incredibly mean and ugly action which none of our friends would have done, which even such a thoroughgoing little rotter as X would have been ashamed of, which we would not for the world allow to be published. At such a moment we really do know that our character, as revealed in this action, is, and ought to be, hateful to all good men, and, if there are powers above man, to them. A God who did not regard this with unappeasable distaste would not be a good being. We cannot even wish for such a God—it is like wishing that every nose in the universe were abolished, that smell of hay, or roses, or the sea should never again delight any creature, because our own breath happens to stink.

When we merely *say* that we are bad, the "wrath" of God seems a barbarous doctrine; as soon as we *perceive* our badness, it appears inevitable, a mere corollary from God's goodness. To keep ever before us the insight derived from such a moment as I have been describing, to learn to detect the same real inexcusable corruption under more and more of its complex disguises, is therefore indispensable to a real understanding of the Christian faith. This is not, of course, a new doctrine. . . . I am merely trying to get my reader (and, still more, myself) over a *pons asinorum*—to take the first step out of fools' paradise and utter illusion.

Laziness

I HAVE RECENTLY come to the conclusion that a besetting sin of mine all my life has been one which I never suspected—laziness—and that a good deal of the high-sounding doctrine of leisure is only a defense of *that*. The Greek error was a punishment for their sin in owning slaves and their consequent contempt for labor. There was a good element in it—the recognition, badly needed by modern commercialism, that the economic activities are not the *end* of man: beyond that they were probably wrong. If I still wanted to defend my old view I should ask you why *toil* appears in Genesis not as one of the things God originally created and pronounced "very good" but as a punishment for sin, like death. I suppose one could point out in reply that Adam was a gardener before he was a sinner, and that we must distinguish two degrees and kinds of work—the one wholly good and necessary to the animal side of the *animal rationale*, the other a punitive deterioration of the former due to the Fall.

Guilt

MANY MODERN PSYCHOLOGISTS tell us always to distrust this vague feeling of guilt, as something purely pathological. And if they had stopped at that, I might believe them. But when they go on, as some do, to apply the same treatment to all guilt feelings whatever, to suggest that one's feeling about a particular unkind act or a particular insincerity is also and equally untrustworthy—I can't help thinking they are talking nonsense. One sees this the moment one looks at other people. I have talked to some who felt guilt when they jolly well ought to have felt it; they have behaved like brutes and know it. I've also met others who felt guilty and weren't guilty by any standard I can apply. And thirdly, I've met people who were guilty and didn't seem to feel guilt. And isn't this what we should expect? People can be *malades imaginaires* who are well and think they are ill; and others, especially consumptives, are ill and think they are well; and thirdly—far the largest class—people are ill and know they are ill. It would be very odd if there were any region in which all mistakes were in one direction.

Some Christians would tell us to go on rummaging and scratching till we find something specific. We may be sure, they say, that there are real sins enough to justify the guilt feeling or to overthrow the feeling that all is well. I think they are right in saying that if we hunt long enough we shall find, or think we have found, something. But that is just what wakens suspicion. A theory which could never by any experience be falsified can for that reason hardly be verified. And just as, when we are yielding to temptation, we make ourselves believe that what we have always thought sin will on this occasion, for some strange reason, not be a sin, shan't we persuade ourselves that something we have always (rightly) thought to be innocent was really wrong? We may create scruples. And scruples are always a bad thing—if only because they usually distract us from real duties.

I don't at all know whether I'm right or not, but I have, on the whole, come to the conclusion that one can't directly *do* anything about either feeling. One is not to believe either—indeed, how can one believe a fog? I come back to St. John: "if our heart condemn us, God is greater than our heart." I sometimes pray not for self-knowledge in general but for just so much self-knowledge at the moment as I can bear and use at the moment; the little daily dose.

Anxiety

SOME PEOPLE feel guilty about their anxieties and regard them as a defect of faith. I don't agree at all. They are afflictions, not sins. Like all afflictions, they are, if we can so take them, our share in the Passion of Christ. For the beginning of the Passion—the first move, so to speak—is in Gethsemane. In Gethsemane a very strange and significant thing seems to have happened.

It is clear from many of His sayings that Our Lord had long foreseen His death. He knew what conduct such as His, in a world such as we have made of this, must inevitably lead to. But it is clear that this knowledge must somehow have been withdrawn from Him before He prayed in Gethsemane. He could not, with whatever reservation about the Father's will, have prayed that the cup might pass and simultaneously known that it would not. That is both a logical and a psychological impossibility. You see what this involves? Lest any trial incident to humanity should be lacking, the torments of hope—of suspense, anxiety—were at the last moment loosed upon Him—the supposed possibility that, after all, He might, He just conceivably might, be spared the supreme horror. There was precedent. Isaac had been spared: he too at the last moment, he also against all apparent probability. It was not quite impossible . . . a sight very unlike most of our religious pictures and images.

But for this last (and erroneous) hope against hope, and the consequent tumult of the soul, the sweat of blood, perhaps He would not have been very Man. To live in a fully predictable world is not to be a man.

At the end, I know, we are told that an angel appeared "comforting" him. But neither *comforting* in . . . English nor . . . in Greek means "consoling." "Strengthening" is more the word. May not the strengthening have consisted in the renewed certainty—cold comfort this—that the thing must be endured and therefore could be?

We all try to accept with some sort of submission our afflictions when they actually arrive. But the prayer in Gethsemane shows that the preceding anxiety is equally God's will and equally part of our human destiny. The perfect Man experienced it. And the servant is not greater than the master. We are Christians, not Stoics.

Psychoanalysis

SINCE CHRISTIAN MORALITY claims to be a technique for putting the human machine right, I think you would like to know how it is related to another technique which seems to make a similar claim—namely, psychoanalysis.

Now you want to distinguish very clearly between two things: between the actual medical theories and technique of the psychoanalysts, and the general philosophical view of the world which Freud and some others have gone on to add to this. The second thing—the philosophy of Freud—is in direct contradiction to Christianity: and also in direct contradiction to the other great psychologist, Jung. And furthermore, when Freud is talking about how to cure neurotics, he is speaking as a specialist on his own subject, but when he goes on to talk general philosophy, he is speaking as an amateur. It is, therefore, quite sensible to attend to him with respect in the one case and not in the other—and that is what I do. I am all the readier to do it because I have found that, when he is talking off his own subject and on a subject I do know something about (namely, languages), he is very ignorant. But psychoanalysis itself, apart from all the philosophical additions that Freud and others have made to it, is not in the least contradictory to Christianity. Its technique overlaps with Christian morality at some points and it would not be a bad thing if every parson knew something about it: but it does not run the same course all the way, for the two techniques are doing rather different things.

When a man makes a moral choice, two things are involved. One is the act of choosing. The other is the various feelings, impulses and so on which his psychological outfit presents him with, and which are the raw material of his choice. Now this raw material may be of two kinds. Either it may be what we would call normal: it may consist of the sort of feelings that are common to all men. Or else it may consist of quite unnatural feelings due to things that have gone wrong in his subconscious. Thus fear of things that are really dangerous would be an example of the first kind: an irrational fear of cats or spiders would be an example of the second kind. The desire of a man for a woman would be of the first kind: the perverted desire of a man for a man would be of the second. Now what psychoanalysis undertakes to do is to remove the abnormal feelings, that is, to give the man better raw material for his acts of choice: morality is concerned with the acts of choice themselves.

Social Morality

THE FIRST THING to get clear about Christian morality between man and man is that in this department Christ did not come to preach any brand-new morality. The Golden

Rule of the New Testament (Do as you would be done by) is a summing up of what everyone, at bottom, had always known to be right. Really great moral teachers never do introduce new moralities: it is quacks and cranks who do that. As Dr. Johnson said, "People need to be reminded more often than they need to be instructed." The real job of every moral teacher is to keep on bringing us back, time after time, to the old simple principles which we are all so anxious not to see; like bringing a horse back and back to the fence it has refused to jump or bringing a child back and back to the bit in its lesson that it wants to shirk.

The second thing to get clear is that Christianity has not, and does not profess to have, a detailed program for applying "Do as you would be done by" to a particular society at a particular moment. It could not have. It is meant for all men at all times and the particular program which suited one place or time would not suit another. And, anyhow, that is not how Christianity works. When it tells you to feed the hungry, it does not give you lessons in cookery. When it tells you to read the Scriptures, it does not give you lessons in Hebrew and Greek, or even in English grammar. It was never intended to replace or supersede the ordinary human arts and sciences: it is rather a director which will set them all to the right jobs, and a source of energy which will give them all new life, if only they will put themselves at its disposal.

People say, "The Church ought to give us a lead." That is true if they mean it in the right way, but false if they mean it in the wrong way. By the Church they ought to mean the whole body of practicing Christians. And when they say that the Church should give us a lead, they ought to mean that some Christians—those who happen to have the right talents—should be economists and statesmen, and that all economists and statesmen should be Christians, and that their whole efforts in politics and economics should be directed to putting "Do as you would be done by" into action. If that happened, and if we others were really ready to take it, then we should find the Christian solution for our own social problems pretty quickly. But, of course, when they ask for a lead from the Church, most people mean they want the clergy to put out a political program. That is silly. The clergy are those particular people within the whole Church who have been specially trained and set aside to look after what concerns us as creatures who are going to live forever: and we are asking them to do a quite different job for which they have not been trained. The job is really on us, on the laymen. The application of Christian principles, say, to trade unionism or education, must come from Christian trade unionists and Christian schoolmasters: just as Christian literature comes from Christian novelists and dramatists—not from the bench of bishops getting together and trying to write plays and novels in their spare time.

Christian Society

THE NEW TESTAMENT, without going into details, gives us a pretty clear hint of what a fully Christian society would be like. Perhaps it gives us more than we can take. It tells us that there are to be no passengers or parasites: if a man does not work, he ought not to eat. Everyone is to work with his own hands, and what is more, everyone's work is to produce something good: there will be no manufacture of silly luxuries and then of sillier advertisements to persuade us to buy them. And there is to be no "swank" or "side," no putting on airs. To that extent a Christian society would be what we now call Leftist. On the other hand, it is always insisting on obedience—obedience (and outward marks of respect) from all of us to properly appointed magistrates, from children to parents, and (I am afraid this is going to be very unpopular) from wives to husbands. Thirdly, it is to be a cheerful society: full of singing and rejoicing, and regarding worry or anxiety as wrong. Courtesy is one of the Christian virtues; and the New Testament hates what it calls "busybodies."

If there were such a society in existence and you or I visited it, I think we should come away with a curious impression. We should feel that its economic life was very socialistic and, in that sense, "advanced," but that its family life and code of manners were rather old-fashioned—perhaps even ceremonious and aristocratic. Each of us would like some bits of it, but I'm afraid very few of us would like the whole thing. That is just what one would expect if Christianity is the total plan for the human machine. We have all departed from that total plan in different ways, and each of us wants to make out that his own modification of the original plan is the plan itself. You will find this again and again about anything that is really Christian: everyone is attracted by bits of it and wants to pick out those bits and leave the rest. That is why we do not get much further: and that is why people who are fighting for quite opposite things can both say they are fighting for Christianity.

Ecumenism

IT IS A LITTLE DIFFICULT to explain how I feel that though you have taken a way which is not for me [his correspondent had left the Episcopal Church to become a Roman Catholic], I nevertheless can congratulate you—I suppose because your faith and joy are so obviously increased. Naturally I do not draw the same conclusions as you—but there is no need for us to start a controversial correspondence! I believe we are very near to one another, but not because I am at all on the Romeward frontier of my own communion. I believe that, in the present divided state of Christendom, those who are at the heart of each division are all closer to one another than those who are at the fringes. I would even carry this beyond the borders of Christianity: how much more one has in common with a *real* Jew or Muslim than with a wretched liberalizing, occidentalized specimen of the same categories. Let us by all means pray for one another: it is perhaps the only form of "work for reunion" which never does anything but good. God bless you.

Other Religions

If you are a Christian, you do not have to believe that all the other religions are simply wrong all through. If you are an atheist, you do have to believe that the main point in all the religions of the whole world is simply one huge mistake. If you are a Christian, you are free to think that all these religions, even the queerest ones, contain at least some hint of the truth. When I was an atheist, I had to try to persuade myself that most of the human race have always been wrong about the question that mattered to them most; when I became a Christian, I was able to take a more liberal view. But, of course, being a Christian does mean thinking that where Christianity differs from other religions, Christianity is right and they are wrong. As in arithmetic—there is only one right answer to a sum, and all other answers are wrong: but some of the wrong answers are much nearer being right than others.

Fascism and Communism

FASCISM AND COMMUNISM, like all other evils, are potent because of the good they contain or imitate. . . . And of course their occasion is the failure of those who left humanity starved of that particular good. This does not for me alter the conviction that they are very bad indeed. One of the things we must guard against is the penetration of both into Christianity—availing themselves of that very truth you have suggested and I have admitted. Mark my words: you will presently see both a Leftist and a Rightist pseudo-theology developing—the abomination will stand where it ought not. . . .

Is Christianity Hard or Easy?

THE ORDINARY IDEA which we all have before we become Christians is this. We take as starting point our ordinary self with its various desires and interests. We then admit that something else—call it "morality" or "decent behavior," or "the good of society"—has claims on this self: claims which interfere with its own desires. What we mean by "being good" is giving in to those claims. Some of the things the ordinary self wanted to do turn out to be what we call "wrong": well, we must give them up. Other things, which the self did not want to do, turn out to be what we call "right": well, we shall have to do them. But we are hoping all the time that when all the demands have been met, the poor natural self will still have some chance, and some time, to get on with its own life and do what it likes. In fact, we are very like an honest man paying his taxes. He pays them all right, but he does hope that there will be enough left over for him to live on. Because we are still taking our natural self as the starting point.

As long as we are thinking that way, one or the other of two results is likely to follow. Either we give up trying to be good, or else we become very unhappy indeed. For, make no mistake: if you are really going to try to meet all the demands made on the natural self, it will not have enough left over to live on. The more you obey your conscience, the more your conscience will demand of you. And your natural self, which is thus being starved and hampered and worried at every turn, will get angrier and angrier. In the end, you will either give up trying to be good, or else become one of those people who, as they say, "live for others" but always in a discontented, grumbling way—always wondering why the others do not notice it more and always making a martyr of yourself. And once you have become that, you will be a far greater pest to anyone who has to live with you than you would have been if you had remained frankly selfish.

The Christian way is different: harder, and easier. Christ says "Give me All. I don't want so much of your time and so much of your money and so much of your work: I want You. I have not come to torment your natural self, but to kill it. No half-measures are any good. I don't want to cut off a branch here and a branch there, I want to have the whole tree down. I don't want to drill the tooth, or crown it, or stop it, but to have it out. Hand over the whole natural self, all the desires which you think innocent as well as the ones you think wicked—the whole outfit. I will give you a new self instead. In fact, I will give you Myself: my own will shall become yours."

Both harder and easier than what we are all trying to do. You have noticed, I expect, that Christ Himself sometimes describes the Christian way as very hard, sometimes as very easy. He says, "Take up your Cross"—in other words, it is like going to be beaten to death in a concentration camp. Next minute he says, "My yoke is easy and my burden light." He means both. And one can just see why both are true.

Teachers will tell you that the laziest boy in the class is the one who works hardest in the end. They mean this. If you give two boys, say, a proposition in geometry to do, the one who is prepared to take trouble will try to understand it. The lazy boy will try to learn it by heart because, for the moment, that needs less effort. But six months later, when they are preparing for an exam, that lazy boy is doing hours and hours of miserable drudgery over things the other boy understands, and positively enjoys, in a few minutes. Laziness means more work in the long run. Or look at it this way. In a battle, or in mountain climbing, there is often one thing which it takes a lot of pluck to do; but it is also, in the long run, the safest thing to do. If you funk it, you will find yourself, hours later, in far worse danger. The cowardly thing is also the most dangerous thing.

It is like that here. The terrible thing, the almost impossible thing, is to hand over your whole self—all your wishes and precautions—to Christ. But it is far easier than what we are all trying to do instead. For what we are trying to do is to remain what we call "ourselves," to keep personal happiness as our great aim in life, and yet at the same time be "good." We are all trying to let our mind and heart go their own way—centered on money or pleasure or ambition—and hoping, in spite of this, to behave honestly and chastely and humbly. And that is exactly what Christ warned us you could not do. As He said, a thistle cannot produce figs. If I am a field that contains nothing but grass-seed, I cannot produce wheat. Cutting the grass may keep it short: but I shall still produce grass and no wheat. If I want to produce wheat, the change must go deeper than the surface. I must be ploughed up and resown.

That is why the real problem of the Christian life comes where people do not usually look for it. It comes the very moment you wake up each morning. All your wishes and hopes for the day rush at you like wild animals. And the first job each morning consists simply in shoving them all back; in listening to that other voice, taking that other point of view, letting that other larger, stronger, quieter life come flowing in. And so on, all day. Standing back from all your natural fussings and frettings; coming in out of the wind.

We can only do it for moments at first. But from those moments the new sort of life will be spreading through our system: because now we are letting Him work at the right part of us. It is the difference between paint, which is merely laid on the surface, and a dye or stain which soaks right through. He never talked vague, idealistic gas. When He said, "Be perfect," He meant it. He meant that we must go in for the full treatment. It is hard; but the sort of compromise we are all hankering after is harder—in fact, it is impossible. It may be hard for an egg to turn into a bird: it would be a jolly sight harder for it to learn to fly while remaining an egg. We are like eggs at present. And you cannot go on indefinitely being just an ordinary, decent egg. We must be hatched or go bad.

May I come back to what I said before? This is the whole of Christianity. There is nothing else. It is so easy to get muddled about that. It is easy to think that the Church has a lot of different objects—education, building, missions, holding services. Just as it is easy to think the State has a lot of different objects—military, political, economic, and what not. But in a way things are much simpler than that. The State exists simply to promote and to protect the ordinary happiness of human beings in this life. A husband and wife chatting over a fire, a couple of friends having a game of darts in a pub, a man reading a book in his own room or digging in his own garden—that is what the State is there for. And unless they are helping to increase and prolong and protect such moments, all the laws, parliaments, armies, courts, police, economics, etc., are simply a waste of time. In the same way the Church exists for nothing else but to draw men into Christ, to make them little Christs. If they are not doing that, all the cathedrals, clergy, missions, sermons, even the Bible itself, are simply a waste of time. God became Man for no other purpose. It is even doubtful, you know, whether the whole universe was created for any other purpose. It says in the Bible that the whole universe was made for Christ and that everything is to be gathered together in Him. I do not suppose any of us can understand how this will happen as regards the whole universe. We do not know what (if anything) lives in the parts of it that are millions of miles away from this Earth. Even on this Earth we do not know how it applies to things other than men. After all, that is what you would expect. We have been shown the plan only insofar as it concerns ourselves.

I sometimes like to imagine that I can just see how it might apply to other things. I think I can see how the higher animals are in a sense drawn into Man when he loves them and makes them (as he does) much more nearly human than they would otherwise be. I can even see a sense in which the dead things and plants are drawn into Man as he studies them and uses and appreciates them. And if there were intelligent creatures in other worlds they might do the same with their worlds. It might be that when intelligent creatures entered into Christ they would, in that way, bring all the other things in along with them. But I do not know: it is only a guess.

What we have been told is how we men can be drawn into Christ—can become part of that wonderful present which the young Prince of the universe wants to offer to His Father—that present which is Himself and therefore us in Him. It is the only thing we were made for. And there are strange, exciting hints in the Bible that when we are drawn in, a great many other things in Nature will begin to come right. The bad dream will be over: it will be morning.

Apologetics

APOLOGETICS MEANS, of course, Defense. The first question is—what do you propose to defend? Christianity, of course. . . .

We are to defend Christianity itself—the faith preached by the Apostles, attested by the Martyrs, embodied in the Creeds, expounded by the Fathers. . . .

The great difficulty is to get modern audiences to realize that you are preaching Christianity solely and simply because you happen to think it *true;* they always suppose you are preaching it because you like it or think it good for society or something of that sort. . . .

Secondly, this scrupulous care to preserve the Christian message as something distinct from one's own ideas, has one very good effect upon the apologist himself. It forces him, again and again, to face up to those elements in original Christianity which he personally finds obscure or repulsive. He is saved from the temptation to skip, or slur, or ignore what he finds disagreeable. . . .

From this there follows a corollary about the Apologist's private reading. There are two questions he will naturally ask himself. (1) Have I been "keeping up," keeping abreast of recent movements in theology? (2) Have I stood firm . . .

amidst all these "winds of doctrine" (Ephesians 4:14)? I want to say emphatically that the second question is far the more important of the two. . . .

I am speaking, so far, of theological reading. Scientific reading is a different matter. . . .

While we are on the subject of science, let me digress for a moment. I believe that any Christian who is qualified to write a good popular book on any science may do much more by that than by any directly apologetic work. . . .

Our business is to present that which is timeless (the same yesterday, today, and tomorrow) in the particular language of our own age. . . .

This raises the question of Theology and Politics. The nearest I can get to a settlement of the frontier problem between them is this:—that Theology teaches us what ends are desirable and what means are lawful, while Politics teaches what means are effective. . . .

Our great danger at present is lest the Church should continue to practice a merely missionary technique in what has become a missionary situation. . . .

(1) I find that the uneducated Englishman is an almost total skeptic about History. . . .

(2) He has a distrust (very rational in the state of his knowledge) of ancient texts. . . .

(3) A sense of sin is almost totally lacking. . . .

(4) We must learn the language of our audience. . . . You must translate every bit of your Theology into the Vernacular. . . .

Do not attempt to water Christianity down. . . .

One last word. I have found that nothing is more dangerous to one's own faith than the work of an apologist. No doctrine of that Faith seems to me so spectral, so unreal as one that I have just successfully defended in a public debate. For a moment, you see, it has seemed to rest on oneself: as a result, when you go away from that debate, it seems no stronger than that weak pillar. That is why we apologists take our lives in our hands and can be saved only by falling back continually from the web of our own arguments, as from our intellectual counters, into the Reality—from Christian apologetics into Christ Himself.

Money

THERE IS ONE BIT of advice given to us by the ancient heathen Greeks, and by the Jews in the Old Testament, and by the great Christian teachers of the Middle Ages, which the modern economic system has completely disobeyed. All these people told us not to lend money at interest: and lending money at interest—what we call investment—is the basis of our whole system. Now it may not absolutely follow that we are wrong. Some people say that when Moses and Aristotle and the Christians agreed in forbidding interest (or "usury" as they called it), they could not foresee the joint stock company, and were only thinking of the private moneylender, and that, therefore, we need not bother about what they said. That is a question I cannot decide on. I am not an economist and I simply do not know whether the investment system is responsible for the state we are in or not. This is where we want the Christian economist. But I should not have been honest if I had not told you that three great civilizations had agreed (or so it seems at first sight) in condemning the very thing on which we have based our whole life.

Gift-love and Need-love

"GOD IS LOVE," says St. John. When I first tried to write [*The Four Loves*], I thought that his maxim would provide me with a very plain highroad through the whole subject. I thought I should be able to say that human loves deserved to be called loves at all just insofar as they resembled that Love which is God. The first distinction I made was therefore between what I called Gift-love and Need-love. The typical example of Gift-love would be that love which moves a man to work, and plan, and save for the future well-being of his family which he will die without sharing or seeing; of the second, that which sends a lonely or frightened child to its mother's arms.

There was no doubt which was more like Love Himself. Divine Love is Gift-love. The Father gives all He is and has to the Son. The Son gives Himself back to the Father, and gives Himself to the world, and for the world to the Father, and thus gives the world (in Himself) back to the Father too.

And what, on the other hand, can be less like anything we believe of God's life than Need-love? He lacks nothing, but our Need-love, as Plato saw, is "the son of Poverty." It is the accurate reflection in consciousness of our actual nature. We are born helpless. As soon as we are fully conscious, we discover loneliness. We need others physically, emotionally, intellectually; we need them if we are to know anything, even ourselves.

Appreciative Love

NEED-LOVE CRIES TO GOD from our poverty; Gift-love longs to serve, or even to suffer for, God; Appreciative love says: "We give thanks to Thee for Thy great glory." Need-love says of a woman "I cannot live without her"; Gift-love longs to give her happiness, comfort, protection—if possible, wealth; Appreciative love gazes and holds its breath and is silent, rejoices that such a wonder should exist even if not for him, will not be wholly dejected by losing her, would rather have it so than never to have seen her at all.

We murder to dissect. In actual life, thank God, the three elements of love mix and succeed one another, moment by moment. Perhaps none of them except Need-love ever exists alone, in "chemical" purity, for more than a few seconds. And perhaps that is because nothing about us except our neediness is, in this life, permanent.

Love of Nature

FOR SOME PEOPLE, perhaps especially for Englishmen and Russians, what we call "the love of nature" is a permanent and serious sentiment. I mean here that love of nature which cannot be adequately classified simply as an instance of our love for beauty. Of course, many natural objects— trees, flowers, and animals—are beautiful. But the nature lovers whom I have in mind are not very much concerned with individual beautiful objects of that sort. The man who is distracts them. An enthusiastic botanist is for them a dreadful companion on a ramble. He is always stopping to draw their attention to particulars. Nor are they looking for "views" or landscapes. Wordsworth, their spokesman, strongly deprecates this. It leads to "a comparison of scene with scene," makes you "pamper" yourself with "meager novelties of color and proportion." While you are busying yourself with this critical and discriminating activity, you lose what really matters—the "moods of time and season," the "spirit" of the place. And, of course, Wordsworth is right. That is why, if you love nature in his fashion, a landscape painter is (out of doors) an even worse companion than a botanist.

It is the "moods" or the "spirit" that matter. Nature lovers want to receive as fully as possible whatever nature, at each particular time and place, is, so to speak, saying. The obvious richness, grace, and harmony of some scenes are no more precious to them than the grimness, bleakness, terror, monotony, or "visionary dreariness" of others. The featureless itself gets from them a willing response. It is one more word uttered by nature. They lay themselves bare to the sheer quality of every countryside, every hour of the day. They want to absorb it into themselves, to be colored through and through by it.

Love of Country

IN REALITY it contains many ingredients, of which many different blends are possible.

First, there is love of home, of the place we grew up in or the places, perhaps many, which have been our homes;

and of all the places fairly near these and fairly like them; love of old acquaintances, of familiar sights, sounds, and smells. . . .

The second ingredient is a particular attitude to our country's past. I mean to that past as it lives in popular imagination; the great deeds of our ancestors. . . .

The third thing is not a sentiment but a belief: a firm, even prosaic belief that our own nation, in sober fact, has long been, and still is markedly superior to all others. . . . I once ventured to say to an old clergyman who was voicing this sort of patriotism, "But, sir, aren't we told that *every* people thinks its own men the bravest and its own women the fairest in the world?" He replied with total gravity—he could not have been graver if he had been saying the Creed at the altar—"Yes, but in England it's true." To be sure, this conviction had not made my friend (God rest his soul) a villain; only an extremely lovable old ass. It can however produce asses that kick and bite. On the lunatic fringe it may shade off into that popular Racialism which Christianity and science equally forbid.

Storge or Affection

AFFECTION . . . is the humblest love. It gives itself no airs. People can be proud of being "in love," or of friendship. Affection is modest—even furtive and shamefaced. Often when I had remarked on the affection quite often found between cat and dog, my friend replied, "yes. But I bet no dog would ever confess it to the other dogs." That is at least a good caricature of much human Affection. "Let homely faces stay at home," says Comus. Now Affection has a very homely face. So have many of those for whom we feel it. It is no proof of our refinement or perceptiveness that we love them; nor that they love us. What I have called Appreciative love is no basic element in Affection. It usually needs absence or bereavement to set us praising those to whom only Affection binds us. We take them for granted: and this taking for granted, which is an outrage in erotic love, is here right and proper up to a point. It fits the comfortable, quiet nature of the feeling. Affection would not be affection if it was loudly and frequently expressed; to produce it in public is like getting your household furniture out for a move. It did very well in its place, but it looks shabby or tawdry or grotesque in the sunshine. Affection almost slinks or seeps through our lives. It lives with humble, undress, private things; soft slippers, old clothes, old jokes, the thump of a sleepy dog's tail on the kitchen floor, the sound of a sewing machine, a gollywog left on the lawn.

But I must at once correct myself. I am talking of Affection as it is when it exists apart from the other loves. It often does so exist; often not. As gin is not only a drink in itself but also a base for many mixed drinks, so Affection, besides being a love itself, can enter into the other loves and color them all through and become the very medium in which from day to day they operate. They would not perhaps wear very well without it. To make a friend is not the same as to become affectionate. But when your friend has become an old friend, all those things about him which had originally nothing to do with the friendship become familiar and dear with familiarity. As for erotic love, I can imagine nothing more disagreeable than to experience it for more than a very short time without this homespun clothing of affection. That would be a most uneasy condition, either too angelic, or too animal, or each by turn; never quite great enough or little enough for man. There is indeed a peculiar charm, both in Friendship and in Eros, about those moments when Appreciative love lies, as it were, curled up asleep, and the mere ease and ordinariness of the relationship (free as solitude, yet neither is alone) wraps us round. No need to talk. No need to make love. No needs at all except perhaps to stir the fire.

Philia or Friendship

[COMPANIONSHIP] IS OFTEN CALLED Friendship, and many people, when they speak of their "friends" mean only their companions. But it is not Friendship in the sense I give to the word. . . .

Friendship arises out of mere Companionship when two or more of the companions discover that they have in common some insight which the others do not share and which, till that moment, each believed to be his own unique treasure (or burden). The typical expression of opening Friendship would be something like, "What? You too? I thought I was the only one." We can imagine that among those early hunters and warriors single individuals—one in a century? one in a thousand years?—saw what others did not; saw that the deer was beautiful as well as edible, that hunting was fun as well as necessary, dreamed that his gods might be not only powerful but holy. But as long as each of these percipient persons dies without finding a kindred soul, nothing (I suspect) will come of it; art, or sport, or spiritual religion will not be born. It is when two such persons discover one another, when, whether with immense difficulties and semiarticulate fumblings or with what would seem to us amazing and elliptical speed, they share their vision— it is then that Friendship is born. And instantly they stand together in an immense solitude.

Lovers seek privacy. Friends find this solitude about them, this barrier between them and the herd, whether they want it or not. They would be glad to reduce it. The first two would be glad to find a third.

In our own time Friendship arises in the same way. For us, of course, the shared activity and therefore the companionship on which Friendship supervenes will not often be a bodily one like hunting or fighting. It may be a common religion, common studies, a common profession, even a common recreation. All who share it will be our companions; but one or two or three who share something more will be our Friends. In this kind of love, as Emerson said, *Do you love me?* means *Do you see the same truth?*—Or at least, "Do you *care about* the same truth?" The man who agrees with us that some question, little regarded by others, is of great importance can be our Friend. He need not agree with us about the answer.

Notice that Friendship thus repeats on a more individual and less socially necessary level the character of the Companionship which was its matrix. The Companionship was between people who were doing something together— hunting, studying, painting, or what you will. The Friends will still be doing something together, but something more inward, less widely shared, and less easily defined; still hunters, but of some immaterial quarry; still collaborating, but in some work the world does not, or not yet, take account of; still traveling companions, but on a different kind of journey. Hence we picture lovers face to face but Friends side by side; their eyes look ahead.

Eros and Venus

BY EROS I mean . . . that state which we call "being in love"; or, if you prefer, that kind of love which lovers are "in". . . . The carnal or animally sexual element within Eros, I intend (following an old usage) to call Venus. . . .

To the evolutionist Eros (the human variation) will be something that grows out of Venus, a late complication and development of the immemorial biological impulse. We must not assume, however, that this is necessarily what happens within the consciousness of the individual. There may be those who have first felt mere sexual appetite for a woman and then gone on to a later stage to "fall in love with her." But I doubt if this is at all common. Very often what comes first is simply a delighted preoccupation with the Beloved—a general, unspecified preoccupation with her in her totality. A man in this state really hasn't leisure to think of sex. He is too busy thinking of a person. The fact that she is a woman is far less important than the fact that she is herself. He is full of desire, but the desire may not be sexually toned. If you ask him what he wanted, the true reply would often be, "To go on thinking of her." He is love's contemplative. And when at a later stage the explicitly sexual element awakes, he will not feel (unless scientific theories are influencing him) that this had all along been the root of the whole matter. He is more likely to feel that the incoming tide of Eros, having demolished many sand castles and made islands of many rocks, has now at last with a triumphant seventh wave flooded this part of his nature also—the little pool of ordinary sexuality which was there on his beach before the tide came in. Eros enters him like an invader, taking over and reorganizing, one by one, the institutions of a conquered country. It may have taken over many others before it reaches the sex in him; and it will reorganize that too. . . .

We must not be totally serious about Venus. Indeed we can't be totally serious without doing violence to our humanity. It is not for nothing that every language and literature in the world is full of jokes about sex. Many of them may be dull or disgusting and nearly all of them are old. But we must insist that they embody an attitude to Venus which in the long run endangers the Christian life far less than a reverential gravity. We must not attempt to find an absolute in the flesh. Banish play and laughter from the bed of love and you may let in a false goddess. She will be even falser than the Aphrodite of the Greeks; for they, even while they worshiped her, knew that she was "laughter-loving." The mass of the people are perfectly right in their conviction that Venus is a partly comic spirit. We are under no obligation at all to sing all our love duets in the throbbing, world-without-end, heartbreaking manner of Tristan and Isolde; let us often sing like Papageno and Papagena instead. . . .

I can hardly help regarding it as one of God's jokes that a passion so soaring, so apparently transcendent, as Eros, should thus be linked in incongruous symbiosis with a bodily appetite which, like any other appetite, tactlessly reveals its connections with such mundane factors as weather, health, diet, circulation, and digestion. In Eros at times we seem to be flying; Venus gives us the sudden twitch that reminds us we are really captive balloons. It is a continual demonstration of the truth that we are composite creatures, rational animals, akin on one side to the angels, on the other to tomcats. It is a bad thing not to be able to take a joke. Worse, not to take a divine joke; made, I grant you, at our expense, but also (who doubts it?) for our endless benefit.

Agape or Charity

WE MUST NOT begin with mysticism, with the creature's love for God, or with the wonderful foretastes of the fruition of God vouchsafed to some in their earthly life. We begin at the real beginning, with love as the Divine energy. This primal love is Gift-love. In God there is no hunger that needs to be filled, only plenteousness that desires to give. The doctrine that God was under no necessity to create is not a piece of dry scholastic speculation. It is essential. Without it we can hardly avoid the conception of what I can only call a "managerial" God; a Being whose function or nature is to "run" the universe, who stands to it as a headmaster to a school or a hotelier to a hotel. But to be sovereign of the universe is no great matter to God. In Himself, at home in "the land of the Trinity," he is Sovereign of a far greater realm. We must keep always before our eyes that vision of Lady Julian's in which God carried in His hand a little object like a nut, and that nut was "all that is made." God, who needs nothing, loves into existence wholly superfluous creatures in order that He may love and perfect them. He creates the universe, already foreseeing—or should we say "seeing"? there are no tenses in God—the buzzing cloud of flies about the cross, the flayed back pressed against the uneven stake, the nails driven through the mesial nerves, the repeated incipient suffocation as the body droops, the repeated torture of back and arms as it is time after time, for breath's sake, hitched up. If I may dare the biological image, God is a "host" who deliberately creates His own parasites; causes us to be that we may exploit and "take advantage of" Him. Herein is love. This is the diagram of Love Himself, the inventor of all loves.

God, as Creator of nature, implants in us both Gift-loves and Need-loves. The Gift-loves are natural images of Himself; proximities to Him by resemblance which are not necessarily and in all men proximities of approach. A devoted mother, a beneficent ruler or teacher, may give and give, continually exhibiting the likeness, without making the approach. The Need-loves, so far as I have been able to see, have no resemblance to the Love which God is. They are rather correlatives, opposites; not as evil is the opposite of good, of course, but as the form of the blancmange is an opposite to the form of the mold.

But in addition to these natural loves God can bestow a far better gift; or rather, since our minds must divide and pigeonhole, two gifts.

He communicates to men a share of His own Gift-love. This is different from the Gift-loves He has built into their nature. These never quite seek simply the good of the loved object for the object's own sake. They are biased in favor of those goods they can themselves bestow, or those which they would like best themselves, or those which fit in with a preconceived picture of the life they want the object to lead. But Divine Gift-love—Love Himself working in a man—is wholly disinterested and desires what is simply best for the beloved. Again, natural Gift-love is always directed to objects which the lover finds in some way intrinsically lovable—objects to which Affection, or Eros, or a shared point of view attracts him, or, failing that, to the grateful and the deserving, or perhaps to those whose helplessness is of a winning and appealing kind. But Divine Gift-love in the man enables him to love what is not naturally lovable; lepers, criminals, enemies, morons, the sulky, the superior, and the sneering. Finally, by a high paradox, God enables men to have a Gift-love toward Himself. There is, of course, a sense in which no one can give to God anything which is not already His; and if it is already His, what have you given? But since it is only too obvious that we can withhold ourselves, our wills and hearts, from God, we can, in that sense, also give them. What is His by right and would not exist for a moment if it ceased to be His (as the song is the singer's), He has nevertheless made ours in such a way that we can freely offer it back to Him. "Our wills are ours to make them Thine." And as all Christians know, there is another way of giving to God; every stranger whom we feed or clothe is Christ. And this apparently is Gift-love to God whether we know it or not. Love Himself can work in those who know nothing of Him. The "sheep" in the parable had no idea either of the God hidden in the prisoner whom they visited or of the God hidden in themselves when they made the visit. (I take the whole parable to be about the judgment of the heathen. For it begins by saying, in the Greek, that the Lord will summon all "the nations" before Him—presumably, the Gentiles, the *Goyim*.)

That such a Gift-love comes by Grace and should be called Charity, everyone will agree.

"Love Thy Neighbor"

IT IS A serious thing to live in a society of possible gods and goddesses, to remember that the dullest and most uninteresting person you talk to may one day be a creature which, if you saw it now, you would be strongly tempted to worship, or else a horror and a corruption such as you now meet, if at all, only in a nightmare. All day long we are, in some degree, helping each other to one or other of these destinations. It is in the light of these overwhelming possibilities, it is with the awe and the circumspection proper to them, that we should conduct all our dealings with one another, all friendships, all loves, all play, all politics. There are no ordinary people. You have never talked to a mere mortal. Nations, cultures, arts, civilization—these are mortal, and their life is to ours as the life of a gnat. But it is immortals whom we joke with, work with, marry, snub, and exploit—immortal horrors or everlasting splendors. This does not mean that we are to be perpetually solemn. We must play. But our merriment must be of that kind (and it is, in fact, the merriest kind) which exists between people

who have, from the outset, taken each other seriously—no
flippancy, no superiority, no presumption. And our charity
must be a real and costly love, with deep feeling for the sins
in spite of which we love the sinner—no mere tolerance or
indulgence which parodies love as flippancy parodies merriment. Next to the Blessed Sacrament itself, your neighbor
is the holiest object presented to your senses. If he is your
Christian neighbor, he is holy in almost the same way, for
in him also Christ *vere latitat*—the glorifier and the glorified, Glory Himself, is truly hidden.

Sex

SEX IN ITSELF cannot be moral or immoral any more than
gravitation or nutrition. The sexual behavior of human
beings can. And like their economic, or political, or agricul-
tural, or parental, or filial behavior, it is sometimes good
and sometimes bad. And the sexual act, when lawful—
which means chiefly when consistent with good faith and
charity—can, like all other merely natural acts ("whether we
eat or drink, etc.," as the Apostle says), be done to the glory
of God, and will then be holy. And like other natural acts it
is sometimes so done, and sometimes not.

Marriage

THE CHRISTIAN IDEA of marriage is based on Christ's words
that a man and wife are to be regarded as a single

organism—for that is what the words "one flesh" would be in modern English. And the Christians believe that when He said this He was not expressing a sentiment but stating a fact—just as one is stating a fact when one says that a lock and its key are one mechanism, or that a violin and a bow are one musical instrument. The inventor of the human machine was telling us that its two halves, the male and the female, were made to be combined together in pairs, not simply on the sexual level, but totally combined. The monstrosity of sexual intercourse outside marriage is that those who indulge in it are trying to isolate one kind of union (the sexual) from all the other kinds of union which were intended to go along with it and make up the total union. The Christian attitude does not mean that there is anything wrong about sexual pleasure, any more than about the pleasure of eating. It means that you must not isolate that pleasure and try to get it by itself, any more than you ought to try to get the pleasures of taste without swallowing and digesting, by chewing things and spitting them out again.

One thing . . . marriage has done for me. I can never again believe that religion is manufactured out of our unconscious, starved desires and is a substitute for sex. For those few years H. [his wife Helen Joy] and I feasted on love; every mode of it—solemn and merry, romantic and realistic, sometimes as dramatic as a thunderstorm, sometimes as comfortable and unemphatic as putting on your soft slippers. No cranny of heart or body remained unsatisfied. If God were a substitute for love, we ought to have lost all interest in Him. Who'd bother about substitutes when he has the thing itself? But that isn't what happens. We both knew we wanted something besides one another— quite a different kind of something, a quite different kind of want. You might as well say that when lovers have one another, they will never want to read, or eat—or breathe. . . .

The most precious gift that marriage gave me was this constant impact of something very close and intimate yet all the time unmistakably other, resistant—in a word, real.

Divorce

CHRISTIANITY TEACHES that marriage is for life. There is, of course, a difference between Churches: some do not admit divorce at all; some allow it reluctantly in very special cases. It is a great pity that Christians should disagree about such a question; but for an ordinary layman the thing to notice is that Churches all agree with one another about marriage a great deal more than any of them agrees with the outside world. I mean, they all regard divorce as something like cutting up a living body, as a kind of surgical operation. Some of them think the operation so violent that it cannot be done at all; others admit it as a desperate remedy in extreme cases. They are all agreed that it is more like having both your legs cut off than it is like dissolving a business partnership or even deserting a regiment. What they all disagree with is the modern view that it is a simple readjustment of partners, to be made whenever people feel they are no longer in love with one another, or when either of them falls in love with someone else.

Intercourse in the Afterlife

THE LETTER AND SPIRIT of Scripture, and of all Christianity, forbid us to suppose that life in the New Creation will be a sexual life; and this reduces our imagination to the withering alternative either of bodies which are hardly recognizable as human bodies at all or else of a perpetual fast. As regards the fast, I think our present outlook might be like that of a small boy who, on being told that the sexual act was the highest bodily pleasure, should immediately ask whether you ate chocolates at the same time. On receiving the answer "No," he might regard absence of chocolates as the chief characteristic of sexuality. In vain would you tell him that the reason why lovers in their carnal raptures don't bother about chocolates is that they have something better to think of. The boy knows chocolate: he does not know the positive thing that excludes it. We are in the same position. We know the sexual life; we do not know, except in glimpses, the other thing which, in Heaven, will leave no room for it. Hence where fullness awaits us we anticipate fasting. In denying that sexual life, as we now understand it, makes any part of the final beatitude, it is not, of course, necessary to suppose that the distinction of sexes will disappear. What is no longer needed for biological purposes may be expected to survive for splendor. Sexuality is the instrument both of virginity and conjugal virtue; neither men nor women will be asked to throw away weapons they have used victoriously. It is the beaten and the fugitives who throw away their swords. The conquerors sheathe theirs and retain them. . . .

I am well aware that this last . . . may seem to many

readers unfortunate and to some comic. But that very comedy, as I must repeatedly insist, is the symptom of our estrangement, as spirits, from Nature and our estrangement, as animals, from Spirit. The whole conception of the New Creation involves the belief that this estrangement will be healed. A curious consequence will follow. The archaic type of thought which could not clearly distinguish spiritual "Heaven" from the sky, is from our point of view a confused type of thought. But it also resembles and anticipates a type of thought which will one day be true. That archaic sort of thinking will become simply the correct sort when Nature and Spirit are fully harmonized—when Spirit rides Nature so perfectly that the two together make rather a *Centaur* than a mounted knight. I do not mean necessarily that the blending of Heaven and sky, in particular, will turn out to be specially true, but that that kind of blending will accurately mirror the reality which will then exist. There will be no room to get the finest razor blade of thought in between Spirit and Nature. Every state of affairs in the New Nature will be the perfect expression of a spiritual state and every spiritual state the perfect informing of, and bloom upon, a state of affairs; one with it as the perfume with a flower or the "spirit" of great poetry with its form. There is thus in the history of human thought, as elsewhere, a pattern of death and rebirth. The old, richly imaginative thought which still survives in Plato has to submit to the deathlike, but indispensable, process of logical analysis: nature and spirit, matter and mind, fact and myth, the literal and the metaphorical, have to be more and more sharply separated, till at last a purely mathematical universe and a purely subjective mind confront one another across an unbridgeable chasm. But from this descent also, if thought itself is to survive, there must be reascent and the Christian conception provides for it. Those who attain the glorious resurrection will see the dry bones clothed again with flesh, and the fact and the myth remarried, the literal and the metaphorical rushing together.

Christmas and Xmas

CHRISTMAS CARDS in general and the whole vast commercial drive called "Xmas" are one of my pet abominations; I wish they could die away and leave the Christian feast unentangled. Not of course that even secular festivities are, on their own level, an evil; but the labored and organized jollity of this—the spurious childlikeness—the half-hearted and sometimes rather profane attempts to keep up some superficial connection with the Nativity—are disgusting.

Three things go by the name of Christmas. One is a religious festival. This is important and obligatory for Christians; but as it can be of no interest to anyone else, I shall naturally say no more about it here. The second (it has complex historical connections with the first, but we needn't go into them) is a popular holiday, an occasion for merrymaking and hospitality. If it were my business to have a "view" on this, I should say that I much approve of merrymaking. But what I approve of much more is everybody minding his own business. I see no reason why I should volunteer views as to how other people should spend their own money in their own leisure among their own friends. It is highly probable that they want my advice on such matters as little as I want theirs. But the third thing called Christmas is unfortunately everyone's business.

I mean of course the commercial racket. The interchange

of presents was a very small ingredient in the older English festivity. Mr. Pickwick took a cod with him to Dingley Dell; the reformed Scrooge ordered a turkey for his clerk; lovers sent love gifts; toys and fruit were given to children. But the idea that not only all friends but even all acquaintances should give one another presents, or at least send one another cards, is quite modern and has been forced upon us by the shopkeepers. Neither of these circumstances is in itself a reason for condemning it. I condemn it on the following grounds.

1. It gives on the whole much more pain than pleasure. You have only to stay over Christmas with a family who seriously try to "keep" it (in its third, or commercial, aspect) in order to see that the thing is a nightmare. Long before December 25th everyone is worn out—physically worn out by weeks of daily struggle in overcrowded shops, mentally worn out by the effort to remember all the right recipients and to think out suitable gifts for them. They are in no trim for merrymaking; much less (if they should want to) to take part in a religious act. They look far more as if there had been a long illness in the house.

2. Most of it is involuntary. The modern rule is that anyone can force you to give him a present by sending you a quite unprovoked present of his own. It is almost a blackmail. Who has not heard the wail of despair, and indeed of resentment, when, at the last moment, just as everyone hoped that the nuisance was over for one more year, the unwanted gift from Mrs. Busy (whom we hardly remember) flops unwelcomed through the letter-box, and back to the dreadful shops one of us has to go?

3. Things are given as presents which no mortal ever bought for himself—gaudy and useless gadgets, "novelties" because no one was ever fool enough to make their like before. Have we really no better use for materials and for human skill and time than to spend them on all this rubbish?

4. The nuisance. For after all, during the racket we still have all our ordinary and necessary shopping to do, and the racket trebles the labor of it.

We are told that the whole dreary business must go on because it is good for trade. It is in fact merely one annual symptom of that lunatic condition of our country, and indeed of the world, in which everyone lives by persuading everyone else to buy things. I don't know the way out. But can it really be my duty to buy and receive masses of junk every winter just to help the shopkeepers? If the worst comes to the worst I'd sooner give them money for nothing and write it off as a charity. For nothing? Why, better for nothing than for a nuisance.

The Ego and the Self

THE SELF CAN BE regarded in two ways. On the one hand, it is God's creature, an occasion of love and rejoicing; now, indeed, hateful in condition, but to be pitied and healed. On the other hand, it is that one self of all others which is called *I* and *me*, and which on that ground puts forward an irrational claim to preference. This claim is to be not only hated, but simply killed; "never," as George Macdonald says, "to be allowed a moment's respite from eternal death." The Christian must wage endless war against the *ego* as *ego:* but he loves and approves selves as such, though not their sins. The very self-love which he has to reject is to him a specimen of how he ought to feel to all selves; and he may hope that when he has truly learned (which will hardly be in this life) to love his neighbor as himself, he may then be able to love himself as his neighbor: that is, with charity instead of partiality.

The other kind of self-hatred, on the contrary, hates selves as such. It begins by accepting the special value of the particular self called *me;* then, wounded in its pride to find that such a darling object should be so disappointing, it seeks revenge, first upon that self, then on all. Deeply egoistic, but now with an inverted egoism, it uses the revealing argument, "I don't spare myself"—and becomes like the centurion in Tacitus, "more relentless because he had endured it himself."

The wrong asceticism torments the self: the right kind kills the selfness. We must die daily: but it is better to love the self than to love nothing, and to pity the self than to pity no one.

The Airplane, the Wireless, and the Contraceptive

"MAN'S CONQUEST of Nature" is an expression often used to describe the progress of applied science. "Man has Nature whacked" said someone to a friend of mine not long ago. In their context the words had a certain tragic beauty, for the speaker was dying of tuberculosis. "No matter," he said, "I know I'm one of the casualties. Of course there are casualties on the winning as well as on the losing side. But that doesn't alter the fact that it is winning." I have chosen this story as my point of departure in order to make it clear that I do not wish to disparage all that is really beneficial in the process described as "Man's conquest," much less all the real devotion and self-sacrifice that [have] gone to make it possible. But having done so I must proceed to analyze this conception a little more closely. In what sense is Man the possessor of increasing power over Nature?

Let us consider three typical examples: the airplane, the wireless, and the contraceptive. In a civilized community, in peacetime, anyone who can pay for them may use these things. But it cannot strictly be said that when he does so he is exercising his own proper or individual power over Nature. If I pay you to carry me, I am not therefore myself a strong man. Any or all of the three things I have mentioned can be withheld from some men by other men—by those who sell, or those who allow the sale, or those who own the sources of production, or those who make the goods. What we call Man's power is, in reality, a power possessed by some men which they may, or may not, allow other men to profit by. Again, as regards the powers manifested in the airplane or the wireless, Man is as much the patient or subject as the possessor, since he is the target both for bombs and for propaganda. And as regards contraceptives, there is a paradoxical, negative sense in which all possible future generations are the patients or subjects of a power wielded by those already alive. By contraception simply, they are denied existence; by contraception used as a means of selective breeding, they are, without their concurring voice, made to be what one generation, for its own reasons, may choose to prefer. From this point of view, what we call Man's power over Nature turns out to be a power exercised by some men over other men with Nature as its instrument.

It is, of course, a commonplace to complain that men have hitherto used badly, and against their fellows, the powers that science has given them. But that is not the point I am trying to make. I am not speaking of particular corruptions and abuses which an increase of moral virtue would cure: I am considering what the thing called "Man's power over Nature" must always and essentially be. No doubt, the picture could be modified by public ownership of raw materials and factories and public control of scientific research. But unless we have a world state this will still mean the power of one nation over others. And even within the world state or the nation it will mean (in principle) the power of majorities over minorities, and (in the concrete) of a government over the people. And all long-term exercises of power, especially in breeding, must mean the power of earlier generations over later ones.

The latter point is not always sufficiently emphasized, because those who write on social matters have not yet learned to imitate the physicists by always including Time among the dimensions. In order to understand fully what Man's power over Nature, and therefore the power of some men over other men, really means, we must picture the race extended in time from the date of its emergence to that of its extinction. Each generation exercises power over its successors: and each, insofar as it modifies the environment bequeathed to it and rebels against tradition, resists and limits the power of its predecessors. This modifies the picture which is sometimes painted of a progressive emancipation from tradition and a progressive control of natural processes resulting in a continual increase of human power. In reality, of course, if any one age really attains, by eugenics and scientific education, the power to make its descendants what it pleases, all men who live after it are the patients of that power. They are weaker, not stronger: for though we may have put wonderful machines in their hands we have preordained how they are to use them. And if, as is almost certain, the age which had thus attained maximum power over posterity were also the age most emancipated from tradition, it would be engaged in reducing the power of its predecessors almost as drastically as that of its successors. And we must also remember that, quite apart from this, the later a generation comes—the nearer it lives to that date at which the species become extinct—the less power it will have in the forward direction, because its subjects will be so few. There is therefore no question of a power vested in the race as a whole steadily growing as long as the race survives. The last men, far from being the heirs of power, will be of all men most subject to the dead hand of the great planners and conditioners and will themselves exercise least power upon the future. The real picture is that of one dominant age—let us suppose the hundredth century A.D.—which resists all previous ages most sucessfully and dominates all subsequent ages most irresistibly, and thus is the real master of the human species. But even within this master generation (itself an infinitesimal minority of the species) the power will be exercised by a minority smaller still. Man's conquest of Nature, if the dreams of some scientific planners are realized, means the rule of a few hundreds of men over billions upon billions of men. There neither is nor can be any simple increase of power on Man's side. Each new power won *by* man is a power *over* man as well. Each advance leaves him weaker as well as stronger. In every victory, beside being the general who triumphs, he is also the prisoner who follows the triumphal car.

Human Pain

WHEN OUR ANCESTORS referred to pains and sorrows as God's "vengeance" upon sin, they were not necessarily attributing evil passions to God; they may have been recognizing the good element in the idea of retribution. Until the evil man finds evil unmistakably present in his existence, in the form of pain, he is enclosed in illusion. Once pain has roused him, he knows that he is in some way or other "up against" the real universe: he either rebels (with the possibility of a clearer issue and deeper repentance at some later stage) or else makes some attempt at an adjustment, which, if pursued, will lead him to religion. It is true that neither effect is so certain now as it was in ages when the existence of God (or even of the Gods) was more widely known, but even in our own days we see it operating. Even atheists rebel and express, like Hardy and Housman, their rage against God although (or because) He does not in their view, exist: and other atheists, like Mr. Huxley, are driven by suffering to raise the whole problem of existence and to find some way of coming to terms with it which, if not Christian, is almost infinitely superior to fatuous content- ment with a profane life. No doubt Pain as God's mega- phone is a terrible instrument; it may lead to final and unre- pented rebellion. But it gives the only opportunity the bad man can have for amendment. It removes the veil; it plants the flag of truth within the fortress of a rebel soul.

If the first and lowest operation of pain shatters the illu- sion that all is well, the second shatters the illusion that what we have, whether good or bad in itself, is our own and enough for us. Everyone has noticed how hard it is to turn our thought to God when everything is going well with us. We "have all we want" is a terrible saying when "all" does not include God. We find God an interruption. As St. Augustine says somewhere, "God wants to give us something, but cannot, because our hands are full—there's nowhere for Him to put it." Or as a friend of mine said, "We regard God as an airman regards his parachute; it's there for emergencies but he hopes he'll never have to use it." Now God, who has made us, knows what we are and that our happiness lies in Him. Yet we will not seek it in Him as long as He leaves us any other resort where it can even plausibly be looked for. While what we call "our own life" remains agreeable, we will not surrender it to Him. What then can God do in our interests but make "our own life" less agreeable to us, and take away the plausible sources of false happiness? It is just here, where God's providence seems at first to be most cruel, that the Divine humility, the stooping down of the Highest, most deserves praise. We are perplexed to see misfortune falling upon decent, inoffensive, worthy people—on capable, hardworking mothers of families or diligent, thrifty little tradespeople, on those who have worked so hard, and so honestly, for their modest stock of happiness and now seem to be entering on the enjoyment of it with the fullest right. How can I say with sufficient tenderness what here needs to be said? It does not matter that I know I must become, in the eyes of every hostile reader, as it were, personally responsible for all the sufferings I try to explain—just as, to this day, everyone talks as if St. Augustine *wanted* unbaptized infants to go to Hell. But it matters enormously if I alienate anyone from the truth. Let me implore the reader to try to believe, if only for the moment, that God, who made these deserving people, may really be right when He thinks that their modest prosperity and the happiness of their children are not enough to make them blessed: that all this must fall from them in the end, and that if they have not learned to know Him, they will be wretched. And therefore He troubles them, warning them in advance of an insufficiency that one day they will have to discover. The life to themselves and their families stands between them and the recognition of their need; He makes that life less sweet to them.

Animal Pain

THE PROBLEM of animal suffering is appalling; not because the animals are so numerous . . . but because the Christian explanation of human pain cannot be extended to animal pain. So far as we know, beasts are incapable either of sin or virtue: therefore they can neither deserve pain nor be improved by it. . . . From the doctrine that God is good we may confidently deduce that the *appearance* of reckless divine cruelty in the animal kingdom is an illusion, and the fact that the only suffering we know at first hand (our own) turns out not to be a cruelty will make it easier to believe this. After that, everything is guesswork.

Suffering

ALL ARGUMENTS in justification of suffering provide bitter resentment against the author. You would like to know how I behave when I am experiencing pain, not writing books about it. You need not guess, for I will tell you; I am a great coward. But what is that to the purpose? When I think of pain—of anxiety that gnaws like fire and loneliness that spreads out like a desert, and the heartbreaking routine of monotonous misery, or again of dull aches that blacken our whole landscape or sudden nauseating pains that knock a man's heart out at one blow, of pains that seem already intolerable and then are suddenly increased, of infuriating scorpion-stinging pains that startle into maniacal movement a man who seems half dead with his previous tortures—it "quite o'ercrows my spirit." If I knew any way of escape I would crawl through sewers to find it. But what is the good of telling you about my feelings? You know them already: they are the same as yours. I am not arguing that pain is not painful. Pain hurts. That is what the word means. I am only trying to show that the old Christian doctrine of being made "perfect through suffering" (Hebrews 2:10) is not incredible. To prove it palatable is beyond my design.

In estimating the credibility of the doctrine two principles ought to be observed. In the first place, we must remember that the actual moment of present pain is only the center of what may be called the whole tribulational system which extends itself by fear and pity. Whatever good effects these experiences have are dependent upon the center; so that even if pain itself was of no spiritual value, yet, if fear and pity were, pain would have to exist in order that there should be something to be feared and pitied. And that fear and pity help us in our return to obedience and charity is not to be doubted. Everyone has experienced the effect of pity in making it easier for us to love the unlovely—that is, to love men not because they are in any way naturally agreeable to us but because they are our brethren. . . .

In the second place, when we are considering pain itself . . . we must be careful to attend to what we know and not to what we imagine. . . . About human pain we know, about animal pain we can only speculate. But even within the human race we must draw our evidence from instances that have come under our own observation. The tendency of this or that novelist or poet may represent suffering as wholly bad in its effects, as producing, and justifying, every kind of malice and brutality in the sufferer. And, of course, pain, like pleasure, can be so received: all that is given to a creature with free will must be two-edged, not by the nature of the giver or of the gift, but by the nature of the recipient. And, again, the evil results of pain can be multiplied if sufferers are persistently taught by the bystanders that such results are the proper and manly results for them to exhibit. Indignation at others' sufferings, though a generous passion, needs to be well managed lest it steal away patience and humility from those who suffer and plant anger and cynicism in their stead. But I am not convinced that suffering, if spared such officious vicarious indignation, has any natural tendency to produce such evils. I did not find the frontline trenches or the C.C.S. more full of hatred, selfishness, rebellion, and dishonesty than any other place. I have seen great beauty of spirit in some who were great sufferers. I have seen men, for the most part, grow better not worse with advancing years, and I have seen the last illness produce treasures of fortitude and meekness from most unpromising subjects. I see in loved and revered historical figures, such as Johnson and Cowper, traits which might scarcely have been tolerable if the men had been happier. If the world is indeed a "vale of soul-making," it seems on the whole to be doing its work.

The Crown and the Cross

MY MEMORIES of the last war haunted my dreams for years. Military service, to be plain, includes the threat of every *temporal* evil; pain and death which is what we fear from sickness: isolation from those we love which is what we fear from exile: toil under arbitrary masters, injustice, humiliation, which is what we fear from slavery: hunger, thirst, and exposure which is what we fear from poverty. I'm not a pacifist. If it's got to be, it's got to be. But the flesh is weak and selfish and I think death would be much better than to live through another war. Thank God He has not allowed my *faith* to be greatly tempted by the present horrors. I do not doubt that whatever misery He permits will be for our ultimate good unless by rebellious will we convert it to evil. But I get no further than Gethsemane: and am daily thankful that that scene of all others in our Lord's life did not go unrecorded. But what state of affairs in this world can we view with satisfaction? If we are unhappy, then we are unhappy. If we are happy, then we remember that the crown is not promised without the Cross and tremble. In fact one comes to realize what one always admitted theoretically, that there is nothing here that will do us good: the sooner we are safely out of this world the better. But "would it were evening, Hal, and all was well." I have even (I'm afraid) caught myself wishing that I had never been born, which is sinful. Also meaningless if you think it out.

The process of living seems to consist in coming to realize truths so ancient and simple that, if stated, they sound like barren platitudes. They cannot sound otherwise to those who have not had the relevant experience: that is why there is no real teaching of such truths possible and every generation starts from scratch. . . .

Death

HUMAN DEATH, according to the Christians, is a result of a human sin; Man, as originally created, was immune from it: Man, when redeemed, and recalled to a new life (which will, in some undefined sense, be a bodily life) in the midst of a more organic and more fully obedient Nature, will be immune from it again. This doctrine is, of course, simply nonsense if a man is nothing but a Natural organism. But if he were, then, as we have seen, all thoughts would be equally nonsensical, for all would have irrational causes. Man must therefore be a composite being—a natural organism tenanted by, or in a state of *symbiosis* with, a supernatural spirit. The Christian doctrine, startling as it must seem to those who have not fully cleared their minds of Naturalism, states that the relations which we now observe between that spirit and that organism, are abnormal or pathological ones. At present spirit can retain its foothold against the incessant counterattacks of Nature (both physiological and psychological) only by perpetual vigilance, and physiological Nature always defeats it in the end. Sooner or later it becomes unable to resist the disintegrating processes at work in the body and death ensues. A little later the Natural organism (for it does not long enjoy its triumph) is similarly conquered by merely physical Nature and returns to the inorganic. But, on the Christian view, this was not always so. The spirit was once not a garrison, maintaining its post with difficulty in a hostile Nature, but was fully "at home" with its organism, like a king in his own country or a rider on his own horse—or better still, as the human part of a Centaur was "at home" with the equine part. Where spirit's power over the organism was complete and unresisted, death would never occur. No doubt, spirit's permanent triumph over natural forces which, if left to themselves, would kill the organism, would involve a continued miracle: but only the same sort of miracle which occurs every day—for whenever we think rationally we are, by direct spiritual power, forcing certain atoms in our brain and certain psychological tendencies in our natural soul to do what they would never have done if left to Nature. The Christian doctrine would be fantastic only if the present frontier situation between spirit and Nature in each human being were so intelligible and self-explanatory that we just "saw" it to be the only one that could ever have existed. But is it?

In reality the frontier situation is so odd that nothing but custom could make it seem natural, and nothing but the Christian doctrine can make it fully intelligible. There is certainly a state of war. But not a war of mutual destruction. Nature by dominating spirit wrecks all spiritual activities: Spirit by dominating Nature confirms and improves natural activities. The brain does not become less a brain by being used for rational thought. The emotions do not become weak or jaded by being organized in the service of a moral will—indeed they grow richer and stronger as a beard is strengthened by being shaved or a river is deepened by being banked. The body of the reasonable and virtuous man, other things being equal, is a better body than that of the fool or the debauchee, and his sensuous pleasures better simply as sensuous pleasures: for the slaves of the senses, after the first bait, are starved by their masters. Everything happens as if what we saw was not war, but rebellion: that rebellion of the lower against the higher by which the lower destroys both the higher and itself. And if the present situation is one of rebellion, then reason cannot reject but will rather demand the belief that there was a time before the rebellion broke out and may be a time after it has been settled. And if we thus see grounds for believing that the supernatural spirit and the natural organism in Man have quarreled, we shall immediately find it confirmed from two quite unexpected quarters.

Almost the whole of Christian theology could perhaps be deduced from the two facts (a) That men make coarse jokes, and (b) That they feel the dead to be uncanny. The coarse joke proclaims that we have here an animal which finds its own animality either objectionable or funny. Unless there had been a quarrel between the spirit and the organism, I do not see how this could be: it is the very mark of the two not being "at home" together. But it is very difficult to imagine such a state of affairs as original—to suppose a creature which from the very first was half shocked and half tickled to death at the mere fact of being the creature it is. I do not perceive that dogs see anything funny about being dogs: I suspect that angels see nothing funny about being angels. Our feeling about the dead is equally odd. It is idle to say that we dislike corpses because we are afraid of ghosts. You might say with equal truth that we fear ghosts and dislike corpses—for the ghost owes much of its horror to the associated ideas of pallor, decay, coffins, shrouds, and worms. In reality we hate the division which makes possible the conception of either corpse or ghost. Because the thing ought not to be divided, each of the halves into which it falls by division is detestable. The explanations which Naturalism gives both of bodily shame and of our feeling about the dead are not satisfactory. It refers us to primitive taboos and superstitions—as if these themselves were not obviously results of the thing to be explained. But once accept the Christian doctrine that man was originally a unity and that the present division is unnatural, and all the phenomena fall into place. It would be fantastic to suggest that the doctrine was devised to explain our enjoyment of a chapter in Rabelais, a good ghost story, or the *Tales* of Edgar Allan Poe. It does so nonetheless.

Judgment

IF THERE IS ANY THOUGHT at which a Christian trembles, it is the thought of God's "judgment." The "Day" of Judgment is "that day of wrath, that dreadful day." We pray to God to deliver us "in the hour of death and at the day of judgment." Christian art and literature for centuries have depicted its terrors. This note in Christianity certainly goes back to the teaching of Our Lord Himself; especially to the terrible parable of the Sheep and the Goats. This can leave no conscience untouched, for in it the "Goats" are condemned entirely for their sins of omission; as if to make us fairly sure that the heaviest charge against each of us turns not upon things he has done but on those he never did— perhaps never dreamed of doing.

It was therefore with great surprise that I first noticed how the Psalmists talk about the judgments of God. They talk like this: "O let the nations rejoice and be glad, for thou shalt judge the folk righteously" (Psalm 67:4), "Let the field be joyful . . . all the trees of the wood shall rejoice before the Lord, for he cometh, for he cometh to judge the earth" (Psalm 96:12,13). Judgment is apparently an occasion of universal rejoicing. People ask for it: "Judge me, O Lord my God, according to thy righteousness" (Psalm 35:24).

The reason for this soon becomes very plain. The ancient Jews, like ourselves, think of God's judgment in terms of an earthly court of justice. The difference is that the Christian pictures the case to be tried as a criminal case with himself as the plaintiff. The one hopes for acquittal, or rather for pardon; the other hopes for a resounding triumph with heavy damages. Hence he prays "judge my quarrel" or "avenge my cause" (Psalm 35:23). And though, as I said a minute ago, Our Lord in the parable of the Sheep and the Goats painted the characteristically Christian picture in another place, He is very characteristically Jewish. Notice what He means by "an unjust judge." By those words most of us would mean someone like Judge Jeffreys or the creatures who sat on the benches of German tribunals during the Nazi regime: someone who bullies witnesses and jurymen in order to convict, and then savagely to punish, innocent men. Once again, we are thinking of a criminal trial. We hope we shall never appear in the dock before such a judge. But the Unjust Judge in the parable is quite a different character. There is no danger of appearing in his court against your will: the difficulty is the opposite—to get into it. It is clearly a civil action. The poor woman (Luke 18:1–5) has had her little strip of land—room for a pigsty or a hen-run— taken away from her by a richer and more powerful neighbor (nowadays it would be Town Planners or some other "Body"). And she knows she has a perfectly watertight case. If once she could get it into court and have it tried by the laws of the land, she would be bound to get that strip back. But no one will listen to her, she can't get it tried. No wonder she is anxious for "judgment."

Behind this lies an age-old and almost worldwide experience which we have been spared. In most places and times it has been very difficult for the "small man" to get his case heard. The judge (and, doubtless, one or two of his underlings) has to be bribed. If you can't afford to "oil his palm," your case will never reach court. Our judges do not receive bribes. (We probably take this blessing too much for granted; it will not remain with us automatically). We need not therefore be surprised if the Psalms, and the Prophets, are full of longing for judgment, and regard the announcement that "judgment" is coming as good news. Hundreds of thousands of people who have been stripped of all they possess and who have the right entirely on their side will at last be heard. Of course, they are not afraid of judgment. They know their case is unanswerable—if only it could be heard. When God comes to judge, at last it will.

Resurrection of the Body

THE OLD PICTURE of the soul reassuming the corpse—perhaps blown to bits or long since usefully dissipated through nature—is absurd. Nor is it what St. Paul's words imply. And I admit that if you ask me what I substitute for this, I have only speculations to offer.

The principle behind these speculations is this. We are not, in this doctrine, concerned with matter as such at all; with waves and atoms and all that. What the soul cries out for is the resurrection of the senses. Even in this life matter would be nothing to us if it were not the source of sensations.

Now we already have some feeble and intermittent power

of raising dead sensations from their graves. I mean, of course, memory.

You see the way my thought is moving. But don't run away with the idea that when I speak of the resurrection of the body I mean merely that the blessed dead will have excellent memories of their sensuous experience on earth. I mean it the other way round: that memory as we now know it is a dim foretaste, a mirage even, of a power which the soul, or rather Christ in the soul (He went to "prepare a place" for us), will exercise hereafter. It need no longer be intermittent. Above all, it need no longer be private to the soul in which it occurs. . . .

At present we tend to think of the soul as somehow "inside" the body. But the glorified body of the resurrection as I conceive it—the sensuous life raised from its death—will be inside the soul. As God is not in space but space is in God. . . .

I don't say the resurrection of this body will happen at once. It may well be that this part of us sleeps in death, and the intellectual soul is sent to Lenten lands where she fasts in naked spirituality—a ghostlike and imperfectly human condition. I don't imply that an angel is a ghost. But naked spirituality is in accordance with His nature; not, I think, with ours. (A two-legged horse is maimed, but not a two-legged man.) Yet from that fast my hope is that we shall return and reassume the wealth we have laid down.

Then the new earth and sky, the same yet not the same as these, will rise in us as we have risen in Christ. And once again, after who knows what eons of the silence and the dark, the birds will sing and the waters flow, and lights and shadows move across the hills, and the faces of our friends laugh upon us with amazed recognition.

Guesses, of course, only guesses. If they are not true, something better will be. For "we know that we shall be made like Him, for we shall see Him as He is."

Purgatory

Our souls *demand* Purgatory, don't they? Would it not break the heart if God said to us, "It is true, my son, that your breath smells and your rags drip with mud and slime, but we are charitable here and no one will upbraid you with these things, nor draw away from you. Enter into the joy"? Should we not reply, "With submission, sir, and if there is no objection, I'd *rather* be cleaned first." "It may hurt, you know"—"Even so, sir."

I assume that the process of purification will normally involve suffering. Partly from tradition; partly because most real good that has been done me in this life has involved it. But I don't think suffering is the purpose of the purgation. I can well believe that people neither much worse nor much better than I will suffer less than I or more. "No nonsense about merit." The treatment given will be the one required, whether it hurts little or much.

My favorite image on this matter comes from the dentist's chair. I hope that when the tooth of life is drawn and I am "coming round," a voice will say, "Rinse your mouth out with this." *This* will be a Purgatory.

Hell

I am not going to try to prove the doctrine tolerable. Let us make no mistake; it is *not* tolerable. But I think the doctrine can be shown to be moral by a critique of the objections ordinarily made, or felt, against it.

First, there is an objection, in many minds, to the idea of retributive punishment as such. . . . Let us try to be honest with ourselves. Picture to yourself a man who has risen to wealth or power by a continued course of treachery and cruelty, by exploiting for purely selfish ends the noble motions of his victims, laughing the while at their simplicity; who, having thus attained success, uses it for the gratification of lust and hatred and finally parts with the last rag of honor among thieves by betraying his own accomplices and jeering at their last moments of bewildered disillusionment. Suppose further, that he does all this, not (as we like to imagine) tormented by remorse or even misgiving, but eating like a schoolboy and sleeping like a healthy infant—a jolly, ruddy-cheeked man, without a care in the world, unshakably confident to the very end that he alone has found the answer to the riddle of life, that God and man are fools whom he has got the better of, that his way of life is utterly successful, satisfactory, unassailable. We must be careful at this point. The least indulgence of the passion for revenge is very deadly sin. Christian charity counsels us to make every effort for the conversion of such a man: to prefer his conversion, at the peril of our own lives, perhaps of our own souls, to his punishment; to prefer it infinitely. But that is not the question. Supposing he *will* not be converted, what destiny in the eternal world can you regard as proper for him? Can you really desire that such a man, *remaining what he is* (and he must be able to do that if he has free will) should be confirmed forever in his present happiness—should continue, for all eternity, to be perfectly convinced that the laugh is on his side? And if you cannot regard this as tolerable, is it only your wickedness—only spite—that prevents you from doing so? Or do you find that conflict between Justice and Mercy, which has sometimes seemed to you such an outmoded piece of theology, now actually at work in your own mind, and feeling very much as if it came to you from above, not from below? You are moved, not by a desire for the wretched creature's pain as such, but by a truly ethical demand that, soon or late, the right should be asserted, the flag planted in this horribly rebellious soul, even if no fuller and better conquest is to follow. In a sense, it is better for the creature itself, even if it never becomes good, that it should know itself a failure, a mistake. Even mercy can hardly wish to such a man his eternal, contented continuance in such ghastly illusion. Thomas Aquinas said of suffering, as Aristotle had said of shame, that it was a thing not good in itself, but a thing which might have a certain goodness in particular circumstances. That is to say, if evil is present, pain at recognition of the evil, being a kind of knowledge, is relatively good; for the alternative is that the soul should be ignorant of the evil, or ignorant that the evil is contrary to its nature, "either of which," says the philosopher, "is *manifestly* bad." And I think, though we tremble, we agree. . . .

Another objection turns on the apparent disproportion between eternal damnation and transitory sin. And if we think of eternity as a mere prolongation of time, it is disproportionate. But many would reject this idea of eternity. If we think of time as a line—which is a good image, because the parts of time are successive and no two of them can coexist; that is, there is no *width* in time, only length— we probably ought to think of eternity as a plane or even a solid. Thus the whole reality of a human being would be represented by a solid figure. That solid would be mainly the work of God, acting through grace and nature, but human free will would have contributed the base line which we call earthly life: and if you draw your base line askew, the whole solid will be in the wrong place. The fact that life is short, or, in the symbol, that we contribute only one little line to the whole complex figure, might be regarded as a Divine mercy. For even if the drawing of that little line, left to our free will, is sometimes so badly done as to spoil the whole, how much worse a mess might we have made of the figure if more had been entrusted to us? . . .

A third objection turns on the frightful intensity of the pains of Hell as suggested by medieval art and, indeed, by certain passages in Scripture. Von Hügel here warns us not to confuse the doctrine itself with the *imagery* by which it may be conveyed. Our Lord speaks of Hell under three symbols: first, that of punishment ("everlasting punishment," Matthew 25:46); second, that of destruction ("fear Him who is able to destroy both body and soul in hell," Matthew 10:28); and thirdly, that of privation, exclusion, or banishment into "the darkness outside," as in the parables of the man without a wedding garment or of the wise and foolish virgins. The prevalent idea of fire is significant because it combines the ideas of torment and destruction. Now it is quite certain that all these expressions are intended to suggest something unspeakably horrible, and any interpretation which does not face that fact is, I am afraid, out of court from the beginning. But it is not necessary to concentrate on the images of torture to the exclusion of those suggesting destruction and privation. What can that be whereof all three images are equally proper symbols? Destruction, we should naturally assume, means the unmaking, or cessation, of the destroyed. And people often talk as if the "annihilation" of a soul were intrinsically possible. In all our experience, however, the destruction of one thing means the emergence of something else. Burn a log, and you have gases, heat, and ash. To *have been* a log means now being those three things. If soul can be destroyed, must there not be a state of *having been* a human soul? And is not that, perhaps, the state which is equally well described as torment, destruction, and privation? . . .

A fourth objection is that no charitable man could himself be blessed in Heaven while he knew that even one human soul was still in Hell; and if so, are we more merciful than

God? At the back of this objection lies a mental picture of Heaven and Hell coexisting in unilinear time as the histories of England and America coexist: so that at each moment the blessed could say "The miseries of Hell are *now* going on." But I notice that Our Lord, while stressing the terror of Hell with unsparing severity, usually emphasizes the idea, not of duration but of *finality*. Consignment to the destroying fire is usually treated as the end of the story— not as the beginning of a new story. That the lost soul is eternally fixed in its diabolical attitude we cannot doubt: but whether this eternal fixity implies endless duration—or duration at all—we cannot say. . . .

Finally, it is objected that the ultimate loss of a single soul means the defeat of omnipotence. And so it does. In creating beings with free will, omnipotence from the outset submits to the possibility of such defeat. What you call defeat, I call miracle: for to make things which are not Itself, and thus to become, in a sense, capable of being resisted by its own handiwork, is the most astonishing and unimaginable of all the feats we attribute to the Deity. I willingly believe that the damned are, in one sense, successful, rebels to the end; that the doors of Hell are locked on the *inside*. I do not mean that the ghosts may not *wish* to come out of Hell, in the vague fashion wherein an envious man "wishes" to be happy: but they certainly do not will even the first preliminary stages of that self-abandonment through which alone the soul can reach any good. They enjoy forever the horrible freedom they have demanded, and are therefore self-enslaved just as the blessed, forever submitting to obedience, become through all eternity more and more free.

Heaven

SCRIPTURE AND TRADITION habitually put the joys of Heaven into the scale against the sufferings of earth, and no solution of the problem of pain which does not do so can be called a Christian one. We are very shy nowadays of even mentioning Heaven. We are afraid of the jeer about "pie in the sky," and of being told that we are trying to "escape" from the duty of making a happy world here and now into dreams of a happy world elsewhere. But either there is "pie in the sky" or there is not. If there is not, then Christianity is false, for this doctrine is woven into its whole fabric. If there is, then this truth, like any other, must be faced, whether it is useful at political meetings or no. Again, we are afraid that Heaven is a bribe, and that if we make it our goal we shall no longer be disinterested. It is not so. Heaven offers nothing that a mercenary soul can desire. It is safe to tell the pure in heart that they shall see God, for only the pure in heart want to. There are rewards that do not sully motives. A man's love for a woman is not mercenary because he wants to marry her, nor his love for poetry mercenary because he wants to read it, nor his love of exercise less disinterested because he wants to run and leap and walk. Love, by definition, seeks to enjoy its object.

I do *not* think that the life of Heaven bears any analogy to play or dance in respect of frivolity. I do think that while we are in this "valley of tears," cursed with labor, hemmed round with necessities, tripped up with frustrations, doomed to perpetual plannings, puzzlings, and anxieties, certain qualities that must belong to the celestial condition have no chance to get through, can project no image of themselves, except in activities which, for us here and now, are frivolous. For surely we must suppose the life of the blessed to be an end in itself, indeed The End: to be utterly spontaneous; to be the complete reconciliation of boundless freedom with order—with the most delicately adjusted, supple, intricate, and beautiful order? How can you find any image of this in the "serious" activities either of our natural or of our (present) spiritual life? Either in our precariousness and heartbroken affections or in the Way which is always, in some degree, a *via crucis?* No. . . . It is only in our "hours off," only in our moments of permitted festivity, that we find an analogy. Dance and game *are* frivolous, unimportant down here; for "down here" is not their natural place. Here, they are a moment's rest from the life we were placed here to live. But in this world everything is upside down. That which, if it could be prolonged here, would be a truancy, is likest that which in a better country is the End of Ends. Joy is the serious business of Heaven.

Bibliography

BOOKS QUOTED IN THE TEXT

The Abolition of Man: Reflections on Education with Special Reference to the Teaching of English in the Upper Forms of Schools.
    London: Geoffrey Bles, 1946.
    New York: Macmillan Publishing Co., Inc., 1947.
    New York: Macmillan Paperback, 1965.
Christian Reflections. Edited by Walter Hooper.
    Grand Rapids: W. B. Eerdmans Publishing Co., 1967.
The Four Loves.
    London: Geoffrey Bles, 1960.
    New York: Harcourt Brace Jovanovich, 1960.
    New York: HBJ Paperback, 1971.
God in the Dock: Essays in Theology and Ethics. Edited, with a Preface, by Walter Hooper.
    London: Geoffrey Bles, 1970; published as *Undeceptions.*
    Grand Rapids: W. B. Eerdmans Publishing Co., 1970.

A Grief Observed.

> London: Faber and Faber Limited, 1961. Published under the pseudonym N. W. Clerk.
>
> New York: The Seabury Press, Inc., 1963. Published under the pseudonym N. W. Clerk.
>
> New York: Bantam Books, 1976. Published under the name C. S. Lewis, with an Afterword by Chad Walsh.

Letters of C. S. Lewis. Edited, with a Memoir, by W. H. Lewis.

> London: Geoffrey Bles, 1975.
>
> New York: Harcourt Brace Jovanovich, 1975.
>
> New York: HBJ Paperback, 1975.

Letters to an American Lady. Edited by Clyde Kilby.

> Grand Rapids: W. B. Eerdmans Publishing Co., 1967.
>
> New York: Pyramid Books, 1971.

Letters to Malcolm: Chiefly on Prayer.

> London: Geoffrey Bles, 1964.
>
> New York: Harcourt Brace Jovanovich, 1964.
>
> New York: HBJ Paperback, 1973.

Mere Christianity. A revised and enlarged edition, with a new introduction, of the three books *The Case for Christianity* (London: Geoffrey Bles, 1942; New York: Macmillan, 1943), *Christian Behavior* (London: Geoffrey Bles, 1943; New York: Macmillan, 1943), and *Beyond Personality* (London: Geoffrey Bles, 1944; New York: Macmillan, 1945).

> London: Geoffrey Bles, 1952.
>
> New York: Macmillan Publishing Co., Inc., 1952.
>
> New York: Macmillan Paperback, 1960.

Miracles: A Preliminary Study.

> London: Geoffrey Bles, 1947.
>
> New York: Macmillan Publishing Co., Inc., 1947.
>
> New York: Macmillan Paperback, 1963.

The Problem of Pain.

> London: Geoffrey Bles, 1940.
>
> New York: Macmillan Publishing Co., Inc., 1943.
>
> New York: Macmillan Paperback, 1962.

Reflections on the Psalms.

> London: Geoffrey Bles, 1958.
>
> New York: Harcourt Brace Jovanovich, 1958.
>
> New York: HBJ Paperback, 1964.

The Screwtape Letters.

> London: Geoffrey Bles, 1942.

New York: Macmillan Publishing Co., Inc., 1943.

New York: Macmillan Paperback, 1959.

The Screwtape Letters, with Screwtape Proposes a Toast. With a new and additional Preface.

New York: Macmillan Publishing Co., Inc., 1964.

New York: Macmillan Paperback, 1962.

Undeceptions. See *God in the Dock*.

Transposition. See *The Weight of Glory*.

The Weight of Glory and Other Addresses.

London: Geoffrey Bles, 1949; published as *Transposition and Other Addresses*.

New York: Macmillan Publishing Co., Inc., 1949.

Grand Rapids: W. B. Eerdmans Publishing Co., 1965.

The World's Last Night and Other Essays.

New York: Harcourt Brace Jovanovich, 1960.

New York: HBJ Paperback, 1973.

BOOKS NOT QUOTED IN THE TEXT

The Allegory of Love: A Study in Medieval Tradition.

London: Oxford University Press, 1936, 1938.

New York: OUP Paperback, 1958.

The Chronicles of Narnia. Boxed set of 7 paperbacks.

New York: Collier Books, 1970.

The Dark Tower and Other Stories. Edited, and with a Preface, by Walter Hooper.

London: Collins Publishers, 1977.

New York: Harcourt Brace Jovanovich, 1977.

The Discarded Image: An Introduction to Medieval and Renaissance Literature.

Cambridge: Cambridge University Press, 1964.

Dymer.

London: J. M. Dent, 1926; published under the pseudonym Clive Hamilton.

New York: E. P. Dutton, 1926.

New York: Macmillan Publishing Co., Inc., 1950.

English Literature in the Sixteenth Century, Excluding Drama.

Oxford: Clarendon Press, 1954.

An Experiment in Criticism.

Cambridge: Cambridge University Press, 1961.

The Great Divorce.
    London: Geoffrey Bles, 1945.
    New York: Macmillan Publishing Co., Inc., 1946.
    New York: Macmillan Paperback, 1963.
The Horse and His Boy. Book 5 in *The Chronicles of Narnia.* Illustrated by Pauline Baynes.
    London: The Bodley Head, 1956.
    New York: Macmillan Publishing Co., Inc., 1954.
    New York: Collier Books, 1970.
The Last Battle. Book 7 in *The Chronicles of Narnia.* Illustrated by Pauline Baynes.
    London: The Bodley Head, 1956.
    New York: Macmillan Publishing Co., Inc., 1956.
    New York: Collier Books, 1970.
The Lion, The Witch, and The Wardrobe. Book 1 in *The Chronicles of Narnia.* Illustrated by Pauline Baynes.
    London: Geoffrey Bles, 1950.
    New York: Macmillan Publishing Co., Inc., 1950.
    New York: Collier Books, 1970.
The Magician's Nephew. Book 6 in *The Chronicles of Narnia.* Illustrated by Pauline Baynes.
    London: The Bodley Head, 1955.
    New York: Macmillan Publishing Co., Inc., 1955.
    New York: Collier Books, 1970.
A Mind Awake: An Anthology of C. S. Lewis. Edited by Clyde S. Kilby.
    New York: Harcourt Brace Jovanovich, 1968.
Narrative Poems. Edited by Walter Hooper.
    London: Geoffrey Bles, 1969.
    New York: Harcourt Brace Jovanovich, 1972.
Of Other Worlds: Essays and Stories. Edited, with a Preface, by Walter Hooper.
    New York: Harcourt Brace Jovanovich, 1966.
    New York: HBJ Paperback, 1975.
Out of the Silent Planet. Book 1 of *The Space Trilogy.*
    London: John Lane, 1938.
    New York: Macmillan Publishing Co., Inc., 1943.
    New York: Macmillan Paperback, 1965.
Perelandra. Book 2 of *The Space Trilogy.*
    London: John Lane, 1943.
    New York: Macmillan Publishing Co., Inc., 1944.
    New York: Macmillan Paperback, 1965.

The Pilgrim's Regress: An Allegorical Apology for Christianity, Reason, and Romanticism.
>London: J. M. Dent, 1933.
>New York: Sheed and Ward, 1935.
>With the author's important new Preface on Romanticism, footnotes, and running headlines.
>London: Geoffrey Bles, 1943.
>New York: Sheed and Ward, 1944.
>Grand Rapids: W. B. Eerdmans Publishing Co., 1958.

A Preface to "Paradise Lost."
>New York: Oxford University Press, 1942.
>London: Oxford University Press, 1942.

Poems. Edited by Walter Hooper.
>London: Geoffrey Bles, 1964.
>New York: Harcourt Brace Jovanovich, 1965.

Prince Caspian. Book 2 in *The Chronicles of Narnia.* Illustrated by Pauline Baynes.
>London: Geoffrey Bles, 1951.
>New York: Macmillan Publishing Co., Inc., 1951.
>New York: Collier Books, 1970.

Rehabilitations and Other Essays.
>Oxford, London: Oxford University Press, 1934.

Selected Literary Essays.
>Cambridge, London: Cambridge University Press, 1969.

The Silver Chair. Book 4 in *The Chronicles of Narnia.* Illustrated by Pauline Baynes.
>London: Geoffrey Bles, 1953.
>New York: Macmillan Publishing Co., Inc., 1953.
>New York: Collier Books, 1970.

The Space Trilogy. Boxed paperback set of *Out of the Silent Planet, Perelandra,* and *That Hideous Strength.*
>New York: Macmillan Paperback, 1975.

Spenser's Images of Life.
>Cambridge, London: Cambridge University Press, 1967.

Studies in Words.
>Cambridge: Cambridge University Press, 1960; second edition, 1966.

That Hideous Strength. Book 3 of *The Space Trilogy.*
>London: John Lane, 1945.
>New York: Macmillan Publishing Co., Inc., 1946.
>New York: Macmillan Paperback, 1965.

They Asked for a Paper.
>London: Geoffrey Bles, 1962.

Till We Have Faces: A Myth Retold.
>London: Geoffrey Bles, 1956.
>New York: Harcourt Brace Jovanovich, 1957.
>Grand Rapids: WBE Paperback, 1966.

The Voyage of the "Dawn Treader." Book 3 of *The Chronicles of Narnia.* Illustrated by Pauline Baynes.
>London: Geoffrey Bles, 1952.
>New York: Macmillan Publishing Co., Inc., 1952.
>New York: Collier Books, 1970.

BOOKS ABOUT C. S. LEWIS

Arnott, Anne. *The Secret Country of C. S. Lewis.* Illustrated by Patricia Frost.
>Grand Rapids: W. B. Eerdmans Publishing Co., 1975.

Carnell, Corbin Scott. *Bright Shadow of Reality: C. S. Lewis and the Feeling Intellect.*
>Grand Rapids: W. B. Eerdmans Publishing Co., 1974.

Gibb, Jocelyn, ed. *Light on C. S. Lewis.* Essays by Owen Barfield, Austin Farrer, J. A. W. Bennett, Nevill Coghill, John Lawlor, Stella Gibbons, Kathleen Raine, Chad Walsh, Walter Hooper.
>London: Geoffrey Bles, 1965.
>New York: HBJ Harvest Book, 1976.

Gilbert, Douglas and Kilby, Clyde S. *C. S. Lewis: Images of His World.*
>Grand Rapids: W. B. Eerdmans Publishing Co., 1973.

Green, Roger Lancelyn and Hooper, Walter. *C. S. Lewis: A Biography.*
>New York: Harcourt Brace Jovanovich, 1974.

Holmer, Paul L. *C. S. Lewis: The Shape of His Faith and Thought.*
>New York: Harper & Row, 1976.

Keefe, Carolyn, ed. *C. S. Lewis: Speaker and Teacher.* Foreword by Thomas Howard. Grand Rapids: Zondervan Publishing House, 1971.

Kilby, Clyde S. *The Christian World of C. S. Lewis.*
>Grand Rapids: W. B. Eerdmans Publishing Co., 1964.

Lindskoog, Kathryn Ann. *C. S. Lewis: Mere Christian.* Foreword by Clyde S. Kilby.
>Glendale, Ca.: G/L Publications, 1973.

————. *The Lion of Judah in Never-Never Land: The Theology*

of C. S. Lewis Expressed in His Fantasies for Children. With a Preface by Walter Hooper.

Grand Rapids: W. B. Eerdmans Publishing Co., 1973.

Montgomery, John Warwick, ed. *Myth, Allegory, and Gospel: An Interpretation of J. R. R. Tolkien, C. S. Lewis, G. K. Chesterton, Charles Williams.* Essays by Edmund Fuller, Clyde S. Kilby, Russell Kirk, John W. Montgomery, and Chad Walsh.

Minneapolis: Bethany Fellowship, Inc., 1974.

Schakel, Peter J., Editor. *The Longing for a Form: Essays on the Fiction of C. S. Lewis.*

Kent, Ohio: Kent State University Press, 1977.

Walsh, Chad. *C. S. Lewis: Apostle to the Skeptics.*

New York: Macmillan Publishing Co., Inc., 1949.

Folcraft, Pa.: Folcraft Library Editions, 1974.

Sources

The page numbers cited below refer to the paperback editions of C. S. Lewis's works currently available in American bookstores.

Affection	*The Four Loves*, 56–57
Agape or Charity	*The Four Loves*, 175–178
Almsgiving	*Mere Christianity*, 81–82
Animal Pain	*The Problem of Pain*, 129–130
Answered Prayers	*Letters to Malcolm*, 57–60
Anxiety	*Letters to Malcolm*, 41–43
Apologetics	*God in the Dock*, 89–96, 98–99, 103
Appreciative Love	*The Four Loves*, 33
Atheism	*Mere Christianity*, 45–46
Begetting and Making	*Mere Christianity*, 138–140
Belief	*Mere Christianity*, 121–124
Belief and Disbelief	*The World's Last Night*, 14–17
Biblical Exegesis	*Letters to Malcolm*, 51–52
Charity	*Mere Christianity*, 115–117
Chastity	*Mere Christianity*, 89–91

Christmas and Xmas — *Letters of C. S. Lewis*, 265
God in the Dock, 304–305

Christian Society — *Mere Christianity*, 79–80
Church Music — *Christian Reflections*, 96–97
Death — *Miracles*, 130–133
Devotions to Saints — *Letters to Malcolm*, 15–16
Divine Goodness — *The Problem of Pain*, 39–41
Divine Omnipotence — *The Problem of Pain*, 26–28
Divorce — *Mere Christianity*, 96
Ecumenism — *Letters to an American Lady*, 11–12

Eros and Venus — *The Four Loves*, 131–134, 140–142
Everythingism — *Miracles*, 171–172
Faith — *Mere Christianity*, 127–128
Faith and Good Works — *Mere Christianity*, 129–130
Fascism and Communism — *Letters of C. S. Lewis*, 176
Festooning Ready-made Prayers — *Letters to Malcolm*, 24–26
First Fervor — *Letters to Malcolm*, 26–27
Forgiveness — *Mere Christianity*, 104–106
Gift-love and Need-love — *The Four Loves*, 11–12
God in Outer Space — *Christian Reflections*, 167, 171
Good Work and Good Works — *The World's Last Night*, 71–72
Guilt — *Letters to Malcolm*, 32–34
Heaven — *The Problem of Pain*, 144–145, 92–93

Hell — *The Problem of Pain*, 120–128
Holy Communion — *Letters to Malcolm*, 101–102, 104–105

Hope — *Mere Christianity*, 118–119
Human Pain — *The Problem of Pain*, 95–97
Human Wickedness — *The Problem of Pain*, 57–59
Humility — *Mere Christianity*, 114
Illustrations of the *Tao* — *The Abolition of Man*, 95–121
Intercourse in the Afterlife — *Miracles*, 166–167
Is Christianity Hard or Easy? — *Mere Christianity*, 166–170
Joy — *Surprised by Joy*, 15–18, 21, 205, 219–221, 230–231

Judgment — *Reflections on the Psalms*, 9–11
Justice and Fortitude — *Mere Christianity*, 76
Laziness — *Letters of C. S. Lewis*, 187–188
Life on Other Planets — *The World's Last Night*, 89–91
Liturgy — *Letters to Malcolm*, 4–6
Love of Country — *The Four Loves*, 40–45
Love of Nature — *The Four Loves*, 34–35
"Love Thy Neighbor" — *The Weight of Glory*, 14–15
Marriage — *Mere Christianity*, 95–96; *A Grief Observed*, 6–7, 20

Mechanics of Meditation   *Letters to Malcolm,* 77–78, 84–85, 80–82

Miracle and the Laws of Nature   *Miracles,* 56–58
Miracle of the Ascension   *Miracles,* 162–163
Miracle of the Raising of Lazarus   *Miracles,* 156
Miracle of the Resurrection   *Miracles,* 148–150
Miracle of the Transfiguration   *Miracles,* 158
Miracle of the Walking on the
    Water   *Miracles,* 155–156
Miracles of Destruction   *Miracles,* 146
Miracles of Fertility   *Miracles,* 141–142
Miracles of Healing   *Miracles,* 144–146
Modern Translations of the Bible   *God in the Dock,* 229–231
Money   *Mere Christianity,* 80–81
Moral Choices   *Mere Christianity,* 86–87
Morality   *Mere Christianity,* 69–71
Mysticism   *Letters to Malcolm,* 63–65
Obedience   *Letters of C. S. Lewis,* 179
On Seeing a Miracle   *Miracles,* 173–174
Other Religions   *Mere Christianity,* 431
Perfection   *Mere Christianity,* 171–172
Philia or Friendship   *The Four Loves,* 96–98
Prayer of Praise   *Reflections on the Psalms,* 90–97
Pride   *Mere Christianity,* 109–112
Prudence   *Mere Christianity,* 74–75
Psychoanalysis   *Mere Christianity,* 83–84
Purgatory   *Letters to Malcolm,* 108–109
"Putting on Christ"   *Mere Christianity,* 160–162
Reading the Gospels   *Letters of C. S. Lewis,* 180–181
Ready-made Prayers   *Letters to Malcolm,* 11–12
Resurrection of the Body   *Letters to Malcolm,* 121–124
Right and Wrong   *Mere Christianity,* 17–18
Screwtape to Wormwood on
    Anxiety   *The Screwtape Letters,* 28–29
    Gluttony   *The Screwtape Letters,* 76–77
    Humility   *The Screwtape Letters,* 62–64
    Irregular Churchgoing   *The Screwtape Letters,* 72–73
    Laughter   *The Screwtape Letters,* 50–52
    Lust   *The Screwtape Letters,* 40–42
    Peaks and Troughs   *The Screwtape Letters,* 36–37
    Prayer   *The Screwtape Letters,* 19–21
    Reinterpreting Jesus   *The Screwtape Letters,* 106–109
    War   *The Screwtape Letters,* 25–27
    Worldly Companions   *The Screwtape Letters,* 45–46
Scripture   *Reflections on the Psalms,* 109–111, 117–119

Scruples   *Letters to an American Lady,* 38

Seeing and Believing   *Miracles*, 7–8
Sex   *Letters to Malcolm*, 14–15
Sins of Thought   *Mere Christianity*, 87
Social Morality   *Mere Christianity*, 78–79
Spirit, Spirits, Spiritual   *Miracles*, 177–179
Spiritual Reading   *God in the Dock*, 201–202
Spiritual Reading   *Letters of C. S. Lewis*, 298–299, 302
                                Letters to an American Lady, 44–45

Storge or Affection   *The Four Loves*, 56–57
Suffering   *The Problem of Pain*, 104–108
Temperance   *Mere Christianity*, 75–76
The Airplane, the Wireless, and
  the Contraceptive   *The Abolition of Man*, 67–71
The Crown and the Cross   *Letters of C. S. Lewis*, 166
The Devil   *The Screwtape Letters*, vii
The Efficacy of Prayer   *The World's Last Night*, 3–8
The Ego and the Self   *God in the Dock*, 194–195
The Fall of Man   *The Problem of Pain*, 69–71
The Incarnation   *Mere Christianity*, 154–155
                                Letters to Malcolm, 70–71
                                Miracles, 112–116
The Moment of Prayer   *Letters to Malcolm*, 142–144
Theology   *Mere Christianity*, 135–138
The Psalms   *Reflections on the Psalms*, 2–5
The Second Coming   *The World's Last Night*, 104–106
The *Tao*   *The Abolition of Man*, 28–30, 56–57
The Three-Personal God   *Mere Christianity*, 141–143
The Trinity   *Mere Christianity*, 149–152
The Universe   *Mere Christianity*, 33–34
The Virgin Birth   *Miracles*, 142–144
                                Letters of C. S. Lewis, 232–233
Thought, Imagination, Language *Miracles*, 72–74
Virtue   *Mere Christianity*, 76–77
What Are We to Make of Jesus
  Christ?   *God in the Dock*, 156–158
When and Where to Pray   *Letters to Malcolm*, 16–18

BY C. S. LEWIS

The Abolition of Man
Mere Christianity
The Great Divorce
The Problem of Pain
The Weight of Glory and Other Addresses
The Screwtape Letters (with "Screwtape Proposes a Toast")
Miracles
The Case for Christianity
The Lion, the Witch and the Wardrobe
Prince Caspian
The Voyage of the Dawn Treader
The Silver Chair
The Magician's Nephew
The Horse and His Boy
The Last Battle
Perelandra
That Hideous Strength
Out of the Silent Planet
The Joyful Christian
George MacDonald: 365 Readings
C. S. Lewis: Letters to Children

About C. S. Lewis:

Through Joy and Beyond: A Pictorial Biography of C. S. Lewis,
    by Walter Hooper
Past Watchful Dragons: The Narnian Chronicles of C. S. Lewis,
    by Walter Hooper
The Letters of C. S. Lewis to Arthur Greeves (1914-1963), edited
    by Walter Hooper
C. S. Lewis at the Breakfast Table and Other Reminiscences,
    edited by James T. Como

Available at your local bookstore or from Macmillan Publishing
Company, 100K Brown Street, Riverside, NJ 08370